The Child

An Introduction to Developmental Psychology

The Child

An Introduction to Developmental Psychology

Deborah Lott Holmes
Loyola University of Chicago

Frederick J. Morrison
University of Minnesota

Brooks/Cole Publishing Company
Monterey, California
A Division of Wadsworth, Inc.

Printed in the United States of America

10 9 8 7 6 5 4 3 2

Library of Congress Cataloging in Publication Data

Holmes, Deborah L.
    The child, an introduction to developmental psychology.

    Includes bibliographies and index.
    1. Child psychology.   2. Adolescent psychology.
I. Morrison, Frederick J., joint author.   II. Title.   [DNLM: 1. Child psychology.   2. Child development.   WS105.3 H749c]
BF721.H593   155.4   78-10711
ISBN 0-8185-0328-9

        Photo on page 36 © Peter Menzel/Stock, Boston. Photo on page 44 (left) courtesy of Carnegie Lab, Davis. Photo on page 44 (right) © Joe Baker/Medical World News. Photo on page 61 © Jerry Howard/Stock, Boston. Photo on page 66 © Hank Lebo/Jeroboam, Inc. Photos on pages 67 (left) and 85 © James R. Holland/Stock, Boston. Photo on page 67 (right) © Gabor Demjen/Stock, Boston. Photo on page 125 © Suzanne Arms/Jeroboam. Photo on page 140 © Foto-Hetzel. Photo on page 144 © René Burri/Magnum. Photo on page 208 (top) © Elizabeth Crews/Jeroboam. Photo on page 208 (bottom) © Patricia Hollander Gross/Stock, Boston. Photo on page 245 © Suzanne Wu/Jeroboam. Photo on page 245 © Ken Heyman. Photo on page 365 © Betsy Cole/Stock, Boston. Photo on page 384 © Jim Pinckney. Photo on page 405 © Peter Vandermark/Stock, Boston.
        Cover photos © Suzanne Arms/Jeroboam (left); © Karen R. Preuss/Jeroboam (right). Part-opening photos © Jim Pinckney.

Acquisition Editor: *Todd Lueders*
Manuscript Editor: *Joan Poole*
Production Editor: *Sally Schuman*
Interior and Cover Design: *Jamie Brooks*
Technical Illustrations: *Boardworks*
Typesetting: *Graphic Typesetting Service, Los Angeles, Calif.*

PREFACE

Our society has witnessed a number of important changes (which some have called revolutions) in the past two decades. In addition to political and racial upheavals, we have seen dramatic shifts in the social organization of our culture. Marriage patterns have altered to such an extent that one of every two or three marriages will now end in divorce. Women are shedding the stereotypic roles of wife and homemaker and are forging new identities. Widespread use of birth control and changes in abortion laws have further altered the fabric of our social and sexual lives. These examples, and many others that can be found in all facets of society, share an important common element: in different ways they all touch the lives of children. Children are all affected by changes in marriage and family structure, divorce rates, social roles, and birth control and abortion. It is, therefore, no exaggeration to state that the deepest and most widespread revolution in our society involves the child.

Concern for the rights of children, heated debate on abortion, and increased awareness of child abuse and childhood problems testify to the central position held by the child in current affairs.

Against this background of concern, we have begun to realize how little we really understand about children and what is crucial in their upbringing. Even defining the beginning of a child's life seems to elude us. We have expressed uncertainty as a society about whether mothers are crucial to their children's normal development, whether daycare centers are bad for children, and whether children need two parents to grow normally.

The field of developmental psychology has traditionally been responsible for studying and understanding children's growth. In recent years an impressive array of information has been gathered on the social, cognitive, and personality development of children, and developmental psychology therefore has much to offer those grappling with some of the important issues we just described.

In the pages that follow we hope to reflect the concern that parents, practitioners, and psychologists have about the development of children. At the same time, we hope to illustrate how the scientific study of child development can

v

contribute to understanding the nature of children and how they develop, thereby contributing to the effort to solve the important problems facing our society.

We have tried to accomplish our purpose in a number of specific ways. First, we have tried to be *thorough* without being encyclopedic. We have attempted to document the many facets of childhood out of respect for the complexity and richness of human development. No simple answers are given where none exist, and at times we express our ignorance more than our understanding.

Second, we have worked to be *integrative*, in two senses. Textbooks in developmental psychology too often present only a mechanical recitation of theories with no attempt to integrate or reconcile them and with little concern for showing how research is used to test theories. In this book, where possible, we have contrasted different theoretical points of view on a particular topic, such as the nature of infant attachment, in the hope that the reader will appreciate how theories relate to one another and how research is used to evaluate the worth of a theory.

In addition, we have tried to be integrative with regard to development itself. Very often textbook chapters are divided into sections on infancy, preschool years, school years, and adolescence. The central topics of each of these chapters often bear little resemblance to one another, leaving the reader with no sense of the continuity of development. By contrast, we have tried to pick up and integrate developmental themes from one age period to the next. For example, our discussion of infant attachment is explicitly connected to our treatment of preschool dependence, which in turn is picked up in our review of the emergence of school-age and adolescent independence. We hope thereby to give the reader a more continuous and integrated picture of the developing child.

Finally, we have tried to adopt a balanced perspective on the important questions we address. Our point of view is first and foremost that of the developmental psychologist, interested in the scientific understanding of human development. However, we recognize that other people have needs and concerns about child development that are more immediate and practical. Thus we have attempted to bring knowledge gained from the study of human development to bear on some important practical questions, in an effort to strike a balance among theoretical, scientific, and practical issues. We have done so in two ways. Each chapter contains a number of special "Issues" that highlight important questions often raised by parents and/or practitioners about children and their development. We have endeavored to reflect how a developmental psychologist would respond to these issues. Second, at the end of each chapter we gather our discussion into some tentative recommendations in a section on providing an optimal environment. We have decided to proffer some ideas, again drawn from the field of developmental psychology, about how to facilitate development within each childhood era. Our goal in making such recommendations is not to dictate how children should be reared. Rather, our purpose is to take the first steps in what we hope will be a growing communication among specialists, practitioners, parents, and all others concerned about the child.

ACKNOWLEDGMENTS

Some years ago at the annual celebration of the Academy Awards, an Italian film received an Oscar for "Best Foreign Film of the Year." The gentleman who stepped forward to receive the award proceeded to deliver a lengthy acceptance speech in Italian. After the audience had listened politely if uncomprehendingly and had applauded enthusiastically, emcee Bob Hope ambled to the podium and explained "Translated, that means 'I did it all myself'!"

The rapid and uproarious laughter that ensued was testimony to how unexpected and absurd Hope's translation was. All endeavors of great complexity and magnitude reflect the efforts of many individuals. We would therefore like to acknowledge and thank those who helped guide this endeavor from an idea to a reality.

To start at the top, Todd Lueders, perhaps more than anyone else, steered this enterprise over its lengthy course. Alternating periods of patience with prodding, he read the authors sensitively and directed them well.

Many professional colleagues added immeasurably to the accuracy, clarity, and richness of the text. We sincerely thank Daphne Bugental, University of California, Santa Barbara, E. Audrey Clark, California State University, Northridge, Dianne C. Draper, Iowa State University, Pauline Gillette, Northern Virginia Community College, Jerome Kagan, Harvard University, Philip Salapatek, University of Minnesota, and Bill Holmes for their careful readings of earlier drafts of the entire manuscript. In addition, we are indebted to several people for their help on specific sections: Tom Trabasso for careful reading of the chapters on preschool and school-age cognition; Jerome Kagan for his comments on the infancy chapters; Cathy Lord for her work on the language and psychopathology chapters; and Michael Maratsos for his comments on the chapter on language development.

We also thank all those who provided invaluable editorial and technical assistance, especially Sally Schuman, Jamie Brooks, Joan Poole, David Dahlgren, Karen LeMay, Kathy Triden, and Fran Albanese.

Finally, special thanks to Marshall Haith and Jerome Kagan.

Deborah Lott Holmes
Frederick J. Morrison

CONTENTS

The Child

An Introduction to Developmental Psychology

1

Perspectives on Childhood

This is a book about children: a description of their behavior and abilities, a discussion of how they develop and mature into adults, and an exploration of how parents and society can best meet the needs of children. The presence of such a book, completely devoted as it is to the development of the child, may not seem unusual in 20th-century North America. However, only a century ago, there were very few books completely devoted to the child, and, prior to that, there were virtually none. The existence of this book—and the hundreds of others written about and for children during the last few decades—shows our current deep concern for the welfare of our children.

During the 20th century, the child has become an important member of our society. Signs of the profound interest that we now show in our children are abundant and can be observed in all the special facilities that have been developed exclusively for children. They can be seen, too, in the increasing number of adults employed purely to serve children: teachers, social workers, child psychologists, pediatricians, child advocates. And they are evident in the growing number of products and services designed exclusively for children: children's books, children's toys, children's clothes, children's movies and television programs. Clearly, 20th-century society has taken a profound interest in its children. The present era has accordingly been referred to by many as "the century of the child." For the first time in history, society wants to understand its children, to help them to develop to their fullest, and to ensure their rights to the liberty and self-fulfillment that we adults have long taken for granted. Unfortunately, this is not to say that 20th-century society has been able to successfully meet this challenge in all respects, for, as we shall see not only in this chapter but throughout this book, there is much that still has to be accomplished. Most importantly, however, we have finally come to realize that the children of our society, like its adults, have special wants and needs that society should recognize and try to meet. In this sense, then, the 20th century truly is a "century of the child."

ISSUE

Even though we have declared this to be the "century of the child," many of our children are not provided with the care and love that they deserve. For example, it has been projected that, during the 1970s, 50,000 children will be murdered by their parents, while nearly 300,000 will be permanently disabled as a result of parental abuse. And millions will be less severely abused, neglected, and poorly educated [Rieman, 1975].

Our newspapers all too regularly provide us with jarring statistics such as those described above. We read of extreme individual cases of abuse. We read of large-scale illiteracy encompassing the majority of children within certain school systems. We read about illegal child labor, child prostitution, and child crime. We even read that the incidence of problems such as child abuse is on the increase, since each year more and more cases of child abuse are reported to the authorities (Rieman, 1975; Bakan, 1971). These problems do, unfortunately, exist, and, by focusing our attention on them, the media perform a clear social service; the problems would not be rectified if we did not know of their existence. Unfortunately, however, the grim reports of the media tend to create a picture of our society as one that has little interest or involvement in the welfare of its children: a society that has somehow "degenerated" and left behind "the golden age of childhood" in centuries past. It has even been suggested that the complexity and frustrations of modern society are causing men and women to actually attack their own helpless children. Possibly. But another explanation seems more likely: we are simply becoming increasingly aware of the fact that *a man or woman does not have the right to abuse and neglect his or her children. Rather, the children themselves have rights, and it is the responsibility of all of us to see that those rights are protected.* This new awareness of the rights of children has sensitized our society to the problems of child abuse and child neglect—hence the growing media attention to these and similar problems. Child abuse and neglect, problems that have existed since humanity's earliest times, have recently come to be viewed as inhuman, immoral, and even illegal. We will no longer allow parents to harm their children. We will no longer look the other way. As a result, the number of *reported* incidents has risen, even though the actual number of cases of child abuse and neglect may well have declined.

This more optimistic view of what is occurring in our society is clearly borne out if one takes the time to actually look at what happened to children in prior centuries. Over the centuries, the lot of the child has not degenerated but has steadily *improved.* Let us, then, briefly consider what prevailed in the attitudes about and treatment of children in ages past, in order to get a better perspective of just what is happening—and what we are accomplishing—today.

CHILDHOOD IN HISTORICAL PERSPECTIVE

Accurate information on the status of children in past centuries is, unfortunately, hard to come by, as any scholar of the history of childhood will readily concede. In past centuries, not only were there no books devoted to the study of child development, but children were rarely mentioned in medical books, philosophical treatises, literature, or even personal letters written from one family member to another. The very absence of historical material pertaining to the child testifies directly to the fact that children were quite simply not considered to be an important part of their society.

When children were mentioned in the literary works of past centuries, the picture that emerged was grim indeed. The limited references show widespread **infanticide** (the deliberate murder of infants), childhood disease, physical abuse, real and near starvation, extreme neglect, and the total absence of any rights for children. The child was considered to be the property of the father, and it was the father who made the ultimate decisions regarding how the child would live—and even if the child would be allowed to live at all.

What little information we do possess reveals that very few children of the past survived, let alone lived well. Until the 19th century, death rates among infants ran as high as 50 to 75% (Brown, Rox, & Hubbard, 1974; Marvick, 1974). Death for the infant came in many forms: disease was a frequent cause of death, due to poor sanitation and ignorance of appropriate medical treatments; other causes of death included starvation, neglect, and even murder. Indeed, infanticide was especially widespread among undesirable and unwanted children: the sickly and deformed, the poor, the illegitimate, the females, and the later-born children in already large families.

Clearly, we cannot here go into great detail in describing the lives of children in centuries past. The sections that follow are therefore meant simply to illustrate children's harsh lot by providing brief glimpses of childhood from ancient Greece to early modern times.

Ancient Sparta

The history of childhood is a nightmare from which we have only recently begun to awaken. The farther back in history one goes, the lower the level of child care, and the more likely children are to be killed, abandoned, beaten, terrorized, and sexually abused [deMause, 1974, p. 1].[1]

Let us begin, then, by going back to Sparta and the ninth century B.C. Sparta was a largely military state, devoted to the waging—and winning—of wars. Spartan citizens lived in a harsh, regimented society. It is not surprising, then, that their children did not escape a harsh existence.

The rigors of Spartan society began at birth. Each newborn infant was carefully examined by a council of elders. This group of men determined whether the infant was strong and healthy enough to live and serve the military state. If the council decided that the child was weak or defective, the sentence was death. Even the death sentence was a harsh one: the infant was taken to the mountains, abandoned, and left exposed to harsh weather, wild animals, and eventual starvation (Despert, 1965).

If the council judged the newborn to be healthy and strong, the infant was allowed to live. However, those infants who were allowed to live were almost immediately required to fit their lives into the highly regimented society. Spartan historians claim that crying was not allowed, but they fail to specify the actual

---

[1]This and all other quotations from this source are from *The History of Childhood*, by L. deMause. Copyright 1974 by Harper & Row, Publishers, Inc. Reprinted by permission.

methods used to prevent it (Despert, 1965). Babies were allowed to nurse only two or three times a day. Even very young infants were "toughened" by cold-water baths and frequent beatings (deMause, 1974).

At 7 years of age, boys were taken from their parents and placed in public barracks. Life in the barracks was extremely harsh. Beatings—often to death—and food deprivation were common.

There can be little doubt that the Spartan treatment of children was extremely cruel. However, it was probably not the result of totally sadistic motives. The Spartans believed that experience with physical hardship was necessary to prepare for the child's later role in the military state (Despert, 1965; deMause, 1974). Thus, the Spartans justified the pain and anguish of their children on the theory that it would be "good for them" in the long run. This idea that painful experiences during early childhood can somehow toughen and prepare the child for the harsh realities of later adult life was, of course, not unique to Sparta. It emerges again and again throughout history.

Ancient Rome

In ancient Rome, we find the beginnings of a strong **patriarchal** (father-dominated) society. Patriarchism has continued to be prevalent in most societies up to the present. In the Roman family, the father's powers were absolute. He examined his infant at birth and decided whether or not the child would be allowed to live. This absolute power over his children continued throughout the father's life, even after his children were grown and married, as long as they continued to live in their father's house. Under the law, the father had the right to "scourge his children, sell them into slavery, banish them from the country or put them to death" [Goodsell, 1934].

The Middle Ages

The Middle Ages have rightfully been called the Dark Ages, since they were a period characterized by extreme superstition, ignorance, brutality, and disease. During this dark period in human history, children fared extremely poorly. Infanticide—both deliberate and "accidental"—was still practiced, and, although it was condemned by the Church as a major sin throughout the Middle Ages, it was not until the 12th century that secular legislation equated infanticide with murder. There are no accurate records of the actual incidence of infanticide during the Middle Ages. However, Church records reveal that few illegitimate children survived to baptism, and the ratio of baptized boys to girls was well over three to two. Certainly, the number of illegitimate and female children murdered and abandoned must have been extremely high. Pope Innocent III was so appalled by the sight of "countless" bodies of newborn infants floating in the Tiber that he established foundling homes or orphanages for the unwanted infants of Italy (McLaughlin, 1974; deMause, 1974).

The life of the medieval child continued to be a hard one even after infancy. Children were beaten, neglected, and afforded no rights whatsoever. Often the father determined the child's life work and marriage partner while the child was still very young. At the age of about 7, most children were taken from their homes and placed in the service of others. Even within the more privileged classes, boys and girls were frequently sent to serve the lords and ladies of nearby castles. These children bore the same duties and hardships as the other servants and slaves of the castle, differing from them only in that their servitude or slavery was of a temporary duration (Despert, 1965).

Among the lower classes, actual child sale was a common occurrence throughout the Middle Ages. The problem in England was serious enough that, in the seventh century the Church ruled that *a man* might not sell *his son* into slavery *after the age of 7*. There is evidence, however, that the English disregarded the edict of the Church and continued to sell even their older children as slaves, at least until the 12th century (deMause, 1974).

Still another form of child abandonment was an **oblat.** An oblat was the religious offering of a child to the Church. The child then served the rest of his or her life in a monastery or a convent. In return, the *parent* received special spiritual consideration. The fate of a child thus given to the Church was sealed. To later leave the monastic life resulted in excommunication, a very harsh penalty in those times (Despert, 1965).

In addition to their hard duties and lack of freedom, children of the Middle Ages were severely beaten and often murdered. In fact, most children living during this period would be considered battered or abused children by 20th-century standards.

It was not until the end of the Middle Ages that there was any real legal or Church concern with childbeating. Thus, one 13th-century law proclaimed, "If one beats a child until it bleeds, then it will remember, but if one beats it to death, the law applies" [quoted in deMause, 1974, p. 42]. Implicit in this edict was the continuing right to seriously beat the child, so that "it" would "remember" and, presumably, learn.

The Renaissance and Early Modern Times

The Renaissance has been viewed as the beginning of modern enlightened civilization: the awakening from the Dark Ages. The "enlightened" attitudes of the Renaissance spread in some degree to attitudes about children. Education came to be viewed as increasingly important and was made available to broader segments of the population. The process of education itself underwent substantial change, as attempts were made through the use of toys and pictures to make education more attractive to the child. Even corporal punishment was condemned, and it was suggested by some that the child should be handled with love rather than fear (Despert, 1965).

In practice, however, these "enlightened" views were not adopted in any widespread fashion. Superstition and brutality remained major forces throughout the Renaissance and well into early modern times.

> Century after century of battered children grew up and in turn battered their own children. Public protest was rare. Even humanists and teachers who had a reputation for gentleness . . . approved of beating children. Milton's wife complained she hated to hear the cries of his nephews when he was beating them, and Beethoven whipped his pupils with a knitting needle and sometimes bit them. Even royalty was not exempt from battering, as the childhood of Louis XIII confirms. A whip was at his father's side at table, and as early as 17 months of age, the dauphin knew enough not to cry when threatened with the

whip. At 25 months regular whippings began, often on his bare skin. He had frequent nightmares about his whippings, which were administered in the morning when he awakened. When he was king he still awoke at night in terror, in expectation of his morning whipping [deMause, 1974, p. 41].

The murder of infants and children was condemned and punished by both the Church and secular authorities during the Renaissance. As a result, outright infanticide of legitimate children diminished somewhat. However, the continued high infant mortality rates indicate that unwanted children were seldom allowed to survive. Their death was ensured by the parents' failure to provide adequate care for them or by subjection to unusual dangers. There is at least one clear record of such a "failure to nurture":

> At eight in the evening my wife delivered a girl who didn't seem capable of surviving. The . . . midwife baptized her in the presence of eyewitnesses as she did have signs of life . . . . The next day she was baptized in the Church . . . and on the following day sent away *en nourrice* [to a wet nurse] at a distance of six leagues and died on the fifth day of life [quoted in Marvick, 1974, p. 282].

Baptism in a church and a long journey to the country hardly seem to be practices geared toward preserving the health of an already sick child.

A more severe form of "failure to nurture" that was sure to seal the infant's fate was abandonment. Although there were many foundling homes or orphanages for abandoned children, the care provided at these facilities was extremely poor. In one such orphanage in France we find that the children " . . . being neither cleaned, cared for nor bedded as their young age requires . . . not a single one was found to have survived to adulthood" [Jacques du Breul, 1636, quoted in Marvick, 1974, p. 286].

In 18th-century Russia, we find still another example of the fate of children sent to foundling homes. In a 20-year period, 37,600 children were admitted to the foundling home in Moscow. Of that number, 1000 were eventually adopted and 6100 remained living at the home. The remaining 30,500 children had died! Even a hundred years later, the situation in Russia was not much improved. We are told that a visitor to the Moscow foundling home accidentally entered a room in which he encountered a terrible sight: "At the end was a stack, composed of the naked bodies of a couple of hundred babies packed like sardines biding their time for internment [sic] in spring" (quoted in Dunn, 1974, p. 390).

Among the wealthier classes, legitimate children were seldom abandoned to the foundling homes. However, the middle and upper classes did engage in a practice shockingly similar to abandonment. This was the practice of sending infants from their birth until 2 to 5 years of age to a **wet nurse** (a woman who breast-feeds and cares for an infant other than her own) who usually resided in the country at some distance from the parents and who was invariably poor and ignorant. Throughout the Renaissance and well into early modern times, parents who could afford it sent their newborn infants out to the homes of these strangers. In the hands of the wet nurses, the children were often abused, neglected, and sometimes even murdered. The survival rate for children sent out to wet-nurse was low indeed. Even though the parents grieved over the loss of their infants at the hands of the wet nurses, later-born children were also sent out nonetheless (deMause, 1974). Children who survived usually spent two to five years with one or several wet nurses.

The common use of wet nurses, even as recently as 1780, is clear in the following statistics provided by the Paris chief of police at that time. He estimated that 21,000 children were born in Paris every year. Of these, 17,000 were sent to the country to be wet-nursed, 2000 to 3000 were abandoned to foundling homes, 700 were wet-nursed at home, and 700 were nursed by their own mothers (deMause, 1974). Clearly, the enlightenment of the Renaissance and even the dawning of early modern times did not greatly improve the fate of most children.

Colonial North America

Lest it be thought that North American children escaped from the "nightmare of childhood," let us now turn to the history of childhood within our own society. Colonial North America differed from the European societies described above in that the family was an extremely strong and important unit. As a result, infanticide and abandonment were relatively rare, and infants were generally raised at home by their own mothers. The European practice of sending infants out to a wet nurse did not become popular in the United States until the 18th century (Illick, 1974; Walzer, 1974).

In most other respects, however, the life of a child in colonial North America did not differ dramatically from that of a child in Europe. Infant death rates, for example, continued to be very high in the American colonies. Although exact population statistics are not available, we do have accurate records on a few families. For example, both Cotton Mather and Samuel Sewall had 14 children. Only six Mather babies survived to adulthood, and only two Sewall children outlived their father (Illick, 1974).

As was the case in Europe, harsh parental practices were undoubtedly responsible in large part for the high infant death rate. For example, parents continued to "toughen" children, moistening their feet in cold water and giving them only thin shoes to wear, while newborn infants continued to be baptized in unheated churches.

Colonial North Americans also shared the European belief in strict discipline for children. Fear and shame tactics were frequent disciplinary measures, and the use of corporal punishment remained widespread. In 1678, John Eliot advised parents in the following manner: "Withhold not correction from the child, for if thou beatest him with the rod he shall not die, thou shall beat him with the rod and deliver his soul from hell" [quoted in Illick, 1974]. Even in 18th-century America, the use of harsh physical punishment was common both in the home and in the school. Moreover, just as was the case in early Sparta, this harsh treatment of children was justified on the basis that it would be good for them in the long run—pain and suffering in childhood would somehow prepare the child for pain and suffering in adult life.

Extreme use of physical punishment of children was further justified in colonial North American society by the social status of children. All available evidence clearly indicates that children occupied the lowest rungs of the social ladder, along with servants and slaves. The legal system provided for severe punishment of servants and slaves—and children—who broke the law. Moreover, the laws were so restrictive and vague that almost any act could be viewed as a violation. For example, the Stubborn Child Law, enacted in 1654 in Massachusetts, punished " . . . divers children and servants [who] behave themselves too disrespectively, disobediently and disorderly toward their parents, masters and governors" (quoted in Katz, Schroeder, & Sidman, 1973, p. 212). For violation of the Stubborn Child Law, a child could be put to death.

The severity of the treatment that children received under the law and the lack of legal restraints on the abusive treatment of children by their parents continued well into the 19th century. Thus, as recently as 1870, when a child was seriously beaten by her mother, the mother was prosecuted under the auspices of the American Society for the Prevention of Cruelty to Animals, not under the normal criminal justice system. The child was, for purposes of the lawsuit, considered to be a maltreated "animal," because animals were given greater protection under the law than were children (Brown et al., 1974). In other words, it was more serious to beat a dog in 1870 than it was to beat a child!

Summary of Historical Perspectives on Childhood

It should be obvious that the history of childhood is a history of shameful behavior on the part of adults toward their children. Modern North America is not without vestiges of this past: children continue to suffer and die from parental abuse and neglect. However, our survey of the history of childhood does reveal a gradual trend away from these neglectful and abusive practices toward better treatment and understanding of our children. We have certainly come a long way from those early societies, and, although we have not yet fully succeeded in protecting all of our children, we are certainly striving in that direction.

PERSPECTIVES ON CHILDHOOD IN 20TH-CENTURY NORTH AMERICA

In 1970, a group of child-care professionals gathered in Washington, D.C., for the White House Conference on Children. One of the products of this conference was a proposal for a Bill of Rights for Children. This Bill of Rights sought to guarantee for all children the following rights:

1. The right to grow in a society that represents the dignity of life and is free of poverty, discrimination, and any other forms of degradation.
2. The right to be born and be healthy and wanted throughout childhood.
3. The right to grow up nurtured by affectionate parents.
4. The right to be a child during childhood, to have meaningful choices of the process of maturation and development, and to have a meaningful voice in the community.
5. The right to have social mechanisms to enforce the foregoing rights (as presented in Brown et al., 1974).

These were the hopes of visionaries and idealists. The 20th-century United States is a long way from realizing these goals. Yet the very fact that this Bill of Rights was proposed as part of a government-sponsored conference suggests that our society is indeed striving to establish rights for our children and to provide adequate means for ensuring their implementation.

What Is a Child?

It has been argued that "childhood" is the invention of modern society. In the past, children were either regarded as infants who "didn't count" or were treated as miniature adults. There were no special facilities, toys, or clothes distinctly for children, as opposed to adults. Even young children were given hard work to perform and in most ways were indistinguishable from the adult slave or servant.

Today's United States, on the other hand, has been described as largely a child's world. There are children's playgrounds, schools, stores, movies, and a multitude of objects and events designed to serve our children. Our children are excused from work and encouraged to play and learn. But what, one may well ask, is a "child"? In what sense does the child differ from the adult—other than in size and shape? And when does one cease to be a child and become a woman or man? Clearly, the answers to these questions are not simple, and in a sense the remainder of this book is an attempt to address these crucial issues. However, let us briefly look at some of the key concepts that characterize our modern understanding of what a child is.

Childhood is Unique and Distinct from Adulthood

Medieval art until about the twelfth century did not know childhood or did not portray it. It is hard to believe that this neglect was due to incompetence or incapacity; it seems more probable that there was no place for childhood in the medieval world. An Ottonian miniature of the twelfth century provides us with a striking example of the deformation which an artist at that time would inflict on children's bodies. The subject is the scene in the Gospels in which Jesus asks that little children be allowed to come to him. . . . Yet the miniaturist has grouped around Jesus what are obviously eight men, without any of the characteristics of childhood; they have simply been depicted on a smaller scale. . . . A painter would not hesitate to give the naked body of a child, in the very few cases when it was exposed, the musculature of an adult [Aries, 1962, p. 33].[2]

The recordings and paintings that are available from the medieval period indicate that the child not only was viewed simply as a miniature adult but was, in many ways, treated as a miniature adult as well. Children's clothing (beyond infancy) was simply a smaller version of that of adults. Even in the areas of work and play, there was little distinction made between the child and the adult. Children and adults worked and played side by side, often engaged in the same activities (Aries, 1962; deMause, 1974).

Modern life has brought with it a clear delineation of "the child's world." We have children's books, children's movies, children's TV programs, children's music, children's games, children's clothing, children's furniture, and even special places for children: separate bedrooms, parks, schools, and clubhouses. The world of the adult and the world of the child have become divided. Less and less do we see children and adults working or playing side by side. Children are clearly considered unique in our contemporary society.

[2]From *Centuries of Childhood,* by P. Aries. Translated by R. Baldick. Copyright 1962 by Alfred A. Knopf, Inc. Reprinted by permission.

The view of a child as unique, valuable, and different from an adult is not, however, something that sprang up suddenly and full-blown in only recent times. As we saw in the previous section, this concept has gradually evolved over the course of several centuries. For example, the laws that govern society have long distinguished between children and adults, with a separate set of legal rules applying to the actions of children. These legal rules have recognized the greater vulnerability of the child and have sought to protect the child from his or her own lack of experience and from the actions of others.

Our criminal laws, in particular, provide a clear example of the gradual recognition of the child as deserving of special attention and protection. In early medieval law, it appears that children were treated as adults and criminally prosecuted as such. One Anglo-Saxon law stated that a boy of 10 ought to know not to steal and could be punished for stealing by death (Kean, 1937).

As society evolved, children continued to be prosecuted for their crimes but were then immediately granted a "pardon," thereby in effect labeling them "guilty" but sparing them from punishment. By the 14th century, pardons were granted to children as a matter of course.

The artificial use of conviction followed by pardons was abandoned by the 15th century, when childhood finally was recognized as being in itself a distinct defense. Judges continued, however, to have considerable discretion in determining when a particular child was old enough to be punished as an adult. Thus, it was argued in a 15th-century English case against a *4-year-old child* that judges could find the child innocent "through their discretion on account of his nonage" [quoted in Kean, 1937]. Implicit in this decision was the judges' right to find a 4 year-old guilty and sentence him to death. By the 17th century, clear age distinctions had been drawn: children below the age of 7 were considered not criminally responsible for their actions; from 7 to 14 years of age, children were assumed to be not responsible, although in individual cases they could be convicted if it was shown that they understood what they were doing; from age 14 on, they were treated as adults (Kean, 1937). This special legal immunity for children continues in modified form in the United States even today.

In recent years, our criminal justice system has gone many steps further in recognizing the unique status of children by establishing separate facilities and procedures for handling children who break the law. For example, an adult who steals a purse is a criminal and is prosecuted in a criminal court. A child who does the same thing is a "juvenile delinquent" and is tried in a special "juvenile court." This distinction is more than a mere game of semantics, since the procedures used differ in many major respects. The juvenile court is much more oriented toward rehabilitating, rather than punishing, the child. Again, the rationale for the separate treatment is the uniqueness of children—they are young and, being young, are still learning, developing, and committing the errors of judgment that come with lack of experience.

The view of the child as unique is, thus, not novel to our present age but part of a gradual evolution of ideas and attitudes toward childhood. Appreciation for the special qualities of the child has, however, greatly accelerated during recent years, largely as a result of our modern educational system. During the latter half of the 19th century, the Education Acts adopted throughout the United States made school attendance compulsory for all children under the age of 12. Prior to that time, most children worked, just as their parents worked. In part, these Education Acts were a reaction to the harsh working conditions that many children faced and an attempt to get the children into a healthier environment. Primarily, however, the Education Acts were an explicit recognition of childhood. Young minds, like young bodies, develop rapidly and benefit from a formal system of education. The Education Acts, recognizing the unique capacity of children for education, sought to ensure that they would receive this education through mandatory school attendance. This, in turn, meant that children for the first time no longer worked side by side with adults, thereby greatly accentuating the difference between "adults" and "children." This difference, already recognized to a limited extent (for example, in the legal defenses discussed above), rapidly came to be reflected throughout our society. "The child's world" quickly came to be a very real, and very clearly delineated, part of our modern world.

The Child Is a Person with Individual Rights

While the child is unique, she or he is also a human being and should be afforded the rights of a human being. True, the child is dependent upon the parents and must rely on them for protection and care. However, the child is not their property.

We have seen how past centuries essentially equated children with slaves and treated them as the property of their parents. Over the years, this view of the child has diminished, although vestiges remain. Together, child-labor laws and compulsory-education laws have severely limited the extent to which children can be put to work in order to provide financial benefits for their parents. But even these laws did not limit the parents' continuing right to control and supervise their children until they reached the "age of majority" (21 in most states), including the right to the child's wages (*American Jurisprudence*). Courts are, however, becoming increasingly willing to limit or sever this right, and **emancipate** (sever parents' rights to control and supervise) the child, under conditions where the child is independent of the parents financially and living away from home (Katz et al., 1973). These changing attitudes within our courts simply mirror changing attitudes within our society toward its young people. Children, like adults, are today viewed as people with rights of their own. The question is no longer whether children have "any" rights at all, for clearly they do in our contemporary society. Rather, the question is now "how many" rights children have.

One relatively recent example of the evolving concept of the child as a person with rights is the recent passage of laws concerning medical treatment for children. Prior to the passage of these laws, it was necessary for children under the age of 21 to obtain parental permission before receiving medical treatment. This requirement often meant that children failed to seek medical treatment for serious medical problems, such as drug problems and venereal diseases, that they wished to hide from their parents. With the passage of these laws, older children now have the legal right in most states to seek medical treatment without parental consent. Such laws reflect a major shift in our attitudes toward older children and their right to make certain decisions independently of their parents.

The concept of the child as a person with distinct rights has appeared, and is evolving, in numerous other ways in the contemporary United States. One of the more striking and widely publicized examples was the 1967 case of *In re Gault*. The Supreme Court held in that case that children are entitled to certain constitutional rights when prosecuted as juvenile delinquents. In the words of the Court, "neither the Fourteenth Amendment nor the Bill of Rights is for adults alone" [quoted in Rodham, 1973, p. 499]. Just as adults have certain fundamental rights, we are coming to increasingly recognize that children, as people, also have rights deserving of special protection.

The Child Is Father of the Man[3]

Give me a dozen healthy infants, well-formed, and my own specified world to bring them up in and I'll guarantee to take any one of them at random and train him to become any type of specialist I might select—doctor, lawyer, artist, merchant, chief, and, yes, even beggarman and thief, regardless of his talents, penchants, tendencies, and race of his ancestors [Watson, 1926, p. 10].

The child is, in a very real sense, the "father of the man," for a person's childhood largely determines the way he or she will develop into an adult. Awareness of the importance of childhood in determining the course of one's later life is not a modern idea. Even in early Sparta there was a clear belief that early childhood experiences were critical in determining the adult personality. Thus, the extremely harsh treatment of children was seen as a means of molding adults who could cope with the harsh realities of military life. It is not surprising, then, that early psychologists, such as Freud and Watson, should incorporate this view in their psychological theories. Both Freud and Watson saw childhood as an especially important period, during which experiences could essentially mold all of later life.

While some of the claims of Watson, Freud, and other early psychologists are today viewed as exaggerated, the impact of childhood experiences should not be underestimated. Modern developmental research reveals that, while it is sometimes possible to reverse the long-term effects of childhood experiences, the process is both slow and difficult. Thus, the unhappy child will, more likely than not, grow up to be an unhappy adult. Children who are abused and beaten by their parents will probably grow up to be parents who abuse their own children. Children who are denied adequate educational experiences will probably remain illiterate in adulthood and deny adequate educational opportunities and incentives to their own children.

This is not to say that the experiences of childhood determine all aspects of human development. In studying childhood, we have become increasingly aware that one cannot completely "mold" the life of an individual by childhood experiences, as Watson claimed in the quotation that began this section. There are certain aspects of human development and personality that seem to be relatively immune to environmental intervention. Those aspects of development and personality that cannot be easily changed by childhood experiences seem to be controlled by the genetic makeup of the particular individual. Thus, for example, childhood experiences have relatively little effect on physical traits such as height—although an environment deprived of adequate stimulation and nutrition will interfere with the normal processes of body growth—since physical traits are largely determined genetically.

Certain aspects of development are, however, strongly influenced by one's childhood. Personality and social behavior, while somewhat influenced by genetic

[3]Quotation from William Wordsworth, a 19th-century poet.

factors, are much more closely associated with childhood experiences. Of course, all of us are aware of exceptional cases when people have turned out differently as adults than would have been predicted from their childhoods—for example, the "self-made" person and the "black sheep." Clearly, however, these special individuals who break away totally from their childhood environments are exceptions. Moreover, some psychologists (following the tradition of Freud) argue that the personalities of even these special individuals are *indirectly* influenced by their childhood experiences. Thus, it is argued that the minister's daughter who becomes a criminal reflects her childhood just as the criminal's daughter who becomes a criminal reflects her childhood. Regardless of whether one accepts this view, there can be little doubt that childhood experiences have a lasting effect on all development. The actual expression of these effects, however, is not always obvious—and is always extremely complex.

Because of this inherent uncertainty and complexity, attempts to construct the "perfect" environment in which our children will develop to their fullest capacity have, to date, had only limited success. Even today, we are not completely sure of what the optimal or ideal environment for our children would be. We do know, however, that certain experiences in childhood are critical for normal, healthy development. The child must grow in an environment that is free of abuse and neglect; the child must be guaranteed adequate care and nutrition; and the child must receive adequate stimulation in the form of attention, play, and education.

THE HISTORY OF DEVELOPMENTAL PSYCHOLOGY

Developmental psychology is the scientific study of children: the study of how children develop and what society can do to help them develop in a normal, healthy way. By its very nature, developmental psychology is committed to a socially worthy and relevant goal: "to better the health, the rearing, the education, and the legal and occupational treatment of children" (Sears, 1975, p. 3).

Developmental Psychology As a Science

Developmental psychology has set as one of its primary goals the study of how "best" to raise our children. The question of what is "best" for the normal and healthy development of our children is an extremely controversial one to attempt to answer. For example, we are all familiar with the old tenet "Spare the rod and spoil the child." Our brief review of childhood in prior centuries showed that the tenet was applied in a merciless, but often well-intentioned, fashion in ages past. Even the parent of today who abuses a child will often do so thinking that the actions are warranted—that they teach the child discipline and self-control.

It is, thus, not enough to simply say that developmental psychology seeks to improve the quality of life for children by showing how best to raise them. Rather, developmental psychology must also provide objective, scientific data to support the suggestions it makes. Only in this way can developmental psychology provide accurate and convincing answers to the riddle of how to raise our children.

The Developmental Perspective

The study of developmental psychology is more, however, than the simple accumulation of objective data about children. Certainly, data collection is the beginning. We need clear, objective data to demonstrate what happens normally in the course of development—what changes occur and when. We also need clear data to demonstrate what changes occur when environmental conditions are altered: what changes in the child's environment will improve the rate and course of development and what changes in the environment will impede the normal course of development. Even more important, however, than the "what" and "when" of child development is the question of "why" these developmental changes occur. Comprehensive *theories* of child development must therefore be formulated to provide explanations for these changes.

In developing these theories, we must, however, keep foremost in mind a consideration that separates developmental psychology from many other scientific disciplines. Developmental psychology is ultimately directed toward the application of developmental facts and theories to social problems. The repercussions of developmental psychology can therefore be very real and very serious. A bad theory may well have disastrous effects upon the actual rearing and treatment of children. The "developmental perspective" thus carries with it considerable social responsibility. It is not enough to develop theories that sound convincing; these theories must be critically tested and retested to ensure their validity. The developmental perspective is thus by no means a fixed set of observations and theories but is an ongoing process of observation, analysis, further observation, and reanalysis.

Research Methods in Developmental Psychology

As is undoubtedly the case in all scientific fields, there is no single way in which children should be studied. Rather, many different types of research methods have been developed for use with children. The particular question under consideration largely dictates which research method should be used. However, whatever the method and whatever the question, the developmental psychologist approaches the task as a scientist and uses objective and controlled methods of observation and measurement.

Cross-Sectional versus Longitudinal Methods

By definition, the developmental psychologist is concerned with children and how they change as they grow older. Therefore, developmental research generally involves comparisons of the behavior of children of different ages. These comparisons are usually made by studying groups of children in different age groups at a single point in time—for example, comparing 3-year-olds to 5-year-olds. Such a comparison is called a **cross-sectional research design.**

Cross-sectional designs are widely used in developmental research because they allow research to be completed quickly. Moreover, cross-sectional designs are more than adequate for those research problems in which the age differences among groups are slight and for those behaviors that one can assume to be relatively immune to environmental and societal changes. For example, there would be no reason to be concerned about the use of a cross-sectional design in a study assessing differences in visual acuity in infants between 6 and 12 months of age. There are, however, many research problems that cannot be addressed adequately by cross-sectional designs—namely, those research areas in which environmental or societal changes may have influenced one group more heavily than the other. For example, cross-sectional studies of changes in intelligence from age 25 to age 64 led to the conclusion that IQ declines with age (Wechsler, 1955). However, in this research, the older groups not only were older but also had been subjected to very different educational and cultural experiences than the younger groups had. Indeed, subsequent research in which the same adults were repeatedly tested over a period of years did not show this decline (Kangas & Bradway, 1971).

When a single group of individuals is studied at several different points in time, the researcher is said to employ a **longitudinal research design.** Because of problems with cross-sectional designs that we have just described, longitudinal designs are sometimes preferable, even though they are expensive and time-consuming. However, there are problems with longitudinal designs, too, that make them less desirable unless one expects to have significant biasing differences among groups in a cross-sectional design. Perhaps the most serious problem with longitudinal designs is that of subject loss: over a period of years many participants will move away or simply refuse to continue to participate. One must then question how representative or normal the remaining group is. In addition, for those participants remaining in the study, one must consider how participation in the study itself has affected the course of their development in general and their performance on specific tasks in particular.

The problems we have just described in both cross-sectional and longitudinal research designs have led many developmental psychologists to develop new methods combining both designs (see, for example, Achenbach, 1978). For example, in a **longitudinal-sequential research design,** one would start with a cross-sectional approach (comparing children of different age groups) and then compare these different groups at intervals over a prolonged period of time. Such designs seem to be especially well protected from bias and problems in interpretation.

Experimental versus Observational Methods

In addition to selecting a research design (for example, longitudinal versus cross-sectional) the developmental psychologist also must choose a method for acquiring the information about the children involved. The psychologist may simply observe the children in their natural environment and record these observations (**observational method**); or the psychologist may devise a special task to be completed by the children in a specified place and time (**experimental method**).

Observational methods attempt to study the child in a natural environment. Therefore, the child is allowed to behave more or less as he or she normally behaves, while being observed unobtrusively by the psychologist. Observational methods allow the psychologist to accurately record naturally occurring behavior, and it is often assumed that the child's behavior is not affected by the fact of being observed. However, because the child is left in his or her natural environment, many things may be happening during the course of the observation, and it is often difficult to determine why a particular behavior occurs.

Experimental methods, on the other hand, allow the psychologist to determine precisely why particular behaviors occur by carefully controlling all of the child's experiences during the course of the experiment. Thus, when experimental methods are used, children are typically taken out of their natural environment and placed in a carefully controlled artificial setting, the laboratory. Experimental methods allow the psychologist to control everything that happens to the child during the course of the experiment and hence to determine more accurately why certain behaviors occur. However, it is difficult to know whether the conditions that operate in this artificial setting also operate naturally. Most psychologists, therefore, use a combination of experimental and observational methods, in an effort to achieve precision and control without sacrificing the naturalness of the environment.

In summary, psychologists use a variety of methods in their study of child development. The particular method chosen is largely determined by the research problem under investigation. All the methods we have described have their advantages and their limitations. It is only through ongoing research in which many psychologists approach the same problem areas using different methods that we can begin to gain a more thorough understanding of the child.

SUMMARY OF PERSPECTIVES ON CHILDHOOD

This chapter has shown how attitudes toward—and the resulting treatment of—children have changed throughout history. There has been a gradual transition from societies in which children were murdered, abandoned, neglected, and abused to a society in which children are increasingly protected, respected, and given special privileges. The recent emergence of interest in providing adequate environments for children has resulted in the birth of a new scientific discipline: the study of child development, known as *developmental psychology*.

The study of child development is a practical science. It is concerned with exploring the mysteries of childhood and with creating comprehensive theories to explain the complex changes that occur during childhood. These theories are then used to help to structure an environment in which our children will be able to develop to their fullest.

SUGGESTED READINGS

deMause, L. *The History of Childhood.* New York: Harper & Row, 1974. This is an outstanding collection of articles on the history of childhood.

Despert, J. L. *The Emotionally Disturbed Child: Then and Now.* New York: Brunner, 1965. An interesting book. It gives nice "nutshell" glimpses of the treatment of children in different societies of the past.

Bakan, D. *Slaughter of the Innocents.* San Francisco: Jossey-Bass, 1971. Bakan provides an interesting—albeit *not* scientific—discussion of the problem of child abuse.

Aries, P. *Centuries of Childhood.* New York: Knopf, 1962. Aries explores the history of childhood as seen in literature and art. Aries has been criticized for painting too rosy a picture of the life of children in ages past.

Kessen, W. *The Child.* New York: Wiley, 1965. This short book is a very interesting collection of papers written by historians, scientists, and politicians on the topic of children. It has the advantage of giving you a firsthand view of the original sources.

GLOSSARY

cross-sectional research design. A research design in which individuals in different age groups are studied at one point in time, as, for example, when a psychologist simultaneously studies a group of 3-year-olds and a group of 5-year-olds.

emancipation. The legal severing of parents' rights to control and supervise their children. Emancipation decrees are usually made when older children are no longer living at home and are financially independent of their parents.

experimental method. Research in which the psychologist devises a special task to be completed by the children in a specified place and time and observes their behavior as they perform the task.

infanticide. The deliberate murder of an infant.

longitudinal research design. A research design in which the same group of individuals is studied at intervals over a period of years, as, for example, when a psychologist studies a group of 3-year-old children and then studies the same group again when they are 5.

longitudinal-sequential research design. A combination of cross-sectional and longitudinal research designs. The psychologist originally creates a cross-sectional sample of different age groups and then repeatedly tests these groups over a period of time.

oblat. The religious offering of a child to the Church. It was common during the Middle Ages.

observational method. Research in which the psychologist observes and records the behavior of children in their natural environment.

patriarchal. A family structure dominated by the father.

wet nurse. A woman who breast-feeds and otherwise cares for another woman's child. The use of wet nurses was common among the upper classes in Renaissance and early modern times.

REFERENCES

Achenbach, T. M. *Research in developmental psychology: Concepts, strategies, and methods.* New York: The Free Press, 1978.

Aries, P. *Centuries of childhood.* New York: Knopf, 1962.

Bakan, D. *Slaughter of the innocents.* San Francisco: Jossey-Bass, 1971.

Brown, R. H., Rox, E. S., & Hubbard, E. L. Medical and legal aspects of the battered child syndrome. *Chicago-Kent Law Review,* 1974, *50,* 45–84.

deMause, L. The evolution of childhood. In L. deMause (Ed.), *The history of childhood.* New York: Harper & Row, 1974.

Despert, J. L. *The emotionally disturbed child: Then and now.* New York: Brunner, 1965.

Dunn, P. P. "That enemy is the baby": Childhood in Imperial Russia. In L. deMause (Ed.), *The history of childhood.* New York: Harper & Row, 1974.

Goodsell, W. *A history of marriage and the family.* New York: Macmillan, 1934.

Illick, J. E. Childrearing in 17th century England and America. In L. deMause (Ed.), *The history of childhood.* New York: Harper & Row, 1974.

Kangas, J., & Bradway, K. Intelligence at middle age: A thirty-eight year follow-up. *Developmental Psychology,* 1971, *5,* 333–337.

Katz, S. N., Schroeder, W. A., & Sidman, L. R. Emancipating our children—Coming of legal age in America. *Family Law Quarterly,* 1973, *7,* 211–241.

Kean, A. W. G. The history of the criminal liability of children. *Law Quarterly Review,* 1937, *3,* 364–370.

Marvick, E. W. Nature versus nurture: Patterns and trends in seventeenth-century French child-rearing. In L. deMause (Ed.), *The history of childhood.* New York: Harper & Row, 1974.

McLaughlin, M. M. Survivors and surrogates: Children and parents from the ninth to the thirteenth centuries. In L. deMause (Ed.), *The history of childhood.* New York: Harper & Row, 1974.

Rieman, R. All the broken children. Series of ten reports aired on WMAQ-AM/WNIS-FM, Chicago. November 10–November 14, 1975.

Rodham, H. Children under the law. *Harvard Educational Review,* 1973, *43,* 487–514.

Sears, R. R. Your ancients revisited: A history of child development. In E. M. Hetherington (Ed.) *Child development research,* Vol. 5, Chicago: University of Chicago Press, 1975.

Walzer, J. F. A period of ambivalence: Eighteenth century American childhood. In L. deMause (Ed.), *The history of childhood.* New York: Harper & Row, 1974.

Watson, J. B. What the nursery has to say about instincts. In C. Murchison (Ed.), *Psychology of 1925.* Worcester, Mass.: Clark University Press, 1926.

Wechsler, D. *Manual for the Wechsler Adult Intelligence Scale.* New York: Psychological Corporation, 1955.

PART ONE
THE BEGINNING OF LIFE

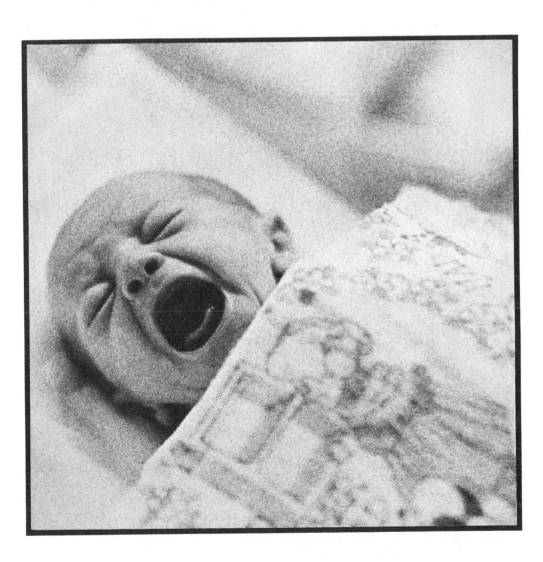

2

Conception, Prenatal Development, and Birth

Each of us began life as a single cell, formed by the union of sperm and egg. This single cell divided to form two cells, the two cells in turn became four, the four became eight, and so on. This process of cell division continues, of course, throughout our lives. However, never again does it occur at the rapid rate that characterizes the prenatal period. By the time we complete the nine-month stay within our mother's womb, the single cell with which our life began will have become literally millions of cells.

Perhaps even more remarkable is the manner in which these cells take on altogether different characteristics. Even though the nucleus and the chromosomes contained in it are identical in all of our cells, the cell bodies themselves take on different shapes and characteristics. Thus, certain of these cells develop into eyes, and still others become our brain, our hair, or our lungs. The entire process of cell division is thus preprogrammed to create a single human being, with the program that generates this human being already intact and complete within the single cell with which life begins.

The material that follows will discuss this remarkable process of prenatal development from three perspectives. First, the chapter will describe the role of genetic factors in the development of the child and the principles whereby these genetic factors operate. Second, the chapter will describe the developmental changes that occur during the prenatal period and the manner in which external factors (such as drugs, disease, nutrition, and the mother's emotional state) can affect the normal growth processes and permanently alter the appearance and functioning of the child. Finally, the chapter will discuss the process of birth and the impact of certain events at birth on later development.

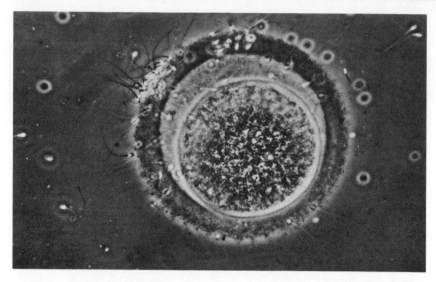

Figure 2-1. The human egg at the moment of conception. The illustration above shows a human egg (the large circular object) surrounded by sperm (the small tadpolelike objects) at conception. The facing illustration is a further enlargement of the contact between egg and sperm membranes as a single sperm fertilizes the egg. (From *Modern Embryology,* by C. W. Bodemer. New York: Holt, Rinehart & Winston, 1968, pp. 57, 61. Reprinted by permission. Photo courtesy of the Carnegie Institution of Washington, Department of Embryology, Davis Division.)

CONCEPTION AND GENETICS

Human life begins when an egg cell and a sperm cell unite to form a single cell, called a **zygote,** or **fertilized egg.** (See Figure 2-1.) Normally, this process is the result of sexual intercourse between a man and a woman, although artificial insemination is of course an exception. During intercourse, the male ejects millions of sperm into the vagina of the woman. Once in the vagina, the sperm swim up the uterus and into the fallopian tubes. If the woman has ovulated (meaning that she has released an egg into the fallopian tube), a sperm may make contact with the egg in the fallopian tube. If such a contact between egg and sperm occurs, the fertilized egg (zygote) thereby formed becomes impenetrable by other sperm. The zygote then travels down the fallopian tube to the uterus, where it attaches itself to the uterine wall and begins its nine-month residence within the womb.

ISSUE

How can some children be so unlike their parents in physical appearance if physical appearance is largely determined by genetic factors?

Genetic factors largely determine our body size and shape, our hair and eye color, and our other physical attributes. Thus, we each look the way we do largely because of the particular genes we acquired from our parents. There is, however, a common tendency to

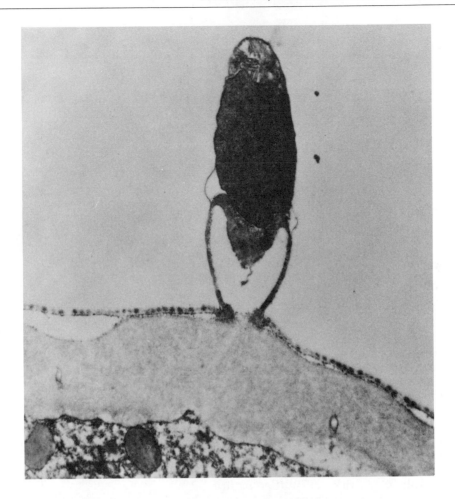

misinterpret the effect of genetics on physical appearance and to conclude that, because appearance is a function of genetics, children will, and necessarily should, resemble their parents.

A striking example of this common and overly simplified expectation is provided by a 1946 paternity case involving the famed comedian Charlie Chaplin, in which it was argued that Chaplin had fathered an illegitimate child. Blood tests had irrefutably shown that he could not have been the father. He was, nevertheless, forced to stand before the jury with the child so that the jury could compare the physical resemblance. Since the child looked like Chaplin, the jury held that Chaplin was the father (Foote, Levy, & Sander, 1966).

The Chaplin case, while extreme, illustrates the danger of oversimplifying the influence of genetics on human development. Physical appearance is, indeed, largely a function of genetic factors. However, a person's appearance is not determined by one or even a few genes but is, rather, a product of many genes interacting with one another. Consequently, the number of possible gene combinations for a particular person is astronomical, and the probability that a child will have the same set of genes, resulting in the same physical appearance, as either parent is virtually zero.

Ironically, the blood test that was disregarded by the jury in the Chaplin case involved one of the few instances in which accurate genetic predictions can be made. A child's blood type is, unlike virtually all other physical attributes, determined by a single gene pair (Goodenough & Levine, 1974). By determining the blood types of the parents, it is thus possible to specify precisely which blood types might occur in their children. This genetic fact of life has, strangely, received only relatively recent recognition outside the scientific community. For example, only a few states have adopted the Uniform Paternity Act, with its rule that, if blood tests reveal that a man could not have fathered a particular child, the tests in themselves are taken as absolute proof. Had that act been in effect in the Chaplin case, Chaplin could not have been held to be the father of the child.

Chromosomes and Genes: The Raw Material of Genetics

The zygote, although only a single, almost infinitely minute cell, contains a complete genetic program for the development of a human being. Thus, we each look the way we do, and are the people we are, largely because of genetic information transmitted from our parents to a zygote and from the zygote to the cells that have become each of us. This genetic information is carried by 46 **chromosomes,** contained in the nucleus of the zygote and transmitted in identical form from the zygote to all of the cells that develop from it.

In physical appearance, the chromosomes are each elongated, threadlike bodies that exist in the nucleus of each cell of the body. Chemically, chromosomes are composed of protein, RNA (ribonucleic acid), and two long strands of DNA (deoxyribonucleic acid) molecules that are twisted around each other in the form of a double helix. A chromosome, thus, has the general appearance of a twisted ladder (Watson & Crick, 1953). (See Figure 2-2.)

The chromosomes serve as the carriers of the actual units of genetic transmission: the **genes.** These genes are arranged end upon end along the length of each chromosome, with each gene having a fixed position, or *locus,* upon a particular chromosome. This means that, in normal individuals, a particular gene always occurs on a specific chromosome and on the same spot (locus) on that chromosome.

In actuality, of course, genes do not stand out on the chromosomes like beads on a necklace. Each gene is simply a particular segment of the chromosome, made up of a set of specific chemical instructions governing development. This can perhaps best be conceptualized by imagining a length of thread that has been measured off into sections. To the eye, the thread appears as a single unit. Once one knows of the measurement, however, it is possible to view the thread as a series of many distinct units. Similarly, a specific gene is not defined by any externally observable physical qualities but, rather, by its effect on development. Through careful observation, science has determined that the chemical instructions contained in particular portions of a chromosome have specific and distinct developmental effects. Some will, for example, affect eye color, while others will affect size.

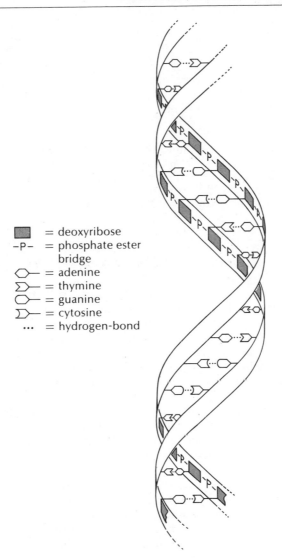

■ = deoxyribose
–P– = phosphate ester bridge
◇— = adenine
∑— = thymine
◯— = guanine
∑— = cytosine
••• = hydrogen-bond

Figure 2-2. A schematic representation of a DNA double helix within a chromosome. The DNA strands that the chromosome comprises have been described as a double helix, which resembles a twisted ladder. The sides of the ladder are composed of alternating molecules of phosphorus and sugar. The rungs of the ladder are composed of combinations of four base chemicals: adenine, thymine, guanine, and cytosine. These four bases always combine in a set manner to form pairs: adenine always pairs with thymine; guanine always pairs with cytosine. The genetic code of the individual is determined by the ordering of these pairs of bases along the DNA strands. (From "Genetic Influences on Behavior and Development," by G. E. McClearn. In P. Mussen (Ed.), *Carmichael's Manual of Child Psychology* (3rd ed.). Copyright 1970 by John Wiley & Sons, Inc. Reprinted by permission.)

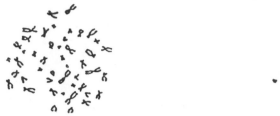 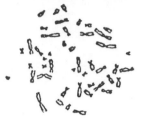

Figure 2-3.   Chromosomes within the nucleus of a human cell. The two pictures show the physical appearance of the 46 chromosomes within a female (left) and a male (right) body cell. (From "Genetic Influences on Behavior and Development," by G. E. McClearn. In P. Mussen (Ed.), *Carmichael's Manual of Child Psychology* (3rd ed.). Copyright 1970 by John Wiley & Sons, Inc. Reprinted by permission.)

Gametes and Chromosome Pairs

The zygote is formed by the union of an **egg** cell (from the female) and a **sperm** cell (from the male). From each of these cells, the zygote receives 23 chromosomes, giving the zygote the normal number of chromosomes: 46. (See typical 46-chromosome body cells in Figure 2-3.) Egg and sperm cells are, thus, distinct from the zygote and all other cells of the body in that they each contain only half of the genetic information needed for the individual's development. Because of this unique characteristic, egg and sperm cells have been termed **gametes** (from *gamos*, marriage; thus, fusion); gametes, unlike all other body cells, possess only half (23) the normal number of chromosomes. (See Figure 2-4.)

When the egg and sperm chromosomes are brought together in the zygote, they operate in so-called *chromosome pairs.* This does not mean that they physically exist in pairs, for in appearance they seem to be randomly placed in the nucleus of the cell. Nonetheless, for each sperm chromosome, there is a corresponding egg chromosome that is closely related functionally. The two members of each such chromosome pair work together to determine particular traits in the child. Thus, two related chromosomes operate as a pair, with one member of each functional pair contributed by the mother's egg and one by the father's sperm.

Twenty-two of these chromosome pairs are called **autosomes.** In the autosomes, each member of a pair perfectly complements the other member; that is, each member carries the same gene types in the same positions on the chromosome. Returning again to our earlier analogy of a thread divided into segments, this means that a chromosome pair, if it is an autosome, would appear as two such threads, divided up in precisely the same way. The bottom segment of each such chromosome "thread" might, for example, consist of a gene affecting eye color, the next segment might consist of a gene affecting hair color, and so on. Note, however, that this does not mean that the two chromosomes are exact mirror images of each other. Rather, it means that the respective genes contained in each of the two chromosomes perfectly complement each other. Thus, returning to our hypothetical example, the eye-color gene comprising the bottom segment of one chromosome might favor blue eyes, while that in the other chromosome might favor brown eyes. The eye-color instructions of each would differ. However, the basic function of each—namely, determining eye color—would be the same. The two would thus perfectly complement each other in function.

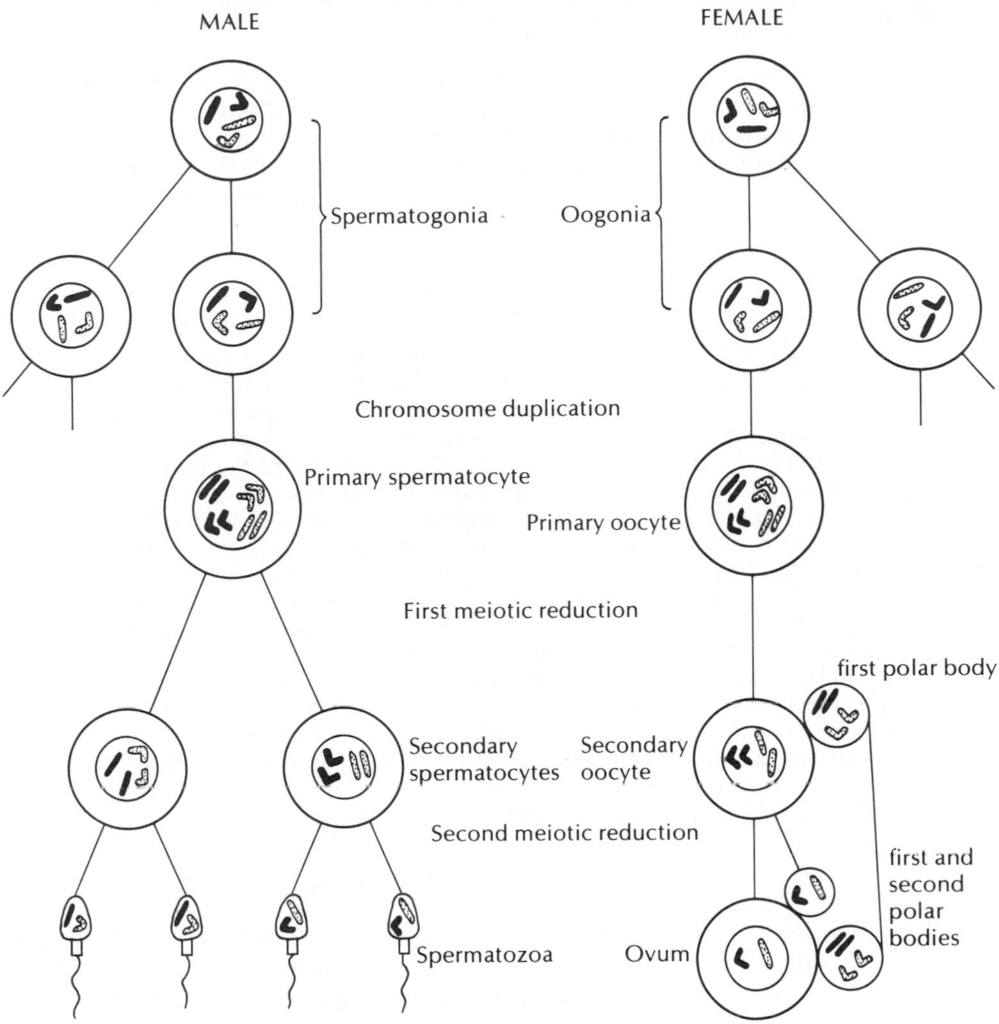

Figure 2-4. The production of gametes. Let us assume that there is an organism whose cells contain only two pairs of chromosomes, instead of the 23 pairs that characterize the human species. In gamete production, the sex cells (the spermatocyte and oocyte) undergo a special type of cell division, called **meiosis,** in which the resulting daughter cells have only half the normal number of chromosomes. Thus, in our hypothetical example above, meiotic divisions produce daughter cells that contain only two chromosomes. At fertilization, the chromosomes of the two gametes combine and produce a normal cell with four chromosomes. (The polar bodies rapidly degenerate and play no part in development.) (From *Life: An Introduction to Biology,* Second Edition, by George Gaylord Simpson and William S. Beck, © 1965 by Harcourt Brace Jovanovich, Inc. and *Fundamentals of Comparative Embryology of the Vertebrates,* rev. ed., by A. F. Huettner, © 1946 by Macmillan Publishing Company, Inc. Reprinted by permission.)

The 23rd of the 23 chromosome pairs is called the **sex chromosome pair,** since it determines the person's sex. The members of the sex chromosome pair *may,* like an autosome, perfectly complement each other, with each member carrying the same types of genes in matching positions; when this occurs, the individual is said to have two **X chromosomes** and will be *female*. Alternatively, the members of the sex chromosome pair *may not* complement each other. One member of the pair (the **Y chromosome**) may have fewer gene types than the other (the X chromosome), so that it appears structurally shorter. When this occurs, the individual is said to have one X and one Y chromosome, and the individual will be *male*.

ISSUE

Why is a woman's age considered to be an important factor in genetics?

Gametes (the egg and sperm cells) are produced by a special type of cell division, called meiosis. In meiosis, the original cell splits into two "daughter cells," each of which normally receives only one chromosome member from each of the cell's chromosome pairs. This gives each daughter cell only half, or 23, of the normal number of chromosomes. In the male, this process of gamete, or sperm, production continues throughout the man's reproductive life. In the female, however, about 400,000 primitive gametes, or egg cells, are present in the ovaries at birth, and *no new egg cells will be produced during the woman's lifetime*. Since the woman, unlike the man, does not continue to produce new egg cells, the possibility of damage to the genetic structure of her eggs from factors such as drugs, disease, or radiation increases as the woman grows older. There is also the possibility that the eggs themselves may become "old" and, hence, more susceptible to genetic damage from such external factors. As a consequence, the children of women over 35 show a higher incidence of such genetic disorders as Down's syndrome (McClearn, 1970; Goodenough & Levine, 1974).

Principles of Genetic Transmission

The basic principles underlying modern genetics have been intuitively understood for centuries. Thus, farmers have, throughout the ages, confidently expected to harvest corn and not wheat when corn was planted, while ancient kings worried when their "sons" did not resemble them. Yet, it is only within very recent history that science has sought to provide scientific explanations for these genetic principles. Science still has a long way to go before finding definitive explanations of the complex process of genetics. Nevertheless, much progress has been made in establishing rules that will link a person's genetic makeup, or **genotype,** with his or her actual appearance and behavior, or **phenotype.** Once such rules are established, the geneticist will be able to make further predictions regarding the phenotype of the unborn child, given the phenotypes of the child's parents. Thus, the study of genetics attempts to scientifically explain why there are often phenotypic similarities between parents and their children and to make predictive statements about the frequencies with which these similarities will be observed.

Basic to any discussion of genotypic/phenotypic relations is the material already covered concerning the basic building blocks of genetics: the genes. Each child has two of each type of gene (except when the gene is sex-linked and the child is male). One of the members of each gene pair is provided by the mother's egg; one is provided by the father's sperm. These genes appear in exactly the same positions in each of the two members of the chromosome pair.

Now let us leave the individual child for a moment and consider genes in general. Any particular gene can exist in either of two (or more) alternative states, with each of these alternative states conveying different chemical instructions affecting development. For example, let us pretend for the moment that height is determined by a single type of gene. Actually, adult height is determined by the extremely complex interaction of several genes and is further complicated by environmental factors. Nonetheless, let us simplify matters, solely for illustrative purposes, and pretend that height is determined by a single gene that can exist in either of two states: gene T is associated with being 6 feet tall, while gene T' is associated with being 5 feet tall.

Now let us go back to our individual child. A particular child, we have pretended, has a single gene pair that will determine her or his height. Both members of the pair could be the same, in which case the gene pair is said to be **homozygous.** Alternatively, the members of the child's gene pair could be different, in which case the gene pair is said to be **heterozygous.** If the two members of the pair are homozygous, and if both are "tall genes" (abbreviated as T/T), then our child will be 6 feet tall. Similarly, if the two members of the pair are homozygous, and if both are "short genes" (T'/T'), then our child will be 5 feet tall. When a child is homozygous for a particular trait, there is, thus, a direct relation between the genotype and the phenotype.

However, what happens when the child is heterozygous—that is, when the child has one tall gene and one short gene (T/T')? Will he or she be tall, short, or somewhere in between? What is the relationship between genotype and phenotype in heterozygous situations? Unfortunately, no single answer to these questions can be given, since the relationship between genotype and phenotype in heterozygous situations is not always completely clear. Instead, there appear to be three different types of relationships that can occur in heterozygous situations between genotype and phenotype: *dominance relationships, incomplete dominance relationships,* and *codominance relationships.* (See Figure 2-5.)

Dominance Relationships

Let us further assume that, in our hypothetical example of height, all people are either 5 feet or 6 feet tall, despite the fact that the parents of some were made up of a mix—that is, perhaps a 5-foot mother and a 6-foot father. Let us also assume that closer examination of the 6-footers reveals that they fall into two distinct groups: those who have two tall genes (homozygous T/T) and those who have one tall gene and one short gene (heterozygous T/T'). In this hypothetical situation, the presence of a single short gene in the heterozygous 6-footer thus has no effect on the person's phenotype (that is, his height). Such genotypic relationships are called **dominance** relationships because one gene (the dominant gene) completely dominates, or masks, the effect of the other gene (the **recessive gene**). Here, the dominant gene is the 6-foot gene, while the recessive gene is the 5-foot gene. In dominance relationships, the only time that the recessive gene can have an effect on the phenotype, or actual appearance of the individual, is when both genes within the individual are recessive.

Although most human traits are not defined by a simple dominance relationship but are determined by the interaction of many genes, there are a few traits that can be described by a dominant/recessive relationship within a single gene pair. Probably the best known of these traits is a disorder called **phenylketonuria.** Children suffering from phenylketonuria tend to be short, light in skin coloring, emotionally disturbed, and severely mentally retarded. All these symptoms have been traced to a single biochemical defect: these children are

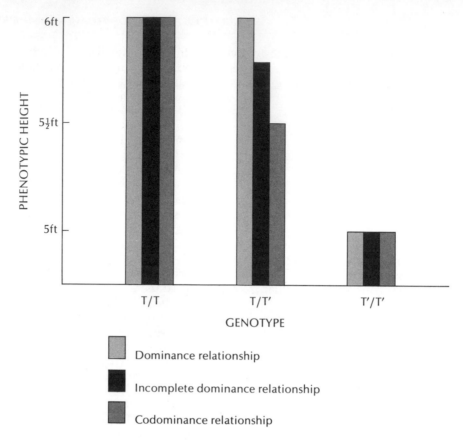

Figure 2-5. Genotypic/phenotypic relationships. The relationship between genotype and phenotype can follow any of several models: dominance, incomplete dominance, or codominance. The graph illustrates the hypothetical example of height used in the text. Note that only when a pure dominance relationship exists would the phenotypes of the homozygous and heterozygous individuals be indistinguishable. (T = 6 ft and T´= 5 ft.)

unable to metabolize the chemical phenylalanine. It is the excess of phenylalanine in the body that causes the problems in growth, coloring, and mental condition. If an excess of phenylalanine is prevented by dietary controls, the symptoms do not occur and the child develops normally. But what causes the biochemical defect in the first place? Phenylketonuria is a disorder based on the presence of one specific gene pair that operates according to the dominance model. Fortunately, the phenylketonuria gene is both rare and recessive: only those individuals who inherit phenylketonuria genes from both parents and, hence, have two recessive phenylketonuria genes will have the disease (McClearn, 1970). (See Figure 2-6.)

Incomplete Dominance Relationships

Let us next assume, in our hypothetical example of height, that some heterozygous people (T/T´) are 5 feet 10 inches tall. For these people, the tall (6-foot) gene is more powerful than the short (5-foot) gene but does not completely mask, or dominate, the short gene's effect. The phenotype, or appearance, of such persons is thus characterized by a blending of the two genes, but with

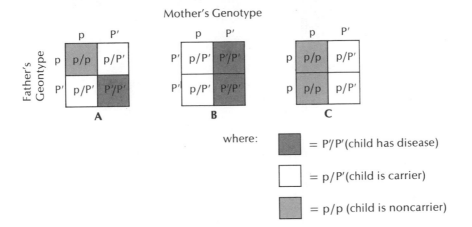

where:

= P'/P'(child has disease)

= p/P'(child is carrier)

= p/p (child is noncarrier)

Figure 2-6. Phenylketonuria: An example of the dominance model. Let's assume that Miss Smith is a carrier of phenylketonuria (p/P'). She is considering marriage but first wishes to understand the probability that she and her chosen spouse, Mr. Jones, might have children suffering from phenylketonuria. If Mr. Jones is also a carrier of phenylketonuria (see part A), then one out of four of their children will have the disease. If Mr. Jones is not a carrier and does not have the disease (see part C), Miss Smith can rest assured that none of their children will have phenylketonuria. On the other hand, should Mr. Jones have the disease (see part B), then fully half of their children will also have it, and the other half will be carriers.

one gene (the dominant gene) playing the major role. Genotypic relationships of this type are called instances of **incomplete dominance.**

Probably the best real-life example of incomplete dominance occurs in the snapdragon. In the snapdragon, homozygous plants of one type (R/R) produce red flowers; homozygous plants of another type (r/r) produce white flowers. If red and white plants are crossed, the heterozygous (R/r) plants thereby produced are all pink (Goodenough & Levine, 1974). The red (R) gene is thus dominant but does not completely mask the recessive white (r) gene. The white gene still has a limited effect, with the resulting color, or phenotype, of the plant being pink.

In humans, an example of incomplete dominance is provided by the sickle-cell trait. Homozygous persons having two sickle-cell genes (s/s) suffer from **sickle-cell anemia** and rarely live to maturity; their bodies produce sickle blood cells instead of normal ones, which causes severe medical problems. Heterozygous persons having one normal gene (S) and one sickle-cell gene (s) also exhibit the sickle-cell trait, but their anemia is not nearly so severe. The overall health of these heterozygous sickle-cell carriers is much closer to that of the normal homozygous noncarrier (S/S) than to that of a person who actually has the sickle-cell disease (s/s). The normal gene is thus incompletely dominant over the sickle-cell gene (Goodenough & Levine, 1974). (See Figure 2-7.)

Codominance Relationships

Let us lastly assume, in our hypothetical example of height, that some heterozygous people (T/T') are exactly 5 feet 6 inches tall. For these people, the tall (6-foot) gene and the short (5-foot) gene each make an equally strong con-

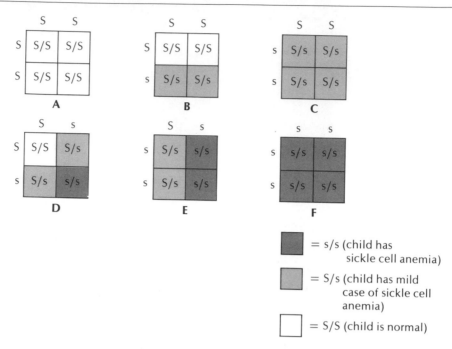

Figure 2-7. Sickle-cell anemia: An example of incomplete dominance. Sickle-cell anemia is a genetic trait that operates according to an incomplete dominance model. Thus, heterozygous individuals (S/s) suffer from a mild case of sickle-cell anemia. The graphs illustrate the frequency with which different types of parents will produce children with either sickle-cell anemia or a mild form of the disorder. It should be noted that the overall health of the heterozygous carriers is much closer to the health of homozygous noncarriers (hence the description of the trait as an example of incomplete dominance).

tribution to the individual's phenotype. Genotypic relationships of this sort, in which phenotype is characterized by an exact compromise between the two genotypes, are termed instances of **codominance.**

A good example of both dominance and codominance relationships is found in the ABO blood types of humans. Blood type is determined by different combinations of three possible genes in a single gene pair: these genes are called L^A, L^B, and 1^O.[1] Of the three genes, 1^O is the clearly recessive one; an individual cannot have O-type blood unless he or she is homozygous for that gene (1^O1^O). Both L^A and L^B are dominant over 1^O. Thus, heterozygous persons with one L^A and one 1^O gene will have A-type blood and will produce only A-antigens in their blood. Heterozygous persons with one L^B and one 1^O gene will have B-type blood and will produce only B-antigens in their blood. But what happens when an individual is heterozygous and has one of each of the two dominant genes (L^A/L^B)? This person will have AB-type blood. Both dominant genes will be fully expressed in the AB blood, and neither gene will mask the effect of the other; hence, both A-antigens and B-antigens will appear in the individual's blood (Goodenough & Levine, 1974). (See Figure 2-8.)

[1]In this genetic description, "L" is used to denote dominant genes, and "l" is used to denote recessive genes.

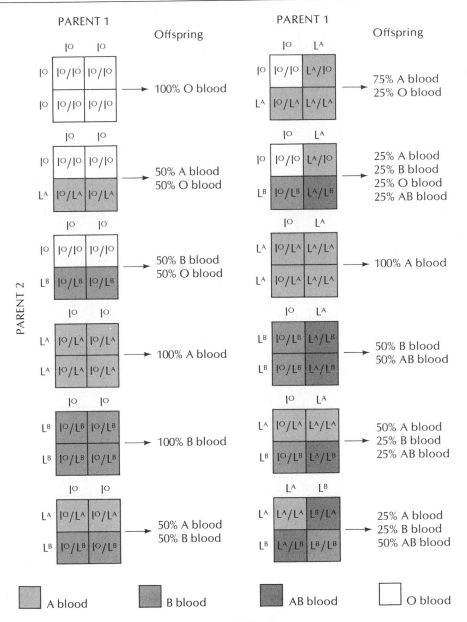

Figure 2-8. The genetic transmission of blood type.

Sex-Linked Traits

The genotypic/phenotypic relationships discussed to this point are subject to one major exception: the **sex-linked traits.** An earlier section of this chapter discussed the distinction between the sex chromosomes and the other chromosomes. The sex chromosomes are different from the others (the autosomes) because, in males, one of the sex chromosomes (the Y chromosome) is structurally shorter than the other (the X chromosome). Females, in contrast, have two long, X chromosomes. Biologists have attempted to specify more precisely just how the shorter Y chromosome found only in the male differs from the X chromosome. While their research remains in an as yet largely preliminary stage, it does indicate that the Y chromosome contains very few (if any) genes that correspond with those found on the X chromosome.

The absence from the Y chromosome of genes that will "match" those found on the X chromosome is particularly significant from a genetic standpoint. Single genes (namely, those found on the X chromosome but absent from the Y chromosome) totally determine certain traits of the male, since there are no corresponding genes on the Y chromosome to "mask" their effect. It is precisely because of this single-gene relationship that male children are more susceptible than females to certain genetically determined disorders, such as hemophilia and color blindness.

Let us take the example of red/green color blindness. Red/green color blindness is determined by a single recessive gene that appears on the X, but not on the Y, chromosome. Since the gene is recessive, color blindness can occur in women only when there are two recessive genes present. Women who are heterozygous and who, therefore, have a matching dominant gene that "masks" the effect of the color-blindness gene will have perfectly normal color vision. But what about men? For men, the Y chromosome does *not* have a gene that affects color blindness. As a result, all men who have the recessive color-blindness gene on their X chromosome will be color-blind. (See Figure 2-9.) The incidence of sex-linked traits such as color blindness is, thus, much higher in men than in women (McClearn, 1970), since a single gene determines these traits in the male while a gene pair determines them in the female.

Composite Traits

In the discussion to this point, genetic relationships have been reviewed in terms of single gene pairs. It was not always easy to come up with examples to illustrate the types of relationships discussed, for the simple reason that most human traits are not determined by a single gene pair but, rather, by the complex interactions of several gene pairs. These multiple interactions are further complicated by the fact that the different gene pairs do not all operate in the same way. Some gene pairs act by masking, modifying, or even enhancing the effects of other gene pairs. For example, human height does not fall into the neat categories we hypothesized above. Rather, it occurs along a continuum of possible heights.

When a trait such as height occurs along a continuum, with individuals falling at all possible values of the continuum, the trait is said to be a **composite trait,** meaning that many gene pairs are responsible for that trait. Good examples of such composite traits include height, intelligence, and hair color. (See Figure 2-10.) Composite traits are extremely complex, since they are determined by many gene pairs. The number of possible gene combinations that could occur in a particular child is virtually astronomical. This makes it well-nigh impossible to make accurate predictions about the composite trait that will occur in a particular child (for example, the child's height or intelligence) by simply measuring these traits in the parents. This is, of course, not to say that science will not one day be able to make such predictions. Rather, it means that the current state of the art is such that these predictions cannot accurately be made.

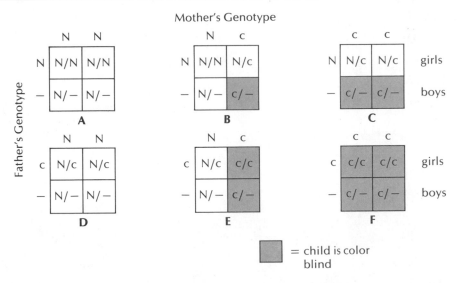

Figure 2-9. Color blindness: a sex-linked trait. Color blindness is a recessive sex-linked trait. This means that, if a boy inherits a color-blindness gene from his mother, he will be color blind, since he does not have a corresponding gene on the Y chromosome that he inherits from his father (see parts B, C, E, and F). A boy cannot, however, inherit the gene from his father, since only girls can get an X chromosome from their fathers (see parts D and E). Girls will be color-blind only when they inherit the color-blindness gene from both parents; hence, they must have fathers who are color blind as well as mothers who carry the gene (see parts E and F).

Genetic Accidents

Many of the so-called genetic diseases are caused by the normal operation of genetic principles. Examples include phenylketonuria, Tay Sachs disease, hemophilia, cystic fibrosis, and sickle-cell anemia. Each of these diseases can be traced to the presence of a particular gene (or genes) within the persons suffering from the disease. Fortunately, these genetic diseases occur with a low frequency in the population as a whole. Also, since these diseases operate according to normal genetic principles, doctors are able to predict with fair accuracy the probability that a particular couple will bear a child suffering from one of these disorders.

There are, however, other genetic disorders that do not follow normal genetic principles but that occur as a result of some form of "accident" in the formation of the gametes. These genetic accidents result in the production of either abnormal chromosomes or an abnormal number of chromosomes.

Nondisjunction

One type of genetic accident is called **nondisjunction.** In nondisjunction, both chromosomes of a given chromosome pair go to the same daughter cell during gamete formation. As a result, one of the gametes, or daughter cells, that is

Figure 2-10. Gradations in hair color. Hair color is an example of a composite trait. Each person's hair color reflects the interaction of many gene pairs. As a result, there are many possible gradations of hair color.

thereby formed has an extra chromosome, whereas the other daughter cell is missing a chromosome.

The best-known example of nondisjunction is **Down's syndrome** (also known as **mongolism),** which occurs an average of about once in every 1000 births (Greenhill, 1960). Down's-syndrome children have 47 chromosomes, rather than the usual 46 (Jacobs, Baikie, Brown, & Strong, 1959). The presence of the extra chromosome results in a whole series of aberrations in the physical appearance and intellectual functioning of these children. Down's-syndrome children have slanted eyes and a flattened forehead and suffer moderate to severe mental retardation. All of these changes can be traced to a single genetic problem: the presence of an extra chromosome.

Although nondisjunction is "accidental" and in a sense impossible to predict or explain, there do appear to be some patterns to its occurrence. For example, the probability of having a Down's-syndrome child increases dramatically in women over 35, while the age of the father appears to be irrelevant. In the United States, only 13.5% of the children born each year are born to women over 35. However, *a full 50% of the Down's-syndrome children are born to this group of women* (Valenti, 1974). The unusually high frequency of Down's-syndrome births in women over 35 suggests that the age of the mother may be the key factor in the appearance of this disorder. Many people have accordingly suggested an "old egg" hypothesis to explain this phenomenon, as stated earlier in this chapter: women, unlike men, do not continue to produce gametes after birth but are born with their full complement of eggs; thus, the older a woman is, the greater the likelihood that her "old eggs" may have been damaged by drugs, disease, radiation, or simply aging, thereby increasing the probability that her child will suffer a nondisjunctive accident such as Down's syndrome.

Other suggestions have also been put forward to explain why older women are more likely to have Down's-syndrome children. Thus, some researchers believe that, at least in some cases, there may be a specific environmental cause. For example, Heinricks, Allen, and Nelson (1963) have found that there are certain geographic areas that have unusually high incidences of Down's-syndrome births. Their data suggest that there may be an external factor, such as a virus, that exists in certain geographic areas and that predisposes certain women to nondisjunctive accidents. It is hypothesized that such a virus in itself would not cause Down's syndrome but might make a woman more susceptible to improper gamete formation during meiosis. This, in turn, would increase the probability that she would have a Down's-syndrome child.

Translocation

A genetic accident can occur not only when an entire chromosome is added or lost (as in nondisjunction) but also when pieces of a chromosome are added, lost, or transferred to an inappropriate position on some other chromosome. Genetic accidents involving pieces of chromosomes are called **translocations.** Children suffering from **cri-du-chat** are an example of translocation: they are missing one end of one member of a particular chromosome pair. This missing piece of chromosome produces children who, in addition to suffering severe mental retardation, make a cry that sounds quite similar to that of a cat.

ISSUE

Should abortion be recommended when a fetus is known to be genetically defective?

The birth of a defective child is a tragedy that every expectant parent worries about: "Will my baby be normal?" "Will my baby develop normally and be able to live a normal, healthy life?" The birth of a child who is either physically or mentally handicapped is an enduring emotional and financial tragedy for all concerned.

Many of these tragic birth defects can now be detected very early in the pregnancy through the use of a medical procedure known as amniocentesis, whereby a needle is inserted into the uterus and some amniotic fluid is removed for examination. Amniocentesis is now used by many hospitals to screen for at least 60 different genetic defects (Ausubel, Beckwith, & Janssen, 1974). If a fetus is thereby found to have one of these genetic defects, the parents are confronted with one of the most, if not the most, difficult decisions they will ever have to make: should the fetus be aborted?

Genetic Counseling

"Do you have diabetes?" "Does your husband have diabetes?" "Are there any members of your family or your husband's family who have diabetes?" Such questions are part of the first step in medical care for a pregnant woman: the completion of a medical history. The physician needs to know not only what medical problems can be expected for the woman during the course of her pregnancy but, in addition, whether or not there are any genetic disorders in the family that may affect the fetus. If the family histories of the prospective parents suggest the possibility that the fetus will suffer from a genetic defect, the physician will quite probably recommend that the parents-to-be see a genetic counselor.

The genetic counselor computes from the family history and other tests the probability that the child will be genetically defective. If the risk is greater than 1%, a recommendation is usually made that the woman have **amniocentesis** performed sometime between the 14th and 20th weeks of her pregnancy. In performing the amniocentesis, the physician inserts a long needle through the abdomen into the uterus and siphons out a few drops of the **amniotic fluid** that surrounds the fetus. As we shall see later in this chapter, the amniotic membranes are actually created from the zygote. As a result, all the cells floating in the amniotic fluid have the same chromosomal structure as the cells of the fetus. It is therefore possible to determine whether the fetus has a genetic defect by examining the chromosomal structure of the amniotic-fluid cells (Macintyre, 1972; Robinson, Puck, Droegemueller, & Goodman, 1972). At least 60 different genetic defects can now be detected through these procedures (Ausubel et al., 1974). If the fetus is found to be genetically defective, most genetic counselors will recommend that the parents consider an abortion.

The increased use during recent years of genetic counseling, amniocentesis, and abortion has produced major, and widely publicized, controversies of legal, moral, and religious scope. One commonly voiced argument has centered on the widespread use of amniocentesis and has objected that amniocentesis is, except under the most extreme circumstances, unwise, due to the risks to mother and unborn child presented by the procedure. It is argued that the placement of a foreign object into the womb always introduces the possibility of infection and that a careless placement of the needle could be fatal to the fetus. Physicians who have studied the use of amniocentesis have, however, concluded that the risks from the procedure itself are quite small and are far outweighed by its benefits (Macintyre, 1972). For example, a study by Robinson and his colleagues (1972) showed complete diagnostic accuracy. Also, of the 51 pregnancies involved in the study, there were only four miscarriages following the administration of amniocentesis, which was about the number that one would normally predict in this particular group of "high-risk" mothers. Moreover, in all four cases in which miscarriages occurred, the amniocentesis had detected a problem indicating that the fetus would not survive.

The main criticism against the use of genetic counseling is not, however, the risk involved in administering amniocentesis but, rather, the fear that abortions will be misused. Parents who are informed that their children will be defective usually opt in favor of abortion (Robinson, 1972; Restak, 1975). This raises the question of whether one can morally deny life to a fetus because of physical or mental defects. How severe must the defect be in order to warrant the use of abortion? It is one thing to perform an abortion where severe mental and physical abnormalities would otherwise result. It would be an altogether different matter to perform an abortion where, for example, the child's eye color would simply not be that desired. Many opponents of genetic counseling have therefore expressed the fear that it will be abused and that parents will choose to abort fetuses on purely whimsical grounds (Restak, 1975).

Summary of Genetics and the Impact of Environmental Factors

A child's development is largely programmed by his or her *genes*. These genes are carried by and are part of 46 *chromosomes*, of which half (23) come from each of the child's parents.

The mechanisms that underlie the functioning of the genes are extremely complex. Thus, individual *gene pairs* may operate according to one of three models: (1) *dominance relationships*, in which one gene (the dominant gene) completely masks or eliminates the effect of the other gene (the recessive gene); (2) *incomplete dominance* relationships, in which the dominant gene largely, but not completely, masks the effect of the recessive gene; and (3) *codominance relationships*, in which both genes are fully and equally expressed.

The complexity of the child's genetic program is further complicated by the fact that most human traits simply are not determined by the presence of a single gene pair but are *composite traits* determined by the complex interaction of many gene pairs. Thus, a particular gene pair may serve to enhance, modify, or mask the presence of another gene pair.

It is, however, becoming increasingly apparent that genetic factors do not, of themselves, determine the course of human development, for they do not operate in a vacuum. Rather, they interact with and are influenced by environmental factors. Genetic factors can be seen as setting the stage: they essentially set the limits on development and determine the extent to which environmental factors will have an effect. (See Figure 2-11.)

Let us take an extremely simplistic example of how this interaction between genetics and environment might occur. We'll assume that an infant is born with a genetic predisposition to be extremely tall. However, during the course of childhood, the child's environment is extremely deprived in terms of both nutrition and stimulation. This poor environment will interfere with the child's normal processes of growth, resulting in an adult who is somewhat shorter than would

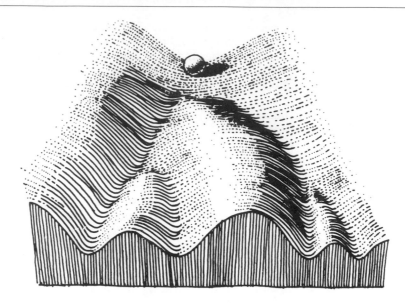

Figure 2-11. The interaction of genetics and environment. This illustration shows Waddington's "epigenetic landscape." The ball at the top can be viewed as the zygote at conception, while the hilly terrain is the child-to-be's genetic predisposition. Thus, the child's genetic predisposition sets the limits on development but does not set up a single route with a single end point. The direction the child will take at any branch in the road is determined by external environmental forces acting upon the child at critical times during development. (From "Genetic Influences on Behavior and Development," by G. E. McClearn. In P. Mussen (Ed.), *Carmichael's Manual of Child Psychology* (3rd ed.). Copyright 1970 by John Wiley & Sons, Inc. Reprinted by permission.)

have been the case had the environment been more adequate. However, this particular child will still grow to be relatively tall: the environment is thus able to alter, but unable to totally eliminate, the effects of the child's genetic predisposition.

The impact of environmental factors on development is particularly dramatic during the prenatal period. For example, even slight drug use can, depending on the drug and the timing of its use, drastically alter the normal genetic program of the affected child and result in severe physical and mental abnormalities. These and other related matters are important subjects of discussion in the material that follows.

BASIC DESCRIPTION OF PRENATAL DEVELOPMENT

The earlier sections of this chapter have been concerned with how the genetic information within the zygote produces the unique qualities of the individual—for example, hair color, height, and blood type. However, most of the genetic information within the zygote is concerned not with unique individual traits but with characteristics shared by all members of the human species. Indeed, one of the more remarkable aspects of our genetic preprogramming is not the minute ways in which one individual differs from another but the many basic similarities in development shared by all humans. By the time of an infant's birth, his or her genetic programming has managed to transform a single cell into a crying, sucking, moving, sensitive, and distinctly human infant. The nine-month period during which this remarkable transformation occurs can be broken down into three stages: the *period of the zygote,* the *period of the embryo,* and the *period of the fetus.*

The Period of the Zygote (0–2 Weeks)

The period of the zygote begins at the moment of conception, with the union of sperm and egg in the fallopian tube of the woman. The resulting zygote begins to grow as it continues its journey down the fallopian tube to the uterus. Sometime between 24 and 60 hours following conception, the first cell division occurs, and the single-celled zygote becomes two-celled. Cell division continues to occur at an extremely rapid rate, so that by the third day the zygote has become a solid ball of cells, called a **morula** (meaning "grapelike cluster").

During the fourth day after conception, a highly significant event occurs: the morula, which was previously an undifferentiated mass of cells, begins to take on form. A cavity begins to develop within the morula, making it somewhat balloon-like in appearance. Also, a small clump of cells (called the *inner cell mass*) begins to develop on one end of the cavity. The thin outer layer of cells will later form the placental connection between the embryo and the mother, while the inner cell mass will later form the embryo and the surrounding membranes. The zygote, in this new form, is now called a **blastocyst.**

On the sixth day, the blastocyst passes from the fallopian tube to the uterus, where it adheres and sinks into the uterine lining. Thus begins the process of **implantation,** which is a complex interaction between the blastocyst and the uterine lining. While the exact nature of this interaction is not yet perfectly understood, it appears that the thin outer layer of cells in the blastocyst produces small tendrils that burrow into the uterine wall. Implantation is complete by two weeks after conception and brings a close to the period of the zygote (Bodemer, 1968). (See Figure 2-12.)

The Period of the Embryo (2–8 Weeks)

The period of the embryo begins at the close of the second week of pregnancy, with the implantation of the blastocyst in the uterine wall. Once implantation is complete, the inner cell mass begins a rapid process of cell differentiation and specialization. Within the inner cell mass, three distinct layers of cells are formed during the third week. Each of these layers is destined to develop into different parts of the body. The outermost layer, or *ectoderm,* will later develop into the outer layer of skin, the hair, the nails, the teeth, and the nervous system. The middle layer, or *mesoderm,* will later develop into the inner skin layer, the muscles, the bones, the circulatory system, and the excretory organs. The innermost layer, or *endoderm,* will later develop into the lining of the gastrointestinal tract, the eustachian tubes, the trachea, the lungs, the liver, the pancreas, the salivary glands, the thyroid glands, and the thymus.

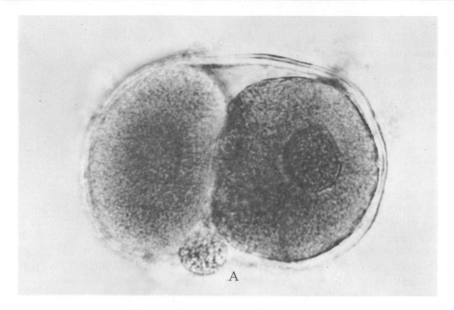

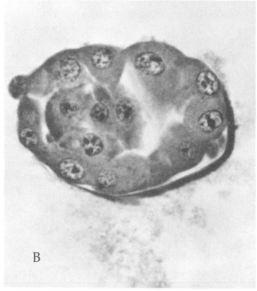
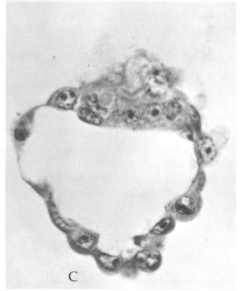

Figure 2-12. The human zygote at various stages of development. Part A shows the first division of the zygote, with the resulting two cells. Part B shows the 58-cell human morula. Part C shows the 107-cell blastocyst. (From *Modern Embryology*, by C. W. Bodemer. New York: Holt, Rinehart & Winston, 1968, p. 377. Reprinted by permission.)

At the same time, the outer layer of cells in the blastocyst also continues to differentiate. Thus, while the inner cell mass is undergoing its division into three distinct layers of cells, the outer layer of cells is transformed into a multilayered sac, to surround the developing embryo. This sac is filled with liquid (amniotic fluid) and protects the developing embryo from external bumps and changes in temperature, much as a house protects us from a sometimes hostile environment.

The fourth week following conception brings the beginning of organ development. The fetus now looks like an elongated creature with head, tail, and primitive arms and legs. A primitive heart develops and begins to beat. A primitive brain is formed. Lungs, thyroid, liver, gall bladder, and the pancreas are all present in primitive form.

The supporting structures of the embryo—namely, the **placenta** and the **umbilical cord**—also become well developed during the fourth week. The umbilical cord (often termed the "lifeline" of the embryo and fetus) serves as a tubelike link between the mother and the embryo. Through the umbilical cord, arteries and veins carry the embryo's blood back and forth between the embryo and the placenta. The placenta itself is rich in spaces in which maternal blood circulates, making it much like a sponge. The two circulatory systems of mother and embryo thus meet at the placenta. Both systems remain distinct, however, because they are always separated by cell walls. These cell walls serve as *semipermeable membranes:* the blood cells themselves cannot pass easily from one system to the other, but other substances, such as gases, salts, and nutrients, are small enough to pass through. Thus, the umbilical cord and the placenta mediate metabolic exchange between mother and embryo; the mother's blood brings nutrition and oxygen to the embryo and then carries off waste products and carbon dioxide.

The placenta additionally serves as a protective screen, filtering out substances that might be harmful to the developing embryo. Some of these substances have difficulty passing across the placental membrane because of their large molecular size and are therefore stopped at the placenta. Other substances, however, are small enough to pass through the placental barrier but, nevertheless, do not. It appears that these latter substances are filtered out by *enzymes* produced by the placenta itself. These enzymes break down some substances before they can be transmitted to the embryo. Thus, the placenta serves a dual role in the life support of the developing embryo: it mediates the metabolic exchange between mother and embryo, and it filters out some potentially harmful substances before they can get to the embryo (Bodemer, 1968).

The Period of the Fetus (8 Weeks to Birth)

Human embryonic development is complete by the eighth week, when the period of the embryo ends and that of the fetus begins. Practically all of the major structures and organs of the body have by then become differentiated, giving the developing organism a truly human form. The period of the fetus, which extends from 8 weeks to birth, is thus not characterized by further structural reorganization but, instead, by general growth and further differentiation of detail. It is also during the period of the fetus that the developing organs begin to actually function.

By 12 weeks after conception, the fetus weighs about 45 grams. This weight is approximately nine times what it was at the close of the embryonic period—only four weeks earlier. The head of the fetus appears too large in proportion to the rest of the body, but, otherwise, the general appearance of the 12-week fetus is definitely human. The face in particular has taken on a more human appearance because of lip, nose, and ear development. Lip movements can even be

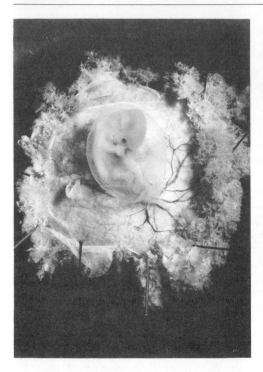 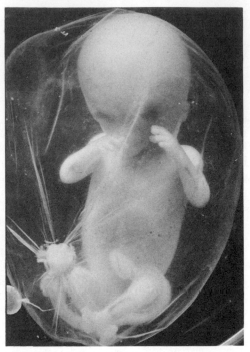

Figure 2-13.   The embryo and developing fetus. The embryo is about 48 days gestational age; the fetus is about 14 weeks gestational age and about 4 inches long. Notice that, although the fetus doesn't yet look completely "human," the appearance is already definitely humanoid.

observed in the fetus at this time, which suggests the presence of a rudimentary sucking reflex.

The fetus has also undergone extensive limb development by the 12th week. Arms and legs are much longer and slimmer than previously. There is clear differentiation of fingers and toes and even the beginnings of nails. Spontaneous movement of the arms and legs also begins to occur. In fact, rudimentary grasp and withdrawal reflexes have been observed in aborted 12-week fetuses (Bodemer, 1968).

The mother usually cannot, however, feel the fetus move until the 16th week, even though the fetus will have been capable of movement since about the 12th week. The movements of the fetus become discernible at about 16 weeks because of both increased fetal size (the fetus now weighs about 200 grams) and increased fetal activity. In addition to the increased size and mobility, the 16-week fetus shows other signs of maturity. For example, by 16 weeks most of the bones are formed and the digestive tract is well on its way to becoming mechanically and chemically functional. (See Figure 2-13 for size of the developing embryo and fetus.)

By 28 weeks, the nervous, circulatory, and respiratory systems of the fetus are mature enough to make survival outside the womb at least possible. Thus, premature infants of this very early age have been known to survive. Their bodily systems have functioned well enough outside the womb to keep them alive.

Moreover, these premature infants have even been found to be responsive to touch, olfactory, visual, and auditory stimulation.

The Effects of External Factors on Fetal Development

The preceding sections have described the normal course of human development, from a single cell to a fully functioning infant. Most of the time, development proceeds according to the schedule that we have described. Sometimes, however, the unborn child's protection against the outside world is penetrated by harmful external factors, and the normal processes of development are interfered with. Some of the more significant factors that are now known to interfere with prenatal development include drugs, disease, poor nutrition, and maternal stress.

It is probably not an exaggeration to say that *any* drug, disease, nutritional deficiency, or stress experienced by a woman during her pregnancy can have an effect on the physical development, and later behavior, of her child. However, medical research has not yet succeeded in clearly delineating just what these effects are. In part, our relative lack of knowledge in this area results from our inability to do carefully controlled research on human subjects. For example, one cannot, of course, randomly dole out potentially harmful medications to perfectly healthy pregnant women; the research subjects in human drug research therefore always consist of women who have a medical problem requiring the use of medication, thereby possibly biasing the test results. Carefully controlled research can be done with animals. However, animal research is unsatisfying, since different animals can react to the same drug in quite different ways.

Still another reason for our relative ignorance concerning the precise effects of external factors on prenatal development is the fact that these effects are not constant. Thus, the particular *type* of drug, disease, or other external factor that is being studied is obviously a key variable: different drugs, diseases, and nutritional deficiencies vary both in the type of effect they produce and in the severity of these effects. Not so obvious is the fact that the time at which the drug is taken or the disease or deficiency occurs can also affect the type and severity of the effect. The picture is still further complicated by recent findings (Joffe, 1969) that some people are, because of genetic differences, more susceptible than others to the effects of certain drugs and diseases. Thus, for example, the same drug may affect one child severely while leaving another child unaffected or affected in a different way, because of genetic differences between the children.

Drugs and Prenatal Development

It has been estimated that 92% of the pregnant women in the United States take at least one potentially harmful drug during their pregnancies; 4% take ten or more such drugs (Peckham & King, 1963). The effect that these drugs will have in a particular case can vary widely as a function of drug type, drug dosage, and the period of pregnancy during which the drug is consumed. (See Table 2-1 for adverse effects on the fetus and newborn that have been attributed to maternal drug use.) The use of drugs can, thus, be like a game of chance—but one in which the stakes consist of the health and development of a future human being.

Table 2-1.   The adverse effects on the human fetus and newborn that have been attributed to maternal drug use.

Agent	Fetal or Neonatal Effect
Antihypertensives	
thiazides	electrolyte imbalance
	thrombocytopenia (?)
reserpine	nasal stuffiness, hypothermia
nitrites	methemoglobinemia
ganglionic blockers	paralytic ileus
Central-nervous-system depressants	
chlorpromazine	sedation, retinopathy
chlordiazepoxide	neonatal depression
narcotic analgesics	neonatal depression
	"withdrawal symptoms"
local anesthetics	fetal bradycardia and acidosis,
	neonatal depression
thalidomide	skeletal anomalies
barbiturate sedatives	neonatal bleeding dyscrasia,
	increased rate of neonatal
	drug metabolism
Antibacterials	
tetracycline	abnormal dentition
streptomycin, gentamycin	deafness (8th nerve toxicity)
nitrofurantoin	hemolysis
chloramphenicol	cardiovascular collapse,
	"gray syndrome"
penicillin (high conc.)	convulsions
sulfonamides	hyperbilirubinemia
Hormones	
androgens	virilization of female
oral progestins	
estrogens	feminization of male
Miscellaneous	
thiouracil	goiter
salicylates (for example, aspirin)	neonatal hemorrhage
quinine	thrombocytopenia, deafness
coumadin anticoagulants	hemorrhage
chloroquine	retinopathy

From "Drug Distribution in Pregnancy," by B. L. Mirkin. In L. Boreus (Ed.), *Fetal Pharmacology.* Copyright 1972 by Raven Press, Publishers. Reprinted by permission.

This makes it particularly important that these effects be measured and determined, to the extent possible.

Research into drugs and prenatal development has shown that drugs can be most harmful if taken during the period of the embryo (2–8 weeks). During this period, cell specialization and organ development are accomplished. Interfering drugs can therefore have disastrous consequences by altering the normal processes of development. In contrast, drugs consumed after the period of the embryo do not cause gross malformation of body organs but may result in smaller birth weights, incomplete brain development, and unusual behavior patterns after birth.

Recent research has additionally shown that drugs can affect development even during the period of the zygote. It was, until quite recently, erroneously believed that the zygote was relatively immune to the influence of external factors such as drugs, since the zygote has not yet formed contact with the mother's tissue. However, recent drug research has found many drugs in high concentrations not only in the uterine fluid but in the free-floating blastocyst as well. Presumably, these drugs, since they are present in the blastocyst, can alter its development. In addition, it is known that certain drugs will prevent normal implantation of the blastocyst in the uterine wall, often resulting in miscarriages. These early miscarriages often go undetected, however, because the blastocyst is so small (only about the size of a pinhead). Drugs can, thus, seriously affect development not only during the later stages of development but during the initial period of the zygote as well (Lutwak-Mann, 1973; Fabro, 1973). Drug use during this early period of pregnancy can be especially dangerous, since the woman is not yet aware that she is pregnant. Thus, women frequently take drugs during this period that they would not have taken had they known of their pregnancy.

The effects of drug consumption on prenatal development can perhaps best be illustrated by means of a few examples. Let us begin, then, with one of the most dramatic examples available.

During the 1960s, many women took a new drug called **thalidomide.** Thalidomide was an over-the-counter drug used in several countries as a sleeping pill and as a nausea reducer. It was a perfect candidate for use as a drug to relieve morning sickness, and many pregnant women used it for that purpose. At about the same time that thalidomide was beginning to be widely used, a strange phenomenon occurred: there was a marked increase in the number of women who were giving birth to children with severe physical deformities. These children had severely stunted limbs, flattened noses, and extensive malformations of the auditory canal, the alimentary tract, the heart, and the circulatory system. The mothers of these children shared something uniquely in common: all had taken thalidomide during the course of their pregnancy. Still, there were many other pregnant women who had also taken the drug and whose children were apparently normal. Because of the inconsistencies in the apparent effects of the drug—and because of the number of tragedies it had apparently caused—widespread research into the effects of thalidomide was begun.

This research indicated that the time at which the drug was consumed was a critical factor in the effects it would have on the developing child. Thus, most of the malformed children were born to mothers who had consumed the drug during the period of the embryo (with the 22nd and 23rd days following conception being particularly critical). Earlier drug consumption, however, also appeared to interfere with normal development in some cases. Thalidomide given to rabbits immediately after conception frequently resulted in failure of implantation and fetal death. Of those blastocysts that did manage to complete implantation, many were already showing signs of malformation, and infant rabbits that survived to birth often showed typical thalidomide malformations of limbs and internal organs (Lutwak-Mann, 1973).

It has even been shown that thalidomide may influence prenatal development when the father takes the drug prior to intercourse. In several studies by Lutwak-Mann (1973), it was shown that, when male rabbits were given large amounts of thalidomide, their subsequent matings produced small, underweight litters, many of which failed to survive. Moreover, some of the infant rabbits produced by these matings exhibited the skeletal and internal malformations that are characteristic of thalidomide. Thus, it appears that the thalidomide consumed by the male coats his sperm and is directly transmitted into the zygote when conception occurs.

Although thalidomide has received more attention than many other drugs, there is an increasing body of evidence to suggest that *most* drugs probably can be transmitted from the mother to the unborn child via the placenta and that *most* of these drugs probably have at least some effect on fetal development. Thus, it has been shown that the nicotine consumed by smoking mothers will increase the incidence of miscarriage and may produce infants with smaller-than-average birth weights who are, as a result, more prone to medical problems (Fabro, 1973). Aspirin, a drug consumed by at least 50% of pregnant women, has been associated with excessive bleeding in the infant (Richards, 1972). Similarly, certain sex steroids, commonly used to maintain full-term pregnancies in women with histories of miscarriages or premature deliveries, have been associated with the birth of female infants whose genitals have male characteristics (Bowes, Brackbill, Conway, & Steinschnieder, 1970). Clearly, drugs can, and do, have a major impact on the normal course of fetal development. The extent of these effects varies considerably according to the stage of development. Thus, drug consumption during the embryonic stage, when there are relatively few cells and little differentiation of function, results in the most widespread damage.

Disease and Prenatal Development

A child's prenatal development can be adversely affected by a number of maternal diseases. The exact role that these diseases play is, however, clouded by the fact that pregnant women, if sick, are usually given drugs to treat their illnesses. Thus, if such a woman later has difficulties in maintaining her pregnancy, or if malformations are present in her infant, it is not always clear whether these problems are due to the drug, the original disease, or some interaction between the two. Clearly, however, some maternal diseases, of themselves, can have adverse effects on the prenatal development of a child, especially if the disease occurs during the second to eighth week of the pregnancy (the period of the embryo).

The most dramatic example of the impact that maternal disease can have on prenatal development involves the disease *rubella* (German measles). Maternal rubella contracted during the embryonic period (2–8 weeks) has been associated with heart damage, blindness, deafness, and other deformities in the infant. Thus, one study (Sheridan, 1964) found that, among the infants of mothers who had rubella during the first 16 weeks of pregnancy, 15% had major abnormalities of the heart, eye, or ear. An additional 16% had minor abnormalities. One encouraging note in the study was that, despite the high incidence of eye, ear, and heart abnormalities, there was little evidence of intellectual, emotional, or social impairment. In other words, the adverse effects seemed to be limited to physical traits.

Venereal diseases can also have marked effects on the development of an unborn child. The most common venereal disease is gonorrhea; the most serious is syphilis. Both gonorrhea and syphilis can be passed from the mother to her fetus. Infants who are infected with gonorrhea may suffer serious infections of the eye, possibly resulting in blindness. Because of the high incidence of gonorrhea in the United States, silver nitrate drops are routinely put in the eyes of all new-borns to prevent eye infections from the disease.

Maternal syphilis is a much more serious problem, frequently resulting in miscarriage, stillbirth, and syphilitic infants. The syphilitic infant may appear normal at birth, but signs begin to appear within a few weeks. Such infants often suffer damage to their bones, eyes, ears, and brain (Barnes, 1965).

Even relatively mild maternal diseases, such as the flu, are suspected of causing birth problems. For example, the Coxsackie B virus, which simply causes a normal case of flu in the mother, has been associated with severe newborn infections of the digestive system, lungs, heart, and brain. In fact, newborn infections of Coxsackie B virus often result in infant death (Barnes, 1965).

Rh Incompatibility and Prenatal Development

The Rh factor is not itself a disease. However, incompatibility between the Rh factor of a mother and her infant can result in **hemolytic disease,** an extremely severe form of anemia.

The Rh factor of the blood is one of the few human traits that is determined by a single gene pair in a dominance relationship (see the discussion of gene pairs and dominance relationships earlier in this chapter). If the infant inherits an Rh-positive gene (a dominant gene) from the father, the infant's blood type will be Rh-positive, regardless of which gene is inherited from the mother. If the mother's blood is also Rh-positive, then the Rh factors of the mother and her infant will be compatible and will not create difficulties. If, however, the Rh factor of the mother's blood is Rh-negative (a recessive gene), the mother and child will have incompatible Rh factors, and problems may develop. If, for some reason (such as injury or disease), the infant's Rh-positive blood mixes with the mother's Rh-negative blood, the mother's blood will begin to produce antibodies. These antibodies can then pass through the placenta into the fetal blood and will attack and destroy the red corpuscles in the blood of the fetus. The resulting destruction of fetal red blood cells produces hemolytic disease, a severe form of anemia.

Usually, interaction between maternal and fetal blood occurs only during birth. Hence, maternal antibodies are not produced until after the birth of the first child. Hemolytic disease, therefore, usually occurs only in later-born children. Identification of a fetus with Rh hemolytic disease is now possible through the use of amniocentesis and the analysis of the amniotic fluid. If the fetus is found to have a severe case of fetal hemolytic disease, the disease can be treated with blood transfusions, either while the infant remains in the uterus or immediately after birth.

During recent years, the incidence of Rh hemolytic disease has been greatly reduced through the use of anti-D gamma globulin. This substance, which is given to a woman within 72 hours of the termination of each pregnancy, retards the formation of maternal antibodies that might otherwise cause hemolytic disease in her later-born children. To date, this treatment appears to be completely successful in about 90% of the cases in which it is used and somewhat successful in the remaining 10% (Douglass, 1972).

Nutrition and Prenatal Development

The rapidly developing fetus is in great need of adequate nutrients, which it receives from the mother through the placenta. Contrary to popular belief, however, the fetus does not have first priority for these nutrients. Rather, the mother takes those nutrients that she needs, and the fetus receives whatever remains. The lower priority given to the fetus of course aggravates for it any nutritional problems that the mother may have. If the nutrients that the mother receives are inadequate or poor, then those actually received by her fetus will be especially poor. Thus, it comes as little surprise that malnourished mothers produce infants who have unusually low birth weights and high mortality rates (especially if malnutrition occurs during the last three months of the pregnancy). Somewhat more startling is the recent suggestion of Myron Winick (1975) that prenatal malnutrition coupled with early malnutrition after birth can result in up to a 60% permanent reduction in the number of cells in the child's brain, resulting in mental impairment. It appears that one of the most important factors in producing a healthy baby is adequate nutrition for the mother during the course of her pregnancy (Winick, 1975; Barnes, 1965).

Maternal Stress and Prenatal Development

Just as drugs, disease, and nutrition can affect a developing fetus, a mother's emotional states can have an effect on her unborn child (Joffe, 1969). These emotional states can cause biochemical changes in the mother's body that, in turn, can easily be passed on to the fetus, in the same manner that externally administered drugs pass from mother to fetus.

It has, in fact, been suggested that maternal stress during a pregnancy can complicate deliveries (Davids & DeVault, 1962), result in miscarriage (Tupper & Weil, 1962), produce newborns with feeding problems (Turner, 1956), and even increase the incidence of cleft palate (Strean & Peer, 1956). These studies do, however, have serious methodological flaws, since most rely on the mother's after-the-fact report. Many mothers may well have forgotten or distorted what actually occurred many months or years in the past. As a result, it is not yet completely clear to what extent maternal stress affects the developing human fetus (Joffe, 1969).

It is clear, however, that extreme stress can affect prenatal development in such lower organisms as the rat. Thus, in the rat, prenatal maternal stress has significant effects on the emotionality, learning ability, and behavior of the offspring. The exact nature of these changes is complexly interrelated with the timing and amount of stress as well as the genetic makeup of the animal. Thus, the effect that appears in a particular offspring may vary dramatically, depending on such complex variables as the genetic makeup of the mother and the fetus and the type, amount, and timing of the stress received (Joffe, 1969).

Summary of Prenatal Development

This section has described the growth of the human infant from conception up to the moment of birth. This growth process is divided into three stages: the *period of the zygote,* the *period of the embryo,* and the *period of the fetus.* The period of the zygote extends from conception until the *blastocyst* completes its *implantation* in the uterine wall at the end of the second week of pregnancy. The period of the embryo extends from the time that implantation is complete (second week) until organ differentiation is completed (eighth week). It is during the period of the embryo, when organ differentiation occurs, that the unborn child is most susceptible to major malformation as a result of external factors such as drugs and disease. The period of the fetus begins when organ differentiation is complete and continues until birth. This period is characterized mainly by overall growth and refinement of detail. Maternal undernutrition and stress during the period of the fetus can affect the birth size and general health of the newborn.

THE BIRTH PROCESS

The final stage of prenatal development is, of course, birth, when the infant leaves the mother's womb and continues the journey down the uterus and into the outside world. It is not yet clear just what triggers the onset of labor and birth. However, it is believed that physiological changes in the fetus affect hormone production in the mother and that these, in turn, cause labor to begin. **Labor** is the process whereby the baby is slowly pushed out of the womb as a result of muscular contractions. The stages of the birth process are illustrated in Figure 2-14.

ISSUE

Is natural childbirth really better?

There has been an increasing tendency during recent years for women to elect to deliver their babies by natural childbirth, with minimal use of medications. In fact, many women seem to feel cheated if medical complications prevent them from doing so. Under normal conditions, it probably is better for infants to be delivered with the use of as little medication to the mother as possible, which would seem to favor natural childbirth. However, there are many other situations in which medication is necessary for the well-being of mother, child, or both, making natural childbirth inadvisable.

The Use of Medications in Childbirth

The process of giving birth is both slow and painful. As a result, many mothers and their physicians have relied on a variety of drugs to either alleviate or completely eliminate this pain. In fact, it has been estimated that over 85% of women giving birth in the United States use some form of anesthetic (Bowes et al., 1970).

Both the type and the amount of this medication vary widely. Some women are given total anesthesia that renders them unconscious throughout the long process of labor and birth. Most women, however, receive some form of a "spinal"—an injection of anesthetic into the spinal cord that anesthetizes the pelvic region but leaves the mother alert and involved.

Obviously, the use of a total anesthesia has direct effects upon the infant, since such drugs are transmitted across the placenta to the infant. Thus, just as

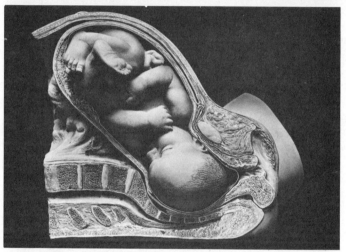

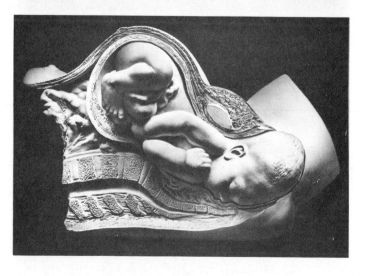

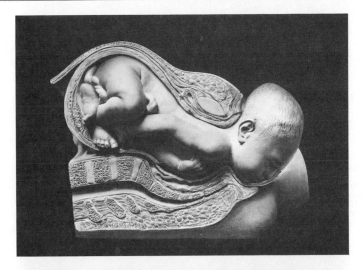

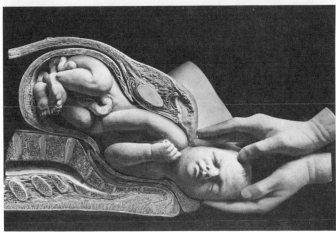

Figure 2-14. The process of birth. (From *Birth Atlas,* by permission of the Maternity Center Association of New York City.)

the mother is rendered unconscious, the infant is also extremely drowsy or even unconscious at the time of birth. The use of spinal anesthesia does not have these direct effects and is generally preferred over the use of total anesthesia (Bowes et al., 1970).

Physicians have, in recent years, tried to minimize the amount of medication used in childbirth. In part, this trend reflects our new awareness of the difficulties that can arise from the use of drugs during pregnancy and the concern that, just as a drug may adversely affect an infant during the prenatal period, it may harm the infant during the birth process as well. The trend away from medication has also occurred as a result of an increasing body of research on medication during childbirth in particular. These studies indicate that, while birth medications do not have dramatic physiological effects on a newborn, more subtle effects can be observed. Thus, mothers who receive medication during delivery tend to have longer labors, and their infants show such signs of mild clinical depression as poor sucking response, poor visual attentiveness, and less prompt and vigorous onset of breathing. These differences between the "medicated" and "nonmedicated" infants can be observed for at least the first month of life (Bowes et al., 1970).

Natural Childbirth

Awareness of the potential risks involved in the use of medication during childbirth has resulted in an increased number of women electing to deliver their children by *natural childbirth*. Natural childbirth refers to the fact that the woman receives either no anesthetic or only a local anesthetic for the final moments of birth. Most women who decide to deliver their child "naturally" will also learn exercises and breathing techniques designed to ease the difficulty and pain of birth (Lamaze, 1970; Read, 1955).

Cesarian Section

Occasionally, infants cannot be delivered in a normal manner because of medical complications. For example, the infant's head may be larger than the mother's pelvic opening, the mother's labor may be irregular or of extremely long duration, or the infant's heart may be beating irregularly. In such cases, the physician must surgically cut into the uterus through the abdomen and remove the infant. When infants are surgically removed in this manner, the procedure is called **cesarian section**—after the historical claim that Julius Caesar was born in this way. Cesarian sections do occur with high frequency in the United States. However, they are usually not used unless there is a medical complication that requires their use, due to the somewhat greater risk to both mother and child. The normal birth process plays a major role in preparing the newborn for life outside the womb by forcing liquid and mucus from the infant's lungs. The lungs of a child born by cesarian section will have far more mucus in them than will the lungs of the child born by normal delivery. As a result, babies born by cesarian section have a somewhat greater incidence of lung complications than do babies born in the normal manner and are, therefore, usually put under close observation for at least 24 hours.

OPTIMIZING THE PRENATAL ENVIRONMENT

The unborn child, although seemingly safe within the mother's womb, is vulnerable. The mother can inadvertently injure the child through disease or the use of drugs. She can also hinder the child's development by failing to provide adequate nourishment. A mother should, therefore, take care to keep herself and her unborn child as healthy as possible. She should avoid exposing herself to potentially dangerous diseases such as rubella. Similarly, she should avoid the use of any drugs, except those prescribed by her physician. Her dietary habits, too, should be of special concern. She should take care to provide adequate nutrition for herself and, hence, her child.

CHAPTER SUMMARY

This chapter has described the course of prenatal development. We have seen how life begins with a single cell, called a *zygote*. The zygote is created by the union of two *gametes* (the *egg* and the *sperm*) and contains all the genetic information that will direct the child's development. This genetic information is carried by 46 chemical strands, called *chromosomes*. The chromosomes exist in 23 pairs, with one member of each pair contributed by each parent.

The chromosomes, in turn, are made up of *genes*, each of which specifies some aspect of development. The mechanisms that underlie the functioning of the genes are extremely complex. In general, individual gene pairs can be described as operating according to one of three models: (1) *dominance relationships*, in which one gene completely masks or eliminates the effect of the other gene; (2) *incomplete dominance relationships*, in which one gene largely, but not completely, masks the effect of the other gene; and (3) *codominance relationships*, in which both genes are fully expressed.

The complexity of genetics is further increased by the fact that most human traits, such as height, are *composite traits* and are determined by the interaction of many genes. Moreover, most human traits are also influenced by environmental factors such as drugs, nutrition, disease, and stress. The impact of the environment can be most dramatic during the prenatal period, even though the child remains largely protected by the mother's womb.

Development during the prenatal period can be divided into three stages: the *period of the zygote*, the *period of the embryo*, and the *period of the fetus*. During the first two weeks of pregnancy, the *zygote* moves down the fallopian tube to the uterus, where it becomes *implanted* in the uterine wall. Once implantation is complete, the *embryo* begins to develop the different organs of the body. The embryo is susceptible to major malformation as a result of external factors such as drugs and disease. For example, "*thalidomide* babies" have severely stunted arms and legs because the drug thalidomide interfered with their normal development during the period of the embryo. Once organ development is complete, the *fetus* continues to grow in size and the different organs of the body begin to function. Poor nutrition during the period of the fetus can result in unusually small infants.

At birth, the infant is slowly pushed out of the womb by muscular contractions, called *labor*. Medication to the mother to reduce the pain of childbirth can have subtle effects on the functioning of the infant. As a result, many women are giving birth to their infants with minimal use of medication—or by *natural childbirth*.

SUGGESTED READINGS

Levine, R. P. *Genetics*, 2nd ed. New York: Holt, Rinehart & Winston, 1968. A thorough and excellent summary of modern genetics. It is written as an introductory text for genetics and should be quite readable for most undergraduates.

Bodemer, C. W. *Modern Embryology*. New York: Holt, Rinehart & Winston, 1968. A thorough and detailed textbook on embryology and prenatal development. It is very technical, however, and probably somewhat difficult for most students.

Read, G. D. *The Natural Childbirth Primer*. New York: Harper & Row, 1955. An interesting and very readable introduction to natural childbirth. It is written for women planning to make use of natural childbirth in their pregnancy.

Lamaze, F. *Painless Childbirth: The Lamaze Method.* New York: Pocket Books, 1970. Another good introduction to natural childbirth—also directed toward the expectant mother.

Boston Women's Health Book Collective. *Our Bodies; Our Selves.* New York: Simon and Schuster, 1971. A thorough and simply written introduction to human physiology and sexuality, childbirth, birth control, and abortion.

GLOSSARY

amniocentesis. A medical procedure whereby a needle is inserted into the uterus and a few drops of amniotic fluid are siphoned out. Fetal cells within the amniotic fluid can then be examined for genetic structure, fetal maturity, and so forth.

amniotic fluid. The fluid that surrounds and protects the unborn child within the womb.

autosomes. All of the chromosomes except the sex chromosomes.

blastocyst. The form of the zygote during the fourth day after conception. It is spherical in shape, with a small clump of cells at one end.

cesarian section. Removal of the infant from the mother by surgically cutting into the uterus through the abdomen.

chromosome. An elongated threadlike body that is made up of genes. In humans, there are 46 chromosomes in the nucleus of each cell.

codominance. A genotypic/phenotypic relationship in which both genes are fully and equally expressed (for example, the A B blood type).

composite trait. A trait determined by the complex interaction of several gene pairs.

cri-du-chat. A condition caused by a genetic accident (translocation) in which one end of one chromosome is missing. It results in severe mental retardation. Children suffering from cri-du-chat make a sound that is quite similar to the cry of a cat.

dominance. A genotypic/phenotypic relationship in which one gene completely masks or eliminates the effect of the other member of the pair (for example, phenylketonuria).

Down's syndrome. A disorder involving an extra chromosome and characterized by severe mental retardation and several abnormalities in physical appearance. (Also known as mongolism.)

egg. The female gamete.

gamete. A special cell (egg or sperm) that contains only half (23) the normal number of chromosomes (one member of each pair). When two gametes combine, a normal body cell is produced and a new organism is formed.

gene. Part of a chromosome. It is functionally a set of chemical instructions regarding some aspect of development.

genotype. A description of the genetic makeup of the individual.

hemolytic disease. A severe form of anemia caused by incompatibility between the Rh factors of mother and fetus.

heterozygous. Condition in which the two members of a particular gene pair are different.

homozygous. Condition in which the two members of a particular gene pair are the same.

implantation. The process whereby the blastocyst attaches itself to the uterine wall by producing tendrils that burrow into the uterine lining.

incomplete dominance. A genotypic/phenotypic relationship in which one gene partially masks the effect of the other member of the pair, thus producing a heterozygous phenotype that is similar, but not identical, to one of the homozygous phenotypes (for example, sickle-cell anemia).

labor. The process whereby the baby is slowly pushed out of the womb as a result of muscular contractions.

meiosis. A special type of cell division that produces "daughter cells" with half the normal number of chromosomes. Gametes are produced by meiosis.

mongolism. *See* Down's syndrome.

morula. The solid ball of cells that is formed on the third day after conception.

nondisjunction. A genetic accident in which both chromosomes of a given chromosome pair go to the same daughter cell during gamete formation. Down's syndrome is one example of nondisjunction.

phenotype. A description of the physical makeup or appearance of the individual.

phenylketonuria. A genetically determined disorder caused by a rare recessive gene. The disease is characterized by an excess of phenylalanine in the blood, which may result in severe mental retardation and other changes in physical appearance. Phenylketonuria can be treated successfully by dietary controls during childhood.

placenta. The site at which the fetus is attached to the mother. Since the two circulatory systems of mother and fetus meet at the placenta, it also serves as the medium for metabolic exchange.

recessive gene. A gene that is dominated or masked by another gene. Thus, in order for a recessive trait to be expressed, the individual must have two recessive genes.

sex chromosomes. The 23rd pair of chromosomes, determining the sex of the individual. The female has two complementary X chromosomes; the male has one X and one Y chromosome.

sex-linked traits. Any traits that are determined by a gene located on the sex chromosomes. Because the male is missing most of the genes on his Y chromosome, sex-linked recessive traits can be expressed in the male on the basis of the presence of a single gene and are, as a result, much more common in males than in females.

sickle-cell anemia. A genetic disorder determined by a rare recessive gene that operates according to an incomplete dominance model. In sickle-cell anemia, the individual's blood cells are shaped like a sickle, the results of which cause serious medical problems.

sperm. The male gamete.

thalidomide. A drug used during the 1960s in several countries as a sleeping pill and nausea reducer. Pregnant women who took the drug had an unusually high incidence of infants who suffered from severe physical deformities. These children had severely stunted limbs, flattened noses, and extensive malformations of the auditory canal, the alimentary tract, the heart, and the circulatory system.

translocation. A genetic accident in which a piece of a chromosome is either lost or appears in the wrong location. Cri-du-chat is an example of translocation.

umbilical cord. The "lifeline" of the embryo and fetus. It serves as a tubelike connection between embryo or fetus and placenta.

X chromosome. The longer of the two sex chromosomes. Females have two X chromosomes; males have one X chromosome (and one Y chromosome).

Y chromosome. The shorter of the two sex chromosomes. It is missing many, if not all, of the gene loci that are present on the X chromosome. Females do not have Y chromosomes; males have one Y chromosome.

zygote. The fertilized egg formed by the union of egg and sperm. It contains all the genetic information for the individual who will develop from it.

REFERENCES

Ausubel, F., Beckwith, J. & Janssen, K. The politics of genetic engineering: Who decides who's defective? *Psychology Today*, 1974, *8* (1).

Barnes, C. G. *Medical disorders in obstetric practice* (2nd ed.). Oxford, England: Blackwell Scientific Publications, 1965.

Bodemer, C. W. *Modern embryology.* New York: Holt, Rinehart & Winston, 1968.

Bowes, W. A., Jr., Brackbill, Y., Conway, E., & Steinschnieder, A. The effects of obstetrical medication on fetus and infant. *Monographs for Society for Research in Child Development*, 1970, *35*(4).

Davids, A., & DeVault, S. Maternal anxiety during pregnancy and childbirth abnormalities. *Psychosomatic Medicine*, 1962, 24, 464–470.

Douglass, C. P. Prenatal risks: An obstetrician's point of view. In S. Aladjem (Ed.), *Risks in the practice of modern obstetrics*. St. Louis: Mosby, 1972.

Fabro, S. Passage of drugs and other chemicals into the uterine fluids and preimplantation blastocyst. In L. O. Boreus (Ed.), *Fetal pharmocology*. New York: Raven Press, 1973.

Foote, C., Levy, R. J., & Sander, F. E. A. *Cases and materials on family law*. Boston: Little, Brown, 1966.

Goodenough, U., & Levine, R. P. *Genetics*. New York: Holt, Rinehart & Winston, 1974.

Greenhill, J. P. *Obstetrics* (12th ed.). Philadelphia: Saunders, 1960.

Heinricks, E. H., Allen, S. W., Jr., & Nelson, P. S. Simultaneous 18-trisomy and 21-trisomy cluster. *Lancet*, 1963, 2, 468.

Jacobs, P. A., Baikie, A. G., Brown, W. M., & Strong, J. A. The somatic chromosomes in mongolism. *Lancet*, 1959, 1, 710.

Joffe, J. M. *Prenatal determinants of behavior*. Oxford, England: Pergamon Press, 1969.

Lamaze, F. *Painless childbirth: The Lamaze method*. New York: Pocket Books, 1970.

Lutwak-Mann, C. Drugs and the blastocyst. In L. O. Boreus (Ed.), *Fetal pharmacology*. New York: Raven Press, 1973.

Macintyre, M. N. Problems and limitations of prenatal genetic evaluation. In S. Aladjem (Ed.), *Risks in the practice of modern obstetrics*. St. Louis: Mosby, 1972.

McClearn, G. E. Genetic influences on behavior and development. In P. H. Mussen (Ed.), *Carmichael's manual of child psychology* (3rd ed.). New York: Wiley, 1970.

Mirkin, B. L. Drug distribution in pregnancy. In L. O. Boreus (Ed.), *Fetal pharmacology*. New York: Raven Press, 1973.

Peckham, C. H., & King, R. W. A study of intercurrent conditions observed during pregnancy. *American Journal of Obstetrics and Gynecology*, 1963, 87, 609–624.

Read, G. D. *The natural childbirth primer*. New York: Harper & Row, 1955.

Restak, R. Genetic counseling for defective parents: The danger of knowing too much. *Psychology Today*, 1975, 9(4).

Richards, I. D. G. A retrospective enquiry into possible teratogenic effects of drugs. In M. A. Klingberg, A. Abramovici, & J. Chemke, *Drugs and fetal development*. New York: Plenum Press, 1972.

Robinson, A., Puck, M., Droegemueller, W., & Goodman, S. Intrauterine diagnosis of birth defects. In M. A. Klingberg, A. Abramovici, & J. Chemke, *Drugs and fetal development*. New York: Plenum Press, 1972.

Sheridan, M. D. Final report of a prospective study of children whose mothers had rubella in early pregnancy. *British Medical Journal*, 1964, 2, 536–539.

Strean, L. P., & Peer, L. A. Stress as an etiologic factor in the development of cleft palate. *Plastic Reconstructive Surgery*, 1956, 18, 1–18.

Tupper, C., & Weil, R. J. The problem of spontaneous abortion. IX. The treatment of habitual abortions by psychotherapy. *American Journal of Obstetrics and Gynecology*, 1962, 83, 421–424.

Turner, E. K. The syndrome in the infant resulting from maternal emotional tension during pregnancy. *Medical Journal of Australia*, 1956, 1, 221–222.

Valenti, C. Perinatal genetic studies and counseling. In S. Aladjem & A. K. Brown (Eds.), *Clinical perinatology*. St. Louis: Mosby, 1974.

Watson, J. D., & Crick, F. H. C. The structure of DNA. *Cold Spring Harbor Symposium on Quantitative Biology*, 1953, 18, 123–131.

Winick, M. Nutrition and brain development. In G. Serban (Ed.), *Nutrition and mental functions*. New York: Plenum Press, 1975.

3

Biological Development in Infancy: Growth of Body and Brain

In the preceding chapter, we described the extraordinary process of growth that occurs during the prenatal period as the infant develops from a microscopic single cell into a sensing, active, and learning infant composed of millions of cells. In the present chapter, we will be concerned with these same processes of growth but at a different stage of development: from the time of the infant's birth until 2 years of age. We will see that these first two postnatal years are no less remarkable than the prenatal period in terms of the growth that occurs. During these first two years, the infant's original birth height nearly doubles, and the birth weight more than triples. During the same period, the totally dependent infant becomes a fairly independent child, able to walk, run, climb, feed himself or herself, and solve problems with very little help from others.

It is on the biological changes in body, brain, and motor behavior that this chapter will focus. The biological and behavioral characteristics of the newborn infant will first be described. We will then turn to a discussion of how the infant's body, brain, and behavior change during these first two years, with special emphasis given to the environmental factors that can influence these normal processes of growth.

THE NEWBORN

Many of you may have never seen a newborn infant. Yet, each of you probably has a very clear mental image of what the newborn looks like. It quite possibly includes a variation of the famous "Gerber's Baby Food" baby, with perfectly smooth and soft skin, a well-shaped head, and bright eyes. Your image may also show the newborn lying on his stomach with his head up (or on his back with his legs up), smiling, and even cooing.

This image of the newborn is one that the media have shown us over and over again, on television, in magazine advertisements, and on the packaging of baby products. The media picture is, however, not a terribly accurate description of the newborn baby; it more aptly describes a baby between 2 and 6 months of age. Most newborns are relatively unattractive—at least to all but their own parents. Instead of soft, smooth skin, a newborn's skin is typically blotchy, wrinkled, and scaly. Instead of a perfectly round head, a newborn's head (unless the delivery was by cesarian section) is generally somewhat flattened and misshapen, because of the great pressure exerted on it during the long and hard process of being born. (See Figure 3-1.) The baby's head is also unusually large in proportion to the rest of the body; in fact, the head comprises nearly a quarter of the newborn's entire body length. When one compares the rest of a newborn's body to the head, the body, arms, and legs seem dwarfed and oddly shaped in comparison.

An additional shock often comes when one realizes how tiny the typical newborn is. It is not unusual for a doctor to be able to hold the newborn's entire body with one hand. Even full-sized newborns in the United States weigh on the average only about 3500 grams at birth, and they average only about 50 centimeters in length. The small size is also exaggerated by the way in which the newborn continues to keep arms and legs tucked in close to the body in the fetal position. Several months will pass before the infant will begin to completely straighten his arms and legs for extended periods of time, let alone before beginning to kick his feet high in the air or lift his head very far from the surface of the crib mattress.

Behavioral Capabilities of the Newborn

The newborn's small size and obvious motor immaturity have led many to think of him as a relatively "incompetent," passive creature who does nothing but eat, cry, and sleep, while remaining relatively oblivious to the environment. Recent research with newborns reveals, however, that nothing could be further from the truth. Rather, the newborn is really quite active and "competent," even from the moment of birth.

State

Infants do not spend all of their time sleeping, crying, and eating. True, newborn infants do sleep a great deal: an average of about 16½ hours a day (Parmelee, Wenner, & Schulz, 1964). However, newborns spend the remaining 7½ hours of wakefulness not only in eating and crying but also in actively exploring their bodies and their world.

During recent years, there has been an increasing attempt to describe more precisely what the newborn does during these periods of sleep and wakefulness. This attempt has resulted in various classifications of the infant's **state,** or level of alertness. These states range from quiet sleep to active crying and arousal. Let us look first at what we know about the more passive of these states: the infant's sleep.

Sleep.   We have known for a number of years that there are at least two distinct stages of sleep: REM (rapid eye movement) and no-REM sleep. **No-REM**

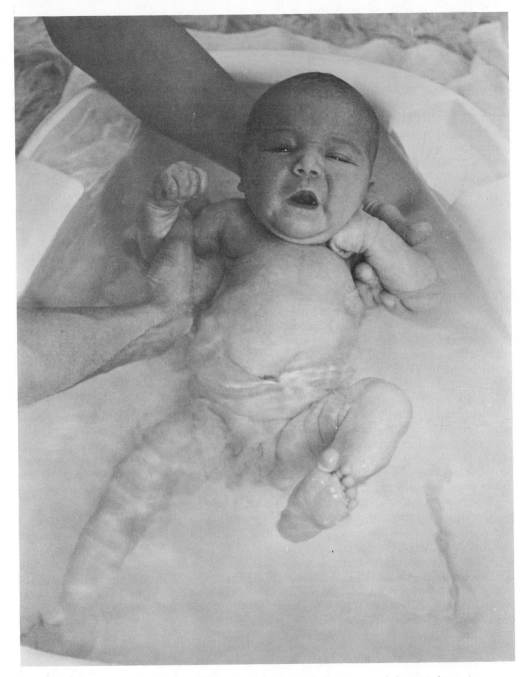

Figure 3-1. The newborn. The actual physical appearance of the newborn infant bears little similarity to the "media" image. Notice the flattened forehead and nose, the large head in relation to the rest of the body, and the way the infant keeps her arms and legs tucked in close to her body in the fetal position.

sleep is quiet sleep, characterized by regular breathing and an absence of body and eye movement. **REM sleep** is active sleep, characterized by small body movements and rapid movements of the eyes under closed eyelids.

Research has determined that REM sleep is when adults dream (Dement, 1965). Given this fact, it is somewhat surprising to learn that newborn infants exhibit both REM and no-REM sleep. It is even more surprising to find that newborns spend a much higher percentage of their total sleeping time in REM sleep (about 50%) than do adults (about 21%) (Dement, 1965; Aserinsky & Kleitman, 1955). Since REM sleep has, at least for adults, been associated with dreaming, the high percentage of REM sleep in newborns poses an intriguing mystery. What could the newborn with no experience in the world be dreaming about? Or is it possible that REM sleep serves a different function for the newborn than it does for adults?

Answers to these questions have not yet been found, although a number of speculations have been put forward. One such speculation is that REM sleep serves the purpose of providing built-in self-stimulation. As the infant grows older, the environment comes to provide increasing levels of external stimulation, and the need for self-stimulation diminishes. Hence, REM sleep comes to occupy less of the infant's total sleeping time (Schaffer, 1977).

While the notion that REM sleep serves the purpose of self-stimulation is a largely speculative one, it is not without support. Thus, research does, indeed, show that as an infant spends increasing amounts of time awake and active, there is a corresponding decline in the proportion of sleep time spent in REM sleep. Even newborns show this inverse relationship between the amount of external stimulation they receive and the amount of REM sleep they exhibit (Emde, Harmon, Metcalf, Koenig, & Wagonfeld, 1971).

Wakefulness.   REM versus no-REM sleep has provided an easy way to assess the newborn's sleep behavior—even though we are not yet completely sure what this assessment means. Classification of the infant's waking state into distinct categories has, however, proved to be more difficult. Indeed, there has been much debate over how many types or states of wakefulness there are, let alone how they should be identified. In part, the difficulty in classifying states of wakefulness stems from the fact that there really is a continuum of wakefulness, with no clear divisions between different states or types. In a sense, then, the psychologist attempting to define different states of wakefulness must more or less arbitrarily draw lines along this continuum and thereby divide it into a small number of categories or states.

Perhaps the most commonly used of these classification systems is that of Prechtl and Beintema (1964, as cited in Schaffer, 1977). This system specifies three states or levels of wakefulness in the newborn: *alert inactivity, alert activity,* and *crying.* When in a state of *alert inactivity,* the infant is fully awake but quiet and not fussing or crying. His body is relatively still and only small movements occur. An infant in a state of *alert activity* is fully awake and actively moving around but is not crying. When in a state of *crying,* the infant is—as the name implies—crying, awake, and actively thrashing about.

Why, you may well wonder, do psychologists such as Prechtl and Beintema bother with labels such as "alert inactivity," "alert activity," and "crying"? Is this simply some form of high-class semantic game? The answer is that these exercises are not a mere game; they do, indeed, have real relevance to our understanding of psychological processes in the newborn. Thus, it is now known that the newborn's behavior and responsiveness to the environment seem to be largely determined by the state he happens to be in at a given time. For example, as early as

1934, Pratt found that an infant's responsiveness to sound was determined more by his state (whether awake or asleep, wet or dry) than it was by any qualities of the sound itself, such as loudness or pitch (as cited in Kessen, Haith, & Salapatek, 1970).

More recent research has verified and expanded Pratt's early findings. Peter Wolff (1965), for example, has found that newborn infants are responsive to sound and visual stimuli *only* when they are in a state of alert inactivity. The lack of responsiveness of newborns to visual and auditory events during states of alert activity and crying suggests that the infants may simply be unable to attend to both external events and their own bodily movements at the same time. In other words, it may be that their bodily activities somehow shut out external visual and auditory events, rendering them unresponsive to the stimuli. After a few weeks, young infants will begin to attend to external events during periods of alert activity as well as during those of alert inactivity. However, infants will only do so when these external events are very simple and familiar. These slightly older infants continue to attend to complex, unfamiliar events only when they are motorically inactive. Thus, even for these somewhat older infants, it is during periods of alert inactivity that they are most actively involved in learning about their world.

We have described the newborn and the very young infant as most responsive to external events such as sights and sounds during periods of alert inactivity. There are, however, certain relationships between external stimuli and behavior that do not appear to be affected by the infant's state in this manner. In fact, in some cases, certain responses are even *stronger* during the unlikely state of deep no-REM sleep than during any of the states of wakefulness. The special class of responses to which we refer are the *reflexes* (Prechtl, 1969), discussed in the following section of this chapter (see Table 3-1). Why many of the reflexes show heightened responsiveness during no-REM sleep is a puzzle for which there are, as yet, no known answers.

Reflex Behavior of the Newborn

Reflex behavior of the newborn is a fascinating subject in its own right, quite apart from its relation to the infant's state. Reflex behavior is, after all, one of the few aspects of newborn behavior that is clearly, obviously, and predictably influenced by external events. In addition, reflexes are *innate* (that is, present from birth), and, hence, intimately connected to the basic physiological functioning of the brain. Finally, some of these reflexes (the newborn reflexes) change as the infant matures, thereby telling us much about the physiological changes that occur as the brain develops. For these and other reasons, reflexes have received considerable attention.

A **reflex** is an innate, unlearned connection between an external event (or stimulus) and a particular behavior (or response) that is triggered automatically by that stimulus. A reflex requires neither "thinking" nor "learning." For example, we are all familiar with the knee-jerk reflex that occurs when a physician taps us on the knee with a rubber mallet. The tapping of the mallet is the stimulus, while the automatic jerk of the lower leg is the reflex response. No thinking or learning is involved in producing this response; it automatically follows from the application of the stimulus.

Table 3-1. The effect of state on the intensity of responses to sensory stimulation in different modalities.

This chart shows how a few common reflexes and visual and auditory orienting are affected by the infant's state. Note that the infant's responsiveness to auditory and visual stimuli is greatest during periods of alert inactivity, while responsiveness to certain reflexes (for example, knee jerk) is greatest during No-REM sleep.

	No-REM Sleep	REM Sleep	Alert Inactivity
Proprioceptive reflexes			
ankle clonus	+++	±	±
knee jerk	+++	±	++
biceps jerk	+++	±	++
lip jerk	+++	±	++
Moro	++	±	++
Tactile reflexes			
rooting	−	−	++
Darwinian	−	++	++
toe reflex	−	++	+++
finger reflex	−	+	++
Nociceptive			
Babinski	++	+++	+++
thigh reflex	++	++	++
abdominal reflex	++	+++	+++
Auditory response			
auditory orienting	±	++	+++
Visual response			
visual orienting	−	−	+++

+++ very strong response; − absent response
Adapted from "Brain and Behavioral Mechanisms in the Human Newborn Infant," by H.F.R. Prechtl. In R. J. Robinson (Ed.), *Brain and Early Behavior.* Copyright 1969 by Academic Press, Inc. Reprinted by permission of the Developmental Science Trust, London.

Reflexes are present from birth in the normal newborn. These reflexes fall into two broad categories: the *permanent reflexes* and the *newborn reflexes.* The permanent reflexes are those that remain with us throughout life, while the newborn reflexes are those that disappear as the infant grows older.

Permanent Reflexes

Most of us have had some experience with our permanent reflexes, since physicians commonly test those reflexes during a medical examination. The first is the already mentioned knee-jerk reflex, known as the **patellar tendon reflex,** which consists of a kick of the lower leg in response to a tap on the knee. Another permanent reflex is the **Achilles reflex,** which is characterized by a contraction of the Achilles tendon of the foot in response to a tap on the heel. Other permanent reflexes include the **pupillary reflexes,** which cause the pupil of the eye to dilate or constrict in response to weak or strong lights. These permanent reflexes are present and observable in the newborn infant and remain through life.

Newborn Reflexes

The newborn reflexes, like the permanent reflexes, are present at birth. Unlike the permanent reflexes, however, the newborn reflexes disappear as the infant matures. They are therefore of greater interest from a purely developmental point of view, for, as we shall see later, the initial presence and the eventual disappearance of these newborn reflexes reveal that major changes are occurring in the organization of the brain. Some examples of the newborn reflexes include the **rooting reflex,** the **sucking reflex,** the **Darwinian reflex,** the **Babinski reflex,** and the **Moro reflex.**

The **rooting reflex** occurs when an infant's cheek is touched. He thereupon turns his head toward the object that touched his cheek, with his mouth wide open. This particular behavior is called "rooting." Once the object touches his lips, the **sucking reflex** is activated, and the infant automatically begins to suck. The rooting and sucking reflexes weaken with time, and usually disappear completely by about the sixth month of age.

The **Darwinian reflex** is also known as the **grasp reflex.** It occurs when an object touches an infant's palm and causes the infant to automatically grasp the object. (See Figure 3-2.) At birth, the Darwinian reflex is so strong that it is possible for infants to completely support their full body weight when clinging to the parent's fingers and being lifted upward. The Darwinian reflex normally disappears by about 3 months of age.

In the **Babinski reflex,** an infant fans and extends his toes outward in response to a slight tickle or stroke on the sole of the foot. The Babinski reflex is gone by about 6 months of age.

The **Moro reflex,** or "embrace reflex," is produced when an infant is surprised (for example, by a loud noise) or is held in such a way as to create a sensation of falling. In the Moro reflex, the infant throws his arms outward and then brings them together at the center of his body, as though trying to put his arms around an invisible object. (See Figure 3-3.) The Moro reflex, like the other newborn reflexes, disappears as the infant matures; it is generally completely gone by the time the infant is approximately 6 or 7 months of age (Bijou & Baer, 1965).

Summary of the Newborn Period

Noteworthy physical characteristics of the newborn include a large head (nearly a quarter of the entire body length), a somewhat flattened forehead and nose, uncoordinated eyes, relatively short arms and legs, and small size. The infant's small size is further exaggerated by the way the arms and legs are tucked against the body in the fetal position.

Noteworthy behavioral characteristics are found not only during the newborn's *states* of wakefulness, but even during the states of sleep. The newborn spends a far greater proportion of total sleep time in *REM* (as opposed to *no-REM*) sleep than does the adult, which suggests that REM sleep in the newborn may be more than a time of dreaming; it may instead be a time of needed self-stimulation. Even the newborn's no-REM sleep reveals fascinating behavioral

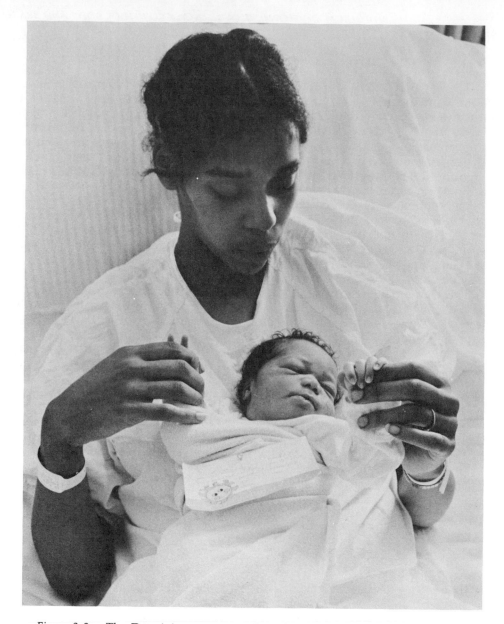

Figure 3-2. The Darwinian or grasp reflex. One of the most interesting of the newborn reflexes is the Darwinian, or grasp, reflex. The infant will grasp any object placed in the palm. This reflex is so strong that an infant can support his own weight while grasping a rope or the fingers of an adult. The picture above shows a newborn infant exhibiting this reflex. The Darwinian reflex is present from birth but disappears by about 3 months of age.

phenomena, for it is during this state of sleep that the newborn is most responsive to many *reflexes*.

Reflexes are innate, unlearned connections between stimulus and response. Several such reflexes are present in the newborn from birth. Some of these, such as the *Achilles reflex*, are *permanent reflexes* that will persist throughout life.

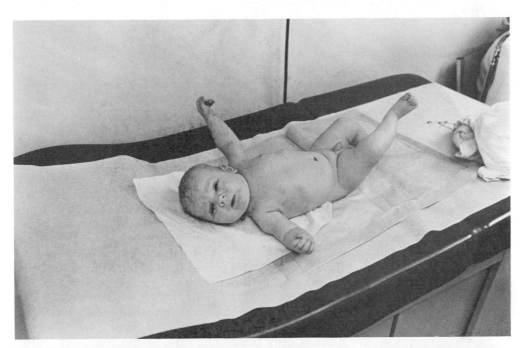

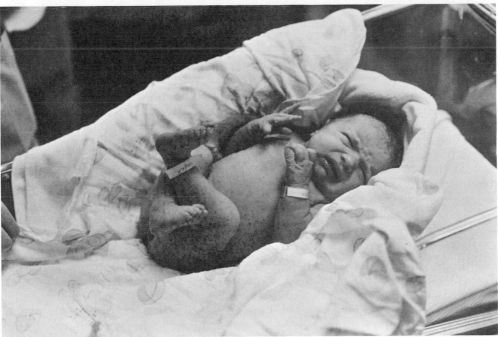

Figure 3-3. The Moro reflex. The Moro reflex is still another of the newborn reflexes. When the infant is startled or has the sensation of falling, he will exhibit the Moro reflex. Notice how the infant throws his arms outward and then brings them together at the center of his body, as though embracing or grasping something for support. The Moro reflex disappears by about the sixth or seventh month of age.

Other, such as the *Darwinian, Babinski, Moro, rooting,* and *sucking reflexes,* are *new-born reflexes* that will disappear as the infant matures.

GROWTH OF THE BODY DURING INFANCY

Babies grow at an extremely rapid rate during their first 2 postnatal years. For example, babies born in the United States grow presently, on the average, to 75 centimeters and almost 10,000 grams during their first year, and to 85 centimeters and almost 13,000 grams during their second year. This growth represents an average height gain during the first year of about 25 centimeters and during the second year of about 10 centimeters. After these first 2 years of extremely rapid growth, the growth process slows to approximately 5 to 10 centimeters per year, until puberty (Tanner, 1970). (See Figure 3-4.)

As the body grows, it does not do so uniformly. Rather, different parts of the body grow at different rates. This results in often dramatic changes in the overall body proportions of the child. The head of the child, which is about one-quarter of the total body length at birth, grows more slowly than do the trunk, arms, and legs. The rest of the body therefore seemingly catches up with the head, so that by two years of age, the head is only about one-fifth of the full body. While overall body proportions are still most definitely not those of an adult, they are certainly much more adultlike than were those of the newborn. (See Figure 3-5.)

Factors That Affect Body Growth

Why are some of us tall, while others are short and still others something in between? This is a question most of us have surely asked ourselves. As we saw in the last chapter, the best predictor of a child's height is the height of the parents, since height is largely determined by genetic factors. However, body growth is also influenced by such other variables as nutrition, health, and stimulation. Let us look first at the genetic factors that influence growth and, in particular, at the role of the endocrine glands. With this as background, we shall then turn to some of the other factors that affect growth.

The Role of Genetics in Body Growth

Body growth and adult height are largely determined by complex genetic factors. (See Chapter 2 for a discussion of genetics.) Studies indicate that body growth is a *composite trait,* determined by a combination of many genes rather than by a single gene pair. Some of these genes are active at birth. Others may be active only during certain periods of development. Still other genes may exist that simply determine how susceptible our growth will be to external environmental factors such as health, nutrition, and stimulation. Thus, for example, two very short parents may produce a baby with an exceptionally long birth height and prematurely conclude that somehow the child has acquired "tall genes." Much to their later surprise, they may well find that the child, like themselves, is short as an adult. This need not mean that something went wrong. It probably means simply that the pertinent genes for determining adult height did not become active until later in the child's development.

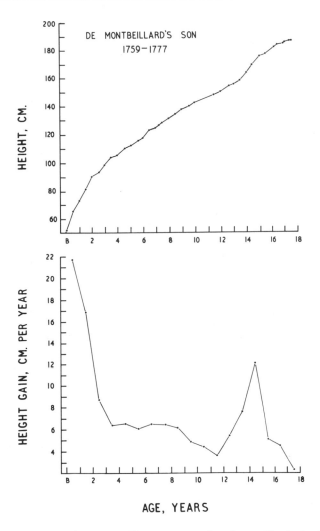

Figure 3-4. The growth curve. The two graphs above illustrate the rate at which one particular child grew in height. The top graph shows his actual height as a function of age. The bottom graph shows the amount of height gain each year. Growth rate is greatest during infancy, declines to a relatively low level of about 6 centimeters per year from ages 2–11, and then shows a spurt of rapid growth during adolescence. (From *Growth at Adolescence,* by J. M. Tanner. Copyright 1962 by Blackwell Scientific Publications, Ltd. Reprinted by permission.)

The Translation of Genetic Factors into Endocrine Factors Controlling Growth

The influence of the genes on the child's body growth largely results from their translation into endocrine production. Thus, the genes instruct the various endocrine glands about what hormones to produce, when, and in what amounts. These hormones in turn directly regulate the processes involved in body growth.

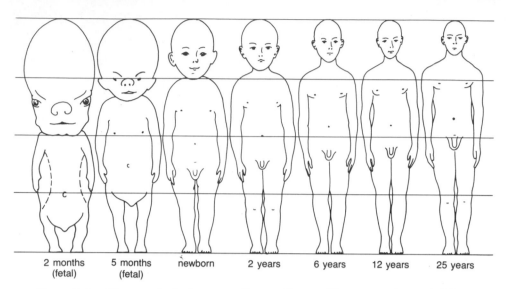

Figure 3-5. Changes in body proportions with age. The proportions of different parts of the body change dramatically with age. The legs get larger and the head smaller in relation to the body as a whole. (From *Growth*, by W. J. Robbins et al. Copyright 1929 by Yale University Press. Reprinted by permission.)

The hormones that appear to be most important in this growth regulation process include thyroxine (from the thyroid gland), cortisol and adrenal androgens (from the cortex of the adrenal gland), testosterone (from the testes), estrogens (from the ovaries), insulin (from the islets of Langerhans in the pancreas), and growth hormone (from the pituitary gland).

In these processes of hormone production, the pituitary gland takes on special importance. It appears that the **pituitary gland** produces a special set of **activating hormones** that in turn stimulate the production of other hormones. For example, thyroxine (from the thyroid) is produced in response to the production of a thyroid-stimulating hormone by the pituitary.

The production of activating hormones by the pituitary is in turn regulated by the presence of other substances, called **releaser substances,** produced by the brain. These releaser substances are triggered by certain *sensors* that monitor the level of different hormones in the blood. This produces a complex feedback chain that controls the growth process: sensor → releaser substance (brain) → activating hormone (pituitary) → hormone (endocrine glands) → change in sensor → , and so on. For example, assume that the sensor has detected a low level of thyroxine in the blood. A releaser substance would be released to trigger the production of thyroid-stimulating hormone by the pituitary. This increased production of thyroid-stimulating hormone would in turn trigger increased levels of thyroxine production by the thyroid gland, thereby bringing the process full circle back to the stage where the sensors measure the amount of thyroxine present in the blood.

Generally speaking, the complex feedback loop just described is ultimately regulated by the child's genetic factors. However, as we shall see in the following sections of this chapter, external factors such as disease, malnutrition, and inadequate stimulation can interfere with the process, thereby interfering with normal body growth (Tanner, 1970).

The Effect of Nutrition on Body Growth

It should come as no surprise that poor nutrition—**malnutrition**—can delay body growth. If the nutritional problem is a temporary one, body growth will simply be delayed; if the child eventually receives proper nutritional care, he or she will temporarily grow faster and catch up with those children who received proper nutrition all along. When, however, severe malnutrition is prolonged, the child will not be able to make this recovery and will continue to grow slowly, and will, as a consequence, be a shorter adult than would have been the case had he or she received a proper diet as a child. Clear evidence of the impact of prolonged malnutrition on body growth can be seen in the drop that occurred in the average heights of schoolchildren in Stuttgart, Germany, during the First and Second World Wars (see Figure 3-6).

The Effect of Health on Body Growth

Minor short-term illnesses have a negligible, if any, effect on body growth. Major diseases that keep a child in bed for several months may cause a slowing of growth, but even these effects are generally only temporary, for, as was the case with short-term nutritional problems, children typically catch up with lost growth after recovery from even a major disease, provided that the disease was only temporary. When, however, the disease is of a relatively permanent or frequently recurring type, it may have a lasting adverse effect upon body growth. This stunting of body growth will likely be further complicated by the fact that major diseases and malnutrition tend to be associated with one another; that is, children who suffer from major diseases or frequently recurring diseases tend also to suffer from nutritional problems, due to bad environmental conditions, the adverse effects of illness on eating habits, or both. For example, children who suffer from continuous colds and other infections tend to be smaller than average. Closer examination of these children reveals that they also tend to live in poor families where proper nutrition and cleanliness are lacking. Thus, it is not clear whether the smaller-than-average size of these children is due to their poor health, the nutritional and environmental problems that they face, or a combination of all of these factors (Miller, Court, Walton, & Knox, 1960; Tanner, 1970).

The Effect of Stimulation on Body Growth

The amount of physical and psychological stimulation that an infant receives, within normal bounds, probably bears little relationship to either growth rate or eventual adult height. In extreme situations, however, it appears that the amount of stimulation that an infant receives may indeed affect body growth. It is known that an extreme deprivation of stimulation clearly can retard growth, and there is some evidence that extreme stress (a form of stimulation) can actually enhance body growth.

ISSUE
___

Is it true that lack of adequate stimulation can result in dwarfism?

During the last 10 years, psychologists and physicians have become increasingly aware of a puzzling phenomenon. There are children who are dwarfed—that is, who have abnormal shortening of the

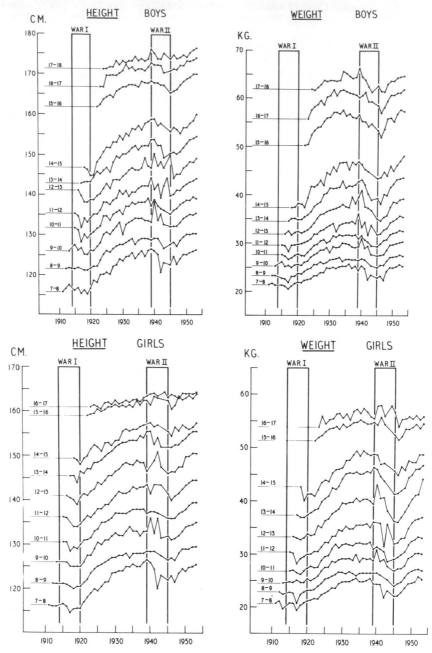

Figure 3-6. The effect of malnutrition on body growth. The above graphs show the average heights of Stuttgart schoolchildren of different ages during the years 1911 to 1953. Notice how the overall trend is for steadily increasing height over the years. This historical trend was, however, reversed during the war years. During the war years, average height actually declined for all age groups. Tanner has suggested that this decline in growth during the war years can be traced directly to the prevalent malnutrition in Germany during these years. (From *Growth at Adolescence,* by J. M. Tanner. Copyright 1962 by Blackwell Scientific Publications, Ltd. Reprinted by permission.)

arms and legs—for no apparent reason. Genetic and hormonal analyses reveal no medical cause for the disorder, and the children appear to have neither health nor nutritional problems. Yet, these children fail to grow normally. The only respect in which these particular children differ from others is in the amount of stimulation provided by their environments. It is generally believed that it is precisely this lack of stimulation that has produced the dwarfed condition. These children are, accordingly, said to suffer from **deprivation dwarfism.**

An extreme deprivation of stimulation may actually retard body growth. This phenomenon, termed *deprivation dwarfism*, has been observed in several clinical cases. Powell and his associates (Powell, Brasel, & Blizzard, 1967; and Powell, Brasel, Raiti, & Blizzard, 1967), for example, documented several such cases involving children raised in very disorganized homes, where the children received little attention. The children were found to be unusually short, despite the absence of any medical, nutritional, or genetic explanation for their dwarfed condition. When, however, the children were removed to stable environments with normal amounts of stimulation, their growth showed a marked improvement, without the need of any form of treatment other than love and adequate stimulation.

A dramatic example of the effects of an inadequate environment on body growth is found in an experiment by Widdowson (1951). Widdowson had originally planned to monitor the growth of two groups of orphans for 6 months and then give one of the groups (Group 1) an improved diet while leaving the other group (Group 2) on standard orphanage fare. She predicted that the growth of Group 1 would pick up, thanks to the change in diet. What she found, however, was that the children in the first group unexpectedly grew at a faster rate during the initial 6 months of observation. These same Group-1 children *actually gained less weight* than did the other group after they were placed on the improved diet. The most plausible explanation of Widdowson's unexpected results followed from the fact that, at precisely the time when the new experimental diet was begun (that is, 6 months into the program), one of the caretakers from Group 2 (the control group) was moved to Group 1 (the added nutrition group). This particular caretaker was extremely strict and nonsupportive. The lack of love, encouragement, and general stimulation that these children now faced, coupled with the presence of frequent emotional distress, apparently interfered with their normal processes of body growth.

Two cross-cultural studies involving worldwide samples have attempted to examine the other side of the same coin—namely, the effects on adult body size of extreme stress during infancy (Gunders & Whiting, 1968; Landauer & Whiting, 1964). Societies in different parts of the world were studied and compared. In some of the harsher societies that were observed, infants were subjected to extreme instances of stress by their parents and others; they were separated from their mothers, tattooed, scarred, and bathed daily in scalding water. The average height of adult males in these extremely stressful environments was found to be about 5 centimeters more than that of males reared in the "control" societies—comparable societies in terms of race, climate, and nutrition where infants were not exposed to such unusual stresses.

More scientifically based evidence on the effects of stimulation on the physical growth of animals comes from an experiment by Seymour Levine (1960) involving rats. Some of the rats in his experiment were left undisturbed during the first 3 weeks following birth; others were handled roughly; others were given electrical shocks. Both the handled rats and the rats subjected to extreme stress (the shocks) showed more rapid rates of development and grew to be heavier, healthier adults than the nonmanipulated rats. Again, it appeared that extreme stress had enhanced body growth.

Admittedly, the studies on the relationship between stress and body growth discussed above are open to criticism. One can't help but wonder whether perhaps another explanation was at work in the two cross-cultural studies; perhaps over time only the strongest survived, with the smaller and weaker members of the harsh societies gradually being eliminated from the genetic pool. An alternative explanation can similarly be given for the seemingly enhanced growth of the rats subjected to stress: the "stressful" environment may simply have been more like the normal habitat of a rat, with the "nonmanipulated" environment actually being a case of stimulation deprivation. The stress and enrichment studies mentioned are, thus, less than conclusive, as are other studies involving this phenomenon.

Significance of Body Growth to the Psychologist

In the preceding material, we have seen that body growth may be affected by several factors, including genetics, endocrinology, nutrition, health, and stimulation. We have seen, too, that these factors can and do interact with one another. The relationship between these factors and body growth is of special interest to the psychologist, since these same factors affect that portion of the body that is of most importance to the psychologist—namely, the brain. For example, a child who suffers retarded growth because of malnutrition, bad health, or deficient stimulation may show additional retardation in intellectual and motor skills. Hence, brain growth and the factors that influence it are of crucial concern to the psychologist.

GROWTH OF THE BRAIN DURING INFANCY

The brain grows far more rapidly than any other organ of the body. At birth, a newborn's brain is already roughly 25% of its full adult weight. By about 1 year of age, it has doubled in size. And by 2½ years of age, the infant's brain is approximately 75% of its full adult weight (Tanner, 1970).

The brain's rapid growth does not follow a single pattern of biological development. Rather, it involves two quite different growth processes. The first form of brain growth involves the rapid division of brain cells, resulting in the actual creation of new brain cells. This growth of brain cells occurs primarily during the prenatal period, but may continue for as long as the first 6 months after birth (Winick, Rosso, & Waterlow, 1970; Kaplan, 1972). By 6 months of age, if not earlier, this cell division is complete, and *no further cells will ever be created.* The second process of brain growth consists largely of the addition of fats and proteins to the existing nerve fibers in the brain (a process known as **myelination**), thereby increasing the size of both the individual cells and the brain as a whole (Winick, 1975 a, b; Kaplan, 1972; Winick et al., 1970).

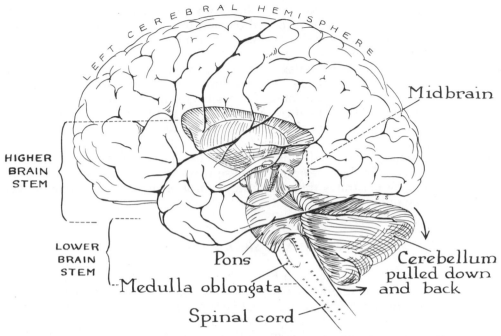

Figure 3-7. The human brain. (From Wilder Penfield and Lamar Roberts, *Speech and Brain-Mechanisms* (Copyright © 1959 by Princeton University Press): Figure II-1, p. 15. Reprinted by permission of Princeton University Press.)

A further characteristic of the brain's growth during infancy is that it is not uniform throughout all parts of the brain. (Figure 3-7, an illustration of the left cerebral hemisphere, diagrams the various parts of the adult human brain.) Different portions of the brain start out at different levels of development and grow at different rates. For example, the **brain stem** is the part of the brain involved in regulating such vital functions as respiration and digestion; at birth, the brain stem is highly developed and already largely responsible for directing the newborn's behavior. In contrast, the infant's **cerebral cortex** (that part of the brain most involved in higher intellectual activities) is less developed at birth, and, hence, less involved in regulating the newborn's behavior.

As the brain matures, different parts of the brain gain increasing control of the infant's behavior, resulting in dramatic changes in behavior. Clear illustrations of these transitions are provided by the disappearance of the newborn reflexes, a major reduction of the proportion of sleep time spent in REM sleep, and changes in the electrochemical activity of the brain.

Disappearance of the Newborn Reflexes

The newborn reflexes have usually disappeared from the infant's behavior by between 3 and 6 months of age. The disappearance of these newborn reflexes occurs as a result of the increasing development of and control by the cerebral cortex and other higher brain centers. Let us consider this interpretation by examining one newborn reflex in particular, the Moro reflex. The Moro reflex is produced whenever a newborn is surprised or held in such a way as to create the sensation of falling. Like other basic reflexes and biological functions, the Moro reflex is regulated by the brain stem. Since the brain stem is already quite well developed at birth, the Moro reflex is present immediately. As the infant grows older, the Moro reflex disappears. The reason for its disappearance is that the cerebral cortex and other higher brain centers begin to take greater control over the infant's behavior. Thus, the increasing activities and functions of the cerebral cortex and other higher brain centers tend in many cases to mask the activity of the brain stem. As a result, between 2 and 6 months of age the Moro reflex becomes increasingly inhibited, until it finally disappears, along with the other newborn reflexes. The disappearance of these newborn reflexes during the early months of infancy illustrates the increasing control of higher brain centers over the infant's behavior.

Changes in Sleep Patterns

At about the same time (3 to 6 months of age) that the newborn reflexes begin to disappear, the infant's sleep patterns also undergo marked changes. As you will recall, the newborn spends about 50% of total sleep time in REM sleep. By 3 months of age, however, the proportion has changed significantly, and the infant now spends almost twice as much time in no-REM sleep as in REM sleep (Schaffer, 1977). As mentioned earlier, it has been hypothesized that this decrease in REM sleep is due to the declining need for self-stimulation as externally provided stimulation increases. Assuming that this explanation is correct, it is quite possible that maturation of higher brain centers such as the cerebral cortex plays a major role in this process. These higher brain centers are responsible for processing external stimulation. Thus, it may well be that as these higher brain centers develop, they make it possible for the infant to "tune in" to the external stimulation, thereby displacing the self-stimulation of early REM sleep. This possible relationship among REM sleep, stimulation, and brain maturation remains, however, only speculative.

Changes in Brain Activity

The behavioral changes that we have just described (disappearance of the newborn reflexes and changes in sleep patterns) are commonly taken as indirect indicators of how the brain itself has changed and matured—a sort of maturational scale by inference from external, observable phenomena. Many psychologists, however, would like to find a more direct index of brain maturation. The electroencephalograph has been used with some success for this purpose.

The **electroencephalograph (EEG)** is a machine that amplifies the electrochemical activity of the brain and records this activity by means of electrodes placed on the infant's scalp. Research on brain maturation during infancy using the EEG has uncovered marked changes in the brain's electrochemical activity indicative of rapid and complex developmental changes in brain functioning. Dramatic shifts in EEG activity occur around the third or fourth month. Moreover, these EEG changes correspond to the time when the newborn reflexes disappear, the infant shows a marked decrease in time spent in REM sleep, and the cerebral cortex and other higher brain centers are assumed to gain control (Eichorn, 1970).

Factors Affecting Brain Development

Like growth in the rest of the body, brain growth is regulated primarily by genetic influences. However, the brain is sensitive to the same environmental influences that affect the body as a whole. Poor nutrition, disease, and inadequate stimulation can both impede the rate at which the brain develops and cause abnormalities in its development. If environmental influences are positive, the brain will develop normally. If, however, they are negative, then the result may well be abnormal brain development.

The Effects of Health and Nutrition on Brain Development

Environmental conditions conducive to poor nutrition and poor health can have a serious impact on the brain. Anoxia, meningitis, encephalitis, convulsions, and severe anemia, to name a few, have all been identified as illnesses that may damage the nervous system of an infant. Similarly, there is evidence that extreme malnutrition, if prolonged over a period of years, can retard physiological maturation of an infant's brain.

Carefully controlled research on the effects of poor health or malnutrition on brain development in humans cannot be done, of course, for children cannot be deprived of food or subjected to severe illness for experimental purposes. Carefully controlled research can, however, be done with animals. Several such studies have been conducted with animals such as rats. In some of these studies, for example, rats were fed diets that were severely deficient during the prenatal and early postnatal periods. Later analyses of brain tissue revealed significantly retarded brain development (Winick, 1975a).

Research with experimental animals has further revealed that the severity (and permanence) of the effects of malnutrition upon brain growth vary, depending upon the type of growth that the brain is undergoing at the time that the malnutrition occurs. If the malnutrition occurs during the first stage of brain development, while brain cells are still dividing to form new cells, then poor nutrition will prevent full cell division and the animal will be left with fewer brain cells than normal. This condition will be permanent if the animal's diet is not improved before the end of the period of cell division (about 6 months after birth for humans). If, however, the malnutrition does not occur until the second stage of brain development (during the addition of proteins and fats to the existing brain cells, or myelination), the animal will have the normal complement of brain cells, but they will be smaller than average. Restoration of a normal diet offsets these adverse effects, resulting in recovery of normal brain size (Winick & Noble, 1966; Winick, 1975).

It is not clear at present how completely we can generalize the results of animal research to human development. Nevertheless, autopsies of children who have died of extremely severe malnutrition before 2 years of age reveal that their brains, like those of the malnourished research animals, have an abnormally low number of brain cells. In some cases, these children were found to have *less than* 40% of the normal number of brain cells (Winick et al., 1970; Winick, 1975a). Such findings strongly suggest that the brains of human infants, like those of experimental animals, are adversely affected by poor nutrition. In particular, it appears that severe and prolonged deficiencies in the diets of pregnant women (and, hence, their infants) that are continued in the child's diet from birth to 6 months of age interfere with the normal processes of cell division. If these nutritional deficiencies are not corrected before the child is 6 months old, they may well result in a permanent reduction in the number of brain cells and, hence, in the size of the brain. There is no current evidence, however, that less severe, even though prolonged, cases of malnutrition have similar adverse effects. Additionally, even severe and prolonged malnutrition after 6 months of age does not appear to have these permanently devastating effects.

The Effect of Stimulation on Brain Development

From a psychologist's perspective, the most provocative research on the development of the brain is that concerned with the effects of stimulation. It is becoming increasingly evident that both the *amount* and *type* of stimulation an infant receives may have dramatic effects on brain development and, by implication, on the complex behavior patterns controlled by the brain. Specific evidence of the importance of stimulation on brain development can be seen in the research of Seymour Levine, which was discussed in our earlier section on body growth. As you will recall, Levine's (1960) study of rats subjected to extreme stress revealed significant changes in body weight. Levine also found that stressed rats showed changes in the size and composition of their brains. Nonmanipulated rats, in contrast, had significantly smaller brains than did those who were handled or subjected to stress. The importance of stimulation on the brain's development was thus compellingly illustrated by Levine's research.

Other studies have produced similar findings by using so-called **enrichment** procedures to test the effects of stimulation upon brain development. In a series of studies by David Krech (1970) and others at Berkeley, the environments of experimental rats were enriched by means of larger cages, playmates, and daily changes in toys. They found that the brains of the enriched animals were larger than those of the nonenriched laboratory animals. Again, it appeared that stimulation, or the lack of stimulation, had a marked effect on brain size. However, as we mentioned in our earlier discussion of the effects of stimulation on body growth, this does not necessarily mean that stimulation enhanced brain size. Rather, it may be that the enriched environments were simply closer to the normally complex environments experienced by rats, while the nonenriched environments may have actually been deprived environments. Thus, while deprivation appears to produce small brains, enrichment may not enhance brain size.

A further finding of the enrichment studies was that the animals that had received stimulation had heavier *cerebral cortices* than the nonenriched animals. This finding was of particular significance, since the cerebral cortex is an area of the brain that is highly involved in intellectual functioning. Other specific changes in the brain's structure were also observed. Thus, it was found that the stressed animals had larger nerve cell bodies. In addition, it was found that the brain cells of the stimulated animals showed more *branching*—a finding that suggested that there were actually more connections formed among cells (Wallace, 1974). In light of these findings, it appears that stimulation may not simply affect the size of the brain; it may also affect the very composition of the brain.

Studies such as those of Levine and Krech illustrate that the general level of stimulation that an individual receives can have dramatic and far-reaching effects on overall brain development. More recent studies have therefore concerned themselves with closer examination of how specific experiences—or the lack thereof—affect aspects of brain development. For example, in one series of studies (Blakemore & Van Sluyters, 1975; Pettigrew, Olson, & Hirsch, 1973; Spinelli, Hirsch, Phelps, & Metzler, 1972), infant kittens were raised in specifically restricted environments. The kittens had special lenses placed over their eyes so that they saw only horizontal, never vertical, lines. When the kittens reached adulthood, the lenses were removed, and it was found that the animals did not respond to vertical lines in a normal manner. Moreover, recordings of their brain activity revealed that their brains contained fewer of the specific cells in the visual cortex that are responsive to vertical lines than did the brains of normal cats. The absence of vertical line stimulation during infancy had in effect prevented normal development of that portion of the brain responsible for seeing vertical lines. (See Figure 3-8.) Their brains had quite literally been modified. Extending this finding to the larger real world, it appears that not simply stimulation but, rather, specific types of stimulation may be necessary for the normal functioning of specific parts of the brain.

Summary of Brain Development in Infancy

At birth, the brain is the most mature part of the infant's body, with the formation of all brain cells completed by 6 months of age, if not earlier. The genetic processes governing brain growth make the brain relatively less vulnerable than other parts of the body to external environmental influences. Nonetheless, extreme environmental factors such as severe malnutrition and extreme deprivation of certain types of stimulation can interfere with the normal development of the brain. Infants who suffer severe malnutrition or extreme deprivation of stimulation during early infancy may have smaller brains than do normal children, with fewer brain cells, smaller brain cells, or both. These children may, as a result, suffer permanent impairment of their later psychological functioning.

ISSUE

What is brain damage?

Brain damage is a very broad term applied to a wide variety of situations. The brain-damaged child is one whose brain has been adversely affected through the influence of genetics, disease, or accident. Typically, this damage to the brain will be reflected in some aspect of the child's behavior—for example, language, reading, motor coordination, or overall cognitive ability.

The Brain-Damaged Child

The brains of some children fail, for one reason or another, to develop normally. A wide variety of terms has been used to describe these children's condition, including brain damage, minimal cerebral dysfunction, developmental disability, perceptual handicap, delayed neural maturation, developmental dyslexia,

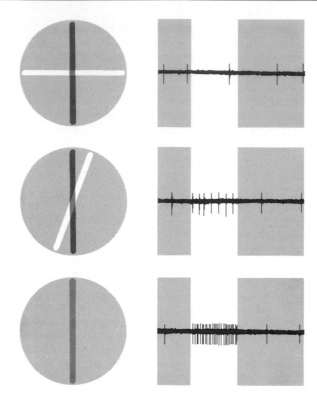

Figure 3-8. The activity of single cells in the visual cortex of the brain. Recent advances in technology have enabled scientists to study the activity of single cells in the brain. Thin glass electrodes are surgically implanted into particular cells in the brain, in particular in the visual cortex. After the animal has recovered from the surgery, it is shown a number of patterns. Certain cells respond only to particular types of patterns, such as vertical lines. This response is then recorded. Research using these "single cell recordings" has shown that each cell is programmed to detect certain features or qualities in the stimulus. The above illustration shows how different stimulus patterns affect the response of a particular cell. Clearly, for this cell, vertical lines are most effective in producing a response. Hence, this cell has been called a "vertical line detector." (From "The Visual Cortex of the Brain," by D. H. Hubel, *Scientific American*, 1963, p. 58. Copyright © 1963 by Scientific American, Inc. All rights reserved.)

hyperkinetic behavioral syndrome, behavioral disorder, Strauss syndrome, and educational handicap. Whatever label happens to be applied, these children share two things in common. First, something either failed to develop or developed abnormally in their nervous systems. Second, these children will have some degree of difficulty in learning. There are approximately 10 million of these children in the United States today (Spears & Weber, 1974).

There is no one simple category of brain-damaged children, as is apparent from the many different labels that have been applied. Most of these children do, however, suffer from some form of impairment in functioning. Also, certain patterns of behavior do occur more frequently in brain-damaged children. These behavioral patterns are used as "soft signs" (that is, indicators but not proof) of neurological damage. Brain-damaged children are more likely to be hyperactive, to have short attention spans, to be uncoordinated, to have perceptual problems, to be behind in achieving certain developmental milestones, and to have difficulty in school. The severity of these disorders may range from very slight problems in coordination and short attention spans to severe mental retardation and emotional disturbance. Thus, the "brain-damaged child" may be anyone from a child with a slight learning disability to a severely retarded child totally dependent upon others for complete custodial care. Obviously, then, when one hears the label "brain-damaged," one must ask, "In what way?" and "To what degree?" In particular, one must keep in mind the fact that severe brain damage is very rare. Most children who are called brain-damaged have only minimal problems.

What Causes Brain Damage?

Ordinarily, when a brain-damaged child arrives in a psychologist's or a physician's office, an attempt is made to find some factors in the past that may have affected the child adversely enough to cause brain damage. For example, the child's mother may report that she was sick or took harmful medications during her pregnancy. The child may have been born prematurely, suffered anoxia at birth, suffered some form of brain infection (such as meningitis or encephalitis), or incurred a head injury in a fall or a car accident. Further probing may reveal that the child comes from an environment which provided neither adequate attention nor proper nourishment. All of these factors, as well as many others, can produce brain damage.

Medical problems of the sort just described do occur more frequently in the histories of brain-damaged children than in those of normal children. There is, therefore, a misguided tendency to jump to the conclusion that any child who has suffered from one or more of these problems will be "at risk"; that is, will be likely to be brain-damaged. Fortunately for those of us who have children who were premature or who suffered serious injury or disease, the probability that these children will be brain-damaged is actually quite low. Most children exposed to the same problems develop quite normally (Broman, Nichols, & Kennedy, 1975; Parmelee, Sigman, Kopp, & Haber, 1975).

ISSUE

How does prematurity affect development of the body and brain?

"Prematurity" has, until recently, been a broad term applied to two quite different situations: to infants who are unusually small at birth because they were born too early ("short-gestation" infants); and to infants who are unusually small at birth even though they have remained within the womb for the full gestation period. The prognoses for the later physical and mental development of these children can vary greatly, depending upon the particular reason for their small size at birth. There is, therefore, a current trend to distinguish between the two groups by referring to the first as *short-gestation-period infants* and the second as *small-for-date infants*.

The Premature Baby

The normal newborn in the United States weighs about 3500 grams and is about 50 centimeters in length. Occasionally, however (about 75 babies per 1000 births in the United States), a baby is born whose size falls dramatically below this average (U.S. Department of Health, Education and Welfare, 1975). Some of these babies are born earlier in the gestation period than normal, and predictably tend to be smaller and less developed than the average full-term baby. Others are born after a full stay in their mother's womb, but are unusually small nonetheless. Until very recently, no distinction was made between these two groups of unusually small babies. Any baby weighing less than 2500 grams at birth was labeled **premature**, regardless of the length of gestation.

Studies of premature babies similarly failed to distinguish between the types of prematurity involved. In some of this research, such a distinction was probably not necessary. However, in a growing number of cases, such a distinction is clearly needed. For example, it has been concluded that many premature babies will be smaller than average even as adults, although they will catch up to some extent during their infancy (Drillien, 1964). It has also been stated that a "premature" baby, as opposed to a "normal" baby, is somewhat more likely to be retarded, brain-damaged or otherwise intellectually impaired, although this does not mean that all or even most premature babies will be thus affected (Drillien, 1964; Braine, Heimer, Wortis, & Freedman, 1966).

Recent studies indicate that such research, though correct, can be somewhat misleading (Tanner, 1970). Specifically, the prognosis for a particular premature baby will vary, depending upon whether he was born too early (short gestation) or whether he was unusually small even after a full gestation period (small for date). If, for example, a baby weighed 2000 grams because he was born too early, his body and brain will probably follow the normal schedule of development. Body and brain will mature in a normal fashion but part of the process that would normally take place inside the womb will occur outside the womb (Tanner, 1970). If, however, a baby weighed 2000 grams at birth even though he had remained within the womb for the full term, the prognosis for future physical and intellectual development is less optimistic. The small size at birth may reflect some underlying genetic or prenatal influence that had an adverse impact on the baby (see Chapter 2 for a discussion of such factors). If so, then the underlying problem that produced the small birth size could, ultimately, result in more serious physical or mental impairment. Note, however, that even for this infant, it is not the fact of being underweight at birth that causes the later impairment. Rather, the small size at birth, like the physical or mental impairment, is produced by some independent factor.

Since different prognoses apply to "short gestation" versus "full term but nonetheless small" babies, there is an increasing tendency to separate premature infants into the two categories. The first category, then, refers to **short-gestation-period infants** and includes all infants, regardless of birth weight, who are born after a gestation period of less than 8½ months. The second category is composed of **small-for-date infants** and includes all infants with a birth weight less than the weight that would be predicted from the length of gestation (Tanner, 1970).

MILESTONES IN MOTOR DEVELOPMENT

As the body and brain mature, the infant is able to do things that he could not do before. In particular the infant acquires new motor skills, such as lifting the head, sitting, crawling, and walking. The exact age at which each of these skills will first appear varies a great deal; however, each skill does tend to appear as the child reaches a certain age. These motor skills can therefore serve as useful cues as to whether a child's development is progressing normally. For this reason, we shall discuss in this section some of the more important of these milestones in the development of the child during the first two postnatal years.

The milestones that we shall examine may, at first glance, seem distinct and wholly unrelated to one another. Closer examination, however, reveals two trends that characterize motor development during infancy. First, most development progresses in a **cephalocaudal** (or head-to-foot) direction, with motor behaviors involving the head and upper extremities developing earlier and motor behaviors involving the feet and lower extremities developing later. Second, most development progresses in a **proximodistal** (or center-to-periphery) direction. Motor behaviors involving "central" parts of the body, such as the shoulders, tend to be perfected before motor behaviors involving "peripheral" parts of the body, such as the fingers. With this background, let us turn now to some specific motor skills that develop during the first two years.

Head Control

At birth, most babies are able to turn their heads from side to side while lying on their backs. When they are turned onto their stomachs, newborns can also usually lift their heads a few centimeters into the air. However, when a newborn is placed in an upright position, his head will wobble uncontrollably if not supported—something that is invariably a cause for alarm in those unaccustomed to holding newborn infants.

As the infant grows older, head control increases to the point where the infant is able to lift the head further into the air while lying down. As neck muscles become stronger and the brain matures, the infant also gains more control over the wobbling of the head. By 6 months of age, the infant usually has full head control and can hold the head in a steady position even while sitting upright.

Sitting

Sitting follows a schedule quite similar to that of head control. Newborns cannot support themselves in a sitting position. However, by approximately 4 months of age, babies can usually sit when propped up, and by 6 months of age, they can sit in a high chair with a fair degree of success. Sometime between 7 months and 1 year of age, they finally perfect the art of sitting. They can then sit alone in the center of the floor with no need for external support.

Locomotion

Babies first learn to roll over from stomach to back at around 5 months of age. Mastery of the back-to-stomach roll does not come until somewhat later, at about 7 months. It is at this time that infants also learn to move themselves from one point to another by a series of body rolls, which they begin to do with amazing determination.

The body roll is not a terribly efficient means of locomotion, and a child will start searching very quickly for a more efficient means of traveling from one point to another. There are several options. The child may learn to *crawl* (or *creep*) on the hands and knees. Alternatively, he may perfect *bear-walking*, which is like crawling, except that the legs are straight and it is the feet, rather than the knees, that touch the floor. Or, the child may learn to *scoot* (or *hitch*). In scooting, the child moves along the floor in a sitting position, pushing himself forward with his arms and legs. (See Figure 3-9.) Whichever form of locomotion a particular child selects, it will probably appear sometime between 8 and 13 months of age.

Even as a child is still perfecting the crawl (or scoot, or bear-walk), he or she is already beginning to learn to walk. If someone lends a helping hand, many babies can stand as early as 8 months. By 9 months, they can normally stand while holding onto coffee tables or crib rails. By 1 year, babies can use these same coffee tables and crib rails to pull themselves into standing positions, and may walk around the tables while holding onto them or even walk across the room if someone takes them by the hand. Walking alone, without the need of external support, usually occurs at about 15 months of age.

TESTS OF PHYSICAL DEVELOPMENT

Children normally acquire the major milestones in physical development with an amazing degree of regularity. Psychologists have therefore been able to develop tests or scales to assess the progress of individual children. These tests include two groups of tests that will be discussed here: the APGAR test and the developmental (DQ) scales.

The APGAR Test

Immediately after birth, and again at 5 minutes of age, most newborns are given a test called the **Apgar test.** This test was developed in 1953 by Virginia Apgar for use by physicians in determining those newborns who will require special medical attention. The test consists of a simple observation by the obstetrician of the infant's vital functions: heart rate, respiration, muscle tone, reflex responsiveness, and skin color. (See Table 3-2.) On each of the five dimensions listed in the Apgar test, the infant receives a score of 0, 1, or 2. The five scores are added together, and the total is the infant's Apgar score.

The maximum possible score on the Apgar is 10. Babies with Apgar scores of 10 are in excellent physical condition at birth: heart and respiration rates are normal, they have good skin color, and they show good muscle tone and reflex responsiveness. Babies scoring 8 and 9 are considered to be in good physical condition. Babies scoring between 5 and 7 may have medical problems requiring some attention. Babies scoring 4 or less have a low chance for survival and require immediate medical attention.

The Apgar was originally developed as a rough index for use by physicians in evaluating the physical condition of infants at birth. However, the test has since been used in attempts to make long-term predictions of future behavior, development, and intelligence. Use of the Apgar for this purpose was based in part on findings that retarded children are likely to have had very low Apgar

Figure 3-9. Learning how to get around. Long before infants actually learn to walk, they are very efficient at getting around. They may accomplish their travels through a variety of techniques: for example, crawling, scooting, and bear-walking.

scores at birth. Moreover, when considering the population as a whole, some researchers have found a significant correlation between Apgar scores at birth and later intelligence (Edwards, 1968; St. Clair, 1978). However, recent research suggests that this relationship may be due to the presence of certain confounding variables. For example, it has long been known that preschool intelligence varies

Table 3-2. The Apgar test.

The Apgar test gives a quick evaluation of an infant's vital functions: heart rate, respiratory effort, muscle tone, skin color, and reflex irritability. Each of these factors is given a score from zero to two. The different scores are then added together to give the Apgar score.

Apgar Score Sign	0	1	2
Heart rate	absent	slow (below 100)	rapid (over 100)
Respiratory effort	absent	irregular, slow	good, crying
Muscle tone	flaccid, limp	weak, inactive	strong, active
Color	blue, pale	body pink, extremities blue	entirely pink
Reflex irritability	no response	grimace	coughing, sneezing, crying

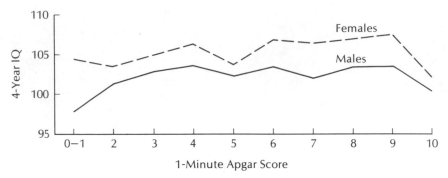

Figure 3-10. The relation of Apgar scores to preschool intelligence. If one simply produces a correlation of Apgar scores with preschool IQ, there appears to be a significant relationship between the two, with lower Apgar scores being associated with lower intelligence. Thus, many psychologists have tried to use the Apgar as a predictor of later intelligence.

However, the work of Broman and her colleagues reveals that, if one is careful to look at the relationship between Apgar scores and IQ within particular racial and sexual groups, the correlation disappears. Notice how flat the different lines are. If Apgar were a good predictor of IQ, the lines would tilt upward, showing higher IQ scores for children with higher Apgar scores. (Adapted from *Preschool IQ: Prenatal and Early Developmental Correlates,* by S. H. Broman, P. L. Nichols, and W. A. Kennedy. Copyright 1975 by Lawrence Erlbaum Associates. Reprinted by permission.)

as a function of socioeconomic status, race, and sex. It has also long been known that birth difficulties—and hence Apgar scores—vary as a function of these same variables. Hence, it has been difficult to determine whether the correlation often obtained between Apgar scores and later intelligence is due to a direct effect of birth condition on mental development or whether both the Apgar scores and the intelligence scores are influenced by other independent factors such as socioeconomic status, race, and sex. A recent extensive study of over 26,000 children in 12 urban medical centers throughout the United States found that, when care is taken to eliminate any effects of socioeconomic class, race, or sex, the Apgar scores of all children (normal as well as abnormal) are not significantly related to their preschool intelligence scores (Broman et al., 1975). (See Figure 3-10.) Thus, unless the Apgar score is extremely low (indicating possible physical damage to the body *and* brain), one need not worry about the psychological well-being and subsequent development of a child simply because the Apgar score is less than perfect.

Developmental Scales

A number of infant *developmental scales* have been constructed for use in identifying mentally retarded children at an early age. Perhaps the best known of these is the Bayley Scale of Infant Development (1969). Another well-known short test is the Denver Developmental Screening Test (see Figure 3-11), which is typically used by physicians and teachers as a quick, rough index of developmental level (Frankenburg & Dodds, 1969). In these tests, the infant is required to per-

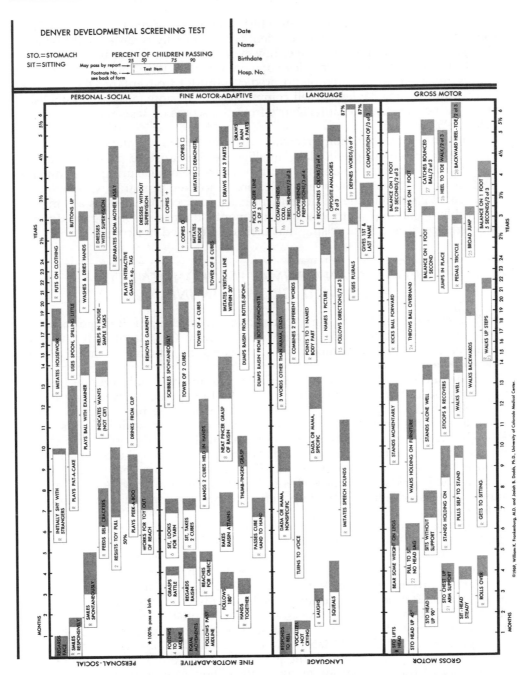

Figure 3-11. The Denver Developmental Screening Test. (Reprinted by permission of the University of Colorado Medical Center, Denver.)

form a number of tasks that may be passed or failed. The infant's **DQ** (or **developmental quotient**) reveals how many items were passed, as compared with the number passed by the "average" child of the same age.

When used for the purposes for which they were originally constructed, the developmental scales are effective in identifying mentally retarded children at an early age. Many psychologists have, however, attempted to predict adult intelligence from performance on the developmental scales. With the exception of the mentally retarded, these attempts to predict adult IQ from infant DQ have been unsuccessful. Nancy Bayley herself commented, "It is now fairly well established that we cannot predict later intelligence from the scores on tests made in infancy" (Bayley, 1955, p. 806).

There are probably many reasons why the developmental scales have not been able to accurately predict later intelligence. Perhaps the principal reason is simply that the infant tests and the adult tests are each measuring quite different aspects of development. The infant scales are concerned primarily with motor and perceptual skills, while the adult tests measure such cognitive skills as language and problem solving. With the measurements themselves being of different characteristics, it is not surprising that their results need not coincide.

CREATING AN OPTIMAL ENVIRONMENT FOR BIOLOGICAL GROWTH IN INFANCY

The secret to providing a good environment for the physical and motor development of an infant should be fairly clear by now. Growth of body and brain, and development of proper motor skills, appear to be intimately related to a few basic variables.

The child's health is one such variable. The infant should therefore receive proper medical attention. Most physicians like to see infants every few months for "well-baby checkups." These examinations enable the physicians to identify potential health problems before they become serious. In addition, it is during these checkups that infants receive immunization shots against some of the more serious illnesses. Timely visits to the doctor are necessary if these important immunizations are to be kept on schedule. During recent years, many communities, realizing the importance of these checkups, have begun to provide free clinics for infants, so that children from impoverished families are not denied adequate medical care.

Obviously, good health care also involves prompt medical attention when an infant is ill. One should not try to second-guess the severity of an illness, but should contact a physician immediately if an infant develops a fever, begins to seem lethargic and out of sorts, or just seems to be behaving in unusual ways.

Part of proper health care involves providing the infant with a good, well-balanced diet. Physicians typically provide parents with diet plans prepared for infants of various ages. These diets are based upon the nutritional needs and digestive capacity of the infant and should be followed closely. Still, there are many parents in the United States who cannot afford to provide adequate nutrition for their children. Although the government has professed an awareness of the severity of the problem (as many as 10 million Americans may be affected) and an interest in its resolution, little progress has been made to date (Kaplan, 1972; Serban, 1975).

Proper health care is, of course, not enough in itself to ensure normal physical and mental development. Children—especially children under 2 years of age—need lots of stimulation. They need to be talked to, held, played with, and given the many other attentions that parents typically give their children. In addition, the *type* of stimulation an infant receives seems to be an extremely important variable affecting proper development. The following chapter, which is concerned with the cognitive development of the infant during the first 2 years, will provide specific suggestions regarding those types of stimulation most effective in promoting the child's development.

SUMMARY OF BIOLOGICAL DEVELOPMENT IN INFANCY

This chapter has been concerned with the biological development of the child during the first two years of life. It has discussed the growth of body and brain and the development of motor skills. Although the development of body, brain, and behavior during infancy is largely determined by genetic preprogramming, it is clear that *extreme environmental influences* can interfere with the normal course of development, producing children who are *physically smaller*, who have *smaller brains*, and who will be *slow in the development of basic motor skills*. The environmental factors that appear to be most responsible for such disturbances in normal development are *severe malnutrition* and *extreme deprivation of stimulation*. It is not clear, however, whether *enrichment* of the diet or of environmental stimulation beyond some adequate level will further enhance development of body, brain, and behavior, although studies of experimental animals suggest that enrichment may have such an effect.

SUGGESTED READINGS

Hirsch, Helmut V. B., & Jacobson, Marcus. The perfectible brain: Principles of neuronal development. In M. S. Gazzaniga & C. Blakemore (Eds.), *Handbook of Physiology.* New York: Academic Press, 1975. This an excellent discussion of the available literature on brain development and of the effects stimulus deprivation has on brain development. It is quite technical but probably the easiest reading in this particular area.

Tanner, J. M. Physical growth. In P. Mussen (Ed.), *Carmichael's manual of child psychology,* Vol. 1. (3rd ed.). New York: Wiley, 1970. Tanner is one of the leading authorities on physical growth. This particular chapter is an extremely thorough review of the area.

GLOSSARY

Achilles reflex. A permanent reflex characterized by a contraction of the foot in response to a tap on the heel (the Achilles tendon).

activating hormones. Hormones produced by the pituitary gland that stimulate hormone production by the other endocrine glands.

Apgar Test. A simple test administered by physicians to all infants at 1 minute and 5 minutes after birth. It provides a quick appraisal of the infant's physiological functioning and adjustment to extrauterine life.

Babinski reflex. A newborn reflex characterized by a fanning and extension of the toes in response to a stroke on the sole of the foot. The Babinski reflex does not occur in children over 6 months of age.

brain stem. Those parts of the brain that are phylogenetically more primitive, such as the spinal cord and the medulla oblongata. These brain stem areas tend to be more involved in regulating basic life-preserving functions (for example, respiration, pulse, digestion) and the basic reflexes rather than the more intellectual functions such as perception, thinking, and language.

cephalocaudal. Literally means "head-to-foot" and is used to describe the general development of motor processes involving the head and upper extremities before those involving the lower extremities.

cerebral cortex. That part of the brain that is phylogenetically most advanced. The size of the cerebral cortex increases as one moves from less intelligent to more intelligent organisms. The cerebral cortex is largely responsible for the more "intellectual" aspects of behavior, such as perception, language, and thought.

Darwinian reflex. A newborn reflex characterized by the infant's grasp of any object placed in his palm. The Darwinian reflex disappears in infants by about 3 months of age.

deprivation dwarfism. Refers to the observation that animals and humans who are raised in an extremely deprived environment show patterns of stunted physiological growth.

developmental quotient (DQ). An estimate of developmental level used with preschool children. It is simply the ratio of developmental age (or maturity) to chronological age.

electroencephalograph (EEG). A device for amplifying and recording the electrochemical activity of the brain.

enrichment. The intentional introduction of certain types of experiences that are believed to be effective in creating an optimal environment for the development of the organism.

grasp reflex. See *Darwinian reflex*.

malnutrition. When an organism receives a prolonged diet that is either insufficient or improper, it is said to suffer from malnutrition.

Moro reflex. A newborn reflex. An infant will exhibit the Moro reflex whenever he is surprised or held in such a way as to create a sensation of falling. In response to this type of stimulation, the infant throws the arms outward and then brings them together at the center of the body. The Moro reflex is gone by 6 or 7 months of age.

myelination. The process whereby fats and proteins are added to nerve fibers in the form of an outer covering, known as the "myelin sheath."

no-REM sleep. A quiet form of sleep, characterized by regular breathing and an absence of body and eye movement.

patellar tendon reflex. A permanent reflex that is characterized by a kick of the lower leg in response to a tap on the knee (that is, on the patellar tendon).

pituitary gland. A gland that plays a central role in endocrine functioning. It produces a special set of activating hormones that stimulate hormone production by the other endocrine glands.

prematurity. Infants weighing less than 2500 grams at birth are considered premature.

proximodistal. Literally means "center-to-periphery" and is used to describe the general development of motor behaviors involving central parts of the body before those involving peripheral parts.

pupillary reflexes. Permanent reflexes that result in dilation and constriction of the pupil of the eye in response to weak or strong lights.

reflex. An innate connection between stimulus and response in which certain types of incoming sensory stimulation automatically release a particular response. For example, a newborn will automatically suck (response) any object placed in his mouth **(stimulus)**.

releaser substances. Substances produced by the brain that trigger production of activating hormones by the pituitary gland.

REM sleep. Active sleep, characterized by small body movements and rapid eye movements. It is generally associated with dreaming in adults.

rooting reflex. One of the newborn reflexes. The rooting reflex has generally disappeared by 6 months of age. It refers to the fact that when an infant's cheek is touched, he will turn his mouth in the direction of the stimulation, with his mouth wide open.

short-gestation-period infants. Infants who are born after a gestation (or pregnancy) of less than 8½ months.

small-for-date infants. Those infants whose birth weights are lower than would be predicted by the length of gestation (the amount of time spent in the womb).

state. An infant's level of alertness, ranging from deep sleep to active arousal and crying.

sucking reflex. One of the newborn reflexes, it refers to the fact that the young infant will suck any object put in his mouth. The sucking reflex has disappeared by 6 months of age.

REFERENCES

Apgar, V. A proposal for a new method of evaluation of the newborn infant. *Anesthesia and Analgesia,* 1953, *32,* 260–269.

Aserinsky, E., & Kleitman, N. A motility cycle in sleeping infants as manifested by ocular and gross bodily activity. *Journal of Applied Physiology,* 1955, *8,* 11–18.

Bayley, N. On the growth of intelligence. *American Psychologist,* 1955, *10,* 805–818.

Bayley, N. *Bayley Scales of Infant Development: Birth to Two Years.* New York: Psychological Corporation, 1969.

Bijou, S. W., & Baer, D. M. *Child development, II.* New York: Appleton-Century-Crofts, 1965.

Blakemore, C., & Van Sluyters, R. C. Innate and environmental factors in the development of the kitten's visual cortex. *Journal of Physiology,* 1975, *248,* 663–716.

Braine, M.D.S., Heimer, C. B., Wortis, H. & Freedman, A. M. Factors associated with impairment of the early development of prematures. *Monographs of the Society for Research in Child Development,* 1966, *31* (4, Serial No. 106.)

Broman, S. H., Nichols, P. L., & Kennedy, W. A. *Preschool IQ: Prenatal and early developmental correlates.* Hillsdale, N.J.: Lawrence Erlbaum Associates, 1975.

Dement, W. C. An essay on dreams: The role of physiology in understanding their nature. In F. Barron & W. C. Dement (Eds.), *New directions in psychology II.* New York: Holt, Rinehart & Winston, 1965.

Drillien, C. M. *The growth and development of the prematurely born infant.* Baltimore, Md.: Williams & Wilkins, 1964.

Edwards, N. The relationship between physical condition immediately after birth and mental and motor performance at age four. *Genetic Psychology Monographs,* 1968, *78,* 257–289.

Eichorn, D. Physiological development. In P. Mussen (Ed.), *Carmichael's manual of child psychology,* Vol. 1. (3rd ed.). New York: Wiley, 1970, pp. 157–286.

Emde, R. N., Harmon, R. J., Metcalf, D., Koenig, K. L., & Wagonfeld, S. Stress and neonatal sleep. *Psychosomatic Medicine.* 1971, *33,* 491–497.

Frankenburg, K. M., & Dodds, J. B. *The Denver Developmental Screening Test.* Denver, Colo.: University of Colorado Medical Center, 1969.

Gunders, S. M., & Whiting, J.W.M. Mother-infant separation and physical growth. *Ethnology,* 1968,*7,* 196–206.

Hubel, D. H. The visual cortex of the brain. *Scientific American,* Nov. 1963.

Kaplan, B. Malnutrition and mental deficiency. *Psychological Bulletin,* 1972, *78,* 321–334.

Kessen, W., Haith, M. M., & Salapatek, P. H. Human infancy: A bibliography and guide. In P. Mussen (Ed.), *Carmichael's manual of child psychology*, Vol. 1. (3rd ed.). New York: Wiley, 1970.

Krech, D. Don't use the kitchen sink approach to enrichment. *Today's Education.* October 1970.

Landauer, T. K., & Whiting, J.W.M. Infantile stimulation and adult stature of human males. *American Anthropologist*, 1964, *66*, 1007–1028.

Levine, S. Stimulation in infancy. *Scientific American*, May, 1960.

Miller, F.J.W., Court, S.D.M., Walton, W. S., & Knox, E. G. *Growing up in Newcastle-upon-Tyne: A continuing study of health and illness in young children within their families.* London: Oxford University Press, 1960.

Parmelee, A. H., Sigman, M., Kopp, C. B., & Haber, A. The concept of a cumulative risk score for infants. In N. R. Ellis (Ed.), *Aberrant development in infancy.* Hillsdale, N.J.: Lawrence Erlbaum Associates, 1975.

Parmelee, A. H., Wenner, W. H., & Schulz, H. R. Infant sleep patterns from birth to 16 weeks of age. *Journal of Pediatrics*, 1964, *65*, 576–582.

Penfield, W., & Roberts, L. *Speech and brain mechanisms.* Princeton: Princeton University Press, 1959.

Pettigrew, J. D., Olson, C., & Hirsch, H.V.B. Cortical effect of selective visual experience: Degeneration or reorganization. *Science*, 1973, *180*, 1202–1203.

Powell, G. F., Brasel, J. A., & Blizzard, R. M. Emotional deprivation and growth retardation simulating idiopathic hypopituitarism, I. Clinical evaluation of the syndrome. *New England Journal of Medicine*, 1967, *276*, 1271–1278.

Powell, G. F., Brasel, J. A., Raiti, S., & Blizzard, R. M. Emotional deprivation and growth retardation simulating idiopathic hypopituitarism, II. Endocrinologic evaluation of the syndrome. *New England Journal of Medicine*, 1967, *276*, 1279–1283.

Pratt, K. C. The effects of repeated auditory stimulation upon the general activity of newborn infants. *Journal of Genetic Psychology*, 1934, *44*, 96–116.

Prechtl, H.F.R. Brain and behavioral mechanisms in the human newborn infant. In R. J. Robinson (Ed.), *Brain and early behaviour.* New York: Academic Press, 1969.

Prechtl, H.F.R., & Beintema, D. J. The neurological examination of the full-term newborn infant. London: William Heinemann Medical Books, 1964.

Robbins, W. J., Brody, S., Hogan, A. F., Jackson, G. M., & Green, C. W. *Growth.* New Haven: Yale University Press, 1929.

Schaffer, R. *Mothering.* Cambridge, Mass.: Harvard University Press, 1977.

Serban, G. *Nutrition and mental function.* New York: Plenum Press, 1975.

Spears, C. E., & Weber, R. E. The nature of learning disabilities. In R. E. Weber (Ed.), *Handbook on learning disabilities.* Englewood Cliffs, N.J.: Prentice-Hall, 1974.

Spinelli, D. N., Hirsch, H.V.B., Phelps, R. W., & Metzler, J. Visual experience as a determinant of the response characteristics of cortical receptive fields in cats. *Experimental Brain Research*, 1972, *15*, 289–304.

St. Clair, K. L. Neonatal assessment procedures: A historical review. *Child Development*, 1978, *49*, 280–292.

Tanner, J. M. *Growth at adolescence* (2nd ed.). Oxford, England: Blackwell Scientific Publications, 1962.

Tanner, J. M. Physical growth. In P. H. Mussen (Ed.), *Carmichael's manual of child psychology*, (3rd ed.). Vol. 1. New York: Wiley, 1970.

U.S. Department of Health, Education & Welfare. *Monthly Vital Statistics Report, Summary Report: Final Natality Statistics, 1973*, 23(11), Supplement, January 30, 1975.

Wallace, P. Complex environments: effects on brain development. *Science*, *185*(4156), 1035–1037. (September 20, 1974, issue.)

Widdowson, E. M. Mental contentment and physical growth. *Lancet*, 1951, *1*, 1316–1318.

Winick, M. Nutritional disorders during brain development. In D. B. Tower & T. N. Chase (Eds.), *The nervous system, Vol. 2: The clinical neurosciences.* New York: Raven Press, 1975a.

Winick, M. Nutrition and brain development. In G. Serban (Ed.), *Nutrition and mental functions*. New York: Plenum Press, 1975b.

Winick, M., & Noble, A. Cellular response in rats during malnutrition at different ages. *Journal of Nutrition*, 1966, *89*, 300–306.

Winick, M., Rosso, P. & Waterlow, J. Cellular growth of cerebrum, cerebellum, and brain stem in normal and marasmic children. *Experimental Neurology*, 1970, *26*, 393–400.

Wolff, P. H. The development of attention in young infants. *Annals of New York Academy of Sciences*, 1965, *118*, 815–830.

4

Cognitive Development in Infancy

Like the last chapter on biological growth, the present chapter deals with development during the first two postnatal years. Unlike the previous chapter, the focus here is more psychological and emphasizes the **cognitive** development of the infant, or the growth of thinking ability. It is the active development of thought processes that will enable the infant to understand the objects around him. We shall follow the gradual development of the child's cognitive abilities through the first two years of life. In the process, we will witness an awesome transition over this period from a newborn with limited, though functioning, sensory capacities to a young toddler who can remember the sights, sounds, odors, and feelings of the past, who can think about these past events, and who can use these memories to plan and direct future behavior.

ISSUE

Can the newborn infant see, hear, and feel the world around him?

Many myths have arisen over the years concerning the cognitive capabilities of young infants. Central to these myths is a general notion of "cognitive incompetence." Thus, many people commonly—and erroneously—assume that the newborn infant has little or no ability to think, feel, or even see. The pervasiveness of these myths was certainly highlighted for me when a teenaged girl recently asked whether the young infant I was carrying could "open her eyes yet?"

In recent years, psychologists have undertaken systematic research to investigate the actual cognitive abilities of the young infant. This research has revealed that the infant has an astounding array of relatively sophisticated cognitive skills. It is upon such skills that this chapter initially focuses.

SENSORY CAPACITIES OF THE NEWBORN

The newborn begins life quite well equipped to learn about his new world. At birth, all of the infant's senses are functioning (Peiper, 1963). The newborn can see his mother, hear her voice, and feel her touch. This is not to say, however, that the newborn can do these things with the same completeness and accuracy as can an adult, for the sensory systems of the newborn are not fully biologically mature at birth. The functioning of one of the newborn's sensory systems (vision) is well illustrated in a study by Robert Fantz (1961)—a study that has since been replicated by many others (for example, Dayton, Jones, Aiu, Rawson, Steele, & Rose, 1964; Salapatek, Bechtold, & Bushnell, 1976).

Fantz first estimated the newborn's precision for seeing detail (or the newborn's **visual acuity**) by the use of a rather clever technique. He showed a newborn two patterns simultaneously: one was a solid gray square, the other was a black and white striped square. The infant's eyes were then carefully observed, and it was determined whether or not the infant spent more time looking at the more interesting striped square than at the gray square. If the infant spent more time looking at the striped square, it was assumed that the infant's acuity was at least good enough to see that amount of detail. Next, the striped square was replaced with another square in which the stripes were narrower. Squares with smaller and smaller stripes were used until the infant began to look at the gray square and the striped square for equally long periods of time. Using this procedure, Fantz and others have estimated that the visual acuity of the newborn is somewhere between 20/150 and 20/800 (normal adult acuity is 20/20). (See Figure 4-1.) This means that adults can see small objects from much greater distances (in fact, 7.5 to 40 times greater) than can newborns. It has been suggested that the newborn is best equipped for seeing objects about 17 to 30 centimeters away, which is the approximate distance between the eyes of the nursing baby and the mother's face (Haith, in press; Schaffer, 1977).

The newborn's capacity to hear has been verified through the use of complicated electrical equipment such as the electroencephalograph (EEG). Studies utilizing this device, which monitors electrical activity in the brain, show clear changes in the newborn's brain waves in response to sound (Weitzman, Fishbein, & Graziani, 1965). In fact, an early study (Bernard & Sontag, 1947) showed responses in fetal activity to sound as early as the third trimester of pregnancy.

The infant's capacity to feel is evident in his clear response to touch. An object that touches the infant's lips will be sucked; a slap or pinprick will produce a cry; a cuddle will often quiet a crying child. That the newborn can thus not only see and hear but feel as well is therefore obvious. This does not mean, however, that infants can, as yet, "understand" what they see, hear, and feel.

In order to understand a particular object or event in the world around him, an infant must first have some sort of memory, or mental representation, with which to compare it. For example, the 2-year-old child, as opposed to the newborn infant, understands that the person standing beside him is his mother because he remembers past experiences with her: experiences in which she cared for him and loved him. The 2-year-old's mental representation for his mother has been gradually created through the literally thousands of times that he has seen her face, heard her voice, and felt her touch.

The newborn, having not yet had the opportunity to build up these mental representations, does not yet possess the necessary tools for understanding the

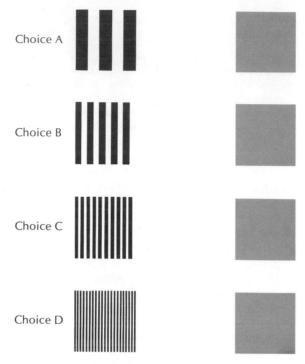

Figure 4-1. A procedure for estimating the visual acuity of the newborn. Fantz (1961) tested the visual acuity of infants by allowing them to look at either striped patterns or gray squares. Four different striped patterns were used that varied in the width of the stripes: (A) 1/8 in. wide; (B) 1/16 in. wide; (C) 1/32 in. wide; and (D) 1/64 in. wide. The smallest striped pattern preferred indicated that the acuity of the infant's eyes ranges from 20/150 to 20/800. Infants under a month could see the 1/8 in. stripes; infants of 6 months could see the 1/64 in. stripes. (From "The Origin of Form Perception," by R. L. Fantz, *Scientific American*, May 1961, *204*, 71–72. Copyright © 1961 by Scientific American, Inc. All rights reserved.)

objects and events in this world. William James thus described the brand-new world of the newborn in the following picturesque manner:

> The baby, assailed by eyes, ears, nose, skin, and entrails at once, feels that all is one great blooming, buzzing confusion [James, 1890, p. 488].

William James' description is of an organism that has sensations but is unable as yet to understand the nature of these sensations. The psychologist describes this distinction in terms of *sensation* versus *perception*. **Sensation** refers to the actual transmission of information about external events from the *sensory receptors* (for example, the eyes and ears) to the brain. Sensations are uninterpreted and, hence, meaningless. **Perception** refers to the processes in the brain that interpret the messages of the senses and give them meaning. Thus, a psychologist would say that the newborn can *sense* the objects of his world but cannot yet *perceive* them. The eyes and ears busily send messages to the brain, but the brain is not yet able to interpret these messages meaningfully for the infant. For this reason, a major part of learning during the first two years of life is *perceptual learning*. During these first two years, the infant must learn how to meaningfully interpret and discriminate the objects and events that he sees, feels, hears, and smells.

ISSUE
_____

Can the infant remember experiences in the womb?

Some psychologists believe that the infant begins to create mental representations or memories for his experiences even before birth. Obviously, the prenatal environment is relatively well insulated from most sources of stimulation. However, there is one stimulus that is continually present: the sound of the mother's heartbeat. Lee Salk (1973) believes that the newborn remembers the sound of the heartbeat and recognizes it after birth. Salk's argument is supported by research that demonstrates that newborns who hear recordings of heartbeat sounds while in the hospital nursery cry less and gain more weight during their first 4 days of life. Other psychologists, however, argue that the infant's tendency to be quiet when exposed to heartbeat sounds need not indicate any sort of memory for the mother's heartbeat. In fact, most rhythmic sounds will effectively reduce crying (Brackbill, Adams, Crowell, & Gray, 1966). Moreover, a more recent attempt to replicate Salk's findings on weight gain was not successful (Palmqvist, 1975). To date, then, the possibility that the infant possesses "womb memories" remains an intriguing, but unproven, hypothesis.

Some Basic Tools for Perceptual Learning

Perceptual learning would, of course, be greatly facilitated if the newborn came equipped with the mental images, or representations, with which to compare and thereby *perceive* incoming *sensations*. However, since it seems unlikely that an infant is born with these mental images already stored away in his head, they must somehow be constructed from experience. In this tremendous task newborns come equipped with a few basic, invaluable tools. First of all, as mentioned earlier, all of the newborn's senses are working from birth. As a result, fairly accurate information about the world is being transmitted to his brain.

Secondly, the newborn can, within the first few weeks of life (and maybe from birth), detect the fact that an object remains the same size even though it "looks" smaller when moved farther away (that is, possesses **size constancy**) and that an object retains the same shape even though it "looks" different when seen from a new angle (that is, possesses **shape constancy**) (Bower, 1965, 1966, 1974). (See Figures 4-2 and 4-3.) Having size and shape constancies is a tremendous asset to the newborn, since it means that he need not construct separate mental images for the same object when seen from a variety of distances and angles on different occasions.

Thirdly, the newborn begins life with certain *attention-directing behavior patterns*. Marshall Haith (in press) has examined some of these patterns by using videotapes to record what newborns look at when they are shown different types of visual displays (see Figure 4-4). From this research, Haith has concluded that

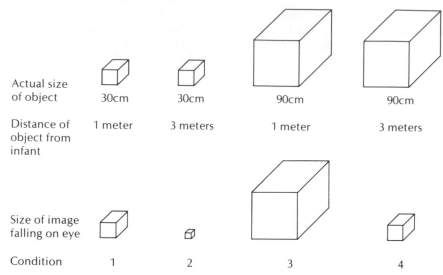

Figure 4-2.   An illustration of size constancy in the infant. In a clever experiment, T.G.R. Bower (1965) taught infants 40 to 60 days old to turn their heads to the left whenever they saw a 30 cm white paper cube from a distance of 1 meter. He then showed them either (1) the same 30 cm cube from the same distance of 1 meter; (2) the same 30 cm cube but from a distance of 3 meters; (3) a new 90 cm cube from a distance of 1 meter; or (4) the 90 cm cube from a distance of 3 meters. The image of these objects that fell on the eye was identical for the cube of 30 cm at 1 meter distance and for the cube of 90 cm at 3 meter distance. However, the infants did not turn their heads to the left when they saw the 90 cm cube from 3 meters away. The images of the objects that fell on the eye for the 30 cm cube from 1 and 3 meter distances, however, were quite different. Nonetheless, the infants continued to turn their heads to the left when they saw the 30 cm cube from 3 meters away. This experiment indicates that 1- to 2-month-old infants exhibit *size constancy.* They are aware that an object remains the same size from different distances even though the size of the image falling on the eye changes. (From "Stimulus Variables Determining Space Perception in Infants," by T.G.R. Bower, *Science,* 1965, *151,* 832–834. Copyright 1965 by the American Association for the Advancement of Science. Reprinted by permission.)

the newborn begins life with a number of attention-directing behaviors or "rules" that govern his looking behavior. These rules all seem to be derived from one basic overriding principle: Keep the level of visual stimulation at a maximal level. The specific behavior patterns or rules that follow from this basic principle are: (1) If you are awake and the light is not too bright, open your eyes. (2) If your eyes are open but you don't see any light, search for it. (3) If you see light but no edges or lines, keep searching for edges. (4) If you see an edge, keep looking at and across it (Haith, 1968; in press).

In other words, the newborn comes already equipped with attention-directing looking patterns designed to help detect visual stimulation and to seek out and maintain levels of visual stimulation as high as possible. Thanks to these behavior patterns, the newborn's attention will be drawn to objects, and his at-

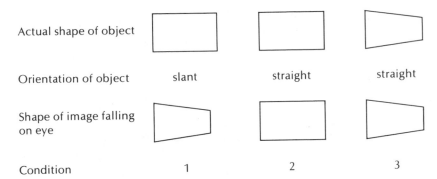

Actual shape of object			
Orientation of object	slant	straight	straight
Shape of image falling on eye			
Condition	1	2	3

Figure 4-3. An illustration of shape constancy in the infant. In another experiment by Bower (1966), infants 50 to 60 days old were taught to turn their heads when they saw a rectangular board presented at a 45-degree slant. The infants continued to turn their heads when they saw the same board in its straight position even though the image falling on the eye in these two conditions was quite different. Moreover, the infants did not turn their heads when they saw a trapezoid that created the same image on the eye as the original board at a 45-degree slant. This experiment indicates that 1- to 2-month-old infants exhibit *shape constancy.* They are aware that an object remains the same shape from different orientations even though the shape of the image falling on the eye changes. (From "Slant Perception and Shape Constancy in Infants," by T.G.R. Bower, *Science,* 1966, *149,* 88–89. Copyright 1966 by the American Association for the Advancement of Science. Reprinted by permission.)

tention and exploration will continue on those objects as long as they provide maximal stimulation. These attention-directing behavior patterns promote efficient learning by keeping the infant looking at objects, rather than at empty spaces, and by predisposing the infant to look at those parts of objects containing the highest level of stimulation (and the greatest amount of information): namely, edges and corners.

Attention-directing behaviors can be seen in the other sensory systems of the newborn, such as hearing and touch. Further, the infant's sensory systems do not operate wholly apart from one another; rather, they interact with and complement one another. Let us consider, for example, the interaction between the newborn's visual and auditory (or hearing) activities.

Certain sounds cause newborns to open their eyes, thereby bringing visual attention into play; other sounds have just the opposite effect, causing infants to close their eyes (Kearsley, 1973). Similarly, young infants who have stopped looking at a checkerboard pattern will start looking at it again if music is turned on (Horowitz, 1974), and young infants spend more time looking at an adult's face (and especially the eyes) when the adult is talking than when the adult is silent (Bergman, Haith, & Mann, 1971). In each of these examples, it appears that there are attention-directing behavior patterns keyed into the infant's hearing; these behavior patterns trigger visual activity designed to bring the source of the sound under visual scrutiny (Mendelson & Haith, 1976)—almost as though the infant is saying, "I hear it. Where is it?" The two sensory systems of vision and audition thus seem to be functionally related from birth, with newborns able to integrate information from both senses in their attempts to learn about the world.

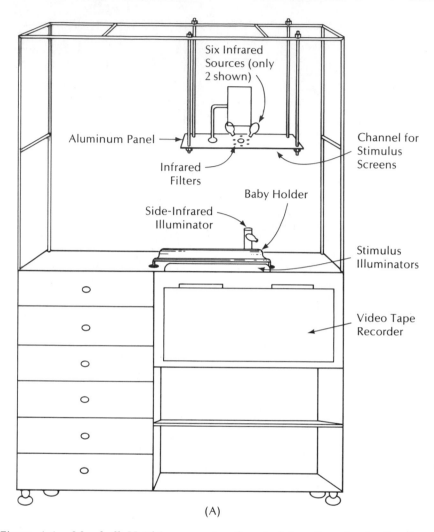

Six Infrared
Sources (only
2 shown)

Aluminum Panel

Infrared
Filters

Side-Infrared
Illuminator

Baby Holder

Channel for
Stimulus
Screens

Stimulus
Illuminators

Video Tape
Recorder

(A)

Figure 4-4. Marshall Haith's apparatus for studying the visual attention-directing behavior patterns of newborns. In this apparatus, the infant lies in a "baby holder." Different pictures are presented directly above while a videotape machine records where the infant is looking (Figure A). Later, observers replay the videotape and score where the infant's eyes are located on successive frames (see Figure B, opposite). (From "The Relation between Audition and Vision in the Human Newborn," by M. J. Mendelson and M. M. Haith, *Society for Research in Child Development Monograph,* 1976, *41* (Whole No. 4). Copyright 1976 by the Society for Research in Child Development. Reprinted by permission.)

In fact, there is some evidence that newborns actually expect sights and sounds to come from the same place (and are upset when they do not), even though they are not yet able to accurately direct their eyes to the location of particular sounds (Aronson & Rosenbloom, 1971; McGurk & Lewis, 1974; Lyons-Ruth, 1975). It may well be that the infant is born not only with certain attention-

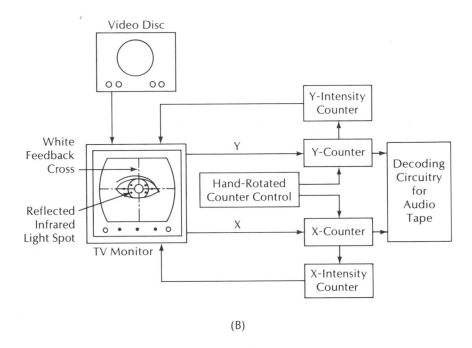

(B)

directing behavior patterns designed to track down the sources of sounds; the infant may even be born with an ingrained expectation as to where the source of a sound can be found (Bower, 1974).

What is true of hearing and vision is true of the newborn's other sensory systems. They, too, reveal the presence of certain inborn attention-directing behavior patterns. Moreover, they, like vision and hearing, interact in directing attention, thereby enabling newborns to more efficiently learn about the sights, sounds, odors, and feelings that surround them.

BEHAVIORAL CAPACITIES OF THE NEWBORN

At birth, the newborn does not yet have the mental capacity to understand, let alone to plan, his behavior. Understandably, then, his behavioral capacities are quite limited. Nonetheless, newborns begin life with a small but very significant set of behaviors. We have already examined some of these **innate** behaviors: namely, the attention-directing behaviors. Other *innate* behaviors that most of us are familiar with include the newborn's ability to cry, to suck, to grasp, to look, and, to a limited extent, to move about. Still other behaviors are ones that we examined in the preceding chapter: the newborn reflexes and the permanent reflexes. **Reflexes** enable the newborn to respond appropriately to certain sensory events without having to actually understand either the meaning of these events or the meaning of his own behavior. For example, if you stroke an infant's cheek with a nipple (or anything else), the infant will root or search for it with her mouth (the rooting reflex). Once attained by the mouth, the nipple will be sucked. Similarly, if you put your finger in a baby's hand, she will grasp it with all her might (the Darwinian reflex). Rooting for an object that touches the cheek, sucking an object placed in the mouth, and grasping an object placed in the hand are all examples of reflexes already present at birth. (See Chapter 3 for a full discussion of infant reflexes.)

COGNITIVE AND BEHAVIORAL DEVELOPMENT: THE LEARNING THEORY MODEL

The infant is born into the world with certain structured behavior patterns: in particular, the permanent and newborn reflexes already present at birth. Other newborn behavior is not so obviously structured but is more spontaneous in nature: for example, the newborn moves, gurgles, and cries when there is no externally apparent reason for the behavior. Together, these structured and spontaneous activities serve as the initial building blocks for learning.

According to the **learning theory** model, learning is said to occur when an infant (or, for that matter, an adult, or any other living creature) changes existing behavior as a result of experience with events that have occurred in the environment. A good example of this process is provided by the sucking reflex. Sucking is not a completely static and unalterable behavior. In fact, sucking is highly adaptable and is readily modified by external factors such as the rate of milk flow, the structure and size of the nipple, and the type of nutrient provided. Even on the first day of life, the infant sucks differently depending on whether milk, corn syrup solution, or an empty pacifier is provided (Schaffer, 1977). This adaptability of the infant's sucking behavior is, thus, one of the earliest indicators that the infant can modify his own behavior, or learn.

Learning can occur in many different ways. For example, the newborn can learn different forms of sucking as a result of getting different types of nipples and liquids. Some psychologists, however, believe that the different approaches to learning boil down to two basic mechanisms: classical conditioning and operant conditioning. These psychologists are called *learning theorists.*

Classical Conditioning

Classical conditioning (also known as **respondent conditioning**) is best illustrated by Pavlov's classic experiment with dogs. Pavlov taught dogs to salivate to the sound of a bell by simply ringing the bell repeatedly while the dogs were being fed. Initially, the dogs salivated to the food, and not to the bell. With time, however, the dogs learned to salivate whenever they heard the bell, even when they received no food.

The classical conditioning model explains learning of the sort that occurred in Pavlov's dogs in the following way. Already present in the dogs is a *reflex* connection between food (the **unconditioned stimulus**) and salivation (the **unconditioned response**). Dogs do not "learn" to salivate when they have food in their mouths; rather, they salivate to food as a reflexive behavior. The sound of a bell, however, is not innately related to salivation. Under normal circumstances, dogs do not salivate simply because they have heard a bell; the bell is therefore referred to as a *neutral stimulus*. After repeated pairings of the bell (the neutral stimulus) and the food (the unconditioned stimulus), the bell begins to elicit salivation by itself. An *association* has thus been formed between the bell and the food. When this happens, the bell is said to have become a **conditioned stimulus,** while salivation in response to the bell is termed a **conditioned response.** This new, learned connection between stimulus and response is called a **conditioned reflex.**

Operant Conditioning

Classical conditioning is a valuable learning tool, for it enables infants to expand their existing reflex behavior. Classical conditioning does not, however, produce totally new behavior; rather, it simply modifies existing behavior by associating an already present reflexive response with a new stimulus. To explain the development of complex new behavior, another type of learning is required: *operant conditioning.*

Operant conditioning (also known as **instrumental conditioning**) involves the modification of behavior as a result of its consequences. These consequences, called **reinforcers,** may be either positive or negative in impact, depending upon whether they increase or decrease the occurrence of the behavior that they follow.

A particular behavior is **positively reinforced** when its consequences cause the behavior to *increase.* The consequences may consist of either the presentation of a reward or the removal of an unpleasant situation. Typical positive reinforcers for newborns are food, a caress, or the removal of wet diapers.

Negative reinforcers have just the opposite effect of positive reinforcers; they result in a *decrease* in the behavior that they follow. One obvious form of negative reinforcement is punishment (an event that hopefully does not occur with newborns). A less obvious form of negative reinforcement is the removal or withholding of rewards.

Most learning theorists have been content to define positive and negative reinforcers by their effects on the child's surface behavior. Other psychologists, however, have tried to look deeper into the child's behavior in explaining just what is occurring. They have theorized that reinforcers affect a child's external behavior (for example, crying) because of the way they change the internal state or *drive level* of the child. For example, when children are hungry, they are presumably uncomfortable. This discomfort produces an intense internal stimulus, called a *drive* (Dollard & Miller, 1950). Feeding them reduces their discomfort and, hence, the accompanying drive. Psychologists who favor this theory argue that it is the decrease in the hunger drive that makes the feeding a positively reinforcing event.

Is Conditioning Possible in the Human Newborn?

If learning theory is correct, then learning in the human newborn occurs as a result of two basic processes: first, the modification of existing behaviors through the pairing of unconditioned stimuli with neutral stimuli (classical conditioning); and second, the creation of new behaviors through the use of positive and negative reinforcers (operant conditioning). Through these processes, the infant supposedly learns not only how to adapt existing behaviors and master new ones but also how to *discriminate* (or distinguish between) different stimuli in the environment—something that he has to know in order to respond appropriately to these stimuli. For example, according to the learning theory analysis, the infant quickly learns to "discriminate" his mother from other objects because of the mother's role as a provider of food and comfort (a few basic positive reinforcers). Thus, "knowledge" of the mother develops as a result of the association between the mother and satisfaction of basic primary drives.

The above model of learning in infancy rests on the assumption that conditioning of the newborn is possible from birth. Studies have found, however, that it is exceedingly difficult to condition the newborn, although the research to date has not been completely conclusive. In fact, it appears unlikely that newborns can be classically conditioned. Operant conditioning, on the other hand, is easier to obtain in newborns, but only under special circumstances.

One experiment neatly illustrates both of the above findings. Siqueland and Lipsitt (1966) examined the head-turning reflex in the newborn. In this reflex, a light touch on the infant's cheek will cause the infant to turn his head (about 25% of the time) to the side that was touched. In their task, Siqueland and Lipsitt first sounded a tone, then touched the infant's cheek. If the infant turned his head appropriately, he was rewarded (positively reinforced) with a swallow of sugar water. This task is interesting because it contains both classical and operant conditioning. Classical conditioning would be demonstrated if the infant learned to turn his head when only the tone was presented. Operant conditioning would be demonstrated if the infant increased the rate of head turning above the normal rate of 25%. The results of the study were both clear and dramatic. Newborns *did not* learn to turn their heads when only the tone was presented. On the other hand, there was an increase from 25% to 80% in the rate of head turning in response to the touch on the cheek. This study clearly demonstrates that, while operant conditioning can occur in the newborn infant, classical conditioning does not. Indeed, prior to about 4 weeks of age, conditioning of any sort is very difficult to establish and to maintain.

Why Can't Newborns Be Classically Conditioned?

A traditional learning theorist might say that the failure of classical conditioning in the newborn may be due to the infant's poor motor control. The study by Siqueland and Lipsitt discussed above eliminates this interpretation, since operant conditioning *of the same response* was demonstrated. Arnold Sameroff (1971) has offered a different, and intriguing, explanation for the absence of classical conditioning in the newborn. Recall that classical conditioning involves the pairing of a previously neutral stimulus with an unconditioned stimulus such as food. Sameroff suggests that a neutral stimulus for a newborn is also a *new* stimulus in that the newborn has had no previous experience with it. The newborn's failure to be classically conditioned might be due, then, to the fact that he has no firm mental representation for the neutral stimulus. Consequently, the newborn simply cannot discriminate the neutral stimulus from other objects and events, thus preventing the formation of a conditioned response to it. Sameroff's analysis implies that the infant must have already developed a mental representation for an object in the environment before he can be classically conditioned. Since the newborn does not come into the world with any well-formed mental representations, classical conditioning is not yet possible.

Note that Sameroff's interpretation essentially turns learning theory on its head, at least with regard to the newborn. The learning theory model argues that "discrimination" comes about through a process of conditioning. Sameroff argues, on the contrary, that, until objects and events have been represented and discriminated from one another, classical conditioning cannot take place. Hence, development of perceptual skills comes first in the life of the young infant.

THE COURSE OF PERCEPTUAL DEVELOPMENT

Infant perception must necessarily remain something of a mystery to both parents and psychologists, for the simple reason that infants cannot describe what they see, hear, and feel. The psychologist must therefore resort to other sources of information in attempting to chart the course of perceptual development during infancy. One source of available information is the looking behavior, or **attention,** of infants.

By observing infants' attention—what they look at, for how long, and how—the psychologist is able to indirectly examine perceptual processes in infancy. For example, if infants of a particular age prefer to look at one object over another (that is, spend more time looking at it when given a choice), it is assumed that there are certain properties inherent in the preferred object that have resulted in the preference for it. When these same infants are then shown a large number of such choices, it is further assumed that the objects that they prefer will share certain properties in common—hence the fact that they are preferred. These shared properties in turn enable the psychologist to generate hypotheses about how infants of a particular age perceive their world. Moreover, when the psychologist finds that different groups of objects are preferred by infants of different ages, this can be taken as evidence that the basic perceptual processes of the infants are different at different ages. Careful examination of which objects are most effective in attracting the attention of different-aged infants can therefore tell us a great deal about the perceptual development of the child.

Kagan's Theory

Jerome Kagan (1971) has used the technique just described to develop a comprehensive theory of perceptual development in the infant. Kagan's analysis of the types of objects most effective in attracting the attention of infants of different ages has led him to conclude that the *perceptual processes* employed by infants in analyzing objects actually change as they grow older, resulting in three stages of perceptual development: the first stage being present from birth, the second stage appearing at about 2 months, and the third stage appearing at about 12 months. Before turning to a description of these three stages, however, it is first necessary to get a solid understanding of two concepts basic to Kagan's theory: the concept of *habituation* and the concept of *schema* (plural form: *schemata*).

Habituation refers to the decrease in attention that occurs with repeated presentation of the same stimulus. A good example of habituation can be seen when a new picture is put on the wall beside an infant's crib. At first the infant seems very interested in the picture and may look at it for several minutes. Over time, however, her interest appears to diminish, and she may start to look at other things. Eventually the new picture is ignored, and the infant's attention is redirected to other objects in the room.

It is assumed that the process of habituation, or loss of interest in an object over time, illustrates several important aspects of perceptual processes in the infant. The infant's initial attraction to the new object illustrates a process called the **orientation reaction.** This is essentially a "what is it?" response to a new object in the environment. The orientation reaction involves a complex set of physiological responses that appear to prepare the child to focus attention on the new object. Once attention is focused, the infant begins to explore the object visually, looking at different parts of the picture, especially those areas that are brightly colored, have high contrast, and have interesting but simple shapes. Having explored all the interesting parts of the picture (for example, its edges and corners), the infant appears to become less interested in the picture and more interested in other things.

Kagan feels that significant learning is occurring while the infant is looking at the object. When the infant looks at different parts of the picture, he is creating mental representations in his memory for them. The mental representations of the people, objects, and events in the infant's environment are called *schemata*.

A **schema,** according to Kagan, is the mental representation or image that the infant constructs for an object. Learning about an object thus consists of constructing a *schema* (mental representation) for that object. This schema is not an exact visual representation of the object (as a photograph would be) but an abstract representation of the basic characteristics of the object (that is, a **prototype** of the object). Thus, the schema for a human face would include eyes, ears, nose, hairline, overall circular shape, and relation of these parts to one another. Whenever the child sees an object that contains the same basic characteristics as his schema, he **recognizes** the object.

Stage 1 of Kagan's Theory: The Infant's Attention Is Determined by the Physical Properties of the Object (0–2 Months)

The infant does not, at birth, possess schemata (mental representations) to perceive and understand the many objects and events that he senses. Rather, the world appears new, unfamiliar, and meaningless—James' "one great blooming, buzzing confusion."

Before the infant can develop these schemata for objects, it is of course first necessary for the objects to catch his attention. For Kagan's Stage-1 infant, it is the *physical properties of objects,* rather than their meanings, that determine which objects will receive attention. For example, in a study by Fantz (1961) involving pictures of faces, it was found that newborns spend almost as much time looking at a scrambled face as they do looking at a realistic face, and they look at both kinds of face pictures longer than at a divided circle. (See Figure 4-5.) The meaning of the two kinds of face pictures is quite different: one is a "face" as we adults understand that term, whereas the other is not. However, the physical properties of both are alike: both contain the same features or segments, although in different arrangements. Since we know that both are equally effective in attracting the infant's attention, we can conclude, then, that it is these physical properties, and not the objects' meanings, that elicit the attention of the Stage-1 child.

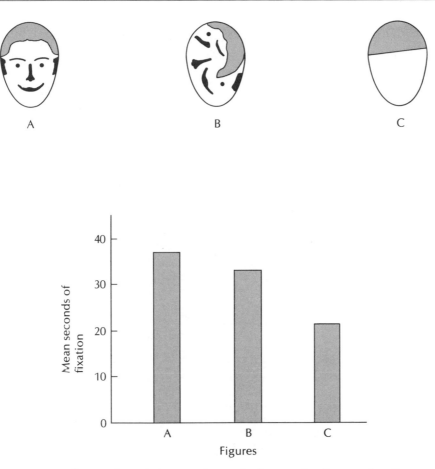

Figure 4-5.   The newborn infant prefers to look at optimally complex figures. Fantz (1966) showed that 2-week-old babies prefer to look at complex figures (A and B) rather than simple figures (C). Although there is a slight preference for the realistic face over the scrambled one, this preference is quite small in comparison to the infants' preferences for both faces over the divided ellipse. (From "The Origin of Form Perception," by R. L. Fantz, *Scientific American*, May 1961, *204*, 71–72. Copyright © 1961 by Scientific American, Inc. All rights reserved.)

Kagan measures the physical properties most important in determining whether a Stage-1 child will attend to a particular object in terms of what he calls the object's *rate of change*. **Rate of change** in an object is a function of the object's speed of movement, amount of contour (that is, the number of dark/light transitions), and contrast (that is, the difference in brightness between the object and the background on which it appears). Thus, moving objects have higher rates of change than stationary ones; objects with a lot of contour (like a checkerboard) have higher rates of change than ones with little contour; and very bright, high-contrast objects have higher rates of change than dull, low-contrast ones (Kagan, 1971; Haith, in press).

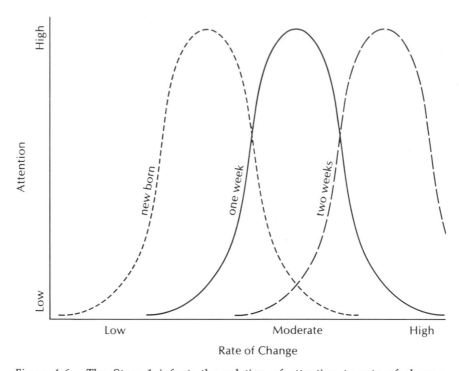

Figure 4-6. The Stage-1 infant: the relation of attention to rate of change. Kagan hypothesizes that the attention of the Stage-1 infant is drawn by objects having moderate rates of change—objects with higher and lower rates of change draw relatively less attention. This figure illustrates both the predicted curvilinear relation between attention and rate of change and the hypothesized increase in "optimal" rates of change as the infant grows older. (Adapted from *Change and Continuity in Infancy,* by J. Kagan. Copyright 1971 by John Wiley & Sons, Inc. Used by permission.)

Kagan argues that once an object with sufficient rate of change has captured the attention of the Stage-1 child, a schema for the object can be formed. For an object having a relatively low rate of change (but not so low as to fail to elicit the child's attention), a schema can be easily created; the amount of time spent looking at that object will be, accordingly, relatively brief. An object having a higher (but not too high) rate of change will be more difficult to handle and, hence, one for which a schema will be more difficult to construct; the amount of time spent looking at this object will thus be longer. Objects with rates of change that are too high will receive relatively little attention, since they will simply be too difficult for the child to handle; the child will not even attempt to create schemata for them. The relation between rate of change and attention is thus *curvilinear*, with highest levels of attention being produced for objects with moderate rates of change. (See Figure 4-6.) As the infant develops during Stage 1, the optimal rate of change increases somewhat—reflecting the infant's ability to deal with increasingly complicated arrays.

In summary, then, Kagan argues that it is the *physical properties* of objects, as measured by their *rates of change,* and the amount of time required to form *schemata* for the objects that determine which objects receive the *attention* of the Stage-1 child.

Stage 2 of Kagan's Theory: The Child's Attention Is Determined by the Similarity of the Object to Existing Schemata (2–12 Months)

Kagan theorizes that at about 2 months of age, a change occurs in the mental processes of the developing child. During Stage 1, the child's attention to objects was determined by their physical properties, with schemata then being formed for the objects that captured the child's attention. By 2 months of age, this Stage-1 mental process will have produced a number of schemata for various common objects in the child's environment.

As the child enters Stage 2, a dramatic change occurs in the types of objects that catch his attention. The Stage-2 child is no longer drawn to objects because of their physical properties. Rather, the child's attention to objects is now determined by *how closely the objects correspond to the child's existing schemata*. Objects that are somewhat different from the child's existing schemata are now the objects that draw the greatest amount of attention.

The mental process that characterizes the child in Stage 2 is thus altogether different from that present in Stage 1. When a Stage-2 child senses an object, he attempts to understand the object by comparing it to his existing stored schemata (mental images). If the object is identical to an existing schema, the comparison task is easy and the amount of time needed to attend to and understand the object will be brief. If the object is totally novel and unlike existing schemata, the comparison is also short, since the object is too unfamiliar for easy comparison. If, however, the object is similar to, but not identical to, an existing schema, the comparison is difficult (but not impossible), and the object will engage the child's attention maximally. Once again, then, a *curvilinear relation* appears to be involved; the Stage-2 child gives highest levels of attention to objects that are moderately different or *discrepant* from the child's existing schemata.

Some evidence for Kagan's view that the Stage-2 infant's attention is no longer determined exclusively by the physical properties of the object may be found in studies of infants' reactions to normal and distorted faces. Recall that the Stage-1 infant attended equally to the normal and distorted faces, since their physical properties were the same (that is, their contour, contrast, and so forth). Infants in Stage 2 (3 to 4 months), however, look longer at a normal schematic drawing of a face than at a distorted or rearranged one (Wilcox, 1969; Haaf & Bell, 1967). Moreover, for these Stage-2 infants, the greater the amount of distortion or rearrangement, the less time spent looking at the picture (Haaf & Bell, 1967). Kagan argues that the Stage-2 infant's preference for the normal over the distorted faces is due to the infant's recent construction of schemata for the faces of the important people in the environment. The normal drawing of a face has many properties in common with the infant's schemata for faces but does not match up perfectly with any of them. Therefore, Kagan would argue, the drawing is optimally discrepant from the infant's existing schemata (Kagan, 1971).

A weakness of studies such as those described immediately above is that we are trying to guess at the schemata that an infant forms for objects from prior experiences without knowing precisely what these experiences were. A true test of Kagan's theory requires that we remove this element of uncertainty by control-

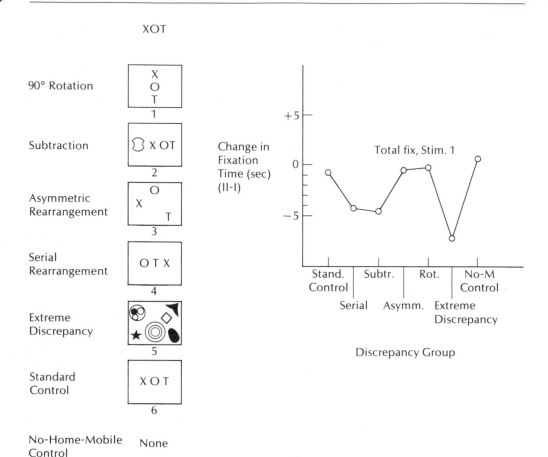

Figure 4-7. A test of the role of discrepancy as a determinant of the Stage-2 infant's attention. At the beginning of this experiment, 4-month-old infants were brought to the laboratory and shown the standard mobile "XOT" (see stimulus 6), and their looking or fixation time was recorded. The infants' mothers were then asked to show their infants one of the discrepant mobiles (see stimuli 1 to 6) at home for 30 minutes a day over a 21-day period. After this period of exposure to one of the discrepant mobiles, the infants were again taken to the laboratory and shown the standard mobile "XOT" (stimulus 6), and their fixation time was again measured. Although the results of this study were not perfectly consistent with Kagan's theory, they do suggest that attention is greatest when stimuli are moderately discrepant with previously experienced stimuli. (From *Change and Continuity in Infancy,* by J. Kagan. Copyright 1971 by John Wiley & Sons, Inc. Used by permission.)

ling these experiences. We can do this by actually giving infants experience with a particular object and, once they have formed a schema for it, carefully noting their attention to different modifications of the object. Research of this type has been done and lends some support to Kagan's view that the Stage-2 infant's attention is greatest for objects with moderate degrees of discrepancy from existing schemata (for example, Super, Kagan, Morrison, Haith, Weiffenbach, 1972). (See Figure 4-7.)

Stage 3 of Kagan's Theory: The Child's Attention Is Determined by the Number of Hypotheses He or She Can Generate about the Object (1 Year On)

Toward the end of the first year, a child moves into the final stage of perceptual development. The most noticeable change that marks this third stage is the ability to actively hypothesize about objects in his world. The Stage-3 child is no longer primarily concerned with matching new objects with existing schemata but rather is concerned with understanding the meaning of the unfamiliar stimulus. The infant now tries to use rules or hypotheses to relate new experiences to memories of past experiences.

An example of this change that occurs as the child enters Stage 3 is in the child's attention to scrambled faces. As explained earlier in the discussion of Stages 1 and 2, Stage-1 children spend the same amount of time staring at both scrambled and normal face pictures, while Stage-2 children stare longer at the normal-face pictures. Stage-3 children, on the other hand, attend *longer* to scrambled faces than to normal faces (Kagan, 1971). They do so, according to Kagan's theory, because they are trying to mentally solve the problem of how the face got into its scrambled state. Examples of this strategy are revealed by Kagan's recordings of the responses of several 2-year-olds to a scrambled face:

> One 2-year-old said, "What happened to his nose? Who hit him in the nose?"
> Another said, "Who that, Mommy? A monster, Mommy?" [Kagan, 1971, p. 73].

Summary of Perceptual Development

Perceptual development during the first two years of human life can be viewed as a gradual transition of the child from a *sensing* organism to a *perceiving* organism and, finally, to a *thinking* organism. The newborn can accurately *sense* objects. He can see his mother's face and the color of her hair. The newborn remains unconcerned, however, if she changes her hair color from one day to the next. This apparent lack of concern simply reflects the newborn's inability to remember the color that her hair was the day before, due to the absence of a *schema* for her face.

The 2- to 12-month-old child is learning to *perceive* objects: to recognize them by matching them with schemata he has already constructed. By 8 months of age, the baby can recognize the color of his mother's hair, because he remembers the color it was yesterday and the day before. Now if the mother changes her hair color, the baby will stare at her for a long time and may even begin to cry. Something is wrong. The person the baby sees no longer matches the mental schema he has constructed, and the baby must change the schema so as to incorporate the change.

One-year-old children can *think* about objects. They can hypothesize about why the objects do not match exactly with their existing schemata. By 1 year of age, the baby can recognize his mother as someone special as she leans over him, regardless of the color of her hair. The baby will not become upset by a change in her hair color, although he will stare at her for a very long time, trying to figure out how the change in hair color might have come about.

This transition from sensing to perceiving to thinking is what psychologists have called *perceptual development.* Perceptual development, however, is only one aspect of the cognitive development that occurs in children during the first two years of life. While infants are learning about the meaning of their sensations, they are also learning new behaviors and how to use these behaviors appropriately in different situations. This behavioral aspect of cognitive development is called *sensori-motor development* and is the subject of the section that follows.

SENSORI-MOTOR DEVELOPMENT

In the preceding section on perceptual development, the infant was in effect treated as an observer who merely lies on his back, looks, listens, feels, and thinks. Obviously this is a rather limited description of a normal, active baby. Even newborns are wiggling, sucking, crying, and grabbing organisms. Older babies are in almost continual motion. A great deal of what an infant must learn during the first two years is therefore necessarily concerned with behavior, for the active, moving infant must learn hundreds of new behaviors and must learn how to use these behaviors appropriately in hundreds of new situations. Some of this learning is surely acquired through the fairly automatic processes of conditioning (as described earlier in this chapter). Other aspects of behavioral (or of *sensori-motor*) development are not so easily explained in terms of conditioning processes and seem to require a more complex interpretation. Just as infants must build up mental representations for objects in their world (that is, "What is it?") if they are to recognize them in the future, they must also build up mental representations for their behavior (that is, "What do I do with it?") if they are to behave appropriately in the future. Thus, a complete description of the infant's development must include an account of the growth of mental representations for *behavior.*

The Course of Sensori-Motor Development

During the first two years of life, one of the infant's main sources of knowledge about the world is his behavioral interactions with that world. Jean Piaget (1951, 1952, 1954), who has done the most extensive analysis of these behavioral and cognitive advances, has called this period in the child's life the **sensori-motor period.** The term *sensori-motor* has been employed because the exchanges between the infant and the world are characterized by connections between incoming *sensory* information (that is not yet fully understood or identified as depicting a particular object) and the *motor behavior* that results from that sensory stimulation.

Piaget's theory (1951, 1952, 1954) of cognitive development focuses on the continual changes that occur in the range and complexity of the infant's behavior during these first years, and Piaget has therefore broken down the developmental process that occurs during this period into six fairly distinct stages. What follows is a brief summary of the child's progress during each of these six stages.

In this summary, approximate ages are given for each stage. However, it should be noted that there is an extraordinary amount of normal variability from child to child in the ages at which successive stages are reached. The ages are provided here only to give the student some idea of the time periods involved.

Any individual child might vary enormously from these guidelines without being in any sense abnormal or retarded. The order in which the stages are achieved is constant, however, for all children, since each stage is constructed from the learning of the earlier ones. Every child must therefore complete all of the earlier stages before moving on to the later ones.

Stage 1: The Use of Reflexes (0–1 Month)[1]

Stage 1 extends approximately from birth through the first month of life. During this stage, the infant's behavior is primarily defined by those reflexes present at birth. The infant can suck, cry, grasp, and wiggle, but can do very little else. True, the infant does apply his reflex behaviors to an increasingly wide variety of situations; he sucks bottles, pacifiers, toys, and fingers and grasps hair, clothing, blankets, and rattles. However, Piaget argues that the infant's behavior is relatively rigid and inflexible; regardless of the nature of the object, his behavior always remains the same. In addition, the infant in this stage fails to exhibit any special behaviors when an object disappears. For example, one infant was seen to inadvertently drop the rattle she was holding. Yet, she continued to hold her fingers curled *as if* the rattle was still there. In the same way, infants at this stage do not cry when their mothers leave the room, although they may continue to stare at the spot where the mother was last seen.

The behavior of the Stage-1 infant is thus characterized by the rigid and persistent application of existing reflex behaviors to new objects. Piaget uses the term **assimilation** to label this phenomenon of applying old behaviors (in Stage 1, the reflexes) to new objects. Thus, Piaget would say that an infant who grasps a new object with which he has not previously come in contact has "assimilated" the new object to an existing behavior: grasping. Assimilation, which is present during Stage 1 and throughout development, is discussed further in the immediately following discussion of Stage 2.

Stage 2: Repetition of Simple Acts for Their Own Sake (1–4 Months)

The infant in the second stage, unlike the infant in the first stage, is characterized by the often seemingly endless repetition of simple acts. For example, an infant of 3 months might be seen repeatedly grabbing her blanket and letting it go. Another infant of the same age might be seen intently watching her fingers as she wiggles them before her eyes.

Piaget believes that the infant's tendency to repeat the same behavior over and over plays an important role in cognitive development. It is through this

[1]Throughout this section, the actual titles used by Piaget for the different stages have not been employed. The authors' reasons for not using these labels reflect Piaget's own inconsistency in his labeling of the stages and the authors' desire not to overly burden the student by introducing a lot of new terminology. However, for the student who wishes to pursue further the study of Piaget, the actual Piagetian titles are given below:

Stage 1: The use of reflexes.
Stage 2: The first acquired adaptations and the primary circular reaction.
Stage 3: The secondary circular reaction and procedures for making interesting sights last.
Stage 4: The coordination of secondary schemes and their application to new situations.
Stage 5: The tertiary circular reaction and the discovery of new means by active exploration.
Stage 6: Invention of new means through mental combinations (Flavell, 1963).

seemingly meaningless repetition that the infant is able to perfect simple skills, for careful examination of the infant's behavior reveals that each repetition of an act is not identical to the one before. Minor modifications are continually introduced. It is these minor modifications that indicate the onset of true learning, or, to use Piaget's term, *adaptation*.

Adaptation, as defined by Piaget, is a two-part process, each part of which complements the other. Adaptation consists first of all of *assimilation:* new objects are assimilated to existing behaviors when they are treated in exactly the same way as old objects. For example, when new objects are placed in the infant's hand, the infant initially responds to all of them in exactly the same way: by grasping. Piaget would say that the infant has assimilated the new object, say a new rattle, to an existing behavior—namely, grasping.

When assimilation occurs in isolation (as during Stage 1 of sensori-motor development), the new object is treated in exactly the same way as old objects. If the new object is identical or extremely similar to old objects, no problem arises. But what happens when the child is given a somewhat dissimilar object? Let us assume, for example, that the infant has just been given a bell for the first time. If the infant tries to grasp the bell in exactly the same way as she grasps a rattle, she will be unsuccessful. The bell will fall to the ground. To successfully manage the bell, the infant must therefore go beyond mere assimilation (the application of an existing behavior to new objects). The second part of adaptation, namely *accommodation*, must first occur.

Accommodation refers to a change or modification of behavior that occurs when an assimilated object cannot fit exactly into an existing behavior pattern. The infant in the second stage of sensori-motor development will, when given a bell for the first time, soon discover that the bell does not fit into her hand in exactly the same way as the rattle with which she is already familiar. If the infant is to successfully grasp the bell, she must make slight changes in her behavior. The infant must learn to curl her fingers around the bell in a slightly different way. When the infant successfully learns to hold a bell as well as a rattle, Piaget would say that she has accommodated her grasping behavior to meet the special demands of a newly assimilated object. The infant has *assimilated* a new object to an old behavior (applied the old behavior to the new object) and has *accommodated* her behavior to the new object (changed the old behavior to fit the new object). Thus, true *adaptation* has occurred.

Piaget theorizes that the modifications that occur in Stage 2, and that result from the child's experience with new objects, are paralleled by corresponding modifications in the child's cognitive, or internal, thought processes. Piaget's term for these internal thought processes is **scheme** (plural form: **schemes**).[2] A *scheme* is the mental representation formed in the infant's mind for a particular sequence of behavioral acts. Thus, each external behavioral act occurs because there is in the child's mind a *scheme* (mental representation) for a particular sequence of actions that directs that particular response. For example, a rattle is grasped because there is an existing grasping scheme that directs the child to close his fingers around any object placed in his hand. Indeed, for the child at this stage, objects are primarily defined by the schemes that can be applied to them.

---

[2]We have chosen to retain the original French word ("scheme") rather than the English translation ("schema") to minimize confusion over differences in the way the term is used by Piaget and Kagan.

In Piaget's theory, the external changes in an infant's behavior that result from assimilation and accommodation are accompanied by internal changes in the infant's *schemes* (mental programs of action). Thus, when the infant accommodates and slightly modifies her grasp in order to be able to hold a bell as well as a rattle, this change in external behavior is accompanied by a corresponding change in the internal scheme for grasping. Similarly, when the infant learns to suck a full bottle of milk in a different manner than a milkless pacifier, this change in external behavior is accompanied by a change in the sucking scheme. Development during Piaget's Stage 2, and all later stages of Piaget's theory, is thus characterized not only by changes in behavior but also by changes in the cognitive structure of the mind.

The similarity between Piaget's term *scheme* (plural: *schemes*) and Kagan's term *schema* (plural: *schemata*) is unquestionably a source of confusion to the student of psychology. Therefore, before turning to Stage 3 of Piaget's theory, it seems advisable first to clarify the distinction. The literature itself unfortunately does not distinguish between these two concepts. However, for the purposes of this text, *schema* (Kagan's concept) refers to a mental representation for perceived objects, whereas *scheme* (Piaget's concept) refers to a mental representation for a behavioral act. In other words, Kagan's *schema* is concerned with the characteristics of the *object itself,* while Piaget's *scheme* is concerned with the *actions available* to the child.

Stage 3: Repetition of Responses to Produce Interesting Results (4–8 Months)

During Stage 2, the child's behaviors were primarily ends in themselves and were not concerned with the results they produced. In other words, the Stage-2 child grabs a blanket not so much for the pleasure of feeling it as for the pleasure of performing the act itself. By Stage 3, this is no longer true. Now, the child's behavior is guided by the effect it has on the environment. The new interest that the child shows in the results of his or her behavior is, not surprisingly, accompanied by a dramatic increase in susceptibility to operant conditioning. However, one need not perform operant-conditioning tasks to see the infant's newly found fascination with the results of his or her own behaviors. For example, one 5-month-old baby was seen knocking over every toy that was placed beside her. This repetition of the "knocking over" response continued dozens of times and was applied to a wide variety of toys, each toy requiring a slightly different method of attack. Indeed, the game terminated only after almost half an hour— and then only because the parent tired of it. The baby's interest appeared insatiable. Another common game played by the child who has reached Stage 3 is that of "toy dropping." In this game, the infant methodically drops his favorite toys from his crib or stuffs them through the bars of his playpen. Once the toys are out of reach, he immediately begins to cry for their return. The toys are then retrieved by an adult—only to be tossed or pushed out again within a few seconds. The toy dropping game usually persists indefinitely—or until the adult simply refuses to continue.

In these examples, it is clear that the baby is not simply repeating an act for its own sake. He or she is repeating an act because that act has interesting results. A toy is knocked over or dropped so that the child may see it fall; a rattle is banged against the crib rail so that the child may hear the clanging sound produced.

It is also during Stage 3 that the child begins to differentiate objects from one another and to give each a special identity. Different objects are now treated differently: a rattle is something to shake; a block is something to bang. If the parent holds a rattle a few feet from the child, the child is likely to shake her empty hand, thereby indicating her recognition of the rattle as something to shake.

Piaget believes that the Stage-3 child who, for example, recognizes the rattle as being something to shake, does *not* recognize the rattle because of its physical characteristics; rather, the child recognizes the rattle because of his or her behavioral interactions with it, as was the case during Stage 2. In other words, it is Piaget's belief that a Stage-3 child, like a Stage-2 child, has *schemes* for actions that do not yet define the objects by their unique physical characteristics (what they look like) but by his or her behavioral interactions with them (what can be done with them). The child may thus remember a behavior he likes to perform and therefore shake his hand back and forth to indicate to his mother that he wants something to shake. Piaget would argue that the child, in so shaking his hand, does not actually remember the physical characteristics of a particular object—he simply wants something—anything—to shake.

Older brothers and sisters are often well aware of the infant's failure to provide a unique identity for objects. If they want a toy the baby is playing with, they simply take it and replace it with something else. For the Stage-3 infant, such switches often go either unnoticed or ignored. As long as the new toy can be readily assimilated into ongoing behavior, the infant remains indifferent to which particular object is available even though he has the perceptual abilities to readily discriminate between these objects.

Another commonplace example that the new parent will appreciate, and no doubt recognize, is the Stage-3 infant's apparent lack of concern when the parent is not present. The infant in Stage 3 seldom cries for her father after he has left on a shopping trip, since she does not yet remember him in his absence. She might cry as the father leaves the room. However, her crying is less an indication that she misses him than that she misses the particular activity in which they were engaged before the father left.

Stage 4: Beginning to Solve Simple Problems (8–12 Months)

It is in Stage 3 that the child's behavior begins to be guided by its results: simple behaviors are repeated since they produce interesting results, not simply for the sake of repetition as in Stage 2. The same fascination with results continues to be present in Stage 4, but to an even greater extent. Now the child will perform one act so as to enable him to perform another act. For example, the 10-month-old baby is likely to knock over a toy in order to reach a rattle that she wishes to shake. One action sequence (knocking over) is employed as a *means*; the other action sequence (shaking) serves as the *goal*.

Piaget argues that such behavior, combining means and goal actions, reflects two very sophisticated advances in internal thought processes. The first such advance is the child's ability to *combine* schemes mentally and use them to *solve simple problems*. During the first three stages, behavior showed a gradual progression from reflexive behavior (for example, a touch on the cheek was followed by rooting and sucking), to repetition for the sake of repetition (for example, re-peatedly grabbing and letting go of a blanket), to repetition to produce interesting results (for example, "knocking over" and "toy dropping"). In all three of these forms of behavior, the child's act resulted from sensory stimulation: either the stimulation that preceded the act (for example, a reflex), or the stimulation that the child sought to achieve (for example, "knocking over"). In Stage 4, however, the child's behavior is no longer solely governed by simple sensory stimulation. The child now develops the ability to combine and coordinate schemes to solve simple problems (such as knocking over a toy to reach a rattle).

The second advance in thought processes that occurs during Stage 4 in-volves the *permanent nature of objects*. Objects begin for the first time to have an existence of their own, independent of the behavior of the child. Searching for lost objects now is much more extensive and intentional. If the 10-month-old sees his sister hide his rattle behind a doll, he will remember where the rattle is and behave appropriately; he will knock over the doll and grab the rattle. Similarly, older brothers and sisters will find, much to their disappointment, that they can no longer get the toy their baby sister is playing with simply by substituting another toy having a similar behavioral use: for example, one rattle for another.

Piaget argues that in exhibiting such behavior, the Stage-4 child shows the beginnings of *object permanence*. **Object permanence** refers to our mental ability to know that an object still exists even though it is not presently visible to us and even though it is not in any other way involved in our current activities. As adults, we take this ability for granted, saying "Of course objects are permanent. Of course they have an existence apart from us." For example, none of us would seriously doubt that our house is still there when we go to school or even when we leave town to go on a vacation. Objects are permanent and enduring. Our involvement with them is not necessary for their continued existence.

For very young infants (in the first three stages), the permanence of objects is not at all obvious, according to Piaget. As far as young infants are concerned, objects are merely extensions of the infants themselves and, as such, they cease to exist when the infants are no longer involved with them. According to Piaget, the infant of Stages 1, 2, and 3 is not at all aware that the rattle she is playing with today is the same as the one she played with yesterday, and that the rattle con-tinued to exist during the time in between. Thus, the Stage 1, 2, or 3 infant shows no apparent concern when an object disappears, for in his or her thought process-es, the following saying applies with real meaning: "Out of sight, out of mind."

By Stage 4, however, the infant is no longer indifferent to the disappearance of an object. The infant will cry for his father after he leaves the room or for the toy that has rolled beneath the sofa. Neither the babysitter nor a new toy will take the place of the lost object, for the child is now able to remember missing objects and to know when they are missing. This ability to remember and miss objects marks a major advance in the cognitive sophistication of the child. In order for a child to remember particular objects in their absence, the child must have ac-quired schemes that include information not present in the schemes of earlier stages of development; namely, the schemes must now contain not only a mental representation, or description, of the child's interaction with an object but also a description of certain *physical features* of the object as well. Thus, for example, a Stage-4 infant's scheme for a rattle might be something like this: a rattle is some-thing to shake, that produces a clanging sound, and that is shaped like two balls connected by a short stick.

Object permanence, although present in Stage 4, remains incomplete. Under certain circumstances, the child's behavior implies that the existence of an object remains very much dependent on his or her behavioral interactions with it. For example, assume that a child's rattle is hidden under her blanket while the child watches. The Stage-4 child will pull the blanket aside and retrieve the rattle. If, however, the rattle is moved to a new hiding place under a pillow before the child can retrieve it, she will continue to persistently search for the rattle behind the doll—even though she watched the entire transaction!

The child at this stage endows each object with a type of permanent identity, as evidenced by persistent search behavior. However, this identity is not quite complete or accurate. Piaget believes that such behavior indicates that the child is still somewhat confused about the permanence of objects.

Stage 5: Trial-and-Error Experimentation (12–18 Months)

In Stage 5, the child continues to show problem-solving behavior. However, the child now takes a much more active role in discovering new and more efficient means to achieve goals. (See Figure 4-8.) The child begins to systematically explore the environment by deliberately varying behavior in order to observe its effects. The Stage-5 child will bang, wiggle, slide, and shove puzzle pieces into their appropriate (or sometimes inappropriate) holes until the goal is achieved. A Stage-4 child, on the other hand, would have persisted in banging the pieces with no deliberate attempt to vary actions and thereby discover a workable solution. *Trial-and-error experimentation* thus characterizes the behavior of the Stage-5 child.

Another example of such trial-and-error Stage-5 behavior may be seen in the child's attempt to get an object that is on a table, slightly out of reach. Whereas the Stage-4 child would have simply persisted in trying to reach the object, the Stage-5 child will quickly turn to new methods of attack. After a few unsuccessful attempts at reaching, she may try to bang the table and knock the toy off. If banging is also unsuccessful, she may climb onto a nearby chair in order to reach her goal.

The Stage-5 child appears, in addition, to have a complete understanding of the nature and permanence of objects. Objects are now viewed not only as permanent and enduring but as having a unique existence of their own. The Stage-5 child is no longer confused when an object is moved from one hiding place to another but will, like an adult, search for the object in the place last seen even if it has been moved several times. Thus, to return to our earlier example, the child will now search for the rattle under the pillow and not under the blanket.

Stage 6: Beginning of Problem Solving through the Use of Mental Imagery (18–24 Months)

While the Stage-5 child undoubtedly could, as already discussed, solve the problem of reaching an object on a table by climbing on a chair already sitting next to the table, he or she would probably not be able to solve the problem if it first required moving a chair to the table. The Stage-6 child can solve this more complex problem; moreover, the child can do so relatively quickly. Stage-6 children are able to solve this problem because, unlike Stage-5 children, they are able

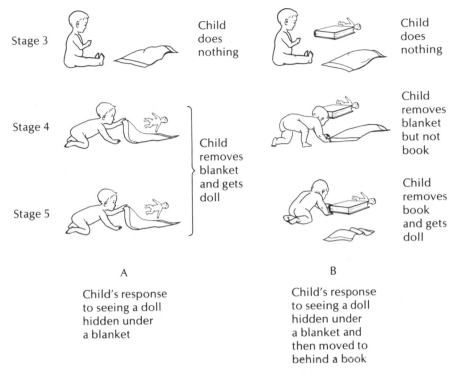

Figure 4-8. The development of object permanence.

to use their imagination to mentally solve problems without first physically employing trial-and-error experimentation.

The onset of this ability to use imagination to solve current problems indicates the close of the sensori-motor period. Objects are now viewed as having a unique and permanent existence of their own. During the earlier stages of the sensori-motor period, the child's thoughts, or schemes, were internal representations of behavior. Particular objects were not represented in thought except as extensions of the particular behaviors in which they were frequently involved. Even at Stages 4 and 5, when the child's schemes first began to include information on the physical features of objects, the behavioral aspects of the schemes continued to control. By Stage 6, however, the child has begun to create separate mental representations for objects, quite apart from behavior. These internal representations for objects in the external world are what Piaget terms *images*. An **image** for an object defines its perceptual characteristics (what it looks like, sounds like, and feels like) without reference to what the child can do with it (the scheme). By the sixth, and final, stage of the sensori-motor period, the *image* for an object has completely broken away from the scheme and functions on its own. Now, the child is said to have an **imagination.** It is, for example, no longer necessary for the child to systematically bang, wiggle, and slide the puzzle pieces into their holes. He or she can now look at the puzzle and the particular piece and *mentally imagine* the outcome of each of these behaviors. Thanks to this new capacity for mental trial and error, the Stage-6 child can often solve a new problem on the very first trial.

Summary of Sensori-Motor Development

In the course of the first two years of life, human infants progress from a state in which their behavior is largely involuntary and reflexlike to a state in which they are able to plan their behavior in advance. Piaget has argued that the advances in behavior that occur during these first two years are the result of the child's creation and modification of internal thought processes, or *sensori-motor schemes*. During the first few months, schemes are simply representations for reflexlike behavior patterns. Later, however, the schemes come to include some form of representation for the results of the behavior and, still later, for the particular objects that are generally involved in these behaviors. Finally, at the close of the sensori-motor period, the objects begin to have unique mental representations of their own, or *images*, that exist apart from the child's mental representations for his or her behavioral interactions with these objects (schemes).

Comparison of the Theories of Piaget and Kagan

Jean Piaget and Jerome Kagan are among the leading theorists of cognitive development in infancy. Their theories have focused on somewhat different aspects of infant development: Kagan on perceptual development, Piaget on sensori-motor development. In addition, Piaget and Kagan have emphasized different techniques in developing their respective theories; Kagan has stressed controlled laboratory research, while Piaget has derived his theory from in-depth, naturalistic observations of his own three children. There are certain points, however, where their theories overlap and conflict.

In comparing their respective theories, it is especially important to emphasize the similarities and differences between Kagan's *schema* and Piaget's *scheme*. Both Kagan and Piaget are concerned with the formation of mental representations in the child. Both Kagan and Piaget assume that these initial mental units are the basis for all later learning. However, Kagan and Piaget differ both in terms of what the basic mental representations are and in terms of how these mental representations are created. Piaget's *schemes* are representations of behavioral acts, created from behavior itself. Kagan's *schemata* are representations of the physical characteristics of objects, created from sensory stimulation.

This distinction between behavior and objects is a very important one and is basic to their respective theories. Piaget believes that the child's knowledge of objects in the world can occur only through behavioral interaction with them. Kagan believes that knowledge of objects can result simply from perceptual exposure to them. For Piaget, mental representations for objects do not develop until the child is in the fifth stage (around 1 year of age). For Kagan, mental representations for objects begin to develop within the first few months.

On at least one point, however, both Kagan and Piaget are agreed: at birth, the infant has no schemata or stored images for external objects in his world. Therefore, although their sensory sytems are working, newborns are unable to recognize, understand, or remember the objects around them. It is only through interaction with the world that infants will create the internal images that will eventually enable them to recognize objects, to behave appropriately with them, and to remember them in their absence.

ISSUE

What happens to the premature baby who is forced to spend weeks or months in a hospital incubator? Is his perceptual or sensori-motor development retarded?

A clear answer to this question is not available. However, research with animals has demonstrated that an animal that spends the first few months of life in a *deprived environment*, with little to look at or do, may suffer severe effects in both its cognitive and its social development. The effects of **deprivation** on human infants are not at all clear, however. Assuming that the prematurity itself has not resulted in some form of biological damage, the human infant, unlike the research animal, may be able to "catch up" with the learning that has been missed. It is not known for certain, however, that this catching up will occur, let alone how complete it will be. There has therefore been a movement in recent years to improve the hospital environment of the premature baby through the use of waterbeds, crib mobiles, and increased handling by nurses and parents. These **enrichment** techniques have been found to be very effective in increasing the health and motor development of premature babies, at least over the short run (Solkoff, Yaffe, & Weintraub, 1967; Scarr-Salapatek & Williams, 1973). The obvious advantage of these enrichment techniques is that, even if it is assumed that premature infants can compensate eventually for learning that they lose while in the incubator, the amount of catching up that they have to do is greatly reduced.

THE EFFECTS OF ENVIRONMENT ON COGNITIVE GROWTH IN INFANCY

Learning in infancy is clearly dependent on the environment of the child. If children are to learn how to use objects and are to form mental representations for these objects, they must have the objects available to them. What, then, are the effects of abnormal and inadequate environments on cognitive development during infancy? How permanent are these effects? These questions, though straightforward and important, yield no simple answers. We do, however, possess a somewhat clearer picture of what happens during infancy itself than we do of what happens later in a person's life. In other words, we are more certain of the short-term effects of environment than we are of the long-term effects. Let us therefore turn first to a consideration of the immediate effects of environment before turning to the more difficult question of long-term effects.

Evidence for the immediate effects of environmental conditions on the cognitive development of the infant is plentiful. For example, Wayne Dennis found as early as 1960 that the severely restricted and inadequate environment of infants in Lebanese orphanages produced children who were severely mentally retarded at the age of 2 years. In fact, the average IQ of this group was only 50 (Dennis, 1960, 1973).

Of course, extreme situations always produce extreme results. Although most psychologists were ready to believe Dennis' findings, many did not accept the implication that less extreme forms of deprivation could affect development in infancy. A recent study by Burton White (1971), however, shows that even relatively minor changes in the infants' environment can have immediate effects on their development. White's experiment was a simple one. He used three groups of orphans in an institution. The first group of children remained in a standard institutional environment. The second group of children received increased stimulation in the form of objects to look at that were very simple initially but gradually increased in complexity. The third group received even greater stimulation in the form of multipatterned crib bumpers and colorful crib mobiles and received this stimulation throughout the experiment. White's findings were striking. The infants in the third group (most stimulation) were able to look at and reach for objects a full month and a half earlier than those in the first group (no extra stimulation). The infants in the second group (middle stimulation), however, were able to look at and reach for objects even earlier than those in the third group (high stimulation).

White's study points to an optimal level of stimulation in infancy; either too much (the third group) or too little (the first group) stimulation can interfere with cognitive development, at least during the period of infancy itself. What, then, happens to these children later on? Does an inadequate environment in infancy permanently retard later learning?

Accurate data on the long-term effects of early experiences are unfortunately not as clear-cut as one would hope. Some psychologists (for example, Burton White, 1976) believe that the effects of early experience are long-lasting, if not permanent. Other psychologists (for example, Clarke & Clarke, 1976) believe that it is possible for children to overcome later the effects of early deprivation and to catch up. Indeed, there are ample data to support both positions.

On the one hand, there is little doubt that children who perform well (or poorly) on cognitive tasks during infancy do so largely because of their environment. Moreover, many of these children continue to perform well (or poorly) throughout their lives (for example, see White et al., 1976). One might add, however, that most children also tend to stay in the same environment. Even those children who are moved from one environment to another often "bring their old environment with them." Thus, their behavior continues to reflect what they have learned—and to affect the way they are treated by others (Schaffer, 1977; Clarke & Clarke, 1976). As a result, the same types of experiences that the child encounters in infancy tend to be repeated throughout his life, and it becomes impossible to determine whether the early experiences alone could have produced the long-term effects.

On the other hand, there are a number of reported case histories to the effect that children who have spent their infancies and early childhoods in severely deprived environments do recover normal cognitive skills when later moved to a normal or "superior" environment (Clarke & Clarke, 1976; Davis, 1947; Koluchová, 1972, 1976). Unfortunately, these individual case histories fail to tell us about the "other children"—the ones who were similarly transferred but continued to show cognitive deficits throughout their lives. Individual success stories no doubt occur. However, there is no guarantee that most, let alone all, cases of deprived environments will have such a happy ending.

Since some children do seem to have the capacity for full recovery, while others do not, it is only natural to search for the key factors that distinguish these children—factors that might help us in arriving at a long-term prognosis for a particular child. Although we have very little definitive evidence of these key factors, the work of Wayne Dennis (1973) is suggestive. Dennis began his investigation of the orphans of Lebanon during the 1950s, just at the time when adoption was first legalized in that country. Thus, he had access to children who had spent their entire lives in orphanages (because adoption was not possible) and to children who were adopted between the ages of 2 and 6 years. Let us first consider the course of development for the children who were not adopted.

Until 1956, all orphans in Lebanon spent their first six years in an infant orphanage or "crèche." At 6 years of age, the average IQ for this group—both boys and girls alike—was 50. When the children reached 6, all were transferred to single-sex institutions. During the years that followed, the cognitive development of the girls remained stable; at adulthood, their average IQ was still 50. During these same years, however, the cognitive development of the boys rapidly accelerated; by adulthood, their average IQ was 80. Since there is no reason to assume that the girls were inherently inferior to the boys, or that they were treated differently up to the age of 6, one must conclude that the older boys' institutional home had a more stimulating environment that enabled them to overcome many of their earlier cognitive deficits.

Dennis' later findings on the course of development of adopted orphans tend to support this conclusion. First, Dennis found that all of the children— regardless of sex—showed gains in IQ as a result of their adoption. Second, he found that the extent of these effects was related to the child's age when adoption occurred. Children adopted before the age of 2 soon showed *full recovery* and achieved an average IQ of *100* by the age of 10 years. Children adopted after 2 years of age grew at a normal rate (that is, one year in mental age for one year of chronological age) but had not overcome their original deficit by the age of 14.

The time for definitive conclusions is not yet here. Nevertheless, it seems that the long-term effects of early experiences in infancy are not as immutable as previously believed. The course of development can change dramatically. Of special importance, of course, is the fact that removing a child from a very deprived environment and placing the child in a very good one can result in major gains in cognitive skills—and in some cases full recovery. The extent of this recovery seems related both to the age at which the change in environment occurs, and the extent to which the new environment is specially structured to the needs of the child.

ISSUE

What is an optimal environment for an infant's cognitive growth?

The child has a great deal of learning to accomplish during the first few years of life. Parents are therefore understandably concerned with how to facilitate this learning. In particular, how can the environment be arranged so as to optimize the child's learning during the first 2 years? In the past, widely discrepant recommendations have been made: keep the child as quiet and unexcited as possible since the lack of confusion will promote learning of basic ideas; versus give the child as much stimulation as possible since wide exposure to different events facilitates learning.

Neither view is quite correct. Certainly, an inadequate environment that provides very little stimulation for the child can produce negative results. How can the child learn about the world if he or she never has the opportunity to experience it? On the other hand, overstimulation can also impede growth. If the environment is too confused and busy, the child has little opportunity to learn much about any particular object. The optimal environment lies somewhere in the middle. The optimal environment is the one that is carefully constructed according to the abilities of the child. Thus, the optimal environment of the child immediately after birth is relatively simple and quiet. As the infant grows older, the environment should grow increasingly complex.

CREATING AN OPTIMAL ENVIRONMENT

The human child is probably able to overcome many unfortunate circumstances in infancy. Nevertheless, it makes good sense to try to create an optimal environment from the start. The optimal environment is one that is geared to the abilities of the child. At each stage of development, the child should be exposed to objects and tasks slightly beyond his or her current abilities. If the tasks are too easy, the child will quickly lose interest in them. If the tasks are too complex, the child will give up and turn to easier tasks.

During the first two months, the infant's environment should be relatively simple. There should be a small number of different objects for the infant to look at that have a few well-defined features. An example of a good "looking object" for this age is the smiling face caricature. (See Figure 4-9.) Objects that are too easy, like a colored circle, will be ignored. Objects that are too complex, like a psychedelic poster, will also be ignored and may upset the child. Similarly, the infant should have a few simple toys to suck and grasp. Examples of good toys during the first two months are rattles and pacifiers. More sophisticated toys that require manipulation of strings and dials will either be ignored or subjected to simple behavior patterns like sucking and grasping. A large number of different toys is also unnecessary, since the child will be relatively inflexible in using them.

From 2 to 4 months, infants are beginning to develop internal representations for objects (schemata) and for behaviors (schemes) and are rapidly expanding their knowledge of the world. At this age, then, it is important to expose the child to simple variations in the environment. The "looking objects" in the environment should be more varied and slightly more complex. For example, more detailed pictures of faces that differ in color, shape, size, and specific features would be appropriate for the child of this age. Toys should remain relatively simple and nonmanipulative, but the child should be exposed to a number of different objects that can be readily adapted to the behaviors of sucking, grasping, and shaking. Rattles, bells, rubber necklaces, and teething rings are good toys for children of this age. Some variety in toys is a good idea, since infants are now able to modify their behaviors to fit the special characteristics of new objects.

From 4 to 8 months, the child's behavior begins to be guided by its results. The child now drops an object to see it fall or pulls a string to see a figure move. At this age, then, the child needs manipulative toys that produce interesting sights and sounds. Crib mobiles with strings to pull and busy boxes with doors to open and knobs to turn are very appropriate for the child of this age. (See Figure 4-10.)

By the next stage (8 to 12 months), the child has made two major advances. He or she is now able to combine different behavior sequences with one another and has a limited ability to remember objects and plan behavior in advance. It is now appropriate to play little games with the child, such as hiding toys under

Figure 4-9.   An example of a good "looking object" for infants during the first few months. The smiling face caricature is a good "looking object" for the newborn. It has a few basic parts (producing an optimal level of complexity) and good contrast between these parts and the background of the face itself. One infant of 1 month was observed staring at such a face for over 15 minutes.

Figure 4-10.   An example of a good toy for the 4- to 8-month-old infant. Between 4 and 8 months, the infant is interested in the results of his behavior. Conventional crib mobiles are usually thoroughly enjoyed by babies of this age.

blankets and behind barriers. Since the child at this age also begins to treat different objects in terms of their own particular characteristics, it is important that a sizable variety of different objects be available. Also, children begin during this stage to integrate behavior sequences; hence, it is useful to have several different objects available for them to play with at the same time. For example, children of this age love to put objects in containers. Buckets full of balls and small toys can engage their interest for a half hour or more. Other good toys for children at this age are simple musical instruments like xylophones and drums.

From 12 to 18 months, children begin to systematically explore their environments. They deliberately vary their own behavior sequences in order to observe what effects these variations will have. The child is now quite able to manipulate objects and should have a variety of manipulative toys. Simple puzzles, form boards, puzzle boxes, stacking toys, nesting toys, and wagons full of blocks would be appropriate at this time. The child of this age will spend many hours trying to fit circular objects into circular holes and stacking blocks on top of one another.

Since the child of 12 months or so has also developed the ability to hypothesize about perceptual objects in the environment, this is also a good time to start showing the child books. Picture books of familiar objects like dogs and cats are especially popular with children at this age.

From 18 to 24 months, children learn to mentally explore their world. They can now figure out solutions to problems in their heads before actually attempting the behavior. Therefore, increasingly complex manipulative toys, puzzles, and games are appropriate at this age. The child's interest in books has also continued to increase. Children of this age seem to be especially interested in make-believe, impossible pictures, such as those used in many of the Dr. Seuss stories. Because the child's language ability (see Chapter 6) has also shown dramatic improvement by this time, many children also are beginning to enjoy listening to the stories as well as looking at the pictures.

The types of environments described for children of different ages have been based on the general rule of structuring the child's world to the cognitive abilities of the child. At each stage, objects and toys should be sufficiently complex to challenge and interest the child and yet not so complex as to be frustrating.

There also appears to be one object in the child's environment that has special properties making it optimally stimulating at all stages of development. This object is, of course, the human being. The human face appears to have an optimal level of complexity, brightness of contour, and movement, and it therefore attracts the attention of the newborn. Similarly, the human face and body are in continual flux and therefore attract the attention of the slightly older child who is interested in novelty. These characteristics of the human face and body are certainly adaptive, for they both facilitate cognitive development in the child and set the groundwork for later social development. As we shall see in the next chapter, normal social development in the child is highly dependent on his or her cognitive advances.

SUMMARY OF COGNITIVE DEVELOPMENT IN INFANCY

This chapter has been concerned with the cognitive development of the child during the first 2 years. Cognitive development was discussed in terms of learning theory, in terms of Kagan's theory of perceptual development, and in terms of Piaget's theory of sensori-motor development. In learning theory, cognitive development is viewed as associations formed between stimuli and behaviors through the mechanisms of *classical and operant conditioning*. In Kagan's theory, the progression from sensing to perceiving and thinking is described as the construction of internal mental representations for external objects, or *schemata*. In Piaget's theory, the progression from reflex behavior to intentional, planned behavior is described as the construction of internal mental representations for behavior, or *sensori-motor schemes*. Although the theories of Kagan and Piaget differ somewhat in their interpretations of cognitive development, they are in agreement in several respects. First, both theories contend that children are *actively* involved in the construction of *mental representations* of their environment. Also, both theories contend that the development of the child requires an adequate environment in which the child may explore and develop new skills.

SUGGESTED READINGS

Kagan, Jerome. *Change and continuity in infancy.* New York: Wiley, 1971. A good description of Kagan's theory and the data to support it. It is somewhat technical at points, but probably not beyond the grasp of the interested student.

Flavell, John. *The developmental psychology of Jean Piaget.* New York: Van Nostrand, 1963. A thorough summary of Piaget's work. It is much more readable for the new student of Piagetian theory than Piaget's own works.

Bower, T. G. R. *Development in infancy.* San Francisco: W. H. Freeman, 1974. A good survey of current research on infant perception. It is somewhat biased toward Bower's own work, however.

Bijou, S. W., Baer, D. M. *Child development, II.* New York: Appleton-Century-Crofts, 1965. Bijou and Baer have created an extremely well-written and easy-to-read introduction to the learning theory interpretation of infant development. It provides excellent descriptions of reflexes, classical conditioning, and operant conditioning in the newborn infant. The major drawback is that the book is somewhat dated.

GLOSSARY

accommodation. In Piaget's theory, one part of the adaptation process. It refers to the infant's ability to change his existing behavior patterns in order to conform to the demands of new objects. For example, the infant must slightly modify or accommodate his grasping behavior in order to learn how to hold a bell as well as a rattle.

adaptation. In Piaget's theory, the process whereby the infant learns to extend his behaviors to new objects by first assimilating those objects to existing behavior patterns and then by accommodating existing behavior patterns in order to conform to the demands of new objects. For example, the infant first assimilates a pacifier to his sucking scheme and then accommodates his sucking scheme in order to take into account the fact that the pacifier does not provide milk.

assimilation. In Piaget's theory, one part of the adaptation process. It refers to the infant's initial tendency to apply existing behavior patterns to new objects. For example, when first given a block, the infant will assimilate it to his shaking scheme.

attention. The focusing of sensory receptors on a particular object in the environment while ignoring other objects also present.

classical conditioning. The process whereby a new "conditioned reflex" can be created through the continued pairing of a neutral stimulus (for example, a bell) with an unconditioned stimulus (for example, food).

cognition. Those internal mental processes that enable individuals to perceive, remember, think, and understand themselves, their behavior, and their environment.

conditioned reflex. A learned connection between stimulus and response. Conditioned reflexes are created through the process of classical conditioning.

conditioned response. A response that has either become associated with an originally neutral stimulus through the procedures of classical conditioning or has increased or decreased in frequency as a function of having been reinforced in operant conditioning.

conditioned stimulus. An originally neutral stimulus that comes to elicit a conditioned response through the procedures of classical conditioning.

deprivation. When certain types of experiences believed to play an important role in the development of an organism are withheld from that organism over a period of time.

enrichment. The intentional introduction of certain types of experiences that are believed to be effective in creating an optimal environment for the development of an organism.

habituation. A gradual decline in attention over time. A novel stimulus originally elicits a great deal of attention. Over time, however, the stimulus elicits less and less attention and interest and attention is redirected to other things.

image. An internal mental representation for an external object.

imagination. The process whereby one uses images to think about an object that is not actually physically present.

innate. Genetically predetermined and independent of experience.

instrumental conditioning. See *operant conditioning.*

learning theory. The theory that explains behavior in terms of experience with events in the environment (that is, operant and classical conditioning). Also known as behaviorism.

negative reinforcement. Any event that results in a decrease in the future probability of occurrence of the particular behavior that it follows. Negative reinforcers include the use of punishment and the withholding of rewards.

object permanence. Piaget uses the term to refer to the older infant's knowledge that an object continues to exist even when the infant is no longer physically interacting with it.

operant conditioning. A form of learning in which behavior changes as a function of its consequences, or its reinforcement.

orientation reaction. A complex set of physiological reactions that occur in the presence of a new stimulus. It consists of directing attention to the new object in an attempt to analyze it.

perception. Those processes whereby one is able to meaningfully interpret sensory experiences.

positive reinforcement. Any event that results in an increase in the future probability of occurrence of the particular behavior that it follows. Positive reinforcers include the use of rewards and the removal of unpleasant stimuli.

prototype. An abstract representation of an object that specifies the invariant or unchanging dimensions of that object as well as the permissible transformations or changes that the object might undergo. Thus, the prototype for a human face must include eyes but not the color of the eyes, since eye color may change without changing the identity of the object as a face.

rate of change. Characteristics of an object that Kagan uses in predicting the object's attractiveness to the newborn. It can be measured in terms of the object's movement, complexity, or contrast.

recognize. To know that an object is familiar, or similar to an object one has seen in the past.

reflex. An innate connection between stimulus and response in which certain types of incoming sensory stimulation automatically release a particular response. For example, a newborn will automatically suck (response) any object placed in his mouth (stimulus).

reinforcer. Any event that changes the future probability of the occurrence of the particular behavior that it follows.

respondent conditioning. See *classicial conditioning.*

schema (plural **schemata**). Kagan's term for an internal mental representation of an external object.

scheme (plural **schemes**). Piaget's term for an internal mental representation of a sequence of behaviors; a mental "program for action."

sensation. A raw, uninterpreted message about external events that has been transmitted from the sensory receptors to the brain.

sensori-motor period. Piaget uses this term as a label for the period of life extending from birth to around 2 years of age. The label indicates Piaget's belief that this period is characterized by sensory and motor experiences rather than perception and thought.

shape constancy. The tendency to see an object as the same shape from different angles even though the incoming sensory information has changed.

size constancy. The tendency to see an object as the same size from different distances even though the incoming sensory information has changed.

unconditioned response. In a reflex, it is elicited by the unconditioned stimulus. For example, babies automatically suck (an unconditioned response) any object (unconditioned stimulus) placed in their mouths.

unconditioned stimulus. In a reflex, a stimulus that automatically elicits the unconditioned response. For example, a bright light (unconditioned stimulus) automatically causes the pupil of the eye to constrict (the unconditioned response).

visual acuity. A measure of the precision with which an individual can see fine detail and small objects.

REFERENCES

Aronson, E., & Rosenbloom, S. Space perception in early infancy: perception within a common auditory-visual space. *Science,* 1971, *172,* 1161–1163.

Bergman, T., Haith, M. M., & Mann, L. Development of eye contact and facial scanning in infants. Paper presented at the meetings of the Society for Research in Child Development, Minneapolis, Minn., April 1971.

Bernard, J., & Sontag, L. Fetal reactivity to tonal stimulation: A preliminary report. *Journal of Genetic Psychology,* 1947, *70,* 205–210.

Bower, T.G.R. Stimulus variables determining space perception in infants. *Science,* 1965, *149,* 88–89.

Bower, T.G.R. Slant perception and shape constancy in infants. *Science,* 1966, *151,* 832–834.

Bower, T.G.R. *Development in infancy.* San Francisco: W. H. Freeman, 1974.

Brackbill, Y., Adams, G., Crowell, D. H., & Gray, M. L. Arousal levels in neonates and preschool children under continuous auditory stimulation. *Journal of Experimental Child Psychology,* 1966, *4,* 178–188.

Clarke, A. M., & Clarke, A.D.B. *Early experience: myth and evidence.* New York: Free Press, 1976.

Davis, K. Final note on a case of extreme isolation. *American Journal of Sociology,* 1947, *52,* 432–437.

Dayton, G. O., Jones, M. H., Aiu, P., Rawson, R. A., Steele, B., & Rose, M. Developmental study of coordinated eye movement in the human infant. *Archives of Ophthalmology,* 1964, *71,* 865–875.

Dennis, W. Causes of retardation among institutional children: Iran. *Journal of Genetic Psychology,* 1960, *96,* 47–59.

Dennis, W. *Children of the crèche.* New York: Appleton-Century-Crofts, 1973.

Dollard, J., & Miller, N. E. *Personality and psychotherapy.* New York: McGraw-Hill, 1950.

Fantz, R. L. The origin of form perception. *Scientific American,* 1961, *204,* 66–72.

Flavell, J. *The developmental psychology of Jean Piaget.* New York: Van Nostrand, 1963.

Haaf, R. A., & Bell, R. Q. A facial dimension in visual discrimination by human infants. *Child Development,* 1967, *38,* 893–899.

Haith, M. M. Visual scanning in infants. Paper presented at regional meeting of Society for Research in Child Development, Clark University, Worcester, Mass., March 1968.

Haith, M. M. Visual competence in early infancy. Revised version to appear in R. Held, H. Leibowitz, & H. L. Teuber (Eds.), *Handbook of sensory physiology* (VIII). Berlin: Springer-Verlag, in press.

Horowitz, F. D. Visual attention, auditory stimulation, and language discrimination in young infants. *Monographs of the Society for Research in Child Development*, 1974, *39* (5–6, Serial No. 158).

James, W. *The principles of psychology*. New York: Henry Holt, 1890.

Kagan, J. *Change and continuity in infancy*. New York: Wiley, 1971.

Kearsley, R. B. Neonatal response to auditory stimulation: A demonstration of orienting and defensive behavior. *Child Development*, 1973, *44*, 582–590.

Koluchová, J. Severe deprivation in twins: A case study. *Journal of Child Psychology and Psychiatry*, 1972, *13*, 107–114.

Koluchová, J. A report on the further development of twins after severe and prolonged deprivation. In A. M. Clarke and A.D.B. Clarke (Eds.), *Early experience: myth and evidence*. New York: Free Press, 1976.

Lyons-Ruth, K. Integration of auditory and visual spatial information in early infancy. Paper presented at the meetings of the Society for Research in Child Development, Denver, April 1975.

McGurk, H., & Lewis, M. Space perception in early infancy: Perception within a common auditory-visual space? *Science*, 1974, *186*, 649–650.

Mendelson, M. J., & Haith, M. M. The relation between audition and vision in the human newborn. *Monographs of the Society for Research in Child Development*, 1976, *41* (4, Serial No. 167).

Palmqvist, H. The effect of heartbeat sound stimulation on the weight development of newborn infants. *Child Development*, 1975, *46*, 292–295.

Peiper, A. *Cerebral function in infancy and childhood*. New York: Consultants Bureau, 1963.

Piaget, J. *Play, dreams and imitation in childhood*. New York: Norton, 1951.

Piaget, J. *The origins of intelligence in children*. New York: International Universities Press, 1952.

Piaget, J. *The construction of reality in the child*. New York: Basic Books, 1954.

Salapatek, P., Bechtold, A. G., & Bushnell, E. W. Infant visual acuity as a function of viewing distance. *Child Development*, 1976, *47*, 860–863.

Salk, L. The role of the heartbeat in the relations between mother and infant. *Scientific American*, 1973, *228*, 24–29.

Sameroff, A. Can conditioned responses be established in the newborn infant? *Child Development*, 1971, *5*, 1–12.

Scarr-Salapatek, S., & Williams, M. L. The effects of stimulation on low-birth-weight infants. *Child Development*, 1973, *44*, 94–101.

Schaffer, R. *Mothering*. Cambridge, Mass.: Harvard University Press, 1977.

Siqueland, E. R., & Lipsitt, L. P. Conditioned head-turning in newborns. *Journal of Experimental Child Psychology*, 1966, *3*, 356–376.

Solkoff, N., Yaffe, S., & Weintraub, D. The effects of handling on the development of premature infants. Paper presented at meeting of Eastern Psychological Association, Boston, 1967.

Super, C. M., Kagan, J., Morrison, F. J., Haith, M. M., & Weiffenbach, J. Discrepancy and attention in the five-month infant. *Genetic Psychology Monographs*, 1972, *85*, 305–331.

Weitzman, E. D., Fishbein, W., & Graziani, L. Auditory evoked responses obtained from the scalp electroencephalogram of the full-term human neonate during sleep. *Pediatrics*, 1965, *35*, 458–462.

White, B. *Human infants: Experience and psychological development*. Englewood Cliffs, N. J.: Prentice-Hall, 1971.

White, B. L., Kaban, B., Shapiro, B., & Attanucci, J. Competence and experience. To be published in I. C. Uzgiris & F. Weizmann (Eds.), *The structuring of experience*. New York: Plenum Press. Manuscript prepared in 1976.

Wilcox, B. M. Visual preferences of human infants for representations of the human face. *Journal of Experimental Child Psychology*, 1969, *7*, 10–20.

5

Social and Emotional Development in Infancy

In earlier chapters, we have examined the biological, perceptual, and cognitive growth of the infant during the first 2 postnatal years. We have seen that this growth occurs at an extremely rapid rate. We have seen, too, that this growth enables the infant to more effectively understand and interact with his environment. In dealing with the environment, the infant quickly learns that there are certain objects that are much more interesting and important than all the rest. These special objects are, of course, *people*.

In this chapter, we will explore how the infant comes to understand and interact with the people in his world. In particular, we will concentrate on two major realms of emotional development in the infant, representing the extremes of normal human emotion. We shall start by examining the infant's first development of a positive love relationship (referred to as *attachment*). We shall then turn to the infant's first experiences with anxiety and fear. As we shall see, the development of attachment and anxiety are intimately related in the emotional life of the young infant.

WHAT IS ATTACHMENT?

If you have ever seen a young infant smiling and cooing as his mother approaches him, or crying and showing signs of distress when his mother leaves the room, you have a sense of the special emotional relationship that exists between mother and child. Psychologists refer to this unique relationship as *attachment*. More formally, **attachment** may be defined as an emotional bond between the infant and some other person. This bond is revealed by the infant's tendency to maintain close contact with that person. Thus, the young infant maintains contact with his eyes; he stares intently at his mother, and his eyes follow her as she moves about. Once the infant is capable of physically following his mother, he will also crawl after her. When his efforts to maintain close proximity to his mother fail, and he is temporarily separated from her, the infant shows obvious signs of distress.

The infant is not simply born with this attachment to his mother or, for that matter, to anyone else. Rather, research has revealed that over the course of the first year and a half of life, infants show increasing signs of the development of this emotional bond. Moreover, this emotional bond influences a wide variety of the infant's behaviors and may have major effects on the subsequent course of emotional and social development.

In the sections that follow, we will trace the course of development of this special emotional bond called attachment. In so doing, we will often refer to the special role of the "mother" and the relationship between "mother" and child. However, it should be made clear at the outset that there is nothing inherently special to infants about mothers nor about mother/infant relationships. A child need not form his initial attachment relationship to his mother—and, in fact, many do not. Rather, this special person in the infant's life can be anyone who cares for the child, is sensitive and responsive to his needs, and is emotionally involved with him—dad, sister, brother, or other caretaker (Schaffer, 1977). For convenience, however, we shall use the term "mother" in the material that follows, not only to refer to real biological mothers, but to any person who has this special attachment relationship to the child.

Milestones in the Development of Attachment

As we mentioned earlier, attachments are gradually created during the infant's first year and a half. In general, the development of attachment follows three basic steps. First, the infant's attention is drawn more to people than to inanimate objects in his environment. Second, the infant learns to distinguish the special people in his world from strangers. Finally, the infant forms a strong emotional bond with specific people, as shown by his active seeking of their company and attention.

Early Signs of the Development of Attachment

Even at a very young age, human infants show clear signs of being extremely social creatures. As we saw in the last chapter, newborns prefer to look at the individual features or dimensions of a visual display, such as contours or angles. In contrast, by 2 months of age infants show a marked preference for patterned stimulation, especially the human face (Fantz, 1961). In particular, their attention seems to be especially drawn to eyes (Bergman & Haith, 1971). Similarly, an infant of even this very young age responds to being picked up and held by an adult by relaxing and molding his body against the adult into a characteristic "cuddly" position (Ainsworth, 1973). Finally, there is evidence that infants respond more positively to the human voice than to other auditory stimuli and that this preference for the human voice increases over the first 4 months of life (Ainsworth, 1973). All of these behaviors reflect the fact that the young infant is especially drawn toward uniquely human interactions. By 4 months of age, the infant obviously derives great pleasure from looking at the human face, listening to the human voice, and being picked up and cuddled by other humans.

The Social Smile

Prior to 4 months of age, infants will smile at a wide variety of stimuli. They will smile upon hearing a human voice or other sounds, at tactile stimulation such as tickling and cuddling (Wolff, 1963), and at attractive visual stimuli such as mobiles. This has been called the phase of *indiscriminate smiling*. At around 4 months of age, a shift occurs in this smiling behavior—a shift that reflects a dramatic change in the infant's relationships with other human beings. The infant now begins to smile more and more at one special person, usually—but not always—his mother. This "special smile" is a clearly visible sign that the infant's earlier preference for human beings in general now includes a special attraction to one person in particular. This shift has been attributed to two factors. First, the infant has begun to develop a schema for his mother's face (see discussion of Kagan's theory in Chapter 4). This schema enables him to discriminate her face from other faces and other visual stimuli. Second, though the ability to recognize objects in general is a pleasurable experience, this recognition of the mother provides an additional source of pleasure. The result is increased smiling toward her in particular.

The appearance of this *discriminating social smile* at around 4 months heralds the true beginning of a unique, positive emotional attachment of the infant to the mother. To be sure, the mother, too, is strongly affected by the developments that take place during this period. The growing responsiveness of her child to her presence, her voice and her physical contact increases the pleasure that she in turn derives from her child. Indeed, a mother will often remark about how much more emotionally positive she feels toward her infant after the appearance of that "special smile" toward her. "For the first time," she may well remark, "my baby seems like a real human being." The pleasure derived by both infant and mother during this period thus serves to bind them together in a unique and mutually satisfying emotional bond.

Stranger Anxiety

By about 4 months, the young infant has established a firm emotional bond with his mother. At approximately 6 to 8 months of age, the child's social behavior again undergoes a dramatic change, which results in strengthening his attachment to his mother. We refer to this change as **stranger anxiety.** Consider the following example. A child is playing contentedly on the living room floor while her mother goes to answer a knock at the door. A stranger (perhaps a salesperson) enters the living room. Seeing the infant, he approaches and greets her enthusiastically. The child stops playing, looks anxiously at the stranger for a moment, then at her mother, and begins to cry and crawl hurriedly toward her mother. The mother goes to the child, picks her up consolingly, and the child quickly stops crying.

This example of stranger anxiety is a not-uncommon occurrence at this age and illustrates several aspects of the child's social and emotional ties to her mother. First, the child shows distinct signs of fear or anxiety in the presence of a strange person. Secondly, the immediate reaction of the child is to seek the security of her mother. Finally, the mother is able to console the child and reduce her anxiety. The consoling effect that the mother has on the child is largely a result of her ability to act as a "secure base" from which the child may now begin to relate to the stranger. The appearance of stranger anxiety is thus a further indication of the special emotional relation that exists between mother and child.

There are large differences in the extent to which individual children seem to experience stranger anxiety. Some children burst into tears at the mere sight of a stranger on the far side of a room; others may remain calm until the stranger actually picks them up; and still others may never actually cry but simply wiggle from the stranger's arms. The child's own temperament is thus one variable that affects the severity of stranger anxiety.

Another equally important factor determining whether an infant will show stranger anxiety is the behavior of the stranger toward the infant. If he or she approaches the child abruptly, speaks in a loud voice, or handles the child roughly, the child is more likely to be afraid (Schaffer, 1966). When the stranger instead approaches slowly and cautiously, with a calm voice and manner, the child is more likely to respond positively.

Separation Anxiety

Anxiety toward strangers begins to wane by the end of the first year, as the child develops more familiarity with strange people and surroundings. However, there is another source of anxiety that emerges dramatically during this period, referred to as **separation anxiety.** Prior to about 10 months of age, an infant shows little distress when, for example, his mother leaves the room in which he is playing. Beginning at about 9 to 10 months of age, however, the infant will frequently cry and be visibly upset when left alone by his mother. This reaction is termed *separation anxiety.* The appearance of separation anxiety is a further indication of the continuing importance of the strong emotional bond between mother and infant—a conclusion that is supported by studies of separation anxiety in other cultures. Infants in Uganda, for example, are in much closer physical contact with their mothers than are North American infants. Ugandan infants are seldom physically separated from their mothers. Not surprisingly, then, they tend to show separation anxiety much earlier than do North American infants. In fact, some Ugandan infants show this reaction as young as 6 months of age (Ainsworth, 1967).

Under normal circumstances, separation anxiety shows a predictable and interesting time course (Kagan, 1976). It first begins to appear at 9 or 10 months of age, peaks at around 14 or 15 months of age, and thereafter gradually declines until 2 years of age (though it crops up again during the preschool years). (See Figure 5-1.) Interestingly, the stable time course of separation anxiety corresponds roughly with important changes in cognitive development that also occur at this time. (See the discussion of cognitive development in Chapter 4.) Indeed, some psychologists have speculated that there is an intimate relation between cognitive and emotional development during this period. For example, recall from the preceding chapter that children at this age are beginning to develop *object permanence;* that is, they have some appreciation of the fact that objects have an existence apart from their own actions and continue to exist despite temporary disappearance (Piaget, 1954). It has been suggested that separation anxiety may appear at this time because the child now knows that his mother still exists after she has left the room, but cannot explain where she has gone or whether she will return. Prior to when the child developed object permanence, he simply did not think

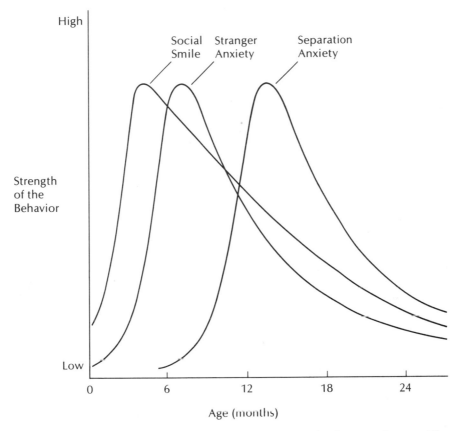

Figure 5-1.   The time course of the major milestones of infant attachment. The social smile peaks at 4 months, stranger anxiety at about 6 to 8 months, and separation anxiety between 12 and 15 months.

about his mother when she left (out of sight, out of mind). Therefore, he was not distressed. Once the child possesses object permanence, however, he can—and does—think about her when she departs. As the child grows still older and develops the cognitive capacity to think about where she might have gone and when she may return, his anxiety level again decreases. A similar view of separation anxiety proposed by Kagan (1976) will be considered later in this chapter.

As the child progresses through infancy, she or he comes to develop attachments to increasing numbers of people in the environment. Fathers, siblings, grandparents—all become objects of attachment, and the child shows similar signs of anxiety when separated from them.

All of the above behaviors (the *social smile, stranger anxiety,* and *separation anxiety*) form major milestones in the emotional and social development of the infant during the first year or so of life (see Figure 5-1). We have seen that the infant develops a strong, unique emotional bond with one person (usually the mother) and that some fears and anxieties experienced by the infant are intimately related to this emotional tie. We now turn to the very important question of how this emotional bond called attachment develops and how it can be facilitated or impeded.

HOW DOES ATTACHMENT DEVELOP?

Several different theories have been offered to explain how the infant becomes attached to his mother. In this section, we will consider each of the theories in depth.

A Learning Theory Explanation

One possible explanation for the development of attachment is derived from learning theory. As you will recall from the preceding chapter, learning theorists argue that the child learns primarily through *classical* and *operant conditioning*. Restated briefly, both classical and operant conditioning result from associations that occur between events in the environment. For example, Pavlov's dogs learned to salivate when they heard a bell because the bell had been previously associated, or paired, with food (classical conditioning). Similarly, circus dogs learn to jump through hoops because in the past, this behavior has been positively reinforced with food (operant conditioning).

According to learning theory, the development of attachment involves both of these types of learning. First of all, a number of things can happen to the infant that are inherently positively reinforcing or negatively reinforcing to him. Getting his diapers changed or being fed are inherently positively reinforcing events— they make the baby feel good—and are likely to increase the frequency of any behavior that they follow. Similarly, being hungry, wet, or cold are inherently negatively reinforcing events—they make the baby feel bad—and are likely to decrease the frequency of any behavior that they follow. Over time, then, the infant should learn to behave in ways that result in positive reinforcement—for example, getting fed or getting a diaper change—and *not* to behave in ways that result in negative reinforcement—for example, being hungry, wet, or cold. Since it is generally in the presence of the mother that positive reinforcement occurs, and since in her absence negative reinforcement occurs, the infant is very likely to behave in ways that will keep him close to his mother.

Operant conditioning is thus used by learning theorists to explain why the infant learns those behaviors that keep him close to his mother—that is, the attachment behaviors previously described. However, attachment is more than just behavior; it is also an emotional bond between mother and child. Thus, the attached infant values and enjoys his mother's presence even when she is not providing positive reinforcers such as food. The development of this emotional bond between mother and infant is described by learning theorists as a result of classical conditioning. When the infant is positively reinforced by being fed (unconditioned stimulus), he feels good (unconditioned response). Since mother (neutral stimulus) is present during these positively reinforcing events, she comes to be associated with them. Over time, her presence alone (conditioned stimulus) produces those good feelings. In essence, then, the mother becomes a valued object whose presence is positively reinforcing and whose absence is negatively reinforcing. She becomes what learning theorists have called an *acquired* or **secondary**

reinforcer. Once the mother has attained the status of secondary reinforcer, the infant will learn to behave in ways that bring him in contact with her simply for the sake of having her present—behaviors such as smiling, cooing, cuddling, and following.

The learning theory view of attachment just described makes some specific predictions about the development of attachment. In particular, it predicts that the intensity of a child's attachment to his mother should be directly related to the mother's history of association with positive reinforcement. Thus, poor or inconsistent caretaking by the mother, for whatever reason, should result in less intense attachment of the infant to the mother. Other negative experiences with the mother, such as severe punishment or neglect of the child, should likewise produce weak attachments. If, however, the attention and care that the child receives from the mother are both ample and positively reinforcing, a strong attachment should develop between mother and child.

Evidence for the Learning Theory Position

Learning theorists point to several studies to support their theory of infant attachment. For example, experimental studies have demonstrated that infant smiling and vocalizing (both indices of social responsiveness and attachment) can be influenced by reinforcement (Brackbill, 1958; Rheingold, Gewirtz, & Ross, 1959). In one study of vocalizations, an adult rewarded 3-month-old infants each time they vocalized by smiling at them and patting them on the stomach. The number of infant vocalizations increased sharply when adult reinforcement was given. Results such as these are certainly consistent with the view that an infant learns to vocalize and smile predominately at his mother since she is the main provider of reinforcement.

Potentially significant support for the learning theory view comes from studies of infants who have been institutionalized from very early in life. Infants in institutions generally receive less overall stimulation (physical and social) than do infants who are reared at home. Institutionalized infants are reared by a variety of different people and are often left unattended for longer periods of time while hungry or wet. To a learning theorist, such an environment not only results in poor and inconsistent reinforcement in general but also fails to consistently associate reinforcement with a particular caretaker. Institutionalized infants would therefore be expected to show less intense attachment behaviors than would home-reared infants. Indeed, studies of institutionalized infants have tended to confirm this prediction: 6-month-old institutionalized infants show very little vocalizing, crying, or typical cuddling reactions (Provence & Lipton, 1962). They show no special reactions to familiar persons as opposed to strangers and exhibit no differential social smile. Finally, there is little evidence in these children of typical stranger anxiety. In short, institutionalized infants show minimal social responsiveness and manifest a distinct lack of emotional attachment and feeling.

Though studies of institutionalized infants can be used to support a learning theory view of attachment, several other factors could also account for the deficits of these infants. Institutionalized children differ from normal home-reared children not only in the lack of a consistent, responsive caretaker, but also in the incidence of medical problems, mild malnutrition, and the amount of general stimulation that they receive. As we saw in Chapters 3 and 4, medical problems,

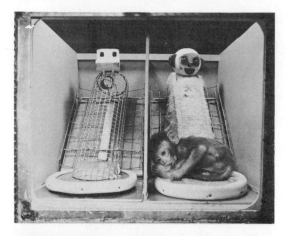

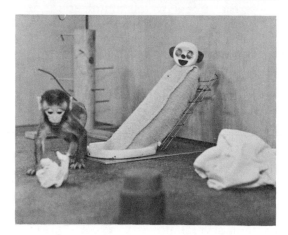

Figure 5-2. Some examples of the behaviors of monkeys in Harlow's "surrogate mother" study: (a) monkey preferring to stay with terry cloth mother; (b) monkey clinging to terry cloth mother in presence of fearful object (a wooden spider); (c) monkey using terry cloth mother as security base while exploring. (Used by permission of the Primate Laboratory, University of Wisconsin.)

malnutrition, and inadequate stimulation all have serious effects on the psychological and physical development of the child. Indeed, studies have shown that given proper nutrition and adequate stimulation, institutionalized infants suffer little, if any, psychological impairment (Bowlby, Ainsworth, Boston, & Rosenbluth, 1956; Rheingold, 1961). Perhaps the problem, then, is not with deficiencies in the caretaker/child relationship in particular but with general deficiencies in the institutions themselves. If so, studies of institutionalized children provide, at best, only possible support for the learning theory view of attachment.

A Direct Test of Learning Theory: The Harlow "Surrogate Mother" Study

Given the uncertainties inherent in interpreting studies of institutionalized infants, a more controlled test of the effects of lack of adequate mothering is needed. This was exactly the goal of a study by Harry Harlow and his colleagues at the University of Wisconsin. Using infant monkeys as his subjects, Harlow separated the infants from their real mothers and placed them with two kinds of mechanical *surrogate mothers*. One "mother" was essentially a wire mesh frame. The other "mother" was identical to the wire mother except that it was covered with soft terry cloth. Although both the wire and terry cloth mothers were available to the infant monkeys, only the wire mother had a feeding bottle. Harlow reasoned that if attachment behavior was produced by an association between positive reinforcers and "mother," monkeys should spend more time in contact with the wire mother—their source of food. The results were quite the opposite. The monkeys spent much more time clinging to the terry cloth mother even though they could get their food only from the wire mother. Further, when a strange object (a large wooden spider) was placed in the cage, the infant monkeys ran to the terry cloth mother rather than to the wire mother (Harlow & Zimmerman, 1959; Harlow & Harlow, 1966). Harlow additionally found that the infant monkeys were more likely to use the cloth mother as a secure base to explore novel or strange objects. When only the wire mother was available, they remained fearful and withdrawn in the presence of the strange object. (See Figure 5-2.)

The implications of Harlow's study are straightforward. Since attachment behaviors exhibited by the infant monkeys (such as clinging and maintaining close body contact) were not directed toward the wire mother who fed them, Harlow's study clearly demonstrated that attachment does not come about through the mother's association with positive reinforcers. Attachment thus cannot be viewed as an example of an acquired reinforcer.

How, then, does attachment develop? Logically enough, Harlow felt that the basis for the infant monkey's attachment lay in the attractiveness of the terry cloth material from which the preferred surrogate mother was constructed. From birth, monkeys raised in a natural environment spend a lot of time clinging with their arms and feet to their mothers who carry them about. This clinging emerges very early in the monkey's life and appears to require little or no learning. The infant monkeys seem drawn to the softness and warmth of the mother's soft, furry belly. In like manner, Harlow felt that the infant monkeys that he studied were instinctively drawn to the warmth and "clinginess" of the terry cloth material. Harlow termed this attraction **contact comfort;** of course, human

Figure 5-3.   The clinging of the monkey and the child's attachment to its blanket point out the similarities between the two species in their attachment behaviors.

mothers do not have furry bellies, and the direct application of Harlow's study to the development of attachment in human infants can be questioned. Nevertheless, everyday observation of children clinging to their teddy bears and their blankets testifies to the applicability of Harlow's ideas that humans, as well as monkeys, derive pleasure from soft, cuddly objects. (See Figure 5-3.)

Harlow's landmark research contains the seeds of a radically different view of the nature of infant attachment. Implicit in Harlow's view is the idea that certain behaviors have been preprogrammed from birth—even such complex behaviors as clinging, smiling, and vocalizing. These preprogrammed behaviors are believed to be intimately involved in the development of attachment and subsequent social and emotional development. Recently, several psychologists have formulated a theory of attachment consonant with Harlow's ideas on the innate bases of attachment behaviors (Ainsworth, 1969; Bowlby, 1969). In developing this theory of attachment, they have also borrowed heavily from the work of *ethologists,* a group of scientists who have uncovered many innate patterns of behavior in lower animals (Lorenz, 1957). Before we can elaborate further upon this theory, we therefore need to acquaint ourselves with some of the fundamental ideas of ethology.

Ethological Theory

Ethology is a branch of behavioral science that studies animal behavior in the natural environment. Ethologists differ from other animal psychologists in emphasizing that the behavior of animals *in their natural surroundings* is quite different from the behavior of animals reared in the artificial environment of the laboratory. Through their naturalistic observations of these animals, ethologists have uncovered a wide variety of animal behaviors that appear to be *innately organized* and to require little learning (Lorenz, 1957). Take, for example, the behavior of squirrels burying nuts (Eibl-Eibesfeldt, 1970). Each fall, the squirrel buries nuts in the ground employing a fixed stereotyped sequence of movements, first digging a hole for the nut with its paws, then shoving the nut into the hole with its snout, and finally covering the nut over and tamping down the dirt. In order to determine to what extent this complex behavior is learned or innate, ethologists have studied the effects of *deprivation* conditions in which squirrels are reared in isolation and given no opportunity to learn or even observe this behavior in other squirrels. Even under these deprivation conditions, adult squirrels raised in isolation mastered the entire burying sequence on the first attempt (Eibl-Eibesfeldt, 1970).

The fact that squirrels can perform this complex behavior sequence on the first try argues persuasively that the nut-burying is not learned but innate. Ethologists view behavior sequences such as these as being genetically "preprogrammed": that is, organized from birth. An enormous variety of innately organized behavior patterns have been uncovered in diverse areas of animal behavior, ranging from the learning of species-specific song behaviors in birds (Eibl-Eibesfeldt, 1970) to maternal feeding behavior (Klinghammer & Hess, 1964), to animal aggressiveness (Lorenz, 1966).

How do ethologists explain these behaviors? According to ethological theory, animals are born with certain innately organized behavior patterns called **fixed action patterns.** In addition, there are certain highly specific stimuli in the environment called **releasers** that trigger these fixed behavior patterns. When a releaser is presented to an animal, the fixed action pattern is triggered, and the complex behavioral sequence is executed in a perfectly organized fashion. In our example of the squirrel, the nut is the releaser and the sequence of nut-burying behaviors constitutes a fixed action pattern.

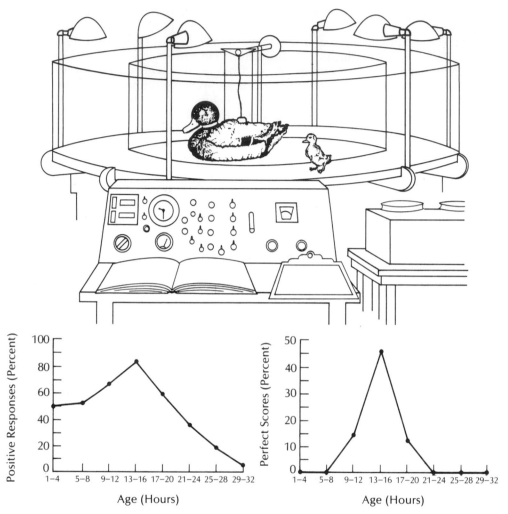

Figure 5-4. An example of imprinting experiments on the critical period is shown above. In this study by E. H. Hess, chicks or ducklings were kept in a dark cage for from 1 to 35 hours after hatching. Following this period of deprivation they were placed on a circular runway (see top picture) along with a mechanical model of an adult male duck. The model moved in a circle around the runway, and observers recorded whether the infant birds followed the model, thus showing imprinting behavior. As shown in the graph at the bottom left, the highest percentage of positive following responses occurred in birds between 13 and 16 hours of age. Following this period the number of following responses declined rapidly, and, by about 30 hours of age, almost no following responses were observed. In addition (see bottom-right graph), birds 13 to 16 hours of age got many more perfect scores than did younger or older birds; that is, they were more consistent in following the model and made fewer errors.

One provocative example of an innately determined behavior sequence bears directly on our discussion of how attachment develops. This phenomenon is called **imprinting** and was discovered by Konrad Lorenz (1935). Soon after birth, a newly hatched mallard duckling will follow along behind its mother wherever she goes. This **following response** has strong survival value for the duckling, since it is the mother who must protect the still-immature infant from prey. Without this behavior, the duckling would almost certainly get separated from its mother and be left vulnerable to attack by predators. Curiously, though, the duckling will develop the following response to other animals, to people, and even to inanimate objects, depending upon which object is presented to the duckling and, more significantly, when the object is first seen (Hess, 1959). If the duckling is presented with the object from 13 to 16 hours after birth, it will follow that object and no others, and if the animal is deprived of seeing *any* objects for as long as 24 hours, the following response will not develop adequately (Hess, 1959). (See Figure 5-4.)

The acquisition of the "following response" is called *imprinting*. Imprinting is viewed by ethologists as a fixed action pattern that is triggered by the sight of some object in the environment. Thus, the duckling will follow the first object that it sees during a certain period in its development. In the natural environment, most often the mother is the first object encountered and, thus, the following response becomes attached to her. As we have already noted, however, the strength of the following response is largely dependent on the age of the duckling when it first sees its mother. If this encounter is delayed, imprinting will be impaired and will not develop adequately. The finding that age affects the strength of imprinting implies that this behavior is dependent upon a *sensitive* or **critical period.** In the case of the duckling, the critical period for imprinting occurs between 13 and 16 hours after birth. Prior to and subsequent to that time, "following behavior" will be weak (Hess, 1959).

The notion of a critical period for imprinting radically distinguishes this behavior from traditional forms of learning based upon reinforcement and conditioning (Eibl-Eibesfeldt, 1970). Learning theorists argue that behaviors can be learned at any time in the life of an animal, being determined solely by appropriate use of reinforcement. The imprinting phenomenon clearly contradicts this view. In fact, if ducklings are given mild electric shocks in the presence of the imprinting object, the strength of the "following response" increases. This is directly opposite to the result predicted from traditional principles of conditioning, which would predict that shocking the animal in the presence of an object should cause avoidance of that object. Imprinting thus seems to be a clear case of an innately organized behavior pattern that develops rapidly and not through a process of conditioning.

One final and potentially important aspect of imprinting should be noted. Here we refer to the *irreversibility* of the effects of imprinting. It has been found that once an animal imprints on a certain object, the animal may prefer that object for the rest of its life (Eibl-Eibesfeldt, 1970). In one dramatic example, Shutz (1968) imprinted male ducks on other males of the same species and then induced them to mate with females of their species. Shutz found that even after the male ducks had mated with females, their homosexual preference for other male ducks remained.

How Would Ethologists Explain Human Attachment?

Most of the work of ethologists has focused on animal behavior. Recently, however, child psychologists like John Bowlby and Mary Ainsworth have put forth a view of human attachment that relies heavily on ethological principles

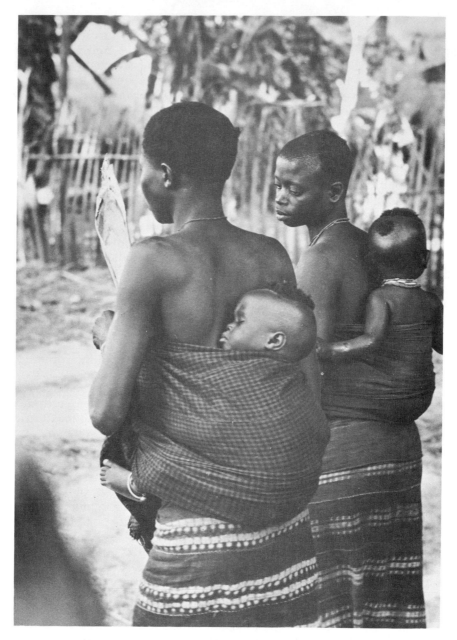

Figure 5-5.   This is the manner in which a typical African infant is carried for the first several months of life. The infants spend most of their time being carried in cloth slings and are nursed on demand. Susan Goldberg, who studied Zambian infants, has pointed out that many newborn reflexes, such as grasping, head lifting, and stepping motions, which serve little purpose for infants in North American society, are quite useful to Zambian infants. Grasping allows the infants to hold on to the mother's back, and head lifting and stepping movements enable them to free themselves when they are in positions where they cannot breathe (Goldberg, 1972).

(Bowlby, 1969; Ainsworth, 1969, 1973). Their view centers around the four main concepts of the ethological theory of imprinting just discussed: the notions of (1) the fixed action pattern, (2) exclusive attachment to one object, (3) a critical period, and (4) irreversibility of the effects of imprinting or attachment.

The Fixed Action Pattern. We have already discussed several examples of fixed action patterns in lower animals. For example, the clinging shown by Harlow's infant monkeys exhibits all the characteristics of a fixed action pattern. What evidence is there for fixed action patterns in human infants that might serve as the basis for an imprinting-like attachment response? Ainsworth (1973) has postulated that the human infant possesses a number of highly developed behavior patterns that are most likely innately organized. For example, the grasp reflex in human newborns (discussed in Chapter 3) seems to be a form of the clinging response observed in monkeys. Similarly, the "cuddling" response shown by human newborns in response to being held in a particular way appears to be an innate response. (See Figure 5-5.) Finally, as we have already noted, the looking behavior of human infants becomes increasingly directed toward objects that have uniquely human characteristics, especially the human face, eyes, and voice; this, too, could be an innately organized response. Although not necessarily conclusive, the examples suggest that the human infant may possess a variety of innately organized behavior patterns that serve to keep him in contact with other human beings and that are analogous to the "following response" in young ducklings. As such, these fixed action patterns provide the foundation for the development of an emotional attachment. The "triggering" of these behaviors by, and toward, the mother could thus be viewed as the attachment process itself.

Initial Exclusive Attachment to One Object. Through the process of imprinting, young animals typically develop a behavioral attachment to one object in the environment and follow only that object. Similarly, the human infant in the first year of life often forms a relatively exclusive attachment relationship with one person—usually the mother. Thus, the mother is usually the first person to elicit a smile; she is usually the one to whom the child rushes when a strange adult approaches; and she alone usually causes anxiety and protest when the child is separated from her (Ainsworth, 1973). Though it is true that subsequent to this initial attachment the child can form attachments to others, there is little doubt that for the first year of life or so, most human infants show attachment behaviors almost exclusively toward one person.

ISSUE

Is attachment to one person necessary for normal emotional development?

This is a very serious question, especially given the growing number of working mothers who leave their infants daily with one or more baby-sitters or in an infant-care center. The question arises whether or not these infants are being deprived of the opportunity to attach themselves to an adult and thus may suffer some psychological harm. This issue is discussed in more detail below. At present, the best answer seems to be that the biological mother need not be the attachment figure, but that if the infant is not given the opportunity to attach himself to one or more people, he may suffer some emotional problems.

The "Critical Period."   Ethological studies of a wide variety of lower animals have shown that there is a well-delineated time period during which attachment-like behaviors are most likely to develop. If the animal has not formed an attachment during this period, attachment does not develop adequately (Hess, 1959). What evidence is there for a critical period in the formation of human attachment? An early study by Goldfarb (1943) suggested that, if infants are kept in an institution until 3½ years of age, it is extremely difficult for them to form attachments to foster mothers upon release from the institution. Other studies have shown that infants who have been reared in institutions and who have not attached themselves to any specific people will develop normally if placed in an adoptive home by the end of the first year (Ainsworth, 1973; Rheingold & Bayley, 1959; Gardner, Hawkes, & Burchinal, 1961), while infants kept in an institution until they are 18 to 24 months of age have great difficulty becoming attached to a foster mother later (Provence & Lipton, 1962). Putting all of these studies together, Ainsworth (1973) has speculated that the period from 1 to 2 years of age might constitute a sensitive period for the development of attachment in human infants. Note that this conclusion does not imply that deprivation has no negative effects on the younger child (1 year or younger). However, it does appear that if there are any negative effects, they are less pronounced, at least for attachment and later social development. (See Figure 5-6 for the effects of isolation on rhesus monkeys.)

Irreversibility of Effects.   The final distinguishing feature of the ethological theory concerns whether or not lack of an adequate opportunity to develop normal attachments has long-term harmful effects that persist into later life. Some evidence does suggest that social deprivation in early life can produce serious problems later on. For example, in the Harlow and Zimmerman (1959) study with the surrogate mothers, even the monkeys raised with the terry cloth mothers showed some abnormal social and sexual behavior when they grew up. In a later study (Harlow & Harlow, 1970), young monkeys were isolated completely from any social contact. They were housed in individual cages that were cleaned by remote control. Food and water were dispensed automatically. They had no normal visual, auditory, or tactile stimulation from the outside world and never interacted with any other creature. Monkeys who had been raised for 6 months in this isolated environment showed very severe behavioral problems when later placed with other, normally raised monkeys in a group playroom. The isolate monkeys were extremely fearful and timid, showed little curiosity or exploration of the environment, and most often crouched in one corner, clutching themselves or rocking back and forth. In fact, one monkey died because of self-imposed starvation, while another survived only because it was force-fed. Harlow reported that female monkeys raised in isolation as infants turned out in adulthood to be exceedingly difficult to breed with adult males, and that those that were bred and produced offspring made exceptionally poor mothers; they were indifferent to their infants, and several were violently abusive. The whole pattern of these behaviors suggested severe emotional and social abnormality.

The above examples document the possibly severe effects that can result from deprivation of normal social contact. Other data involving human children suggest similarly that the adverse effects of a socially deprived environment can be both severe and long lasting. These studies, involving children raised initially in institutions who were then placed in adoptive homes, show that a disproportionately large number of the adopted children, compared with children in the

(a)

(b)

(c)

Figure 5-6.   The devastating effects of total isolation can be seen in these pictures from Harlow and Harlow (1962). Monkeys isolated as infants become extremely withdrawn and passive. Above, a comparison of mothers who grew up normally (a and b) versus one who had been isolated in her infancy (c). As you can see, the previously isolated monkeys were very rejecting and even aggressive toward their infants. (From "The Effect of Rearing Conditions on Behavior," by H. F. Harlow and M. K. Harlow, *Bulletin of the Menninger Clinic*, 1962, *26*, 213–224. Reprinted by permission of the Menninger Clinic and the Primate Laboratory, University of Wisconsin.)

general population, are treated for mental illness (Bostock, 1961). A study by Menlove (1965) reported higher incidences of hyperactivity, aggressiveness, and, later, juvenile delinquency among adopted children than among children raised by their biological mothers.

The evidence reviewed above paints a very different picture of the nature and development of attachment from that derived from learning theory. In ethological theory, the infant is viewed as entering the world with a set of innately programmed behaviors (looking, smiling, cuddling) that prepare him to seek out and maintain contact with other human beings. Increasingly, his responses become ever more directed toward one specific person, his mother or other primary caretaker. The end result of this sustained interaction with the mother is the development of a strong emotional attachment toward her. Lack of adequate opportunities to become attached to one person (through deprivation or institutionalization), if carried beyond a specified critical period, will in most cases have serious and long-lasting negative effects on the emotional well-being and social development of the child.

Critique of Ethological Theory

While the evidence cited above certainly supports the ethological viewpoint, other observations and experimentation cast some doubt on certain aspects of the theory. Consider, for example, the case of institutionalized children. These children commonly both lack a single mother figure and suffer from severe emotional and social problems; this has been interpreted by some as suggesting that the absence of a mother causes the social and emotional problems. Other factors, however, may contribute equally to their problems. Thus, to the extent that these children suffer from congenital abnormalities or malnutrition, there could be a purely biological or nutritional cause of their developmental retardation (Pinneau, 1955). Similarly, some problems can be traced to the fact that institutionalized infants do not generally receive the quantity or quality of stimulation (visual, auditory, and tactile) needed for normal development (Casler, 1961). An additional contributing factor could be the fact that their deprived environments tend to be "self-perpetuating," thereby continually reinforcing any original deficits (Clarke & Clarke, 1976). Stated bluntly, some of these children suffer from warped social behavior that tends to bring out the worst in other people. Thus, even when these children are taken out of the institution and placed in foster or adoptive homes, their new "parents" may find them extremely exasperating and hard to deal with. Even well-meaning adults may therefore find it difficult to establish strong positive emotional ties to these children, thereby reinforcing the children's original social deficits. A final consideration undercutting the ethological theory of attachment—again involving institutionalized children—is that not all studies have found negative effects of institutionalization (Tizard, 1977; Thompson & Grusec, 1970; Rheingold, 1956; Rheingold & Bayley, 1959).

What conclusions, then, can we draw? First, it appears that while institutionalized infants often suffer from emotional and social damage, this result is not inevitable; they may in certain instances survive the experience emotionally intact. Second, it appears that even when some impairment is shown, it is impossible to pin down "the" source of the problem. In particular, we cannot attribute their social and emotional disorders completely to the lack of a consistent mothering figure; several other factors may be involved. The ethological theory thus does not provide a complete explanation of why certain children—institutionalized children in particular—are socially and emotionally impaired.

Other aspects of the ethological theory can also be criticized. For example, evidence has been gathered that casts doubt on the hypothesis that exclusive attachment to a single person is a necessary condition for normal social development. Indeed, it appears that once an infant is able to form specific attachments, he is also capable of forming several attachments at once. In one study, Schaffer and Emerson (1964a) found that 29% of the infants studied initially formed multiple attachments—and that 10% of the infants formed five or more! Moreover, the number of attachments the babies had did not affect the strength of their individual attachments. To quote Schaffer (1977, p. 100):

> Being attached to several people does not necessarily imply a shallower feeling toward each one, for an infant's capacity for attachment is not like a cake that has to be shared out. Love, even in babies, has no limits.

The work of Schaffer and Emerson argues persuasively against the ethological notion that the presence of a single exclusive attachment figure is necessary for the development of a secure emotional attachment.

Still a further area in which ethological theory has come increasingly under attack is the notion of critical periods and the supposed irreversibility of the effects of early experience. Even for lower animals early experience no longer seems so critical and irreversible as previously believed. For example, in one laboratory study, Hess (1972) imprinted newly hatched ducklings on human beings. Later, these ducklings were put in the company of a female mallard that had recently hatched several ducklings. After only 1½ hours of exposure to her, the ducklings followed the female mallard, thereby showing a reversal of their initial imprinting on a human being.

Similarly, a recent study by Suomi and Harlow (1972) shows that under proper conditions, the initial effects of extreme deprivation in infancy can later be reversed. Recall that earlier studies of monkeys by Harlow and his colleagues demonstrated severe, lasting damage following early social isolation. Suomi and Harlow wondered whether these monkeys could ever be rehabilitated. They therefore conducted a study in which monkeys were first isolated for 6 months and then placed with a group of "therapist" monkeys: specifically, 3-month-old female monkeys. The choice of the therapists was a critical feature of the study. Prior to this particular study, isolate monkeys had typically been placed with normal 6-month-old monkeys—monkeys who are typically well socialized, quite strong, aggressive, and vigorously playful. When confronted with their normal—and very lively—peers, the isolate monkeys had little chance to explore and develop normal social responsiveness. Three-month-old females, in contrast, are less aggressive and initiate playful social contact, making them far less overwhelming to the isolate monkeys. The isolate monkeys received 26 weeks of therapy (2 hours per day, 3 days a week). Initially, they showed the typical pattern of severe emotional and social abnormality. Following the period of therapy, however, they exhibited significant and dramatic recovery from their behavioral deficits. In fact, their behavior became virtually indistinguishable from that of normally reared monkeys.

The Suomi and Harlow study is a key study for several reasons. First, the fact that the monkeys were able to recover runs counter to a strict critical period notion of the development of social attachments. Further, the success of the re-habilitation indicates clearly that the effects of early deprivation are not irreversi-ble, at least in higher animals like monkeys (and, presumably, man). Finally, and most importantly, the nature of the therapeutic experience was shown to be vital to successful recovery. If the therapeutic environment is too demanding, the so-cially deprived infant is likely to be overwhelmed, making recovery impossible. If, however, the environment allows the infant to explore and initiate play behavior and social contact on a less intense level, full recovery is quite possible.

ISSUE

How can one best overcome the effects of early social deprivation?

Clear data on how to overcome early social deprivation in human children are not available. Nevertheless, it seems likely that two principles derived from research with animals are helpful. The first is that the deprived child must be placed in the company of other children at his level of development: most likely children who are somewhat younger. Secondly, the child must be given the oppor-tunity to explore his environment and the security that will enable him to do so. The combination of these two factors, a simple envi-ronment and feedback that is positive and not fear-inducing, ap-pears to be major ingredients in overcoming early childhood depri-vation.

Summary of Ethological Theory

The ethological description of attachment stresses four key concepts taken from imprinting research with lower animals: (1) attachment is a kind of innate fixed action pattern, (2) attachment is, at least initially, exclusive to one object, (3) there is a critical or sensitive period for attachment to occur, and (4) attachment, if impaired during the critical period, can have long-term, irreversible effects on the emotional well-being and social development of the child. Research indicates that while the first of these assumptions (namely, the "innate" nature of attachment) is plausible the other three assumptions are open to some doubt. Attachment to a single mother figure appears not to be necessary for normal social development; in fact, multiple attachments are quite possible in human infants. Also, there is little evidence for a critical period for attachment beyond which normal social development is rendered incapable of occurring. Finally, the devastating effects of early deprivation or isolation can, under certain circumstances, be reversed with the appropriate therapeutic techniques.

THE DYNAMICS OF MOTHER/CHILD INTERACTION

As we have seen, neither ethological theory nor simple learning theory can explain all facets of attachment in infants. Indeed, no single theory to date has been successful in encompassing all of the known facts about early social and emotional development in infants. In an attempt to probe more deeply into the factors that influence this development, psychologists have looked more closely at the complex interaction occurring between mother and infant during the first year of life. As a result of this in-depth examination, they have found that the process of mother/infant attachment cannot be studied by examining either the behavior of the mother or of the infant in isolation. Rather, one must concentrate simultaneously on both mother and child. Attachment should thus be viewed not only as the infant's emotional bond for his mother, but also as a reciprocal bond of the mother for her infant.

In the complex interaction between mother and infant, each member makes a separate important contribution. The contributions of each are woven together in determining the course of the mother/infant attachment. Let us therefore look specifically at those characteristics that are known to affect the types of contributions made by each member of the pair. We will first examine the factors that influence what the mother brings to the relationship.

Maternal Hormonal Condition

An extremely interesting factor that may affect the normal development of attachment by affecting the mother's sensitivity to her child's needs is the mother's hormonal condition. It has been suggested (Ainsworth, 1973; Klaus & Kennell, 1976) that after giving birth, mothers experience a physiological or hormonal change (called the **maternal condition**) that acts to make the mothers more responsive and sensitive to their infants. For example, animal studies (Trause, Klaus, & Kennell, 1976) have shown that for rats, cats, and goats, the maternal condition diminishes rapidly if the mother is separated from her litter shortly after birth. When their litters are later returned to them, these mothers do not respond as adequately to their offspring.

It has been suggested that mothers of human infants who are separated from their infants for prolonged periods due to prematurity or early severe illness may be similarly adversely affected (Klaus & Kennell, 1976). For example, Leifer, Leiderman, Barnett, and Williams (1972) reported that mothers of full-term babies who were allowed to take their babies home after a few days showed more positive mothering behavior when the infants were older than did a group of mothers whose children, because of prematurity, had to stay in the hospital for several weeks. Moreover, mothers of premature babies who were only allowed to look at their infants in the incubator, without holding them, showed an unusually high incidence of giving up their babies for adoption and of turning over the child's custody to the father in cases of divorce. In the group of mothers who were allowed to handle their premature babies as well as look at them, none gave up their babies. These findings have important practical implications for hospital practices. In particular, the practice of "rooming in" (placing the newborn in the mother's hospital room instead of in an isolated nursery) may directly enhance mother/child interaction by stimulating very early the hormonal sensitivity of the mother to her child.

Birth Order

Still another factor that affects the mother's behavior is whether or not she has had any other children. Mothers frequently report that they are more anxious and make more mistakes with their first child than with subsequent children. It has also been reported that first-born children often have difficulty in later social adjustment (Adams, 1972). These two findings suggest that the mother's behavior toward her first-born child may produce a less emotionally secure infant and may influence his later adjustment (Ainsworth, 1973).

The Feeding Situation

Of course, the mother's role in the development of mother/infant attachment does not stop when she brings her baby home from the hospital. Rather, the mother's role pervades all aspects of the child's development during the many years to come. Any attempt to isolate specific aspects of the mother's role will therefore not be completely satisfactory. Nonetheless, it does seem that there is one aspect of her role that does require some special attention: her behavior in the feeding situation.

From the earliest months of life, one of the most frequent and important sources of interaction between mother and child occurs when the child is being fed. It is not surprising, then, that methods of feeding have been found to be significantly related to the quality of the attachment relationship that infants establish with their mothers (Ainsworth, 1967). Mothers who respond sensitively to the infant's needs during the feeding situation (namely, the timing of the feedings, the determination of the amount of food eaten, and the pacing of the rate of the baby's intake) tend to have infants who are more strongly attached to them (Ainsworth & Bell, 1969). Of particular importance is the quality of the interaction between mother and child during feeding. Mothers who seem to enjoy feeding their infants likewise tend to have more securely attached infants (Ainsworth, 1967).

Characteristics of the Infant

By now, it is apparent that the mother's attitudes and experience greatly affect the type of relationship she will have with her child. However, as we mentioned earlier, the infant is also actively involved in the development of the attachment bond. Indeed, infants have their own unique temperaments or early personalities that they bring to the relationship. They differ from one another not only in such obvious ways as their sex and age but in such less obvious ways as activity level and "cuddliness." These differences in temperament in the infant can have very significant effects on how mothers respond to their children (Schaffer & Emerson, 1964b; Thomas & Chess, 1977).

Activity Level

Anyone who has been around infants will readily agree that infants differ widely from one another in their overall level of activity. Some infants sleep a lot and others less; some cry more than others; some infants are very active and others passive. Obviously, the infant's level of activity has dramatic effects both on his own behavior and on the responses he elicits from others. For example, an active baby is more often capable of interacting with his mother—and of demanding that opportunities for interaction be provided (Schaffer, 1977).

Cuddliness

Closely related to an infant's activity level is his degree of cuddliness. Some infants (especially relatively inactive ones) seem to love to be held, soothed and stroked—to be "cuddled" for hours on end. Other babies (especially relatively active ones) seem to hate to be cuddled; they cry and struggle during even momentary embraces (Schaffer & Emerson, 1964). A child's degree of cuddliness will have dramatic effects on how the mother interacts with that child later on. A warm and responsive child is more apt to bring out warmth and responsiveness in his mother, while the child who rejects his mother is more likely to in turn be rejected by her.

Sex

Also believed to be related to a child's activity level is the child's sex. For example, it has been suggested (Moss, 1967) that infant boys sleep less than girls and are more irritable. As a result, mothers seem to shower more attention on boys and to hold them more often. A more obvious way in which the child's sex affects the mother/child relationship is its impact on the mother's expectations of what the child should be like and her responses to what he or she *is* like. For example, many people believe that infant boys should be more active than infant girls. Thus, the mother of an inactive son may try to stimulate him more. "Wake up, you," she may playfully say, "Where's that rowdy son of mine?" Maybe he's not, by inclination, a "rowdy." Nevertheless, precisely because he is a "son," rather than a daughter, his mother may expect him to be lively and active.

Age

Of course, babies behave differently at different ages, and mothers must be responsive to these changes as they develop. For example, 3-week-old infants sleep more and cry more than they will when they are 3 months old; mothers are generally attuned to this; they normally rock and cuddle their 3-week-olds more than they do their 3-month-olds (Moss, 1967). Age, with the behavioral changes that it brings, is thus one more factor that very clearly affects the nature of the interaction between mother and child.

Summary of the Dynamics of Mother/Child Interaction

The study of the development of attachment cannot be accomplished by looking at either mother or child in isolation. Each member of the pair brings something unique to the relationship and ultimately affects the behavior of the other. What seems to be crucial to the formation of a strong mother/infant bond is a situation where there is a good "match" between mother and infant: where mother is sensitive and responsive to baby's needs, and where baby conforms at least to some degree to what mother expects baby to be like.

SEPARATION FROM THE MOTHER

To this point, we have focused on those factors that influence the development and strength of the infant's attachment to his mother. However, once an attachment is firmly established, there are times when the mother simply has to be away from her child: at work, at the store, or somewhere else. What happens to the child when separation occurs? This issue is certainly one of the most complex and important issues in the field of developmental psychology. It is complicated by the fact that there are as many kinds of separation as there are children. For example, separations can be short, long, or even permanent, and they can be from one parent or from the entire family. Separations can be handled well by the temporary caretaker or they can be handled poorly. They can occur in families where the relationship between parents and child is strong and healthy or in families where the relationship is weak and distorted. And separations can occur when the child is 1 day old, 6 months old, 5 years old, or even 18 years old. Certainly *all* of these factors—and undoubtedly many others—will affect the child's immediate and long-term reaction to separation. Keeping these complicating factors in mind, let us consider the *immediate* effects of prolonged separation (several weeks or more) of the young child from his family.

The Immediate Effects of Prolonged Separation

There is little question that prolonged separations produce extreme emotional upset in the child—emotional upset that is far more severe than the "separation anxiety" associated with temporary separations (see above discussion of separation anxiety). John Bowlby (1969) has suggested that this upset can be divided into three distinct phases: *protest, despair,* and *detachment.* The first phase, known as *protest,* begins immediately after the separation. At this time, the child is obviously extremely distraught; he cries, calls for his mother, tries to follow her, and searches for her. If the mother returns during this phase, the child may alternately cling to her and push her away, as if to show his unhappiness and anger at her for leaving him.

If, however, the mother does not return within a few days, the child will move into a second phase called *despair.* This phase is signaled by the fact that the child stops crying or actively searching for his mother. He becomes passive and withdrawn and spends much of his time by himself, whimpering quietly on and off. If the mother returns during this phase, he will still recognize and accept her.

Should the separation be prolonged over several weeks, the child moves into the final phase of his reaction, *detachment.* Outwardly the child seems to adapt to the separation and even begins to form new attachments to the people around him. However, if the mother now returns, the child will not seek her out or interact with her. He will, in fact, actively avoid her.

A direct test of Bowlby's account of the child's reaction to prolonged separation is provided by Heinicke and Westheimer (1965). In this study, observations were made of 2-year-olds who were separated from their families and placed for about 2 weeks in a residential nursery. As Bowlby has suggested, these children were extremely upset when the separation occurred, and they cried and searched for their mothers. Later, they appeared less upset and began to interact with the adults at the nursery. However, their distress was apparent in their unusually aggressive behavior. Upon being reunited with their mothers, the children at first rejected them, and although typical attachment behaviors gradually reemerged, the children still showed some upset and ambivalence even after 3 months. When the children were evaluated 20 months later, however, there was "no obvious and overt effect of the separation."

One possible criticism of the Heinicke and Westheimer study is that the children were not only separated from their mothers, but were also placed in a rather sterile and unsupportive environment. Thus, it is not clear whether the children's distress was caused by separation from the mother or simply by the unfamiliar and possibly frightening nursery environment. Robertson and Robertson (1970) attempted to examine the effects of separation under more favorable circumstances. They took four children into their home while the children's mothers were in the hospital. Much effort was given to make the environment as much like their own homes as possible for the children, and they were frequently reminded of mother and her imminent return. The Robertsons report that while the children showed far less distress than is the case when children are separated and placed in a less friendly environment, they nevertheless showed clear signs of emotional upset.

The Long-Term Effects of Prolonged Separation

Clearly, the child is unmistakably upset during the course of a prolonged separation from his parents. But what—if any—are the long-term effects of such separations on the social and emotional development of the child? Many studies (for example, Ainsworth, 1962) have shown that children who have experienced prolonged separation from their parents early in life are somewhat more likely to have emotional disturbances later on. In fact, Bowlby (1946) suggested that "prolonged separation of a child from his mother (or mother substitute) during the first five years of his life stands foremost among the causes of delinquent character development and persistent misbehavior."

More recently, however, psychologists have begun to take a more optimistic view of the long-term effects of prolonged separation (for example, Rutter, 1971). It appears that while prolonged separations may have long-term effects on a child's social and emotional development, this need not occur. Children most likely to suffer long-term adverse effects of separation are those whose families are tense, cold, and disorganized. Those whose families are warm and nurturant, however, are much more likely to recover from the immediate effects of even prolonged separations.

The Effects of Short-Term Separations

Prolonged separations of a child from his family have severe immediate effects—and, in some cases, prolonged effects—on the child. This has led many people to believe that separations of any kind should be avoided at all costs. However, demonstrating that prolonged separations can be upsetting to the child does not necessarily imply that short-term separations will have a comparable result.

With an increasing number of mothers taking on full-time employment, it is important to ask whether very young children are adversely affected by the short, daily separation from their mothers. Happily, the evidence suggests that little, if any, damage is done, provided that the alternative care offered to the child provides a stimulating and emotionally secure environment. For example, a study by Caldwell, Wright, Honig, and Tennenbaum (1970) compared the characteristics of 30-month-old home-reared children with similar-aged children who had entered a modern, stimulating day-care program at 1 year of age. No differences were observed between the two groups in emotionality, dependence, hostility, or other personality traits. Other studies have shown that the nature of the substitute care is critical to the security of the child (Moore, 1963). Constantly changing babysitters or unpredictable day-care arrangements can produce anxious and overly dependent children. Mothers who want to work or who have to work should therefore take care to secure the best caretakers or day-care programs for their children and stick with them.

THE ROLE OF THE FATHER

Fathers have been conspicuously absent in our discussion thus far. And, until very recently, little attention was given by psychologists generally to the father's role in early infant social development. To some extent, there was good reason for this lack of attention. During the 1950s and 1960s the typical role of the father as the family's "breadwinner" kept him away from the home for long periods of time each day, and the care of young infants was left almost exclusively with the mother. A study by Rebelsky and Hanks conducted in 1971 documented just how little interaction some fathers have with their young infants. Rebelsky and Hanks attached a microphone to the infant's shirt and recorded the amount of verbal interaction that fathers engaged in with their children. Startlingly, they found that during the first 3 months of the infant's life, the fathers in the study spent an average of only 37.7 seconds a day talking to their infants. Assuming that most kinds of interaction involve some degree of talking, it seems clear that these fathers spent very little time interacting with their infants.

It would appear, then, that the influence of the father in the typical North American home may be quite minimal, at least for very young infants. In contrast to the mother's absence, the absence of the father seems to be the rule, rather than the exception, and seems to produce little direct effect (either positive or negative) on the infant's development.

Nevertheless, recent years have witnessed a gradual change in the structure of the "average" North American household and, often, in the amount of time that fathers spend with their infants. In some households, both parents hold jobs and each spends half a day caring for the infant at home. Some men have taken on the role of "househusband," a situation where they do not hold jobs and their wives do. These recent changes in infant caretaking have prompted psychologists to take a closer look at some of the more serious forms of family disruption that can occur as a result of father absence. Such cases include divorces and broken homes as well as cases where the father has died. What happens to families in general, and to infant emotional development in particular, when fathers are separated from the family?

Studies of children from fatherless homes have concentrated mainly on older children. In general, it has been found that children from such homes show a higher incidence of juvenile delinquency and extramarital pregnancy, have lower intellectual ability and school achievement scores, and in general appear to be less well adjusted psychologically and socially (Herzog & Sudia, 1973). It is important to note that most of the effects on children of coming from fatherless homes emerge later in life, during late childhood and early adolescence. In general, however, most studies have found that factors *other* than the simple absence of the father are more important in determining the social adjustment of children. Two major factors are the general family climate and the degree of supervision of the child that is exercised by the mother. For example, one study examined the families of juvenile delinquents. Although fathers were absent from a large number of these families (61% compared with 34% in a control group), of greater importance seemed to be the degree of discipline exercised by the mother. In 96% of the juvenile delinquent cases, the mothers were judged to discipline the child unsuitably (Glueck & Glueck, 1962). Other studies have shown that the home climate (happiness at home, amount of friction) is more important than father's absence per se (Nye, 1957; Slocum & Stone, 1963).

It appears, then, that the father may play a minimal role in early infant social development. The absence of the father through death or divorce has its effects most strongly on older children and depends equally strongly on the family climate existing in the home and the degree of discipline and supervision of the child exerted by the mother. Note, however, that these conclusions apply to the "typical" family situation—one in which the "mothering figure" is the mother herself. In those situations where principal attachment is instead between the child and the father (for example, where the father is the primary caretaker), separation of the child from the father can then be extremely upsetting to the child.

COGNITIVE FACTORS IN EMOTIONAL DEVELOPMENT

To this point, we have stressed the role of environmental and maternal influences on the emotional growth of infants. However, there is growing evidence that the child's social responsiveness, and especially his anxiety reactions, may be affected by his level of cognitive sophistication. Jerome Kagan (1976) has recently put forth a view emphasizing the cognitive bases of the child's emotional reactions. He feels that many of the child's emotional and social behaviors are influenced primarily by the child's cognitive schemata and memory processes and develop quite independently of any environmental influences, following, as it were, a biological or maturational timetable.

Take, for example, the appearance of the distinctive social smile to the mother (or other primary caretaker) when the baby is 4 months of age. Kagan has theorized that by this age, the child has developed a well-articulated schema (mental image) for his mother's face. The mother's face is the first face for which the child creates an integrated, fully developed memory. Hence, the distinctive smile to the mother is a sign that the infant recognizes her. Though it is true that the infant responds to his mother's face by smiling (a sign of emotional satisfaction), Kagan's point is that a necessary prerequisite for smiling is the prior cognitive capacity to form a schema for his mother's face.

In like fashion, Kagan has tried to find a cognitive basis for such phenomena as stranger anxiety and separation anxiety. Stranger anxiety, he feels, arises from the fact that the stranger represents an extreme discrepancy from the schema that

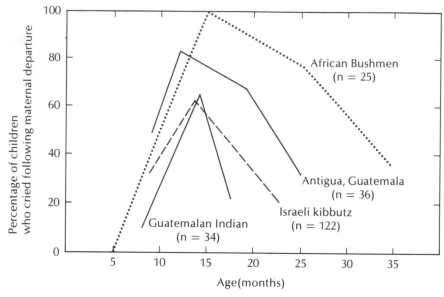

Figure 5-7. Comparison of the time course of separation anxiety in different cultures. Studies of "separation protest" as a function of age yielded remarkably similar results in four independent samples outside the United States. In all studies, the values represent the percentage of children in each age group who cried when their mothers left them alone with an unfamiliar woman. The response seems to be the result of a new competence that emerges in the last third of the first year, when the child is mature enough to raise questions about the consequences of an unexpected event such as the mother's departure but not mature enough to resolve them. (From "Emergent Themes in Human Development," by J. Kagan, *American Scientist*, 1976, *64*, 189–196. Reprinted by permission.)

the child possesses for the familiar people in his environment. As you will recall from the last chapter, extreme discrepancies cause decreased attention in young infants, since they cannot assimilate the strange event into their already existing schema. With the added hypothesis that decreased looking at a strange event or person could be caused by fear of that object, Kagan posits that stranger anxiety is primarily due to the inability of the child to understand an extremely novel event. Support for his position comes from a series of studies by Hebb (1946), which showed that monkeys show extreme fear to very novel objects, such as snakes and severed monkey heads, even though they have never seen these objects before.

Kagan has similarly interpreted separation anxiety in cognitive terms. His view is that separation anxiety reveals the emergence of a new cognitive process—namely, the infant's ability to *retrieve* from memory a representation of his mother when she is away. The anxiety is caused since he can think about his mother but cannot yet understand completely where she has gone or whether she will return (Kagan, 1976). Prior to the age at which separation anxiety emerges, Kagan feels the child has no memory for her and, therefore, does not miss her. As the child grows older, there is a decline in separation anxiety as the child is able to comprehend where she has gone and to predict that she will return.

The predictable timetable of many of the milestones in infant social development appears to Kagan to reveal a strong maturational determinant of these behaviors. Comparing data from a wide variety of cultures with extremely different child-rearing practices, Kagan has shown a striking similarity in the appearance and disappearance of separation anxiety (see Figure 5-7). For Kagan, this similarity despite strong cultural differences argues forcefully that many aspects of social responsiveness in infants follow a predictable maturational course and are under the influence of the changing cognitive capacities of the growing infant.

At present, it is unclear to what extent the social and emotional development of infants is under the influence of maturational and cognitive factors and to what extent it is influenced by the specific experiences and interactions that the child undergoes with his mother. No doubt, however, both maturation and experience play a complementary and interacting role in determining the time course and strength of different attachment behaviors.

CREATING AN OPTIMAL ENVIRONMENT

The principles discussed in this chapter allow us to make some recommendations to ensure the optimal social and emotional growth of the infant.

As soon as the child is born, every effort should be made to maximize the amount of time mother and infant spend together. Rooming-in practices should be encouraged wherever possible. If the infant is in an incubator, the parents should be allowed to visit and handle their baby as often as possible. Maximal interaction between parent and child will permit the child to exercise those behaviors (cuddling, looking) upon which later attachment is based. Additionally, interaction with her child may serve to stimulate the mother's *maternal condition*, thereby increasing her sensitivity and responsiveness to her infant.

Although attachment to a single mother figure is not necessary, it seems prudent to suggest that there should be some consistency in the caretakers looking after the infant. Efforts should be made to secure the same baby-sitters to care for the child when the mother is away. The same attendants in infant day-care centers should consistently care for the infant. These practices will allow the infant to become securely attached to a few significant people in his environment and, thus, to develop the security and trust necessary for normal social development.

The characteristics of the people caring for the infant are extremely important. Caretakers should be sensitive to the infant's needs and signals, and they should genuinely enjoy interacting with the infant. Care should therefore be taken in the selection of baby-sitters or alternate care facilities—particularly for working mothers or mothers away from home a good deal.

Major, prolonged separations of the infant from the mother should be avoided, if at all possible. If separation is unavoidable, as in cases where the child has to be hospitalized, the parent should attempt to be with the child as much as possible. Prolonged vacations away from the child are risky, especially if adequate alternate care cannot be ensured. And if the parent must leave the child for any reason, the child should, if possible, be cared for in familiar surroundings by people he knows.

SUMMARY OF EMOTIONAL DEVELOPMENT IN INFANCY

Our discussion of emotional development during infancy has covered a number of interesting issues. We explored the major milestones in infant social development and considered two theoretical attempts to explain how infant attachment develops: the learning theory view and the ethological theory. We saw how a number of environmental and other factors influence the strength and quality of the infant's attachment to his mother as well as some of the sources of anxiety that can disrupt the normal course of emotional attachment. Finally, we considered some recent evidence linking the cognitive growth of the infant with his emerging social behaviors. In conclusion, we would like to summarize the main points of our discussion and point out some practical implications of our analysis.

First, human infants enter the world with a complex set of innately organized behaviors (looking, sucking, smiling). These behaviors appear to form the basis for the early social interaction between mother and child. Thus, there may be some instinctual or innate components to the growth of infant attachment. Lack of opportunity to display these behaviors and to develop a secure attachment, either through institutionalization, inadequate mothering, or some other form of deprivation, may cause serious psychological damage to the young infant. The presence of a single mother figure, however, does not appear to be a necessary condition for the development of a strong and secure attachment. More important are the sensitivity of the caretakers to the child, the quality of their interaction with him, and the genuine enjoyment that they seem to derive from the infant. Though a single mother figure is no guarantee of normal emotional development, it is most likely true that the characteristics of a normal, stimulating home environment provide at present the best circumstances for healthy emotional development.

Second, in humans at least, the effects of inadequate mothering or deprivation, though severe, need not be permanently damaging. The right kind of therapeutic environment can compensate for early deprivation. However, it is critical that the therapy be geared to the needs of the child. Simply placing the child in a "normal environment" is no guarantee that he will become "normal." Moreover, massive enrichment programs may actually have harmful consequences if the child is unable to cope with the complexities of his new surroundings. Gradual emergence into a secure, controlled environment that allows the child ample opportunity to adjust and explore is more likely to provide the right kind of therapeutic setting.

SUGGESTED READINGS

Ainsworth, M.D.S. The development of infant-mother attachment. In B. M. Caldwell & H. N. Riccuiti (Eds.), *Review of child development research* (Vol. 3). Chicago: University of Chicago Press, 1973. An excellent overview of the current state of knowledge on the nature and development of infant attachment.

Bowlby, J. *Attachment and loss.* Vol. 1: *Attachment.* London: Hogarth; New York: Basic Books, 1969. A somewhat lengthy but comprehensive statement of Bowlby's position on infant attachment. It clearly delineates the ethological framework upon which many of his ideas are based.

Clarke, A. M., & Clarke, A.D.B. *Early experience: Myth and evidence.* New York: Free Press, 1976. This recent book reviews current research and thinking on the importance of early experience on later development. It presents a strong challenge to the notion that early experience produces long-lasting, irreversible effects in later life.

Harlow, H. F. The maternal affectional system. In B. M. Foss (Ed.), *Determinants of infant behavior II.* London: Methuen; New York: Wiley, 1963. A comprehensive statement of Harlow's basic position on the nature and development of infant/mother attachment.

Kagan, J. Emergent themes in human development. *American Scientist,* 1976, *64,* 186–196. The most recent statement by Kagan detailing his maturational/cognitive view of the emergence of some milestones in the emotional development of infants.

Schaffer, R. *Mothering.* Cambridge, Mass.: Harvard University Press, 1977. A very readable and exciting summary of infant development. It is especially helpful in elucidating the complex interaction of mother and child in the development of attachment.

GLOSSARY

attachment. The emotional bond that develops between an infant and another person (usually the mother) by which the infant seeks close contact with that person and will show signs of emotional upset if separated from that person.

contact comfort. Term used by Harlow to describe the pleasure which infant monkeys derived from clinging to soft, warm material (such as the terry cloth mother). Harlow believes that the need for contact comfort is innate.

critical period. A relatively well delineated time period in the life of an organism during which certain experiences or environmental stimuli will have more pronounced effects than either prior to or subsequent to that period. Ethologists were first to see the importance of critical periods in early social and emotional development.

fixed action pattern. A complex, innately organized behavior pattern which runs itself off automatically with little or no prior learning. Ethologists have uncovered a number of fixed action patterns in lower animals, and psychologists have speculated that some behaviors of very young infants (such as clinging, cuddling and looking) may resemble these innately organized fixed action patterns.

following response. The behavior of young mallard ducklings who will follow an object upon which they have become imprinted, if the object is presented to them during a given critical period (13 to 16 hours after birth).

imprinting. The phenomenon whereby an attachment is formed, typically between the young of some species and other members of that species. The following response of young mallard ducklings is an example of the imprinting process. Some psychologists feel that the attachment of a human infant for its mother resembles the imprinting process.

maternal condition. A hormonal change that, it is hypothesized, mothers experience immediately after giving birth that predisposes them to be more responsive and sensitive to their infants.

releaser. Some stimulus or aspect of a stimulus that triggers a fixed action pattern. For example, a nut is a releaser that triggers nut-burying behavior in the squirrel.

secondary reinforcer. A reinforcer that is learned on the basis of its association with some basic or primary reinforcer. Learning theorists view infant attachment as a situation in which the mother comes to be a reinforcer as a consequence of being the person most closely associated with primary reinforcers such as food.

separation anxiety. The anxiety that the infant experiences when he is separated from an attachment figure. Separation anxiety first appears at around 9 months of age, peaks between 13 and 16 months of age, and gradually declines thereafter.

stranger anxiety. The anxiety that an infant experiences in the presence of "strange" or novel people. Stranger anxiety first appears at around 5 or 6 months of age, continues typically through the eight or ninth month, and disappears thereafter. Not all children show stranger anxiety, and the behavior of the stranger toward the infant is an important factor in determining whether the infant will show anxiety.

social smile. The smiling behavior of an infant toward other human beings. At first, infants show "indiscriminate social smiling" toward many humans and even toward objects. However, at about 4 months of age, infants show smiling predominantly toward the person to whom they have formed an attachment, typically the mother.

REFERENCES

Adams, B. N. Birth order: A critical review. *Sociometry,* 1972, *35,* 411–439.

Ainsworth, M.D.S. The effects of maternal deprivation: A review of findings and controversy in the context of research strategy. In *Deprivation of Maternal Care: A reassessment of its effects,* Public Health Paper. Geneva: World Health Organization, 1962.

Ainsworth, M.D.S. *Infancy in Uganda: Infant care and the growth of love.* Baltimore: Johns Hopkins University Press, 1967.

Ainsworth, M.D.S. Object relations, dependency and attachment: A theoretical review of the mother-infant relationship. *Child Development,* 1969, *40,* 969–1025.

Ainsworth, M.D.S. The development of mother-infant attachment. In B.M. Caldwell & H. N. Riccuiti (Eds.), *Child Development Research* (Vol. 3). Chicago: University of Chicago Press, 1973.

Ainsworth, M.D.S., & Bell, S.M.V. Some contemporary patterns of mother-infant interaction in the feeding situation. In J. A. Ambrose (Ed.), *Stimulation in early infancy.* London: Academic Press, 1969.

Bergman, T., & Haith, M. M. Development of eye contact and facial scanning in infants. Paper presented at the biennial meeting of the Society for Research in Child Development, Minneapolis, March 1971.

Bostock, J. Thieving in childhood. *Medical Journal of Australia,* 1961, *1,* 813–815.

Bowlby, J. *Forty-four juvenile thieves: Their characters and homelife.* London: Bailliere, Tindall & Cox, 1946.

Bowlby, J. *Attachment and loss: Attachment* (Vol. 1). London: Hogarth Press, 1969.

Bowlby, J., Ainsworth, M.D.S., Boston, M., & Rosenbluth, D. Effects of mother-child separation. *British Journal of Medical Psychology.* 1956, *29,* 211–247.

Brackbill, Y. Extinction of the smiling response as a function of reinforcement schedule. *Child Development,* 1958, *29,* 115–124.

Caldwell, B. M., Wright, C., Honig, A., & Tennenbaum, J. Infant day-care and attachment. *American Journal of Orthopsychiatry,* 1970, *40,* 397–412.

Casler, L. Maternal deprivation: A critical review of the literature. *Monographs of the Society for Research in Child Development,* 1961, *26*(2, Serial No. 80).

Clarke, A. M., & Clarke, A.D.B. *Early experience; Myth and evidence.* New York: Free Press, 1976.

Eibl-Eibesfeldt, I. *Ethology: The biology of behavior.* New York: Holt, Rinehart & Winston, 1970.

Fantz, R. L. The origin of form perception. *Scientific American,* 1961, *204,* 66–72.

Gardner, D. B., Hawkes, G. R., & Burchinal, L. B. Non-continuous mothering in infancy and development in later childhood. *Child Development,* 1961, *32,* 225–234.

Glueck, S., & Glueck, E. *Family environment and delinquency.* Boston: Houghton Mifflin, 1962.

Goldberg, S. Infant care and growth in urban Zambia. *Human Development,* 1972, *15,* 77–89.

Goldfarb, W. Effects of early institutional care on adolescent personality. *Journal of Experimental Education,* 1943, *12,* 106–129.

Harlow, H. F., & Harlow, M. K. Social deprivation in monkeys. *Scientific American,* 1962, *207,* 137–146.(a)

Harlow, H. F., & Harlow, M. K. The effect of rearing conditions on behavior. *Bulletin of the Menninger Clinic*, 1962, *26*, 213–244. (b)

Harlow, H. F., & Harlow, M. K. Learning to love. *American Scientist*, 1966, *54*, 244–272.

Harlow, H. F., & Harlow, M. K. The young monkeys. In P. Cramer (Ed.), *Readings in developmental psychology today*. Del Mar, Calif.: CRM Books, 1970. Pp. 58–63.

Harlow, H. F., & Zimmerman, R. R. Affectional responses in the infant monkey. *Science*, 1959, *130*, 421–432.

Hebb, D. O. On the nature of fear. *Psychological Review*, 1946, *53*, 259–276.

Hebb, D. O. *The organization of behavior*. New York: Wiley, 1949.

Heinicke, C. M. & Westheimer, I. *Brief separations*. New York: International Universities Press, 1965.

Herzog, E., & Sudia, C. E. Children in fatherless families. In B. M. Caldwell & H. N. Riccuiti (Eds.), *Review of child development research*. Chicago: University of Chicago Press, 1973.

Hess, E. H. Imprinting. *Science*, 1959, *130*, 133–141.

Hess, E. H. Imprinting in a natural laboratory. *Scientific American*, 1972, *227*, 24–31.

Kagan, J. Emergent themes in human development. *American Scientist*, 1976, *64*, 186–196.

Klaus, M. H., & Kennell, J. H. *Maternal-infant bonding*. St. Louis: Mosby, 1976.

Klinghammer, E., & Hess, E. H. Parental feeding in ring doves (Streptopelia roseogrisea), innate or learned? *Zeitschrift fuer Tierpsychologie*, 1964, *21*, 338–347.

Leifer, A. D., Leiderman, P. H., Barnett, C. R., & Williams, J. A. Effects of mother-infant separation on maternal attachment behavior. *Child Development*, 1972, *43*, 1203–1228.

Lorenz, K. Der Kumpan in der Umwelt des Vogels; die Artgenosse als auslosendes Moment sozialer Verhaltungaweisen. (Companions as factors in the bird's environment: The conspecific as the eliciting factor for social behavior patterns). *Journal für Ornithologie*, 1935, *83*, 137–213; 289–413.

Lorenz, K. Companionship in bird life. In C. H. Schiller (Ed.), *Instinctive Behavior*. New York: International Universities Press, 1957.

Lorenz, K. *On aggression*. New York: Bantam Books, 1966.

Menlove, F. L. Aggressive symptoms in emotionally disturbed adopted children. *Child Development*, 1965, *36*, 510–532.

Moore, T. W. Effects on the children. In S. Yudkin & A. Holme (Eds.), *Working mothers and their children*. London: Michael Joseph, 1963.

Moss, H. A. Sex, age and state as determinants of the mother-infant interaction. *Merrill-Palmer Quarterly*, 1967, *13*, 19–36.

Nye, F. I. Child adjustment in broken and in unhappy unbroken homes. *Marriage and Family Living*, 1957, *19*, 356–361.

Piaget, J. *The construction of reality in the child*. New York: Basic Books, 1954.

Pinneau, S. The infantile disorders of hospitalism and anaclitic depression. *Psychological Bulletin*, 1955, *52*, 429–452.

Provence, S., & Lipton, R. C. *Infants in institutions*. New York: International Universities Press, 1962.

Rebelsky, F., & Hanks, C. Fathers' verbal interactions with infants for the first three months of life. *Child Development*, 1971, *42*, 63–68.

Rheingold, H. L. The modification of social responsiveness in institutional babies. *Monographs of the Society for Research in Child Development*, 1956, *21*(2, Serial No. 63).

Rheingold, H. L., & Bayley, N. The later effects of an experimental modification of mothering. *Child Development*, 1959, *30*, 363–372.

Rheingold, H. L. The effect of environmental stimulation upon social and exploratory behavior in the human infant. In B. M. Foss (Ed.), *Determinants of infant behavior*. London: Methuen; New York: Wiley, 1961.

Rheingold, H. L., Gewirtz, J. L., & Ross, H. W. Social conditioning of vocalization in the infant. *Journal of Comparative and Physiological Psychology*, 1959, *52*(1), 68–73.

Robertson, J., & Robertson, Joyce. *Young children in brief separation*. A series of films. London: Tavistock Child Development Research Unit. New York: New York University Film Library, 1970.

Rutter, M. Parent-child separation: Psychological effects on the children. *Journal of Child Psychology and Psychiatry*, 1971, *12*, 233–260.

Schaffer, R. Activity level as a constitutional determinant of infantile reaction. *Child Development*, 1966, *37*, 595–602.

Schaffer, R. *Mothering*. Cambridge, Mass.: Harvard University Press, 1977.

Schaffer, R., & Emerson, P. E. The development of social attachments in infancy. *Monographs of the Society for Research in Child Development*, 1964, *29* (3. Serial No. 94). (a)

Schaffer, R., & Emerson, P. E. Patterns of response to physical contact in early human development. *Journal of Child Psychology and Psychiatry*, 1964, *5*, 1–13.(b)

Shutz, R. Sexuelle Pragungserscheinungen bei Tieren (The appearance of sexual characteristics in animals). In H. Giese (Ed.), *Die Sexualitat des Menschen (Sexuality of man)*. Stuttgart: Enke, 1968.

Slocum, W. L., & Stone, C. L. Family culture patterns and delinquent type behavior. *Marriage and Family Living*, 1963, *25*, 202–208.

Suomi, S. J., & Harlow, H. F. Social rehabilitation of isolate-reared monkeys. *Developmental psychology*, 1972, *6*, 487–496.

Thomas, A., & Chess, S. *Temperament and development*. New York: Brunner/Mazel, 1977.

Thompson, W. R., & Grusec, J. E. Studies of early experience. In P. H. Mussen (ed.), *Carmichael's manual of child psychology* (3rd ed. Vol. 1). New York: Wiley, 1970.(a)

Tizard, B. *Adoption: A second change*. New York: Free Press. 1977.

Trause, M. A., Klaus, M. H., & Kennell, J. H. Maternal behavior in mammals. In M. H. Klaus & J. H. Kennell (eds.), *Maternal-infant bonding*. St. Louis: Mosby, 1976.

Wolff, P. H. Observations on the early development of smiling. In B. M. Foss (Ed.), *Determinants of infant behavior II*. London: Methuen, 1963.

PART TWO
THE PRESCHOOL YEARS

6

Language Development

A young child, bundled in heavy winter coat and cap and clutching a snow shovel, rings the doorbell. When the door is opened, he looks up and asks, "Hey, mister, d'ya want your snow tooked off?"

A little girl, seated in the back seat of a car that has been moving in stop-and-go fashion, through rush-hour traffic, exclaims in an annoyed tone, "Gee, mom, what a traffic jelly!"

"What is a knife—the fork's husband?" [Chukovsky, 1971, p. 22].

The above examples illustrate some important principles underlying a fascinating aspect of early child development: the acquisition of language. As the examples illustrate, the language of young children is not identical to that of adults. Nevertheless, the child's language is not simply a poor copy or garbled version of adult speech. Careful scrutiny of sentences such as those above reveals that the speech of young children is surprisingly complex and creative, often producing some startling and amusing results, such as the child who exclaimed, "Mommie, I'm so sorry for the baby horses—they cannot pick their noses" (Chukovsky, 1971, p. 2).

In this chapter, we shall focus on how the child comes to acquire the basic language of the culture around him. It is not a simple task, though to all appearances most children accomplish it rather effortlessly. To gauge the enormity of the task confronting the young child, consider the number of years in school it took you to master the rudiments of a second language, such as French, Spanish, or German. Although you had the benefit of direct instruction, teachers, drills, and textbooks (not to mention your knowledge of English, with which you could compare the second language), it still took you several years of painstaking study. The young child has none of these aids, yet by approximately 5 years of age, he will be using a language that in many ways is almost as sophisticated as that of an adult.

This chapter will chart the course of language acquisition during the first few years of life. We will first describe the gradual development of the basic speech sounds that the child uses to produce words. We will then trace the child's speech from simple words to the development of complex multiword sentences. While reviewing these later stages of language acquisition, we will discuss the rules the child uses in arranging and combining words to form sentences (**syntax**) and the child's understanding of the meaning of these words and sentences (**semantics** and **semantic relations**).

THE DEVELOPMENT OF BASIC SPEECH SOUNDS

Most children do not utter their first intelligible "word" until around 1 year of age. Nevertheless, the 1-year-old child has already made significant advances in his basic ability to produce a wide variety of sounds. He or she does not forever lie quietly in the crib, but produces a broad range of cries, coos, and babbling sounds. These early sounds are forerunners of the child's eventual production of still another type of sound: the basic **speech sounds** that make up the actual "words" of the child's language.

The gradual progression of these early sounds (called *vocalizations*) into actual words follows a relatively set order. Thus, the child cries before she coos, coos before she babbles, and babbles before she speaks in words (Kaplan & Kaplan, 1971). In our discussion, we shall provide rough age estimates of when each of these vocalizations typically appears—but with the strong reminder that there is a great deal of normal variability in the ages at which different vocalizations may emerge in individual children.

Crying

From the moment of birth until about 1 month of age, most of the sounds that an infant produces are best described as **crying**—that is, cries and other sounds of distress. These cries consist of alternately high- and low-pitched sounds that are produced with a regular rhythm and are repeated about once every second. Like a siren, the cries are therefore well-nigh impossible to block out of consciousness and disregard. In short, they are a highly effective means of getting the attention of other people.

Each infant produces a variety of slightly different crying sounds. It appears that these different forms of crying are used by the infant to indicate different states of distress. Thus, for example, the infant's cries when he is hungry differ from his cries when his diapers are wet. Many parents believe that they are able to interpret these cries, thus indicating the presence of a primitive communication system between parent and child. However, a recent study (Muller, Hallien, & Murry, 1974) revealed that when parents were asked to listen to tapes of their infant's cries, they were not very accurate in identifying the "cause" or the "message" that the infant seemed to be communicating. The study did not, however, negate the fact that the cries differed; rather, it simply showed that parents are generally not very good at picking up the cues.

Cooing

At around 4 weeks of age, the infant begins to produce new sounds that are more associated with pleasant states than with distress. The onset of these new pleasure-related sounds moves the child into the second phase of his early vocalizations: **cooing.** Most of these new sounds have a characteristic "u" or "oo" sound, much like the sound of a dove. In fact, it is probably because of this predominant "u" sound that the label "cooing" was originally coined.

Babbling

The third phase (called **babbling**) emerges during the middle months of the first year, when the infant's vocalizations finally begin to sound similar to some of the speech patterns of adults.

One of the more interesting aspects of the infant's babbling is the apparent regularity in the order in which certain types of babbling sounds emerge. Thus, the babbling stage begins with the production of a variety of sounds like consonants. Later, the child will produce consonant/vowel combinations such as "pa," "ba," and "ma." Finally, repetitions of the basic combinations emerge, with the child making such sounds as "pa pa" and "ba ba." The term "babbling" probably reflects the fact that the infant's vocalizations at this stage consist primarily of consonant/vowel combinations, making them close in sound to adult words. Most of these sounds, however, are clearly not real words and are largely unintelligible to adults.

As the infant acquires the basic speech sounds and sound combinations, he also acquires patterns of pitch, stress, and rhythm (called **intonation patterns**). Like the speech sounds themselves, these intonation patterns approximate those of adults. As a result, children in the babbling stage often seem to be engaged in a long dialogue with their parents and other adults—a dialogue, however, in which neither participant can understand what the other is trying to say. Thus, children at this time produce long strings of sounds, their voices rising and falling in intonation and their facial expressions reflecting that they actually think they are communicating.

Patterned Speech

The final phase in the development of the child's basic speech sounds begins at about 1 year of age. This fourth phase, called **patterned speech,** heralds the onset of "true language," for the child now begins to produce sounds that consistently take on the characteristics of intelligible adult-like words and, most importantly, are used by the child to communicate with others. Sounds such as "mama," "dada," "me," and "no" appear and are used to convey messages to other people, showing that they have become more than mere sounds and are now truly words.

As the child's speech sounds gradually begin to approximate the speech of his parents and other adults, a further change occurs: some of the sounds produced during the babbling stage begin to disappear. This dropping-out of sounds not normally heard by a child in his parents' speech formerly led many psychologists and linguists to hypothesize the following explanation of early language development: they speculated that perhaps all children, regardless of the language into which they happen to be born, come to produce *all* possible speech sounds of *all* languages during the babbling phase, and that producing the correct sounds of a particular language during the phase of patterned speech simply involves the dropping-out of unnecessary sounds. This interpretation is, however, not quite correct. Recent research has demonstrated that during the phase of patterned speech, children also acquire new speech sounds that they have not previously produced (Oller & Richards, 1973). Thus, the period of patterned speech is not simply a time when unnecessary speech sounds are eliminated; it is also a period when children add to their basic stock of sounds in creating their first words.

ISSUE

How do children learn to produce the basic speech sounds?

More intriguing to the psychologist than the order in which speech sounds are produced is the question of how the child learns to produce these sounds. Is the child simply imitating the sounds produced by his parents? Are his speech sounds molded by the rewards and punishments received from the parents? Or is the child genetically preprogrammed to produce certain speech sounds—and to produce them in a particular order—and relatively immune to what he hears and experiences in his environment?

Theoretical Explanations of the Development of Basic Speech Sounds

We have seen that from the very beginning of life, the infant produces sounds—sounds that form the nucleus of the child's first words. As the infant develops, new types of sounds appear in four relatively ordered periods. Thus, the initial period of crying gives way to periods of, respectively, cooing, babbling, and, finally, patterned speech. Just how and why the infant progresses in this systematic fashion are at present little understood, though some explanations have been attempted. One interpretation, derived from *learning theory principles*, argues that when an infant produces a sound that occurs in the language he is learning (that is, the language he hears spoken around him), his parents are quick to reward, or *positively reinforce*, the infant with praise and attention. These positively reinforced sounds therefore occur more and more frequently in the child's vocalizations, eventually becoming an established part of his language. Similarly, the learning theory view argues that when the child produces a sound that does not occur in the language he is learning, he is not reinforced, and, therefore, such sounds eventually disappear.

Intuitively reasonable as it appears, this simplistic learning theory view seems incorrect—or at least less than completely correct. In particular, the learning theorists' assumption that parents selectively reinforce "correct" language sounds does not appear to be valid. Studies of how mothers actually respond to their infants' vocalizations reveal that mothers are *not* more likely to reward sounds that occur in their language than they are to reward sounds that do not occur in their language (Wahler, 1969).

Thus, the early development of speech sounds does not seem to be molded in any simple way by selective reinforcement. A different explanation is necessary. At present, no alternative view has been proven definitely correct. Some evidence, however, suggests that much of early sound production (especially through the babbling stage) is strongly linked to *maturational* and *genetic factors* (for example, Jakobson & Halle, 1956). This evidence has led many theorists to argue that infants may be born with a genetic predisposition to learn language and will begin to produce speech sounds as soon as their brains and vocal apparatus are sufficiently mature physiologically. Theorists who favor a maturational/genetic view argue that the early stages of language production—at least up through the babbling stage—are fairly independent of the language environment into which the child happens to be born. Clearest support for this notion is found in studies of deaf children. Research reveals that deaf children do indeed babble, and that their babbling is relatively indistinguishable from the babbling of children who can hear. It is only with the onset of patterned speech, when hearing children begin to produce speech sounds increasingly like those of their parents, that the deaf child stops babbling and becomes mute (Lenneberg, 1962).

Research with deaf children implies that the onset of early speech sounds is, in part, genetically controlled. As the child reaches different maturational levels, his genetic programming may cause him to produce certain sounds, with environmental influences becoming critical when he reaches the stage of patterned speech. Again, however, it must be emphasized that the genetic/maturational view is, like the learning theory view, only a calculated guess. We do not yet know for certain just how or why the infant progresses from one phase to the next, let alone how and why certain types of sounds appear during each of the phases.

Summary of the Development of Basic Speech Sounds

Even prior to his first meaningful words, the human infant produces a wide variety of sounds, called *vocalizations*. The gradual progression of these sounds into actual *speech sounds* follows a relatively set order, from *crying*, to *cooing*, to *babbling*, and, finally, to *patterned speech*. Research with deaf children indicates that the onset of these sounds is, at least in part, genetically controlled, with environmental factors becoming critical during the fourth, and final, stage of patterned speech.

THE FIRST WORDS

Most children begin to utter their first intelligible words at around 1 year of age, during the period of patterned speech. These first words are, however, often intelligible only to the child and to those with whom he lives, since the child frequently mispronounces his first words. For example, he may say "gog" for "dog" or "wankey" for "blanket." These early attempts at human language are, of course, what is commonly known as "baby talk."

First words are relatively simple, consisting of one or two syllables at most. For example, common first words are "dada," "mama," "hi," "baby," and "go." In addition, first words generally refer to concrete objects that are important to the child (such as "ball," "doggie," and "mama"). In particular, the names of objects that the child frequently plays with or manipulates are typically learned first. Thus, words such as "blanket" and "key" are common first words, while words for other common objects that the child does not manipulate ("table," "stove," "window") are missing (Nelson, 1973a). Finally, objects that move or change themselves in some way—cars, animals, and so forth—are more common as first words than are objects that are just "there" ("table," "tree," "window"). In short, words that are relatively simple and that concern objects with which the child commonly interacts or that are active and moving, rather than static, are most likely to be among the child's first words.

For the first few months following the emergence of his first words, the child simply expands his vocabulary. Language development during this time occurs quite literally "one word at a time" (Bloom, 1973). Nevertheless, the first words the child uses are not simply labels used to describe some object or event, but are often used to communicate fairly complex messages. For example, if the child says "milk" while being fed, we normally interpret this to mean "I want some milk." Similarly, if the child uses the word "no" when her mother tries to feed her, she may be expressing a quite complex message, such as "I don't want any more food" or "Please mother, I'd rather do it myself!" The important point is that the child is trying to convey a more complex idea than is expressed in the simple word or words he uses. We will return to this issue of the relation between the child's thought and his language later in the chapter.

Summary of the One-Word Stage

Language development during the first few months following the appearance of the child's first words occurs "one word at a time," as the child expands his vocabulary to describe objects and events in his immediate environment. These first words tend to be simple (one to two syllables) names for concrete objects and events in the child's immediate environment. Objects that move or change, or that the child plays with or otherwise manipulates, are particularly strong candidates for early acquisition. While these first words thus tend to consist of "names," children do not use language simply to label things in their environment. Rather, the words are tied to the child's thoughts and wishes, and the words often appear to be abbreviated expressions of fairly complex thoughts.

FROM WORDS TO SENTENCES: AN OVERVIEW OF SEMANTICS, SYNTAX, INFLECTIONS, AND SEMANTIC RELATIONS

Children first begin to combine words to produce simple sentences at about 18 to 20 months of age. These first sentences are short—usually only two or three words in length—and their structure is relatively simple. Over the next several years, however, the child's sentences will become increasingly longer. With this increase in length, the child's sentences will also become ever more complex. Thus, for example, a child only 3 years old produced the following sentence:

> Our Granny killed the geese in the wintertime so that they would not catch cold [Chukovsky, 1971, p. 2].

Let us consider what a child must know before he can produce a sentence such as this. First, the child must have a large vocabulary. Our example alone uses 14 different words. In order to produce the sentence, the child must thus be able to pronounce these 14 words *and* know their approximate meaning. We have already described how the child learns to pronounce the basic speech sounds that make up the words of his language, but we have not yet touched upon the processes involved in just how the child learns to understand the actual meanings of these words (a task called *semantic learning* by psychologists).

Learning the meanings of individual words is an extremely complex task that will be discussed in great detail later in this chapter. However, let us briefly examine the process at this time, so as to prepare at least a foundation for the more detailed discussion that follows. Consider the words "Granny" and "geese" used in the sentence given above. These are labels for *concrete objects* that can be seen, heard, touched, and even smelled. The child's task of learning these labels is therefore relatively straightforward, since the words involve concrete objects with which the child has had direct experience. But what about such words as "in," "so that," and "our"? These words involve concepts that cannot be so easily seen, pointed to, or described. Obviously, the task of learning to use and understand the meaning of *abstract words* such as these is a much more difficult one. Not surprisingly, then, abstract words tend to be learned and used at a much later age than are concrete words.

Learning meanings of individual words is, however, just the beginning. In order to produce a correct and intelligible sentence, the child must also know how to arrange and combine words correctly to form a sentence. This process of systematically organizing words into sentences is called **syntax.** For example, since in our sentence, it was the "geese" who were killed and not "Granny," the child must know that he has to say "Granny killed the geese" and not "The geese killed Granny." Of course, the child does not say to himself: "The rules of syntax require that I put 'Granny,' the subject, before my verb, and 'the geese,' the object, after the verb." Nevertheless the child must at some level "know" these rules in order to produce the sentence correctly and thereby communicate effectively to his listener.

Interestingly, the child seems to have a basic and intuitive understanding of word order from the moment that he first puts two words together to form a sentence. The child's earliest sentences are consistently organized to follow a relatively set word order, and this word order is used by the child to convey meaning. Later in this chapter, we will discuss how the child learns these first rudimentary rules of syntax.

Knowledge of proper word order is, however, still not enough. Consider, for example, the word "killed" in our example of Granny and her unfortunate geese. To produce this sentence, the child had to know how to create the past tense of "kill" by adding the word ending "ed" to it. The rules that tell us how to use word endings to change the tense of verbs or to make a noun plural are called **inflections.** Inflections can change the overall meaning of a sentence, and the child must therefore master the rules of inflection in order to communicate properly.

Even sophisticated knowledge of individual word meanings, word order and word endings is not sufficient to fully explain how we produce complex sentences. The child must further master **semantic relations** before he or she can understand the complete meaning of a sentence. A semantic relation is a relationship between a word and another word or words in a sentence that gives the word added meaning. Consider, for example, the sentences: "The man kicked the girl" and "The man loved the girl" (Maratsos, personal communication). In these two sentences, the word "man" acquires additional meaning that it would not have when used by itself, and it acquires this added meaning because of its interaction with other words in the sentence. Thus, we know that the "man" in the first sentence is a man who kicked a girl, while the "man" in the second sentence is a man who loved a girl. Knowing this, we make certain assumptions concerning the character and personality of each of these men. Semantic relations are therefore the understandings that each of us has concerning the ways that words in a sentence interact to modify or build on their individual meanings. These concepts, too, are ones that children must master before they can produce sentences that other people can understand.

This brief look at what the child needs to know to produce a sentence will give you some feeling for the complexity of the task facing the child when he progresses beyond the one-word stage. Sentences do not involve simply stringing together single words in any haphazard way. In order to eventually produce adultlike sentences, the child must master an enormously complex set of grammatical rules and semantic relations. In the discussion that follows, we will first focus on the problem of distinguishing different stages in the child's gradual acquisition of adult speech. We will then examine each of these stages and the type of sentences that are typically found in each.

THE BASIC STAGES OF LINGUISTIC DEVELOPMENT

There are large discrepancies in the rates at which different children learn language, for some children simply take longer than others to accomplish this difficult task. It is therefore not particularly meaningful, and is extremely difficult, to try to pin down, say, the "typical language" of a "typical 2-year-old." Psychologists have found that it is more appropriate to group children according to the level of linguistic skill that they have attained, regardless of their chronological age. Thus children are grouped in terms of whether they use only single-word utterances, or utterances two or three words in length.

Roger Brown (1973) has developed such a technique for measuring the level of a child's linguistic skill by comparing the language of children who use sentences of different lengths. This measure of sentence length is called the child's **mean length of utterance** (or **M.L.U.**), with the M.L.U. being simply the mean number of *morphemes* used in the sentences produced by the child. A **morpheme** is a unit of meaning. Thus, words like "car," "boat," "mommy," "dog," "hi," and "bye-bye" are each comprised of a single morpheme. You might well ask, then, "Why not simply count up the number of words in the sentence?" The reason for using morphemes, rather than words, is that some words have two or more units of meaning. The word "cars" is one word but contains two units of meaning: one for the word "car" and one for the plural inflection "s," which changes the meaning of the word "car" from a singular to a plural form. Thus, "cars" is said to be comprised of two morphemes.

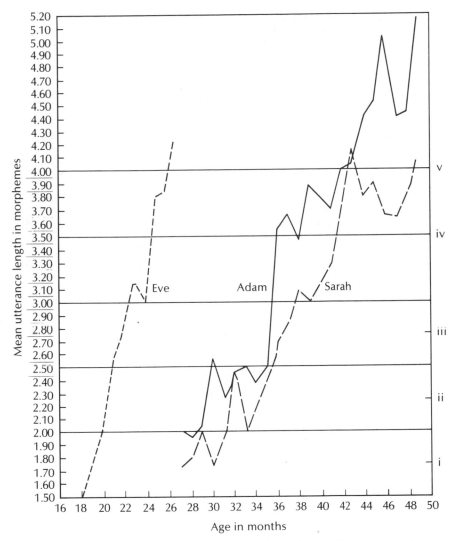

Figure 6-1. Mean length of utterance (M.L.U.) for three children up to 4 years of age. The horizontal lines mark the different stages defined by M.L.U. (From "The Child's Grammar from I to III," by R. Brown, C. Cazden, and U. Bellugi-Klima, *Minnesota Symposium on Child Psychology,* Vol. 2, 1969. Reprinted by permission of the University of Minnesota Press.)

Using *mean length of utterance (M.L.U.)* as a rough index, it is possible to distinguish different groups of children, and then study the structure of the language that characterizes each group. Roger Brown has used this method to define five such groups, which he has called "stages." In the discussion that follows, we will examine the first two of these stages and see how the child's language at these stages has been described by Roger Brown and other psycholinguists (see Figure 6-1).

In studying the material presented, it is important to understand that the stages are, by definition, arbitrary. They are used as handy reference points and do not necessarily have any psychological significance. The child's language development does not always fit nicely and neatly into these stages. Rather, it progresses in a step-by-step fashion throughout the different stages, with each stage itself being in a state of constant flux.

Stage 1 (M.L.U. = 1.1 to 2.0)

During Stage 1, the child produces sentences that have an average length of only one to two morphemes. Thus, the child is speaking predominantly one- and two-word sentences, although longer sentences (sometimes as many as six morphemes long) do occasionally occur (see Table 6-1).

Several attempts have been made in recent years to describe the typical speech of the child during Stage 1. All of these attempts have focused on slightly different aspects of the child's language, and all have come up with slightly different conclusions. There are, however, two general characteristics of Stage 1 speech that emerge in all descriptions of the child's language at this stage. First, Stage 1 speech is *simple*. In one sense this discovery is not surprising, since the child's sentences are quite short. In addition, however, the words used in the sentences are themselves linguistically simple, consisting of words such as nouns, verbs, and adjectives. The more linguistically complex words (such as articles, conjunctions, and prepositions) are missing from Stage 1 speech.

The second characteristic of Stage 1 speech is that it is *creative*. The child produces sentences that he has never heard before—sentences like "Johnny goed" or "Me want." Stage 1 speech is the unique creation of the child; it is neither identical to adult speech nor even a simplified version of adult speech.

Table 6-1. Typical utterances of the child in Stage 1 (child is 2 years old).

Mother	Child
Would you like to look at a book?	
	No.
	I see dat. *(looking at tape recorder)*
What is that?	
	Huh?
Who's here?	
	Car.
Who is here?	
	A truck.
What are you doing? I haven't seen you crawl in a long time.	
	Here truck. *(crawls to door)*
Where do you want to go? Where do you want to go?	
	Outside.
Huh?	
	Outside. I want outside. Go outside.

From "Language Acquisition and the Linguistic Environment," by C. E. Lord. Used by permission of the author.

Telegraphic Speech

Some early attempts at describing the child's speech during Stage 1 noted that it often sounds like a telegram (Brown, 1973); thus, it is often referred to as **telegraphic speech.** For example, if you wanted to send a telegram to your mother asking for money, you would probably say "Send money" instead of "Mother, please send me some money." In composing your telegram, you would retain the important content words (the nouns and verbs), but would delete the less important words (such as articles, prepositions, and auxiliary verbs). The child in Stage 1 appears to do much the same thing.

The telegraphic nature of Stage 1 speech is especially apparent in the child's imitation of adult speech. If you ask a Stage 1 child to repeat the sentence "I am going to the store," he is likely to say "I go store." Like a telegram, the essential message carried by the nouns and verbs is present, but the less essential words and morphemes are missing.

The Appearance of Syntax and Semantic Relations during Stage 1

Describing Stage 1 speech as telegraphic captures some aspects of the child's utterances at this early stage. However, it does little more. In order to really understand Stage 1 speech, we need to know *why* the child produces the sentences that he does. Thus, we need to have some idea of the nature of the grammatical rules that the child is using in forming sentences.

Pivot-Open Grammar. In the early 1960s, Martin Braine suggested that the early word combinations of young children indicated that they had developed a simple syntactical rule about the positions of certain words in sentences, and that this syntactical rule explained why the children organized their sentences in the way that they did. He noted that the two-word utterances of young children often contain the same word, repeated over and over with other words that change. For example, a child in Stage 1 might say "more milk," "more daddy," "more read." In this example, "more" is always used in the first position in the utterance, and the child seems to try out a variety of different words with it.

On the basis of his observations, Braine proposed that the Stage 1 child uses a simple syntactical rule that instructs him to always use certain words in a constant or fixed position in an utterance: some of these words always occur in the first position; others always occur in the second position. Braine further argued that these fixed-position words comprise a primitive grammatical category, which he called the *pivot class.* In Braine's formulation, there are also other words that appear to be free to appear in either the first or the second position, depending upon the pivot word being used. He argued that these words that do not have a fixed position in the utterance comprise a second primitive grammatical category, which he called the *open class.*

Many early Stage 1 utterances do, indeed, seem best described by a simple syntactical rule about the position of certain words, as Braine suggested. However, more careful recent observations (for example, Bloom, 1970; Brown, 1973; Braine, 1976) have shown that only a small part of Stage 1 speech is of this rigid **pivot-open grammar** variety. Many children do not always place pivot words in only one position. For example, a child may say "mommy bye-bye" but still say "bye-bye cat." Thus, it appears that the pivot-open explanation is not enough. Some further explanation is needed.

Semantically Based Grammars.   Perhaps the most successful attempt to date at a viable explanation has been that offered by Lois Bloom (1970). Bloom observed the early utterances of young children and kept extensive records of the contexts in which the utterances were made. She concluded that if one could reliably decide from the context what it was that the child intended to say, one could gain insight into the rules the children were using to produce their early word combinations. For example, suppose that a child says "Mommy sock." What does the child mean by this simple utterance? "Mommy" may be the subject of the sentence and "sock" the object with some verb left out, as in "Mommy is putting on my sock." Alternatively, "mommy" may be a possessive adjective and "sock" a noun, as in "That's my mommy's sock." The same utterances can thus be used to convey alternative meanings, making it essential that we know the context in which the utterance was made.

In the above examples (recorded by Bloom, 1970), the utterance "Mommy sock" was first spoken by the child when her mother was putting a stocking on the child's foot. The identical utterance was later used when the child picked up her mother's sock. In the first instance, the utterance was thus used to express a simple relationship between an *agent* and an *object* ("*Mommy* is putting on my *sock*"), while in the second instance, the same statement was used to express the idea of *possession* ("That's *mommy's sock*").

Bloom's explanation, unlike Braine's early pivot-open formulation, did not use only concepts of syntax to explain the rules underlying Stage 1 sentences. Bloom argued that *semantic relations* also play a very important role in the child's first sentences. You will recall from our earlier discussion that a semantic relation is the relationship between a word and another word or words in a sentence that gives the word added meaning.

According to Bloom, the Stage 1 child has a surprisingly firm grasp of several semantic relations. She argued that most of the sentences of Stage 1 children can be viewed as an attempt to express these semantic relations in their speech. Thus, two such types of semantic relations are reflected in our above example of "Mommy sock." The first is the relationship between a possessive ("Mommy's") and the object that it possesses ("sock"); this relationship of *possession* adds to the meaning of the object being possessed (it is not simply a "sock" but is more particularly "mommy's sock"). The second type of semantic relation reflected in our "Mommy sock" example is the relation of *agent* to *object*, as in "Mommy is putting on my sock"; this relationship adds to the meaning of both the agent ("Mommy") and the object ("sock"). Through careful observation of the utterances of Stage 1 children, and of the contexts in which these utterances were made, Bloom hypothesized the existence of several other types of semantic relations that she concluded are found in Stage 1 speech.

The second part of Bloom's explanation of why Stage 1 children structure their sentences in the way that they do relied, like Braine's explanation, on the notion of *syntax*. Bloom argued that Stage 1 children use a basic syntactical rule based upon word order to actually express the semantic relationships reflected in their sentences. Thus, the child who wishes to say her own version of the adult sentence, "That is Mommy's sock," uses *word order* to accomplish this task. The front position of "Mommy" in her sentence "Mommy sock" tells us that

Table 6-2. Basic semantic relations present in Stage 1 speech, illustrating the predominance of relations characteristic of the sensorimotor intelligence of the child at this stage. "N" refers to noun; "V" refers to verb.

Semantic Relation	Form	Example
1. Nomination	that + N	that book
2. Notice	hi + N	hi belt
3. Recurrence	more + N, 'nother + N	more milk
4. Nonexistence	allgone + N, no more + N	allgone rattle
5. Attributive	Adj + N	big train
6. Possessive	N + N	Mommy lunch
7. Locative	N + N	sweater chair
8. Locative	V + N	walk street
9. Agent-Action	N + V	Eve read
10. Agent-Object	N + N	Mommy sock
11. Action-Object	V + N	put book

From "The Child's Grammar from I to III," by R. Brown, C. Cazden, and U. Bellugi-Klima, *Minnesota Symposium on Child Psychology*, Vol. 2, 1969. Reprinted by permission of University of Minnesota Press.

"Mommy" is here being used as a possessive. Similarly, when the child says her equivalent of the adult sentence "Mommy is putting on my sock" (still "Mommy sock"), she is again using word order to actually express the semantic relationship between an agent, "Mommy," and an object, "sock."

Bloom's observations have been extended in studies by Roger Brown (1970). Brown, like Bloom, carefully studied the language of several children in Stage 1. From his observations, Brown has compiled a list of several different types of semantic relations that he argues are commonly used in Stage 1 speech. These basic semantic relations are shown in Table 6-2.

Explanations of the Semantics and Syntax of Stage 1 Speech

The work of Bloom and Brown provides a clearer picture of the nature of the child's utterances in Stage 1. The Stage 1 child seems to have a fairly firm grasp of the meanings of words that he uses (*semantics*). In addition, the Stage 1 child's use of these words indicates that he largely understands how these words interact and, through this interaction, change their individual meanings. In expressing these *semantic relations*, the child uses a primitive *syntactical rule* based upon word order (for example, placing "Mommy" in the first position in the sentence "Mommy sock," to indicate that it is either a possessive or an agent). Since the child understands and tries to express several semantic relations but with sentences that contain only a very few words, the child's sentences are often ambiguous and can be understood only if we know the actual contexts in which they are made.

The observations of Bloom and Brown help us in understanding *how* Stage 1 children put their words together to form sentences. However, this knowledge still leaves unanswered the key questions of *why* certain semantic relationships are typically the first to appear and *why* the child uses word order to express these semantic relationships.

The answer to the first question—why certain semantic relationships are the first to appear—seems to be found in the level of *sensorimotor intelligence* that the Stage 1 child has reached. When we examine the types of semantic relations that, according to Bloom and Brown, are typically expressed during Stage 1, we see some striking regularities. Those relations expressed in the child's early utterances reflect primarily his knowledge of the world around him—namely, his knowledge of the existence of objects apart from himself and their permanence, his knowledge of the spatial/temporal relationships between objects, and his notions of what causes these relationships to change (that is, causality). These relations are the same ones that characterize the child during Piaget's "sensorimotor period" of development. The strong similarity between the child's level of sensorimotor intelligence and the semantic relationships that the child first expresses seems more than merely coincidental. The semantic relations appearing in the speech of the Stage 1 child appear to be shaped and limited by the level of cognitive development that he has attained.

The second question—why the Stage 1 child uses word order to express these semantic relationships—is more difficult to answer. One possibility is that the child simply mimics and adopts a primitive version of the word order rules heard in adult speech—in other words, the child simply *imitates* adults. Though this **imitation** explanation seems logically appealing, it is open to some doubt in light of studies of languages other than English. The so-called inflectional languages, such as Latin, Russian, Korean, and Finnish, do not rely as rigidly as does English upon word order to tell us what role a particular word is performing in a sentence. Rather, *inflections*, or word endings, are heavily used for this purpose. Take, for example, the sentence, "Man bites dog" (this example is drawn from Dale, 1976). In Latin, this sentence could be expressed using *many* different word orders and yet still convey the same meaning. Thus, "Vir mordet canem," "mordet canem vir," and "canem mordet vir" are all acceptable versions of "Man bites dog" that would *not* be confused with "Dog bites man," thanks to the use of inflections to tell the listener which word is the subject, which is the verb, and which is the object of the sentence.

Studies of children learning inflectional languages indicate that children do not simply imitate their elders in forming their own early word-order rules. If they did, then we would expect children learning Russian, Korean, and Finnish (inflectional languages) to use many different word orders—imitating their parents. One study of a Russian boy (in Slobin, 1966) found, however, that although he heard his parents use many different word orders, he himself used only one or two word orders. Moreover, he appeared to use word orders to identify the roles of the different words in his sentences (initially subject-object-verb and later subject-verb-object). Bowerman (1973) studied two Finnish children and found that while one picked up the many word orders used by his mother, the other consistently used a word order rule that put the subject of his sentences first, the verbs second, and the objects third.

Taken together, the studies of children learning inflectional languages suggest a tentative answer to why children use word order to convey meaning during Stage 1. In part, the process appears to be based upon simply picking up the importance of word order in the speech of the child's parents. Additionally, however, the process appears to involve a cognitive strategy that the child adopts independently of his parents' language. Thus, even though his parents may use many different, seemingly inconsistent word orders, the child may nevertheless create his own relatively rigid word order rule to convey meaning.

Summary of Stage 1

The early sentences of Stage 1 children are short (averaging 1½ to 2 morphemes in length) and simple. Their basic structure is often like a telegram, with the important content words included but the less important words omitted. In using these words, the Stage 1 child seems to understand quite well how they interact and alter their respective meanings. This fundamental knowledge of *semantic relations* appears to be shaped and limited by the level of sensorimotor intelligence that the child has reached. English-speaking children seem to use *syntactical rules* based upon *word order* to express semantic relations and thereby convey meaning. This special emphasis upon word order can be found even among children learning languages more dependent on inflection to convey meaning. Thus, the use of word order by Stage 1 children may be a process that involves not simply imitation of adult language but, in addition, the creation by the child of strategies for communicating meaning *independently* of his parents' language.

Stage 2 (M.L.U. = 2.0 to 2.5): The Appearance of the First Grammatical Morphemes

As the child's language develops, it progressively becomes more and more complex, until sentences containing two or more morphemes become common. When this occurs, the child is said to have entered Stage 2 of Brown's five stages of linguistic development. At first, the Stage 2 child simply links together a larger number of words, still using the same semantic relations and word order rules that he used in Stage I. Thus, a three-word sentence such as "I read book" is simply an agent-action-object combination, constructed from the two previously learned semantic relations of agent-action ("I read") and action-object ("read book") present in Stage 1. Eventually, however, as the child progresses into Stage 2, completely new grammatical rules begin to appear.

Roger Brown (1973) has studied the development of 14 such rules, which he has called **grammatical morphemes.** Many, but not all, of these grammatical morphemes first appear in Stage 2, while others appear later. Brown argues that the child, like the adult, uses these grammatical morphemes to change the meanings of words and thereby convey meaning in a more discriminative way. For example, the plural inflection "s" (one of the 14 grammatical morphemes) is used to change a noun from singular to plural; the " 's" inflection is used to express possession; and addition of the inflection "ed" to a verb changes it from present to past tense. By use of such rules, the child is able to express meaning far more successfully than during Stage 1. Thus, the Stage 2 statement "Mommy's sock" is much more informative than the Stage 1 utterance "Mommy sock," thanks to the addition of the possessive inflection " 's." The 14 grammatical morphemes observed by Brown are listed in Table 6-3. As you can see, they include a number of different grammatical forms—indefinite and definite articles ("a," "the"), two prepositions ("on," "in"), nouns (plural inflections), and a variety of verb forms.

Two recent studies have examined the order in which the grammatical morphemes first appear in the language of children and have found a strikingly regular pattern (Brown, 1973; de Villiers & de Villiers, 1973). The present progressive was found to appear first, with the prepositions "in" and "on" appearing next,

Table 6-3. The 14 grammatical morphemes studied by Roger Brown, listed according to their order of acquisition.

Morpheme	Order of Acquisition	Example[a]
Present progressive	1	play*ing*
On	2.5	*on* the table
In	2.5	*in* the kitchen
Plural	4	toy*s*
Past irregular	5	*went, came*
Possessive	6	Daddy*'s* chair
Uncontractible copula	7	*Is*n't she little?
Articles	8	*the* dog, *a* bird
Past regular	9	walk*ed*
Third person singular regular	10	Billy run*s*.
Third person singular irregular	11	Mommy *does*.
Uncontractible auxiliary	12	The girls *are* sleep*ing*.
Contractible copula	13	They*'re* happy.
Contractible auxiliary	14	It*'s* rain*ing*.

[a]The relevant morpheme is in italics.

From *A First Language: The Early Stages*, by R. Brown. Copyright © 1973 by the President and Fellows of Harvard College. Reprinted by permission of Harvard University Press.

and so on. This pattern of acquisition was quite consistent in most of the children studied.

What factors explain this pattern? One possible explanation is that the first morphemes learned are simply the ones that children hear most often. If so, then we would expect the morphemes that appear most frequently in the language of a child's parents to be the first morphemes that the child uses. Brown (1973) found, however, that the grammatical morphemes learned earliest by children are no more frequent in their parents' speech than are the morphemes acquired last. The order in which the grammatical morphemes are learned is thus *not* simply a function of the frequency with which the child hears the different morphemes being spoken by parents.

Brown next considered the possibility that the grammatical morphemes learned later are in some sense more complex than those learned earlier. If so, the uniform order in which the morphemes appear may simply be a result of learning the simpler, less complex morphemes first. Careful analysis of the relative syntactic and semantic complexity of different morphemes revealed that this assumption was, indeed, correct. The order of acquisition of the 14 grammatical morphemes was highly correlated with the relative complexity of the morphemes.

Brown's findings do not, however, answer the question of *how* the morphemes are actually learned. Certainly, parents do not sit down with their children and explain to them the rules that underlie the various morphemes. Rather, the child must somehow *abstract* or *create* these basic grammatical rules by listening to his parents' speech and by experimentation. This creative process, like many others in the field of psycholinguistics, remains largely a mystery to us. We know that the process somehow occurs, but we are not certain how it occurs.

Overregularization

All that we have said to this point strongly suggests that in learning language, children do not simply mimic what they hear. Rather, they are actively involved and creative in their acquisition of language. This fact is dramatized by a fascinating phenomenon called *overregularization*. **Overregularization** refers to the child's tendency to go overboard, or *overregularize*, in applying appropriate grammatical rules to special "irregular" cases. For example, a child at Stage 2 might say "he comed," "he goed," or "he taked," even though he has never heard these words spoken by anyone else. In so doing, the child is simply applying the general rule concerning the formation of a past tense (namely, addition of the inflection "ed") to irregular verbs as though they were regular.

Even more fascinating is the fact that generally the child does not overregularize until *after* he has already correctly used some of the irregular forms. Thus, a Stage 2 child may first use phrases such as "she *went*," "she *saw*," "she show*ed*," and "she ask*ed*," in which he correctly forms the past tense for both regular and irregular verb forms. Later, however, the child appears to regress in his use of the verb forms and produces phrases such as "she go*ed*," "she se*ed*," "she show*ed*," and "she ask*ed*." This apparent regression actually reflects a major advance in the child's mastery of grammatical rules. The earlier correct use of irregular cases probably involved mere imitation of both the regular and irregular cases without any real understanding of the rules underlying their use. The onset of overregularization indicates that the child has mastered an inflectional rule. Since he then applies this rule in novel ways that he would not have heard in adult speech ("she goed" and "she seed"), simple imitation alone no longer explains what is occurring. It appears that the child has, indeed, constructed a grammatical rule that he actively and creatively applies.

Summary of Stage 2

Many of the 14 *grammatical morphemes* begin to appear during Stage 2. In mastering these initial grammatical morphemes, the Stage 2 child seems to be learning the *less complex* morphemes first. Children's mastery of at least some of these morphemes is shown by the fact that they apply them not only in ways that they have heard them used by adults, but, in addition, to even the "irregular" cases (*overregularization*).

ISSUE

How does the progression to more complex grammatical forms occur?

A common thread that runs throughout the preceding material on Stages 1 and 2 is the fact that language development is a gradual, and *progressive*, process. Children progress from using relatively simple grammatical forms to the use of forms that allow them to more precisely and clearly express themselves. How does this progression occur? What are the factors that influence this process?

How Are the Grammatical Forms Acquired?

The above question really asks: "How does the child progress from relatively primitive, less grammatical utterances to the production of more sophisticated grammatical utterances that are closer to the adult forms?" A number of hypotheses have been proposed. Let us look closely at each of them.

Imitation

One simple hypothesis is that children learn by imitating their parents' speech. In its simplest form, this hypothesis states that children, in wanting to be more like their parents, come to produce more adultlike utterances by simply copying the utterances that they hear their parents using. However, evidence that we reviewed earlier in this chapter suggests that simple imitation of adult speech cannot explain much of the child's early language development. Utterances such as "all-gone daddy" and "I goed" don't appear in adult speech, so a child's use of these forms could not have come about through simple imitation. Direct imitation is therefore not a complete answer.

Reinforcement

Another enticing hypothesis is that the child progresses from less grammatical to more grammatical utterances through the operation of some kind of selective reinforcement. Thus, it may be that correct utterances are simply being reinforced by signs of approval from parents (saying "good," nodding approval, and so forth), whereas grammatically incorrect utterances are being discouraged by signs of disapproval (saying "no," correcting the child, and so forth). This hypothesis has been tested by careful comparison of the reactions of parents to the grammatical, versus ungrammatical, utterances of their children. To quote the conclusion of one group of investigators, "there is not a shred of evidence that approval and disapproval are contingent on syntactic correctness" (Brown, Cazden, & Bellugi-Klima, 1969, p. 71). Approval and disapproval seemed to follow only the truth or falsity of the content of the sentence. Thus, when one child said about her mother, "He a girl," her mother said, "That's right." The mother implicitly understood the child's real meaning and responded to it. The fact that the grammar was wrong was inconsequential. However, when another girl said, "There's an animal farmhouse," her mother did correct her (since the building was a lighthouse), although her sentence was grammatically perfect (Brown et al., 1969). In general, parents seem to pay little attention to their children's early grammar. They are engaged in conversation with their children, and "meaning" is what counts.

Simple reinforcement theory thus does not seem adequate to explain the child's early acquisition of grammatical rules. There is, however, a somewhat more complex version of reinforcement theory. This alternative version argues that the child has a need to communicate his thoughts, feelings, and needs to others. Each successful communication is therefore automatically reinforcing to the child. According to this view, then, the reinforcing mechanism is not something affirmative that the child's parents have done (such as saying "good") but, instead, simply whether the child has successfully gotten his message across.

If this hypothesis is correct, we would expect the following to be true. First, we would expect the child's grammatically correct utterances to be more likely than his grammatically incorrect utterances to be followed by appropriate responses from his parents, indicating that they have understood just what it is that he is trying to say. Similarly, we would expect grammatically incorrect sentences to be more likely to be followed by inappropriate responses that indicate that the parents have not understood the child's message.

Brown and Hanlon (1970) tested this hypothesis by comparing how often a child's well-formed and ill-formed utterances were followed by appropriate responses by the parents (responses indicating understanding and communication) and by inappropriate responses (indicating misunderstanding or miscommunication). Put simply, no differences were found. Instead, they found that reinforcement of grammatical correctness simply does not appear to occur. Parents are very good at understanding what their children are trying to communicate and, therefore, respond appropriately to even their children's ill-formed utterances. In fact, it sometimes seems surprising that children's speech gets better at all. Dale (1976) reports that his son at 26 months said " 'gain" in urging his father to repeat some action. Nevertheless, at 31 months his son said "Do that again, Dad." If his son were attempting solely to communicate his needs or desires, he would never have had to go beyond " 'gain." For other reasons, then, his son decided that " 'gain" was not good enough.

ISSUE

Does it help to correct a child when he makes an error in grammar?

Thus far, we have seen that the progress of the young child toward producing better and more sophisticated grammatical utterances is not wholly explained through the use of selective reinforcement by the parents. But *can* correcting the child facilitate this process? Although we don't have all the answers to this question at present, there is some evidence that negative reinforcement, for the normal child, can actually be harmful to normal language growth. If parents want to help their children, they should therefore concentrate on positive encouragement and on setting the right example, and not on constantly correcting the child's mistakes.

The Role of Negative Feedback in the Child's Language Learning

In a study of children learning various vocabulary words, Nelson (1973a) found that "directive" mothers, namely those who felt they had to "teach" their children language by correcting the children's mistakes, actually had children who learned words more slowly than children whose mothers accepted their utterances even if they were wrong. In an instructive example, Braine (1971) relates the futility of his attempts to stop his daughter from saying "other one" in front of a noun:

"Want other one spoon, Daddy."
"You mean you want the other spoon."

"Yes, I want other one spoon, please, Daddy."
"Can you say 'the other spoon'?"
"Other . . . one . . . spoon."
"Say 'other.' "
"Other."
"Spoon."
"Spoon."
"Other spoon."
"Other spoon. Now give me other one spoon."

The above example illustrates that correcting the child's mistakes may have little positive impact and over the long run may actually impede the child's progress. It seems imperative to let the normal child actively generate his own language. Nelson (1973a) conjectures that "a directive maternal style imposes the mother's views and expectations and prevents the child from effectively formulating and naming his own concepts." Constantly correcting mistakes may serve to discourage the child from taking an active part in acquiring language.

Simple notions of reinforcement thus do not appear to provide a complete answer to what guides the child from more primitive to more sophisticated grammatical forms. At this point you may well be saying, "But surely the environment must have some effect! The child doesn't speak like an adult from the beginning!" In saying this, you are of course quite correct. A more complex description of language learning is needed that takes into account the active tendencies of the child, but at the same time tries to search for possible ways that the environment could play a role in language acquisition. Recently, psychologists have begun to recognize the complex nexus of factors influencing a child's language acquisition. In particular, they have begun to explore more deeply the relation between the child's cognitive abilities and his language production (Bowerman, 1977). In addition, recent studies have looked in depth at the nature of the language and social environment to which the child is exposed (Snow, 1972; Lord, 1976). We will discuss the findings of some of these studies in detail later in the chapter. Before we can fully appreciate these studies, however, we first need to consider a facet of language acquisition that we mentioned at the outset of the chapter: namely, the development of meaning, or *semantics*.

Summary of How Grammatical Forms Are Acquired

A number of hypotheses have been put forward to explain the child's gradual progression from simple to ever more complex grammatical forms. *Imitation* alone does not explain this progression, for the child produces utterances that he could not have heard in adult speech. Similarly, *reinforcement* does not seem to provide the answer, for studies show that children's parents respond appropriately, and reinforcingly, to even children's grammatically incorrect utterances. Finally, negative feedback, correcting a child's mistakes, may actually be harmful to language learning. The answer to how language progresses will more likely be found in a complex interaction between the child's own cognitive processes and his language environment. The interraction between these factors is discussed in depth later in the chapter.

SEMANTIC DEVELOPMENT

Recall from our earlier discussion that in addition to syntax, language acquisition requires that the child learn both the meanings of words (*semantics*) and the *semantic relations* that exist between words. Thus, before a child can meaningfully use the word "jump," she must learn the meaning of the word itself, and before she can meaningfully use the word in sentences, she must come to know how its meaning affects, and is in turn affected by, the meanings of other words. The learning of individual word meanings and of semantic relations is thus an integral part of the child's language development.

The Meaning of Meaning

Thus far, we have been using the term "meaning" as if its own meaning were clear. This, however, is far from the case. The definition of *meaning* has been discussed for centuries by philosophers, psychologists, and linguists, with little agreement. However, in order to understand semantic development, we do nevertheless need to have at least a rudimentary idea about the meaning of *meaning*.

If you were asked "What is the meaning of the words 'the table'?" your answer would probably run something like this: "Well, it's an object that has four legs—well, not always four—that has legs anyway, and the legs support a top. Tables vary in size and shape. They are often made of wood or metal. You use them for putting things on, or writing on, or eating on. That's about it. That's what the word 'table' means." Most adults tend to describe the meaning of words in much this way. If, however, they are questioned in greater detail, they can usually come up with other meanings. For example, if pressed for a further answer, you might say "Well, you're not talking about just any old table. You're talking about a particular table—'the' table." These descriptions of the phrase "the table" contain the essential elements of what most of us mean by *meaning*. If you look closely at the descriptions, you find that when you describe the meaning of a word you really *enumerate a set of characteristics* or *features* that belong to that word. The characteristics belonging to a word are called *semantic features* (Katz & Fodor, 1963; Clark, 1973). The meaning of a word can therefore be described as a *list of its semantic features*.

There are several types of semantic features by which a word is assigned meaning. First, there are *perceptual features:* namely, those features that can be seen, heard, touched, smelled, and tasted. For "table," perceptual features would include "having legs," "having a top," and "being made of wood or metal." There also are *functional features:* namely, those that define how the object is used. For "table," such functional features include "You put things on it, or eat on it, or write on it." Finally, there are other kinds of features that are more *abstract* than perceptual and functional features, and usually describe how a particular word or object interacts with other words or objects and changes or adds to their meaning. In our example of "the table," the word "the" has features that add to the meaning of the word "table" by telling us that we are talking about a particular table.

The idea that words are comprised of semantic features accounts for a substantial part of what we mean by *meaning*. To be fair, we must admit that the question of meaning is really far more complex than this, but for the present, our definition of meaning will suffice—with one exception. In defining some of the features underlying a word's meaning, we often have the sense that some features are more *critical* than others. Thus, we may know that a table must have legs, but the *number* of legs is less important, as is the material from which a table is constructed. Even for features that are not critical, some are more typical, or more *central*, in defining a word. For example, size is not very critical in the definition of the word "dog." But most people, when asked to rate certain dogs on the basis of size, typically say that a "good" dog does have a certain size (about cocker spaniel size). Thus, some notion of *critical defining features* as well as *centrality of features* is needed in our concept of meaning.

In summary, what we mean by the "meaning of a word" usually consists of a complex set of semantic features (perceptual, functional, and abstract), some of which are more critical than others in defining the word's meaning, and some of which are more central in defining the word's meaning even if they aren't critical.

The Development of Word Meanings

Now that we have some perspective of what is meant by *meaning*, let us turn to the important question of how children learn the meanings of different words in their language. This task is an enormously complex one. Try, for a moment, to consider this task from the child's point of view. Let's assume that a mother is taking her young child for a walk. Suddenly, the mother says "Look, Alice, there's a little doggie!" Now, Alice is faced with a whole series of problems if she is to successfully interpret this statement. First, she has several other words to decipher in addition to the key word "doggie." Second, there is a vast and confusing array of objects around her—houses, trees, cars, people, and a dog. Somehow, she must make an association between the word "doggie" and a particular small, four-footed, furry creature.

Let's next assume that Alice has been successful in her task and has made the association between "doggie" and the small, four-footed, furry creature. Only a few minutes later, however, she is told that another small, four-footed, furry creature is a "kitty." Alice must now try to learn just what it is that makes one of these creatures a "kitty" and the other a "doggie." The task is complicated still further when the mother later refers to the dog as a "cocker spaniel" or says to it "Come here, Ralph." When one considers the complexity of the task and the amount of conflicting information that the child often receives, it is truly remarkable that the child is ever able to learn the meanings of words in his language.

In our attempt to understand how children learn word meanings, we will first examine some common errors that children commit while learning the meanings of individual words. You may well ask "Why look at the errors first? Isn't that putting the cart before the horse?" The answer is that the nature of the errors provides valuable insight into just how the child goes about learning the meanings of words.

Overextension

A common phenomenon of early childhood utterances involves the misuse of a word to refer to a wider range of objects or events than the word covers in the adult language. This behavior, called **overextension,** occurs when, for example, a child uses the word "doggie" to refer to dogs, cats, and even cows. In so doing, the child is simply overextending the meaning of the word beyond the boundaries set by adult language. Another common example of overextension is the tendency of some children to say "daddy" to all adult males or "mommy" to all adult females. In these examples, the use of the word indicates that the child has learned some of its semantic features, but not all of them. Thus, the child who uses "doggie" to refer to cats, dogs, horses, and cows has learned that dogs are animals with four legs, but has not learned some of their finer distinctions or features, such as body sizes and body proportions. One can, therefore, say that the presence of *overextension* indicates that the child's meaning of the word seems to *exclude* semantic features that are present in the adult definition.

Underextension

Underextension is the opposite of overextension and refers to the child's tendency to use a particular word to refer to a smaller range of objects or events than does the adult. For example, a child may use the word "doggie" only to refer to the family pet, and use some other word—or no word at all—to refer to all other dogs. Similarly, a child may use the words "mommy" and "daddy" appropriately to refer to her own parents, but then fail to use the words to refer to the parents of other children. In these examples, the child has learned the appropriate semantic features that define the words, but has also included an additional feature (in our examples of "doggie," "mommy," and "daddy," the extra feature of personal possession) that is not present in adult usage. Thus, just as overextension involves the omission of needed semantic features, *underextension* occurs when the child *includes* extra features in the meaning of a word that are not present in the adult definition.

Overlap

At times, a child's word meanings seem to be both overextended and underextended at the same time. This phenomenon is called **overlap** (Anglin, 1975). For example, a child might call all *small*, living, furry, four-footed creatures "dogs" and all *large*, living, furry, four-footed creatures "horses." The child's concept of "dog" is here simultaneously both overextended (since he would call cats and guinea pigs "dogs") and underextended (since he would not call large dogs such as sheep dogs, St. Bernards, and Great Danes by the word "dog").

The explanation of *overlap* is rather straightforward. The child has *included* features that are not included in the adult definition (for example, size in the above example). At the same time, he has *excluded* features that would normally be present in the adult definition (for example, features specifying head shape and body proportions).

The Early Mastery of Semantics

Overextension, underextension, and overlap suggest a likely explanation of how the child gradually masters the semantics of individual words. Psychologist Eve Clark (1973) argues that a child's first words contain only a small set of the correct semantic features that define the meaning of a word. If the small set of features has excluded some relevant features, then *overextension* will occur and the child's word definition will not jibe with that of an adult. Through trial and error, the child gradually *adds* features to his definition, until it finally coincides with that of adult language.

If we somewhat modify Clark's theory to assume that the child's word meanings can also change by *subtracting* features, then we can explain *underextension* as a further instance of how the child gradually learns correct word meanings through experience. For example, if the child defines the word "muffin" to include the feature "blueberry" (Dale, 1976), then the child may find himself requesting, and getting, "muffins" that he neither expected nor wanted. Eventually, then, he will learn through experience to delete the feature "blueberry" from his definition of "muffin." In like fashion, the phenomenon of *overlap* can be explained as an initial misunderstanding of just what features to include in and exclude from the word definition, with the child's definition gradually changing through trial and error until it coincides with the adult definition.

Though our explanation seems logical, it may give you the erroneous impression that the learning process is purely hit and miss. The process is not random, however, as we can tell by examining the child's overextensions during the one-word stage and asking on what basis the child overextends his usage of a particular word. What we find is that the child most often overextends his words on the basis of *perceptual features* (Bowerman, 1977), such as shape, size, and movement. For example, one child studied by Bowerman used the word "moon" to refer to the real moon but also to refer to half-grapefruits, lemon slices, and a ball of spinach (Bowerman, 1977). These other objects were round in shape, like the moon, and the child appeared to use this perceptual feature of shape as the basis for her overextensions. We find, too, that the child sometimes overextends meaning on the basis of *functional features,* though in general this occurs less frequently (Nelson, 1974; Bowerman, 1977). Often it is difficult to know exactly on what basis the child is overextending use of a word. If a child uses the word "cherry" to refer to both cherries and grapes, he could do so on the basis of their perceptual similarity (roundness) or on the basis of their functional similarity (both are edible). However, in those instances where the distinction is more clear-cut, the child most often tends to overgeneralize on the basis of perceptual features.

In acquiring early word meanings, then, the child relies heavily on the *perceptual* attributes of things. Size, shape, texture, and movement appear to be particularly salient in determining word meaning for the child. Since the child initially stresses perceptual features over other possible features, it is not surprising that his early word definitions often differ from those of adults. With his perceptually oriented word definitions as a base, he must learn through experimentation to add or subtract other features until he finally arrives at the definitions of adult language. We will consider this process again when we discuss the relation between the child's cognitive activity and his mastery of language.

Sentences and the Appearance of Abstract Features

The meanings of words during the one-word stage seem to revolve around the perceptual, and to a lesser extent the functional, features that define these words. However, when the child begins to combine words into sentences, he must additionally come to understand more abstract features that exist between words. An important part of semantic development after the one-word stage is thus learning these basic interword relations.

The gradual mastery of these interword relations is an extremely complex process. Nevertheless, we can gain some understanding of what the child is learning by considering a concrete example. Consider the articles "the" and "a." What must the child know in order to use these two articles properly with other words? First, the child must realize that "the" is specific, while "a" is nonspecific. If the child wants to refer to a specific class of things, he uses "the." If, for example, he wants a particular book, he must say "I want *the* book." If he will take any book, he must say "I want *a* book."

The knowledge that "the" is specific and "a" nonspecific is still not enough, however. Maratsos (1974) provides an illustrative example of what else is needed. Suppose that someone has just entered a room full of people after he has been bitten by a dog outside. Since none of the people know of the incident, he must start off by saying "*a* dog just bit me," using the indefinite article. Though it was a specific dog, he can't say "*the* dog just bit me," since "the" would imply that the other people already know which dog he is referring to. This example illustrates that correct usage of the word "the" also implies *shared knowledge* on the part of both the speaker and the listener about the event being discussed. Thus, for a child to correctly use the articles "the" and "a," he must have knowledge of both the specificity/nonspecificity distinction and the shared knowledge implied in the article "the."

Psycholinguists who have studied children and their use of the articles "the" and "a" have found that by 3 years of age most children correctly use "the" as specific and "a" as nonspecific but do not yet understand the "shared knowledge" requirement for correct use of "the" (Brown, 1974; Maratsos, 1974). For example, the children in a study by Brown correctly referred to "the mailman" when a particular mailman was present. Similarly, one child appropriately requested "a Band-Aid," since any one would do. Thus, the children knew the distinction between specific and nonspecific. However, they incorrectly used "the" when they knew precisely what they were asking about but the listener did not. For example, one child said "the monkey hit the leopard," even though his listener did not know "which leopard" the child was talking about. Children do not make use of the "shared knowledge" requirement for the use of "the" until around 4½ years of age—fully a year and a half after correct usage of the specific/nonspecific distinction.

Our example of the articles "a" and "the" neatly illustrates the principle of *gradual feature acquisition*. Certain features are mastered first (in our example, the specific versus nonspecific distinction). Others (such as shared knowledge) are mastered later. Indeed, the child only gradually comes to adopt correct word usage in sentences by adding (and perhaps subtracting) the proper features to those he already knows. This is in some cases a slow process, and semantic development therefore continues well beyond the time when syntactic development is generally completed (Gentner, 1975).

Summary of Semantic Development

We define the *semantics*, or meanings, of words in terms of three general categories of semantic features: *perceptual features* (how the object or event to which the word refers looks, sounds, feels, smells, and tastes); *functional features* (what the object or event does or is used for); and *abstract features* (how the object or event interacts with, and changes the meaning of, other objects or events). Certain of these features may be more *critical* or *central* in defining the meaning of a particular word. Common childhood errors, such as *overextension* (omitting needed features and, hence, using the word to cover too broad a class of objects), *underextension* (including too many features and, therefore, using the word to cover too small a class of objects), and *overlap* (a mix of both overextension and underextension) provide insight into how the child goes about gradually defining the meaning of a word. Through trial and error, the child learns to *add* needed features and *subtract* unnecessary features, until his own word definition finally coincides with that of adult language. The child begins to master *perceptual* and, to a lesser extent, *functional features* during the *one-word stage*. Abstract features, however, do not begin to appear until he begins to *combine words into sentences*. Since an individual word may have many features, the process of semantic development can be slow, and it may take literally years for the child to correctly learn all of the features of a single word.

THE CAUSAL BASES OF LANGUAGE ACQUISITION

Throughout the chapter, we have concentrated on describing the structure of the child's language and how this structure changes as the child becomes more sophisticated in his use of language. At several points, we have touched upon the question of why and how the child learns language in the first place but have not really attempted to answer this obviously complex question. In this section, we will address this question squarely. We will first consider the contribution of the child himself: how his general cognitive abilities to perceive and understand his world influence the language he produces. We will also consider the role of the child's environment: how the language he hears spoken to him by his parents influences the language he produces himself.

Cognition and Early Language Acquisition

In an earlier section, we discussed how the child's first two-word sentences tend to express semantic relationships (such as existence, disappearance, reappearance, spatial/temporal characteristics, and causality relations) that bear a strong resemblance to the sensorimotor skills described by Piaget. Thus, the early development of linguistic skills often mirrors the development of more general cognitive abilities. This similarity strongly suggests a causal connection but does not actually tell us which skill precedes and directs the development of the other. Does a child first learn a concept nonlinguistically and then later learn to express that concept in language? Or does a child learn to understand a concept nonlinguistically only after the child can express the concept in language?

In a recent attempt to answer the question of "which comes first," Bowerman (1977) examined the language of her two daughters to see if she could discern the extent to which they used words based on concepts that they had acquired primarily through hearing language. She found that for some words, the two children initially developed quite different meanings, despite the fact that their verbal environments must have been relatively similar. One daughter used the word "off" to mean only "things coming off the body," while the other daughter used the word to refer to many different situations, including some that were not appropriate in adult usage. Bowerman argued that in such situations, where one sees different word usage by different children despite relatively similar verbal environments, one can infer that the children have first learned a nonlinguistic concept that they have later expressed in their usage of a word.

Other examples, however, can be cited where language use by the child seems to be molded by the speech that he hears. Brown (1958) analyzed the first words that children use to name things and found that many of these words depend heavily upon the words that their parents use to describe the same things. For example, children often use the word "dog" to refer to any and all types of dogs. More specific words such as "collie" and "cocker spaniel" simply don't appear in their vocabularies. The apparent explanation is that their parents don't make these fine, and confusing, distinctions when talking to them but simply refer to these animals as "dogs." This, then, is the label that the children hear being applied to certain animals. The children intuitively search for the characteristics shared by these animals, thereby forming a definition of the term that they themselves adopt. The child's use of a word can thus be strongly influenced by the words he hears, especially from his parents.

We have evidence, then, that the language of a young child is molded *both* by his own cognitive structures and by the language that he hears. The child himself contributes through his cognitive abilities to perceive and interpret the world around him. At the same time, the child's environment contributes by establishing language models for the child to perceive and adopt. For some words, the child's own cognitive abilities may dominate, causing him to define the words in a unique way inconsistent with adult usage. For other words, the environment may dominate, causing the child simply to adopt the adult usage. This process may vary greatly from one child to another. Nevertheless, some psychologists (Bowerman, 1977) have speculated that during early language acquisition, children's words are governed primarily by their own cognitions. As the children grow older and mature, they become increasingly sensitive to the social environment and begin to acquire concepts on the basis of the language they hear.

The Linguistic Environment

Thus far in our discussion, we have speculated about what the language environment *might* be like and how it *might* influence language acquisition. But what is the language environment actually like? How do parents talk to their children? Several recent studies have looked at the speech between mothers and their children (Lord, 1976; Snow, 1972; Phillips, 1973). These studies show that, in general, a mother's speech tends to be much simpler when she is speaking to her child than when she is speaking to another adult. The length of her utterances is shorter, and she uses fewer verbs, modifiers, conjunctions, and prepositions. Also, her vocabulary is more concrete and repetitious. A sample from Catherine Lord's (1976) study of one mother's speech to her child is given in Table 6-4. As you can see, the mother uses short, simple sentences with mostly concrete words. There is also a lot of repetition, presumably for the child's benefit; and the mother seems to spend a good deal of time eliciting language from her child (asking questions like "What's that?" or "Where's the keeper?"

Table 6-4. A sample of one mother's speech to her child, indicating the simple, concrete, repetitive nature of her utterances as well as her attempts to elicit language from the child.

Mother	Child
What's that? A tiger.	
	Roar.
Roar! He roars. What's that?	
	(Kanga) roo.
What's he in? Is he in his mother's pocket? Does the mother keep him in the pocket?	
Oh, look at . . . . Where's the keeper? Do you see him?	
	Keeper.
Where's the keeper?	
	The keeper.
Where is he? Where is he? I know where he is. Do you know where he is? What's he doing?	
	Working. Working.
Right. Do you work? Hey, do you work?	
	No.
You don't!	

From "Language Acquisition and the Linguistic Environment," by C. E. Lord. Reprinted by permission of the author.

What effect could this kind of language have on the language that the child learns to use? Some psychologists feel that the simple, concrete, and repetitive nature of a mother's speech provides an ideal model for the child to use in learning the rules of adult speech. Since children must extract or construct their knowledge of these rules from the speech that they hear, to the extent that this speech is simple and repetitious, it should be easier for children to understand and construct the necessary rules. Thus, the language environment serves as a simplified *model* of adult speech from which the child can construct his own rules.

Studies of the manner in which mothers speak to their children reveal how the linguistic environment can influence other aspects of the child's own speech. Lord (1976) studied three children and found that their speech differed in the proportion of questions and imperatives that they used. The mothers of these children showed exactly the same differences in their own speech. For example, the child who asked questions more had a mother who asked questions more. Clearly, then, there is an intimate relationship between the language that children hear and the language that they use. The language that children hear provides the models that they use in learning speech, and different models can produce striking differences in the child's language.

Summary of Causal Bases of Language Acquisition

Learning language is a complex process involving the child's own active *cognitive strategies* as well as input from the *linguistic environment*. Children appear to cognitively formulate their own concepts about words and how they are to be used. Some of these concepts coincide with those found in adult speech. Others, however, do not. The language spoken to the child, if simple and repetitive, will provide an optimal model for the child to formulate and test these concepts and, ultimately, to modify incorrect ones.

PROVIDING AN OPTIMAL ENVIRONMENT

We have discussed the complexity of the task of language acquisition. We have also seen how creative the child is in learning language. In light of such considerations, it is difficult to state "the" type of environment that would be most effective in stimulating language development, since we must always remember that the child himself is the master builder of his language. Nevertheless, we can suggest some basic techniques that should help the child along.

First, and most importantly, children must be exposed to language. This "language" must, however, be one that they can effectively deal with and that will encourage them to further expand their own language. Like other forms of stimulation, speech to children should be neither too simple nor too complex. If the parents' speech to the child is too simple, it could retard the child's acquisition of more complex syntactic and semantic forms by failing to provide the necessary model for mastery of these forms. If it is too complex, it could impede the child's job of discovering and constructing new forms by confusing him. In general, speech is optimal to a child if it is slightly beyond his own current level of understanding and use. Parents should therefore stay in tune with the actual language abilities of their children. They should not put unreasonable demands upon their children ("Johnny can do it. Why can't you?"), but, at the same time, they must encourage their children to master language to the full extent of their own capabilities.

Second, it must be remembered that positive reinforcement and setting the right example are far more effective than negative feedback in teaching the child language. In fact, as we saw earlier, negative feedback can actually impede learning by forcing the view of the parents on the child and by discouraging him. If the child appears to be formulating a language concept on his own, it appears that trying to forcibly change it to conform to the "correct" adult view will not be very effective. Rather, it is far better to channel the process by providing a correct model that the child can observe and integrate into his own language. In addition, parents can further help the process along by making a point of being responsive to the child. If the child indicates an interest in some new object, parents should encourage him by naming the object and by discussing with him what it is and what it does. Naming will not only add to the child's vocabulary but will help him develop basic language concepts that enable him to use this and other words effectively and correctly.

CHAPTER SUMMARY

In this chapter we studied a number of phenomena important in the acquisition of language. We examined the gradual development of the basic *speech sounds* used to produce words. In addition, we discussed a number of linguistic skills that the child must master in order to use these words in a meaningful manner: *semantics* (the meanings of the words themselves); *semantic relations* (the way in which the interaction between words adds to their meanings); *syntax* (the rules governing the order in which we organize our words); and *inflections* (the word endings that change the meanings of words). We explored some theories that have tried to explain how these skills evolve during different *stages* of linguistic development. Our review led us to conclude that neither *environmental factors* nor *cognitive factors* alone explain the gradual acquisition of language. Thus, children do not simply imitate adult speech but are actively involved in developing their own cognitive structures for creating and combining words. Linguistic development is thus a very intricate and complex process in which both environment and cognitive development play major roles.

SUGGESTED READINGS

Brown, R. *A first language: the early stages*. Cambridge, Mass.: Harvard University Press, 1973. Currently considered "the Bible" on early language acquisition, this is a difficult book for beginning students, but it presents the most detailed, comprehensive look at child language available.

Chukovsky, K. *From two to five*. Berkeley: University of California Press, 1971. A delightful and informative book on the creative and often witty sentences of preschool children.

Dale, P. *Language development: Structure and function* (2nd ed.). Holt, Rinehart & Winston, 1976. An excellent introduction to child language acquisition, this book covers most important topics in a thorough and comprehensible manner.

Morehead, D., & Morehead, A. (Eds.). *Directions in normal and deficient child language*. Baltimore, Md.: University Park Press, 1977. This book not only gives a very up-to-date account of our current state of knowledge on language acquisition; it extends to a consideration of more practical issues such as pathologies in learning language.

GLOSSARY

babbling.   The third phase infants pass through in their early vocalizations. Babbling consists of the production of vowels and consonants that sound similar to adult speech but that are as yet not real words.

cooing.   The second phase of vocalization infants typically go through on their way to producing the basic speech sounds of actual words. During this phase, which begins at around 4 weeks of age, infants produce a variety of vocalizations containing a characteristic "u" or "oo" sound.

crying. The first phase of early infant vocalization. During this phase, infants predominately vocalize with crying behavior, alternating high- and low-pitched sounds in a regular rhythm.

grammatical morphemes. Those morphemes that make word meanings more distinctive or in other ways modify the meaning of a word. Fourteen morphemes studied by Roger Brown revealed that children are quite consistent in the order in which they learn the morphemes.

imitation. With regard to language development, the child's repeating of an utterance that he has heard. Once thought to be "the" basis for language acquisition, simple imitation now appears to be only one factor that contributes to the child's language learning.

inflections. The word endings attached to words to change their meanings. The study of "inflectional languages" has helped us to understand the nature of the early rules that children employ in constructing sentences.

intonation pattern. The patterns of pitch, stress, and rhythm by which we can change basic speech sounds. For example, rising pitch at the end of a sentence signals the listener that a question is being asked. Infants first begin to use intonation patterns during the final, fourth stage of vocalization.

M.L.U. Mean Length of Utterance (in morphemes). It is a global measure of the child's linguistic ability and provides a better index of the child's language than does his age. Changes in M.L.U. form the basis for defining the five basic stages in early language acquisition.

morpheme. A unit of meaning. A morpheme may be a word but also a part of a word: for example, the plural "s" changes the meaning of a word (from singular to plural).

overextension. The tendency of young children to often inappropriately apply words to too many objects—for example, "dog" to all four-footed, furry creatures.

overlap. The child's simultaneously "overextending" use of a word on some dimensions and "underextending" use of the word on other dimensions.

overregularization. Occurs when a child applies a grammatical rule in a consistent manner to even the "irregular" cases—for example, "I go*ed*." Overregularization provides dramatic evidence that the child is not simply mimicking the words of adult speech but has mastered basic grammatical rules and is applying these rules to create new words.

patterned speech. The fourth and final stage of infant vocalization, when the infant begins to utter his first intelligible words and adopts some of the characteristic adult intonation patterns.

pivot-open grammar.   An early attempt (Braine, 1963) to describe the syntax of the child's earliest two-word utterances. This theory relied wholly on word order rules to describe the child's syntax in this early stage. Recent work has shown, however, that early word combinations are not as rigid as pivot-open grammar would suppose and that the theory is therefore only partially correct.

semantic relation.   A complex set of features (perceptual, functional, and abstract) that are thought to make up the meaning of a word.

semantics. The actual meanings of words.

speech sounds. The actual sounds that make up speech.

syntax. The rules that govern how words are organized to form meaningful sentences.

telegraphic speech. Stage 1 of language acquisition, when the child often speaks like a telegram, producing the important content words of a message and omitting less important words.

underextension. The tendency of young children to inappropriately apply words to too few objects—for example, "dog" to only small dogs.

REFERENCES

Anglin, J. The child's first terms of reference. In S. Erlich & E. Tulving (Eds.), Special issue of the *Bulletin de Psychologies,* 1975.

Bloom, L. *Language development: Form and function in emerging grammars.* Cambridge, Mass.: MIT Press, 1970.

Bloom, L. *One word at a time: The use of single word utterances before syntax.* The Hague: Mouton, 1973.

Bowerman, M. *Early syntactic development: A cross-linguistic study with special reference to Finnish.* Cambridge: Cambridge University Press, 1973.

Bowerman, M. Semantic factors in the acquisition of rules for word use and sentence construction. In D. Morehead & A. Morehead (Eds.), *Directions in normal and deficient child language.* Baltimore, Md.: University Park Press, 1977.

Braine, M.D.S. The ontogeny of English phrase structures: The first phase. *Language,* 1963, *39*(1), 1–14.

Braine, M.D.S. On two types of models of the internalization of grammar. In D. I. Slobin (Ed.), *The ontogenesis of grammar.* New York: Academic Press, 1971.

Braine, M.D.S. Children's first word combinations. *Monographs of the Society for Research in Child Development,* 1976, *41* (1, Serial No. 164).

Brown, R. How shall a thing be called? *Psychological Review,* 1958, *65*(1), 14–21.

Brown, R. *Psycholinguistics.* New York: Free Press, 1970.

Brown, R. *A first language: The early stages.* Cambridge, Mass.: Harvard University Press, 1973.

Brown, R. The development of the human child's native language. In A. Silverstein (Ed.), *Human communication: Theoretical explorations.* Hillsdale, N.J.: Erlbaum, 1974.

Brown, R., Cazden, C., & Bellugi-Klima, U. The child's grammar from I to III. In J. P. Hill (Ed.), *Minnesota symposium on child psychology* (Vol. 2). Minneapolis: University of Minnesota Press, 1969.

Brown, R., & Hanlon, C. Derivational complexity and order of acquisition in child speech. In J. R. Hayes (Ed.), *Cognition and the development of language.* New York: Wiley, 1970.

Chukovsky, K. *From two to five.* Berkeley: University of California Press, 1971.

Clark, E. What's in a word? On the child's acquisition of semantics in his first language. In T. M. Moore (Ed.), *Cognitive development and the acquisition of language.* New York: Academic Press, 1973.

Dale, P. *Language development: Structure and function* (2nd ed.). New York: Holt, Rinehart & Winston, 1976.

de Villiers, J. G., & de Villiers, P. A. A cross-sectional study of the acquisition of grammatical morphemes in child speech. *Journal of Psycholinguistic Research,* 1973, *2*, 267–278.

Gentner, D. Evidence for the psychological reality of semantic components: The verbs of possession. In D. A. Norman & D. E. Rumelhart, *Explorations in cognition.* San Francisco: W. H. Freeman, 1975. Pp. 211–246.

Jakobson, R., & Halle, M. *Fundamentals of language.* The Hague: Mouton, 1956.

Kaplan, E., & Kaplan, G. The prelinguistic child. In J. Elliot (Ed.), *Human development and cognitive processes.* New York: Holt, Rinehart & Winston, 1971. Pp. 359–381.

Katz, J. J., & Fodor, J. A. The structure of a semantic theory. *Language,* 1963, *39*, 170–210.

Lenneberg, E. H. Understanding language without the ability to speak. *Journal of Abnormal and Social Psychology,* 1962, *65*, 419–425.

Lord, C. E. *Language acquisition and the linguistic environment.* Unpublished doctoral dissertation, Harvard University, 1976.

Maratsos, M. P. Preschool children's use of definite and indefinite articles. *Child Development,* 1974, *45*, 446–455.

Muller, E., Hallien, H., & Murry, T. Perceptual responses to infant crying: Identification of cry tapes. *Journal of Child Language,* 1974, *1*, 89–95.

Nelson, K. Structure and strategy in learning to talk. *Monographs of the Society for Research in Child Development,* 1973, *38*(149).(a)

Nelson, K. Some evidence for the cognitive primacy of categorization and its functional basis. *Merrill-Palmer Quarterly,* 1973, *19*, 21–39.(b)

Nelson, K. Concept, word and sentence: Interrelations in acquisition and development. *Psychological Review,* 1974, *81*(4), 267–285.

Oller, J. W., & Richards, J. C. *Focus on the learner: Pragmatic perspectives for the language teacher.* Rowley, Mass.: Newbury House, 1973.

Phillips, J. R. Syntax and vocabulary of mothers' speech to young children: Age and sex comparisons. *Child Development,* 1973, *44*, 182–185.

Slobin, D. I. The acquisition of Russian as a native language. In F. Smith & G. A. Miller (Eds.), *The genesis of language: A psycholinguistic approach.* Cambridge, Mass.: MIT Press, 1966. Pp. 129–248.

Snow, C. E. Mothers' speech to children learning language. *Child Development,* 1972, *43*, 549–565.

Wahler, R. G. Infant social development: Some experimental analyses of an infant-mother interaction during the first year of life. *Journal of Experimental Child Psychology,* 1969, *1*, 101–113.

7

Learning and Cognitive Development in the Preschool Child

A precocious young 3-year-old child was out trick-or-treating one Halloween when she came to the house of an elderly lady with a basket of lollipops. "What's your favorite color?" the lady asked. "Yellow," the child responded. "Then take two yellow lollipops," the lady said. The child carefully selected two yellow lollipops, and, as she took each one, she said aloud—seemingly to no one—"One pop. Two pops!"

This brief story illustrates a number of aspects of cognitive development in the preschool child that we shall explore in this chapter. So as to set the basic framework for our discussion, we shall begin the chapter with an examination of Jean Piaget's theory as it applies to the preschool child, since a great deal of our insight into the intellectual growth of the preschool-aged child comes from the work of Piaget. We shall then examine the development during the preschool years of a number of highly significant cognitive skills—two of which are illustrated in the above story: learning about color and learning about numbers. The preschooler's language, too, is a subject we will explore, and we shall explore some leading theories of why the child in our story counted aloud when selecting her candies. In so doing, we will witness how language and thought merge toward the end of the preschool period, so as to become virtually indistinguishable. Finally, we will discuss the problems of "disadvantaged" children—children who begin as preschoolers to show the first signs of several intellectual deficits—and we will describe some recent attempts to help these disadvantaged children.

INTELLECTUAL GROWTH IN THE PRESCHOOL CHILD

We owe to Jean Piaget much of our knowledge of the preschool period and the advances that occur during it. Recall that Piaget concluded that a major shift occurs in the child's intellectual functioning at the end of the second year or so.

199

(See Chapter 4 for a review of Piaget's theory of the *sensorimotor period* of infancy.) This shift was significant enough that Piaget felt it heralded the dawn of a wholly new period of development: the *preoperational period*.

Piaget's Theory: The Preoperational Period (2 to 7 Years)

By the close of Piaget's sensorimotor period (see Chapter 4), the child is beginning to show signs of real thought. For the first time, the child seems to think about things before he acts on them and to anticipate the outcomes of events without seeing them directly. Piaget provides an illustrative example of this new ability (Piaget, 1952). Piaget is playing a familiar game with his daughter Lucienne (at this time about 16 months old) in which he hides objects and his daughter tries to find them. Formerly, the games had been relatively simple, such as when Piaget put a watch on a chain in a matchbox and closed the box only part of the way. Lucienne could easily solve this problem by sticking her hand in the slit and pulling out the chain. Now, Piaget complicates things by closing the matchbox almost all the way, so that she cannot insert her hand so easily without first opening the box further. Lucienne has not had experience with opening and closing boxes. In other words, she does not have a ready-made *scheme* for solving the problem. When Piaget presents this new problem, Lucienne at first fails, but then something very striking happens. She pauses for an instant, looks at the box, and then opens and closes her mouth. She repeats this sequence several times, opening and closing her mouth, wider and wider. Finally, she sticks her finger in the small slit and pulls the box open.

Lucienne's behavior reveals that she is mimicking the action of opening with her mouth. She is in a sense trying to solve the problem in her head, since she cannot readily solve it with familiar behavioral schemes. She has to invent a new means to get to the desired end. She therefore thinks about the problem, creates the solution in her head, and acts out the solution with her mouth.

Behavior such as the above first appears near the close of the sensorimotor period. For Piaget, it is a prelude to the emergence of a major shift in the young child's behavior, away from a dependence on action in dealing with the world toward utilization of mental representations of those actions—what we call *thought*.

Perhaps the classic example of this new sophistication is the child's attainment of complete *object permanence* (see Chapter 4 for a review). For the first time, the child understands that objects have an existence of their own and that this existence does not cease when the objects disappear. The child with object permanence will continue to search for an object no matter how it has disappeared. "It must be somewhere," she appears to be saying: "It can't just disappear." Moreover, the child entering the **preoperational period** can evoke the memory of the lost object and keep its image in her mind even though it may have disappeared from her view. As we said, this ability to retrieve and use mental representations defines the beginning of preoperational thought. Piaget felt that this newly acquired ability, which he called **representation,** changed the child's abilities so dramatically that the child could be said to have entered a whole new period of development.

What has really happened at this stage is that the child's schemes for dealing with objects have become **interiorized.** This means that the preschool child is now able to internally evoke schemes at will—to think about behavior without actually behaving overtly. During the sensorimotor period of infancy, the child's schemes had been evoked only externally, in response to some stimulus, and the scheme was always accompanied by an overt expression of the behavior. In a sense, the child's intelligence—which was visible in his behavior as an infant— goes "underground" during the preschool period and hence becomes less visible to outsiders. This new ability to think about and manipulate objects and events in his head has important consequences for the child, since it frees him from dominance by the environment. The capacity for mental manipulation also enables the child to understand the environment without interacting with it. Thus, being able to solve problems in his head, albeit at a primitive level, makes the child's behavior more adaptive, economical, and flexible, since he is not tied to his immediate surroundings. In this sense, the preoperational child can progress far beyond the sensorimotor child.

Aside from the above advantages, the capacity for representation actually makes possible a number of significant new abilities. The first of these Piaget calls **deferred imitation.** The child can now imitate someone else's actions long after he has seen or heard them. The newly acquired ability to carry over and evoke the memories of the previous event makes this development possible and also gives the child the freedom and flexibility to retrieve those earlier experiences whenever he wishes. Another new ability of the preoperational child is a primitive kind of **insight learning.** The child can look at a problem and solve it without having to actually do anything. He can deduce what the outcome will be by considering various alternatives in his head and "realizing" (like the proverbial light bulb going on) in his head what the outcome will be.

A third very significant advance made possible by the capacity for representation is the child's ability to *pretend and make believe.* These behaviors involve the ability to use an object for a purpose for which it was not originally designed. For example, one of Piaget's daughters used a piece of cloth as a pillow. She would pick up the cloth, put her thumb in her mouth, lie down with her head on the cloth, and pretend to go to sleep. Children play these kinds of make-believe games constantly, and during the preoperational period make-believe forms a large part of their activity. Piaget feels that the emergence of make-believe during this period stems directly from the child's representation skills. The child can now relate objects to each other in his head. Therefore, objects that resemble each other in some way can come to substitute for each other and thus, for example, allow the child to use a cloth *as if* it were a pillow.

Finally, the capacity for representation underlies and makes possible the child's developing use of *language.* Language, for Piaget, is comprised of "words" that stand for objects and events. The child's appropriate use of such words to describe objects and events not actually physically present requires the presence of mental representations for both the objects or events and the words used to describe them. Not surprisingly, then, the capacity for representation and the child's first multiword utterances emerge during similar time periods. For Piaget, there is a causal connection between the two. Representation makes possible the acquisition and use of language.

Summary of the Preoperational Child's Abilities

As we have seen, the preoperational child has made some enormous advances over his sensorimotor capabilities. Complete object permanence, the abilities to defer imitation, pretend and make-believe, and some degree of skill at solving problems in his head all flower during this period. For Piaget, these accomplishments all stem from a basic source: the ability to represent objects and events mentally in his head as well as the consequent ability to retrieve and manipulate those mental images at will. This capacity for representation in turn is believed to be responsible for the emergence and growth of sophisticated language skills.

Limitations in the Preoperational Child's Abilities

Despite his many new achievements, the preschool child is still quite limited relative to older children in many ways. Although the preschool child shows signs of thinking, his thinking ability is restricted and immature. Stated generally, the preoperational child lacks the ability to coordinate and control different thoughts in an integrated and systematic way. Though he has thoughts, they are isolated and not generally governed by an overall plan or system. This general limitation reveals itself in several important ways.

Egocentrism.   By **egocentrism,** we mean that the preoperational child is centered around his own viewpoint. When he is thinking about something and describing it from his viewpoint, he does fine. However, he has great difficulty when required to think about and describe something from another viewpoint—one which he is not experiencing immediately or with which he is less familiar. An experiment by Piaget and Inhelder (1956) helps to illustrate this. A child is shown a model on a large table of three mountains arranged in a triangle. The mountains differ in size and shape and each has different familiar toy objects on it. The child walks around the table to see all sides of the three mountains. He then sits on one side of the table facing one of the mountains. A doll is placed sitting in a chair on another side of the table facing a different mountain. The child is shown a series of pictures, each of which depicts different viewpoints of the scene. If the child is asked to pick the picture that shows what he sees, he answers correctly. However, if he is asked to pick what the doll sees, he consistently chooses his own viewpoint. This is egocentrism: namely, the inability to see things from another perspective. The preoperational child seems locked into his own rigid viewpoint. Moreover, this egocentrism is not restricted to simple perceptual activities. As we shall see in the next chapter, it extends to the child's social and emotional behavior as well.

Concatenative Thinking.   A second limitation characteristic of preoperational thought is better illustrated than described. A 3-year-old girl wanted to compose a song about expecting a new baby. Her mother wrote down the song verbatim (Millar, 1973):

> Happy news the baby is born, dear baby cannot contrary. We cannot play as rain. Some rain melts. Each rain sows a plain of lessons Rome [p. 139].

In addition to a certain egocentrism in the song, notice how the different sentences are connected. Although the child starts out with the central idea, a song about the baby, she soon gets sidetracked by individual words or ideas in one sentence and carries those words or ideas into the next sentence with little regard for the original idea or the overall unity or theme of the song. Thus "cannot" in the first sentence gets carried over into "We cannot play as rain." The idea of rain takes over and leads to the next sentence about rain melting and finally to "rain" and "plain" in the next phrase; it probably would have been Spain except that the child suddenly remembered they were going on a trip to Rome. In all, we might say that the baby got thrown out with the rainwater!

This song neatly illustrates what we call **concatenative thinking,** namely, the tendency for the child to string successive ideas together, each individual idea triggering another idea with little regard for overall unity and little concern for adhering to a central integrating theme or idea. This concatenative thinking pattern can be viewed as another instance, like egocentrism, of a failure to coordinate individual ideas or thoughts into an integrated, controlled sequence. Each individual image is quite coherent, illustrating that the child can represent simple images and thoughts. What he cannot do very effectively is put those individual thoughts into a general coherent system.

Anthropomorphism. **Anthropomorphism** means projecting human characteristics onto nonhuman objects. Chukovsky (1971) provides some humorous examples of this phenomenon:

> George cut a worm in half with his toy spade—
> "Why did you do that?"
> "The worm was lonesome. Now there are two of them—it is more cheerful that way" [p. 2].
>
> "Daddy, look how your pants are sulking" [p. 2].

As seen in these examples, the preoperational child often tends to project human feelings and emotions onto inanimate objects and animals. In this tendency, the child seems to manifest an inability at times to clearly distinguish human beings from objects. He behaves as if he really believes that pants could sulk or that worms could be lonely. Though adults can and do perceive human characteristics in objects (an ability often forming the basis of great art), they also realize the metaphorical nature of this perception. Pants looks *as if* they were sulking. In other words, adults can keep apart different thoughts about the world and exercise control over those thoughts, depending on the appropriate circumstances. The preoperational child has less control over how his thoughts are organized and will thus tend to get human and nonhuman characteristics mixed up.

Although the child's anthropomorphism is readily apparent in his actions and words, it may not be only the child's primitive mental abilities that contribute to this characteristic. The adult world constantly bombards the child with anthropomorphic pronouncements, encouraging him to blur the distinction between human and nonhuman. As Millar (1973) puts it:

> It is hardly surprising that a child who is told that the sun will be sad if he does not go out and play, or who hears the stories of talking trains, elephants' fancy dress parties, and naughty winds who blow when they ought not to . . . should have some difficulty in stating criteria for the concept "alive" [p. 141].

Egocentrism, concatenative thinking, and *anthropomorphism* represent different facets of a common underlying problem. The preoperational child does not coordinate his thoughts into an integrated system or direct those thoughts via an overall plan or organization. He is egocentric, since he cannot coordinate different perspectives. His thinking, like so much chain-link fence, is put together in concatenative strings without benefit of any unifying concept or consistent direction. He tends often to confuse human and nonhuman characteristics, since he lacks the control and organization to distinguish them appropriately.

It may be apparent from the above description in what direction the preschool child is headed. In order to make progress, the child must begin to move beyond separate, isolated thoughts and begin to put those thoughts into some coherent system. If this pattern is familiar, it is because the same developmental pattern characterized the sensorimotor infant. Recall that during the sensorimotor period, the infant progressed across stages by systematically integrating and coordinating separate, isolated schemes into ever more organized, higher-order schemes. This process of progressive integration and intercoordination also characterizes the developmental path of the preoperational child, but at a higher level. For the preoperational child, this growth is occurring at the level of mental schemes or ideas, whereas for the sensorimotor infant, it was occurring at the specific behavioral level. Nevertheless, the more basic developmental pattern remains the same. The development of the preoperational child recapitulates, at a higher level, the same pattern of development that takes place in the sensorimotor infant.

LEARNING ABOUT THE WORLD: CONCEPTUAL GROWTH IN THE PRESCHOOL CHILD

During the preschool years, the child advances his knowledge of the world in many different domains. He learns to recognize and name colors and, to some extent, letters. He learns to count and develops a rudimentary understanding of the concept of numbers. His knowledge of objects and how they are related becomes more sophisticated. He even begins to gain some understanding of the concept of time, reflected in his growing use of certain words specifying time. In this section, we will survey the child's progress in these skills, illustrating what the preschool child knows (and doesn't know) about colors, numbers, objects, and time. In so doing, we will try to highlight how developments in each skill reflect the general form of conceptual growth outlined in the previous section.

Learning about Colors

Colors come to play an increasingly prominent role in the life of the preschool child. Popsicles, candy, and other attractive goodies come to be distinguished partially on the basis of their color differences. Consequently, the child begins to pay attention to different colors and starts to learn their names. At first glance, this might seem to be a relatively easy task. The child sees the color red, learns the word "red," and subsequently uses the word when he sees the color. However, things are not quite this simple.

ISSUE

How does the child learn to name colors?

The difficulty in learning about colors is that the same label, "red," applies to many different shades of color. Think of the scores of different shades of lipsticks that are all called "red." Color is actually a category or a concept. Many different and distinguishable colors fall into the category "red." How does the child learn color concepts; and, specifically, how does he learn to group certain colors together to form a single category for each one?

Research has yielded some fascinating insights about color concepts and how the child comes to name colors. If you ask English-speaking adults to point out the color "red," most adults agree on the range of colors to which the term applies. In this sense, adults in our culture have very similar color concepts. More fascinating is the fact that adults also agree on what constitutes the "best red" or the "best green" (that is, the color that seems to best exemplify the concept). These best examples have been termed **focal colors** (Berlin & Kay, 1969). Moreover, adults in widely different cultures seem to agree on what the best focal colors are, even though different languages don't always agree on the whole range of colors falling into a given category. The concept of a focal or best color thus seems to be universal among human adults. But what about children?

An experiment by Heider (1971) examined children's color choices and found that even 3-year-old children who aren't yet using color words systematically find the focal colors more appealing. Heider simply asked the children to show her a color; the children most often chose a focal color. She then took a group of 4-year-olds and asked them to pick out a specific color from a larger array that matched a given color. The 4-year-olds were much better at matching focal colors than nonfocal colors. When she asked the children "Show me a red one," though many of the 3-year-olds couldn't do it, those that could frequently chose the focal color red.

These are surprising and tantalizing findings. They hint that perhaps there is an innate basis for defining focal colors that shows up in the color preferences of the young children and in the naming practices of adults in widely different cultures. Indeed, recent studies have examined color preferences in 4-month-old infants (Bornstein, 1975; Bornstein, Kessen, & Weiskopf, 1975). They found that infant and adult color preferences were very similar, with most-preferred shades near the center of a color category and least-preferred shades near the boundary of the color category. In another study (Bornstein, 1975), infants looked at one color until they *habituated* or quit paying attention to it. The infants were then shown a different color. Attention to the second color was less if it remained within the adult-defined color category than if it crossed over into a different category of color, even though both new colors were the same physical distance (in wavelengths) from the original color. These studies suggest that even young infants are sensitive to color, that they prefer to look at focal colors and that they may even possess primitive color categories akin to those of adults. In this sense, it may be said that our ability to distinguish colors, our preference for focal colors, and even our color categories are innately based.

How, then, might the child come to learn color names? It is very probable that the child's color words may be learned by being attached first to the focal colors and then gradually generalized to other colors within the same category. Although we do not yet know with certainty that this is the case, if it is true, it has some immediate implications for the best way to teach color words to young children.

Learning the Number Concepts

Another salient skill that begins to develop during the preschool years centers around numbers. Children are sensitive to numbers from a very early age. Anyone who has ever tried to divide up candies among a group of preschoolers will testify to that! Children begin to learn the rudiments of counting during the preschool years. Nevertheless, their knowledge of numbers is quite limited, and their concept of "number" is primitive relative to school-age children and adults. A mature concept of number is quite complex and includes much more than the ability to count, since included in the adult concept of number are such essentials as the cardinal, ordinal, and invariant aspects of numbers.

Cardinal Aspects

The cardinal aspect of numbers refers to the ability to know that a given number of objects has a particular name. The child is said to possess a cardinal sense of number if he can pick out a specific number of objects when asked, or if he can accurately tell how many objects there are in a pile.

Ordinal Aspects

The ordinal aspect of numbers refers to the ability to know that numbers can be ordered and that, for example, 2 is greater than 1, 3 is greater than 2, and so on.

Invariant Aspects

Knowing that numbers can be changed by performing certain operations (like adding and subtracting), and likewise knowing that certain operations do *not* change numbers (for example, lengthening or compressing a row of candies does not change the actual number), is referred to as "a sense of invariance of numbers under certain transformations."

As we shall see, the preschool child possesses some of these essential elements to a surprisingly sophisticated degree. However, he still lacks a complete and integrated concept of number at this time and will not attain this level of sophistication until the concrete-operational period, around 7 years of age.

ISSUE

How much does the preschool child know about counting?

It is a relatively easy procedure to get children to count, simply by asking them. Many preschool children in fact can easily count to 10 and beyond. However, does this mean that the child knows those numbers in the senses that we have just described (cardination, ordination, and invariance)? Most probably not. The ability to count to 10 by rote memory doesn't reveal any real knowledge on the child's part, just as memorizing a passage in French does not reveal any real knowledge of the meaning of the passage. As we shall see, the preschool child's firm knowledge of numbers is limited to the first few in the number series.

Children's Counting Abilities

A better way to test how firm a grasp the child has of numbers would be to arrange a test so that he could respond on the basis of numbers only. For example, we might place a whole bunch of toys or other objects in a box and ask the child to take out a specific number. (See Figure 7-1.) By successively probing for different numbers, we could estimate how well the child could count and which numbers he really understood. Using tasks similar to these, a number of investigators many years ago assessed the ability of 2- to 6-year-old children to estimate numbers accurately (Beckmann, 1924; Descoeudres, 1921; reported in Gelman, 1972). Their findings are presented in Table 7-1. As the table shows, the youngest children, between 2 and 3 years of age, typically could produce the number "2" with accuracy but not the number "3," with the number "3" being used to refer to anything greater than "2." Not until 3½ to 4 years of age could "3" be produced with great reliability, and it was only the 5- and 6-year-olds who could count higher and truly comprehend the meaning of what they were doing.

Thus, although the youngest children seemed to know the number "2," they did not appear to know numbers greater than "2" and they loosely used "3" to refer to these greater numbers. This has been referred to as the "1, 2, 3, many" phenomenon to capture the young child's knowledge of numbers at this point. We might view these results with some caution, however, since the studies were conducted over 50 years ago. With the advent of nursery schools, day-care centers, *Sesame Street* and similar television programs, which often specifically teach preschoolers to count, it would not be surprising to find that present-day youngsters know higher numbers than did the children in the studies.

The Significance of Counting

Once the child has achieved a primitive sense of number, his counting ability takes on a whole new significance. No longer merely repeating rotely memorized sequences, the child now has the ability to gain more stable knowledge about the

Table 7-1. Percentage of children in different age ranges who could successfully estimate given numbers.

	Number				
Age	1	2	3	4	5
2.0	40	40	0	—	—
3.0	100	100	19	4	4
4.0	100	97	78	25	11
5.0	100	100	96	81	33
6.0	100	—	100	100	93

Figure 7-1.

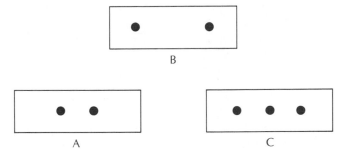

Figure 7-2. Example of the kind of stimulus arrangement used to test the child's knowledge of number. (Adapted from Gelman, 1972).

world. By counting things, the child can gain certainty about them—at least about how many there are. This may seem like a trivial accomplishment, but, without the number concept and the ability to count, the child's behavior is prey to all kinds of errors and miscalculations. An experiment by Gelman (1972) reveals how the child's knowledge of number (or lack of it) can influence the child's ability to solve problems. Gelman's study is illustrated in Figure 7-2. Gelman presented 4- and 5-year-old children with three cards. Two of the cards (A and B) contained the same number of dots, but with the dots on one of the cards more widely spaced than on the other. In addition, the dots on two of the cards, though they differed in number, were spread the same total distance apart (B and C). The child was asked, "Give me the cards that have the same number." Gelman found that when the test was given with two versus three dots, the 4- and 5-year-old children always responded correctly, giving her the cards that were equal in number. However, when she used cards with five versus nine dots, the children very often gave her the cards that were spaced equally, even though the number of dots differed. Gelman's results revealed that preschool children would solve problems on tests using numbers that they could count. However, once the numbers exceeded the child's counting ability, errors were frequent. Interestingly, Gelman found that when preschoolers failed to use numbers in their judgments, they most often used the length of the display. Specifically, when asked to select the card with more dots, they chose the card that was longer, indicating that they were judging the number of dots on the basis of the overall distance that they covered.

We can see how having a concept of number and being able to count helps the child. It gives him a firm basis to compare objects and does not force him to rely on more global, less accurate bases such as overall length. Bryant (1974) has referred to these different modes of responding as "absolute" and "relative" codes. Having a given number concept indicates use of an absolute code for numbers and allows the child to count. Responding to the length of a string of objects indicates use of a relative code. Other relative codes include the density of the objects and whether the objects can be placed in a one-to-one correspondence. In some instances, relative codes can be useful. We often estimate number on the basis of length or density without actually counting, as, for example, when deciding which line to get into in a grocery checkout counter. But relative codes are clearly less beneficial in the long run than are absolute codes. For this reason, it is obviously to the child's advantage to advance his conceptual knowledge of the number system.

Number concepts play a central role in how the child deals with certain day-to-day problems. The development of simple number concepts also paves the way for development of more sophisticated aspects of the number concept, particularly appreciation of the invariance of number across certain spatial transformations. Gelman (1972) investigated this aspect of the child's knowledge of numbers in a very ingenious experiment. There were two phases to the experiment. In the first phase, the child played a game with the experimenter. First, the child was shown two cards, one with two green mice on it and the other with three green mice. The experimenter pointed to the latter card and simply said "This is the winner." The cards were then hidden under two large cans; the experimenter mixed them up and asked the child to lift up a can and say if that card was the winner. This continued until the child consistently chose the card with three mice as the winner and knew that the other card was the loser. Then the next phase occurred, during which the experimenter did one of two things; out of sight of the child, she either added or subtracted one mouse from the winning card, or she lengthened or shortened the row of the winner. Gelman felt that the child's reaction to these two surreptitious changes would test whether the child had an invariant sense of number. If so, he should react with surprise at the addition and subtraction but not at the lengthening or shortening, since the actual number did not change. In fact, Gelman did find exactly that result when two or three mice were used in the test: children were very surprised to see the number of mice change but not at all surprised by the position changes. However, in another test using three versus four mice, many 3- and 4-year-old children did not perform as well. Here, the results revealed that children who could count the mice in the first phase performed better than children who did not yet evidence counting behavior.

Together, these studies provide some compelling evidence for the importance of being able to count. Under conditions where counting occurred, the children revealed a fairly sophisticated sense of invariance of number. Where counting did not occur, the children reverted to more relative modes of responding.

What can we say of the preschool child's concept of number? At present, we can say that he has a firm concept for probably only the first few numbers—perhaps only the first two or three. Nevertheless, this rudimentary conceptual base has some important consequences for how the child deals with his world. He is less prone to estimate number in a global and relative way; he can estimate precisely and give more certainty to his judgments and behavior.

On a more general plane, the child's developing sense of number illustrates two important things. First, the child possesses an increased *analytic ability*. He has a growing appreciation for how complex phenomena can be broken down into elements and then recombined to reconstitute the original phenomena. A complex array of objects can be broken down, counted, and added up to total the whole array. Second, the child is beginning to appreciate the importance of *absolute measurement* in dealing with objects. Numbers provide absolute measuring sticks that result in invariant and certain knowledge about objects. To the degree that measurement can be applied to objects, the child can gain better information about the state of the world.

Our survey of the child's concept of number illustrates the importance of representation in the development of this skill. Before children can progress in their conceptual development, they must develop mental representations for numbers. These absolute codes, as we've called them, pave the way for the growth of a more sophisticated sense of number. The preschool child's knowledge of number is by no means complete. Coming to grips with certain higher-order relations does not emerge fully until the school years. Nevertheless we cannot fail to be impressed with the wide range of abilities that his number concepts permit.

Learning More about Objects: Elementary Function Relations

As we saw in Chapter 4, the sensorimotor period culminates in the development of some specific knowledge about objects and the world. By the end of the second year, the child has an object concept, object permanence, size and shape constancy, and some behavioral understanding of causality. As we have just seen for colors and numbers, an important part of the early preschool years is spent in developing symbolic, or mental, representations for objects. It is later in the preschool years that the child begins to show an appreciation for certain relations between objects. We will discuss two of these relations: **function relations** and **semiclasses.**

Function Relations

If you give a preschool child a rubber band and metal pieces of different weights that can be attached to it, the child will be able to tell you that the heavier weights will stretch the rubber band more than will the lighter weights. In a rough way, he may even be able to predict how far the band will stretch when different weights are placed on it. This relation between the length of the rubber band and the size of the weights is called a *function relation* (Fischer, 1978). That is, the length of the band will vary *as a function of* the weight of the metal. For Piaget, the late preoperational child has a kind of intuitive grasp of certain function relations that exist between objects and/or events. Thus, as a further example, the preschool child knows that if you pour water from a wide beaker into a thinner beaker, the water level in the thinner beaker will be higher. In this case, the function relation specifies that variations in the width of the beaker will produce variations in the height of the water. Thus, the child has an intuitive understanding of certain relations concerning events. However, his understanding is not yet very precise or quantitative. This limitation stems in part from the child's as yet poor grasp of numbers. He is only just beginning to appreciate the quantitative relations that can exist between things. Hence, his knowledge of function relations necessarily remains rather imprecise and qualitative, rather than quantitative.

A further limitation lies in the child's inability to combine and coordinate individual function relations into a coherent system. Though he can tell you that changes in the height of the liquid in a beaker can be predicted from changes in the width of the beaker, and though he can equally well predict the opposite relation, if you now ask him if these two facts tell him anything about the amount of water involved, he will be unable to tell you that the amount of water stays the same. In order to do this, according to Piaget, the child must be able to consider the two function relations together. His inability to do so indicates a lack of integration and coordination. This inability prevents the child from demonstrating *conservation*, an attainment we will discuss when we look at the concrete operational child in Chapter 9.

Semiclasses

Another type of relation between objects that begins to emerge involves the child's ability to form higher-order classes or categories. For example, if you ask a child to sort a variety of objects into piles that go together, he can sort them by color or shape or even at times into such categories as different animals or vehicles. In so doing, he reveals a rudimentary awareness of the classes or categories into which objects may be grouped. Again, though, the child's awareness of classes or categories is not yet complete. If you show the child three horses and four dogs and ask him if there are more horses or dogs, he will respond correctly. If you now ask him if there are more animals or more dogs, he will likely say that there are more dogs. His knowledge of classes is not yet quite as stable or complete as it will become. Hence, the child is said to possess knowledge of *semiclasses* only, as opposed to the complete classes that he will master later.

A Sense of Time

The following conversation occurred between an adult and a young child who had recently moved and was being enrolled in a new day-care center:

Adult: "So you just moved here. When exactly was it?"
Child: "Well, it wasn't yesterday."
Adult: "When was it?"
Child (after long pause): "About 20 years ago!"

Knowing time concepts and how to judge and name various time intervals is very difficult for the preschool child. Relative to other concepts, acquisition of the concept of time is mastered relatively late. At present, we know very little about the developmental course of time concepts, but we do have some clues to suggest that "time" must be a difficult concept for the child.

Clues from the Child's Language

One way to assess what the child knows about time would be to see how well he uses words that refer to time concepts. Compare, for example, the child's use of the "wh-questions" (what, where, when, why, and how). Questions using "when" refer to time, as in "When daddy come home?" Studies have shown that of all the wh-questions, those beginning with "when" are usually among the last to occur in the child's language.

Many other words refer to temporal events or concepts. Words like "until," "about to," and "ready to" all imply some knowledge of temporal relations. These words, too, appear very late in the child's speech and not until well into the child's fourth year (Cromer, 1971). Words expressing more complex senses of time, such as "never," "always," and "sometimes," likewise do not appear until well after the child reaches 4 years of age.

It would appear, then, that the concept of time, at least as expressed through language, develops much later than do other concepts. Why this is so we do not at present understand. It may have something to do with the fact that time, as a subjective dimension, appears more continuous than do other dimensions, like color and number, that seem more discrete and analyzable into units. Time seems to flow indistinguishably, without noticeable breaking points. For this reason, it may be more difficult for the child to grasp concepts like "hour," "day," "yesterday," and "tomorrow."

In many cases, parents find it helpful to first illustrate time concepts by associating them with concrete events. One father, for example, tried to explain the notion of 1 hour of time as equal to "one *Happy Days* show and one *Laverne and Shirley* show." Such an approach may, indeed, provide useful models for learning time concepts. Children may need to anchor time notions to discrete events about whose duration they have some intuitive understanding. Coupled with their just-emerging ability to count, they can then begin to analyze and measure time more accurately. In this way, they can begin to conceive of time as less continuous and more like other discrete and countable concepts.

Summary of Preschool Conceptual Growth

The preschool child is learning a great deal about the world. As we have seen, most of this learning is going on inside his head, in contrast to the infant whose knowledge was acted out in his behavior. We chose several different conceptual skills on which to focus, including colors, numbers, objects, and time. For each skill, we emphasized slightly different phenomena. Nevertheless, we saw that each skill reflected a general pattern of forming mental representations for events and, in some instances, combining these representations into newer, higher-order concepts. If a dominant theme emerges from the above discussion, it is that the preschool child is beginning to build and construct his knowledge of the world, first through simple concepts and gradually through more complex, connected, coordinated, and controlled ones.

THE INTERPLAY OF LANGUAGE, THOUGHT, AND BEHAVIOR

Language and thought become increasingly intertwined during the late preschool years. For us, as adults, language and thought are virtually indistinguishable; thinking often seems like subvocally talking or communicating with oneself. But as we have seen, language and thought are not so inextricably bound in the young child. The prelinguistic infant can solve problems and has concepts that are independent of language. Moreover, the early language of the child seems to lag somewhat behind his level of cognitive sophistication. As the preschool years pass, and the child's linguistic sophistication increases, language begins to assume a greater role in the child's thoughts and behavior. Not surprisingly, psychologists have been particularly intrigued with this aspect of preschool development. Some, like Piaget (1952), see language development as a further extension of the child's cognitive growth. Others, including many Russian psychologists, see language as taking on a far more significant and distinct role—indeed, to the point of arguing that language begins to play a major role in controlling the child's actual behavior.

The Function of Language

Piaget, in a book called *The Language and Thought of the Child* (1962), reported studies of the speech of groups of kindergarten children. He was interested in how the children used language and what this could tell him about their cognitive processes. He distinguished two broad classes of speech that, he argued, roughly showed a developmental progression from one to the next. The two were called **egocentric speech** and **socialized speech.** Egocentric speech is speech spoken to oneself or spoken in the presence of others without any intent by the child to actually communicate to others. Socialized speech is speech directed at others for the purpose of communication. Egocentric speech can include simple *repetition* of an utterance, presumably for the simple pleasure of producing the sounds. A second variety of egocentric speech, called *monologue*, occurs when the child talks to himself while doing something—say, playing with a puzzle. ("I'll put this one here and that one . . . no, this goes over there, dummy!") Still a third type of egocentric speech is labeled **collective monologue,** in which individual children each comment on something but seemingly with little intent to communicate to anyone else in the room.

In Piaget's view, socialized speech emerges somewhat after egocentric speech and is characterized by the child's asking direct questions of another child, giving commands, or in some way modifying his speech to accommodate to someone else. In socialized speech, the child acts as though he is aware of the speaker and adapts his own speech in order to accommodate to the needs of other people.

Basic to Piaget's analysis of how speech operates in the young child is the notion of *egocentrism.* Recall that we defined egocentrism as the inability to consider something or someone from a perspective other than one's own. For Piaget, egocentrism is a general cognitive deficit stemming from the child's inability to coordinate different perspectives. Thus, the egocentric language of the child follows directly from his cognitive egocentrism. Since the preschool child finds it difficult to consider another's perspective, he feels no real need to adapt his speech so that another person can understand. Piaget's overall view can be seen in the following example. A boy is playing in the garage and imitating his father doing some carpentry. All of a sudden, the boy looks over at a large pile of broken pieces of wood and says:

"Dad, hand me that piece of wood there."
"Which one?" his father patiently asks.
"The calm one," the boy says.

For Piaget, cognitive structures are always paramount in the behavior of the child. They make possible the very learning of language in the first place, and the child's use of language to communicate is primarily molded by his cognitive egocentrism. Once egocentrism begins to wane, near the end of the preoperational period, the child's language follows suit, speech becomes increasingly adapted, and the child's communicative skills increase accordingly.

An Alternative Viewpoint

Some Russian psychologists have quarreled with certain of Piaget's notions, particularly that egocentric speech is not really intended for communication with others. Psychologists L. Vygotsky and, more recently, A. R. Luria have put forth a different perspective of the functional role of language in thinking, one that emphasizes the increasingly causal role that language purportedly plays in the child's behavior.

This view was first propounded by Lev Vygotsky (1962). Vygotsky felt that Piaget had missed the true meaning and ultimate fate of egocentric speech. For Vygotsky, egocentric speech implied nothing about the child's lack of awareness of other people's perspectives. Rather, Vygotsky believed that egocentric speech simply has a different purpose from socialized speech. The function of egocentric speech is, according to Vygotsky, self-regulation or self-guidance. The child uses speech to direct his behavior. At first, this self-directing speech is external and audible to others. Over time, however, speech goes underground and becomes internalized. Vygotsky termed this later internalized speech "inner speech." At this point, he argued, language and thought intertwine; thought becomes verbal and speech rational. Thus, what to Piaget looked like a disappearance of egocentric speech was to Vygotsky merely a sign that speech had become covert, or internalized, and had fused with the thought processes. Vygotsky took pains to point out that inner speech isn't just subvocally talking to oneself. Rather, it is a very rapid-fire sequence of ideas fleeting across the mind, some of which momentarily get translated into words that one says to oneself, others into images. The important point is that, in Vygotsky's view, inner speech, like earlier egocentric speech, is directed at oneself for the purpose of regulating and controlling one's own behavior.

Both Piaget and Vygotsky cite studies to support their respective points of view. These studies, however, are difficult to evaluate, since the data contained in the studies do not lend themselves to any in-depth review. Further exploration of the provocative proposals of Piaget and Vygotsky is, therefore, much needed.

One aspect of Vygotsky's theory has been explored in some depth by A. R. Luria (1932, 1961). This aspect concerns the increasingly powerful role played by language in controlling the behavior of the child. Vygotsky and Luria took as their starting point the work of their predecessor I. Pavlov. Recall that Pavlov discovered that certain "signals" (conditioned stimuli), like tones or lights, could come to control behavior when paired appropriately with certain "unconditioned stimuli." Physical stimuli were in some sense primary or first signals. Vygotsky and Luria felt that language constituted a "second-signal system" that could also come to control behavior. For Luria, the young child progresses through a series of stages in his ability to control his behavior. In very young children (1½ to 3 years of age), control of behavior resides in the words of adults who issue commands and guide the child's attention. At this first stage, verbal commands can initiate the behavior of the child but cannot inhibit behavior. If you tell a 1½-year-old to do something and then while he is doing it tell him to stop, he is likely to continue nonetheless. At the second stage, around 4 or 5 years of age, after the child has acquired some language, he begins to show some elementary self-regulation, though most control still rests with adults. At this stage, the child's own speech may influence behavior, but only in an excitatory way—not an inhibitory way. For example, a child will perform correctly if asked to press one button and simultaneously say the word "press." The child cannot yet, however, say "don't press" and refrain from pressing the button. The verbal utterance "don't press" serves to initiate the action and the child will actually press. It is not until the final stage, when language is more fully internalized, that the child can use language to control his behavior completely. Hence, around 5 years of age the child can tell himself to press or not press and behave accordingly.

Luria considers the above phenomena as evidence that language comes to control the child's behavior, first in an excitatory and later in an inhibitory fashion. If Luria is correct, his conclusion has important implications for our view of the functions of language, as well as our understanding of some important features of the preschooler's behavior. Unfortunately, the picture painted by Luria is in reality not so clear.

Several studies in recent years have attempted to replicate Luria's results and have failed (Jarvis, 1963; Wilder, 1969; Miller, Shelton, & Flavell, 1970; Bloor, 1977). For example, in one study (Miller et al., 1970), very young children were given a typical task of making specific responses to a sequence of colored lights. To one color (the positive bulb), the child had to press a rubber bulb; to the other color (negative bulb), no response was required. Some children were to respond without saying anything; others were to say "squeeze" while they pressed the positive bulb; a third group was told to say "don't squeeze" while refraining from squeezing the negative bulb; and a final group was instructed to say the appropriate thing for both positive and negative bulbs. In this experiment, Luria would have predicted that children around 3½ would be more likely to squeeze the bulb when verbal statements were used, regardless of whether they said "squeeze" or "don't squeeze." That is, both groups of children should squeeze. However, there was no evidence of any effect at all of either verbal utterance.

This study lends little support to what initially appeared to be an enticing idea. Failure to replicate Luria's work, however, does not automatically prove him wrong. As one psychologist has pointed out (Wozniak, 1972), the many differences in technique and style of conducting these experiments in two different cultures (Russia and the United States) could account for the discrepant findings. Moreover, while Luria's theory of self-regulation may be incorrect, there is little question that language and thought begin to play more interdependent roles as the child reaches the end of the preschool years. Our society relies heavily on verbal communication, and young children no doubt are sensitive to the importance of developing sophisticated verbal skills. Little wonder, then, that our thinking in time comes to be occupied more and more with forms of "talking to ourselves." Over time, this verbal thinking receives ever-increasing priority, if not absolute supremacy.

Summary of Language and Thought

As the preschool child progresses in both language skills and cognitive abilities, psychologists have wondered what function language continues to play in the cognition and behavior of the child. Piaget sees language as the handmaiden of cognition, with preschool speech a natural outcome of the child's basic egocentrism. Certain Russian psychologists, in contrast, stress the growing importance of language in controlling the child's behavior. Vygotsky feels that the child's egocentric speech did not disappear, as Piaget had suggested, but rather became internalized as "inner speech" and progressively came to merge with thought, thereby controlling the child's behavior. Luria continued this line of thinking and proposed a series of three stages in the child's verbal control of his behavior: from no control, to an excitatory-only control, to, lastly, total control, inhibitory as well as excitatory. Though Luria's own experiments appeared to corroborate these three stages and, thus, provided support for Vygotsky, recent studies in the United States have either failed to replicate Luria's basic results or even contradicted his view of the supremacy of verbal control over behavior. Nevertheless, regardless of which dominates which, late preschool development shows an increasing interplay and coordination among language, thought, and behavior.

THE DISADVANTAGED CHILD

Up to now, we have been talking about the child's development and learning in an abstract, idealized way. Unfortunately, normal learning and growth are not guaranteed to every child. There are large numbers of children in our society who do not progress as well as other children in learning the basic intellectual skills necessary for success in school. Sometimes this lack of progress results from problems inherent in the child, such as biologically based mental retardation or brain damage. Often, however, this lack of progress results from problems within the child's environment—problems such as malnutrition and inappropriate stimulation. This latter group of children (the ones with environmentally based problems) has been termed "disadvantaged" in the quite literal sense that they are at a disadvantage in terms of having access to the resources that stimulate and foster cognitive growth.

ISSUE

What causes the disadvantaged child?

This simple question cannot be answered with an equally simple, straightforward answer. As we shall see, numerous factors contribute to producing learning and intellectual deficits in certain children. However, probably the single most obvious factor common to disadvantaged children can be summed up in one word: *poverty*. In 1970, it was estimated that roughly 10 million (or 14%) of all children in the United States under 18 were living in families whose income was less than $3000 a year—certainly a level of poverty by anyone's standard. Although overall there are more poor people who are white (6 million whites versus 4 million nonwhites), there is a much higher proportion of nonwhite people who are poor (40% of nonwhites versus 10% of whites). Nevertheless, as we shall see shortly, it appears that poverty of itself and not race is the most crucial factor causing a child to be disadvantaged. Since poverty tends to go hand in hand with level of education and social standing, the families of disadvantaged children tend to cluster in the lower economic classes.

Characteristics of Poor Children

It has become increasingly clear over the last few decades that poor children do not do as well as other children on a variety of intellectual and scholastic measures. Thus, poor children tend to do more poorly on standardized tests of intelligence, to perform more poorly in school, and to show deficits in specific cognitive skills.

General Intellectual Ability

Nearly every study conducted has found that the average intelligence of poor children (as measured by standardized IQ tests) is substantially lower than the intelligence of their nonpoor counterparts. Moreover, the differences in intelligence between low-income children and other children tend to increase as the children grow older. Thus, studies to date have shown that prior to about 2 years of age, low-income children do not show any cognitive deficits relative to other children (Bayley, 1965; Golden, Birns, Bridger, & Moss, 1971). The differences do not begin to show up until the early years of elementary school. Furthermore, children from poor families appear to show steady and progressive declines in IQ throughout their school years (Klaus & Gray, 1968; Deutsch, 1967). One study of a group of poor rural black children in the South reported that between 5 and 13 years of age, some children's IQs dropped 21 points, a very significant amount. The impact of being poor is thus potentially devastating. This detrimental effect is not, however, limited to intelligence scores only but shows up in other ways.

School Performance

Poor children do less well in school than do other children—a fact that has now been very well documented (Coleman, 1966). By grades 3 or 4, poor children tend to lag several months behind their peers in reading, arithmetic, and other basic subjects. The detrimental impact of poverty thus shows up not only in standardized tests of intelligence, but in the harsh light of how these children perform in school.

Specific Cognitive Skills

We know less about the impact of poverty upon specific areas of cognitive functioning, but here, too, there is some evidence that poor children lag significantly behind other children in certain cognitive abilities. Take, for example, the development of classification categories that we discussed earlier in the chapter. If you give a child a large group of objects and ask him to choose those that somehow "go together," very young children will put the objects together on the basis of their functions or what you can do with them (Vygotsky, 1962). For example, "boy" and "house" go together, since the boy lives in the house. Older children can additionally group objects on the basis of higher-order classes, such as animals, vehicles, or foods. This ability appears to unfold at a slower rate for poor children than it does for other children. Other studies provide further evidence of a developmental lag in poor children on developmental milestones observed by Piaget (Overton, Wagner, & Dolinsky, 1971; Gaudia, 1972).

In general, then, poverty and lags in development tend to go hand in hand, with poverty manifesting itself in a host of problems in general and specific intellectual abilities and school performance. These problems get worse as the child moves through the school system. The fact that the problems did not seem as severe in the very early years has prompted some to speculate that the first significant period of disadvantage is probably that just prior to entry into school; namely, the preschool period. As we shall see, most attempts to help disadvantaged children have therefore focused on this period.

We have thus far spoken in general terms about how poverty and developmental lags are related. However, we have not directly answered our earlier question, "What causes this disadvantage?" What is it about living in poverty that acts to impair the intellectual growth of children? There are, in fact, a number of actual and potential influences, all of which interact to produce a kind of vicious cycle in which the conditions and outcomes of poverty perpetuate themselves.

Factors Associated with Poverty and Lags in Development

We turn now to some of the factors associated with poverty that may hamper the intellectual growth of the child. As we discuss these factors, you will hear echoes from our earlier discussion of factors affecting prenatal and infant development. Health, nutrition, family size, and prematurity all crop up again in the present discussion. These factors, it seems, operate on not only the young infant; their reach can extend to the older child and into the realm of learning.

Biological and Health Factors

We reviewed earlier evidence that premature babies are more likely to die and to suffer brain damage. It turns out that the incidence of prematurity is higher in poor families than it is in higher income groups. Some investigators have hypothesized that this apparent link between poverty and prematurity may result from the general nutritional and health conditions of low-income mothers (Knobloch & Pasamanick, 1960). Indeed, studies have shown that the nutritional habits and diets of poor pregnant mothers tend to be less adequate than those of middle-income pregnant mothers (Knobloch & Pasamanick, 1963). Studies with animals reviewed in Chapter 3 have shown us how severe malnutrition can affect the anatomy of the brain. The brain being the organ of learning and cognition, it is not unlikely, then, that the nutritional problems of the poor could have serious, damaging effects on the intellectual growth of children reared in low-income families. Our knowledge in this area is still very limited. Nonetheless, it does appear that nutritional deficits can affect cognitive growth. A recent study, for example, used a battery of cognitive tests to compare a group of children hospitalized for severe malnutrition with their siblings and with well-nourished classmates (Hertzig, Birch, Richardson, & Tizard, 1972). They found that the severely malnourished children performed most poorly. Although other factors admittedly could account for this difference, the finding is consistent with the work done with animals in showing that malnutrition can adversely affect basic cognitive skills.

In addition to nutrition, other health factors such as disease and injury are implicated in the link between poverty and learning. In general, poorer families are at a higher risk for many infections and chronic diseases associated with closer living quarters and less adequate heating and sanitary facilities. There is, in addition, a higher risk of accidental injury, and certain neurological diseases are almost wholly associated with urban poverty, as, for example, lead poisoning caused by ingesting paint fragments. Since the risk of serious illness and injury is thus higher among the children of the poor, these children are more likely to be hospitalized or to be confined in their homes for prolonged periods of time. Psychologists have speculated that periods of illness or hospitalization provide a kind of wasted time period during which the child's learning is stalled. It is little wonder, then, that the added problems of disease and injury that confront poor children would show up in retarded learning skills.

There are, finally, a host of other factors surrounding poverty that affect biological, psychological, and economic life. Poorer families tend to have more children and tend to have them earlier and in closer succession. The drain that this places on the mother, both physiologically and in the psychological stress of caring for a large family, and the economic drain of feeding, clothing, and otherwise providing for larger families (with much less in the way of income to start with), cannot but adversely affect the general atmosphere and learning environment of the child.

Psychological Factors Surrounding Poverty and Development

The numerous biological and health problems discussed above would, of themselves, constitute condition enough to impair a child's intellectual growth. These are not, however, the only factors linking poverty and impaired intellectual development. Other factors pertain to the quantity and quality of environmental stimulation available to the child in the home.

It is extremely difficult to design a study that will accurately measure the amount and quality of environmental stimulation that children receive in their homes. With this qualification, researchers have tried to characterize different homes on the basis of a *deprivation index* of such factors as the size of the family, the physical condition of the home, the quantity and nature of conversations between children and adults, and the parents' aspirations for the children (Whiteman & Deutsch, 1968). They found that children from homes rated high in deprivation showed definite declines in school performance between first and fifth grade. In contrast, children from nearby homes rated low in deprivation showed no such declines. These findings suggest that a key factor separating these groups of children may be the amount and type of stimulation that they receive. The "high-deprivation" family may provide less appropriate stimulation for the child and, therefore, less opportunity to learn and develop basic cognitive skills. This in turn may adversely affect his academic performance in school.

Of Vicious Circles and Cycles

As we have just seen, numerous factors are implicated in the relation between poverty and lowered intellectual performance in children. At present, we have been able to identify many potential factors but do not yet have a clear idea of which factors play the greatest role. Probably all play some significant part, and none in itself is paramount. In this sense, then, the child of poverty enters a kind of "vicious circle" in which he is surrounded by these factors. Over the years, this circle becomes a repeating, self-reinforcing "vicious cycle." The child plagued by certain economic, environmental, and possibly even biological deficits does not learn certain fundamental intellectual skills. This in turn prevents him from coping with his environment, which serves to further retard his intellectual ability and scholastic achievement. This is the "vicious circle." The "vicious cycle" enters when that same child grows up and tries to find a job. Lacking certain requisite skills and possessing a poor academic record, the adult finds only a poor-paying job—if any job at all—with little hope of advancement. This adult of poverty marries, has children, and those children start the cycle all over again. Though oversimplified, this description illustrates the frustration and the elusiveness of the problem of poverty. How can we break these vicious patterns? For psychologists and those concerned primarily with the child, the answer has been to concentrate on breaking the vicious circle of factors that hold back the children of the poor by providing these children with the things needed to grow and learn. Several programs of compensatory education have been devised, of which the best known is Head Start. In the following section, we shall examine some of these programs and discuss some of their successes and failures.

Compensatory Education Programs

Most attempts to date to help the disadvantaged child have focused on the preschool period. This focus stemmed primarily, though not exclusively, from findings already discussed that differences in basic skills between poor and middle-income children do not begin to show up until about the time that the children enter school. It was assumed that because poor children had been denied certain opportunities available to wealthier children, they simply were not yet ready to meet the expectations of the educational system. Special preschool programs were therefore set up to make these opportunities available to the children of the poor. In this way, it was argued, the children would no longer be at a disadvantage by the time they entered school. The argument seemed appealingly straightforward in its logic. Unfortunately, experience has since shown us that the problem of the disadvantaged child is not so easily resolved. Special preschool programs can help, but these structured programs cannot alone be expected to break the vicious circles and cycles of poverty.

Head Start: A Nationwide Experiment

Perhaps the best-known and certainly the biggest endeavor in the United States was Project Head Start. Launched officially in 1965 by the federal government, this project mounted a massive program of summer and later of full-year education for 3-, 4-, and 5-year-old children. The goal was to correct the health problems and prevent the educational incapacitation found among poverty-level children. Numerous centers were set up around the country to administer and evaluate the project. In the areas of cognitive enrichment, Head Start concentrated on providing experiences for young children that would encourage certain types of intellectual achievement and increase school readiness. Some of the initial programs were somewhat hastily devised, with little attention to problems of evaluation. Nevertheless, preliminary results showed that children who attended the Head Start programs made significant gains in various measures of intellectual performance over the course of the summer. Children attending the year-long program also showed significant gains in IQ, though most gains were modest (in

the range of 5 to 10 points). These early findings prompted some initial enthusiasm for the project and hope that it would achieve its laudable goals.

The gains in performance and IQ were not, however, viewed as spectacular.
In addition, whatever gains there were appeared to be short-lived; in follow-up
studies of some of the Head Start children, the early gains seemed to soon disappear. For example, later research showed that the summer Head Start children
remained ahead of comparable low-income children who had not been in the
program at the end of the first school year, but, after the second school year, the
control group caught up. Even for those children who had a full year of Head
Start experience, only marginal effects on cognitive development could be seen in
grades one through three (Eisenberg & Conners, 1966). In general, then, the results of the early Head Start efforts have revealed that short-term gains in intellectual ability could be obtained, but that these gains were not maintained over any
substantial period of time and did not measurably improve children's performance in school.

Head Start programs are still operating and are changing and refining their
procedures in light of new evidence and a better understanding of the difficulties
of projects of this type. The early programs were often not clearly thought out,
nor were evaluation techniques adequately devised. These and other problems
have since been recognized, including in particular a major shortcoming of Head
Start as it was originally structured. Specifically, though all children in the program were from poor families, many of the children were from poor black
families, while teachers were white. Head Start did not adequately see the importance of this distinction in selecting teachers and programs, and hence differences
in culture between blacks and whites were not given any serious attention. The
cultural barriers that separate blacks from whites in themselves may well have
hampered effective cooperation, communication, and, ultimately, learning.

Nevertheless, the basic Head Start results of short-term gains without long-
term maintenance have since been found in other compensatory education projects with better design and evaluation procedures. There are a number of such
programs that have been conducted and are still ongoing (Klaus & Gray, 1968;
Wiekart, 1972; Bereiter & Engelmann, 1966; Deutsch & Deutsch, 1968; as well as
others). We will describe one, the Early Training Project (Klaus & Gray, 1968).
This project enrolled four groups of black children in the South. One group entered the project at 3½ years of age and received three successive summers of
a 10-week preschool. Other groups either received slightly different experiences
or served as control groups with which to compare the effects of the preschool
experience. Results showed that on several tests of cognitive abilities, groups
that had received the preschool experience were superior to control children at the
end of the first grade. By fourth grade, however, there were no differences
between the preschool group and the control group. The initial gains had not
held up, and both groups, in fact, began to show the characteristic pattern of deterioration.

What are we to make of these discouraging results? Different people have
placed different interpretations on these findings. On the one hand, some have
realized, as did Gray and Klaus (1970), that "an intervention program, such as
ours, cannot carry the entire burden of offsetting progressive retardation" (p.
923)—programs such as Head Start may simply be insufficient to offset other
factors that not only hold the child back but eventually pull him down. Others
have not been so sanguine about the results (Jensen, 1969; Herrnstein, 1973). In
their view, the results point to a more dire implication that poor people may in

fact be genetically inferior in intelligence and that no amount of intervention can overcome that genetic limitation. Because of the complexity and the gravity of this claim, we will reserve full discussion of it until Chapter 10 when we review the concept of intelligence.

Most people have seen the discouraging results as further evidence for the power of the vicious circles that entrap poor people. With the benefit of hindsight, it is easy to see how a few weeks at a preschool camp could hardly overcome the enormous economic, social, health, and cultural factors weighing down on the poor family and the child. Nevertheless, the question still remains of how best to help the disadvantaged child.

Programs for Parents

One approach has been to direct attention to parental behavior, especially that of the mother. Programs are attempting to teach mothers about hygiene, family planning, and other skills. In addition, many of these programs are attempting to engage mothers in direct tutoring of their children, in the belief that the extra teaching will help the child. Many of these programs are still developing, and precise evaluations of their efficacy are not yet available. Nevertheless, some problems have already been encountered. These include poor attendance at parent education groups and mothers who are often so overwhelmed by hard work, many children, and fathers absent from the home that they have no time to act as tutors for their children.

As you can see, ameliorating the problems of poverty and disadvantage is difficult, complex, and often discouraging. Tackling any one problem clearly is not enough. But tackling all of them at once is well-nigh impossible.

Another Approach: The Lure of Television

> In a rural town, a mother walks into her kitchen and finds her retarded 5-year-old playing with three spoons and a knife and singing to herself "One of these is not like the others. One of these doesn't belong."

The song the child was singing is from *Sesame Street*, a television program for preschool children. *Sesame Street* began as another kind of experiment: to see what impact, if any, an educational television show could have on young preschoolers' learning, especially that of disadvantaged children. The program began in November 1969, and an evaluation was set up to assess how much various children watched the show and whether or not it had any substantial effect on their knowledge of letters, numbers, and forms, as well as on their classifying and sorting skills (Bogatz & Ball, 1971). The program has become enormously popular; children love to watch it and hate to miss it, and *Sesame Street* characters and by-products have become famous.

But does *Sesame Street* have any effect on the child's mind? Some initial evaluations recently conducted have shown that the program can have an enormous positive impact on children who watch it frequently. For example, a comparison was made of disadvantaged children of 3, 4, and 5 years of age. It was found that 3-year-old children who watched the show frequently (more than five times a week) performed better in certain cognitive skills than many of the 4- and 5-year-olds who did not watch the program. Other comparisons similarly disclosed significant gains in basic cognitive skills for children of all ages who watched *Sesame Street* on a frequent, regular basis (Bogatz & Ball, 1971).

The success of *Sesame Street*, even with disadvantaged children, raises the possibility that television programs aimed at teaching basic skills may have a better chance of success than do preschool programs. Just why this is the case is not obvious, but some factors suggest themselves: children like to watch television; *Sesame Street* is entertaining and holds their interest; they can watch it at home where they are comfortable and not as anxious as they might be at a preschool. These are but a few of the possible special strengths of *Sesame Street*. The important point is that television may play a more significant role in helping disadvantaged children than was initially supposed and predicted. We are only now beginning to realize the importance of television in the child's life. As we shall see in the next chapter, though, television can be a mixed blessing.

PROVIDING AN OPTIMAL ENVIRONMENT FOR COGNITIVE DEVELOPMENT DURING THE PRESCHOOL YEARS

We have seen how important the environment of the preschool child is for his current and future cognitive development. The nutrition, health care, and level of stimulation that he receives can affect the actual structure of his brain and along with it the normal development of his cognitive skills. Thus, the first step in providing an optimal environment for cognitive development is to ensure that children have adequate nutrition, health care, and stimulation throughout the preschool years. For many, this means somehow breaking the vicious cycle of poverty—a task that society has not yet been able to master.

Once these critical basics have been met, attention can be turned to more specific matters. Children should be given ample opportunity and encouragement to explore their environments, use their imaginations, and talk about their discoveries and fantasies. Aid should also be given to children in learning about the world of objects that surrounds them. Here, some concrete psychological observations can be helpful. Since focal colors are most salient for children as well as adults, concentrate on teaching the child about these colors; focal colors can then serve as an anchor for learning other members of color categories. Similarly, the child will find it much easier to learn number concepts if her parents use concrete examples, instead of simply forcing rote memorization on her ("one head," "two ears," "three brothers," rather than simply "1, 2, 3"). This same technique can be successfully used with other quantitative concepts, such as length, volume, and time. A final specific suggestion is that the parent devise games that will teach the child how different objects relate to one another (for example, the *Sesame Street* game of "one of these is not like the others" or pouring liquid from a wide into a narrow container).

SUMMARY OF COGNITIVE DEVELOPMENT IN THE PRESCHOOL CHILD

Piaget has called the preschool period the period of "preoperational thought." It is during this period that the child shows the first signs of real internalized thought. A characteristic of this internalized thinking is *representation*, or the ability to create and make later use of memories of objects not physically present. This ability makes possible *deferred imitation, insight learning,* and *make-believe*. It is also assumed that the child's developing mastery of representation makes possible his growing mastery of language.

According to Piaget, the preoperational child is still limited in cognitive skills, due to inability to coordinate his many thoughts in an integrated and systematic way. As a result, the child's cognitive activities are *egocentric* (that is, centered around his own viewpoint), *concatenative* (his thoughts are linked mechanically without coordinating them as a whole), and *anthropomorphic* (there is a tendency to perceive human traits in inanimate objects).

Numerous factors can affect the normal development of cognitive skills during this period. The most dramatic effects seem to be linked to a cluster of problems associated with poverty: poor nutrition, poor health care, and inappropriate stimulation. Although the visible effects of such factors generally do not show up until the child reaches school age, it is generally assumed that the damage is done during the earlier, preschool period—if not before. A number of attempts have been made to counteract these problems through preschool compensatory education programs such as Head Start. To date, however, the results have been discouraging. A promising alternative is the use of special, learning-oriented television programs such as *Sesame Street*. These television programs have seemingly proved beneficial for all children, but most especially for the disadvantaged child.

SUGGESTED READINGS

Caldwell, B. M., & Riccuti, H. N. (Eds.). *Review of child development research* (Vol. 3). Chicago: University of Chicago Press, 1973. A series of papers on issues directly related to discussions in this chapter, including social class and child development, environmental intervention programs, and programs for disadvantaged parents.

Gelman, R. The nature and development of early number concepts. In H. Reese (Ed.), *Advances in child development and behavior* (Vol. 7). New York: Academic Press, 1972. A straightforward and clear, if occasionally technical, monograph describing a series of ingenious studies on number development.

GLOSSARY

anthropomorphism. Attributing human qualities to nonhuman things; characteristic of preoperational thought.

collective monologue. A type of egocentric speech, according to Piaget, in which individual children comment on something but with little intent to communicate to one another.

concatenative thinking. A characteristic of the preoperational child in which words in sentences are related to the immediately preceding or following word but with no overall unity or theme.

deferred imitation. A major accomplishment of the preoperational period, whereby the child gains the ability to imitate others even though they are not present.

egocentric speech. An early form of child speech, according to Piaget, in which the child speaks to himself in the presence of others with little intent to communicate to others.

egocentrism. One of the limitations of the preoperational child's thought in which the child is unable to see things from another person's perspective.

focal colors. Colors that are regarded as the best examples of a particular color. Evidence suggests that we may be innately sensitive to focal colors.

function relations. A later accomplishment of the preoperational period in which the child begins to appreciate that changes in one variable are a function of changes in another variable; for example, changes in the height of water in a beaker are a function of changes in the width of the beaker.

insight learning. One of the accomplishments of the preoperational period in which the child becomes capable of solving problems intellectually without having to act them out.

interiorized. A late development of the sensorimotor period whereby schemes "go underground" and are activated internally, allowing the child to solve simple problems in his head.

preoperational period. The second period of cognitive development, according to Piaget's theory, in which the child advances beyond the sensorimotor level and begins to have genuine thoughts.

representation. The signal accomplishment of the preoperational period whereby the child becomes capable of retrieving and relating schemes in his head without having them activated externally.

semiclasses. The label used to describe the classification skills of the preoperational child. Though the child understands classes to some extent, he is limited in his ability to group or classify things.

socialized speech. The later speech of the child, used with the intent to communicate with others.

REFERENCES

Bayley, N. Comparisons of mental and motor test scores for ages 1–15 months by sex, birth order, race, and geographical location and education of parents. *Child Development,* 1965, *36,* 379–411.

Beckmann, H. Die Entwicklung der Zahlleistung bei 2–6 jährigen Kindern. *Zeitschrift fuer Angewandte Psychologie,* 1924, *22,* 1–72.

Bereiter, C., & Engelmann, S. *Teaching disadvantaged children in the preschool.* Englewood Cliffs, N.J.: Prentice-Hall, 1966.

Berlin, B., & Kay, P. *Basic color terms: Their universality and evolution.* Berkeley: University of California Press, 1969.

Bloor, D. The regulatory function of language: An analysis and contribution to the current controversy over the Soviet theory. In J. Morton & J. C. Marshall (Eds.), *Psycholinguistics: Developmental and pathological.* Ithaca, N. Y.: Cornell University Press, 1977, pp. 73–79.

Bogatz, G. A., & Ball, S. Some things you've wanted to know about "Sesame Street." *American Education,* 1971, *7*(3), 11–15.

Bornstein, M. H. Qualities of color vision in infancy. *Journal of Experimental Child Psychology,* 1975, *19,* 401–419.

Bornstein, M. H., Kessen, W., & Weiskopf, S. Color vision and hue categorization in young human infants. *Science,* 1975, *191,* 201–202.

Bryant, P. *Perception and understanding in young children.* New York: Basic Books, 1974.

Chukovsky, K. *From two to five.* Berkeley: University of California Press, 1971.

Coleman, J. S. *Equality of educational opportunity.* Washington, D.C.: U.S. Government Printing Office, 1966.

Cromer, R. F. The development of the ability to decenter in time. *British Journal of Psychology,* 1971, *62*(3), 353–365.

Descoeudres, A. *Le développement de l'enfant de deux à sept ans.* Paris: Delachaux and Niestlé, 1921.

Deutsch, C. P., & Deutsch, M. Brief reflections on the theory of early childhood enrichment programs. In R. D. Hess & R. M. Baer (Eds.), *Early education: Current theory, research and action.* Chicago: Aldine, 1968. Pp. 83–90.

Deutsch, M. (Ed.). *The disadvantaged child.* New York: Basic Books, 1967.

Eisenberg, L., & Conners, C. K. Series of studies on Head Start. Report from Johns Hopkins Hospital, Baltimore, to Research and Evaluation, Project Head Start, Washington, D.C., 1966.

Fischer, K. W. *Piaget, learning and cognitive development.* Manuscript in preparation, 1978.

Gaudia, G. Race, social class and age of achievement of conservation on Piaget's tasks. *Developmental Psychology,* 1972, *6,* 158–165.

Gelman, R. The nature and development of early number concepts. In H. Reese (Ed.), *Advances in child development and behavior* (Vol. 7). New York: Academic Press, 1972.

Golden, M., Birns, B., Bridger, W., & Moss, A. Social class differentiation in cognitive development among black preschool children. *Child Development,* 1971, *42,* 37–45.

Gray, S. W., & Klaus, R. A. The early training project: A seventh year report. *Child Development,* 1970, *41,* 909–924.

Heider, E. R. Focal color areas and the development of color names. *Developmental Psychology,* 1971, *4,* 447–455.

Herrnstein, R. J. *IQ in the meritocracy.* Boston: Little, Brown, 1973.

Hertzig, M.E., Birch, H. G., Richardson, S. A., & Tizard, J. Intellectual levels of school children severely malnourished during the first two years of life. *Pediatrics,* 1972, *49,* 814–824.

Jarvis, P. E. The effect of self-administered verbal instructions in simple sensory-motor performance in children. Unpublished doctoral dissertation, University of Rochester, New York, 1963.

Jensen, A. R. How much can we boost I.Q. and scholastic achievement? *Harvard Educational Review,* 1969, *39,* 1–123.

Klaus, R. A., & Gray, S. W. The early training project for disadvantaged children: A report after five years. *Monographs of the Society for Research in Child Development,* 1968, *33*(4, Serial No. 120).

Knobloch, H., & Pasamanick, B. Environmental factors affecting human development after birth. *Pediatrics,* 1960, *26,* 210–218.

Knobloch, H., & Pasamanick, B. Predicting intellectual potential in infancy. *Journal of Diseases of Children,* 1963, *106,* 43–51.

Luria, A. R. *The nature of human conflicts.* (Trans. by W. Horsley Gantt.) New York: Liveright, 1932.

Luria, A. R. *The role of speech in the regulation of normal and abnormal behavior.* New York: Boni & Liveright, 1961.

Millar, S. *The psychology of play.* Baltimore, Md.: Penguin, 1973.

Miller, S., Shelton, J., & Flavell, J. A test of Luria's hypothesis concerning the development of self-regulation. *Child Development,* 1970, *41,* 651–665.

Overton, W. F., Wagner, J., & Dolinsky, H. Social class differences and task variables in the development of multiplicative classification. *Child Development,* 1971, *42,* 1951–1958.

Piaget, J. *The origins of intelligence in children.* New York: International Universities Press, 1952.

Piaget, J. *The language and thought of the child.* London: Routledge and Kegan Paul, 1962.

Piaget, J., & Inhelder, B. *The child's conception of space.* London: Routledge and Kegan Paul, 1956.

Vygotsky, L. S. *Thought and language.* Cambridge, Mass.: MIT Press, 1962.

Whiteman, M., & Deutsch, M. Social disadvantage as related to intelligence and language development. In M. Deutsch, I. Katz, & A. R. Jensen (Eds.), *Social class, race, and psychological development.* New York: Holt, Rinehart & Winston, 1968.

Wiekart, D. P. Relationship of curriculum, teaching and learning in preschool education. In J. C. Stanley (Ed.), *Preschool programs for the disadvantaged.* Baltimore, Md.: Johns Hopkins University Press, 1972. Pp. 22–66.

Wilder, L. The role of speech and other extra-signal feedback in the regulation of the child's sensory motor behavior. *Speech Monographs*, 1969, *36*, 425–434.

Wozniak, R. H. Verbal regulation of motor behavior—Soviet research and non-Soviet replications. *Human Development*, 1972, *15*, 13–57.

8

Social and Emotional Development in the Preschool Child

The child emerging from our preceding discussions has learned many things about the nature of objects in his world. He can construct internal mental representations, or concepts, for objects that enable him to remember them in their absence and to think about novel ways of manipulating and using them. Further, his increasingly sophisticated use of language permits him to communicate with others about this world of objects—both the world that he sees and the world of his fantasies. In short, he has developed an impressive array of adaptive and creative skills. Our treatment of these skills has, however, been somewhat lopsided thus far, having focused primarily on children's interactions with inanimate objects. Not surprisingly, the most important—and in many ways the most complex—objects about which preschoolers must learn are not inanimate objects but people: their parents, their peers, and indeed themselves.

In this chapter, we shall focus upon the social and emotional development of the preschool child. We will explore the child's growing understanding of himself and others and how this understanding affects his relationships with others. In so doing, we will begin by describing the nature of the preschooler's interactions with others: with parents, with peers, and with that almost-human object, the television set. We will then examine how interactions between the child and others, coupled with advances in his cognitive skills, allow the preschooler to develop a rudimentary understanding of himself: in particular, a self-concept and a sex-role identity. Similarly, we will examine how the preschool child begins to understand others. We will see that this understanding of others involves primarily developing the ability to consider another person's point of view (called *perspective taking*). Finally, we will consider how different factors affect the social development of the preschooler, with an eye to understanding what combination of factors may be critical in promoting social development.

229

INTERACTIONS WITH OTHERS

The preschool child, like the infant, spends a great deal of time with other people and derives pleasure from their company. Unlike infants, however, preschoolers are no longer content to spend all of their time with their parents but begin to actively seek the companionship of other children who might loosely be called "friends." Most preschoolers also spend increasing amounts of time watching television, a rather one-sided form of social interaction but certainly an important one. There is little doubt that all three of these "others" (parents, peers, and television) contribute significantly to preschoolers' social development.

Importance of Parents and Other Adults

The child's parents—and other important adults—remain the primary focus of the child's interactions and continue to play a central role in the child's social development throughout the preschool years. In large part, this continued interaction, particularly with the mother, is a product of the enduring attachment of the child to the mother, formed during infancy. During the preschool years, however, the parents take on an additional role, as *socializers* or shapers of the child's behavior.

The Continuing Course of Attachment

We saw (Chapter 5) how the young infant and the "mothering figure" (usually but not necessarily the biological mother) come to establish a strong and reciprocal emotional bond, or **attachment.** The infant's attachment to his mother is most apparent in those behaviors that serve to keep the mother close at hand, such as looking, smiling, following, and crying.

In contrast, the preschooler's increasing independence frequently draws him away from his mother's presence. Nonetheless, the emotional bond between mother and child is far from over. For example, preschoolers continue to use their mothers as a secure base from which to explore their environment; they are more likely to explore a strange environment when their mothers are close by than when they are not. Similarly, the preschooler is still very likely to show signs of distress when separated from the mother for prolonged periods.

ISSUE

Has the preschool child achieved enough independence from his parents that he can be separated from them without becoming upset?

The preschool period is marked by increasing independence and an increased willingness on the part of the child to accept short separations of several hours from his parents. However, the preschooler, like the year-old infant, does not react well to longer separations from the parents. The preschooler remains strongly attached to his parents and is still very dependent upon them. When lengthy separations of the child from the parents cannot be avoided, they should be handled with extreme care lest the child suffer undue psychological distress.

The Preschooler's Reaction to Separation

Under most circumstances, the preschooler can tolerate short separations from his parents, as in a nursery school or day-care center. Even these short separations, however, do not go totally unnoticed by the young child, who is likely to cry when the mother leaves and may periodically ask for her during the day. In most cases, though, behavior is not seriously disrupted by the separation, despite some minor crying and whining. The picture is altogether different, however, when a preschooler is separated from the parents for many days or weeks. In fact, the reaction of the preschooler to prolonged separation is very similar to that of the older infant: she shows signs of protest, despair, and detachment. (See Chapter 5 for a discussion of these reactions.) There are, however, some differences. The older the child is, the more quickly she will regain her equilibrium during the course of the separation, thereby making the separation easier to take. Unfortunately, there is a trade-off, for, the older the child, the more likely she is to act with ambivalence upon reunion with her parents (Heinicke & Westheimer, 1965).

A good illustration of the differing reactions of younger and older children comes from a recent observation of the reactions of two girls (aged 2 and 5 years) to separation from their mother for a four-day period. During the course of the separation, the 2-year-old child showed many signs of distress: crying for her mother, loss of appetite, and regression to bed-wetting. The 5-year-old, on the other hand, after being reassured that "mommy" would return in a few days, showed little sign of distress. Upon reunion, however, the 2-year-old rushed to her mother, expressed her happiness at her mother's return, and, with the exception of a little extra clinging for a few hours, showed complete and immediate readjustment. The 5-year-old, in contrast, initially rejected her mother by refusing to kiss her or even talk to her. Even several days later, the 5-year-old continued to show ambivalence and anger toward her mother and repeatedly told her that she had not wanted her to return.

The differing responses of younger and older preschoolers during separation and at reunion should not, however, be interpreted solely in terms of the respective ages of the children. While it has been suggested that older children suffer fewer long-term or permanent effects from prolonged separation (Bowlby, 1973), age is much less important in determining a child's reaction to separation than are the *quality of the parent-child relationship* prior to separation and the *quality of substitute care* during the course of the separation (see, for example, Bowlby, 1973; Robertson & Robertson, 1971; Rutter, 1971). The child whose family is tense, cold, and disorganized, and who spends a two-week separation in a strange and cold residential nursery, is likely to suffer long-term effects no matter what her age. In contrast, the child whose family is warm, calm, and organized, and who spends a two-week separation with his favorite grandmother, is not likely to suffer major long-term effects regardless of his age.

Changes in Attachment during the Preschool Period

The distress of preschoolers during separations from their mothers reveals that they are still strongly attached to and dependent upon them. However, the child's emotional reactions undergo rather significant changes during the preschool period, in the direction of increasing diversity. Specifically, the preschool child extends his emotional responsivity to an ever-widening circle of adults and peers, manifesting this attachment in increasingly diverse ways.

Perhaps the most significant change in attachment during the preschool period is the child's extension of attachments to other adults and even to other children. One particularly important extension is to the father. In part, this new attachment is nurtured by the increasing interaction that occurs between pre-schoolers and their fathers. The father is also likely to take on the role of disciplinarian during the preschool period. This combination of increased time spent together, and increased responsibility of the father in the child's upbringing, serves to greatly strengthen the emotional bond between father and child. The father, however, is not the only other person to take on new importance during the preschool period. As the child spends increasing time away from his parents and under the care of other adults, such as nursery school teachers and the parents of friends, these adults, too, come to develop important emotional bonds with the child. Finally, feelings for other children begin to flower, as friendships develop between the child and his peers.

A second major change occurs in the type of attachment behaviors exhibited by the preschool child. These attachment behaviors, often called **dependence,** serve the purpose of keeping the child in contact with others. Such behaviors are manifested in diverse ways in preschool children, making attachment relationships much more difficult to identify.

The attachment of the infant shows up in a few easily identifiable behaviors, and most infants show the same kinds of attachment responses: smiling, stranger anxiety, and separation anxiety. In the preschool child, however, attachment tends to be less predictable from one child to the next and hence more difficult to identify and interpret. Different indexes of attachment in the preschooler tend to be relatively independent of one another, and children who display very different patterns of behavior may all be rated as highly dependent. Moreover, some or all of these "highly dependent behaviors" may not be positively related to the strength of the parent-child bond (or attachment) but may be related to how secure the child feels about his parents' love for him. For example, one preschool child may demonstrate his dependency by the same *proximity-seeking* behaviors used by the infant. However, another preschool child may show her dependency through **positive-attention-seeking** behaviors, behaving in ways designed to get her parents' approval and attention. Still another child may use **negative-attention-seeking** behaviors, such as crying, whining, having tantrums, and destroying things to attract the parents' attention, albeit disapproval. The behavior of the negative-attention-seeking child seems to point to some insecurity in the child, while the underlying motivation for the dependent behavior of the other two children is less clear. In all three cases, however, the goal remains the same: getting the parents' attention, regardless of whether that attention takes the form of a hug, a word of praise, a reprimand, or a spanking (Martin, 1975).

In general, dependent behaviors such as those described above tend to decrease in frequency as the child passes through the preschool period. Between 2 and 4½ years of age, children spend less time clinging to adults, acting out, and seeking the attention and approval of adults. Not surprisingly, this same time period shows corresponding increases in the amount of time children spend seeking attention and approval from other children (Sears, Rau, & Alpert, 1965; Heathers, 1955). This growing bond to the child's peers will be explored more fully later in the chapter.

The Gradual Emergence of Independence

For a variety of reasons, the preschool child's behavior becomes more and more self-initiated and self-directed. This emerging **independence** stems initially from the child's increasing physical coordination, which results in greater freedom of movement. Other factors facilitating the growth of independence are the preschooler's burgeoning curiosity and imagination and the increasing role that motives such as pride and self-accomplishment come to play in behavior.

Increased Freedom of Movement. As preschoolers mature physically, they become better coordinated and more agile. They develop the ability to walk, run, climb, open doors, and manipulate objects with ever-increasing skill and dexterity. This increased motor coordination enables them to execute many behaviors by themselves that were previously impossible without the aid of adults. For example, they no longer need to seek help from adults in order to reach objects on counters or to climb onto a chair.

Increased Curiosity. Coupled with increases in physical dexterity are advances in the preschooler's mental control of his environment. For example, he can remember objects even in their absence, and he can remember where they are and how to get them. Similarly, he can use his imagination to think about all the possible objects hiding behind a closet door, and he can use his physical skills to open the door and test these imaginary hypotheses. These increased mental and physical skills result in active exploration of the unknown—behavior commonly known as *curiosity.*

Motives for Competence or Mastery. The child's increased mobility, fine motor control, and curiosity work together to get him actively involved with the environment and to decrease dependence on the parents. In reality, parents themselves encourage this independence, and they become less willing to do things for the child. "You can do it" becomes a common household phrase. The main impetus for this increasing independence, however, appears to come from the child himself. The child wants to do things himself; he wants to master and control the environment. "Me do it!" becomes the preschooler's battle cry, as he adamantly refuses to allow parents to help him tie his shoes or pour his milk.

From where does this internal impetus for independence come? One reasonable answer, according to R. W. White (1959), is that the preschool child has a primary drive to master and understand his environment. This drive is as primary or fundamental as hunger or thirst. According to White, each successful independent act is in itself positively reinforcing or rewarding to the child, regardless of whether or not he receives praise or other external rewards for the behavior. This basic motive, called **effectance motivation** by White, keeps children oriented to new and different aspects of their environment and hence increases the variety and range of objects and events with which they interact.

THE SOCIALIZATION OF THE CHILD: THE ROLE OF PARENTS AND OTHER ADULTS

The increasing mobility and independence of the preschooler have problems, of course, and the curious, inquiring preschooler develops a knack for getting into mischief and even outright danger. We have all seen cartoon pictures of the young child at the cookie jar. Anyone who has a child knows that this actually does happen and that there is a very real risk that the child will fall, will break the jar, or will otherwise hurt himself. If the preschooler is to continue to behave independently, he must therefore learn to control his behavior so as to minimize dangers to himself and others. In short, he must learn **self-control.** He must accept and adopt the restrictions placed upon him by his parents and by society, including the ability to delay gratification, inhibit excessive behavioral displays, and generally control impulses. Coupled with this need to exert controls upon himself is the need to learn his society's more positively valued **prosocial behaviors.** Obvious prosocial behaviors include sharing, cooperation, and helping. The process whereby the child learns to inhibit antisocial behaviors (self-control) and to show positively valued social behaviors (prosocial behavior) is called **socialization.** Socialization is the process by which the child internalizes the behaviors, rules, standards, motives, values, and opinions of his parents and his society. Obviously, parents and other important adults are central figures in the child's socialization. Their influence operates in at least three important ways: (1) as providers of rewards and punishments; (2) as models for imitation; and (3) as models for identification.

Parents as Providers of Rewards and Punishments

Parents actively shape the social behavior of their children through the administration of rewards and punishments. Children are frequently given praise or more tangible rewards such as toys, candy, or privileges when they behave in ways that are socially acceptable. As a result, these rewarded behaviors tend to increase in frequency. Similarly, children frequently are shown disapproval and are given tangible punishments such as removal of privileges and spankings when they behave in ways that are socially unacceptable. These punished behaviors therefore tend to diminish in frequency.

There is increasing evidence that several factors can influence the effectiveness of these rewards and punishments, causing some to be more effective than others. Three important parameters are: (1) parental disciplinary style; (2) the timing of rewards and punishments; and (3) the consistency of rewards and punishments.

Parental Disciplinary Style

A fascinating area of research has looked at the types of rewards and punishments used by different parents, called **parental disciplinary style.** There can be little doubt that the types of rewards and punishments administered to a child differ greatly in their effectiveness. For example, laboratory studies have shown that giving children noxious punishment for their behavior produces very different effects than does withholding of rewards—although both are forms of negative reinforcement (Bandura & Walters, 1963).

However, before we look closer at the effectiveness of different types of parental disciplinary practices, it is important to keep in mind that the effectiveness of particular forms of reward and punishment is also greatly influenced by the relationship that exists between the parents and the child. Parents appear to differ in this respect in at least two dimensions: (1) love/hostility, or the degree of

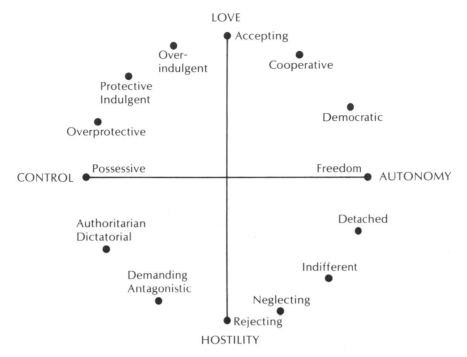

Figure 8-1. This figure illustrates the two basic dimensions of parental interactions with their children. (From "A Circumplex Model for Maternal Behavior," by E. S. Schaefer, *Journal of Abnormal and Social Psychology*, 1959, *59*, 226–235. Copyright 1959 by the American Psychological Association. Reprinted by permission.)

love and warmth in the relationship; and (2) control/autonomy, or the degree to which parents are restrictive or permissive in their control of the child's behavior (see Figure 8-1). Where a particular parent falls on the scale of these two dimensions can greatly influence the effectiveness of his disciplinary style.

Theoretically, the degree of warmth in a parent/child relationship should be independent of the type of discipline used. Thus, parents who physically punish their children need not be less "loving." However, in our culture, the situation is complicated by the fact that the relative warmth and strictness of parents *are* correlated with their use of particular disciplinary styles. In particular, the use of praise and reasoning occurs more frequently in families high in warmth, while the use of physical punishment occurs more frequently in families high in hostility (Becker, 1964). Thus, when we find differences between the behavior of children whose parents use physical punishment and children whose parents use praise and reasoning, we cannot say definitively just what is causing the differences. Is it the disciplinary differences themselves, or is it the degree of accompanying warmth or hostility between parent and child (Becker, 1964)? We will try to disentangle these factors while examining three general disciplinary styles: (1) **power-assertive** (physical punishment, yelling, threatening); (2) **love-withdrawal** (threatening loss of love, isolation, disappointment); and (3) **love-oriented** (praise and reasoning). In our attempt to assess the effectiveness of these three disciplinary styles, we will consider their effects on specific aspects of the preschool child's behavior: namely, aggression by the child, the child's resistance to temptation, the child's reactions to transgression, and the child's prosocial behaviors, such as helping and cooperating with others. We shall attempt to compare the effectiveness of different disciplinary styles in discouraging, or encouraging, each of these types of behavior.

Let us turn, then, to the first of these forms of behavior: *childhood aggression*. The relationship between parental disciplinary style and a child's aggressiveness is an extremely complex one. One might expect that a power-assertive parent using physical punishment would be particularly effective in discouraging aggressive behavior, as operant conditioning would predict. However, there is evidence that just the opposite is true: power-assertive parental techniques are associated with *high* levels of aggression in preschool children (Hollenberg & Sperry, 1951; Becker, Peterson, Luria, Shoemaker, & Hellmer, 1962; Sears, Maccoby, & Levin, 1957; Eron, Banta, Walder, & Laulicht, 1961; Martin, 1975). The work of Bandura (1963) discussed later in this chapter suggests a plausible explanation of this phenomenon. Bandura found that children who observed an adult strike a large toy were more likely to strike the doll themselves. Possibly, then, the preschooler who regularly receives harsh punishment from his parents will simply imitate his parents' aggressive behavior and become aggressive himself.

Aggression is probably the most common form of socially unacceptable behavior in young children. It is not, however, the only form, as any parent or teacher will readily attest. The young child can also do many other things that are forbidden (for example, taking candy from a store counter). Many of these socially unacceptable behaviors can be described as *failures to resist temptation*. How, then, do parental disciplinary styles affect the child's ability to resist temptation? As was the case with aggression, we find that power-assertive techniques are usually the *least* effective in producing children who are able to resist temptation. Preschool children who are most able to control their behavior and resist temptation tend to have parents who use love-oriented methods of discipline—parents who make extensive use of praise and reasoning in a generally nurturant and nonpunitive atmosphere (Baumrind, 1967).

Of course, no matter what the type of discipline, every preschooler *transgresses* on occasion: she hits her brother, he steals a cookie or tells a lie. How does the preschooler react to these transgressions? There is ample evidence that the preschooler has at least two possible reactions. He can be anxious and fearful that his transgression will be discovered and that he will be punished; or he can feel guilty about behaving in a manner that he believes is wrong. Not surprisingly, parents who use power-assertive techniques of discipline are more likely to produce children whose main reaction to transgression is fear of punishment. In contrast, parents who use love-oriented techniques such as praise, affection, and reasoning tend to produce children who feel guilty when they transgress (Martin, 1975; Becker, 1964).

Thus far, we have focused on the negative aspects of the preschooler's behavior: aggressiveness, failures to resist temptation, and reactions to his transgressions. We have seen that differences in parental disciplinary styles do seem to affect these negative facets of the child's behavior. Let us turn now to the positive side of the preschooler's behavior. Do differences in parental disciplinary styles affect the development of prosocial behaviors, such as helping and cooperating with others?

Unfortunately, there is relatively little information currently available on this question. The information we have indicates that the relationship between parental disciplinary style and the child's prosocial behavior does not fall neatly into the categories already described: power-assertive, love-withdrawal, and love-oriented. We must therefore resort to other methods of distinguishing between different disciplinary practices. In one study, Olejnik and McKinney (1973) categorized parents of 4-year-old children into those who administered rewards and punishments on the basis of a **prescriptive value system** (one that stressed teaching the child what he ought to do) and those whose value system was **proscriptive** (one that stressed teaching the child what he ought *not* to do). Parents with prescriptive values were found to have more generous children than did parents with proscriptive values.

What conclusion can we draw from the above? It appears that love-oriented disciplinary practices with an emphasis on teaching the child what he ought to do, rather than what he ought not to do, are the most effective in helping the preschool child inhibit antisocial behavior and develop prosocial behavior.

The Timing of Reward and Punishment

Some of the most interesting research on the effectiveness of reward and punishment has looked at the importance of timing, for much of this research goes directly against common parental practices. Most parents tend to reward or punish their children some time after the fact. Often, there may be a delay of several hours before the parents finally get around to administering the punishment or giving the reward. Research shows, however, that rewards and punishments delivered to a child after the child has actually done something are relatively *ineffective* in altering the child's future behavior. In fact, reward and punishment are far more effective if they occur when the child has just begun to initiate the behavior in question. The timing of rewards and punishments is thus a key factor in changing the child's social behavior.

A classic study by Aronfreed and Reber (cited in Bandura & Walters, 1963) provides an excellent illustration of the effects of timing upon the effectiveness of punishment. In this study, boys were asked to choose several times between a highly attractive toy and a relatively unattractive toy. One group of boys was punished by verbal reprimand each time they started to reach for the more attractive toy; a second group was punished by reprimands after they had selected the attractive toy and had begun to play with it; and a control group was not punished at all. Following this training session, the children were once again given a choice between an attractive and an unattractive toy. During this later test, only 26% of the boys who had previously been punished *when reaching for* the attractive toy now chose it. On the other hand, 71% of the children who were punished *after* taking the attractive toy continued to pick the attractive toy. This 71% figure was quite similar to the performance of those in the unpunished control group, who selected the attractive toy on 80% of the later trials.

We do not yet fully understand why punishment is more effective when used at the start of a behavior than it is when used after the behavior has been completed. One possible explanation points to the timing of the "anxiety" that the punishment produces. If a child is punished when just initiating a particular behavior, this creates an anxiety that the child will again feel if he later starts to behave in the same way. The anxiety will thus prevent the child from repeating the behavior. Punishing the child after he has completed the act may still produce anxiety—but not until after he has completed the act. Thus, if he later starts to repeat the behavior, he will not feel anxiety until the behavior is complete, so that the anxiety will come too late to be effective in preventing the behavior itself.

Regardless of why the timing of reward and punishment is so important in the child's socialization, it is clear that these findings have important implications for parental disciplinary techniques. The research suggests that if parents wish their rewards and punishments to be most effective, they should try to provide the punishment or reward early in the child's behavioral sequence, rather than after the behavior has been completed.

Consistency of Reward and Punishment

Another reason that parental disciplinary practices are often ineffective is that the parents may punish the child for some behavior on one day, and ignore—or even reward—the same behavior on another day. When this happens, the parental behavior is said to be *inconsistent*; as such, it can have chaotic effects on the parents' disciplinary programs. It is not hard to imagine how such inconsistencies might affect proper socialization of the child. If a child is on one occasion rewarded for taking her sister's doll—simply by the parents' lack of intervention—but on another occasion is punished for exactly the same behavior, it will be difficult for the child to learn which behavior is acceptable and which is not. Existing research on the impact of inconsistent parental discipline is surprisingly sparse. However, the limited research that is available indicates that inconsistencies in discipline may not only undermine the effectiveness of discipline; these inconsistencies may be even worse than no discipline at all. Thus, it has been found that children who are punished in an inconsistent fashion, as opposed to those who are not punished or disciplined at all, tend to be most aggressive and least "socialized" (Martin, 1975; Read, 1945).

Parents as Models for Imitation

While differences in parental disciplinary styles play an important role in a child's socialization, they do not tell the whole story. Other mechanisms are also involved.

One such mechanism is **imitation.** Not only do parents dispense rewards and punishments to their children; they also show their children how to behave by setting an example. Thus, imitation can explain the fact that parents who physically punish their children for aggression tend to have very aggressive children. By using physical aggression to discipline their child, these parents provide an aggressive model for the child.

The importance of imitation has been very compellingly demonstrated by a series of experiments by Bandura, Ross, and Ross (1963; see also Bandura & Walters, 1963, for a survey of this research). In these experiments, preschool children saw live or filmed adult models who behaved aggressively or nonaggressively toward a large inflated "Bobo" doll. It was found that children who observed the aggressive model were likely to precisely imitate the model's behavior when later

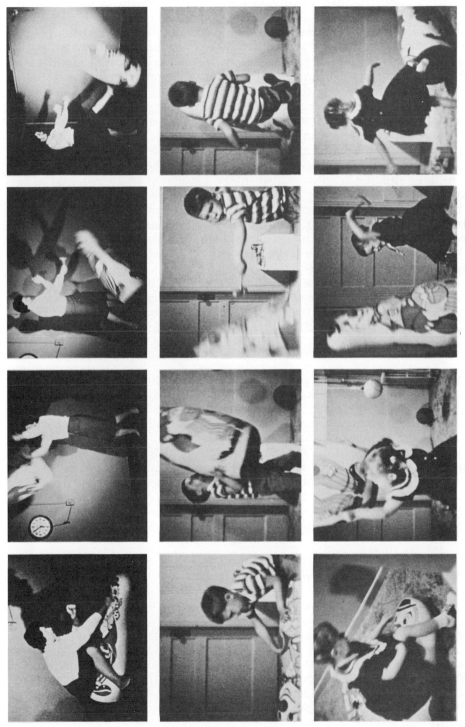

Figure 8-2. These photographs show nursery school children imitating the aggressive behavior of the female model they first observed in a film. (From "Imitation of Film-Mediated Aggressive Models," by A. Bandura, D. Ross, and S. A. Ross, *Journal of Abnormal and Social Psychology,* 1963, 66, 3–11. Copyright 1963 by the American Psychological Association. Reprinted by permission.)

put in a room with the doll. In contrast, those children who had observed the nonaggressive model tended to be nonaggressive toward the doll. (See Figure 8-2.)

Admittedly, the experiments with a Bobo doll were far divorced from reality, so that one might legitimately question whether a child's actions toward such a doll really tells us anything about real-life socialization. However, Bandura's results in the laboratory have been generally confirmed by more naturalistic studies. For example, Bandura (1960, cited in Bandura & Walters, 1963) compared the behavior patterns of parents of highly aggressive children with those of parents of very quiet and inhibited children. He found that the parents of the inhibited children were generally likewise inhibited and restrained. On the other hand, the parents of the aggressive children were relatively expressive and impulsive. Similarly, Levin and Baldwin (1959) found that parents who were socially retiring tended to have children who were also shy and inhibited when required to perform in public.

Children obviously are not, however, carbon copies of their parents, let alone of anyone else. Although children may imitate many aspects of their parents' behavior, they will not imitate all of them. Moreover, some children will imitate more of their parents' behavior than will other children, causing considerable divergence among children. What, then, determines whether or not the behavior of a particular model in a particular situation will be imitated by a particular child? In answering this question, we need to consider three different factors: the characteristics of the child, the model, and finally the nature of the situation.

Characteristics of the Child

One characteristic that appears to be involved is the child's history of rewards. Children who are seldom praised and rewarded for their behavior are more likely to imitate the behavior of others (Bandura & Walters, 1963). It seems that these children somehow believe that if they carefully copy the behavior of others who have power or who receive many rewards, they will also come to receive rewards and attention. Another characteristic commonly shared by some children most susceptible to a model's influence is that they have histories of being rewarded for imitating others. Thus, imitation becomes more and more frequent as the child comes to view imitation in itself as a means of getting rewards (Bandura & Walters, 1963). "Isn't that cute," the child hears as he imitates the behavior of others. Hearing this, his tendency to imitate becomes all the greater.

Characteristics of the Model

Obviously, however, even very susceptible children do not imitate everyone. Certain models are more likely to be imitated than others. For example, children are more likely to imitate models whom they perceive as similar to themselves. The child's same-sex parent is thus frequently imitated, since this parent is of the same sex, has the same last name, and probably shares certain physical similarities with the child, such as similar hair and clothing styles (Bandura & Walters, 1963; Janis, Mahl, Kagan, & Holt, 1969). Other characteristics of the model that tend to increase imitation are nurturance, rewarding power, and status. Thus, the parent or teacher who controls whether the child's behavior will be rewarded or punished is likely to be imitated. Similarly, high-status models such as television heroes or older brothers or sisters also tend to be imitated (Bandura & Walters, 1963; Hetherington, 1965; Hetherington & Frankie, 1967).

Characteristics of the Situation

We have already noted that children are likely to imitate high-status models or models who hold the power to dispense rewards and punishments. This imitation may occur because the child assumes that his imitation of such models is likely to be rewarded. It is almost as though the child were saying to himself "I know Daddy and Mommy like big brother. If I'm like big brother, they will be especially good to me, too." Studies do, indeed, support such an interpretation, for they indicate that a child is more likely to imitate when he *knows* that he will receive a reward for his behavior or that his model has been rewarded in the past for similar behavior.

A good illustration of the importance of the situation comes from a study by Walters, Leat, and Mezei (1963). In this study, kindergartners were shown some attractive toys but were forbidden to play with them. The children were then placed in one of three groups. The first group (model-rewarded) saw a film in which a child played with the forbidden toys and was rewarded through his mother's gentle and nurturant interactions. The second group (model-punished) saw a film in which the mother scolded the child for playing with the forbidden toys. The third group (control) saw no model at all. The children were then tested for "resistance to temptation" by being left alone in the room with the toys for 15 minutes. It was found that children who had seen the model being rewarded were much more likely to play with the forbidden toy. If their model had been treated well, then the children were more likely to imitate him. The situation surrounding the model's behavior—and especially the consequences of the behavior—was thus found to be a further factor influencing the likelihood of imitation.

Parents as Models for Identification

The material on imitation that we have just examined suggests that children are really quite sensible: they do *not* imitate the behavior of strangers when they have observed the strangers being punished for their behavior. One might expect, then, that the same rational approach would characterize the interaction between parent and child. The child who sees the misery and unhappiness of his alcoholic father should not imitate these behaviors. Similarly, the child who has experienced the tortures of child abuse would not be expected to subject her own children to such torment. And yet we know that this rational reaction is often not likely to prevail. The son with an unhappy alcoholic father all too often grows up to be an unhappy alcoholic himself, and the child who was physically abused by her parents is likely to abuse her own children. It seems, then, that we have less control over our imitation of our parents than some would like to believe.

There are psychologists (for example, Freud and Kagan) who believe that this lack of control means that a different process of socialization is controlling the child's behavior; according to this view, we do not simply imitate the behaviors of our parents and others—we *identify* with these people and actually incorporate their personality traits into our own personalities. By this process of **identification,** the child acquires the personality characteristics of another person—in particular, of his or her same-sex parent. Those who favor the notion of identification often assume that it is an all-or-nothing process; the child takes on the parent's personality more or less as a whole—the bad traits as well as the good ones. Hence the son of an alcoholic identifies with his father and becomes an alcoholic himself.

Many psychologists (especially behaviorists) do not believe in the existence of a process such as identification and argue that the child's behavior simply reflects the principles of imitation and reinforcement. Even among those psychologists who do believe in the process of identification, there are many who are at a loss to explain how and why it occurs. One recent attempt to explain the process of identification is that proposed by Janis, Mahl, Kagan, and Holt (1969).

According to this theory, identification consists of four interrelated processes. The first process is called *perceived similarity.* In this process, children discover that they share physical or psychological attributes in common with their same-sex parent. For example, a young girl notices the *real* similarities between herself and her mother, such as the fact that they have the same last name, the same sex, the same skin color, and many other physical features in common. In addition, the child is frequently told of how similar she or he is to the parent: "You look just like your mother," "You're a chip off the old block."

Once a child perceives himself as similar to his or her parent (the first process), the second process, **vicarious affect,** is activated. Kagan argues that when we see ourselves as similar to others, we tend to share vicariously in their emotional states—that is, we feel the same way they do. For example, when mommy receives a pleasant gift, daughter shares her happy feelings. Similarly, when mommy burns her hand badly, daughter feels the pain and unhappiness. Anyone who has been sexually aroused or driven to tears by a movie can understand how real these vicarious emotions can be.

The third process in the theory is called *shared privileges and goals.* This process occurs independently of the other processes and is not triggered by them. Rather, it occurs right alongside even the first process (perceived similarity). This third process involves the child's growing desire to obtain the positive attributes, such as power, wealth, intelligence, happiness, and kindness, that the same-sex parent possesses. This desire in turn leads to the fourth process, in which the child *imitates* the parent as a way of acquiring the parent's positive attributes. The child adopts the behaviors and attitudes of the same-sex parent since he believes that, by increasing his similarity to his parent, he may share the parent's desirable attributes. An interesting side effect of this imitation is that it increases the child's perceived similarity to the parent and, as a result, increases the vicarious affect experienced. The processes thus feed into and upon one another.

ISSUE

Can the boy who is reared without a father develop normally?

Identification with the same-sex parent is generally assumed to be an important process in socialization. Thus, it is logical to assume that children unable to form such an identification—as is the case of boys reared without a father in the home—would be incompletely socialized. Early research seemed to indicate that this was true: father-absence during early childhood, for example, was found to be associated with high levels of juvenile delinquency in adolescence. More recently, however, it has become apparent that the early results were rather misleading, since usually when the father is absent from the home, the family's financial status also suffers. The delinquency of boys without fathers seems to stem more from family poverty than from the fathers' absence, for, as we saw in the last chapter, the effects of poverty are extremely pervasive (Herzog & Sudia, 1973).

Summary of Parental Roles in Preschool Socialization

The parents remain an extremely powerful force in the preschooler's social life, for the preschool child remains very attached to and dependent upon the parents. The continuing importance of this parental *attachment* shows up quite clearly in children's poor adjustment to prolonged separations from their parents. The attachment of children does change, however, in the direction of increasing diversity. Thus, preschoolers expand their emotional ties to an increasing number of people within and outside the family, and they come to express these attachments with an increasing variety of behaviors, such as proximity-seeking, positive-attention-seeking, and negative-attention-seeking behaviors. At the same time, the preschool period is also a period of increasing *independence*, as children become more physically competent, more curious, and more motivated to go off on their own and explore the environment.

The preschool period is a time when the parents take on new roles in their relationship with their child, as *socializers* or shapers of the child's social behavior. Parents come to mold their child's behavior through the use of *reward and punishment*, by providing a model for *imitation*, and by providing a model for *identification*. Parental disciplinary style can have especially important consequences on the child's socialization. *Love-oriented* disciplinary techniques (based on praise and reasoning) tend to be more effective than *love-withdrawal* (isolation and expressions of disappointment) or *power-assertive* (physical punishment) disciplinary techniques. Similarly, telling children what they ought to do (assigning *prescriptive* values) tends to be more effective than telling them what they ought not to do (assigning *proscriptive* values). Most important, setting the right example can be critical to proper socialization of the child. Children may be told in no uncertain terms "Do as I say, not as I do." Nevertheless, most children are likely to go right ahead and imitate their parents' behavior. In short, the old adage "Like father, like son" is often true.

INTERACTIONS WITH PEERS

Since much attention is paid to the role of the child's parents in early social development, an often-neglected but key influence on the child's social growth is the child's *peers* or age-mates. Even the child's own parents frequently forget the important role of peers in their child's development. Thus, one recent study (Lewis, Young, Brooks, & Michalson, 1975) found that fewer than 20% of the first-born 1-year-olds surveyed were consistently given the opportunity to play with another child.

Even the 1-year-old, however, likes to be around and play with children his own age and can form rudimentary friendships with other children (Lewis et al., 1975; Mueller & Lucas, 1975; Lee, 1973). By preschool age, the child's interest in and involvement with other children are continually expanding and changing in important ways. The preschool child actively seeks out his peers, and certain peers are clearly preferred over others. The preschooler is thus becoming an active social being with interests and friends of his own.

The Nature of Peer Interactions

Like the younger infant—or the much older adult—the preschool child is generally somewhat apprehensive when meeting a new child. For example, a little girl may clutch her mother's skirt, lower her head, or show other signs of nervousness. Soon, however, the child's shyness gives way to curiosity and she may begin to stare intently at the new person. She may even reach out to touch and poke him. After several minutes of this reciprocal staring, children will often get down to the more serious business at hand—playing, talking, and, of course, fighting. Throughout the preschool period (from 2 to 5), the child's interactions with peers change both *quantitatively* and *qualitatively*. On the quantitative side, there is a marked increase with age in the total amount of actual interaction. Younger children spend more time doing nothing, playing alone, or just watching other children; older children participate more in group activities, cooperative activities, and group play (see Figure 8-3). Similarly, the older the child, the less time he spends seeking the attention of adults, and the more time he spends seeking the attention of other children (Hartup, 1970).

On the qualitative side, this period also shows a transition from interactions that are basically "self" oriented to interactions that are basically "other" oriented. The self-oriented emphasis that prevails at the start of this transition shows up in the **egocentrism** of the 2-year-old's peer interactions. That is, the young preschooler often behaves as if he were the center of the universe, while viewing other children as simply objects or extensions of himself. Thus, 2- and 3-year-olds often engage in **parallel play.** In parallel play, two or more children play side by side, interacting with the same objects, but not interacting with one another (see Figure 8-4).

The young preschooler's conversations with his peers likewise indicate a high degree of egocentrism. These conversations are often nothing more than **collective monologues,** in which each child carries on his conversation independently of what the other child is saying or doing. In a sense, collective monologues can be described as parallel conversations: the children can give the appearance of a real dialogue, but there is no actual interchange of information. An example of a collective monologue is seen in the following "conversation" between two 3-year-olds.

Melissa:	"I got two new kitties."
Patrick:	"Ooh-ooh, I a train."
Melissa:	"Named Snowball and Butterball."
Patrick:	"Chug-a-chug-a. Ooh-ooh. Train coming home."
Melissa:	"Snowball scratched me."

Figure 8-3.   Older preschool children, like the children in this photo, spend more time interacting with their peers and also spend more of their play time in group activities.

Figure 8-4.   This photograph shows two young children engaged in parallel play.

The egocentric quality of the young preschooler's interactions and conversation with peers has led many psychologists to conclude that the young preschooler is essentially "asocial," with little understanding of or interest in peers as other human beings. Such an interpretation, however, appears too harsh. Even the very young preschooler has moments of true social interaction and cooperative play. And even the very young preschooler does at times engage in meaningful dialogue with peers. In fact, at least 60% of the preschooler's speech is made up of meaningful conversations with other people (Piaget, 1926). The young preschooler is thus not really a social isolate. He feels a clear need to be with others, apparent in the fact that the 2-year-old will go out of his way to play *beside* another child, even if he doesn't play *with* him. Nevertheless, egocentrism constitutes a prominent part of the preschooler's early behavior.

Development of Friendships

All of us show marked preferences for particular people, called our *friends*. Research shows that the same is true of even very young preschoolers. By preschool age, friendships come to bear striking similarities to the adult form. First, preschool friends like to be with one another and behave in ways that bring them into close physical contact. These behaviors, which we have called *proximity-seeking* behaviors, include such things as sitting beside a friend, following a friend, calling a friend, and hugging and kissing a friend.

Preschoolers also show their desire to be physically close to their friends through their *reactions to separation.* Young children react to separation from their friends in much the same way as they react to separation from their parents. Surveys of parents reveal that their children become "moody," "depressed," or "at loose ends" when they are separated from their friends (Hartup, 1975). Similarly, children may play less when alone, while making every effort to persuade their parents to let them see their friends: "Mommy, see Lauren? Please, please, please!"

These external and observable reactions to separations are also reflected in the child's *mental activity.* The child who has been separated from his friend talks about him, thinks about him, and even has fantasies about him. The real strength of preschool friendships is perhaps best reflected in these cognitive activities. For example, one girl, named Dawn, was permanently separated from her best friend, Kimmy, when the family moved several thousand miles away. This separation occurred when Dawn was only 3 years old. Even at age 5, however, Dawn still talked about Kimmy, named her dolls "Kimmy," and frequently asked when she would be able to see Kimmy again. Many adult friendships would appear weak in contrast to this child's long-enduring love of her friend.

There can be little doubt, then, that friendship is important to the preschool child and that childhood friendships usually endure and in some cases remain remarkably stable. There are, however, several ways in which the friendships of the preschooler differ from those of the older child. First, the *stability* of friendships is generally lower in younger children. Two-year-olds' friendships are usually much less stable than are 4-year-olds' friendships. Second, younger children's friendships often seem to change depending upon the particular situation. Thus, Johnny may be Mary's best friend during nursery school art projects, but not when they are out on the playground. Older children, however, show greater *consistency* in their friendships, regardless of changes in situations (Hartup, 1975).

ISSUE

How important is peer contact for preschoolers?

Peers play an important role in the child's social development. In fact, available research suggests that the opportunity to interact with other children of the same age is not only a desirable but may be a *necessary* condition for normal social development. Too much peer interaction, however, can be bad if it occurs to the exclusion of adult interaction. The key, then, is a balance between peer and adult interaction; young children should be given the opportunity to interact regularly with both adults and other children.

The Importance of Peers in Social Development

We have seen that preschool children can and do form friendships with their peers, and that separation from these peers can be painful. We have not, however, addressed the question of whether such peer relations are *necessary* for normal social development. To answer this question, we need research data—data that we cannot obtain by simply observing preschool-aged children, since it fortunately is true that very few children are totally deprived of peer companionship. Research animals such as rhesus monkeys must therefore be used to assess the importance of peer interactions on normal social development.

We cannot meaningfully discuss what happens to the social development of rhesus monkeys raised in abnormal peer environments until we know something about the normal course of socialization of infant rhesus monkeys. Suomi and Harlow describe this normal socialization process as follows:

> The rhesus monkey infant typically spends most of its first month in ventral contact with its mother. Initial behaviors, chiefly clinging and sucking, are primarily reflexive and are directed toward maintenance of close physical contact with the mother. The infant monkey acquires voluntary control over most of its behavior gradually, and by one month of age, it begins to leave its mother for brief periods to explore the surrounding environment. During the second month of life the infant rhesus spends an increasing proportion of time away from its mother, being exposed for the first time to other monkeys, including those its own age. Initially it does not differentiate between social and nonsocial objects in its environment, exploring each with equal frequency, both tactually and orally. . . . As the baby monkey acquires greater sensory-motor integration, however, it begins to prefer mobile, animate playmates to static inanimate playthings. . . . By three months of age it is initiating contact and elementary play behaviors and is actively reciprocating similar initiations from other monkeys. By four months of age it has developed remarkable agility, ingenuity and versatility in its repertoire of social activities [Suomi & Harlow, 1975, p. 155].

Earlier, in Chapter 5, we saw how this normal course of social development is seriously impaired when monkeys are raised in total social isolation. We also described how these serious impairments could later be reversed under special therapeutic conditions—namely, under conditions where the isolates were given the companionship of somewhat younger peers. Thus, we have already seen how important appropriate social contacts can be for the monkey's social development.

In subsequent studies, Suomi and Harlow (1975) looked more particularly at the need for peer contacts by studying what happens to monkeys who are reared only by their mothers and are thus denied the opportunity to interact with and form "friendships" with other young monkeys. This research has revealed that monkeys who are raised only by their mothers, and in the complete absence of peers, fail to show normal social development, with longer periods of isolation from peers resulting in more serious problems. Specifically, these monkeys are extremely shy; they avoid playing with other young monkeys; and when they do interact with peers, they are often hyperaggressive. Early contact with peers thus appears to be necessary if normal social development is to occur in the monkey.

Research with monkeys supplies a reasonable model of what probably occurs with human beings: we may assume, therefore, that human children, like young monkeys, probably need the companionship of peers for normal social development. However, this conclusion raises further questions. How much peer companionship is optimal? Should preschool-aged children spend most of their day interacting with peers—as in a day-care center? Before discussing possible answers to these questions—particularly the effects of day-care settings on social development—let us look first at the most extreme form of peer togetherness: the child raised only in the company of his peers.

Here, too, the research of Harry Harlow provides valuable insight—in this case into the effects of excessive peer contact. In an ingenious study, Harlow separated several infant monkeys from their mothers at birth and put them together in an environment where they had no one to interact with but one another for several months. These "peers-only" or "together-together" monkeys showed clear disturbances in their social behavior when returned to a normal group but different types of disturbances from those of the "mother-only" monkeys just described. The problem with the "together-together" monkeys was not failure to establish contact and affectionate bonds with age-mates, but the opposite. These "together-together" monkeys became hyperattached to one another and spent most of their time huddled together. Consequently, they did not spend much time exploring the environment, so that their social development was retarded. As they grew older, some of the clinging subsided, and more normal social behavior appeared. Certain problems did remain, however. The "together-together" monkeys continued to be disturbed by the mildest of stresses. Also, they never developed normal social behavior with other peers outside their original rearing group; in fact, they often behaved with extreme aggression toward these "other peers" (Harlow, 1969). (See Figure 8-5.)

Intuitively, Harlow's work would seem relevant to certain human children. Freud and Dann (1951) studied six war orphans who were neglected by adults and shifted from camp to camp from birth until about 3 years of age. During these three years, their environment was constantly changing. Their treatment by adults was detached and inadequate. The only constancies in their lives were one another.

At age 3, the behavior of these children was disturbed in many ways. They were aggressive and wild, destroying furniture and attacking attendants. They were cold and indifferent to adults and to other children outside the group of six. Finally, they were extremely attached to one another and could not bear separation. As Freud and Dann succinctly described them:

Figure 8-5.   Notice how the young monkeys cling together in this photograph. These are Harlow's "together-together" monkeys—young monkeys raised only in the company of their peers. (From "The Role and Reason of Peer Relationships in Rhesus Monkeys," by S. J. Suomi and H. F. Harlow. In M. Lewis and L. A. Rosenblum (Eds.), *Friendship and Peer Relations.* Copyright 1975 by John Wiley & Sons, Inc. Reprinted by permission. Courtesy University of Wisconsin Primate Laboratory.)

The children's positive feelings were centered exclusively in their own group. It was evident that they cared greatly for each other and not at all for anybody or anything else. They had no other wish than to be together and became upset when they were separated from each other, even for short moments. No child would consent to remain upstairs while the others were downstairs, or vice versa, and no child would be taken for a walk or on an errand without the others. If anything of the kind happened, the single child would constantly ask for the other children while the group would fret for the missing child [Freud & Dann, 1951].

ISSUE

Is day care good or bad?

Whether good or bad, day care has taken the families of this country by storm. The number of children enrolled in day care ranges from about 1% of the children under 1 year of age to about 24% at age 4 years (National Childcare Consumer Study, 1975). And the number seems sure to increase in the future.

Of course, the fact that day care is being used by more and more parents does not necessarily mean that it is good for the child. Many psychologists who have concentrated on the importance of the mother-child bond believe that day care can have disastrous effects on the social and emotional growth of the child (for example, Bettelheim, 1969; Bowlby, 1951). However, there is a growing number of psychologists (for example, Lewis et al., 1975; Swift, 1964) who believe that day care probably has little effect on the social/emotional development of the child—and what effects there are may well be positive instead of negative.

Experiments in Group Upbringing

Over the last few decades, this country and many others have been engaged in what can best be described as experiments in group upbringing. Many countries have instituted widespread day-care programs in which the child spends eight to ten hours a day with a group of peers and a few adult supervisors. Day care is very different from conventional babysitting (because of the increased numbers of peers and adults) and from nursery school (because of the prolonged time periods). However, even though we know day care to be a departure from other, more traditional forms of child care, we know surprisingly little about what effects it will have on our children.

In 1951, John Bowlby wrote a book called *Maternal Care and Mental Health*. He cited evidence of the disastrous effects of rearing a child in the total absence of his mother (as in institutions) and of multiple short-term separations of the child from his mother. He described studies in which it was shown that infants and young children raised in institutions became social misfits, unable for life to interact normally with others or to feel real emotional bonds to others. Based on his findings under these extreme circumstances, Bowlby concluded that the continual presence of the mother is paramount for normal child development. Although Bowlby did not discuss day care in his writings, there is no doubt that he would have viewed it as an extreme threat to the child's mental health, since it removes the child from the presence of his mother during most of the day.

During the 1950s and early 1960s, psychologists continued to stress the special importance of the mother in social development. No one, however, had yet really thought about considering the importance of peers. Some psychologists did begin to argue that not all mothers are "good" mothers and that, at least in some cases, the child might be better off away from his mother. These "socially disadvantaged" children tended to be the same children as the "cognitively disadvantaged" children, and both conditions seemed to be associated most often with poverty. As a result, day-care programs were begun to provide disadvantaged children with more appropriate social and cognitive environments.

The Kibbutz Experience

Meanwhile, in Israel, a number of *kibbutzim*, or communal living groups, were being established. In these kibbutzim, children are raised communally by adults who specialize in child rearing, the **metaplet**, rather than by their own parents. The concept of family is thus replaced by the concept of the **kibbutz**, or larger communal living group.

What are the results of the kibbutz experience in group child care and communal living? With regard to the parents, they are relieved from many special responsibilities to their children—both economically and in their role as socializers. The dependence of the child upon the parents is thus reduced. In addition, when parents are with their children—usually for a few hours a day—they may be able to fully enjoy and interact with them, having avoided many of the responsibilities and frictions that normally accompany family life (Rabin, 1971).

Beyond the simple descriptions of family life in the kibbutz listed above, relatively little is known about its effects on the child. Moreover, the evidence that exists is often incomplete and contradictory. Thus, children of the kibbutz have been described by some as mature, courageous, unselfish, and ethical (Rabin, 1965; Shapiro & Madsen, 1969). Others have described them as rigidly opinionated, having a low self-concept, being overly conforming, hostile, introverted, insecure, and incapable of intimacy (Spiro, 1958; Bettelheim, 1969). However, more carefully controlled research in the area does not seem to show any strong evidence that the kibbutz children are in any way harmed by their experience. Thus, Eleanor Maccoby and Shirley Feldman (1972) found no differences among kibbutz and United States children at 3 years of age in their reactions to their mothers or in their reactions to separation from their mothers. Similarly, Robert LeVine (1970) has concluded that kibbutz children are within normal ranges in intelligence and mental health. The currently prevailing view is thus that childrearing in a kibbutz probably does not have any major adverse effects upon the child.

The Day-Care Experience

The prevailing opinion that child rearing in a kibbutz does not have devastating effects on the mental health of the child has important implications for a different experience in group upbringing closer to home: the day-care center.

Day care accounts for the care of only about 1% of the children in the United States less than 1 year of age. For older age groups, enrollment in day care climbs steadily, until it levels off at about 24% at age 4 years. These enrollment figures tell us something very important about United States day care—namely, that while it is extensively used with older children, it is only rarely used with children during their first year or two of life, when attachments to parents are usually formed and when the child is most sensitive to separations from his parents.

Another important fact is that it is *day* care. Children go to the day-care centers for about seven to ten hours a day, but they go home every night, and they live at home every weekend. The day-care child thus spends much more time with his parents than does the kibbutz child, who spends his nights and weekends in the kibbutz.

Studies of day care and its effects on the child are not yet conclusive. Nevertheless, it is noteworthy that research to date has failed to consistently show that day care causes any social or emotional problems in children (Swift, 1964; Heinicke, 1956). Moreover, a few studies have shown significant gains in social behavior, independence, and maturity (see Swift, 1964, for a discussion of these studies).

While these conclusions may at first seem inconsistent with Bowlby's findings, the two can be reconciled. Day-care children, unlike the institutionalized children involved in Bowlby's studies, are able to form attachments to their parents, since they normally are not placed in day care until after their first year or two of life. In addition, day-care children, unlike institutionalized children, spend considerable time with their parents. This interaction between parents and child is thus one of the major reasons that day-care children probably do not experience the severe psychological strains felt by children separated from their parents and placed in an institutional setting (Heinicke, 1956). Finally, day-care children enjoy far more interaction with their peers and the adult staff than do children placed in institutions.

Summary of Interactions with Peers

Peer relations during the preschool period are one of the most frequently overlooked and neglected topics in psychology. This neglect has stemmed from a theoretical and empirical bias toward the parent-child relationship. However, there is little question that preschoolers want and need to be with other children their age—as perhaps best exemplified by Harlow's research with monkeys reared only with their mothers. Too much contact with peers can likewise be a bad thing, however. Thus, the work of Harlow with "together-together" monkeys and of Freud and Dann with "together-together" children illustrates how peer contact to the complete exclusion of adult contact can interfere with normal social development. The key, of course, is to find a reasonable balance between too much and too little peer and parental contact. There is considerable debate about whether the kibbutz experience meets this need. There is no debate over whether institutionalized child-rearing meets this requirement; it does not. And while there is debate over whether day care provides a reasonable balance, existing data fail to show any social or emotional problems resulting.

INTERACTIONS WITH TELEVISION

To say that the preschool child "interacts" with television might be somewhat misleading. After all, a television set is just another inanimate impersonal object. Or is it? Some preschool children spend more hours per day watching television than in any other activity except sleep. One study found that preschoolers average 5 to 88 hours a week in front of the television set (Stein & Friedrich, 1972). Though these long hours of TV viewing are relatively passive experiences for the child, they can have a major impact on his behaviors at other times. Since many of the child's behaviors and beliefs are influenced by television, it is important to consider its effects very carefully.

Television as a Social Teacher

In the last chapter, we discussed the effectiveness of educational programs such as *Sesame Street* in teaching basic cognitive skills to preschool children. All television is, in a sense, educational. A child cannot help but learn through watching television. Thus, even in watching so-called noneducational programs, children are exposed to events that they never experience in their daily lives. They see people walking on the moon, working with complex machines and computers, and living in foreign countries.

Much of what the child sees on television can best be described as learning about people—how they behave, how they feel, and, to a certain extent, how they think. Unfortunately, as we shall see, much of what children learn about social skills by watching television is not what most of us would consider balanced or appropriate, since much television has been devoted to violence and aggression. The child who watches a lot of television may occasionally see characters caring for one another or helping one another, but the same child is continually bombarded by television characters who maim and kill one another. A recent survey by Gerbner and his associates (1972) revealed that the incidence of such physically aggressive acts on television is extremely high: *80%* of the programs surveyed contained at least one incident of overt physical aggression. On the average, they found that one can expect to see about eight violent acts during each hour of television viewing. Programs aimed particularly at the child audience were found to be especially violent, with cartoons having the highest frequency of violence of any programs on the air (30 violent incidents per hour in 1969; 17 such incidents per hour in 1972). What, then, are the effects of viewing long hours of television—which is predominantly violent—on the social development of the preschool child?

As television becomes an increasingly major part of modern life, more and more research has been dedicated to surveying its effects on all of us, and on young children in particular (see Stein & Friedrich, 1975, for a review). This research indicates that the behavior of young children can be affected by television viewing in at least two major ways. First, television influences the child's emotions and motivations. When children watch an extremely violent program, their level of arousal increases. If they see violence rewarded by approval and physical gains such as money and power, they may be motivated to behave aggressively themselves. Second, television viewing provides children with models of *how* to behave. These models provide specific training on particular behavioral sequences.

Televised Violence and the Learning of Aggression

Televised violence can have wide-reaching effects on the social behavior of children, often producing devastating results. A particularly shocking example occurred in 1975:

> A mother in Tokyo left her 14-day-old baby asleep in a crib and told her 9-year-old son she would be back after a ten-minute trip to the grocer. When the mother returned, the baby had been tortured to death and her son was hysterical.
> The boy, who later told police he was inspired to torture by two children's television programs, whimpered, "The baby on television didn't die; the baby on television didn't die" [*Chicago Tribune*, December 1, 1975].

Fortunately, events such as this occur very infrequently. This has led many proponents of television violence to argue that these extreme incidents are special cases that cannot be explained purely in terms of television programming. There are, however, numerous less dramatic examples that illustrate equally well the adverse effects of television violence on children.

The early work of Bandura and Walters (1963) demonstrates quite clearly that televised models can be as effective in social learning as live models, and that the same principles of imitative learning apply. We have already discussed Bandura's now-classic study, in which preschool children saw a film of adults attacking a large inflated Bobo doll. When these children were later left alone with the Bobo doll, they, too, attacked it—and many of them imitated exactly the behavior of the filmed models.

Bandura's findings have since been corroborated by an increasing body of evidence that televised violence increases aggression in young children. Thus, several studies have shown that even a single viewing of one violent cartoon results in increased levels of interpersonal aggression (for example, Ellis & Sekyra, 1972; Lovaas, 1961; Ross, 1972; as cited in Stein & Friedrich, 1975). Moreover, the more that a child watches violent cartoons, the more aggressive he becomes (Steuer, Applefield, & Smith, 1971).

Television and the Learning of Prosocial Behavior

Of course, all television is not bad, and television's capacity as a social teacher is not limited to violence and aggression. There are some television programs, such as *Mr. Rogers' Neighborhood,* that attempt to model prosocial behaviors such as helping and cooperation. There is some evidence to suggest that these programs are effective in achieving this goal. Thus, viewing of *Mr. Rogers' Neighborhood* has been found to be effective in increasing sharing, helping, and cooperation while reducing interpersonal aggression in preschool children (studies reviewed in Stein & Friedrich, 1975).

ISSUE

What should be done about television violence?

There can no longer be much question about the impact that television programming has on children. The long hours spent by American children in front of the television set make it one of the major "social teachers" of our society. This raises the question of what sorts of controls should be placed on television programming in general and on children's programming in particular. After all, we carefully police the qualifications of the human teachers employed by our schools. Why not the inhuman, and often inhumane, teacher called television?

Many parents and other interested people have requested government censorship of television violence—especially during daytime and early evening hours when children are most likely to be watching. Other interested parties have responded that such censorship would be a violation of First Amendment rights and that parents should take on the responsibility for supervising their children's viewing practices.

The claim that censorship would violate First Amendment rights is beyond the scope of this book. However, First Amendment rights are not unlimited, and even constitutional rights must occasionally give way if they interfere with valid, overriding public interests. The opinion that parents should regulate their children's viewing has merit, but this simply does not work in real-life settings. Too many parents use television as a babysitter, while too many other parents do not care or cannot monitor every program. Society as a whole, then, must evidently take some responsibility for these children if our society is to solve its problems of aggression and crime. Supervision of a child's television viewing may help to prevent the child from behaving antisocially, but it cannot protect him from becoming a victim of someone else's antisocial behavior.

UNDERSTANDING ONESELF

We have seen that the preschool period is one of growing social sophistication. The preschool child comes into increasing contact with other people and learns how to interact and communicate effectively with them. This growing sophistication reveals in part that he has gained considerable insight into the nature of people—their identity, their behavior, and their motives. Besides other people, he is beginning to gain greater understanding of himself. Hence, the preschool period is characterized in part by the beginnings of children's self-concept—their image of themselves, what they are, and how each of them differs from other people.

The Emergence of a Self-Concept

The notion of a **self-concept** is difficult to define—even in adults—and even more difficult to study. However, most of us would agree that a "self-concept" includes at the very least an awareness that "I" am a separate entity, different from all other entities, and that "I," like other entities, am permanent and do not pass back and forth between existence and nonexistence (for example, when I go to sleep I do not simply cease to exist). Beyond these characteristics, however, the self-concept has certain other qualities. For example, it includes the knowledge that certain things belong to "me," and that I can assert "my" existence by demanding "my" rights or by refusing to do certain things that I don't want to do.

We really don't know just what kind of self-concept the preschooler has. The child's egocentrism at this age does at least tell us that the preschooler has some sense of himself as a unique and separate person but does not yet completely understand his own boundaries—where he leaves off and others begin.

Other factors likewise tell us that a primitive form of self-concept exists and is evolving in the preschool child. Provocative evidence of this emerging self-concept is found in the preschooler's use of certain linguistic terms that refer to himself. Such terms as possessives ("my," "mine," "myself") and negatives ("I don't need pants off" or "I don't eat it") reflect the child's awareness of himself as a separate person who can assert his own desires and will. It is during the preschool years that these linguistic forms begin to emerge and develop. Though learning some of the forms depends on some purely linguistic factors (for example, syntactic or semantic complexity), it is difficult not to see their existence in the child's vocabulary as evidence that the child possesses a self-concept to some degree.

Another area in which we can discern the gradual emergence of self-concept during the preschool period lies in the child's developing knowledge that "I am a girl" or "I am a boy."

The Emergence of Sex-Role Identity

The first words a woman hears after the birth of a baby girl are, "It's a girl." After these vitally important words, the doctor tells the mother about such secondary matters as the baby's health. The baby is then cleaned up, wrapped in a blanket (pink, because of her sex), and sent to the nursery. Seven years later, this same child will state with absolute conviction that she is a "girl," that she will always be a "girl," and (maybe) that she should engage only in activities meant for "girls." During this seven-year period, the child will thus have learned one of the most important things she will ever learn about herself: her **sex-role identity.**

The Course of Development of Sex-Role Identity

Boys and girls are different from the moment of birth. These differences range from obvious differences in genital form to subtle differences in temperament. For example, newborn females react more to the removal of a blanket and have less tolerance to air jets applied to their stomachs (Bell & Costello, 1964). Male infants are larger and heavier (Bijou & Baer, 1961), and they can raise their heads higher (Bell & Darling, 1965).

As children grow older, the differences between the sexes increase, with boys in our culture generally becoming more active and aggressive, more competitive, less verbal, higher in visual-spatial ability, and better in mathematics. Similarly, boys are more conforming to peer pressures, while girls are more conforming to adult pressures. (See Maccoby & Jacklin, 1974, for an excellent survey of what we know about sex differences.)

Accompanying these increased differences in the behavior of girls and boys is an increased awareness by the child of his or her own sex—and of what sorts of behaviors are typically considered appropriate for his or her sex. Of course, the process of developing a sex-role identity requires that the child come to note these differences and to recognize that "boys" are one thing and "girls" another. This process begins with the child's hearing and learning the verbal labels "boy" and "girl." Next, the child must learn that "he is a boy" or "she is a girl." Learning one's own gender label usually occurs quite early, at around 2 years of age. Thus, Gesell (1940) reports that two-thirds to three-fourths of the 3-year-olds interviewed correctly answered the question "Are you a little girl or a little boy?"

At 2 years of age, the child's correct use of gender labels does not, however, extend much beyond himself. Thus, Kohlberg (1966) says of a little boy named Tommy, aged 2½:

> Tommy . . . would go around the family circle saying, "I'm a boy," "Daddy boy," "Mommy boy," "Joey (brother) boy." After correction he eliminated his mother from the list, but did not label people outside the family correctly [p. 94].

By 3 or 4 years of age, the preschooler has improved his ability to label the sex of others, though he still will make mistakes. Also, the majority of 3-year-olds still don't accept the *constancy* of gender; they don't realize that they cannot grow up to be a "mommy" (for boys) or a "daddy" (for girls) (Rabban, 1950). A good illustration of the child's failure to comprehend gender constancy is provided by a young friend of Kohlberg's (1966). Jimmy, just 5 years old, said "I can be a girl, you know. I can. I can wear a wig and have my throat so I can talk like a girl" (p. 97). It is not until the age of 5 to 7 that the child will be able to completely and accurately identify the sex of others and will realize that sex cannot be changed by wearing a wig or changing one's voice.

Biological Differences between the Sexes

An intriguing question is whether the increasingly divergent behavior of boys and girls (commonly called *sex differences*) is caused by biological factors, environmental factors, or a combination of both. For most children, however, any such attempt to disentangle biological from environmental factors and seek out ultimate causes is almost impossible. At birth, a child is given a sex label, and this sex label is usually completely determined by the appearance of the genitals. Henceforth, this label is constantly reinforced by both words and deeds. Thus, there is a complete confounding of biological factors (such as genetic sex) and environmental ones (such as how the child is labeled and treated). There are, however, a few children for whom this confounding of factors does not occur— these are the mis-sexed children.

During the 1950s, hormones were sometimes prescribed for pregnant women who were in danger of having a miscarriage. If these hormones were taken by the mother during the period of embryonic development when sex organ differentiation was occurring, then genetically female children (that is, children who had two X chromosomes) were often masculinized and developed male sex organs. (See Chapter 2 for a fuller discussion of drug effects on embryonic development.) During the years when these hormones were first on the market, many of these masculinized girls were mislabeled as boys and reared as boys during their early years of life. These genetic girls developed typical male behaviors and attitudes. The development of male behaviors and attitudes in genetic girls who were labeled and treated as boys led early researchers (who assumed that *only* the external genitals had been affected) to conclude that sex differences in behavior are entirely learned by the child—an environmental explanation (Money, 1961; Hampson & Hampson, 1961; Money, Hampson, & Hampson, 1957).

More recent research has, however, tended to contradict this early view. Thus, John Money and Anke Ehrhardt (1972) have studied 25 masculinized girls whose condition was diagnosed and surgically corrected at birth. These girls were thus both genetically and physically female and were always treated as female. However, the effects of the sex hormones were not completely eliminated from their behavior. The treated masculinized girls were—in comparison to normal girls—more "tomboyish" (more active and more competitive) and less interested in "female" activities such as dolls, babies, marriage, and dating. Thus, hormonal activity—which is usually regulated by genetic sex—also seems to play a very important role in the development of behavioral sex differences.

Probably the most accurate view of sex differences takes into account both biological and environmental factors. How the two factors might interact in the development of sex differences is far from clear. However, a potentially reasonable view is one which describes the child's environment not in terms of its shaping forces on the child but as something with which the child interacts (for example, Schaffer, 1977). Thus, one might well argue that the differences in behavior of boys and girls present at birth cause them to be treated differently. These differ-

ences in treatment, in turn, tend to increase the magnitude of the initial differences. As the child develops, the two forces (biological and environmental) thus
reinforce one another, further solidifying the child's sex-role identity.

Mechanisms in the Learning of Sex-Role Identity

The research of Money and Ehrhardt (1972, discussed above) illustrates the
importance of biological factors in the development of sex differences. It does not,
however, rule out the importance of experience and learning. Let us, therefore,
consider how the differential treatment of boys and girls might be expected to
affect their behavior.

Over the years, a number of theories have been proposed to explain how the
child learns his sex-role identity and sex-role behavior. These different theories
tend to rely on processes of learning, such as reinforcement, imitation, identification, and cognitive activity. All of these processes are no doubt involved. However, there is major controversy regarding which processes are more crucial and
which come first.

Reinforcement.   There is little question that boys and girls are treated differently, almost from the moment of birth. Even with very young infants, parents in
the United States spend more time interacting with their little boys, especially in
rough and tumble play, while time spent with their little girls is more likely to be
spent soothing and talking to them (for example, Lewis, 1972; Minton, Kagan, &
Levine, 1971; Moss, 1967; Parke, O'Leary, & West, 1972; Yarrow, Waxler, & Scott,
1971). As children grow older, more direct reinforcements are applied to appropriate sex-typed behaviors. Little boys are generally discouraged from and even
punished for playing with dolls; little girls are encouraged and rewarded for the
same behaviors. Thus, early in the development of sex-role identity, the types of rewards available influence the child's behavioral choices. Reinforcement, then, is
certainly one of the processes shaping a child's sex-role identity.

Imitation and Identification.   Two other factors molding sex-role identity
are **imitation** and **identification.** The little boy who observes other boys or his father
engaged in rough and tumble play imitates their rowdy behavior, while the little
girl who observes her older sister playing quietly with dolls imitates her sister's
more demure behavior. Similarly, the little boy who identifies with his father will
incorporate his father's personality into his own, thereby coming to share his
father's "masculinity" in behavior and attitudes.

Imitation and identification, like reinforcement, are crucial determinants of
the child's sex-role identity. However, unlike reinforcement, they emerge too late
in the child's development to be responsible for the child's initial adoption of a
particular sex identity. As mentioned earlier, one factor that influences whether or
not a child will imitate a particular model is the extent to which he perceives the
model as being similar to himself. Thus, before a child can imitate his same-sex
parent, he must first be able to accurately identify both his own sex and that of
his parent. The same is true of identification: before identification can occur, the
child must already have a grasp of the sex identity of both himself and his parent. Perhaps the best attempt to explain how the child comes to apply these sex
labels accurately and to learn to behave as society would have him behave is
Lawrence Kohlberg's (1966) theory of cognitive activity.

ISSUE

Is the presence of the father necessary for normal development of sex-role identity in male children?

One of the most commonly voiced fears of women raising boys without a father in the home is that the child will become a "sissy," or "mommy's boy," or put more technically, a boy with a poor masculine identity. Since imitation and identification seem to play a role in the development of sex-role identity, how can the young boy without a father present develop normally?

Scores of studies have sought to address this. Results of these studies are often inconsistent. However, it does appear that on a variety of measures, father-absent boys have been found to be slightly less "masculine" (for example, Biller, 1971; Biller & Davids, 1973; Carlsmith, 1964; Hetherington, 1960; Herzog & Sudia, 1973).

The really surprising aspect of this research is not, however, that the father-absent boys are slightly less masculine, but that the effect is so small and inconsistent. It seems that the reason that the sexual identity of so many of these boys appears normal lies in the fact that the father is not the only male model for the child. Indeed, even in father-present homes, other males appear at least as important as the father as a model for the child's behavior (for example, grandfathers, uncles, older brothers, neighbors, TV stars, sports figures, and so on). Thus, the child's concept of masculinity and femininity are more influenced by the "total environment" of adults than by a single parent (Kohlberg, 1966; Herzog & Sudia, 1973).

Cognitive Activity. Kohlberg's theory of cognitive activity is perhaps best introduced by way of an example, consisting of the following exchange between a professional woman and her 5-year-old daughter:

Mother:	"What are you going to be when you grow up?"
Daughter:	"A nurse."
Mother:	"Why not a doctor?"
Daughter:	"Everyone knows girls can't be doctors."
Mother:	"I'm a doctor."
Daughter:	"No, you're not a real doctor. You're a teacher."

The mother was a university professor: both a doctor and a teacher. She had never given particular emphasis to feminine over masculine behavior, and she certainly had not provided a traditionally feminine role model for her child. Nonetheless, her daughter had adopted the more general stereotype for female-appropriate behavior and attitudes. So as to bring her mother's occupation into line with this stereotype, she chose to interpret her mother's profession according to a sex-appropriate standard and chose as this standard *not* the model set by her own mother but, rather, the standard that prevails in society at large.

In so doing, the child was acting in a perfectly normal manner. The sex-appropriate behavior of young children conforms more closely to the general picture of what society says is appropriate than it does to the specific examples set by the children's parents. To use Kohlberg's words, the explanation for the girl's behavior does not lie in rewards or in particular models but in her awareness of her sex-role identity:

"I am a *girl*, therefore I want to do *girl* things, therefore the opportunity to do *girl* things (and to gain approval for doing them) is rewarding" [Kohlberg, 1966, p. 89—*girl* replaces *boy* in original quote].

Kohlberg's model for the development of the child's cognitive awareness of his sex-role identity goes something like this. First, the child must learn his gender identity. This gender identity is learned by observing the basic physical and behavioral features associated with the concepts of "male" and "female" and then comparing these with the child's own features. Once this gender identity has been mastered, it in turn serves as a basic organizer of sex-role attitudes and behavior. It also determines which children and adults will be imitated and identified with. It is as if the child were saying to himself: "He is a boy and he is doing this. I am a boy. Therefore I can do what he does." Thus, once the child has learned his gender identity, he goes on to selectively imitate and identify with others who share his gender identity. This, in turn, leads to ever-increasing levels of sex-appropriate behavior and attitudes.

Summary of Understanding Oneself

The preschool period is a time when the child first begins to understand himself. He shows the beginnings of a *self-concept*, as reflected in his egocentrism and his use of language that refers specifically to himself. He also shows an increasing awareness of a particularly important aspect of his self-concept: namely, his *sex-role identity*. Thus, he shows an increasing ability to label himself and others by sex, and he engages in sex-appropriate behavior to an ever increasing degree. Although social learning mechanisms of reinforcement, imitation, and identification are undoubtedly involved in the child's acquisition of a sex-role identity, the child's cognitive activity and awareness seem to be especially important.

UNDERSTANDING OTHERS

When a child learns to understand himself, he also learns to understand others. This process of understanding others is called **perspective-taking.** Perspective-taking includes both learning how to think about other people and learning how to understand the thoughts, emotions, intentions, and viewpoints of others.

Perspective-taking is, to some extent, a cognitive skill. As such, it is related to the child's overall level of cognitive ability. Since the cognitive ability of the preschool child remains immature and limited in certain regards, his capacity to understand others is necessarily limited. These limitations stem predominantly from the child's *egocentrism:* his tendency to view himself as the center of the universe and the resulting inability to realize that others have different perspectives, beliefs, and attitudes.

Piaget's Theory of Egocentrism

Until very recently, psychologists have relied heavily on Piaget's early research and theory concerning egocentrism. Piaget's theory suggested that throughout the preschool years the child remains in the period of preoperational thought, with one of the characteristics of preoperational thought being the child's predominant egocentrism and a corresponding lack of perspective-taking ability. Piaget's belief in the predominant egocentrism of the preschooler stemmed from a rather ingenious experiment (Piaget & Inhelder, 1956). In this experiment, preschoolers were shown a model landscape consisting of three different-sized "mountains" placed on a table top. The child sat at one side of the table and a large doll was placed at another side. The child was first asked to describe the scene from where he sat—a task completed quite easily. However, when the child was asked to describe the same scene as it looked to the doll, he simply repeated his earlier description of what he saw from his own perspective. The preschool child thus projected his own point of view or perspective inaccurately onto another. In contrast, school age (concrete operational) children were able to accurately describe the scene from the doll's perspective as well as from their own.

Recent Research on Egocentrism and Perspective-Taking

Piaget's original work was exciting in that it highlighted a significant limitation on the preschooler's social skills: namely, his egocentrism. It was misleading, however, in that it suggested very high levels of egocentrism throughout the preschool period Further observation, however, suggests that this interpretation cannot be completely correct. Hide-and-seek and many other play activities that are very characteristic of preschool children require some ability to know the perspective of others. In order to hide effectively, the child must know that the seeker's perspective does not allow him to see the child.

Recent research has, indeed, demonstrated that while children remain largely egocentric throughout the preschool period, significant gains are made during this time in the child's understanding of "what the other is seeing" (**visual perspective-taking**). John Flavell (1974) has suggested a series of stages in the child's learning of "what the other is seeing" that roughly correspond to the child's learning the correct answers to the following questions: "Does the other see something?" "Can an object look differently?" "What does the other see?" "How does it appear to him?" (Shantz, 1975).

The earliest beginnings of visual perspective-taking occur in infancy, with the child's awareness that an object remains the same even when seen from another perspective. Thus, the infant who recognizes his bottle when he sees its bottom and not its nipple has some awareness that objects can be seen from other points of view and still stay the same. As the child grows older, he will also begin to be able to describe objects from those other points of view. However, this ability to describe objects from other points of view remains quite fragile, as exemplified in the following study (Masangkay, McCluskey, McIntyre, Sims-Knight, Vaughn, & Flavell, 1974). Two- to 5-year-olds were shown cards with pictures on both sides. Each child then sat facing one side of the card, while the experimenter faced the other side. When the experimenter asked "What do *I* see?" the children responded egocentrically by describing their own side of the card. However, when asked "What picture is on *my* side of the card?" the children were sometimes able to respond correctly. Thus, the children did realize that another point of view was possible and were sometimes able to express this other point of view.

The fact that even very young preschoolers do have some awareness that objects look differently from different perspectives is also well illustrated in a study by Shantz and Watson (1970). In this study, 3- to 5-year-olds looked at an array of objects inside a covered box from both ends of the box. Unknown to the children, the array was sometimes completely rotated, so that the children saw the same perspective from both ends of the box. About half of the children were surprised when this happened, indicating quite clearly that they expected the objects to change in appearance when viewed from another perspective.

It appears, then, that even very young children realize that objects have different perspectives—although they cannot yet infer what those perspectives are. From this, it seems reasonable to hypothesize that these young children also have the cognitive ability to realize that other people are different from themselves—with different attitudes, beliefs, motives, and fantasies—even though they may not be able to infer exactly what these differences are.

Summary of the Child's Understanding of Others

We have seen that the child's ability to understand others through *perspective-taking* is rather limited during the preschool period, due to his predominant *egocentrism*. This limitation is nicely illustrated in the work of Piaget. However, since the time of Piaget's classic study of this phenomenon, we have come to learn that the preschooler is not so completely egocentric as Piaget originally believed. Even the preschool child has some perspective-taking ability, and this ability improves significantly throughout the preschool period.

PROVIDING AN OPTIMAL ENVIRONMENT FOR SOCIAL DEVELOPMENT DURING THE PRESCHOOL YEARS

We have seen that the child's parents continue to play a major role in the social and emotional development of the preschool child. Thus, it is primarily to the parents that we must turn in making our recommendations about an optimal environment. One of the most important aspects of the parents' interactions with their child centers around their disciplinary style. The best results—in terms of socialization—appear to occur when parents primarily utilize love-oriented methods of discipline that make extensive use of praise and reasoning. In addition, explaining to a child what he should do (prescriptive style) rather than what he should not do (proscriptive style) is most effective in producing prosocial behaviors such as cooperation, helping, and sharing. Two specific points regarding parental disciplinary style are concerned with timing and consistency. Rewards and punishments are most effective if delivered at the outset of a behavior, rather than after the behavior has been completed. Similarly, rewards and punishments are most effective if they are applied in a consistent manner.

Parental disciplinary style is by no means the only way in which parents influence the socialization of preschool children. Of special importance is the way in which the parents themselves behave. Thus, the optimal environment is the one in which the parents behave prosocially, thereby providing good role models for their children. The optimal environment is not the home in which the child is told: "Do as I say, not as I do."

Because the preschool period is also a time when the child's environment begins to extend beyond the family, the optimal environment should not be exclusively parent-dominated. Peers begin to take on special importance at this time. The preschooler should thus be given ample opportunity to play with other children and form friendships with them. Visits with other children, play groups, nursery schools, and day-care centers all provide excellent opportunities for these peer interactions.

Finally, the optimal environment is one in which great care is taken regarding still a further socializing force present during the preschool period: television. Young children should be encouraged to watch educational programs (for example, *Sesame Street*). Programs that emphasize prosocial skills should also be encouraged (for example, *Mr. Rogers' Neighborhood*). And other programs should be screened regarding their content before the child is allowed to watch them, since they may have a very real impact not only on what he learns but on how he behaves.

In short, the optimal environment for the social development of the preschool child is one in which the child has ample opportunity to interact with parents, peers, and even television. Great care should be taken, however, to ensure that these three socializing forces provide models of well-socialized behavior for the child to emulate. Ultimately, the question is how these three forces will interact with the child to help shape his behavior. If they are positive, prosocial forces, then they will foster prosocial behavior in the child as well. But if they are negative, antisocial forces, they can have a devastating impact on the child's social development.

CHAPTER SUMMARY

This chapter has discussed both the nature of the preschool child's interactions with others and the child's understanding of these interactions. We have argued that the preschool child's interactions center around three significant "others": parents, peers, and television.

The preschooler's interactions with his parents continue to reflect his strong *attachment* to them—as evidenced in his reaction to separation. These interactions change, however, as the parents take on an altogether new role as "socializers" of the child. This socialization occurs primarily through the use of *reward and punishment, imitation,* and *identification.* The way in which parents use reward and punishment, called *parental disciplinary style,* can differ greatly between different parents: some use *power-assertive* techniques: others use *love-withdrawal* styles of discipline: and still others stress *love-oriented* methods. The *role model* that parents set by their own behavior can likewise differ greatly. Studies show, however, that the most effective socializers are love-oriented disciplinary styles coupled with prosocial parental role models that the child can *identify* with and *imitate.*

The second major socializing force during the preschool period is the child's peers, as evidenced by Harlow's research with monkeys. This research showed that monkeys raised only with their mothers do not develop normally—thus strongly indicating that at least some peer contact is critical for the development of normal social skills. Too much peer contact, however, can also be destructive, as shown by Harlow's research with "together-together" monkeys and Freud and Dann's research with "together-together" children. A reasonable balance is thus needed.

The third principal socializing force in the preschool period is television. Television directly affects the child's emotions and motivations, while supplying him with detailed role models as to how he should behave. Thus, just as care should be taken to regulate the role models that the child's parents and peers provide, stress should be placed on regulating the types of television programs that the child is allowed to view.

The preschool period is characterized not only by changes in the child's social behavior. It is also marked by changes in the child's social understanding. He acquires a greater understanding of himself—reflected in his emerging *self-concept*. This self-concept in turn shows up in his increasing ability to talk about himself and in his developing *sex-role identity*. The child's understanding of others, however, remains incomplete during the preschool period. The child still remains largely *egocentric* and can take the perspective of others (called *perspective-taking*) only in very simple, familiar situations.

SUGGESTED READINGS

Bandura, A., & Walters, R. H. *Social learning and personality development*. New York: Holt, Rinehart & Winston, 1963. An excellent introduction to social learning theory with special emphasis on the effects of imitation on social development.

Lewis, M., & Rosenblum, L. A. (Eds.). *Friendship and peer relations*. New York: Wiley, 1975. A series of very interesting articles on peer relationships in infancy and early childhood.

Maccoby, E. E. *The development of sex differences*. Stanford, Calif.: Stanford University Press, 1966. An interesting series of articles on the development of sex differences.

Piaget, J. *The language and thought of the child*. London: Routledge & Kegan Paul, 1926. A rather difficult book for the beginning student, but provides invaluable information on Piaget's concept of egocentrism.

Shantz, C. U. The development of social cognition. In E. M. Hetherington (Ed.), *Review of child development research*. Chicago: University of Chicago Press, 1975. An excellent summary of our existing knowledge of the development of social cognition.

GLOSSARY

attachment. The emotional bond that develops between an infant and another person (usually the mother). This bond is reflected in the infant's tendency to seek close physical contact with that person and to be upset when they are separated.

collective monologues. Activity whereby each child carries on his own conversation, independently of what the other person is saying or doing.

dependence. A trait that describes the extent to which the child performs behaviors that serve the purpose of keeping him in close physical contact with others. It is similar to "attachment."

effectance motivation. The child's desire or motive to master and control his environment.

egocentrism. Term used by Piaget to describe the child's self-centered tendency to project his own perspectives, beliefs, motives, and so forth onto others.

identification. The process whereby the child acquires the personality characteristics—behaviors, attitudes, beliefs, and so forth—of another person.

imitation. The copying of the behaviors of others.

independence. The ability to initiate and direct one's own behavior.

kibbutz. A form of communal living group common in Israel.

love-oriented discipline. Disciplinary techniques tending to rely heavily on praise and reasoning.

love-withdrawal discipline. Disciplinary techniques tending to use "love" as a reward for good behavior and "removing love" as punishment. Specific forms include isolation, threat of loss of love, and expression of disappointment.

metaplet. The community care-takers in charge of the children living in a kibbutz.

negative-attention-seeking. Behaving in ways that are designed to result in disapproval, anger, punishment, or generally negative attention from others.

parallel play. Two or more children playing side by side, interacting with the same objects but not interacting with one another.

parental disciplinary styles. The ways in which parents reward and punish their children. Parental disciplinary styles are generally characterized as power-assertive, love-withdrawal, and love-oriented.

perspective-taking. The opposite of egocentrism—refers to the child's ability to understand the point of view, beliefs, motives, and so forth of others.

positive-attention-seeking. Behaving in ways that are designed to result in praise, nurturance, and positive rewards or attention from others.

power-assertive discipline. Disciplinary techniques tending to rely heavily on threats, yelling, and physical punishment.

prescriptive value system. An orientation that stresses positive values and behaviors (that is, what one "ought to do").

proscriptive value system. An orientation that stresses the avoidance of negative values and behaviors (that is, what one "ought not to do").

prosocial behaviors. The socially valued behaviors of a society (for example, helping, sharing, cooperation).

self-concept. A person's sense or image of himself. It includes what he looks like, what he believes, and what he can and cannot do.

self-control. The ability to delay gratification, inhibit excessive behavioral displays, and control impulses. In acquiring self-control, the child must internalize the restrictions of his parents and society.

sex-role identity. The child's ability to label his (or her) sex appropriately and to acquire the behaviors and beliefs culturally appropriate to his sex.

socialization. The process by which children internalize the behaviors, rules, standards, motives, values, and opinions of their parents and their society.

vicarious affect. The ability to share the emotional states of some other person.

visual perspective-taking. The ability to *see* things from another person's point of view.

REFERENCES

Bandura, A., Ross, D., & Ross, S. A. Imitation of film mediated aggressive models. *Journal of Abnormal and Social Psychology,* 1963, *66,* 3–11.

Bandura, A., & Walters, R. H. *Social learning and personality development.* New York: Holt, Rinehart & Winston, 1963.

Baumrind, D. Child care practices anteceding three patterns of preschool behavior. *Genetic Psychology Monographs,* 1967, *75,* 43–83.

Becker, W. C. Consequences of different kinds of parental discipline. In M. L. Hoffman & L. W. Hoffman (Eds.), *Review of child development research.* New York: Russell Sage Foundation, 1964.

Becker, W. C., Peterson, D. R., Luria, Z., Shoemaker, D. J. & Hellmer, L. A. Relations of factors derived from parent-interview ratings to behavior problems of five-year-olds. *Child Development,* 1962, *33,* 509–535.

Bell, R., & Costello, N. Three tests for sex differences in tactile sensitivity in the newborn. *Biologia Neonatorium,* 1964, *7,* 335–347.

Bell, R., & Darling, J. The prone head reaction in the human newborn: Relationship with sex and tactile sensitivity. *Child Development,* 1965, *36,* 943–949.

Bettelheim, B. *The children of the dream.* New York: Avon Books, 1969.

Bijou, S. W., & Baer, D. M. *Child Development*. New York: Appleton-Century-Crofts, 1961.

Biller, H. B. *Father, child, and sex role*. Lexington, Mass.: Heath, 1971.

Biller, H. B., & Davids, A. Parent-child relations, personality development, and psychopathology. In A. Davids (Ed.), *Abnormal child psychology*. Monterey, Calif.: Brooks/Cole, 1973.

Bowlby, J. *Maternal care and mental health*. New York: Schocken Books, 1951.

Bowlby, J. *Attachment and loss: Separation*. New York: Basic Books, 1973.

Carlsmith, L. Effect of early father-absence on scholastic aptitude. *Harvard Educational Review*, 1964, *34*, 3–21.

Ellis, G. T., & Sekyra, F. The effect of aggressive cartoons on the behavior of first grade children. *Journal of Psychology*, 1972, *81*, 37–43.

Eron, L. D., Banta, T. J., Walder, L. O., & Laulicht, J. H. Comparison of data obtained from mothers and fathers on child-rearing practices and their relation to child aggression. *Child Development*, 1961, *32*, 457–572.

Flavell, J. H. The development of inferences about others. In T. Mischel (Ed.), *Understanding other persons*. Oxford: Blackwell, Basil & Mott, 1974.

Freud, A., & Dann, S. An experiment in group upbringing. In R. Eissler, A. Freud, H. Hartmann, & E. Kris (Eds.), *The psychoanalytic study of the child* (Vol. 6). New York: International Universities Press, 1951.

Gerbner, G. Violence in television drama: Trends and symbolic functions. In G. A. Comstock & E. A. Rubinstein (Eds.), *Television and social behavior*. Washington, D.C.: U.S. Government Printing Office, 1972.

Gesell, A. The first five years of life: A guide to the study of the preschool child. New York: Harper, 1940.

Hampson, J., & Hampson, J. The ontogenesis of sexual behavior in man. In W. C. Young (Ed.), *Sex and internal secretions*. Baltimore, Md.: Williams & Wilkins, 1961.

Harlow, H. F. Age-mate or peer affectional system. In D. S. Lehrman, R. A. Hinde, & E. Shaw (Eds.), *Advances in the study of behavior* (Vol. 2). New York: Academic Press, 1969.

Hartup, W. W. Peer interaction and social organization. In P. H. Mussen (Ed.), *Carmichael's manual of child psychology*. New York: Wiley, 1970.

Hartup, W. W. The origins of friendship. In M. Lewis & L. A. Rosenblum (Eds.), *Friendship and peer relations*. New York: Wiley, 1975.

Heathers, G. Emotional dependence and independence in nursery school play. *Journal of Genetic Psychology*, 1955, *87*, 37–57.

Heinicke, C. M. Some effects of separating two-year-old children from their parents: A comparative study. *Human Relations*, 1956, *9*, 105–176.

Heinicke, C. M., & Westheimer, I. *Brief separations*. New York: International Universities Press, 1965.

Herzog, E., & Sudia, C. E. Children in fatherless families. In B. M. Caldwell & H. N. Ricciuti (Eds.), *Review of child development research*. Chicago: University of Chicago Press, 1973.

Hetherington, E. M. Effects of paternal absence on sex typed behavior in Negro and white preadolescent males. *Journal of Personality and Social Psychology*, 1960, *1*, 87–91.

Hetherington, E. M. A developmental study of the effects of sex of the dominant parent on sex-role preference, identification and imitation in children. *Journal of Personality and Social Psychology*, 1965, *2*, 188–194.

Hetherington, E. M., & Frankie, G. Effects of parental dominance, warmth and conflict on imitation in children. *Journal of Personality and Social Psychology*, 1967, *6*, 119–125.

Hollenberg, E., & Sperry, M. Some antecedents of aggression and effects of frustration in doll play. *Personality*, 1951, *1*, 32–43.

Janis, I. L., Mahl, G. F., Kagan, J., & Holt, R. R. *Personality*. New York: Harcourt Brace Jovanovich, 1969.

Kagan, J., & Moss, H. A. *Birth to maturity*. New York: Wiley, 1962.

Kohlberg, L. A cognitive-developmental analysis of children's sex-role concepts and attitudes. In E. E. Maccoby (Ed.), *The development of sex differences.* Stanford, Calif.: Stanford University Press, 1966.

Lee, L. Social encounters of infants: The beginnings of popularity. Paper presented at the International Society for the Study of Behavioral Development, Ann Arbor, Mich., August 1973.

Levin, H., & Baldwin, A. L. Pride and shame in children. In M. R. Jones (Ed.), *Nebraska Symposium on Motivation.* Lincoln: University of Nebraska Press, 1959.

LeVine, R. A. Cross-cultural study in child psychology. In P. H. Mussen (Ed.), *Carmichael's manual of child psychology* (3rd ed.). New York: Wiley, 1970.

Lewis, M. State as an infant-environment interaction. *Merrill-Palmer Quarterly,* 1972, *18,* 95–121.

Lewis, M., Young, G., Brooks, J., & Michalson, L. The beginning of friendship. In M. Lewis & L. A. Rosenblum (Eds.), *Friendship and peer relations.* New York: Wiley, 1975.

Lovaas, O. Effect of exposure to symbolic aggression on aggressive behavior. *Child Development,* 1961, *32,* 37–44.

Maccoby, E. E., & Feldman, S. S. Mother-attachment and stranger-reactions in the third year of life. *Monographs of the Society for Research in Child Development,* 1972, *37*(1, Serial No. 146).

Maccoby, E. E., & Jacklin, C. N. *The psychology of sex differences.* Stanford, Calif.: Stanford University Press, 1974.

Martin, B. Parent-child relations. In F. D. Horowitz (Ed.), *Review of child development research.* Chicago: University of Chicago Press, 1975.

Masangkay, Z. S., McCluskey, K. A., McIntyre, C. W., Sims-Knight, J., Vaughn, B. E., & Flavell, J. H. The early development of inferences about the visual percepts of others. *Child Development,* 1974, *45,* 357–366.

Minton, C., Kagan, J., & Levine, J. A. Maternal control and obedience in the two-year-old. *Child Development,* 1971, *42,* 1873–1894.

Money, J. Sex hormones and other variables in human eroticism. In W. C. Young (Ed.), *Sex and internal secretions.* Baltimore, Md.: Williams & Wilkins, 1961.

Money, J., & Ehrhardt, A. A. *Man and woman, boy and girl.* Baltimore, Md.: Johns Hopkins University Press, 1972.

Money, J., Hampson, J., & Hampson, J. Imprinting and the establishment of gender role. *Archives of Neurology & Psychiatry,* 1957, *77,* 333–336.

Moss, H. A. Sex, age and state as determinants of mother-infant interaction. *Merrill-Palmer Quarterly,* 1967, *13,* 19–36.

Mueller, E., & Lucas, T. A developmental analysis of peer interaction among toddlers. In M. Lewis & L. A. Rosenblum (Eds.), *Friendship and peer relations.* New York: Wiley, 1975.

National childcare consumer study: 1975. Office of Child Development, U.S. Department of Health, Education, and Welfare, 1975.

Olejnik, A. B., & McKinney, J. P. Parental value orientation and generosity in children. *Developmental Psychology,* 1973, *8,* 311.

Parke, R. D., O'Leary, S. E., & West, S. Mother-father-newborn interaction: Effects of maternal medication, labor and sex of infants. Proceedings of the Eightieth Annual Convention, American Psychological Association, 1972.

Piaget, J. *The language and thought of the child.* London: Routledge & Kegan Paul, 1926.

Piaget, J., & Inhelder, B. *The child's conception of space.* London: Routledge & Kegan Paul, 1956.

Rabban, M. Sex-role identification in young children in two diverse social groups. *Genetic Psychology Monographs,* 1950, *42,* 81–158.

Rabin, A. I. *Growing up in the kibbutz.* New York: Springer, 1965.

Rabin, A. I. *Kibbutz studies.* East Lansing: Michigan State University Press, 1971.

Read, K. H. Parents' expressed attitudes and children's behavior. *Journal of Consulting Psychology,* 1945, *9,* 95–100.

Robertson, J., & Robertson, J. Young children in brief separation: A fresh look. *Psychoanaly-*

tic Study of the Child, 1971, *26*, 264–315.

Ross, L. B. *The effect of aggressive cartoons on the group play of children*. Unpublished doctoral dissertation, Miami University, 1972.

Rutter, M. Parent-child separation: Psychological effects on the children. *Journal of Child Psychology and Psychiatry*, 1971, *12*, 233–260.

Schaefer, E. S. A circumplex model for maternal behavior. *Journal of Abnormal and Social Psychology*, 1959, *59*, 226–235.

Schaffer, R. *Mothering*. Cambridge, Mass.: Harvard University Press, 1977.

Sears, R. R., Maccoby, E. E., & Levin, H. *Patterns of child rearing*. Evanston, Ill.: Row, Peterson, 1957.

Sears, R. R., Rau, L., & Alpeft, R. *Identification and child rearing*. Stanford, Calif.: Stanford University Press, 1965.

Shantz, C. U. The development of social cognition. In E. M. Hetherington (Ed.), *Review of child development research*. Chicago: University of Chicago Press, 1975.

Shantz, C. U., & Watson, J. S. Assessment of spatial egocentrism through expectancy violation. *Psychonomic Science*, 1970, *18*, 93–94.

Shapiro, A., & Madsen, M. C. Cooperative and competitive behavior of kibbutz and urban children in Israel. *Child Development*, 1969, *40*, 605–618.

Spiro, M. E. *Children of the kibbutz*. Cambridge, Mass.: Harvard University Press, 1958.

Stein, A. H., & Friedrich, L. K. Television content and young children's behavior. In J. P. Murray, E. A. Rubinstein, & G. A. Comstock (Eds.), *Television and social behavior*. Washington, D. C.: U. S. Government Printing Office, 1972.

Stein, A. H., & Friedrich, L. K. Impact of television on children and youth. In E. M. Hetherington (Ed.), *Review of child development research*. Chicago: University of Chicago Press, 1975.

Steuer, F. B., Applefield, J. M., & Smith, R. Televised aggression and the interpersonal aggression of preschool children. *Journal of Experimental Child Psychology*, 1971, *11*, 442–447.

Suomi, S. J., & Harlow, H. F. The role and reason of peer relationships in rhesus monkeys. In M. Lewis & L. A. Rosenblum (Eds.), *Friendship and peer relations*. New York: Wiley, 1975.

Swift, J. W. Effects of early group experience: The nursery school and day nursery. In M. L. Hoffman & L. W. Hoffman (Eds.), *Review of child development research*. New York: Russell Sage Foundation, 1964.

Walters, R. H., Leat, M., & Mezei, L. Response inhibition and disinhibition through empathetic learning. *Canadian Journal of Psychology*, 1963, *17*, 235–243.

White, R. W. Motivation reconsidered: The concept of competence. *Psychological Review*, 1959, *66*, 297–333.

Yarrow, M. R., Waxler, C. Z., & Scott, P. M. Child effects on adult behavior. *Developmental Psychology*, 1971, *5*, 300–311.

PART THREE
THE SCHOOL YEARS

9

Learning and Cognitive Development during the School Years

There is a striking sensation that grips most child psychologists, as well as students learning about children, at periodic intervals. It could be called "the developmentalist's syndrome." You might be experiencing it at about this point in the book. Simply put, the syndrome usually hits after you have read about, absorbed, and marveled at the complexity, intricacy, and infinite variety of the experiences, tasks, and skills that developing humans must master. You begin to wonder how any of us ever makes it, given the pitfalls and problems to which we as children were prey. Then you realize that with all this, you've only gotten the child to the point where he is starting grade school!

The importance of those early years notwithstanding, the child's intellectual growth and learning are by no means complete when he enters the school years. In fact, they are only beginning to develop in the sense that the child is just now starting to develop adult-like thoughts, behaviors, and attitudes. Also, the tasks set before the child in school come to approximate ever more closely those skills we foster and need in adulthood.

Psychologists view the early school period as one of major upheaval and change in the child's cognitive abilities. Throughout the school years on toward adolescence, the child is acquiring and perfecting a vast new array of competencies for understanding and dealing with the world.

In this chapter, we will trace the child's cognitive development through the school years. We shall see how numerous changes are brought about in how the child attends, perceives, remembers, and thinks. We will also consider the difficult question of why the school years, in particular, are a time of such rapidly accelerated cognitive growth.

THE 5 TO 7 SHIFT

Many different segments of our society acknowledge that at about the age of 5 to 7 the child undergoes a rather profound "shift" in his behavioral and intellectual capabilities (the so-called **5 to 7 shift**). As we shall see, Piaget feels that the child actually jumps at about this time to a new, more sophisticated level of cognitive organization (*concrete operational thinking*). Closer to home, this is the time when society at large recognizes that the behavioral and intellectual capabilities of the child are undergoing marked change. It is at age 5—the approximate start of this period of change—that children in the United States and many other countries begin school. Similarly, the criminal codes in most of our states assume that the child is first capable of knowing right from wrong and is, hence, first capable of being "guilty" at about the age of 7. Catholic Canon Law makes similar presumptions, stating that the child is first capable of committing sin, of truly knowing right from wrong, and of confession and communion at age 7.

Research psychologists, too, have documented an impressive array of important changes during this age period in the child's cognitive functioning (White, 1965). We will document a number of these changes in the ensuing pages of this chapter. In general the child's mind is seen as becoming progressively more like that of the adult. The child is becoming more *planful* in his behavior, thinking about things and evaluating their probable outcomes before he takes action. The child is becoming less impulsive, less dominated by environmental stimuli: he appears to be able to step back from the world and examine and evaluate it.

One simple explanation of these changes would be that they all occur because the child is going to school, where he is taught these new skills. While not denying that school is an impetus to cognitive growth in the child, the answer is not quite that simple. There are signs that profound psychological—and even physiological—reorganizations may be taking place that underlie a significant portion of the evolution across this age period. In fact, one could argue that the reason our society decided to send children to school at this age was precisely because of a greater readiness for formal schooling brought about by these changes. At least some support for this latter view is found in the fact that the legal and church rules that set young children apart for special treatment, presuming their legal innocence and incapacity for committing sin, evolved at a time well before the development of universal school systems. However, regardless of the precise causes of the 5 to 7 shift, there do appear to be a host of changes in the child that occur at about this time across a wide spectrum of cognitive abilities. Let us therefore examine some of these changes.

Learning Theory Evidence of the 5 to 7 Shift

Much of the early research on the development of intellectual abilities during the early school years relied on a learning theory approach. Hence, much of this early research utilized different types of classical and operant conditioning tasks to assess the changes in intellectual capacities that were occurring. While the research left largely open the key question of why certain intellectual changes occur during the early school years, it did clearly demonstrate major advances in the child's intellectual performance between the ages of 5 and 7.

Classical Conditioning

As you know from an earlier discussion in this text, in *classical conditioning* a neutral stimulus is continually paired with some unconditioned stimulus until the neutral stimulus alone comes to elicit some reflexive response (for example, pairing a bell with food until the bell alone elicits salivation). As we discussed in Chapter 4, classical conditioning is probably not possible until about 2 months of age. Thereafter, the child's susceptibility to classical conditioning (that is, the ease with which classically conditioned responses are established) steadily increases, up to about the age of 5 or 6 years. Strikingly, however, around the age of 5 or 6, the child becomes *less and less* susceptible to classical conditioning (Razran, 1933; White, 1965).

Although we do not yet know with certainty *why* the child at 5 or 6 becomes more difficult to classically condition, one possible explanation is that at this age the child begins to interpose thought processes between the environmental stimulus and the response. As a result, the child becomes increasingly more capable of controlling his own behavior and resisting the forces of the environment when they conflict with his own thoughts or intentions.

Simple Discrimination Learning

Another area in which a significant shift can be seen between the ages of 5 and 7 is in simple *discrimination* tasks. In a discrimination task, the child is presented with two or more alternatives and is rewarded for choosing the "correct" one. After a number of such trials, the child learns which is the correct one and thereafter picks it. Performance on such tasks improves steadily with age. However, when the discrimination problem is extremely simple (for example, learning which of several animal pictures are correct), there is evidence to suggest that after the age of 5 or 6, performance actually begins to *decline* (Weir & Stevenson, 1959; White, 1965). Observation of the behavior of older children in these simple tasks suggests that their poor performance is often due to the fact that they generate solutions to the problem that are more complex than they need be. They can't believe that the answer is so obvious and simple!

Transposition Tasks

A more complicated form of discrimination task is called **transposition.** In transposition tasks, the child is first taught a simple discrimination, such as picking the larger of two circles. Once the child has mastered this discrimination, he is then given a choice between the originally "correct" large circle and a still larger one. Which one will he choose? The child's answer depends upon two factors: (1) his age, and (2) the extent of the difference between the originally correct stimulus and the new stimulus. Children of all ages (and indeed animals such as rats and pigeons) will pick the new largest stimulus if the difference between it and the originally correct stimulus is small. However, if the difference between the originally correct stimulus and the new stimulus is a large one, age becomes an important factor. In this case, children under the age of 5 (and lower animals) will continue to pick the originally correct stimulus, the one for which they have been rewarded in the past. Children over the age of 7 (and adults), however, pick

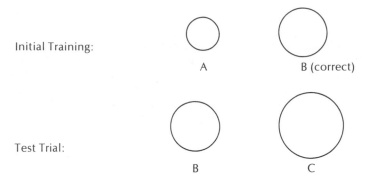

Initial Training:

A   B (correct)

Test Trial:

B   C

Figure 9-1.   Transposition task. This illustration shows a transposition task in which the difference between the initially "correct" stimulus (*B*) and the new stimulus (*C*) is quite large. In a task such as this, children 5 years of age and younger would continue to pick stimulus *B* on the test trial, whereas children 7 years of age or older would be more likely to pick the new stimulus, *C* (the "larger" one).

the new larger stimulus (Kuenne, 1946; White, 1965). (See Figure 9-1.) Thus, the young child's response seems to be determined by the physical identity of the particular stimulus ("It's *that* one!"), while the older child's response is determined by the concept "larger" ("It's the *larger* one!")—a concept that the older child generates when he solves the original discrimination problem. Moreover, instructing the younger children to say "larger" when picking the correct stimulus does not alter their performance. Unlike older children, the younger children somehow cannot or do not generate the same type of concept for distinguishing between objects (Marsh & Sherman, 1966; McKee & Riley, 1962).

Reversal-Nonreversal Shifts

One final type of discrimination task that has frequently shown interesting changes in performance between the ages of 5 and 7 is the *reversal-nonreversal shift* task. In this task, children are initially trained on a two-dimensional discrimination task in which only one dimension is relevant. For example, they are shown either a small circle and a large square or a large circle and a small square. Initially, they are trained to always pick the *larger* stimulus, regardless of whether it is a circle or a square. In other words, the size dimension, but not the shape dimension, is relevant, with "large" being the correct "value" of the size dimension.

Once the children have mastered the above task, the rules change and the children must learn to make a new response. For half of the children, the change is a **reversal shift;** for the others, a **nonreversal shift.** In a reversal shift, the relevant dimension remains the same while the value changes (for example, the new correct response is now the *smaller* stimulus, regardless of whether it is a circle or a square). In a nonreversal shift, the whole dimension changes (for example, shape now becomes the correct dimension: the new correct response is now the *square*, regardless of whether it is large or small). (See Figure 9-2.)

Depending on how the child solved the original discrimination task, his response to these changes can be quite different. If the child's solution during the

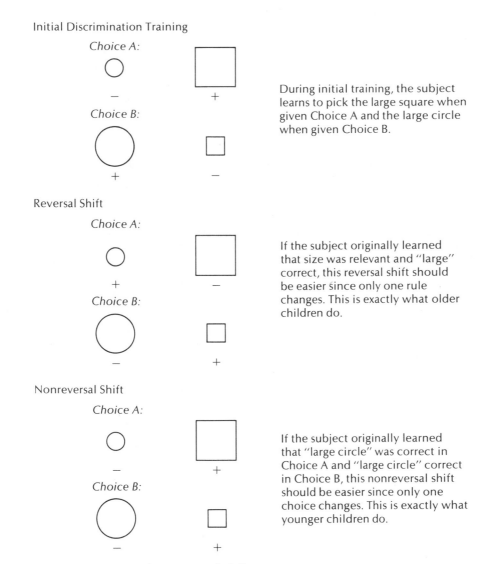

Initial Discrimination Training

Choice A:

Choice B:

During initial training, the subject learns to pick the large square when given Choice A and the large circle when given Choice B.

Reversal Shift

Choice A:

Choice B:

If the subject originally learned that size was relevant and "large" correct, this reversal shift should be easier since only one rule changes. This is exactly what older children do.

Nonreversal Shift

Choice A:

Choice B:

If the subject originally learned that "large circle" was correct in Choice A and "large circle" correct in Choice B, this nonreversal shift should be easier since only one choice changes. This is exactly what younger children do.

Figure 9-2.   Reversal-nonreversal shifts.

original discrimination was determined by some conceptual strategy that told him to *ignore* shape as a dimension, he will find the reversal task to be easier than the nonreversal task. Children over 7 do, indeed, perform better on reversal shifts than they do on nonreversal shifts, indicating that their performance in the new task is determined by a strategy adopted during the earlier task that allows them to concentrate on size differences and ignore shape differences.

Now, assume, however, that the child learned the initial discrimination task by simply remembering the actual stimuli that were correct for each choice, and not by learning a general rule such as "It's the larger one." If this were the case, the nonreversal shift (picking squares instead of circles) should be easier to learn, since the answer to only one of the two choices changes. (See Figure 9-2 and note that the square in the first choice is also the larger object.) In contrast, both choices change in the reversal shift task. Interestingly, children under 5—and animals—tend to perform better on nonreversal shifts than they do on reversal shifts (Kendler, 1963; Kendler, Kendler, & Wells, 1960), indicating that they simply learn the identity of the correct stimulus for each choice and do not attempt to apply a general strategy such as "size comparison" or "shape comparison."

Much research in recent years has attempted to explain why younger and older children differ so markedly in their performance on reversal-nonreversal shift tasks (Stevenson, 1974; Kendler & Kendler, 1975). While precise answers have not yet been found, it is known that training young children to verbalize their solutions ("It is the larger one"; "It is the square") does not always change their performance. Hence, it seems that the "conceptual" solution used by the older children is not simply a matter of applying the correct verbal label, but is related to use of more general cognitive strategies and skills. Younger children can be taught to correctly "mouth" the correct verbal labels but somehow cannot—or do not—utilize the actual cognitive strategies used by older children in distinguishing between the objects.

Summary of Learning Theory Evidence of the 5 to 7 Shift

In a number of ways the intellectual performance of children younger than about 5 to 7 differs from that of older children. Specifically, older children's solutions on typical learning problems, such as classical conditioning, discrimination, transposition, and reversal-nonreversal shifts, are more "strategic" and "conceptual," while younger children's solutions seem more "mechanical" and bound to the physical properties of the particular stimuli.

Piaget's Theory: The Concrete Operational Period

Though we have seen that somewhere between 5 and 7 years of age children become more "conceptual" in the way that they think and solve problems, we have not attempted to explain in any detail either what we mean by more "conceptual" or precisely why these changes occur. In an attempt to answer these difficult questions, let us again turn to one of the leading theorists on the subject: Jean Piaget.

Piaget has long been a major proponent of the view that the early school-aged child undergoes profound qualitative changes in his cognitive capacities (Piaget, 1970). Around the age of 6 or 7, the child jumps from the intuitive, semilogical mode of the preoperational child (see Chapter 7 for a discussion of the preoperational child) to a more systematic and strategic way of thinking, the **concrete operational period** (Fischer, 1978). On a more obvious level, this change is reflected in the child's behavior, as he visibly becomes better and more efficient in handling complex problems. Modifications in external behavior, according to Piaget, are produced by an internal restructuring of mental activity. The child develops new mental schemes, called *operations*, that enable him to solve problems in ways that are qualitatively different from those of the preoperational child.

Piaget's explanation of these "qualitative" differences in internal thought is one of the more difficult parts of his theory. We shall try to capture the essence of

Phase 1:

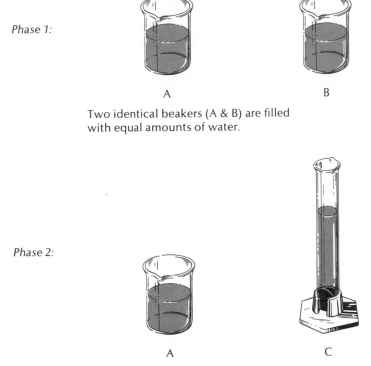

A   B

Two identical beakers (A & B) are filled
with equal amounts of water.

Phase 2:

A   C

Then water from beaker B is poured into beaker C (which is
narrower and taller). The pre-operational child is deceived by
the physical appearance of the beakers and concludes that
beaker C contains more water.

Figure 9-3. Typical conservation-of-liquid quantity problem.

Piaget's explanation by focusing on three important domains of intellectual growth identified by Piaget: conservation, addition of classes, and seriation/ transitivity.

Conservation

Consider the problem depicted in Figure 9-3. Two identical beakers (beakers *A* and *B*) are filled with equal amounts of water. Water is then poured from one of the two beakers (beaker *B*) into a third beaker (beaker *C*) that is both taller and narrower than the other two. Since beaker *C* is narrower than the other two beakers, the water in beaker *C* will rise to a level higher than that in beaker *A*. Does this mean that the two beakers have different amounts of water? "Obviously not," you will say. "We didn't do anything to change the amount of water, just the shape of the container." Despite how obvious this answer may seem to us as adults, Piaget has found that prior to about age 7, children will say that the tall, thin beaker—the one with the higher water level—*does* contain more water.

This example illustrates a cognitive ability that Piaget believes is central to intellectual functioning in the school-aged child: **conservation.** Conservation in this particular case means the understanding that the amount of liquid does not change when it is merely poured from one beaker into another. More generally, conservation is the understanding that certain "transformations" do not change some of the basic properties of objects. We saw an earlier example in Chapter 7 involving conservation of number: the understanding that altering the length or density of a row of objects does not change the number of objects. Why does Piaget believe that conservation is so important? For Piaget, the emergence of conservation is of special importance since it means that the child can now see underlying *regularities* in an environment that otherwise appears to be fluctuating and irregular. Put more formally, conservation is the ability to see invariance in the face of apparent variance or change. Conservation permits the child to see past the apparent changes in his environment (for example, the higher water level in the tall, thin beaker) and appreciate those aspects of objects that remain the same despite these apparent changes: quantity, number, and volume. The child comes to distinguish appearance from reality—although to the eye the amount of water appears to change, in reality the amount does not change. For Piaget, conservation is thus a leap forward in the child's dealings with the world. The child has a deeper, more fundamental, and higher-order knowledge of the principles governing objects and how they function.

The Transition to Concrete Operations

The preoperational child possesses some rudimentary knowledge required to understand conservation. What the preoperational child cannot do, according to Piaget, is coordinate these individual pieces of knowledge and create the integrated system of knowledge required for conservation. Specifically, we saw in Chapter 7 that the preoperational child can predict accurately what will happen to the water when it is poured from the short fat beaker (B) into the tall thin one (C). It will rise higher in beaker C. We called this "knowledge of functional relations." What the preoperational child cannot do, according to Piaget, is to integrate and coordinate different functional relations into a single system. In order to "conserve," the child must be able to simultaneously put together his thoughts about the length and width of the liquid in the first beaker, the length and width of the liquid in the second beaker, and the change brought about by pouring the liquid from the first beaker into the second (Fischer, 1978). The preoperational child cannot do this. He focuses only on the *state* of the liquids in each beaker and is seduced by the appearance of the tall, thin beaker, which appears to contain more. The concrete operational child with "conservation of liquid quantity" focuses not on the liquid's state but on the **transformation** that occurs as the liquid is poured. He puts that knowledge together with his knowledge about the height and width of the containers. It is this ability to simultaneously consider several different features of the display that underlies the acquisition of conservation.

With this general idea of what is involved in conservation, let us take a deeper look at the important changes behind the transition from preoperational to concrete operational thought. Probably the most important change centers on a concept called the **operation,** the mental structure that enables us to perform correctly in such higher level problem-solving tasks as conservation.

An *operation* is a special kind of scheme with the following three critical components: it is **interiorized;** it involves a *transformation;* and it is **reversible.**

Thus, *an operation is an interiorized transformation that is reversible*. By interiorized, we mean that the child can carry out the thought process in his head and does not have to act it out in his behavior. By transformation, we mean that the thought process is concerned with changing objects from one state to another. And by reversible, we mean that the child can mentally "reverse" the transformation in his head and return objects to their original state. Let us relate each of these terms to our earlier example of the beakers and the water. The child who understands conservation can mentally consider the act of pouring (interiorization) without having to actually pour the liquid. He can mentally figure out the two different states that would result from pouring the liquid (transformation). Finally, he can return the liquid to its original state by mentally imagining that he is pouring it back into the original beaker (reversibility). The mental structure composed of these three skills—referred to by Piaget as an *operation*—underlies the child's mastery of conservation (Fischer, 1978).

Liquid quantity is just one domain in which conservation ability is acquired. The child must master such diverse notions as conservation of number, length, volume, quantity, and weight. These basic abilities are shown in Figure 9-4. The different types of conservation are not mastered all at once. The child may be struggling with one type of conservation long after he has mastered other types. Thus, complete conservation in all of its aspects is not fully mastered until well into adolescence, and sometimes beyond (Piaget, 1970).

Addition of Classes

We saw in Chapter 7 how even the preoperational child possesses certain primitive category or class relations; we called these *semiclasses*. According to Piaget, the development of complete knowledge of classes does not, however, occur until the school years. To illustrate this point, let us again use the example that we used in Chapter 7—remembering, of course, that classification skills encompass a broad variety of different abilities in addition to those reflected in the example. Recall that in our example, when the preoperational child was shown four dogs and three cats, he could say accurately that there were more dogs than cats, but when he was asked whether there were more dogs or more *animals*, he would say "more dogs." The concrete operational child, in contrast, will answer this last question correctly: "more animals." This classification ability—found in the older child but not in the younger child—is called **addition of classes**: the ability to add classes together to form a higher-level class. For Piaget, successful performance in this task involves several things: first, an awareness of the subclasses (dogs and cats); next, knowledge that these subclasses can be added together to form a third, higher-order class (animals); and finally, knowledge that the higher-order class can be broken back down into its subclasses. Thus, this task involves the use of mental operations similar to those involved in conservation. The two subclasses can be combined (via *transformation*) into a third class that can be broken back down (via *reversibility*) into the two subclasses. And, all this can be done in the head (*interiorization*).

As with conservation, the ability to add different types of classes develops at different rates. Even very young children can add up classes of items with which they are very familiar, such as types of clothes or candy. For less familiar, and

Type of Conservation	Child initially sees:	Experimenter then transforms display:	Child is asked conservation question:
Length	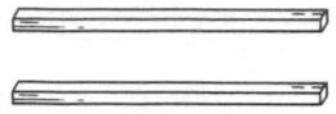 Two sticks of equal length and agrees that they are of equal length.	 Moves stick over.	*Which stick is longer?* *Preconserving* child will say that one of the sticks is longer. *Conserving* child will say they are both the same length.
Number	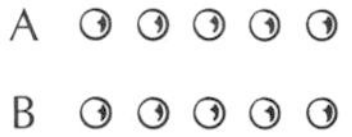 A ⊙ ⊙ ⊙ ⊙ ⊙ B ⊙ ⊙ ⊙ ⊙ ⊙ Two rows of beads and says that they have the same number of beads.	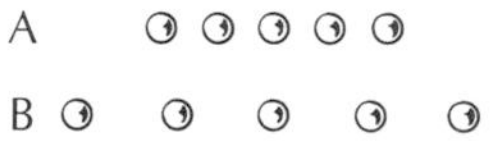 A ⊙ ⊙ ⊙ ⊙ ⊙ B ⊙ ⊙ ⊙ ⊙ ⊙ Spreads out beads on bottom row to increase length of row.	*Which row has more beads?* *Preconserving* child will say that row *B* (the longer row) has more beads. *Conserving* child will say they both have the same number of beads.
Liquid Quantity	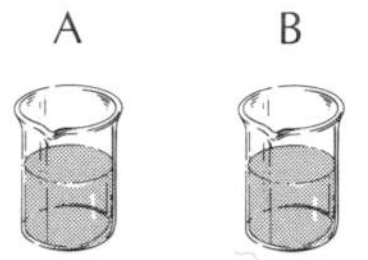 Two beakers filled with water and says that they both contain the same amount of water.	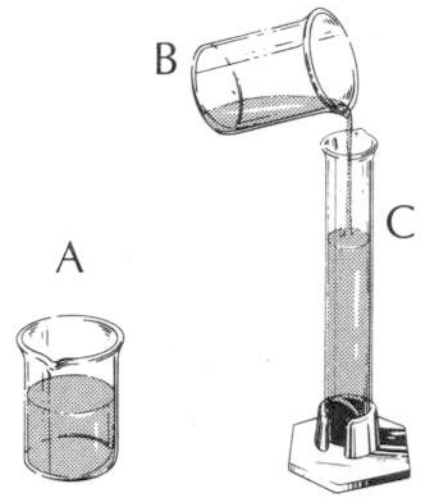 Pours water from *B* into a tall, thin beaker (*C*), so that water level in *C* is higher than in *A*.	*Which beaker has more water?* *Preconserving* child will say that *C* has more water: "See, it's higher!" *Conserving* child will say that they have the same amount of water: "You only poured it!"
Volume	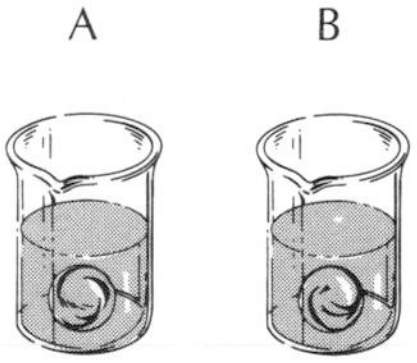 Two balls of clay placed in two beakers containing equal amounts of water. Child sees that water level rises equally in both beakers.	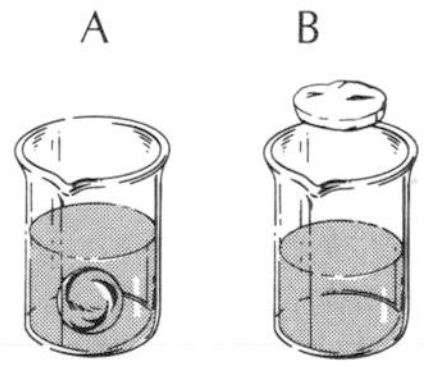 Molds clay ball *B* into a different shape and holds it above the beaker.	*When clay ball B is placed in the beaker, will the water level be higher or lower or the same as in beaker A?* *Preconserving* child will say that the water level will be lower because the ball is flattened out. *Conserving* child will say that the water level will be the same as in beaker *A* because nothing was really changed.

Figure 9-4.   Visual depiction of several conservation tasks and how preconserving and conserving children typically respond in each situation.

more difficult, concepts, such as biological classifications of animals, the ability to add classes does not occur until later in the school years.

Seriation/Transitivity

The last major accomplishments of the concrete operational period we will focus upon are seriation and transitivity—actually two separate but related skills. **Seriation** refers to the ability to string together a series of objects according to some given relation—that is, to organize them in some orderly series. Figure 9-5 shows a typical Piagetian task to assess seriation by length. If you ask a preoperational child to organize a group of sticks according to length, he will be able to do this to a limited degree, most often organizing two sticks correctly but then not aligning the third stick with the first two, and so on. In this sense, he could be said to have *semiseriation* akin to his semiclassification skills. The child at this stage has some but not all of the operational skills needed to successfully seriate all the sticks. It is not until the child develops the necessary mental *operations* during the school years that complete seriation emerges.

Transitivity is a skill that builds on seriation. You can see in Figure 9-5 a typical example of the development of transitivity. The child is first shown several sticks, two at a time, and is asked which stick is the longer of each pair ("Which is longer? *A* or *B*? *B* or *C*?"). After he responds to this phase, he is asked to compare the lengths of the two sticks that were not originally paired ("Which is longer? *A* or *C*?"). The preoperational child performs very poorly on this task, according to Piaget, whereas the concrete operational child performs correctly. For Piaget the crucial ability needed to solve this problem is the ability to cross the bridge between the two pairs—that is, to conceptually bring together two separate seriations. Clearly, one must be able to seriate the sticks in order to do this. In addition, however, one must be able to coordinate two isolated relations (for example, "*A* is longer than *B*" and "*B* is longer than *C*") into a system in order to make the *transitive inference* that "*A* is longer than *C*." For Piaget, the preoperational child cannot coordinate these two relations. He knows "*A* is longer than *B*" and separately that "*B* is longer than *C*," but he cannot coordinate these two facts via the middle linking term "*B*" to solve the problem. Again we see that the preoperational child lacks the mental operations needed to integrate and coordinate separate pieces of information into a coherent, unified and logical system (Trabasso, 1977).

ISSUE

Is the 5 to 7 shift an abrupt change in cognitive functioning or does it evolve gradually?

As we have seen, Piaget views the changes in cognitive ability that appear between the ages of about 5 and 7 as happening relatively rapidly—in the nature of a sudden "jump" to higher-level thought processes, which he terms operations. Others view the process quite differently. They see the 5 to 7 shift as being a gradual change that builds upon skills acquired during the preschool years and that is not completed in some cases until adolescence. Those in this latter group have found increasing evidence that the process is more gradual than Piaget believes. Some of this evidence is discussed in the section that follows.

SERIATION

Child is shown a group of sticks of different lengths and asked to put them in order.	Preoperational child will order two sticks at a time correctly but not the whole sequence.	Concrete-operational child will order all the sticks correctly.

TRANSITIVITY

Child is first shown a series of sticks: Then child is asked which stick is longer—*A* or *B*? *B* or *C*? *C* or *D*?—and so on. In each case the preoperational child responds correctly. But when asked which stick is longer— *A* or *C*? *B* or *D*?—	Preoperational child responds incorrectly and/or inconsistently (says, for example, that *A* > *C* or *B* > *D* or sometimes *A* > *C* and other times *C* > *A*.	Concrete-operational child responds correctly in all cases.

Figure 9-5. Typical seriation and transitivity tasks showing the constructions of younger and older children.

An Evaluation of Piaget

Throughout this discussion, and in describing Piaget's theory in earlier chapters, we have avoided any critical comments in order to give a clear, uncomplicated picture of Piaget's views. Nevertheless, Piaget's ideas have not gone unchallenged, and especially in recent years, many criticisms of his theory have appeared (see Liben, 1977; Trabasso, 1977). Some criticisms focus on Piaget's methodology (the *clinical method*), while others strike directly at the heart of his theoretical explanations.

Methodological Critique

In arriving at his theory, Piaget utilized a clinical method that consisted of informal observation, on-the-spot experimentation, detailed descriptions of small numbers of children, and in-depth verbal questioning of children about the reasons for the answers they gave him. As a scientific strategy, many psychologists have criticized Piaget's method. They point out that since he uses only a small number of children, we really don't know how representative his conclusions are of the population at large. Also, the unsystematic and subjective nature of his observations, they caution, could easily lead to bias. Some bias seems likely, since Piaget favored a particular philosophical view of human nature and, as a result, may have looked only for confirmation of his views, thereby failing to notice equally valid but contradictory observations. Still others have criticized Piaget for his heavy reliance on what the children tell him about their solutions to his problems. For example, in the conservation of number problems, the child may say that the longer row has "more" not because he lacks conservation but because he has not fully mastered the meaning of the word "more." To the child, the word "more" in this particular circumstance may mean "longer." If nonverbal assessment procedures could be used, they contend, the child might indeed show conservation. In fact, you will recall from our discussion in Chapter 7 of Gelman's research on the number concept that even 4- and 5-year-olds (presumably preoperational) showed conservation of number in a nonverbal, surprise situation, at least with small numbers.

In general, these methodological criticisms have attempted primarily to show that certain logical abilities can appear much earlier than postulated by Piaget. At present, these arguments are being hotly debated, and we cannot, with certainty, state whether the age norms postulated by Piaget are accurate or representative of the majority of children in Western culture. There is a growing body of evidence, however, that suggests that Piaget's norms are somewhat misleading and that many children do show evidence of conservation, classification, and transitivity much earlier than Piaget predicted (Gelman, 1972; Trabasso, 1977).

The methodological criticisms just described—focusing as they do upon the question of when certain logical abilities normally appear—do not quarrel with the fundamental theoretical ideas of Piaget about the processes underlying cognitive development. Other criticisms, however, have focused on these more theoretical aspects of Piaget's work.

Theoretical Critique

Several studies have recently challenged Piaget's claims that possession of basic logical operations determines whether the child will show conservation, classification, and transitivity. These studies have attempted to show that the younger child's failure on Piagetian task is not due so much to defects in his logic as to other deficits, such as improperly directed attention, poor memory skills, or a lack of familiarity with the test materials.

Deficits in Attention. Gelman (1969) tested one of these other possible deficits: improperly directed attention. She reasoned that very young children may be focusing their attention on the wrong dimension. For example, if they are asked to look for the object(s) with "more" in a conservation task, they may look at the "longer" row or the "higher" beaker in conservation of number or liquid quantity tasks, since in most instances in the child's life, "more" usually means longer or taller. Gelman hypothesized that, if she could train young nonconserving children to focus on the more relevant dimension by applying appropriate reinforcement techniques, she could get them to conserve. For example, in one condition she presented children with three cards, two of which had the same number of items but were different in length, and one of which had a different number of items but was similar in length to one of the other two cards (see Figure 9-6). She asked the children to pick the cards that had the "same number."

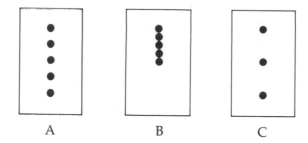

Figure 9-6. Reinforcement technique used by Gelman to train young children to perform correctly on a conservation of number task. Children were shown three cards, two of which had the same number of items on them but were different in length (*A* and *B*) and one of which had a different number of items but was similar in length to one of the other two cards (*C*). The children were asked to pick the cards with the "same number." If they correctly picked cards *A* and *B*, they were rewarded. If they incorrectly picked cards *A* and *C*, they were told that they were wrong. Using this training, Gelman was able to redirect their "attention" from the more dominant, but incorrect, cue (length) to the correct cue (number), so that even the supposedly preoperational children were then able to solve conservation of number problems. (Adapted from Gelman, 1969.)

Every time a child responded correctly (to number), he was rewarded. Every time he responded incorrectly (to length), he was told that he was wrong (nonreward). In this way, she redirected the child's attention away from the more dominant perceptual cue (length) and toward the correct cue (the number of items). Gelman's procedure was highly successful. Children who were initially unable to conserve "number" showed conservation when tested after this training. They even transferred the conservation abilities acquired in this number task to other conservation problems, such as conservation of quantity. And even more remarkably, they retained the conservation ability even one month after the original training.

Gelman's study provides provocative evidence that in many instances, children who appear not to have the operational systems of conservation do indeed possess them but are prevented from demonstrating those abilities by deficient attention.

Deficits in Memory. Still other psychologists have suggested that the poor performance of children under 5 on tasks such as transitivity may be due more to the child's forgetting the problem than it is to deficient logical operations. To illustrate this possibility, try to solve the following problem after reading it once and without the aid of pencil and paper:

> John is taller than Mary; Mary is taller than Jane; Jane is taller than Sally; Sally is taller than Sue. Is Sally taller than Mary?

In attempting this problem, you will probably have forgotten where Sally and Mary came in the series—and hence will fail to show transitivity. Obviously, this doesn't mean you don't possess transitivity. Rather, your failure simply means that you couldn't remember all of the data you needed to solve the problem. Tom Trabasso and his associates (that is, Bryant & Trabasso, 1971; Riley, 1975; Riley & Trabasso, 1974; Trabasso, 1977) have suggested that this kind of memory problem may exist for young children.

To test this hypothesis, Trabasso and his colleagues asked children not only about the critical transitive inference judgment (for example, "Is *A* greater than *C*?") but also about the individual seriation judgments needed to successfully perform the transitivity task (for example, "Is *A* greater than *B*?" "Is *B* greater than *C*?"). They reasoned that if the children had forgotten one of the original pairs (for example, that *B* is greater than *C*), they would not show correct transitive inferences due to this memory problem. Indeed, it was found that in the majority of instances where children under about 6 years of age failed the transitive inference task, they also failed to remember at least one of the original pairs. When the children remembered the original pairs, they were very likely to correctly complete the transitive inference. These studies point up that memory deficits may play a crucial role in whether or not a child demonstrates transitivity. The preoperational child may be unable to handle transitivity tasks not so much because he lacks the necessary cognitive structures (Piaget's "operations") but, instead, because he simply can't remember the needed information.

Deficits in Familiarity with the Task. One final factor that may well influence the young child's performance in various Piagetian tasks is his familiarity—or lack of familiarity—with the test situation. For example, a recent study of conservation abilities in rural, unschooled Guatemalan children found that although the children failed many traditional Piagetian conservation tests, over half of them showed conservation on the area of a farm, something with which the children were familiar (Lester & Klein, 1972).

Similarly, the kind of question asked in a classification problem may result in errors because children are not used to being asked to make such obvious and "silly" comparisons that span two hierarchical levels. And, in some cases, the young child may simply not be familiar with the higher-level concept. For example, when one supposedly preoperational child was asked whether there were "more dogs or more animals" after being told that there were "three dogs and two cats," she responded, "What's an animal?" Once the term *animal* had been defined in a way she could apparently grasp, she said, "more animals." Like the conservation example involving the Guatemalan children, her performance in a classification task seemed to be not so much a function of her cognitive thought processes as it was a function of her familiarity with the concepts involved.

Summary of Piaget's Theory of the Concrete Operational Child

According to Piaget, dramatic changes occur in the mental structures of children at about the ages of 6 to 7. Children master systems of logic called *operations* that are *interiorized* (done mentally and without the necessity of acting them out in behavior), involve *transformations* (the changes of objects from one state to another), and are *reversible* (can be mentally reversed, putting the objects back into their original states). These logical systems in turn enable the children to correctly analyze such difficult conceptual tasks as *conservation, addition of classes, seriation,* and *transitivity.*

Having set out these basic points in Piaget's theory, we cast a critical eye at several aspects of his theory. Certain criticisms focused on methodological weaknesses in Piaget's approach, including excessive reliance on verbal assessments, lack of systematic and objective observations, and the possibility of biased information. More important criticisms centered on theoretical issues. We saw how attentional, memory, and familiarity factors might have distorted Piaget's interpretations. Indeed, age-related changes in these other factors, rather than the use of logical operations, may explain many of the cognitive changes involved in the 5 to 7 shift.

AN ALTERNATIVE VIEW OF COGNITIVE DEVELOPMENT DURING THE SCHOOL YEARS: INFORMATION PROCESSING THEORY

Over the last several years, some psychologists have developed an extremely complex and sophisticated view of mental activity—for example, perception, memory, and thinking—as it normally occurs in human adults. This view, known as **information-processing theory,** argues that all forms of mental activity are really composed of a relatively large number of individual processes, each of which can influence behavior in significant ways. Take, for example, the processes involved in reading this book. In order to read successfully, you must be able to perform and coordinate very rapidly an enormously large number of individual behaviors. You must be able to control and focus your attention on a limited portion of the text, identify the words you are looking at, decide where to move your eye to focus on the next piece of text, and then integrate the new information with the information already read. Surprisingly, normal adult readers can carry out all these behaviors in less than a quarter of a second. Even more surprisingly, most children master this extremely complex skill during their first few years of school.

The skills involved in tasks such as reading—and indeed all complex thinking—are part of a highly complicated and varied cognitive system. This system is composed of many different components, each with unique characteristics. In order to understand the complexity of the changes that occur in the school child's intellectual growth, we therefore first need to look at the intricate complexity of the adult mind. Once we know more about the adult mind, we can ask more meaningfully just what changes take place in the child's mind during the school years.

A Microscopic Look at the Mind

In recent years, psychologists have gained considerable insight into the varied and complex workings of the mind. Figure 9-7 gives a schematic view of some important components of the mind. There are two things to notice initially: (1) what we call the *mind* or *cognition* is really a general term for a large number of individual processes or components; and (2) the component processes are linked to each other temporally. This last feature means that each act of thinking requires some finite amount of time, since each individual component takes some time to execute before it sends information to the next processing stage. Psychologists, working with the appropriate research tools, have attempted to "dissect" the mind and examine the individual components in isolation, as if under a microscope, to see how each works. Although some of the components and their operations are not yet fully understood, the present model will serve our purposes.

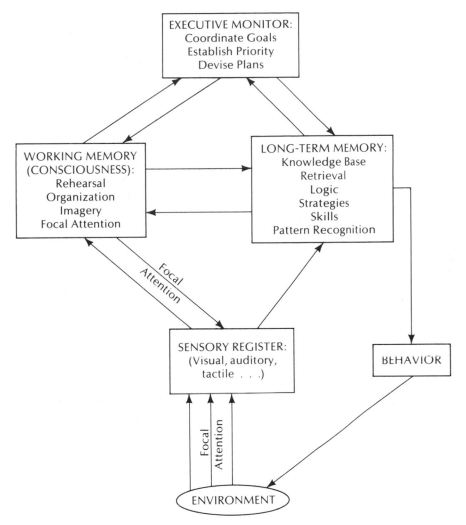

Figure 9-7.   A schematic drawing of one theory of the components of the mind and their temporal connections.

A 5-Cent Tour

It will be helpful to take a brief tour through the model to get a feeling for how it works. Let's take a simple example: how would we describe a woman looking up a phone number and making a phone call? In simple terms, we would say the person opens the phone book, finds the number, closes the book, picks up the phone, and dials the number. However, this seemingly simple sequence actually involves the execution and coordination of a large number of processes. Let us begin at the point where the person starts looking up the number.

The many numbers in the book constitute a complex array of environmental stimuli (represented by the "Environment" in Figure 9-7). In order to correctly search through the book, the person must know how phone books are organized—knowledge that will already be stored in her **long-term memory.** Once she finds the right page, she is still confronted with a huge array of information. At this point, she must begin to focus her attention on selected parts of the page (again aided by her long-term memory of how names are organized on a page). This we call *focal attention,* the process by which we focus on relevant information and filter out irrelevant information.

When our hypothetical person gets close to the name she desires, she will begin to look at each name in turn until she hits the correct one. This is known as *pattern recognition*—the process whereby we match incoming environmental stimuli with information stored in long-term memory. The information first passes through a **sensory register,** where it is held for only a brief period ($\frac{1}{4}$ second). Information from the sensory register then passes to **working (conscious) memory,** into which other information from long-term memory is likewise pulled, and the pattern-recognition process is executed.

If she does not find the desired match, she will keep searching, moving her eyes systematically down the page until the desired name is found. Once this is done, she moves her eyes laterally to look at the person's phone number. Looking at the number involves a pattern-matching process to numbers stored in long-term memory; simultaneously, the number is transferred to the working memory, which is really our conscious experience of having the number in mind. If at this point she closes the telephone book, she will almost automatically begin to **rehearse** the number—that is, say it over and over again so that it will not be forgotten or lost from working memory. She may also refrain from talking or listening to anyone for fear these activities might interfere with her remembering the number. With the number firmly fixed in working memory, she begins dialing the telephone (which involves more complicated matching between the digit in memory and locating its match on the telephone dial). Finally, if the desired person answers, the *executive function* directs her to immediately switch from one strategic plan—for simplicity, let's call it the "telephoning plan"—to still another strategic plan: the actual phone conversation.

You can see from this simple example how complicated our thoughts and behaviors are when viewed in this microscopic way. Just about any cognitive act involves the execution, sequencing, and coordination of many different processes, only a small number of which have been described here. It is evident that any one of these processes could change with age, especially during the school years. In addition, the control and coordination of these individual components (the so-called *executive monitor*) could show major age changes. It has been the goal of developmental psychologists over the last decade or so to chart the nature and extent of development of many of the processes described above and to show how they interact with and influence each other. As we shall see in the next section, some of these processes show little development during the school years; others show major changes.

We are going to divide our discussion into two major sections, each corresponding to a significant portion of the model outlined above. The first section deals with the development of processes and strategies for getting information from the environment into the mental system. The second section examines some of the age trends in working and long-term memory. Although we will discuss these sections separately, we will see how they are all interrelated.

We should first insert one important note: the work to be discussed is, in many instances, quite recent; therefore, our conclusions about some aspects of development are tentative. At present, these conclusions should be regarded as the best guesses of some—but by no means all—psychologists about the extent and nature of the child's cognitive growth.

Getting the Information into the System

The environment bombards us with a vast array of information—sounds, sights, tastes, smells. To meaningfully process this information, we have to be able to attend to, perceive, and search out the relevant from the irrelevant information. In the language of psychology, successful acquisition of information brings into play such mental processes as *sensory registers, processing speed,* and *selective attention,* as well as effective strategies for searching out and utilizing the various items of information. We shall discuss each of these processes in turn.

The Sensory Register

Many visual events occur so rapidly that we can only see them with a "single glance." When this happens, we have only a limited ability to report what we have seen. In fact, we can usually report only about five to seven different items (Miller, 1956; Sperling, 1960). Nevertheless, we often have the feeling that we saw more but simply can't "get at it." This intuitive feeling that we can see more than we can report led to the hypothesis of the existence of *sensory registers* by George Sperling in 1960.

In his now-classic experiment, Sperling devised an ingenious procedure to examine what happens to those items shown to subjects but not reported. In this procedure, called a *partial-report procedure,* an array of letters (or other figures) is displayed very briefly. However, subjects are not required to report everything in the display, but only one or a few letters. What the subject has to report on any particular trial is determined by a *cue* (for example, an arrow) that occurs at some time *after* the original array. (See Figure 9-8.)

This clever technique has produced some very interesting results. In particular, if the cue appears immediately after the original array has disappeared, subjects perform perfectly, as if the array or some precise image of it were still present in their visual memory. This finding led Sperling to suggest that the subject retains a full and detailed mental image of the exact stimulus for some period of time after the external stimulus has disappeared—sort of a temporary mental photograph. This short persistence of detailed visual information is called a *sensory register.*

The second major finding of Sperling's research was that if one gradually increases the amount of time between the array and the cue (out to about ¼ second), the subject's ability to report the desired item decreases quickly. This drop in performance suggests that although the visual information in the sensory register is initially detailed and complete, it loses detail and accuracy very quickly—or *decays.*

Finally, Sperling found that further increases in the time between the array and the cue beyond ¼ second had no effect on performance. This finding revealed that the sensory register is no longer operating, and that the information has been *processed* (or *coded*) and transferred into another, more permanent, memory store: the *working memory.*

Sperling's findings and interpretations have interesting implications for the psychologist studying the development of cognitive processes. Recall that when

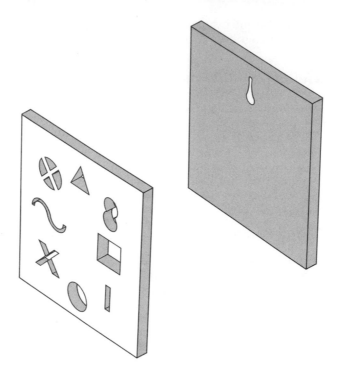

Figure 9-8. Schematic drawing of a partial-report procedure. Initially, an array of figures is flashed briefly and then disappears. Fractions of a second later, a teardrop indicator appears near where one of the figures had appeared. Subjects are required to say which figure the indicator was pointing to (here it is the triangle).

adults are briefly shown an array of items and asked to report everything they can, adults can usually report four or five different items. Interestingly, 5-year-old children can report only about two items (Haith, Morrison, Sheingold, & Mindes, 1970). It seems, then, that 5-year-old children are not as efficient as adults in the way they handle or process information.

In an attempt to understand why young children are able to remember fewer items than are adults, recent research with children has utilized partial report studies of the type just described. (Morrison, Holmes, & Haith, 1974; Sheingold, 1973). This research reveals that when the cue comes on immediately after the display, 5-year-olds can perform *as well* as adults. When, however, the cue is delayed beyond approximately ¼ second, adults perform much better.

This research suggests the following tentative conclusions. The difference between the performance of adults and of 5-year-olds seems not to be due to differences in their sensory registers. For both, the same amount of information apparently gets into the sensory register, and the sensory register lasts for about the same amount of time (approximately ¼ second). Our best guess is that the differences between 5-year-olds and adults reside in the way in which they code or transfer the information to working memory. Adults seem to be using a complex strategy for systematically processing and coding the items in the array and transferring them to working memory—hence their ability to recall much of the information even after it has decayed from the sensory register. Five-year-olds, in contrast, do not seem as strategic or systematic in coding the information as it decays from the sensory register—hence their reduced efficiency in recording and retrieving the information.

In sum, the results of these studies have suggested that some aspects of "getting the information into the system" do not change with age. Both the capacity and the duration of the sensory register appear to be equivalent in even young children and adults. However, children do appear deficient in coding information and transferring it to working memory.

Processing Speed

One possible explanation for the children's poorer performance at greater delays in the partial report task is that, in some sense, they process information more slowly. Recall that processing information takes time, even though subjectively we "feel" that perceiving and recognizing objects are almost instantaneous. Psychologists have devised a technique for studying the amount of time it takes to process a single piece of information (see Figure 9-9). In this technique, called a *masking procedure,* a stimulus (for example, a letter or geometric form) is flashed onto a screen very quickly, followed by a "masking stimulus." This masking stimulus is simply a sudden display of irrelevant information right where the stimulus had appeared, the effect of which is to overpower and obliterate the subject's perception of the earlier stimulus—much as a sudden loud noise would disrupt your ability to think about the sentence you're now reading. By varying the amount of time we give the subject to process the first stimulus before presenting the masking stimulus, we can estimate the time a person needs to process and recognize the first stimulus.

Using procedures such as these with young, grade-school children and adults, some researchers have found that children under age 6 or 7 need significantly more time to process and recognize a stimulus than do older children and adults (Bosco, 1972; Holmes, Olsho, & Nagy, in preparation). Other researchers have found no differences in this respect between young children and adults (Blake, 1974; Liss & Haith, 1970). Thus, at present we cannot say with certainty whether processing speed increases with age during the school years, since the available data are not consistent.

Processing speed remains a potentially important variable, however, especially when large amounts of information are to be taken in. If young children indeed process individual stimuli more slowly (as indicated by at least some of the research), then the cumulative effect of this deficit across large numbers of stimuli could be quite dramatic, with the result that the young child simply may not have available as much information for later processing. This, then, would at least in part explain their poorer performance in tasks that require them to retrieve and report the information.

Selective Attention

Another important process involved in processing information is **selective attention.** The environment contains a vast array of stimuli that would soon overwhelm us if it were not for our ability to "attend selectively." Selective attention refers to the reciprocal abilities to *focus on* relevant information and *filter out* irrelevant information. For example, in reading this page, you must be able to

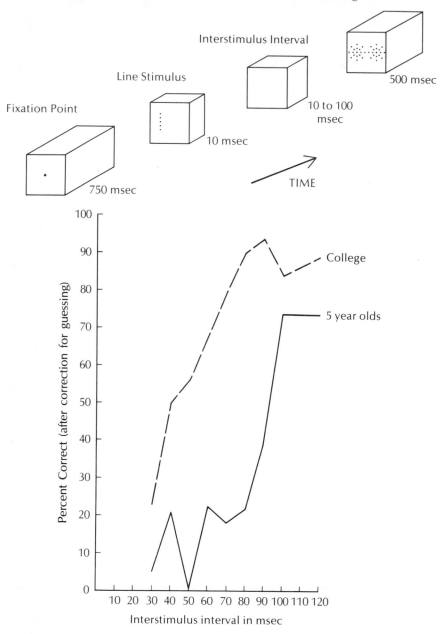

Figure 9-9. An illustration of visual masking. Basically the experiment comprises three sequential events: (1) *Stimulus*—each trial begins with a short presentation of a line stimulus (| or —); (2) *Interstimulus interval or Delay*— after the stimulus, a blank field appears. This blank field remains for a variable amount of time; and (3) *Mask*—after the specified delay, a masking stimulus appears.

The data from this study (Holmes, Olsho, & Nagy, in preparation) suggest that 5-year-olds take longer to process information than do adults. Note, for example, that it takes about 50 msec longer for the children than for the adults to reach a 50% accuracy point.

focus selectively on particular words and at the same time ignore, or filter out, the many other words on the page.

Although our knowledge of selective attention in children is still limited (Pick, 1975), the evidence we do have suggests tentatively that young children (under 8 years) are somewhat less able than adults to control their attentional processes (Hagen, 1967; Hale, 1975; Pick, 1975). They are more easily distracted and less flexible in shifting their attention between different items of relevant information. In one study (Pick, Christy, & Frankel, 1972), for example, second-grade and sixth-grade children were shown two colored wooden animals and had to make a judgment about some aspect of the animals: for example, whether they were the same color or the same shape. To perform this task efficiently, the children had to focus on the relevant aspect (for example, color) and ignore other, irrelevant aspects of the animals (for example, shape). The older children responded more quickly than did the younger children, indicating that they could make this judgment faster. Moreover, in one condition of the test, the children were told the relevant aspect *before* the animals were shown. This clue should have helped the children to focus immediately on the relevant aspect and to ignore everything else. In this case, the older children responded even faster than they had before; the younger children, however, showed *little change*. The older group, then, was able to use the clue to help focus their attention on the relevant feature and ignore the irrelevant features. The younger children continued to process some irrelevant aspects, and their response times were slowed down as a result.

Although the above study indicates that younger children are less able to focus attention (that is, are less selective than are older children), this is not always the case. In some instances, young children appear to be *more* selective in the sense that they are less able to shift from one item of relevant information to a new one. In one study (Pick, 1975), children 7 to 12 years of age were presented with a large box full of multicolored letters of the alphabet. The children were asked to search through the box to find all the As, Ss and Ls. Unknown to the children, all the instances of a particular letter were in the same color. Only the older children noticed this clue and used it to their advantage in searching through the pile. The younger children were more selective—they rigidly focused their attention on the relevant information (As, Ss and Ls) and thus failed to pick up the unmentioned clue (color). Thus, the older children showed greater flexibility in the way they directed their attention.

Our knowledge of just how attention works is far from complete. However, it appears that as children grow older, they become better able to control attention and to adapt it to the demands of different tasks. When a high degree of selectivity is called for, older children can more readily focus on the relevant and ignore the irrelevant. When less selectivity is appropriate, older children seem likewise better able to broaden their focus and take in more relevant information. Selective attention thus progresses in schoolchildren toward both greater control and greater flexibility.

Visual Search

When an adult—or a young child—"looks around" for something, he is engaged in what is called a *visual search*. He is visually searching the environment for relevant items of information. In these visual search tasks, the younger child (below approximately 7 years) is again hampered by deficiencies in his attentional skills. In general, young children do not seem to adopt a systematic plan in visually searching their environment: they instead focus on less informative parts of the environment, and they are less thorough and efficient in doing the search (Day, 1975).

An experiment by Vurpillot (1968) illustrates these points. In her study, Vurpillot showed two houses to children between 3 and 9 years of age. Each house contained six windows, each with different features. In some cases, all of the windows in the two houses were identical; in other cases, one or more windows in one house were different from those in the other house. The child had to decide whether the two houses were "identical." Vurpillot recorded the children's eye movements as they moved their eyes back and forth, comparing the two houses. Though even the youngest children (3-year-olds) could perform the task, there were marked changes with age in their search-and-comparison behavior. The youngest children (aged 3 to 6 years) appeared to scan the windows of the houses nonsystematically, making few close comparisons of corresponding windows. The older children (aged 7 to 9 years), in contrast, tended to make systematic comparisons between corresponding windows. Thus, the older children were more systematic and logical in their search behavior. In addition, the older children searched more exhaustively and efficiently—they continued to compare windows until they reached the end and were certain that all windows were the same, or they stopped immediately upon finding a difference. The youngest children, on the other hand, often gave up too early after finding that the first few windows were the same, or continued to search even after finding a difference.

In all, this study and others have shown that in searching for and gathering information, there is an increase with age in the use of systematic, planful, and efficient strategies. Older children appear better able to determine what to look for and how to look for it.

Encoding and Transfer to Working Memory

The final processes we will consider are those directly involved in placing information in *working memory* and, in some instances, in *long-term memory*. We have already alluded to the greater use of strategies by older children in transferring information from the sensory register to working memory. There is a further aspect of this transfer process that also appears to develop with age.

Whenever we look at a complex stimulus, there are a number of dimensions or features that we can focus on and commit to memory. We call this process **encoding,** to refer to the fact that in our memories we do not keep a literal copy of the stimulus we see. We *code* or transform the stimulus in some way, so as to retain what is important, while "forgetting" those aspects that are not important—sort of a "memory shorthand." For example, in looking at a complex stimulus, we could focus on and encode its color, shape, size, or distance, or we could encode its name or we could list some objects it is associated with.

Some psychologists have hypothesized that children perhaps differ from adults in the kinds of encodings they normally utilize. In general, research tends to bear this hypothesis out: young children tend to encode only one or a few dimensions; as children grow older, they increase the number of dimensions that they include in their mental shorthand and engage in *multiple encoding*. The net result is that older children get more information concerning the object into their memory.

The procedure psychologists have used to examine these encoding processes is basically as follows. Children are first shown a number of different stimuli (for example, words). Then they are shown these same words mixed together with a lot of other new words and are required to say for each word whether or not it was previously shown. Some of the new words are completely different from the old words, while others are similar. For example, if one of the original words was "dog," a new word might be "log" or "cat." If a child erroneously says that he saw "log" on the original list, we can assume from this error that when he saw "dog" originally, he encoded the word's sound, and when tested with a similar-sounding word, became confused and made an error. Similarly, if he falsely recognized the new word "cat" on the test, we can assume that he encoded the old word "dog" semantically (as an *animal*) and thus confused it with the semantically similar word "cat."

Several experiments have used this technique to examine encoding differences in children (Bach & Underwood, 1970; Felzen & Anisfeld, 1970; Freund & Johnson, 1972; Hall & Halperin, 1972). In general, they have found that the older the child, the more likely he is to make a wide variety of different kinds of errors, while younger children (up to about 7 years of age) tend to err predominantly on only one or two dimensions. Thus, older children may make errors on items that look the same, sound the same, or are related in meaning. Younger children's errors tend to predominate on only a few features. These results suggest that older children are indeed engaging in a richer, more elaborate encoding operation (multiple encoding), resulting in a greater number of relevant features being stored in memory.

Summary of Getting the Information into the System

The material that we have discussed in the immediately preceding pages suggests that young children under the age of 5 or 6 differ in several respects from school-aged children (over 7) and adults in how they acquire information from the environment and in the mental processes they use for coding and interpreting that information. Their *sensory registers* (a temporary persistence of detailed information), at least in the visual system, appear to be no different from those of adults. However, older children and adults seem to be much more effective at getting information from the sensory register into *working memory*. A number of factors may contribute to and account for this difference. Differences in *processing speed* (the time it takes to process the information) may be partially responsible. A further likely factor is *selective attention* (the ability to focus on relevant information and filter out irrelevant information), with attention being both more flexible and better controlled in older children. Similarly, in searching about the environment (*visual search*), older children seem to be more efficient in searching for relevant information. Finally, older children *encode* (record in working memory) more relevant information, with these *multiple encodings* providing them with a richer, more detailed storage of information to work from later.

Working and Long-Term Memory

We have talked about how information gets from the environment into the mental system: after first being attended to and recognized, vital pieces of the information are encoded from the sensory register and transferred into the mental system. But what is this "mental system" into which the information flows? Different psychologists have referred to it with different terms; thus, it has been called *short-term memory, primary memory, conscious memory,* and *working memory.* We prefer the terms *working memory* or *conscious memory,* since these better express the crucial aspect of this cognitive activity: working memory is that portion of our cognitive activity of which we are most aware, since it is (probably) in working memory that our *conscious* intellectual work is carried out. As such, working memory differs from what we call *long-term memory,* this being the actual storehouse of information into which working memory feeds, and from which it draws, specific items of information.

Imagine long-term memory as a recording of a Beethoven symphony. Working memory is the portion of the record that we hear at a given moment in time; it is meaningful and pleasing to the ear. If, however, we were to hear all of the sounds on the record simultaneously, the result would be an overwhelming cacophony of sound. Working memory thus serves the vital function of keeping the amount of information being processed within reasonable bounds—in fact, as we noted earlier, the maximum number of unrelated items of information that working memory seems to be able to handle simultaneously is in the neighborhood of five to seven items (Miller, 1956).

Our analogy is not completely accurate, however, for working memory is not simply concerned with the playing back of information from long-term memory. It is also actively involved in the feeding of information into long-term memory and the processing of current information that does not actually get into long-term memory. Discussion of three processes associated with working and long-term memory helps clarify this point: *rehearsal, organization,* and *retrieval.*

Recall from our earlier example of dialing the telephone that after closing the telephone book, the person repeated the number over and over to herself, so as not to forget it. This process of repetition is called **rehearsal** and, as in our telephone example, serves to keep information in memory. Without adequate rehearsal, much information would be quickly lost. Thus, rehearsal is a process that facilitates remembering.

Another memory process is **organization,** which is best explained with another example. Suppose the number the person had looked up in the phone book was 234-5678. If she realized that the number was composed of the seven consecutive digits starting with the number "2," she probably could have formulated this rule in her head and dispensed with rehearsing the individual numbers. Thus, by organization, we mean the tendency to find higher-order relations or rules between seemingly distinct objects or events. As we shall see, the tendency to utilize sophisticated organizational techniques to facilitate remembering increases during the school years.

Finally, there are a group of processes called **retrieval.** Distinct from rehearsing and organizing information in memory, retrieval processes occur at the time you are trying to remember something: that is, pull it out of long-term memory and get it back into working (conscious) memory. We have all had the experience of misplacing some object and trying to remember where we left it. We search through our memories trying to recall the last time we saw it, or the last time we had it in our possession, thereby trying to reason where it could be or where it could not be. In attempting to remember, we engage in a vast assortment of search procedures, logical arguments, and decisions. All these processes constitute sophisticated retrieval strategies and, as we shall discuss later, they become increasingly more prevalent in children of school age.

Rehearsal

There is a great deal of evidence that suggests that 4- and 5-year-old children have an extremely limited ability to remember things for even short periods of time (for example, Haith et al., 1970; Ornstein, Naus, & Liberty, 1975). Although a number of explanations for this deficit have been offered, one of the most reasonable explanations centers on the process of *rehearsal*. Early research led some psychologists to the conclusion that young children do not rehearse at all (Flavell, 1970).

For example, in some early experiments, John Flavell and his associates (Flavell, Beach, & Chinsky, 1966; Keeney, Cannizzo, & Flavell, 1967) watched the lip movements of 5- to 10-year-old children who were trying to remember some pictures. The results of these studies showed dramatic increases in the amount of lip movement (presumably rehearsal activity) in the older children, as opposed to the younger ones. In fact, only about 10% of the 5-year-olds seemed to rehearse. Moreover, within any particular age group, those children who showed lip movements—and who were therefore assumed to be rehearsing—could remember more pictures than those who showed no lip movement. From these observations, Flavell and his colleagues concluded that most 5-year-olds do not spontaneously rehearse information when trying to remember it, and that it is this lack of rehearsal that accounts for their generally poor memory.

More recently, however, psychologists have found that in certain situations, children as young as 4 or 5 do seem to engage in spontaneous rehearsal (for example, Garrity, 1975). However, even when they do rehearse, these young children seem not to rehearse as *effectively* as older children and adults; the rehearsal strategies of younger children are less systematic and organized.

For example, a recent series of studies by Ornstein, Naus and their colleagues (Ornstein, Naus, & Liberty, 1975) used a very ingenious "overt rehearsal" technique—in which children said the words to be remembered aloud as they were presented—to examine the rehearsal strategies of children in the third and eighth grades. Table 9-1 shows the typical rehearsal patterns of younger and older children. As you can see, they are quite different. The third-graders rehearsed each successively presented word in isolation or with the immediately preceding word. The eighth-graders, in contrast, rehearsed more actively, mixing several different words together in each rehearsal and making sure the earlier-presented words continued to be rehearsed. Thus, the third-grade children's rehearsal was less organized and more tied to the specific word present, whereas the eighth-grade children showed a more active, organized *cumulative rehearsal* strategy.

These observations provide one explanation for why older, school-aged children are more effective than preschoolers at "remembering." The older children use more efficient, sophisticated methods of rehearsing desired information, thereby not only doing a better job of keeping the information in working (conscious) memory but, quite likely, also doing a better job of getting the information into long-term memory for later retrieval.

Organization

The development of sophisticated rehearsal strategies is just one of the skills that develop during the school years. A second, equally important skill involves the ability to recognize and utilize the "rules" that link various events together.

Table 9-1.   Typical rehearsal pattern of third and eighth graders.

The third graders predominantly repeat and rehearse the last presented word, whereas the eighth graders incorporate and keep rehearsing words presented earlier (a strategy known as *cumulative rehearsal*).

Word Presented	Third Graders' Rehearsal	Eighth Graders' Rehearsal
Dog	Dog, dog, dog	Dog, dog, dog
Pen	Pen, pen, pen, dog	Pen, dog, pen, dog
Book	Book, book, book	Book, pen, dog, book, pen, dog
Flag	Flag, flag, flag	Flag, book, pen, dog, flag, book, pen, dog
Cup	Cup, cup, cup	Cup, flag, book, pen, dog, cup, flag, book, pen, dog

We call this ability *organization*. During the school years—and perhaps throughout life—the child becomes better able to organize material that he wants to remember.

In order to clarify the concept of organization, consider the following example. Suppose you were shown the following two lists of words and asked to recall each of them. Which could you recall more easily?

1. Chair, train, farmer, dish, year, clock, paper, grass, word.
2. Apples, oranges, bananas, shirt, pants, tie, car, truck, boat.

The second list is easier to recall once you realize that the nine words in it are composed of three separate "categories" (fruits, clothes, and vehicles). By recognizing that the words are grouped into categories, you form a higher-order rule and then use the rule to help you at the time of recall. Indeed, experiments have shown that recall of such categorized lists is much easier than recall of lists of unrelated words (Flavell & Wellman, 1977).

Is this true for young children? In general, studies have shown that up to about the third grade, children's recall of categorizable items is not much better than their recall of unrelated items. Older children, in contrast, recall categorizable items much better than unrelated items (Lange, 1973; Vaughn, 1968). These findings imply that older children make better use of organization to help them remember things.

One possible way to help even younger children organize material might be to present the material in a "blocked" fashion (that is, all items from one category first, from the next category second, and so on). To test this possibility, one experiment (Yoshimura, Moely, & Shapiro, 1971) presented children 4 to 10 years of age with categorizable stimuli. For some of the children, the stimuli had been blocked into categories, while for other children, items from different categories were all mixed together. It was found that the older children benefited from having the items blocked, but the younger children did not. Other studies have shown some slight improvement by blocking items for younger children (Cole, Frankel & Sharp, 1971; Kobasigawa & Middleton, 1972), but, in general, the results reveal that young children appear not to notice or utilize the categorical structure of materials presented to them.

Skill at organization thus appears to be another ability that makes older, school-aged children more adept at remembering things than their younger, preschool counterparts. As children progress through school, they become increasingly more effective at noticing and utilizing higher-order relations among stimuli and more likely to organize or group items together on the basis of such higher-order relations. Like rehearsal, this growing organizational ability in turn makes the older children more effective at keeping the information in working memory and getting it into long-term memory in a form that can later be retrieved.

Retrieval

As mentioned earlier, working or conscious memory can be filled not only by items currently or recently available, but also by items that occurred long in the past. This process of searching for and transferring past experiences from long-term memory (our mental storehouse of information) into working memory is called *retrieval.*

Successful retrieval depends heavily on our ability to find what we are looking for. Moreover, studies show that we are much more likely to be successful in this search if our original experience was categorized or organized at the time it occurred (Cole, Frankel, & Sharp, 1971). Since young children seem not to effectively organize information at the time they experience it, it is not surprising that they also have later difficulties in retrieval.

Interestingly, however, a recent study by Morrison and Lord (1978) suggests that the relationship between age, organization, and retrieval is not as straightforward as simple logic might suggest. Logically, we would expect that if deficiencies in organization skills keep young children from efficiently getting information into memory (as suggested by the studies discussed in the preceding section), this would mean that the information simply would not be there for later retrieval. In their study, however, Morrison and Lord found that organization skills may play an especially significant role not simply at the time of information input but also, perhaps even more importantly, at the time of retrieval.

In this study, 5- and 8-year-old children and adults were shown three categories of pictures, with five pictures in each category. First, the pictures were presented in either a "blocked" fashion (by category) or a random fashion, and subjects were free to recall the items in any order they chose. As expected, the 8-year-olds and adults recalled more items in the blocked condition than they did when items were randomly presented, while 5-year-olds did not benefit much from the categorized list. However, it was possible to dramatically improve the performance of the 5-year-olds if, at the time of recall, the children were *reminded* of the categories and forced to recall items category by category. This forced use of categories produced only small increases in the performance of the older children and adults, however, since they already were spontaneously making use of categories in their recall strategies.

Similar findings have been made by other researchers (Halperin, 1974; Scribner & Cole, 1972). What do these findings suggest? A provocative possibility is that the memory difference between young, preschool children and older, school-aged children rests not so much in whether the information is getting into memory as it does in how the children get the information back out—that is, retrieval. Somehow, even the very young children seem to be getting at least some information into memory—hence their ability to retrieve the information when "forced" to use sophisticated retrieval strategies. Unlike the older children and adults, however, the young children are apparently unable to make *spontaneous* use of organizational strategies at the time of retrieval.

If this interpretation is correct, organization and retrieval do not appear as distinct processes. Rather, organization appears as a vehicle to aid memory by facilitating retrieval, and their coordination becomes increasingly mastered as children progress through the school years.

ISSUE

Why can't we remember much about our experiences prior to the age of about 5?

Psychologists have long been intrigued by the phenomenon of *infantile amnesia*, or the inability to remember much of our life before the ages of 4 or 5. Although the exact reason for this phenomenon is unknown, it may be intimately related to some of the major changes in cognitive ability—and especially memory—that we have just discussed. One common argument is that the child's failure to use active, planful, and spontaneous organization strategies in remembering events makes such events essentially unavailable for later retrieval. Such a view argues that although we have retained memories of early childhood, these memories are so disorganized that we can no longer find them. In a sense, we can draw an analogy between early childhood memory and a large box filled with millions of slips of paper, each bearing the description of a particular experience. Since all the slips are mixed up, it is extremely unlikely that we could ever find the one we are looking for.

The "Can't/Doesn't" Controversy

Up to now, we have been describing how the young child in a variety of circumstances fails to use sophisticated rehearsal, organizational, and retrieval strategies that older children routinely draw upon in helping them to remember. Initially, researchers thought that children younger than 6 or 7 did not possess the requisite knowledge or skills and, therefore, *could not* behave in a strategic way. However, more recent studies suggest that even 4- and 5-year-old children may indeed have some knowledge of rehearsal and organization but simply may not activate or utilize that knowledge or skill. Rather than saying that young children *can't* rehearse or organize, it may therefore be more accurate to say that they *can but don't*, **the can't/doesn't controversy.**

One way to test this idea directly is through "training" studies. If you can train a young child to rehearse more actively or organize more efficiently than he otherwise would, you have evidence that he does indeed possess the requisite capability (he "can") but that for some reason he doesn't utilize it.

A number of such training studies have been done, and almost uniformly, they have succeeded. For example, one study (Naus, Ornstein, & Aivano, 1977) tried to improve the rehearsal skills of young children. Recall that third-graders typically rehearse only one or two items at a time. In this study, the third-graders were trained to rehearse in the more active, organized fashion of older children; namely, to rehearse three items together—the word just presented and any two previous items. They found that the young children, when so trained, followed the instructions, rehearsed more actively, and increased their memory performance. This study showed that third-graders could utilize the more mature rehearsal pattern, but only when prompted or instructed to do so.

Why Don't Children When They Could?

Several possible factors may contribute to the young child's failure to utilize memory strategies that he possesses. One possible explanation is that the younger the child, the less "knowledge" he possesses about his memory skills and about when it is appropriate to use them. (The study of what children know about their memories has been called *metamemory*—Flavell & Wellman, 1977). For example, if you ask children to guess how many words they expect to remember in a memory test, 8- and 10-year-old children are fairly accurate at estimating their actual performance. Five- and 6-year-old children, on the other hand, estimate that they will recall far more than they actually can (Kreutzer, Leonard, & Flavell, 1975). Although there is the possibility that the younger children may be trying to show off or impress the adult experimenter, this result implies that young children simply don't know as much about their memory abilities as do older children.

Similarly, children of different ages approach memory tasks differently. If an older child knows his memory will be tested, he makes special efforts to retain as much information as he can. For example, in one study (Appel, Cooper, McCarrell, Sims-Knight, Yussen, & Flavell, 1972), 5- to 10-year-old children were told to look at some materials. Some of the children were told in advance that their memory of the materials would be tested, while others were not. Older children showed distinctly different behaviors when preparing for what they knew would be a memory test; they studied more and recalled more.

Younger children, however, did not show any different behavior even when they were told that a memory test was coming—indicating that they did not realize that active study and utilization of strategies could help their memories. Thus, a further possible reason the younger child does not use the strategies of which he is capable is that he doesn't realize that these strategies would improve his performance.

These "metamemory factors" are not, however, the only possible contributing causes. Another possible explanation is that the use of sophisticated memory strategies may simply require too much *effort* for the young child. Although the young child may be able to learn and perform at a higher level, it may take much more effort for him to do than it would take an older child. We know that the early stages of learning in any task, such as driving a car, require a lot of concentration and effort; in contrast, after having learned the skill, we can perform even complex actions seemingly effortlessly. Perhaps for the young child, utilizing the more mature strategies requires too much effort. For example, we do know that left to his own devices, the young child will often revert to his less strategic behavior after successfully using a more mature strategy (Keeney et al., 1967). It may be that the mature strategy requires more effort than he is willing to give.

Summary of Working and Long-Term Memory

We have examined several processes associated with working and long-term memory. *Working (conscious) memory* we have defined as that portion of our cognitive activity in which our conscious intellectual work is carried out. *Long-term memory* we have defined as the actual storehouse of information into which working memory feeds, and from which it draws, specific items of information.

The specific memory processes that we have examined are *rehearsal, organization,* and *retrieval.* We have examined these particular processes in an attempt to not only clarify the differences—and the interactions—between working and long-term memory but, in addition, to show how these processes change as children pass through the school years, thereby producing changes in the children's memory abilities. We have seen that *rehearsal* becomes progressively more active and organized as children pass through the school years; older children rehearse more items together in a coherent plan than do younger children. We have seen, too, that *organizational strategies* increase during the school years; older children are better able to see and utilize higher-order categorical relations between items and thereby aid their memory. Additionally, we have seen that with increasing age comes an increase in the use of more sophisticated *retrieval strategies*—strategies for retrieving information from long-term memory—and that these retrieval strategies are closely intertwined with the child's organizational skills. Finally, we have seen that while the younger, preschool child has at least a limited capacity for using the more sophisticated rehearsal, organizational and retrieval skills of his older, school-age counterpart, he for some reason fails to effectively utilize this capacity, due in part to *metamemory factors* (the child's limited awareness of his own capabilities and the significance of these capabilities) and to the greater amount of effort required by younger children in using these developing skills.

Information Processing Theory: An Alternative Explanation of the 5 to 7 Shift

The material that we have discussed in connection with information processing theory suggests that the term 5 *to 7 shift* is actually something of a misnomer. As children mature during the school years, changes gradually evolve in their methods of processing information. Thus, they become progressively more adept at using mental strategies such as rehearsal, organization, and retrieval to encode information from their sensory registers into working and long-term memory in a form that will stay intact and from which desired information can later be efficiently retrieved.

Viewed in this light, the so-called 5 to 7 shift is neither a sudden shift in abilities nor limited to the ages of 5 to 7. Rather, it is a process of change that progressively evolves well beyond the age of 7. Moreover, it is a process of change that seems to be due not so much to differences in underlying capacities as to differences in what the children actually do with their capacities.

A CLOSING QUESTION: WHICH CAUSES WHICH?

In a way, the material we have just discussed brings us full circle back to a question we asked at the outset of this chapter: does school "cause" the 5 to 7 shift, or does the shift instead make successful schooling possible? The training studies discussed earlier—in which young children through training came to rehearse and remember as well as older children—suggest that it is perhaps school that is the impetus; school may somehow "train" children to effectively use their latent mental abilities.

Several other findings, however, can be cited to support the opposite conclusion. We shall mention two of the more interesting of these: the first based upon cross-cultural research, and the second upon biological research.

Cross-Cultural Evidence

One possible way of approaching the question of whether training in school causes the 5 to 7 shift is by examining the cognitive development of children in cultures where children do not receive much formal schooling or begin school at a much later age. If the same basic developmental patterns are observed at approximately the same ages as here in the United States, we would have at least some evidence for a fundamental and universal developmental sequence *independent* of schooling. If, however, children in these other cultures lag far behind the formally schooled children of our own culture, or fail to develop certain higher-order skills, we would have evidence of a direct influence of formal schooling upon cognitive growth.

Several such cross-cultural studies have been conducted and have found that the kinds of basic cognitive changes seen in school children in our own society seem to emerge at about the same age in even "unschooled" populations of children. For example, Price-Williams (1962) studied *classification* skills among a group of unschooled children in Nigeria and found them to be about the same as comparable-aged Western children. Similarly, Goodnow (1969) worked with unschooled children in Hong Kong and found that their lack of schooling did not adversely affect their ability to *conserve* weight or volume. In another large series of studies of the *memory* skills of a group of unschooled children in Liberia (Cole & Scribner, 1974), it was found that while the children did not "organize" material according to semantic categories in the same manner as Western children, they did possess other sophisticated memory skills and memory strategies, particularly in telling stories or dealing with familiar objects or events.

There is thus cross-cultural evidence that certain fundamental skills like memory, conservation, and classification develop independently of formal education. However, this evidence may be somewhat misleading insofar as it rests on the assumption that lack of a "formal," Western-style education makes the children "unschooled"; it may be that the lack of formal schooling in these other cultures is, at least for purposes of developing basic cognitive skills, amply offset by the informal schooling that these children receive at home and in the community.

Moreover, other studies have shown that regardless of whether or not formal education is a must for the development of basic cognitive skills (which it apparently is not), formal education does *accelerate* the emergence of skills such as conservation (Bruner, Olver, & Greenfield, 1966) and higher levels of reasoning and thinking (Goodnow & Bethon, 1966). In addition, it is clear that beyond basic cognitive skills, formal schooling plays a direct role in fostering arithmetic and reading skills—skills that themselves come to later influence how children reason, think, and gain access to information about the world.

Biological Changes

Of parallel significance has been recent research concerned with biological changes that occur in children during the early school years. If dramatic biological changes occur at about this time, then perhaps the cognitive changes already discussed are in effect signposts of biological changes that facilitate the 5 to 7 shift.

There is indeed evidence of what is sometimes called a mid-growth spurt that occurs in some aspects of body growth during the early school years. In particular, measures of weight and body width (for example, hip width in females) show a marked acceleration around 6 or 7 years of age.

Even more provocative are certain biological changes that occur at about this time in the brain itself. One of these changes involves **myelination.** Myelination is the process whereby a fatty substance (myelin) surrounds neurons in the brain. This process begins at the lower brain centers and proceeds gradually to the higher brain centers. While the process continues for many years in humans—possibly well into adulthood (Campbell & Spear, 1972)—those brain centers responsible for higher-order thinking (the association cortex) begin to be heavily myelinated *during the school years.* This latter fact seems especially suggestive for our purposes, since neural impulses travel much *faster* in myelinated than in nonmyelinated neurons.

Another change that occurs during this period involves *arborization.* Arborization is the process whereby individual nerve cells develop more and more connections (or branches) with other nerve cells, thereby increasing the number and diversity of connections between cells. There is suggestive evidence that arborization occurs most predominantly during periods of rapid developmental progress (Campbell & Spear, 1972). The early school years would be such a period.

It is certainly intriguing that major changes in the brain appear to occur across the same age span as major changes in cognitive ability. Indeed, it is not hard to imagine how changes in myelination and arborization might facilitate some of the psychological processes discussed elsewhere, such as information-processing speed and memory skills. Nevertheless, it must be emphasized that we cannot tell from these biological observations alone whether there is a causal connection between the two, let alone which may come first and "cause" the other. For example, one could argue either that myelination and arborization of the higher brain centers make possible the rapid cognitive advances of the early school years *or* that the accelerated mental stimulation of the early school years produces this myelination and arborization *or* that these processes occur independently of one another. In short, though we have some highly provocative findings, they must be pursued further before definitive conclusions can be drawn.

PROVIDING AN OPTIMAL ENVIRONMENT

How does one provide an optimal environment for cognitive development during the early school years? This question cannot be answered in any simple form, because of the extreme complexity of the changes in learning and cognition that take place at this time. This extreme complexity is reflected in the fact that this chapter has, for the sake of keeping our discussion within reasonable bounds, been limited to more general concepts, rather than an examination of specific skills. Thus, we have examined such basic issues as conservation, classification, and memory, while not discussing such specific skills as reading and arithmetic. This is not to say that the specific skills are less important but simply that a line had to be drawn somewhere, and the line that was drawn was between the general and the specific. We shall draw a similar line in this discussion of providing the optimal environment and shall, therefore, suggest some of the ways in which the general skills discussed in this chapter can be fostered and promoted.

Stated generally, the optimal environment during the early school years is one that takes into account three particularly important factors. The first is the fact that the child's thought processes during the school years are characterized by a marked shift toward conceptual, generalized strategies and away from mechanical strategies tied to the physical properties of particular objects; in fact, it is the development of these conceptual strategies that accounts for most of the cognitive changes that occur at this time. The second key factor is the fact that these conceptual strategies are not as firmly developed if they are forced on the child; rather, they develop best if the child is able to discover them for himself. The third and final factor that we shall mention here concerns the child's memory skills; initially, these memory skills are quite weak, for the child has not yet developed the more sophisticated techniques for remembering used by older children and adults.

How, then, can we best go about taking these factors into account when working with the child? With respect to the first two factors (inducing the child to "discover cognitive strategies" for himself), we should keep in mind the following basic rule: The tasks and instructions that the child is given should, in the beginning, be kept simple and involve objects and concepts with which he is already familiar. For example, if the child is being taught to add up classes of objects, the objects themselves and the classes into which they fall should be those he is familiar with (for example, clothing such as pants and socks), not exotic, never-before-seen animals (such as llamas and camels). If the child is presented with a conservation of liquid task, care should be taken to make sure he understands just what is meant by the question "Which has more in it?"

With respect to the third factor (weaknesses in his memory skills), some specific suggestions can be made from our discussion of information processing theory. The child should be encouraged to *rehearse* items he is trying to remember and, especially, to rehearse several items at a time. He should be given plenty of time to look at the objects he is trying to remember, so that he can adequately rehearse and organize them. Finally, his attention should, whenever possible, be drawn to the relationships between items, with one especially effective way of doing this being the *blocking* technique discussed earlier (organizing the objects category by category), coupled with attempts to prod the child into using organizational strategies when retrieving the information from his memory.

SUMMARY OF LEARNING AND COGNITIVE DEVELOPMENT DURING THE SCHOOL YEARS

The early school years are a period of cognitive change so dramatic and rapid in their apparent onset that a special phrase has been coined to refer to this period: the *5 to 7 shift*. We have examined some learning tasks (*classical condition-*

ing, discrimination, transposition, and *reversal-nonreversal shifts*) that have been used to test the nature of these changes and have seen that the following common theme runs through them: a shift away from the "mechanical" mental processes of the preschool period, toward mental processes that are more conceptual and strategic.

We examined the views of one of the leading theoreticians on the subject: Jean Piaget. According to Piaget, dramatic and relatively sudden changes occur in the mental structures of children at about the ages of 6 or 7. They master logical systems of thought (called *operations*) that sharply distinguish their thinking from that of the preoperational period. Through mastery of these operations, the concrete operational child (unlike the preoperational child) is able to handle such complex analytical tasks as *conservation, classification,* and *seriation/transitivity.*

In evaluating Piaget's theory, we saw that shifts in thinking between 5 and 7 years of age appear neither so abrupt nor so focused on logic as Piaget hypothesized. We therefore examined an alternative explanation (information-processing theory) of at least some of the changes that are taking place. We looked at a number of studies that reveal basic differences between preschool children and older, school-age children in how they get information from the environment through the *sensory registers* and into *working memory* (conscious thought) and *long-term memory* (differences in *selective attention, visual search, encoding,* and possibly even *processing speed*) and in the actual mechanisms of their memory (*rehearsal, organization,* and *retrieval*). Finally, we explored some evidence that these differences in "mental strategies" may be due not so much to differences in underlying mental capacities (what the child "can" do), but instead, to *metamemory factors* and to the initial difficulty of mastering these developing strategies—a difficulty that possibly may be overcome eventually through *biological* maturation of brain cells that occurs during the early school years.

SUGGESTED READINGS

Brainerd, C. J. *Piaget's theory of intelligence.* Englewood Cliffs, N. J.: Prentice-Hall, 1978. A thorough look at Piaget's theory that includes a good deal of recent research replicating and/or contradicting Piaget's work.

Estes, W. K. (Ed.). *Handbook of learning and cognitive processes* (Vol. 1). Hillsdale, N.J.: Erlbaum, 1975. A difficult though valuable series of papers on recent information-processing research on human cognition.

Kail, R. V., & Hagen, J. W. (Eds.). *Perspectives on the development of memory and cognition.* Hillsdale, N.J.: Erlbaum, 1977. A series of papers reviewing most current work on the development of memory and thought, including chapters on metamemory, encoding, organization, and retrieval. There is a particularly valuable chapter by Trabasso on the role of memory in making Piagetian-type inferences.

GLOSSARY

addition of classes. One advance made by the concrete operational child whereby the child develops the ability to fully classify a group of objects.

can't/doesn't controversy. A phenomenon shown by young children who appear to possess a sophisticated memory skill (like rehearsal or organization) but who, unlike older children, do not normally use the skill to improve memory.

concrete operational period. The third period of cognitive development, according to Piaget's theory, in which the child attains the ability to coordinate thoughts into a system.

conservation. A major accomplishment of the concrete operational period whereby the child learns that certain properties of objects (for example, number, quantity, and volume) remain the same across more observable changes (in length or shape).

encoding. The process whereby incoming information is transformed for processing by later stages (for example, short-term or long-term memory).

5 to 7 shift. The widespread and seemingly rapid shift in cognitive functioning between 5 and 7 years of age. May be due to maturational effects as well as to schooling.

information-processing theory. A framework for describing human cognition that emphasizes that thinking is made up of a large number of processes occurring over time.

interiorized. A property of an operation whereby transformation of objects can be carried out in the head.

long-term memory. The memory system that serves as repository for our world knowledge.

myelination. The process whereby a fatty substance (myelin) surrounds neurons in the brain. Neurons become heavily myelinated during the school years, suggesting that part of the 5 to 7 shift may be due to biological changes such as myelination.

operation. An interiorized transformation that is reversible; a central accomplishment of the concrete operational period.

organization. The ability to recognize and utilize a rule that links various objects or events together. Organization skills improve with age and are responsible in part for age differences observed in memory capacity.

processing speed. The rapidity with which we attend to, perceive, and encode an object or event, may be responsible for age differences in certain tasks.

rehearsal. Repetition of a sequence of words, images, and so on, to maintain them in memory. Differences in rehearsal skills are responsible in part for age differences found in memory capacity.

retrieval. Bringing back to conscious working memory some information stored in long-term memory. Differences in retrieval strategies are partly responsible for age differences in memory ability.

reversal-nonreversal shift. A type of discrimination problem demonstrating that older children use more sophisticated strategies than do younger children to solve problems.

reversibility. A property of an operation by which an interiorized transformation on some object may be changed back to its original state—for example, imagining pouring liquid from a tall thin beaker back into a short fat beaker.

selective attention. The process of focusing on relevant information and filtering irrelevant information. Differences in control of selective attention are responsible for age trends seen in certain cognitive tasks.

sensory registers. A large-capacity short-duration memory system that processes incoming information. There appear to be minimal age differences in the visual sensory register between 5 years of age and adulthood.

seriation/transitivity. Two related accomplishments of the concrete operational period whereby the child develops the ability to fully order objects (seriation) according to a rule or relation (for example, length of a group of sticks) and hence to infer a transitive relation; that is, if $A > B$ and $B > C$, then $A > C$.

transformation. One property of an operation in which an object is changed from one state to another (for example, changing the height in two beakers that differ in width).

transposition. The ability to respond on the basis of a relation between events (for instance, larger than) rather than to an absolute stimulus. Transposition skills develop between 5 and 7 years of age.

working memory. The memory system whereby we consciously operate or work on information.

REFERENCES

Appel, L. F., Cooper, R. G., McCarrell, M., Sims-Knight, J. Yussen, S. R., & Flavell, J. H. The development of the distinction between perceiving and memorizing. *Child Development*, 1972, *43*, 1365–1381.

Bach, M. J., & Underwood, B. J. Developmental changes in memory attributes. *Journal of Educational Psychology*, 1970, *61*, 292–296.

Blake, J. Developmental change in visual information processing under backward masking. *Journal of Experimental Child Psychology*, 1974, *17*, 133–146.

Bosco, J. The visual information processing speed of lower-class and middle-class children. *Child Development*, 1972, *43*, 1418–1422.

Bruner, J. S., Olver, R. R., & Greenfield, P. M. *Studies in cognitive growth.* New York: Wiley, 1966.

Bryant, P. E., & Trabasso, T. Transitive inferences and memory in young children. *Nature*, 1971, *232*, 456–458.

Campbell, B. A., & Spear, N. E. Ontogeny of memory. *Psychological Review*, 1972, *79*, 215–236.

Cole, M., Frankel, F., & Sharp, D. Development of free recall learning in children. *Developmental Psychology*, 1971, *4*, 109–123.

Cole, M., & Scribner, S. *Culture and thought.* New York: Wiley, 1974.

Day, M. C. Developmental trends in visual scanning. In H. W. Reese (Ed.), *Advances in child development and behavior* (Vol. 10). New York: Academic Press, 1975.

Felzen, E., & Anisfeld, M. Semantic and phonetic relations in the false recognition of words by third and sixth grade children. *Developmental Psychology*, 1970, *3*, 163–168.

Fischer, K. W. *Piaget, learning and cognitive development.* Manuscript in preparation, 1978.

Flavell, J. H. Developmental studies of mediated memory. In H. W. Reese & L. P. Lipsitt (Eds.), *Advances in child development and behavior* (Vol. 5). New York: Academic Press, 1970.

Flavell, J. H., Beach, D. H., & Chinsky, J. M. Spontaneous verbal rehearsal in a memory task as a function of age. *Child Development*, 1966, *37*, 283–299.

Flavell, J. H., & Wellman, H. M. Metamemory. In R. V. Kail & J. W. Hagen (Eds.), *Memory in cognitive development.* Hillsdale, N.J.: Erlbaum, 1977.

Freund, J. S., & Johnson, J. W. Changes in memory attribute dominance as a function of age. *Journal of Educational Psychology*, 1972, *63*, 386–389.

Garrity, L. I. An electromyographical study of subvocal speech and recall in preschool children. *Developmental Psychology*, 1975, *11*, 274–281.

Gelman, R. Conservation acquisition: A problem of learning to attend to relevant attributes. *Journal of Experimental Child Psychology*, 1969, *7*, 167–187.

Gelman, R. The nature and development of early number concepts. In H. Reese (Ed.), *Advances in child development and behavior* (Vol. 7). New York: Academic Press, 1972.

Goodnow, J. J. Research on culture and thought. In D. Elkind & J. H. Flavell (Eds.), *Studies in cognitive development.* New York: Oxford University Press, 1969.

Goodnow, J. J., & Bethon, G. Piaget's tasks: The effects of schooling and intelligence. *Child Development*, 1966, *37*, 573–582.

Hagen, J. W. The effects of distraction on selective attention. *Child Development*, 1967, *38*, 685–694.

Haith, M. M., Morrison, F. J., Sheingold, K., & Mindes, P. Short-term memory for visual information in children and adults. *Journal of Experimental Child Psychology*, 1970, *9*, 454–469.

Hale, G. A. *Development of flexibility in children's attention deployment: A colloquium.* Research memorandum. Princeton, N.J.: Educational Testing Service, April 1975.

Hall, J. W., & Halperin, M. S. The development of memory-encoding processes in young children. *Developmental Psychology*, 1972, *6*, 181.

Halperin, M. S. Developmental changes in the recall and recognition of categorized word lists. *Child Development*, 1974, *45*, 144–151.

Holmes, D. L., & Olsho, L. W. *The child's perception and memory of the orientation of a line.* Unpublished manuscript, Loyola University, 1977.

Keeney, T. J., Cannizzo, S. R., & Flavell, J. H. Spontaneous and induced verbal rehearsal in a recall task. *Child Development,* 1967, *38,* 953–966.

Kendler, H. H., & Kendler, T. S. From discrimination learning to cognitive development: a neobehavioristic odyssey. In W. K. Estes (Ed.), *Handbook of Learning and Cognitive Processes.* Hillsdale, N.J.: Lawrence Erlbaum Associates, 1975.

Kendler, T. S. Development of mediating responses in children. In J. C. Wright & J. Kagan (Eds.), Basic cognitive processes in children. *Monographs of the Society for Research in Child Development,* 1963, *22*(2), 33–51.

Kendler, T. S., & Kendler, H. H. Inferential behavior in children as a function of age and subgoal constancy. *Journal of Experimental Psychology,* 1962, *64,* 460–466.

Kendler, T. S., Kendler, H. H., & Wells, D. Reversal and nonreversal shifts in nursery school children. *Journal of Comparative and Physiological Psychology,* 1960, *53,* 83–88.

Kobasigawa, A., & Middleton, D. B. Free recall of categorized items by children at three grade levels. *Child Development,* 1972, *43,* 1067–1072.

Kreutzer, M. A., Leonard, C., & Flavell, J. H. An interview study of children's knowledge about memory. *Monographs of the Society for Research in Child Development,* 1975, *40*(159).

Kuenne, M. R. Experimental investigation of the relation of language to transposition behavior in young children. *Journal of Experimental Psychology,* 1946, *36,* 471–490.

Lange, G. The development of conceptual and rote recall skills among school age children. *Journal of Experimental Child Psychology,* 1973, *15,* 394–406.

Lester, B., & Klein, R. E. Unpublished manuscript. Institute of Nutrition of Central America and Panama, Guatemala City, 1972.

Liben, L. S. Piagetian investigations of the development of memory. In R. V. Kail & J. W. Hagen (Eds.), *Memory in cognitive development.* Hillsdale, N.J.: Erlbaum, 1977.

Liss, P., & Haith, M. M. The speed of visual processing in children and adults: Effects of backward and forward masking. *Perception and Psychophysics,* 1970, *8,* 396–398.

Marsh, G., & Sherman, M. Verbal mediation of transposition as a function of age level. *Journal of Experimental Child Psychology,* 1966, *4,* 90–98.

McKee, J. P., & Riley, D. A. Auditory transposition in 6-year-old children. *Child Development,* 1962, *33,* 469–476.

Miller, G. A. The magical number seven, plus or minus two: Some limits on our capacity for processing information. *Psychological Review,* 1956, *53,* 81–97.

Morrison, F. J., Holmes, D. L., & Haith, M. M. A developmental study of the effect of familiarity on short-term visual memory. *Journal of Experimental Child Psychology,* 1974, *18,* 412–425.

Morrison, F. J., & Lord, C. E. *Age differences in recall of categorical material: Organization or retrieval?* Manuscript in preparation, 1978.

Naus, M. J., Ornstein, P. A., & Aivano, S. Developmental changes in memory: The effects of processing time and rehearsal instructions. *Journal of Experimental Child Psychology,* 1977, *23,* 237–251.

Ornstein, P. A., Naus, M. J., & Liberty, C. Rehearsal and organizational processes in children's memory. *Child Development,* 1975, *45,* 818–830.

Piaget, J. Piaget's theory. In P. H. Mussen (Ed.), *Carmichael's manual of child psychology* (Vol. 1). New York: Wiley, 1970. Pp. 703–732.

Pick, A. D. *The development of strategies of attention.* Paper presented at the biennial meeting of the Society for Research in Child Development, Denver, 1975.

Pick, A. D., Christy, M. D., & Frankel, G. W. A developmental study of visual selective attention. *Journal of Experimental Child Psychology,* 1972, *14,* 165–175.

Price-William, D. R. Abstract and concrete modes of classification in a primitive society. *British Journal of Educational Psychology,* 1962, *32,* 50–61.

Razran, G.H.S. Conditioned responses in children: A behavioral and quantitative critical review of experimental studies. *Archives of Psychology,* 1933, No. 148.

Riley, C. A. *Representation and use of comparative information and inference making by young children*. Unpublished doctoral dissertation, Princeton University, 1975.

Riley, C. A., & Trabasso, T. Comparatives, logical structures and encoding in a transitive reference task. *Journal of Experimental Child Psychology*, 1974, *17*, 187–203.

Scribner, S., & Cole, M. Effects of constrained recall training on children's performance in a verbal memory task. *Child Development*, 1972, *43*, 845–857.

Sheingold, K. Developmental differences in intake and storage of visual information. *Journal of Experimental Child Psychology*, 1973, *16*, 1–11.

Sperling, G. The information available in brief visual presentations. *Psychological Monographs*, 1960, *74*, 11.

Stevenson, H. *Children's learning*. New York: Appleton-Century-Crofts, 1974.

Trabasso, T. The role of memory as a system in making transitive inferences. In R. V. Kail & J. W. Hagen (Eds.), *Perspectives on the development of memory and cognition*. Hillsdale, N.J.: Erlbaum, 1977.

Vaughn, M. E. Clustering, age and incidental learning. *Journal of Experimental Child Psychology*, 1968, *6*, 323–331.

Vurpillot, E. The development of scanning strategies and their relation to visual differentiation. *Journal of Experimental Child Psychology*, 1968, *6*, 632–650.

Weir, M. W., & Stevenson, H. W. The effect of verbalization in children's learning as a function of chronological age. *Child Development*, 1959, *30*, 143–149.

White, S. H. Evidence for a hierarchical arrangement of learning processes. In L. P. Lipsitt & C. S. Spiker (Eds.), *Advances in child development and behavior* (Vol. 2). New York: Academic Press, 1965.

Yoshimura, E. K., Moely, B. E., & Shapiro, S. I. The influence of age and presentation order upon children's free recall and learning to learn. *Psychonomic Science*, 1971, *23*, 261–263.

10

Intelligence: Measuring Mental Capacity

Compensatory education has been tried and it apparently has failed.

Compensatory education has been practiced on a massive scale for several years in many cities across the nation. It began with auspicious enthusiasm and high hopes of educators. It had unprecedented support from Federal funds. It had theoretical sanction from social scientists espousing the major underpinning of its rationale: the "deprivation hypothesis" according to which academic lag is mainly the result of social, economic, and educational deprivation and discrimination—an hypothesis that has met with wide uncritical acceptance in the atmosphere of society's concern about the plight of minority groups and the economically disadvantaged.

The chief goal of compensatory education—to remedy the educational lag of disadvantaged children and thereby narrow the achievement gap between "minority" and "majority" pupils—has been utterly unrealized in any of the large compensatory education programs that have been evaluated so far [Jensen, 1969, p. 2].

In our earlier discussion of compensatory education (Chapter 7), we contrasted several viewpoints on why programs such as Head Start have had only limited success. One view stressed the importance of the concept of intelligence: namely, that compensatory education has failed because intelligence is determined more by heredity than by environment. If this view were correct, and intelligence were genetically fixed, then one would be forced to the pessimistic conclusion that attempts to raise the IQs (and thus the academic achievement) of children in compensatory education programs are automatically doomed to failure.

311

At the very heart of the controversy over the success or failure of compensatory education lies the concept of **intelligence,** or in its more particular form, the concept of **IQ.** There are few concepts in psychology or society that arouse such extreme ideological and political battle lines. Yet, few people really understand the concepts of intelligence or IQ as they are used by psychologists and educators. Even specialists have misconceptions about the terms. In this chapter, we shall try to obtain a clearer picture of the concept of intelligence and its importance in human development. We will first discuss the history and development of intelligence testing to learn just how and why intelligence tests came about. We shall then describe two of the most respected and widely used IQ tests: the **Stanford-Binet** test and the **Wechsler Scales.** After this brief survey of the "mechanics" of IQ testing, we will turn to some practical, theoretical, and ethical issues that currently surround the use of IQ tests. In particular, we shall ask: "What is intelligence?" "Is intelligence one or many things?" "What does your IQ score predict about your life?" "What are the respective roles of heredity and environment in determining IQ scores?" "Are there racial or other group differences in IQ?" And "How are IQ tests used and potentially abused?" (Brody & Brody, 1976).

ISSUE

What is intelligence?

The concept of intelligence is an extremely important one in our society. Few conversations can go on for very long without someone making an evaluation of some other—usually absent—person's intelligence. We continually describe people as smart or dumb, brilliant or stupid, average in intelligence or above or below average. Even very young preschoolers seem to realize that being called "dumb" is an insult and will use the term in that way.

   Since all of us seem willing to evaluate the intelligence of others so quickly and effortlessly, we might assume that psychologists know exactly what intelligence is. Unfortunately, nothing could be further from the truth. The concept of intelligence has been so difficult to define that many psychologists have essentially given up and define intelligence simply as that which an IQ test measures.

THE HISTORY OF MENTAL TESTING

To say that intelligence is that which an IQ test measures is hardly a satisfactory definition. Certainly, intelligence must have some role outside mere performance on IQ tests if it is assumed to be a valid and useful concept. Let us look back historically to see why psychologists attempted to measure *intelligence* in the first place.

Darwin

In an indirect way, the notion of intelligence and intelligence testing can be traced to Charles Darwin and the theory of evolution. In particular, we find in Darwin's theory three basic concepts that are central to our current views on intelligence. First, Darwin brought attention to the fact that individual members of a species differ in certain ways from other members of that species. Second,

Darwin noted that many of these *individual differences* stem from differences in the genetic makeup of these individual members. Finally, Darwin suggested that certain members of a species are in some way "better" than others in the sense that they are more able to adapt to their environment and hence survive and propagate.

The application of Darwin's theory to human beings, and to human intelligence in particular, is not difficult to understand. Individual humans, like any other species, differ from one another in certain ways. For example, humans differ in skin color, eye color, height, weight, and physical appearance. Not so obviously, people also differ in psychological characteristics, such as temperament, emotionality, energy level, and thinking ability. Many of these individual differences in humans also could be genetically determined since family members often share such physical characteristics as hair color, height, and general physical appearance.

Galton

It was, however, not Darwin himself but his younger cousin, Francis Galton, who first attempted to apply evolutionary theory to the study of human intelligence. Galton noted that people differ in mental ability and that family members tend to be more similar than nonfamily members in their mental ability, suggesting hereditary transmission. For example, scientists, poets, and eminent politicians are through the generations often related by blood. This suggested to Galton that intellectual ability might be largely an inherited trait little molded by the environment. Galton's was thus one of the first modern statements on the heredity/environment issue. His commitment to hereditary influences was so extreme, in fact, that it led him to propose the idea of *eugenics*: a science that seeks to change genetically determined characteristics through selective breeding.

Galton went further, however, than mere armchair theorizing in his study of mental ability. In 1882, he set up a laboratory in London where he tried to measure mental ability objectively. He again took his cue from evolutionary theory. Since the study of evolution had suggested that the higher species possessed keener senses (could perceive finer detail more accurately) and could respond more quickly, Galton figured that intelligence might also be embodied in faster reaction times and finer sensory discrimination abilities. If so, then those particular abilities could be used as yardsticks of intelligence. He turned out to be wrong—keenness of sense and quickness of reaction time did not seem to discriminate those generally believed to be "bright" from the "dull."

Much more important, however, than the failure of Galton's test of intelligence was the fact that for the first time someone had tried to *measure mental capacity*. Galton thus launched the mental testing movement, and his influence is still very much felt today.

Binet

Though Galton launched the mental testing movement, it was a French psychologist, Alfred Binet, who gave the movement substance, direction, and practical importance. Along with a colleague, Victor Henri, Binet wrote an article in 1895 calling for a redirection of mental testing procedures away from the restricted set of sensory functions espoused by Galton and toward a wider, more comprehensive set of processes, including memory, imagination, attentiveness, esthetic appreciation, and moral sensitivity. These processes, he felt, were more relevant to the acts of thinking that occur in everyday life. He felt that mental tests, therefore, ought to try to capture these qualitites of mind in some objective way. Moreover, the tests should be practical and relevant and not harnessed to any particular theory of intelligence. In the years that followed, Binet tried out numerous tests on children, until he eventually developed a stockpile of tests that appeared to discriminate "smart" from "dull" children.

The Age Connection

The use of children of different ages was a critical aspect of the early testing movement. Binet noted that whatever "intelligence" or "mental ability" might be, older children had more of it than younger children, at least until 15 or 16 years of age. For example, if you ask children of various ages to remember a sentence read to them, 12-year-olds will remember more of it than will 8-year-olds. Twelve-year-olds thus possess more mental ability than do 8-year-olds. By inference, Binet assumed that if two children *of the same age* recall different amounts, they could also be said to *differ in mental ability.* Notice carefully that the connection between age and ability allowed Binet to finesse the whole question that most often stymies people—namely "What *is* intelligence?" By tacking the definition onto the generally accepted notion that older children are more "intelligent" than younger children, Binet wasn't compelled to define the term—merely to measure it.

ISSUE

Is faster better?

Indirectly, however, Binet did end up defining intelligence. He defined it as the *speed of cognitive development.* Thus, he assumed that the child who develops the ability to solve complex problems at an earlier than average age (that is, who is "faster") will continue to develop more rapidly and, as an adult, will be able to solve problems that are more *complex.* Although this notion that "faster is better" appears highly plausible, there is only limited evidence that it is in fact the case. Indeed, one might as easily believe the opposite to be true. Thus, consider the following statement made by Jean Piaget during a 1967 lecture in New York:

"If we accept the fact that there are stages of development, another question arises which I call 'the American question,' and I am asked it every time I come here. If there are stages that children reach at given norms of ages can we accelerate the stages? Do we have to go through each one of these stages, or can't we speed it up a bit? Well, surely, the answer is yes . . . but how far can we speed them up? . . . I have a hypothesis which I am so far incapable of proving: Probably the organization of operations has an optimal time . . . For example, we know that it takes 9 to 12 months before babies develop the notion that an object is still there even when a screen is placed in front of it. Now kittens go through the same sub-stages but they do it in three months—so they're six months ahead of the babies. Is this an advantage or isn't it?

"We can certainly see our answer in one sense. The kitten is not going to go much further. The child has taken longer, but he is capable of going further so it seems to me that the nine months were not for nothing . . . It is probably possible to accelerate, but maximal acceleration is not desirable. There seems to be an optimal time. What this optimal time is will surely depend upon each individual and on the subject matter. We still need a great deal of research to know what the optimal time would be."[1]

The Binet Test

Binet got his first real chance to try out his new tests in 1904. During the late 19th century, public education had expanded considerably throughout most of Europe. Compulsory education had placed many more children in school, and since classes were age-graded, some children fell behind their peers in school performance. The Minister of Public Instruction in France became concerned and wished to find out who the "dull" children were, so that special classes could be set up for them. He turned to Binet and his colleague Simon to apply their techniques to develop objective measurements of differences in mental ability.

On the first of their attempts, Binet and Simon drew up a group of 30 tests ranging from the rudimentary ability to follow a moving, lighted match, through simple naming of objects, repeating sentences, arranging objects by weight, and using three words in a sentence, up to such analytically difficult tasks as distinguishing abstract words like "character" and "reputation." The tests were given to both normal children and to children diagnosed by other clinical techniques to be *idiots* or *morons*. Through numerous refinements and revisions of these basic tests, Binet successfully collected a battery of tests to distinguish "dull" children from normal children and even different groups of normal children.

Binet's success established mental testing as a fruitful objective approach. With a test that could be given in just over an hour, Binet was able to distinguish among "dull" and "bright" children more quickly, economically, and possibly more accurately than ever before.

At this juncture, we should carefully note the differences between Galton's approach and that of Binet. Galton started from a theoretical point of view: his belief that evolution and heredity caused differences in intelligence. In sharp contrast, Binet's approach was pragmatic. Additionally, Galton had a working definition of intelligence as *sensory keenness*. Binet let his tests discover what intelligence might be and did not attempt to define the concept theoretically. Finally, Galton's tests were experimentally rigorous and exact, at least for the time. Binet's tests were global, ill-defined, and lacked rigor and exactitude. In the end, however, Binet succeeded where Galton had failed!

Binet's emphasis on relevance and pragmatism produced a workable test of intelligence that appeared to distinguish bright, average, and dull children. And Binet's method left a very important legacy for us today. Tests of intelligence do not as a rule provide a definition of intelligence, thereby opening themselves to the criticism that they do not capture all or some important aspects of intelligence. Though the definition of intelligence is still hotly debated, mental tests go their

[1]From "Giant in the Nursery: Jean Piaget," by D. Elkind, *New York Times Magazine*, May 26, 1968. Copyright © 1968 by the New York Times Company. Reprinted by permission.

own way disregarding the issue of definition. Secondly, the pragmatism of the tests leaves always in doubt the question of the hereditary or environmental basis of what is being measured. No attempt was made by Binet, as was made by Galton, to tie the tests necessarily to one or the other (or yet some third) point of view. As we shall see shortly, this ambiguity poses serious problems for modern psychologists. Finally, in contrast to Galton's tests, Binet's tests were global and vague in that they tapped a wide variety of cognitive and other processes. Psychologists would still like to know what processes define "high intellectual ability," but Binet's tests were simply not designed to tell us.

Thus, we have been left with a concrete, demonstrably successful test that captures important differences between people but about which we really know very little. It is this ignorance that has created much of the confusion and controversy that have arisen in recent years. Before we examine these issues, we need to become more acquainted with the tests and how they are constructed.

THE IQ TESTS

There are literally hundreds of tests that purport to measure intelligence. We shall focus on two of the most respected and widely used: the Stanford-Binet test and the Wechsler Scales.

The Stanford-Binet Test

Once the Binet test had been developed in France, it was only a matter of a few years before it was brought to the United States. In 1916, Louis Terman of Stanford University translated and published a version of Binet's test for use with American children from 3 years of age until adulthood.

Like the Binet test, the Stanford-Binet test is comprised of a series of age-graded tasks, or items. Figure 10-1 gives some examples of the kinds of items that are used. For example, 2-year-old items on the test include tasks like having the child place blocks in a three-hole board, identify common objects by their use, and repeat two unrelated words. Test items for 4-year-olds place more emphasis on verbal or linguistic production. The 4-year-old is asked to perform tasks like naming objects from memory, repeating sentences, and completing analogies.

In general, as children get older the test probes more abstract cognitive skills. For example, 7-year-olds are given a "similarities" test in which the child is read a pair of common words and asked how they are similar: for example, "wood and coal," "ship and automobile." The key to answering such a question correctly is to come up with some abstract property, function, or relation common to the two words. Thus, for coal and wood, answering that they both burn or they're both used for fuel would be correct. However, saying "coal is black and wood is brown" would not be correct. For still older children, the similarities test uses three words; for example, "book, teacher, and newspaper." Very young children and severely mentally deficient people cannot do this part of the test.

We shall see in the next section how each child's performance is graded and scored. However, you can see from this brief survey and from Figure 10-1 that as age increases the test items get progressively harder in that they require larger memory span, more abstract reasoning ability, and greater facility and flexibility with language and concepts. These abilities seem, at least in a general sense, to resemble the sorts of cognitive skills that we have discussed in previous chapters.

Test Items for 2-year-olds
A. Form board

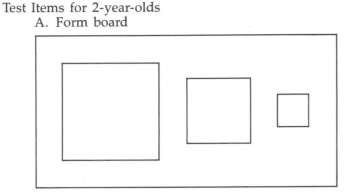

B. Picture vocabulary
The child is asked to name each picture.

C. Memory
The child is asked to repeat unrelated words:
(1) "Say dog, carrot"
(2) "Say car, banana"

Figure 10-1.   The items above are analogous to some of the items provided on the Stanford-Binet. These items increase in difficulty as one moves through the test. Thus, one is able to compute a child's mental age (and, hence, IQ) by noting how far he or she is able to progress through the test.

The Wechsler Scales

The other widely used tests of intelligence are those devised by David Wechsler of New York University-Bellevue Medical Center (Wechsler, 1949, 1958, 1974). Wechsler is responsible for three separate tests: the WAIS (Wechsler Adult Intelligence Scale); the WISC (Wechsler Intelligence Scale for Children); and the WPPSI (Wechsler Preschool Primary Scale of Intelligence). All three of these Wechsler Scales are basically similar to the Stanford-Binet test in that they sample a variety of different abilities. However, the Wechsler Scales have, unlike the Stanford-Binet test, attempted to look separately at the different types of skills that go into the general concept of intelligence. For example, the most recent revision of the children's intelligence test, called the WISC-R (Wechsler, 1974), is divided into two main scales: Verbal and Performance. The Verbal Scale is then further divided into six subscales: information, similarities, arithmetic, vocabulary, comprehension, and digit span. These verbal subscales all involve some degree of language use and facility—hence the designation *Verbal Scale*. The Performance Scale is likewise broken into different subscales: picture completion, picture arrangement, block design, object assembly, and coding. These performance subscales, unlike the verbal subscales, are devised to be relatively independent of language use and facility.

IQ Scores and Their Characteristics

Now that we have some idea of what intelligence tests are like, we can look directly at how a child's performance on them is translated into a meaningful score.

Calculating a Child's IQ

Calculating a child's IQ on the Stanford-Binet test involves determining the child's *mental age* (MA). Since items on the Stanford-Binet are age-graded, the child's mental age simply reflects the age level of the items he is able to pass correctly. For example, if a child passes all the items up to and including the 6-year-old level, he is said to have a mental age of 6 years. Similarly, assume a child passed all the items up to the 5-year-old level, three of the five items at the 6-year-old level, and two of the five items at the 7-year-old level. This child would be given credit for 0.2 additional years for each item passed beyond the age level at which he was able to pass all items (in our example, the 5-year-old level). Thus, this child also would have a mental age of 6 years.

Obviously, however, mental age alone does not tell you how "bright" or "dull" a particular child is; you must also know how old the child actually is—the child's score must somehow relate his mental age to his *chronological age*. This relation between mental age and chronological age is expressed as the *intelligence quotient* (IQ). To obtain the IQ score, mental age (MA) is simply divided by chronological age (CA) and multiplied by 100:

$$IQ = \frac{MA}{CA} \times 100$$

The IQ measure just described has some very interesting properties. First, the child who is completely average—that is, who passes all items at his age level and no other items—has a chronological age equal to his mental age; hence, his IQ value equals 100. However, a 6-year-old with a mental age of 9 receives an IQ score of 150 (9/6 × 100) and is considered to be as "bright" as an 8-year-old with a mental age of 12 (12/8 × 100). Thus, calculating the ratio of mental age to chronological age allows a more reasonable comparison of children's ability at different ages.

Another interesting property of IQ tests is that the scores are "normally distributed." (See Figure 10-2.) This means that the most common value of IQ is 100 and that approximately equal numbers of people have IQs of, say, 90 and 110, or of 80 and 120. Thus, an IQ score of 100 divides the population roughly in half. This fact stems not from anything intrinsic to the IQ but, rather, to the way the tests were constructed. Binet and his followers carefully selected items that the "average" child at each age could pass, thus establishing that the average child's mental age would equal his chronological age, so that his IQ would be 100.

ISSUE

What happens to IQ measures in adulthood?

It is known that beyond about 15 or 16 years of age, absolute performance on certain IQ test items does not continue to increase. For

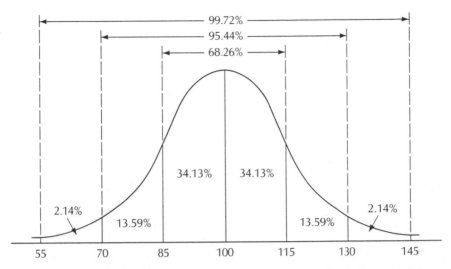

Figure 10-2. The distribution of IQ scores, showing the classic "normal" (bell-shaped) distribution. The figure shows the mean score of 100 for the population and the percentage of people above and below the mean by a given score. For example, approximately 34.13% of people score 15 points above and below the mean (115 and 85), making a total of 68.2% of the people who fall between these two scores. In contrast, only about 2.14% of the people obtain scores above 130 or below 70.

example, immediate memory span is about seven digits at age 15 and remains the same at age 50. Notice, however, that dividing a constant mental age by a growing chronological age necessarily would result in a decrease in IQ score. Thus, an IQ of 100 at age 15 (15/15 × 100) would be an IQ of 50 at 30 years of age (15/30 × 100) and a miserable 25 at 60 years of age (15/60 × 100). Since, clearly, 30-year-olds are not less intelligent than teenagers, Wechsler (1974) decided to use another measure of relative ability. This new measure is expressed in terms of the percentage of scores that a particular score exceeds. For example, an adult with an IQ of 125 scores better than about 94 percent of all adults tested. This *index of relative standing* measures how much one's score deviates from the norm. Hence Wechsler called his measure a *deviation IQ*. Since the deviation IQ is dependent on how IQ scores are distributed in the population, rather than the ratio of mental age over chronological age, one can continue to measure adult IQ reliably without penalizing adults for their increasing chronological age.

Reliability, Standardization, and Validity

Up to this point, we have simply described the history of IQ testing and what currently used tests are like. We have not really asked whether the tests do what they were designed to do: namely, measure individual differences in mental ability. In order to address this difficult issue, it is necessary to examine IQ tests in terms of their reliability, their methods of standardization, and their validity.

Reliability

On the simplest of levels, in order for an IQ test to be a useful measure of mental ability, the test must have **reliability** or stability. If a test is reliable, an individual child who is given the test several times over the course of a few days, should receive quite similar scores on all testings. If, however, a child received a score of 75 on one day and 150 on the next, we would not have much confidence that the tests were a very reliable measuring instrument. We would have no more confidence in them than in a thermometer that gave two radically different temperature readings when used two minutes apart. We would assume that something was wrong with the thermometer—that it wasn't very reliable. The same goes for IQ tests. In order to be confident that the test accurately measures IQ, we must assure ourselves of its reliability in repeated testings over short periods of time. Happily, most IQ tests are pretty reliable, though not perfect. For the Stanford-Binet, the correlation between scores on repeated testings (called *test-retest reliability*) is about .90. Thus, whatever the test is measuring, we can be reasonably confident that it consistently measures the same thing, at least if testings are administered within a relatively short period of time.

Standardization

Obviously, for an IQ test to be useful, it must be reliable, but reliability alone is not enough. If, as an extreme example, one decided to define intelligence in terms of "height," the measure would be quite reliable—that is, a person's score would remain predictably constant—but the score would not be very useful; it simply would not help us to distinguish "bright" from "dull" children. Thus, a useful IQ test, in addition to being reliable, must also measure what it is supposed to measure, and it must measure the same qualities in all children. In determining whether the IQ tests that we have discussed meet this additional requirement, let us first consider how the tests were originally *standardized*.

Since the IQ score represents a child's relative standing among his age peers, it is crucial to know the characteristics of the particular population to which the test applies. The Binet IQ tests were originally tried out on a group of French children who shared a common language and also, it was assumed, a relatively common environment and upbringing. The test then reflected a child's relative standing among a group of children with similar experiences. Obviously, an IQ score derived for a child who spoke a different language, or who came from a radically different environment, would not be indicative of his "intelligence" or mental ability. Thus, in constructing tests like IQ tests, one needs to be confident that the sample on which the test is originally used is fairly representative of the population as a whole. This procedure is referred to as **standardization**. The 1908 Binet and Simon scale was standardized on only 300 children. The 1937 Stanford-Binet was standardized on 3000 people from all over the United States—but all 3000 were native-born Whites.

The question of whether a test has been properly standardized, and on what population it has been standardized, has important implications regarding the "generalizability" of the test. The generalizability of a test simply refers to how well it measures what it is supposed to measure in all people who take the test. Thus, an intelligence test is supposed to be measuring intelligence in the sense of cognitive or mental abilities. If, however, the test for some children simply measures how well they use the English language, it is obviously not a useful test of *intelligence* for those children. Thus, to take an extreme example, a child who spoke no English would do very poorly on the test; however, his performance would not be a measure of his mental ability, but only of his knowledge of English.

A further issue concerns the Stanford-Binet test itself. Since this test was standardized on only U.S.-born Whites, the important question arises whether the test is useful or appropriate for foreign-born or Black children—children raised in different environments who may not have had equivalent experiences.

Although we might reasonably conclude that a Samoan child and a child in the United States have not had equivalent experiences, what about the experiences of a Black child and a White child in the United States? In some respects, these children share the same environments and experiences; in others, they do not. For IQ tests to be appropriate for both of these children, we must assume roughly equivalent opportunities and experiences. But we really don't know how equal the two children's experiences have been. Hence, there is some doubt about the appropriateness of presently existing IQ tests for Black children in the United States. Some psychologists have therefore devised more "culture-fair," "culture-free," or "culture-reduced" tests that try to eliminate the influence of different experiences and to test "basic intellectual capacity." An example of such a test is given in Figure 10-3. As you can see, the items in this test rely less on common information or verbal production than do items of the Stanford-Binet or Wechsler tests. The items are assumed to be "culture-reduced," because the mental processes used are presumably equally available to all members of the culture and, also, since the tasks are relatively novel for everyone taking the test. Nevertheless, if you try the test yourself, you'll see that it requires certain skills that are very much related to school learning, especially learning to read. One must be able to follow the instructions. One must know that the items are to be processed in a linear fashion. And one must have learned how to control eye movements and how to hold prior information in memory while scanning other information. As we discussed in Chapter 9, many of these cognitive skills are developed during the school years—very possibly as an outgrowth of learning to read. A child not attending school, or having trouble learning to read, could easily do poorly on this test, not because of poor mental ability but because he hasn't yet mastered certain information-processing skills.

In truth, determining the culture-fairness of a test is a very complex matter. On the one hand, IQ tests must use some of the cultural information learned by children, or they cannot adequately assess how well the child has assimilated his environment. On the other hand, assuming cultural equivalence, or constructing tests that eliminate only obvious cultural biases, does not guarantee that the test is truly fair in all respects. Unfortunately, there is at present no real solution to this dilemma, and any statement about how standardized and unbiased such tests are must be made with extreme caution.

Validity

The question of whether or not IQ tests measure the same sorts of abilities in children of different backgrounds brings us to one of the critical questions with which we began this chapter: namely, what are IQ tests measuring anyway? And, is what IQ tests measure what we want them to measure, or is it something else?

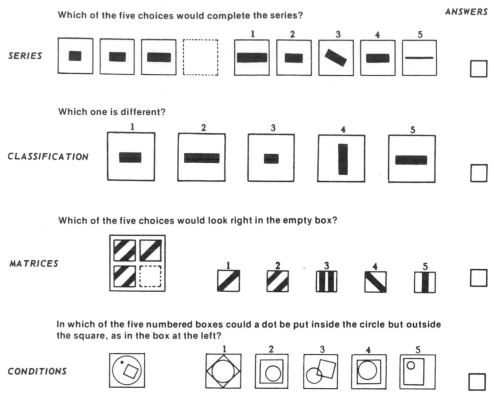

Figure 10-3. Sample items from the IPAT Culture Fair Intelligence Test are shown here. Note how these items require visual, logical, and problem-solving abilities without relying on language skills or specific school and cultural experiences. (Copyright 1949, 1957 by the Institute for Personality and Ability Testing. Reproduced by permission.)

The question of whether or not a test measures what it is supposed to measure is a question of test **validity.** How valid a test of intelligence is the IQ test? This, however, brings us back to still another of our original questions: What is intelligence? Some have tried to skirt the issue by stating that "Intelligence is what IQ tests measure." But most of us are not happy with this answer. We would prefer an independent definition of intelligence by which IQ test measurements could be evaluated and thereby validated (or invalidated).

We must admit that at present, we do not have an agreed-upon definition of intelligence. In part, this is a consequence of Binet's pragmatism in constructing a wide range of tests tapping numerous psychological processes, thereby precluding any easy assessment of the specific abilities that underlie performance on these tests. Nevertheless, our ideas of intelligence have always depended more on preconceptions than on scientific data. For something practical to work with we have usually defined intelligence in terms of "those mental abilities that make for success in our Western culture." We value abstract thinking, good memory, sophisticated verbal and problem-solving skills, and similar mental abilities. IQ tests focus on those abilities and, hence, have usually been assumed to be useful predictors of success in our culture. If we were a society of hunters, no doubt intelligence would be defined by keenness of eye and fleetness of foot. The definition of intelligence is thus shaped by the demands of any culture. Promoting the welfare of our particular society is more dependent on thinking or problem-solving ability than on visual acuity. Thus, any definition of intelligence is subjective, based on intuition and a society's relatively shared consensus. It was this intuition that guided Binet and the early mental testers. Without this intuitive consensus, measuring intelligence the way we do would be fruitless (Herrnstein, 1973).

We cannot yet (or maybe ever) define intelligence "objectively." However, this does not necessarily refute the validity of IQ tests. For years, scientists were able to measure electricity without being able to define it. Lack of definition thus does not preclude validity. Validity can simply be defined by how well a measurement instrument does its job. An IQ test does its job if it consistently measures differences between people that relate to important differences in our society and culture. Thus, in order to evaluate the validity of IQ tests, we need to examine if IQ is related to anything *important* in life. This is called *predictive validity*—that is, the ability of scores on IQ tests to predict some other important aspect of a person's life. As we shall see, IQ scores do predict to some degree features of human life and accomplishment that most of us consider important.

WHAT DOES IQ PREDICT ABOUT YOUR LIFE?

Early IQ and Later IQ

One of the first questions regarding the predictive validity of IQ tests can be stated as "Does present IQ predict future IQ?" or "Does a person's IQ remain the same throughout life?"

Figure 10-4 shows mean IQ score changes for a group of children who were part of a longitudinal study done at the University of California, Berkeley. The figure shows the differences between the IQ scores taken at age 17 and those obtained at several earlier ages. Several things should be noted about these data. First, individual IQ scores—especially those taken at an early age—were subject to quite dramatic fluctuations. The mean change in IQ from tests given before age 6 in comparison with tests given at age 17 was greater than 10 points. For some children, changes in IQ scores over this period were quite dramatic, on the order of 25 points or more. Thus, a young child's IQ score can change substantially. As he grows older, however, and comparisons were made with increasingly older children, the average amount of change dropped dramatically. For example, between 12 and 17 years of age, the average change was only about 7 points. This variability in IQ scores obtained at different testings can be seen more graphically in Figure 10-5, where individual IQ scores for five males from the same study are depicted from birth through 36 years of age (Bayley, 1970). As you can see, the various children showed different patterns of IQ score changes over the period studied. Some individuals (Cases 8M and 13M) showed marked drops in IQ over the first ten years, while others (5M and 22M) increased over the same period and still another (7M) zigzagged up and down.

We readily see from the data that IQ scores for individual people can and do fluctuate over time. In some cases, quite large changes occur. In fact, for most of

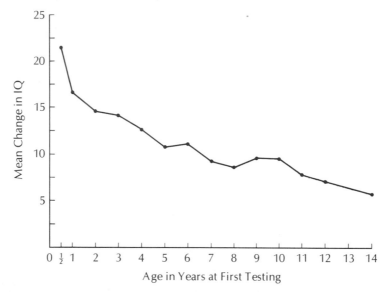

Figure 10-4. In the Berkeley Growth Study, IQ scores obtained from 6 months of age to 14 years of age were compared with IQ scores obtained at age 17. Subjects first tested at age 14 showed little IQ score change when tested at age 17. However, scores obtained at a very early age (under 6 years) changed dramatically by age 17. (From "Development of Mental Abilities," by N. Bayley. In P. H. Mussen (Ed.), *Carmichael's Manual of Child Psychology*. Copyright 1970 by John Wiley & Sons, Inc. Reprinted by permission.

us, our IQ score changes over time. Life experiences do not remain constant and neither does the IQ. Many factors probably contribute to changes in IQ scores. Short-term influences like diseases or changing homes or schools can influence IQ scores, as can longer-term changes in one's personality and/or social circumstances.

In summary, then it appears that while IQ remains fairly stable in most people (at least after age 7), large changes in IQ scores can occur in an individual child. Averaging across all children, one sees relative stability in the IQ scores. Looking at individual children, in contrast, presents a less uniform picture of the stability of IQ scores. For this reason, one should use caution in using an individual child's IQ score to predict his IQ in adulthood, though on the *average* that prediction would not be far off. Similarly, it is risky to use data on groups of individuals to make predictions or inferences about a single individual, as we shall see when we discuss the controversial issues of genetics and of racial differences in IQ.

IQ and School Achievement

In constructing the early IQ tests, Binet purposefully eliminated tests that did not show any relation to how well children did in school. Thus, it comes as no shock that IQ scores correlate well with measures of success in school. The correlation between IQ scores and school grades is about .50. Moreover, until the last few years of high school, this correlation between IQ score and school grades tends to increase with age, probably because the skills acquired in school—for

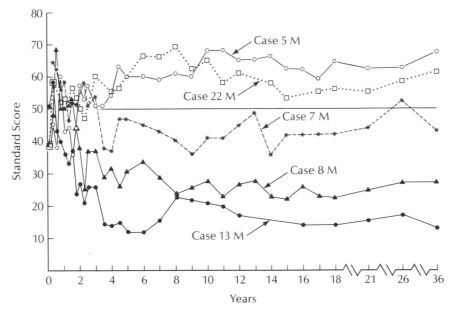

Figure 10-5. This figure shows the IQ scores obtained by five males on different tests administered between birth and age 36. (From "Development of Mental Abilities," by N. Bayley. In P. H. Mussen (Ed.), *Carmichael's Manual of Child Psychology.* Copyright 1970 by John Wiley & Sons, Inc. Reprinted by permission.)

example, information or knowledge, abstract reasoning, and vocabulary—are also the skills required on IQ tests.

The correlation of .50 between IQ scores and school grades thus suggests that IQ score is an important factor in predicting *school achievement*. This relationship is, indeed, borne out by actual observations. Children with high IQs do tend to do better in school and to stay longer in school (Brody & Brody, 1976). However, we have to add a precautionary note: the correlation between IQ score and school performance is far from a perfect one, and there are obviously many other factors that influence how well one will do in school.

IQ and Occupational Status

One of the most significant links yet obtained in studies was between IQ scores and male occupational status. A study of a large sample of enlisted men in the Air Force in World War II compared the intelligence test scores of recruits from 74 different civilian occupations (Harrell & Harrell, 1945). Independent assessments had been made of the prestige of each occupation. Table 10-1 shows the rank order of some of the occupations (from most prestigious to least prestigious), along with IQ score data of the men from each occupational group. As you can see, the *mean* (the arithmetic average) IQ score increases in a rather straightforward way with increases in the prestige ratings of the jobs. Thus, more prestigious jobs tended to be held by more intelligent men. Notice, however, the column that shows the *range* of IQ scores for the different occupations. For the

Table 10-1.   The relation between IQ and occupational status.

The table below shows the mean and range of IQ scores obtained by enlisted men from several different occupations during World War II. Note how, as one goes down the list, both mean IQ for the groups and minimum IQ for the groups decline while maximal IQ remains relatively stable. In other words, as one moves down in occupational status, the amount of individual variability in IQ increases dramatically as people with lower IQs enter the lower status groups.

Occupation	Mean IQ	Range in IQ
Accountant	128.1	94–157
Lawyer	127.6	96–157
Engineer	126.6	100–151
Chemist	124.8	102–153
Reporter	124.5	100–157
Teacher	122.8	76–155
Bookkeeper	120.0	70–157
Photographer	117.6	66–147
Clerk, general	117.5	68–155
Radio repairman	115.3	56–151
Salesman	115.1	60–153
Artist	114.9	82–139
Manager, retail	114.0	52–151
Laboratory assistant	113.4	76–147
Stock clerk	111.8	54–151
Musician	110.9	56–147
Electrician	109.0	64–149
Mechanic	106.3	60–155
Butcher	102.9	42–147
Plumber	102.7	56–139
Bartender	102.2	56–137
Carpenter, construction	102.1	42–147
Chauffeur	100.8	46–143
Painter, general	98.3	38–147
Cook and baker	97.2	20–147
Truck driver	96.2	16–149
Barber	95.3	42–141
Lumberjack	94.7	46–137
Farmer	92.7	24–147
Miner	90.6	42–139
Teamster	87.7	46–145

Adapted from T. W. Harrell & M. S. Harrell. Army General Classification Test scores for civilian populations. *Educational and Psychological Measurement,* 1945, *5,* 229–239. Used by permission.

high-prestige jobs, most men had a relatively high IQ (for example, 94–157 for accountant). In contrast, the IQ scores of men in low prestige jobs tended to vary more widely. For example, one teamster had an IQ of 145. This pattern of scores suggests that the more prestigious occupations require a certain minimum IQ, but that IQ alone does not determine occupational status; many people with very high IQs hold less prestigious occupations.

Since the prestige of a job is often highly correlated with the amount it pays, it is not surprising to find there has been a further correlation involving IQ: the correlation between the IQ and the income level of white males in the United

States. This correlation, however, has been somewhat weaker than the other correlations that we have already discussed, being about .30 (Jencks, 1972). Clearly, there are other factors, in addition to IQ, that work to determine income level.

An important observation to raise at this point in our discussion is that all of the above variables—IQ, school success, income, job prestige—are correlated with each other to some degree. It is therefore a tantalizing question whether one particular variable is the *real* or principal cause of all the others. Some have pointed to IQ and argued that this factor determines success in school and later life. Others feel that since high-income families can afford better schools, their children usually get better educations, attain higher IQs, get better jobs, and perpetuate the cycle; low IQ children, they contend, are shut off from high education and good jobs through reduced economic opportunities. The data we have at present, however, are only correlations and do not prove causality of one sort or another. Some recent attempts have been made through the application of sophisticated statistical techniques to tease apart the causal relations among these factors (Duncan Featherman, & Duncan, 1972). Though tentative, these attempts have shown that intelligence does seem to be causally related to school success and that success in school directly affects occupational status. Thus, IQ may influence job prestige primarily through the education system. The conclusions of these studies are bound to be controversial, but we offer them to point out that attempts are indeed being made to zero in on the causal status of one's IQ.

IQ and Success on the Job

More intelligent people are, as we have observed, generally found in more prestigious jobs. But what about performance in the job itself; does intelligence really matter? This is an important social issue, since many organizations use IQ or similar test scores as selection criteria for job applicants. What is the relation between IQ and job performance? This is a difficult question to research for a number of reasons. One obvious problem is the difficulty of deriving an agreed-upon measure of "good" or "bad" performance in an occupation. Another problem is that some occupations, such as medicine, are open to *only* relatively high-IQ people. Thus failure to find a relation between IQ and job performance may only mean that the range of IQs selected was too small to see a difference, since all doctors probably have a high enough IQ to be successful. If it were possible for people with low IQs to become doctors, one might see a very strong correlation between IQ and job performance.

Keeping these qualifications in mind, though, there are at least some studies of the relation between IQ and job success (cited in Brody & Brody, 1976). Not surprisingly, these studies tend to show that the relation between IQ and job performance is complicated by other factors, some of which we just mentioned. For example, Matarazzo (1972) correlated IQ scores of policemen with their job performance and found no connection. However, since policemen's jobs, like medical-school admissions, are open to only applicants with reasonably high IQ scores, it is not clear whether or not some relation might have been found if lower IQs had been included. Other studies have shown that, in those professions where IQ scores range widely, there may be a connection between IQ and job performance. Hay (1943) found a correlation for machine bookkeepers of .59 between IQ and number of clerical transactions completed. Other studies found no such relations for certain sales jobs (Kenagy & Yockum, 1925). These latter studies are suspect, since it also appears that more intelligent people tend to be more dissatisfied with repetitive clerical jobs and to leave the job earlier than low IQ people (Brody & Brody, 1976).

What conclusions can we draw from these seemingly divergent results? At the very least, it appears that IQ does not predict job performance in any simple way. For jobs demanding a high IQ, intelligence test scores are not related to subsequent performance, for the apparent reason that IQ has already had its effect in limiting the job to those able to handle it. For other jobs, however, high IQ will result in better performance. And for still others, high IQ will actually work against performance by making the person more readily dissatisfied with the job.

IQ and Accomplishment

The last IQ connection we will discuss concerns the relation between tested intelligence and accomplishments other than getting a prestigious job or a large salary. Does IQ relate to really important contributions to society? Is IQ related to a sense of achievement and creativity? In essence, this question asks "You may be smart, but are you leading a happy and productive life?" Unfortunately, no recent data exist to address this question (Brody & Brody, 1976). Only one study begun in the 1920s by Terman (1925) provides any clues; nevertheless, the findings of that study are quite revealing.

The plan of the study was simply to find a large group of people with exceptionally high IQs, record what they were doing and what they were like, and follow the normal course of their lives. For the study, Terman observed 1528 children (857 boys and 671 girls) with an average IQ of about 150.

Terman gathered an enormous amount of information on these people over the years. As children, they tended on a physical scale to be taller, heavier, stronger, and earlier in sexual maturity than children in the general population. They did better in school and were advanced in reading, arithmetic, and other indices of normal development. The adult group, now about 50 years old, shows the predicted IQ correlations. The men hold prestigious jobs, and are earning good salaries. But what about the quality of their lives? All indications are that their lives are indeed rich. The death rate in the sample is one-third less than in the general population, and fatal accidents are very rare. The productivity of the group by their mid-forties was prodigious and spread over all walks of life. Collectively, the men and women at that time had produced 2000 scientific and technical articles, some 60 books, 33 novels, 375 short stories or plays, 265 miscellaneous articles on various subjects, and 230 patents.

Clearly, by commonly accepted criteria these people were leading lives of accomplishment and productivity. Moreover, when asked about their own feelings, over half reported "deep satisfaction" with their lives, and almost 90% reported being fairly content.

Although the exact relation between IQ and life accomplishments is not fully understood, the findings of Terman's study suggest that there is a connection. As two commentators recently said, "It is doubtful that the attempt to select children scoring in the top 1% of any other single characteristic would be as predictive of future accomplishment" (Brody & Brody, 1976, p. 109). Further, it is hard not to marvel that "an IQ test can be given in an hour or two to a child and from this infinitesimally small sample of his output, deeply important predictions follow—about schoolwork, occupation, income, satisfaction with life, even life expectancy" (Hernnstein, 1971, pp. 11–12).

Summary of Characteristics of IQ Tests and Scores

Numerous tests have been developed to measure "intelligence." We examined two: the *Stanford-Binet test* (which derives IQ as a function of *mental* and *chronological age*), and the *Wechsler Scales* (a battery of tests that, unlike the Stanford-Binet test, attempt to look separately at the different types of skills that go into the general concept of intelligence). We have seen that in terms of *reliability*, these tests seem sound; performance on the tests by a given child remains relatively stable if tests are administered within a few days or weeks of each other. In terms of *standardization*, however, the tests raise serious questions concerning the "generalizability" of their appropriate application; specifically, since the tests were standardized for particular children sharing particular types of experiences (in the case of the Stanford-Binet test, American-born Whites), there arises the serious question of whether they can meaningfully be applied to other groups of children. Attempts have been made to meet this problem with so-called "culture free" or "culture-reduced" tests, but examination reveals that even these tests are largely tied to at least some of the very same environmental conditions that arguably separate different groups of children. Finally, although precise determination of the complete *validity* of the tests that we have discussed is impossible (due to the lack of any universally accepted definition of "intelligence" itself), the tests do show *predictive validity* for certain groups in our culture—particularly White males—for those accomplishments commonly accepted as being signs of intelligence in our culture: school achievement, occupational status, job success (depending on the nature of the job), and productivity.

IS IQ ONE OR MANY DIFFERENT THINGS?

The fact that IQ has seemed to be so important in predicting the course of many people's lives leads us back to the question we have already asked several times in this chapter: "What does IQ measure anyhow?" Although we have admitted that we do not have any very good answer to this question, perhaps some answer can be obtained by asking a simpler, related question: "Is IQ one or many things?"

As you recall from our discussion of the development of IQ tests, Binet did not concern himself with this question. The original Binet test was developed neither to prove a specific theory nor to empirically examine isolated psychological processes, such as selective attention, rehearsal strategies, or processing speed. Psychologists were therefore left in the dark about exactly what the tests were measuring, let alone whether a small set of abilities or processes accounted for most of a person's performance on the test.

The question of whether IQ is one or many things was, however, probed by a number of psychologists soon after Binet's IQ tests were introduced into the United States. The starting point in their inquiry was a simple one. They noted that performance on one test of intelligence often correlated with performance on another test, though not perfectly. For example, the correlation between two separate forms of the 1937 Stanford-Binet was .91. In addition, correlations were often found between different items within a single test. Performance on the information test on the WAIS, for example, correlated .70 with performance on the comprehension test and .66 with performance on the arithmetic test (also part of the WAIS). Why did these correlations exist? Among other reasons, it was felt that possibly performance on the different items was an outward manifestation of some underlying common ability (or abilities). It was to the discovery of that underlying ability that some psychologists turned their attention.

Spearman's Two-Factor Theory of Intelligence

Charles Spearman (1904) was one of the pioneers in studying the components of mental capacity. Before we consider his **two-factor theory,** however, we need to look at the method he chose to study the problem—a method that practically all others since have followed. The method is called *multiple-factor analysis* (Thurstone, 1947).

Factor Analysis Technique

Multiple-factor analysis involves a special and complicated application of the statistical technique of *correlation.* The following is a simplified example of the basic process of **factor analysis.** Suppose that a number of people are all given four items in an IQ test: items A, B, C, and D. The psychologist then looks at the performance of the people on these four items in order to see if the different items are related to one another in any way.

Scores on these four items might be related to each other in a variety of ways. First, they might not be related at all, in which case we might assume that each item measures some *independent* ability, and that these abilities are not related to one another. On the other hand, items A and B might correlate with each other and items C and D with each other, but performance on A and B might be unrelated to performance on C and D. In this case, we would say that two different *factors* or abilities seem to be operating—one for items A and B, and one for items C and D.

Factor analysis attempts (1) to analyze the pattern of correlations among a group of scores, (2) to then find out which scores cluster together with each other and not with other scores, and, finally, (3) to identify some general factors or abilities that describe the scores. For example, if information, comprehension, and similarities items correlate highly, we might want to infer some general kind of verbal ability—or verbal "factor." Note here an important distinction. Steps 1 and 2 in factor analysis are relatively objective, statistical procedures, but Step 3 is less so; it represents an attempt on the part of the psychologist to give a meaningful *label* to a set of statistical correlations. It is something like a concept-formation task: namely, trying to find a common higher-order label that unites, in this case, a diverse set of items that happen to be correlated. Different psychologists in Step 3 could conceivably interpret the findings of Steps 1 and 2 in quite different ways.

Spearman's early work focused on various complex correlations among tests of ability and schoolwork. He noted, for example, that grades in the classics (Latin and Greek) correlated very highly with performance in many other areas—in particular, schoolwork, and some of Spearman's own tests. However, grades in the classics correlated very poorly with tests of sensory discrimination. Spearman reasoned that where scores were correlated, this was because of some common mental capacity or ability. He called this ability "**g**," for "general," and thought it to be whatever the tests had in common. Individual tests, however, clearly required their own particular skills, and Spearman therefore postulated a separate factor, "*s*," for "special." Thus, any test required some amount of general ability *(g)* and some amount of various specific abilities *(s)*. Although Spearman tried to avoid calling his "*g*" factor intelligence—he preferred *mental energy*—he did believe that tests of intelligence in fact measured "*g*," or general ability.

Spearman's *two-factor theory of intelligence* was the first real effort to probe the structure of mental capacity. His view was relatively straightforward: namely, that only two factors defined performance on a given test. Furthermore, he believed that the more a test was infused with "*g*," the better a test of intelligence it was, since it measured general mental ability.

Group Factors

Soon after Spearman's formulation, criticisms of his procedures and theory appeared. The most fundamental problem surrounded the issue of defining one and only one factor—Spearman's "*g*" factor—as the basis for an intercorrelation between scores. Specifically, it was pointed out that two tests could correlate with each other not due to a common "*g*" or even an identical "*s*," but rather due to an *intermediate* group of skills, like verbal ability or visual imagery. Though these intermediate skills might themselves be correlated with "*g*," they could legitimately be considered separate abilities. In fact, Thurstone identified a number of such intermediate skills, which he called "Primary Mental Abilities"; these included Spatial, Perceptual, Numerical, Verbal Relations, Words, Memory, Induction, Deduction, and Arithmetic Reasoning (Thurstone, 1938).

Research has tended to support Thurstone's contention that one or two factors alone cannot account for the pattern of correlations among the various subtests on the WAIS. Thus, although Thurstone found substantial correlations among all items (supporting Spearman's notion of a general ability), he also found identifiable "groups" of correlations that went together. For example, he observed that vocabulary, information, comprehension, and similarities all correlated with each other highly and much less with other items like object assembly and block design. Though these four tests involve many different specific "*s*" abilities, the items can be grouped into a "verbal" component of ability. Likewise, object assembly, block design, picture completion, and picture arrangement correlate highly and may be grouped as a separate "visual" component. Thus these intermediate-level abilities came to be called "group factors." There are other group factors as well, suggesting other possible components.

The result of these early factor-analysis procedures was to increase the number of abilities or components beyond the simple two-factor theory of Spearman. It was felt that there may be a number of different factors at different levels of abstraction. At the highest level is "*g*"—some general ability that plays a role in most tests and, indeed, in most thinking. At an intermediate level there may be a number of as yet undetermined general abilities, like verbal skills or the ability to use visual imagery, on which people may differ and that will manifest themselves on the appropriate tests. At the most specific level are skills ("*s*") related only to that test (Brody & Brody, 1976).

Fluid and Crystallized Intelligence

The analysis of mental structure did not end with Spearman and Thurstone. Raymond B. Cattell carried Spearman's observations a step further (Brody & Brody, 1976). He noted that tests involving perceptual classifications and analogies were highly correlated and were good measures of "*g*." In contrast, tests like vocabulary or information did not reflect "*g*" very well and seemed to depend more on knowledge acquired in school. The first set of tests seemed to be pure measures of ability uncontaminated by cultural factors. From considerations such as these, Cattell attempted to devise a "culture-fair" test.

Cattell (1971) proposed that the general ability "*g*" is actually composed of two separate components: "*g_f*" for **fluid intelligence** and "*g_c*" for **crystallized intelligence.** Fluid intelligence was presumed to be that aspect of intelligence that did not depend on cultural influences but was related more to general learning ability—perhaps, he suggested, to the size of the individual's neural substrate for learning. Crystallized intelligence was that component thought to reflect a person's schooling and acculturation.

According to Cattell's theory, factor analysis of performance on different IQ test items should result in two factors. Those items most obviously related to school learning should fall together on one factor ("*g_c*"), while those items least dependent on schooling should fall together on the other factor("*g_f*"). This distinction has not, however, been definitely established—at least not in factor analytic studies to date (Brody & Brody, 1976). Some of these studies seem to support Cattell's g_f/g_c distinction, but others do not. Thus, although Cattell's notion is logically appealing, acceptance (or rejection) of his ideas awaits further research.

J. P. Guilford

The theorists we have considered to this point are, despite their differences, all pretty much committed to the view that there exists a relatively small number of abilities that comprise intelligence. A radically different view has been proposed by Guilford (1967), who feels that there are a great number of mental abilities (120 in fact) that are called into play in different ways at different times.

Basically, Guilford feels that, to understand mental structure, one must assess three kinds of information: (1) what does a thinker think about (*content*); (2) what process does he utilize in that thinking (*operation*); and (3) how do these thoughts manifest themselves (*product*)?

Guilford further breaks down each of the three kinds of thought into subcomponents. Thus, he divides the *content* of thought into:

1. Figural—specific features of things we see, hear, and touch, such as color, loudness, or texture.
2. Symbolic—letters, digits, or other symbols.

3. Semantic—ideas.
4. Behavioral—mental ability manifested in social situations.

Guilford also describes five different thought *operations,* including:

1. Cognition—recognition, discovery, and so forth.
2. Memory—retaining and recalling a cognition.
3. Divergent thinking—producing a variety of ideas or solutions to a problem.
4. Convergent thinking—producing the best, most elegant idea or problem solution.
5. Evaluation—deciding how good or bad an idea is.

Finally, Guilford suggests five different possible *products* of thought:

1. Unit—a single digit, letter, or word.
2. Class—a higher-order concept.
3. Relation—a connection between ideas or concepts.
4. Transformation—changing an idea in some way.
5. Implication—drawing an inference from a set of different pieces of information.

The result of crossing the various subcategories of contents, operations, and products with each other yields a 4 by 5 by 6 "cube" of intellectual structure (hence the 120 different abilities that Guilford postulates). Guilford has devised individual tests to, presumably, measure each cell in the structure. For example, an item (called *Hidden Print*) is used to test Cognition of Figural Units; this item involves finding a digit or letter formed by a group of dots among a random matrix of dots. The task involves cognition (an "operation"), since the person is supposed to discover something; the "content" is a visual one—that is, figural; and the "product" is a unit (a letter or digit). As a further illustration, in a test of Memory for Symbolic Classes, a person is presented with names like IRIS, IRENE, IRVING. He is then shown another word (like IRA or IDA) and asked if the word belongs with the other words. The "operation" of memory is involved, the "content" is symbolic (names), and the "product" is a class.

On the basis of test results from many different people, Guilford has concluded that mental abilities are extremely diverse and therefore cannot be captured in the simplistic theories of either Spearman or Cattell. Specifically, Guilford noted that, based upon his own calculations, 24% of the correlations between his various tests did not reach any level of statistical significance. From this, he argued that there was no evidence—at least from his own studies—for general underlying factors in intellectual ability.

Despite Guilford's assertion, it is evident that 76% of Guildford's own correlations were, in fact, significantly high. In this sense, then, there is a good degree of correlation among various tests and test items. Therefore, those who argue for a small number of components of intelligence appear to be closer to the truth.

Problems with the Factor Analytic Approach

The study of intelligence through the use of factor analysis has borne some fruit, but one is often left with a sense of uneasiness about the technique. Indeed, there are several problems with the factor analytic method that hamper its usefulness. The first problem with the factor analytic method is a purely methodological one. This problem centers on the choice of tests on which the data are originally collected. Since inferences about mental abilities are determined by the correlations among tests, abilities cannot show up in the results unless appropriate tests for those abilities are used in the first place.

Other interpretive criticisms can be made. For example, factor analysis assumes that a high positive correlation between two items means that the same mental ability is involved in the two items. This assumption may be false. For example, if you give the "digit-span backward test" to a group of people, some report that they do it verbally (by silently repeating the digits forward and then saying the last digit aloud), and others report that they do it visually (by projecting the digits onto a mental screen and reading them off backward). If the digit-span backward test were to correlate with the information test, one might be tempted to state that both tests involve verbal ability, when clearly the digit-span need not—at least for those who use the "mental screen," rather than the "verbal," memory technique. Hence, the general assumption that correlation implies underlying similarity cannot be uncritically accepted.

Finally, even if one could assume that these correlations indicate the presence of some basic ability, it is no easy task to discover just what the basic ability is. Psychologists have tended to give labels (like "verbal ability" or "imagery") to different clusters of correlations. However, it must be remembered that these labels are only arbitrary descriptions and not true explanations for test performance. To say, for example, that scores on various subtests correlate and thus represent verbal ability is to beg the question of what we mean by verbal ability. In short, we can and do derive labels for the various correlations that we observe, but these labels are simply our best guesses of the meaning of what we have observed.

A Newer Approach

Given the problem of the factor analytic approach, some psychologists have attempted to examine intelligence more directly (Keating & Bobbitt, 1978). They argue that intelligence may be embodied very directly in the basic processes by which we attend to, remember, and process information. In one study, groups of children of above-average mental ability and below-average mental ability were shown a series of digits (for example, 6, 1, 4). Once they had the digits fixed in memory, they were shown another digit (for instance, 4) and had to decide as quickly as possible whether it was part of the original series. In order to solve this problem, subjects had to rapidly scan their memories to see if the digit was there. Children of above-average mental ability performed this mental scanning much more rapidly and efficiently than children of below-average mental ability (Keating & Bobbitt, 1978).

The approach taken here represents a radical departure from more traditional factor analytic techniques. The goal of this newer approach is to identify as precisely and carefully as possible the processes of thinking that distinguish highly intelligent from less intelligent children. As such this approach is very much like the information-processing approach to cognition that we discussed in the last chapter. How successful it will be, in understanding either development or intelligence, must await further research.

Summary of Whether Intelligence Is One or Many Things

Psychologists have used a statistical method called *multiple-factor analysis* to probe the question of whether intelligence comprises one, a few, or many basic mental abilities. Using this method, different psychologists have postulated widely different answers to the question. Spearman argues that two basic types of abilities are involved in measurements of intelligence: a *general ability* ("*g*") that is involved in different skills and *specific abilities* ("*s*") uniquely associated with each of these skills. Thurstone and others, in contrast, have postulated *intermediate general abilities* (such as "verbal skills" and "visual imagery") that, together with the "*g*" and "*s*" factors, seem to be involved in tests of intelligence. Still a further orientation is that of Cattell, who argues that the various mental abilities involved in intelligence can be divided into two basic categories: *fluid intelligence*, meaning those aspects of intelligence not dependent on cultural influences, and *crystallized intelligence*, meaning that component of intelligence resulting from a person's schooling and acculturation. Finally, Guilford, unlike the other theorists mentioned in our discussion, argues that intelligence is made up of many different basic mental abilities, rather than only a few.

Available data seem to support the notion of a relatively small number of components of intelligence, although the precise nature of these components remains unclear at present.

WHAT ARE THE ROLES OF HEREDITY AND ENVIRONMENT IN DETERMINING IQ?

The question of *heredity* versus *environment* brings us into an area of great controversy. Ever since "mental testing" began and the IQ score was established as a fairly reliable, fairly predictable characteristic of a person, the question of whether one's IQ is determined predominantly by nature or by nurture has been of central importance. There are those who argue that heredity and environment are inextricably bound in determining the IQ of any one individual, so that attempts to separate their relative contributions are fruitless. This, however, is true only in a limited sense. For though it is difficult to separate the contributions for any one individual, it is possible to estimate the strengths of heredity and environment in the population as a whole. Biologists do this quite frequently, and the results have been applied successfully to, for example, animal breeding programs. Geneticists and population biologists, in fact, have mathematical formulas for estimating the comparative potency of heredity versus environment. This field, called *population genetics*, attempts to portion out the various influences into percentages and to compare the percentages for heredity and environment. Basically, the formula used is:

$$\text{Individual's IQ Score} = \text{Genetics} + \text{Environment} + \text{Covariance}$$
$$\text{of genetics and environment}$$

Let us consider each component separately. The influence of genetics is called **heritability** (and is symbolized by "h^2"). Heritability represents the amount of variability in some outward characteristic (like height, weight, IQ score) in a population that is attributable to variations in the genes possessed by individuals belonging to that population. Thus, if h^2 for IQ scores is .80, this means that 80% of the variability of scores for the particular population being examined is due to differences in their genes.

Note that statements about heritability are statements about populations—not individuals. Thus we cannot say that 80% of a particular person's IQ score is determined by his genetic makeup. This is a critical distinction. IQ scores vary in a population, as we have seen, with these variations being approximately normally distributed. Heritability estimates how much of this variability can be accounted for by genetic differences among individuals. For example, assume that the heritability figure for IQ within a particular population were 1.0. This would mean that almost all the variability in IQ for the population is caused by differences in genes, rather than by differences in environment. Nevertheless, if an individual child within this population had been locked up in a closet for the first five years of his life, we can quite safely predict that his IQ would be miserably low. With adequate care and stimulation, however, his IQ would rise, though maybe not to a normal level. His low IQ would not affect the overall heritability figure for the population as a whole, since heritability says nothing about how much the environment may affect any one individual.

Before discussing further the question of the relative influences of genetic and environmental factors on intelligence, let us briefly describe how these two factors operate. Recall from Chapter 2 that genetic traits are determined by the interaction of gene pairs. When a trait, like intelligence, has many possible values, it is determined by many different gene pairs and is called a *composite trait*. Since there are so many different possible combinations of genes for a composite trait, it is virtually impossible to make useful predictions about any particular child.

The complexity of the genetic factors involved in intelligence is compounded by the fact that human beings do not mate randomly. Rather, there is a tendency for people to mate with others who are similar to themselves, and who have similar genes. This tendency is called *assortative mating*. Intelligence is a variable that often produces assortative mating, with intelligent people tending to seek out and mate with other intelligent people. The result is that their children acquire genes that more closely resemble those of their parents than would be the case if matings occurred randomly.

Environmental influences on intelligence are also numerous. For example, biological factors such as prenatal environment, early nutrition, and health are known to influence the development of cognitive abilities and intelligence (see Chapters 2 and 3). Social influences, too, such as family structure, home environment, and peer group, are also important. Again, then, we find that the number of possible factors involved is so numerous as to make it impossible to make valid predictions about any particular child.

Our problem of determining the specific effects of environment and heredity on intelligence is further compounded by the fact that genetic and environmental factors do not operate in isolation; rather, they interact with one another. The relationship between genetic and environmental factors is known as the "covariation of genetics and environment." For example, intelligent people, being more likely to "succeed," will as a consequence be able to provide their children with better environmental conditions. Thus, intelligent genes and better environments tend to go together (covary), while the opposite is likewise true.

With these basic concepts in mind, we turn now to the factor most in controversy: the heritability factor (h^2). We will deal first with the evidence in favor of heritability, and then present the counterarguments.

The Influence of Heredity

There are three main sources of evidence on the heritability of IQ: **twin studies, adoption studies,** and studies of **kinship correlations.**

Twin Studies

The study of twins is a particularly intriguing way to get at the role of heredity in IQ, since it is known that *monozygotic* (identical) twins share identical sets of genes. *Dyzygotic* (fraternal) twins, in constrast, are like normal siblings in genetic similarity. Differences in the genetic relationships between monozygotic twins on the one hand and dyzygotic twins and normal siblings on the other hand thus provide a basis for comparing the relationship between genetic makeup and intelligence.

The IQ correlation of monozygotic twins reared together is about .90, while the IQ correlations for dyzygotic twins and normal siblings are about .60 and .55, respectively (Brody & Brody, 1976). Thus, it is argued by some that IQ must be largely genetically determined, since the more genetically similar children are, the closer together are their IQ scores. However, one could also argue (and correctly) that monozygotic twins are not only genetically more similar but also share more uniform environments; this environmental similarity could work to produce more similar IQ scores.

In order to demonstrate that it is their identical genes—and not their identical environment—that is responsible for these high correlations, one must therefore examine the degree of similarity in IQ scores of monozygotic twins *not* reared together. One study, by Sir Cyril Burt in England, did just that. Burt studied the IQ correlations of monozygotic twins who were reared apart in homes that he claimed were not similar at all. He found a correlation of .86 in IQ scores for the separated monozygotic twins. When this figure is converted into a heritability score, it becomes .80. Hence, Burt concluded that 80% of the variation in IQ in the population is due to genetic variation between individuals (Burt, 1955, 1966).

Adoption Studies

Another source of evidence on heredity comes from studies of the IQ correlations of parents with children whom they had given up for adoption at an early age. The logic of these studies is that if environment is all-important in determining IQ, then the child's IQ ought to correlate more highly with the adopting parents than with the biological parents. In contrast, if the correlation between the biological parents and the child is higher than that of the adopting parents and the child, this constitutes evidence for a strong influence of heredity—an influence that maintains itself even in very different environments. On the basis of a number of studies (for example, Jencks, 1972), it has been estimated that the correlation between biological parent and child is around .55, while the correlation between adopting parent and child is only about .28. Thus, even though the biological parents had little contact with the child, their IQ correlates more strongly with the child's IQ than does that of the adopting parents, again suggesting a strong role of heredity in determining intelligence.

Kinship Correlation

The last source of evidence concerning heredity derives from calculating IQ correlations as a function of the "blood relationship" between two individuals. In a sense, identical or monozygotic twins are at one extreme (with a correlation of .90), while at the other extreme are two unrelated children who are reared in the same home (they correlate about .24 with each other in IQ). In between there are various degrees of relatedness: parents, grandparents, uncles, cousins. Geneticists have worked out predictions for how closely blood relatives should correlate with one another on the assumption that intelligence is a purely heritable trait. They have found that the actual correlations agree quite well with the predicted correlations, implying that intelligence must therefore be a largely heritable trait. For example, if intelligence were purely genetic, the predicted average IQs of first cousins in a population would correlate about .18 and second cousins about .14 (Herrnstein, 1971). The actual correlations from the studies were .26 and .18—too large to explain by genetic factors alone but quite close. The predicted correlation in IQs between grandparent and grandchild was .31; the correlation actually found was .27. Finally, parent and child should correlate, by genes alone, about .49, whereas the actual figure is .50. Since the actual correlations are so close to the correlations predicted for a purely genetic trait, it is argued, intelligence must be more a matter of genetics than of environment (Herrnstein, 1971).

Critique

The above studies represent the primary evidence favoring a genetic explanation of IQ. Almost as soon as the evidence was advanced, however, criticisms poured forth. Let us therefore look at each source of evidence and the kinds of criticisms advanced. As we shall see, the controversy that has resulted takes us beyond the realm of objective debate into some of the darker corners of scientific inquiry.

The Twin Studies. There have been numerous studies of twins (Juel-Nielson, 1965; Newman, Freeman, & Holzinger, 1937; Shields, 1962). However, the most important and controversial ones are those of Sir Cyril Burt, discussed above. Not only did Burt report the largest monozygotic twin correlation (.86), but his is the only study in which it is purported that the environments of the separated twins were not similar. Because of its significance, Professor Leon Kamin (1974) undertook an extensive review of Burt's studies—studies that spanned several decades of research. Kamin uncovered some puzzling aspects in Burt's data. First, Kamin found a lack of consistent information about the conduct of Burt's studies. Burt sometimes reported that he administered the English version of the Stanford-Binet. In other instances, however, Burt emphatically denied using the Binet tests. On occasion, when questionable results were obtained about the scores of twins, Burt retested them, relying on the judgments of their teachers if they felt that the obtained scores did not reflect the children's "true" scores.

Other anomalies turned up in Kamin's examination. For example, the size of Burt's actual sample of twins kept changing over the years, as new twins were added and some were dropped. However, in three separate reports, published in 1955, 1958, and 1966, the IQ correlation reported for monozygotic twins reared apart never changed out to the third decimal place (.771), nor did that of monozygotic twins reared together (.944). Kamin felt that stability of this magnitude strains credibility (Kamin, 1974).

In other places, Burt was extremely inconsistent. For example, in two separate papers, he gave different estimates of the numbers of twins of professional parents who were reared in institutions. There are other procedural ambiguities and methodological anomalies in Burt's studies. There is even evidence that the people Burt cited as coauthors may not have, in fact, existed. In summing up his evaluation of Burt's work, Kamin concludes that "The numbers left behind by Professor Burt are simply not worthy of serious scientific consideration" (Kamin, 1972, p. 11).

What of the other, non-Burt, twin studies? Kamin reviewed three other major studies and found various problems with all of them. The most troublesome problem is that separated twins were most often placed in very similar environments. Consequently, one cannot know whether the observed similarities in IQ scores came from a common heredity or from the very similar environments. The general conclusion that has been drawn by critics of the twin studies is that the data on which these studies are based leave a good deal to be desired; thus, critics argue, deriving estimates of heritability is not justified.

The Adoption Studies. Kamin also undertook a review of the adoption studies that, as you will recall, have shown much higher IQ correlations between biological mother and child (.55) than between adopting mother and adopted child (.28). Kamin noted a serious omission in the data. What about the correlation, he asked, between the adopting parents and their own biological children? When Kamin examined those correlations, he found a surprising result; the correlation between the IQs of adopting parents and their own children is only .35, significantly lower than the same correlation in the general population. Kamin concluded that, for a variety of reasons, adopting parents are a special group of people whose characteristics or actions result in lower correlations, both with their own children and with their adopted children. For this reason, he argued, it is not fair to use the correlations obtained from adopting parents to their natural and adopted children to make inferences about the strength of hereditary influences.

Despite Kamin's argument (which is in this instance valid), there are other kinds of evidence on adopted children that suggest at least some genetic determination of IQ scores (Brody & Brody, 1976). For example, why does the biological mother's IQ correlate with her child's at all if genetics is irrelevant? Kamin argues that the *apparent* connection is due to selective placement (that is, children being placed in foster home environments that are similar to the biological mother's home environment). But this is stretching the notion of "similarity" beyond reasonable boundaries. In fact, very little correlation has been found between characteristics of the biological mother and those of the adopting mother. In a recent study, Munsinger (1975) looked at correlations between IQ scores of adopted children and the social and educational status of their biological parents. Social status of the biological parents correlated .70 with the child's IQ. The corresponding correlation involving the adopting parents was −.14, essentially no correlation. Significantly, there was no selective placement in this sample.

Kinship Correlations.   As we have seen, the actual IQ correlations between relatives of different degrees of kinship appear in some studies to approximate those that would be predicted if IQ were a purely genetic trait. This suggests some "genetic" determination of IQ. Nevertheless, it can be—and has been— argued that the environmental similarities between relatives closely approximate the genetic similarities; that is, relatives tend to share similar environments, making it impossible to say which (environmental or genetic similarity) is "the" causal factor (Brody & Brody, 1976). Hence, it is argued, no clear estimate can be made of the relative strengths of genetics versus environment in explaining the kinship correlations.

Summary of the Roles of Genetics and Environment

The issue of IQ and "heredity versus environment" is one that has generated great controversy and debate. Presently there are those who argue that the cumulative evidence (twin studies, adoption studies, and kinship correlations) is overwhelmingly in favor of a genetic determination of IQ and, further, that the data translate into a *heritability* score of about .80. In contrast are others who argue that the data are neither clear nor strong enough to permit any statements at all about heritability, let alone about the magnitude of the supposed influence.

At this point, we must all make up our own minds. Genetic influences on IQ scores do appear to exist, but the degree of influence is very much in debate. Be it .10, .50, or .80, however, the numbers refer to populations, and not to particular individuals. One cannot use these numbers to infer what kind of effect any particular environmental intervention would have on any particular child.

ARE THERE RACIAL (OR OTHER GROUP) DIFFERENCES IN IQ?

We return at this point to the quote by Arthur Jensen with which we began this chapter. Jensen concluded that compensatory education had failed. His argument was straightforward: intervention programs have tried to raise IQ scores through environmental efforts; IQ scores are most strongly determined by genetics (Jensen accepted the heritability figure of .80); hence, attempting to raise IQ through intervention programs was doomed to inevitable failure (Jensen, 1969).

Jensen's assertions and conclusions were assailed at all levels. Some criticized him for prematurely concluding that compensatory education had failed at a time when most programs were still only developing. Others criticized his acceptance of the 80 percent figure for genetic determination. Perhaps his most serious error, however, was in using the heritability figure to infer that environmental intervention was necessarily doomed. As we have seen, heritability (h^2) in a population bears no necessary relation to the effectiveness of environmental intervention with a particular child. As Brody and Brody have noted, "It is an egregious error to derive conclusions about the validity of a program of environmental intervention from estimates of h^2" (1976, p. 112).

At the heart of the controversy over Jensen's article was not, however, the issue of genetic influences on IQ or even the "failure" of compensatory education. Rather, the controversy arose in large part because of the intimate relation of Jensen's position to racial issues that predominated in the United States in the late 1960s and early 1970s. At a time when Blacks were struggling for recognition of their rights and dignity, Jensen's conclusion seemed to many a kind of racist backlash, because most of the disadvantaged children in compensatory education programs were Black. It seemed to many that Jensen was in effect arguing that Blacks were genetically inferior to Whites in intelligence.

Black-White Differences
in IQ Scores

It is true that, on the average, groups of Black children have scored an average of 15 points lower on traditional IQ tests than have groups of White children (Brody & Brody, 1976). However, it seems highly inappropriate to jump from these bare data to the fatalistic conclusion that the difference results from genetic causes, as Jensen has done. There are many other possible explanations for these differences in performance. Probably the most important alternative explanation involves the cultural biases inherent in the IQ tests themselves. We have already seen that commonly used IQ tests, such as the Stanford-Binet, were designed for and standardized on middle-class White children raised in the United States. Many of the items on these tests therefore *assume* the shared experiences of White middle-class children—experiences that the Black child (especially the *poor* Black child) has not had. The Black child's "failure" on these culturally biased items, far from showing a lack of inherited mental capacity, may simply reflect lack of these experiences. Not even the supposedly "culture-reduced" and "culture-free" tests have escaped this problem. While these tests have tried to reduce the problem of cultural bias, they, too, have not been wholly successful in this attempt. Cultural bias thus appears to be a serious confounding factor in all of the tests—a factor that should cause us to view any purported "genetic" explanation of IQ differences between the races with extreme caution.

A second major criticism of Jensen's position is that, *even if* the perfect "culture-free" test could be designed and *even if* this test still showed IQ differences between Black and White children, one still could not automatically conclude that these differences are "genetically" determined. We know that environmental factors—in particular nutrition, health, and the quality of stimulation—all influence the course of cognitive development. We also know that inadequate nutrition, poor health, and inappropriate stimulation generally go hand-in-hand with poverty and that Blacks in our society are more likely than Whites to live in conditions of poverty (see discussion of these relations in Chapter 7). The poor Black child whose environment is more likely to be deprived in these environmental aspects is also more likely to suffer deficiencies in cognitive development, reflected in poorer performance on IQ tests. The 15-point difference in IQ observed in traditional IQ tests may thus be explained by environmental factors, as well as by cultural bias in the tests. Certainly, the difference need not necessarily—as Jensen asserts—be attributed to genetics alone.

At most, what we seem to have, then, are data that do show IQ differences but that are silent on the critical question of what has basically caused these differences. Any attempt to categorically assert the relative strengths of the many different possible contributing factors—environmental as well as genetic—is, at best, still extremely premature.

FAMILY SIZE
AND BIRTH ORDER

To round out our picture of group differences in IQ, we will mention briefly two other factors that relate to intelligence test scores: family size and birth order.

Children belonging to large families have, on the average, tended to score lower on intelligence tests than children from smaller families (Brody & Brody, 1976). Just what has caused this difference is not yet known, but there are a number of now-familiar possibilities: a presumed thinner spreading of parental attention; presumably poorer economic, nutritional, and health care; and other social conditions. Clearly, more study is needed before we would be able to pinpoint the true cause(s).

Similarly suggestive but inconclusive are the available data concerning birth order and IQ. A 1973 study in Holland (Belmont & Marolla, 1973; in Zajonc & Markus, 1975) reported the IQ test scores for 386,114 Dutch Selective Service registrants. When these scores were plotted according to birth order, the results came out as shown in Figure 10-6. As you can see, on the average, later-born children showed lower scores than those born earlier. And, somewhat surprisingly, the last child born in the family showed the largest drop in IQ of all. (Also note that the larger the family, the lower the overall IQ score of the children.) Again, however, these data simply suggest a starting point for further research; they do not tell us which of the many possible variables may be contributing to these results.

WHAT IS THE POTENTIAL USE (AND ABUSE)
OF IQ TESTS?

In this final section, we would like to consider just what use IQ tests have been put to and to point out some potential sources of abuse. IQ tests have penetrated the lives of children in two areas: schools, and clinical settings, such as hospitals and guidance centers.

IQ Tests in the Schools

Most children in the United States at one time or another receive some kind of individual or group IQ test. Though the practice seems to have decreased in recent years, partly because of the controversies we have just discussed, IQ information is generally still obtained and is available to teachers and counselors. In what ways are the test results used and, possibly, abused (Brody & Brody, 1976)?

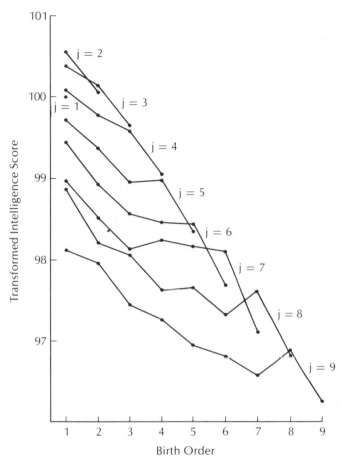

Figure 10-6. Birth order, family size, and intelligence. Note that j = number of children in family. (From Zajonc, R. B., & Markus, G. B. Birth order and intellectual development. *American Psychologist*, 1975, *82*, 75. Copyright 1975 by the American Psychological Association. Reproduced by permission.)

Identification of Low Achievers

One common use of IQ tests is to spot students who for one reason or another are not achieving their full academic potential. A child who is failing in the third grade and yet receives a score of 130 might be cause for concern or special attention. Without the IQ test, one probably would not have known that the child was capable of higher achievement—hence the tests' potential for constructive use. By the same token, however, an IQ score can be misused to "justify" a student's poor performance. If a student is performing poorly and also gets a low IQ test score, the child's poor performance may easily be blamed on a supposed low potential, resulting in a fatalistic assumption that nothing can be done to help the child and, hence, that attention should be directed to other, more promising children. What if, however, the child's poor performance is due not to irreparable genetic factors but to environmental problems—problems that could, with time and effort, be overcome? For this child, the low IQ test score, far from being a help, will prove a substantial hindrance. Care must therefore be taken not to make unwarranted assumptions about IQ test scores, lest the IQ tests be used as vehicles of abuse (even unwittingly), rather than as constructive tools.

Academic Tracking and Grouping

A related use of IQ test scores is in channeling students into classes based on their presumed mental abilities. One reason for this practice is the supposed predictive validity of IQ scores. If IQ score predicts school success (it is argued), why not channel or group students into areas in which they will be "best suited"? One problem here is that although IQ scores after the fact have been shown to correlate highly with school achievement, occupational status, and other measures of "success," it is a different matter to make that decision beforehand for any one individual. IQ scores can fluctuate widely during the lifetime of any one person, as we discussed earlier. Making a decision that may affect the course of a person's life on the basis of one IQ test score (or even several) is risky at best.

Interpretation of Scores

Having IQ scores available at all to influential adults may pose hazards, since even many supposed experts don't really understand the nature and limitations of the tests (Brody & Brody, 1976). Some educators believe that intelligence is fixed and unchanging across age. Ignorance about the basic characteristics of the tests, and consequent misinterpretation of the meaning (and importance) of a test score, can have serious consequences for a child in school.

IQ Tests in Clinical Settings

IQ test scores are usually obtained in clinical settings as part of a large battery of tests assessing a child's cognitive, emotional, and social skills. IQ scores, particularly the pattern of scores, are sometimes used to diagnose a particular disorder. For example, a child who is given a WISC and receives a high verbal IQ score and a low performance IQ score might be diagnosed as having a "specific learning disability." In the absence of other confirming evidence, this is a risky procedure, since many non-learning disabled or even normal children may show the same kind of pattern. The pattern of scores on an IQ test may be used inappropriately to infer a diagnostic category like "learning disabilities" when studies so far suggest that patterns of scores on IQ tests do not predict at all well the kind of problems a child may have (Brody & Brody, 1976).

The Positive Uses of IQ Tests

By themselves, IQ tests serve only a limited purpose. They provide only *potentially* valuable information about a child. When taken together with information from various other sources, they may help to provide a clearer picture of a child's strengths or weaknesses. The IQ score should not, however, serve as some end in itself; rather, the score should only be considered a starting point for further inquiry and action. If IQ tests indicate that a child has particular weaknesses, then steps should be taken to identify the sources of the weaknesses and to find methods of counteracting them. Similarly, if the tests indicate that a child has special strengths, these results should serve only as a starting point for further efforts (if appropriate) designed to bring him up to his full potential.

CHAPTER SUMMARY

In this chapter we have attempted to examine in some depth the concept of *intelligence* and the IQ tests used to assess it. We saw that traditional IQ tests do not provide a specific a priori definition of intelligence. They rest on the assumption that intelligence increases with age and that children whose mental abilities (as revealed by the test) develop earlier than average are somehow more intelligent.

Even though the IQ tests do not provide a specific definition of intelligence, they are not without value. Thus, IQ tests such as the Stanford-Binet and the Wechsler are *reliable* and have historically had high *predictive validity* for certain population groups about school performance and later accomplishments. Moreover, although a given individual's score may change rather dramatically over his life, the IQ tests do have some stability for populations as a whole.

During the years since IQ tests were first developed, a number of psychologists have attempted to define more precisely what the tests measure. As a result of this research, some psychologists have argued that performance on IQ tests is determined by a few basic *factors* or abilities. Other psychologists have argued that many different factors or abilities are involved. Although the issue is far from resolved, the evidence to date suggests to the authors that IQ test performance is probably determined by a relatively small number of basic abilities.

Related to the question of what abilities underlie performance on IQ tests is the question of what causes individual differences in these abilities. Although the relative importance of genetic and environmental factors in determining individual IQ scores remains unknown, there is little doubt that both are involved.

SUGGESTED READINGS

Brody, E. N., & Brody, N. *Intelligence: Nature, determinants, and consequences.* New York: Academic Press, 1976. An excellent and through survey of various facets of the study of intelligence, including a history of intelligence testing, the nature of IQ tests, and a balanced consideration of the questions surrounding genetics and intelligence and racial differences in intelligence.

Jensen, A. R. How much can we boost IQ and scholastic achievement? *Harvard Educational Review,* 1969, *39,* 1–123. The original article that ignited the controversy about genetics, IQ, and race. Jensen's claim is relatively comprehensible to the beginning student.

Kamin, L. J. *The science and politics of IQ.* Hillsdale, N.J.: Erlbaum, 1974. Partly in response to claims such as Jensen's, Kamin's review of work on the genetic basis of IQ provides a contrasting perspective to Jensen's and draws on some social and political factors in the controversy.

GLOSSARY

adoption studies. Studies that compare the correlation on some characteristics (for example, height or intelligence) between biological parent and child and adopting parent and the same child; one way to assess the role of heredity in determining the characteristic.

crystallized intelligence. One component of intelligence, according to Cattell, that reflects a person's schooling and acculturation.

factor analysis. A complicated statistical technique devised to find correlation among a variety of tests or items or other factors.

fluid intelligence. The other component of intelligence identified by Cattell; thought to be relatively independent of schooling and related to general learning ability.

"g." The term used by Spearman to capture the correlation that showed up among tests of ability and achievement. Spearman felt that some "general" ability was responsible for performance on all of these tests.

heritability. A term used in population genetics to refer to the amount of variance in a trait that could be attributed to hereditary or genetic influence.

intelligence. An ill-defined term used to describe mental ability; depends heavily on societal consensus about skills important to a culture.

IQ. Intelligence quotient, a score obtained by dividing mental age (determined by scores on a test like the Stanford-Binet) by chronological age and multiplying by 100. Average IQ is 100.

kinship correlations. Correlation on some characteristic between people who are related to each other in differing degrees, such as parents, grandparents, uncles, or cousins. Such correlations for IQ scores support the view that IQ is largely an inherited trait.

reliability. The requirement that a child given a particular test score on one day will obtain a similar score if tested a short time later.

standardization. The procedure for assuring that the sample from which a test is originally constructed is fairly representative of the population as a whole. Some IQ tests have been criticized for not having been properly standardized.

Stanford-Binet. A widely used test of intelligence that comprises a series of age-graded tasks assessing a variety of skills.

twin studies. Studies that compare the correlation on some characteristic (for example, height or IQ) between identical-twin, fraternal-twin, and sometimes nontwin siblings. Correlations have been used to estimate the role of heredity on the characteristic.

two-factor theory. The theory proposed by Spearman that intelligence is composed of two factors, general ability ("g") and special ability ("s"). Any test requires some amount of "g" and some amount of "s." The best tests of intelligence are those requiring lots of "g."

validity. The requirement that a test measure what it purports to measure. One kind of validity, *predictive validity*, refers to how well a test predicts something important in our society. The predictive validity of IQ tests refers to their ability to predict such things as school achievement and vocational success. In this sense IQ tests are valid measures of important differences between people in mental ability.

Wechsler Scales. A series of widely used tests of intelligence devised by David Wechsler. The tests sample a variety of different abilities that have been divided into two scales: a verbal scale and a performance scale.

REFERENCES

Bayley, N. Development of mental abilities. In P. H. Mussen (Ed.), *Carmichael's manual of child psychology.* New York: Wiley, 1970. Pp. 1163–1209.

Belmont, L., & Marolla, F. A. Birth order, family size, and intelligence. *Science,* 1973, *182,* 1096–1101.

Brody, E. N., & Brody, N. *Intelligence: Nature, determinants, and consequences.* New York: Academic Press, 1976.

Burt, C. The evidence for the concept of intelligence. *British Journal of Educational Psychology,* 1955, *25,* 158–177.

Burt, C. The genetic determination of differences in intelligence: A study of monozygotic twins reared together and apart. *British Journal of Psychology,* 1966, *57,* 137–153.

Cattell, R. B. *Abilities: Their structure, growth and action.* Boston: Houghton Mifflin, 1971.

Duncan, O. D., Featherman, D. L., & Duncan, B. *Socioeconomic background and achievement.* New York: Seminar Press, 1972.

Elkind, D. Giant in the nursery: Jean Piaget. *New York Times Magazine,* May 26, 1968.

Guilford, J. P. *The nature of human intelligence.* New York: McGraw-Hill, 1967.

Harrell, T. W., & Harrell, M. S. Army General Classification Test scores for civilian occupations. *Educational and Psychological Measurement,* 1945, *5,* 229–239.

Hay, E. N. Predicting success in machine bookkeeping. *Journal of Applied Psychology,* 1943, *27,* 483–493.

Herrnstein, R. J. I.Q. *Atlantic Monthly,* 1971, *228*(3), 43–64.

Herrnstein, R. J. *I.Q. in the meritocracy.* Boston: Little, Brown, 1973.

Jencks, C. *Inequality: A reassessment of the effect of family and schooling in America.* New York: Basic Books, 1972.

Jensen, A. R. How much can we boost I.Q. and scholastic achievement? *Harvard Educational Review,* 1969, *39,* 1–123.

Jensen, A. R. *Educability and group differences.* New York: Harper & Row, 1973.

Juel-Nielson, N. Individual and environment: A psychiatric-psychological investigation of monozygotic twins reared apart. *Acta Psychiatrica et Neurologica Scandinavia,* Monograph Supplement, 1965, 183.

Kamin, L. J. Heredity, intelligence, politics and psychology. Unpublished manuscript, Princeton University, 1972.

Kamin, L. J. *The science and politics of IQ.* Hillsdale, N.J.: Erlbaum, 1974.

Keating, D. P., & Bobbitt, B. L. Individual and developmental differences in cognitive-processing of mental ability. *Child Development,* 1978, *49,* 155–167.

Kenagy, H. G., & Yockum, C. E. *The selection and training of salesmen.* New York: McGraw-Hill, 1925.

Matarazzo, J. D. *Wechsler's measurement and appraisal of adult intelligence* (5th ed.). Baltimore, Md.: Williams & Wilkins, 1972.

Munsinger, H. Children's resemblance to their biological and adopting parents in two ethnic groups. *Behavior Genetics,* 1975, *5,* 239–254.

Newman, H. H., Freeman, F. N., & Holzinger, K. J. *Twins: A study of heredity and environment.* Chicago: University of Chicago Press, 1937.

Shields, J. *Monozygotic twins brought up apart and together.* London: Oxford University Press, 1962.

Spearman, C. The proof and measurement of association between two things. *American Journal of Psychology,* 1904, *15,* 72–101.

Spearman, C. *The abilities of man.* New York: Macmillan, 1927.

Terman, L. M. (Ed.). *Genetic studies of genius. Volume 1: Mental and physical traits of a thousand gifted children.* Stanford, Calif.: Stanford University Press, 1925.

Thurstone, L. L. *Primary mental abilities.* Chicago: University of Chicago Press, 1938.

Wechsler, D. *Wechsler Intelligence Scale for Children.* New York: Psychological Corporation, 1949.

Wechsler, D. *The measurement and appraisal of adult intelligence.* Baltimore: Williams & Wilkins, 1958.

Wechsler, D. *Wechsler Intelligence Scale for Children.* New York: Psychological Corporation, 1974.

Zajonc, R. B., & Markus, G. B. Birth order and intellectual development. *Psychological Review,* 1975, *82,* 74–88.

11

Social and Emotional Development during the School Years

We have all heard the logical dilemma of "which came first, the chicken or the egg?" Psychologists attempting to understand the school-aged child face a similar dilemma: namely, which comes first, school or the onset of maturity? As we saw in Chapter 9, the child's entrance into school is accompanied by a host of changes in his intellectual abilities. These changes, in turn, are reflected in numerous advances in the child's commerce with his environment. Do these changes mean that the child has somehow become more mature and, hence, is now ready for school? Or does going to school somehow bring about these changes, thereby making the child more mature?

Though we may never find a satisfactory resolution to this question, some things are apparent. We do know that the tremendous gains in social and emotional development that take place during the school years are reflected in almost everything the child says and does. Perhaps most noticeable is the child's increasing independence from parents and other adults, accompanied by a parallel dependence upon peers—peers with whom children spend many of their waking hours. We know, too, that the quality of the relationships that children form with their peers changes rather dramatically when children enter school. School-aged children are much less egocentric in their dealings with others. They are therefore more likely to form adult-like relationships. We shall see that many of the changes in social behavior at this age go hand in hand with the child's progress in understanding himself and others: the ability to take the perspective of another person, the ability to relate empathetically to another person's emotions, and the ability to evaluate the morality of other people and of oneself.

INTERACTIONS WITH OTHERS

Children's social interactions undergo major alterations and expansions when they enter school. No longer are these interactions limited to the parents or a few other adults and children. Children must now learn to deal effectively with several teachers and administrators and a whole classroom full of other children. As they spend more and more time with these other people, school-aged children necessarily spend less and less time with their parents.

The Role of the Parents

In Chapter 8, we described the preschool child as beginning to show independence from his parents, although the preschool child's attachment to and dependence on his parents are still quite strong. By school age, however, the child's independence from his parents is more obvious and extreme. School-aged children continually assert their independence to "do their own thing," even though often it is not what their parents tell them to do and sometimes it is the exact opposite. This is not to say that the emotional ties between parent and child disappear, for the school-aged child continues to feel strongly toward his parents. This bond is not, however, primarily one of dependency.

The school-aged child still spends a substantial amount of time with his parents, during late afternoons, evenings, weekends, and holidays. During this time, parents continue to play an active role in shaping the child's social behavior. However, the push toward independence felt by the child at this time means that he or she spends much less time in the parents' company, and more and more waking hours with friends or in school. These two factors (a growing sense of independence and spending less time with parents) work to restrict the direct impact of the parents on the child's behavior. Nevertheless, even in their absence, parents normally continue to exert an indirect influence on the child's actions. Patterns of socialization begun during the preschool period—through *reward* and *punishment, imitation,* and *identification*—continue to direct the child's behavior. Parental attitudes about acceptable and unacceptable behavior have been largely *internalized* by the child to the point that they now represent his own standards of social acceptability. When school-aged children violate these standards, they feel guilt, even when they know that their parents will not discover the transgression.

The Role of the Teacher

Though the school-aged child spends far less time than formerly in the presence of his parents, he is seldom left completely in charge of his own actions. Teachers now come to take on a major role as socializers of the school-aged child. Like the parents of the preschooler, teachers now have the power to reward and punish; teachers act as *models* for the child's imitation and, in some cases, as models for identification. A sense of the importance of teachers in the child's life at this time can be obtained by remembering how many of your friends from 7 to 11 years of age claimed they would be teachers when they grew up! Teachers are very salient people in the lives of school-aged children.

ISSUE

What effect is there on young boys of having all female teachers?

Ours is a society in which teachers of young children have been predominantly women. It is also a society in which young boys have a harder time adjusting to school. Boys are more likely to be disruptive and behave unacceptably in school; they are also more likely to have trouble academically and to be recommended for classes for the educationally handicapped. Some psychologists have wondered whether the problems faced by young boys in school could be due, in part, to the fact that most of their teachers are women. Since young boys may have trouble identifying with a female teacher, they may be less inclined to acquire school-based values and attitudes. Although we are far from answering this question, there is some evidence that the predominantly female teaching establishment in the United States contributes to the school problems of young boys. In the island of Hokkaido in northern Japan, the proportion of male elementary school teachers is about 60%. In Hokkaido, the number of boys suffering from learning disorders is equal to the number of girls—a situation that contrasts sharply with our own society, in which the number of boys suffering from learning disabilities far outweighs the number of girls suffering from these problems (Dr. Kuzuo Miyake, as cited by Janis, Mahl, Kagan, & Holt, 1969).

What Makes a Good Teacher?

Since children's teachers serve as one of the primary socializers of children's behavior, it is important to know what characteristics are associated with success in this capacity. In other words, what kind of teacher is likely to help children to learn about themselves and others and to learn to behave in ways that are valued in our society?

Though we don't have a complete answer to this important question, available evidence does suggest that more effective teachers have basically similar characteristics to good parents (see discussion in Chapter 8). As with parents, the best teachers are those who are **love-oriented**—who rely heavily on praise and reasoning and who create a warm and nurturant environment for the children. The least effective teachers are those who are **power-assertive**—who stress threats and punishment when the child misbehaves (for example, see Anderson & Anderson, 1954; Gage, 1965). In addition, teachers, like parents, are most effective in shaping the child's behavior when they have the ability to "read" the child's behavior in advance and take appropriate action before the child has actually acted. In short, the best teacher is the one who can sensitively guide the child toward appropriate avenues of behavior, rather than punishing the child after he has gotten onto the wrong track.

The Role of Peers

In large part, the school years can be described as a period when teachers come to take on much of the parents' role in the socialization of the child. However, school-age socialization cannot be ascribed solely to the replacement of two adults, the parents, by several others, the teachers. One must also consider the crucial impact exerted by schoolchildren on one another. Reasons for the increasing influence of peers during school age are not hard to discover. First and foremost, school-age children spend much of their day in school. In class, they are surrounded by 30 to 40 other children and usually one adult teacher. The sheer amount of time spent interacting with these other children cannot help but have an impact on children's attitudes and behavior.

Coupled with this quantitative increase in interaction with peers, there is a qualitative difference in interactions among children versus among children and adults. In child/adult interactions, the adult assumes higher status and power with the resulting tendency to control the way things are done. In child/child interactions, however, children meet on relatively equal ground, and each member of the group can contribute to group decisions and activities.

Peer Conformity

The favored status of peers during this period can be seen clearly in the *imitative* tendencies of children. As every parent and teacher knows, children will imitate almost anything they see another child do (Hartup & Coates, 1967; Hicks, 1965). An interesting demonstration of this *peer conformity* is provided by Berenda (1950).

Berenda studied the conformity of children aged 7 to 13 to inaccurate responses made by either peers or a teacher. The children were first shown a single line (the "standard") and then three "choice" lines. The task was to say which of the three choice lines was the same length as the standard line. However, before responding, each child heard either five peer "stooges" or a teacher answer incorrectly. The results showed that children of all ages tested were very likely to "conform," or give the wrong answer, and that they conformed more to a group of peers than to a teacher.

Peer Cooperation and Competition

Schoolchildren also influence one another through the manner in which they interact. Two particularly interesting forms of this interaction are *cooperation* and *competition*.

Somewhat surprisingly, research (see Bryan, 1975, for a review) on these two topics suggests that cooperation and competition are inextricably linked, with both being related to the child's age. As a child progresses through the early school years, his interactions with peers seem to become increasingly competitive and decreasingly cooperative. Unfortunately, however, this conclusion is based on research in a game situation that typically does not allow children to behave both competitively and cooperatively at the same time. For example, in one task (Kagan & Madsen, 1971), two children play a game in which they take turns moving a marker to adjacent circles in a 7 by 7 array of circles. When the marker reaches one child's side, he is given a prize. Since each child can only move the marker once per trial, competitive behavior results in neither child winning. On the other hand, if the children cooperate and move the marker first to one child's side and then to the other's, both can win a prize. In this task, Kagan and Madsen found that 4- to 5-year-olds were more likely to cooperate than 7- to 9-year-olds.

One should keep in mind, however, that game situations, such as the one described above, are natural grounds for competitive interaction. The fact that children become increasingly competitive—and decreasingly cooperative—in such situations may tell us little about competitiveness and cooperation in other situations. It seems likely that the child's tendency to be either competitive or cooperative with his peers is strongly colored by whether or not they are close friends and also by the social situation in which they find themselves (Bryan, 1975). For example, in settings where cooperation is essential, as in team sports, it may well increase with age.

How Are Friendships Formed during the School Years?

Since friends are so important in the child's life, let us consider for a moment on what basis children form friendships. One obvious basis is *proximity;* children are more likely to form friendships with other children who live nearby, since they are most likely to be in regular contact. However, proximity is not the only basis for friendship. Like adults, children do not form friendships with every child who happens to be around. The girl next door may not become a friend, even though she is close at hand, for numerous other factors, such as *similarity, status*, and *social qualities*, also seem to determine who will and who will not become friends. Thus, schoolchildren prefer to play and be friends with children who are similar to themselves—the same sex, the same age, and with similar backgrounds and interests. They prefer to be friends with children who enjoy high status due to attractive physical appearance or special skills. Finally, school-children prefer to be friends with other children who possess certain social graces, such as outgoingness, generosity, kindness, and friendliness (see Campbell, 1964; Hartup, 1970).

An Experiment in the Formation of Children's Friendships. Much of our current knowledge about how children form friendship groups comes from some ingenious research by Mazafer Sherif and Caroline Sherif (Sherif & Sherif, 1953, 1964; Sherif, Harvey, White, Hood, & Sherif, 1961). Though their work formed a series of studies, one experiment in particular, called the Robber's Cave (Sherif et al., 1961), is very revealing.

The Robber's Cave experiment took place at a summer camp for boys. Twenty-two fifth-grade boys were divided into two matched groups. Prior to the beginning of camp, all the boys were strangers, and at the outset, neither group knew of the other's existence. Once the two groups had discovered one another, there were several contrived instances of competition and, finally, of cooperation.

In the course of this experiment, many observations were made about the structure of the two groups. First, friendship and leadership patterns developed very quickly in both groups. When the two groups discovered one another, each group's solidarity increased, with expressions of aggression and hostility being directed primarily at the "other" group. When, however, the two groups were required to work together cooperatively, old group lines diminished; there was less "other-group" hostility, and friendships were formed that crossed group lines. Thus, although group and friendship patterns may initially evolve through physical proximity, similarity, and status, *situational factors* are also important. Competitive situations appear to make people in a group close ranks, which prevents the formation of new friendships, whereas cooperative situations help to break down old barriers and foster the development of new friendships.

ISSUE

Can "gang" and "racial" barriers be diminished through cooperative activities?

The results of the Robber's Cave experiment suggest a possible means of reducing the extreme barriers that separate certain groups of children, such as "gangs" and sometimes racial groups. The intergang rivalry and competition that characterize these groups probably increase hostility and aggression. What would happen, then, if these hostile gangs could be somehow channeled into cooperating, instead of competing, with one another? The Robber's Cave findings suggest that gang violence might be substantially reduced. The key, however, is in finding a way to convince or coerce such groups into working together. No ready technique has, as yet, been discovered.

Summary of Interactions with Others

The school years are characterized by both quantitative and qualitative changes in the child's interactions with others. The child spends less time with parents and more time with teachers and peers. The role of parents thus becomes increasingly _indirect; internalization_ of his parents' attitudes and beliefs—rather than the parents themselves—comes to guide the child's behavior. Direct socialization pressures on the schoolchild do continue to come from parents, but to a much greater degree they now come from teachers and peers. Peers, in particular, play a major role in influencing the child's social behavior. Pressure to _conform_ with the behavior and attitudes of peers becomes especially great. Additionally, _friendships_ are formed that provide models of behavior for the child to emulate. The nature and course of these friendships are influenced substantially by _peer proximity, similarity, status,_ and _social qualities,_ as well as _situational factors._

UNDERSTANDING ONESELF

Schoolchildren discover a great many things about themselves through interacting with one another. They begin to see themselves as others see them and to construct a more realistic and articulated self-concept. For perhaps the first time, they see their strengths and weaknesses and attitudes and values in a clearer light. This knowledge helps them to deal more effectively not only with others but also with themselves.

Advances in the Child's Self-Concept

In Chapter 8 we saw how the preschool child began to construct a feeling for himself as a separate entity. This early **self-concept** was, however, still rather poorly articulated. In contrast, the school-aged child shows an ever-increasing awareness of feelings about himself, as he comes to see himself more clearly. As his self-concept becomes better known and articulated, he begins to formulate values for himself and to make value judgments about himself. This tendency to judge himself heralds the development of **self-esteem** (Coopersmith, 1967).

Obviously, how a child comes to define himself (self-concept) and to judge himself (self-esteem) influences not only his current behavior but, more critically, the course of his future social development. Children who value themselves positively (high self-esteem) tend to behave in ways that result in positive evaluations by others. As one commentator describes these children:

> They have confidence in their perceptions and judgments and believe that they can bring their efforts to a favorable resolution. Their favorable self-attitudes lead them to accept their own opinions and place credence and trust in their reactions and conclusions. This permits them to follow their own judgments when there is a difference of opinion and also permits them to consider novel ideas. The trust in self that accompanies feelings of worthiness is likely to provide the conviction that one is correct and the courage to express those convictions. The attitudes and expectations that lead the individual with high self-esteem to greater social independence and creativity also lead him to more assertive and vigorous actions. They are more likely to be participants than listeners in group discussions, they report less difficulty in forming friendships and they will express opinions even when they know these opinions may meet with a hostile reception. Among the factors that underlie and contribute to these actions are their lack of self-consciousness and their lack of preoccupation with personal problems. Lack of self-consciousness permits them to present their ideas in a full and forthright fashion; lack of self-preoccupation permits them to consider and examine external issues [Coopersmith, 1967, p. 70].[1]

On the other hand, children who judge themselves negatively (have low self-esteem) act in ways that will prevent positive evaluations by others:

> These persons lack trust in themselves and are apprehensive about expressing unpopular or unusual ideas. They do not wish to expose themselves, anger others, or perform deeds that would attract attention. They are likely to live in the shadows of a social group, listening rather than participating, and preferring the solitude of withdrawal above the interchange of participation. Among the facts that contribute to the withdrawal of those low in self-esteem are their marked self-consciousness and preoccupation with inner problems. This great awareness of themselves distracts them from attending to other persons and issues and is likely to result in a morbid preoccupation with their difficulties. The effect is to limit their social intercourse and thus decrease the possibilities of friendly and supportive relationships [Coopersmith, 1967, p. 71].

In short, the child's self-concept and self-esteem are of special importance since they affect not only the child himself but the way he interacts with others. Let us consider, therefore, what factors are especially important in developing a self-concept and self-esteem. Not surprisingly, research has revealed that the child's parents and his peers both play a critical role in this regard (Coopersmith, 1967; Sears, Maccoby & Levin, 1957; Sears, 1970). First, a child whose parents are

---

[1]From *The Antecedents of Self-Esteem*, by S. Coopersmith. Copyright 1967 by W. H. Freeman & Company. This and all other quotations from this source are reprinted by permission of the author.

forever criticizing him is unlikely to develop feelings of self-worth, while a child whose parents are warm and supportive is clearly more likely to develop a strong sense of self-esteem. Not so obvious is the fact that a child's attitudes toward himself are shaped by his parents' own self-esteem: the way they view themselves. Thus, parents who have high self-esteem are more likely to produce children with high self-esteem, while parents who have low self-esteem create those same feelings in their children (Coopersmith, 1967).

Peers also have an impact on a child's self-concept and self-esteem. As he spends more and more time with friends, the child comes to perceive what they think of him and, in some cases, to think of himself in the same light.

The association between the child's self-concept and his peers' concept of him has been demonstrated in a number of studies. These studies have shown that children who are evaluated negatively by their peers tend to have a negative self-concept and low self-esteem; they want to be "different" than they are. Children who are popular and well-liked by their peers tend to have a positive self-concept and high self-esteem; they are content with themselves "as they are" (Horowitz, 1962; Rosen, Levinger, & Lippitt, 1960).

These findings may be somewhat misleading, however, if they appear to suggest that a poor evaluation by one's peers will somehow "cause" a poor self-concept. In reality, we do not know which comes first: does popularity lead to a positive self-concept, or does a positive self-concept lead to popularity with peers (or are both related to some third factor)? Something we do know is that the self-concept of the school-age child includes much more than a reflection of his popularity with others. It reflects a fairly accurate picture of his own behavior and the reasons he acts as he does. Let us look at some of these underlying reasons, or *motives*, guiding the behavior of the school-aged child.

What Motivates the School-Aged Child?

Before examining specific motives, however, we must understand the concept of motivation itself. A **motive** is an internalized goal that activates and directs behavior. Thus, if you are hungry, you will be motivated to obtain food, and you will behave in ways that will likely get you food. Obviously, the behavior of even very young children is activated and directed by a variety of different motives, encompassing satisfaction of basic biological needs (hunger, thirst, avoidance of pain) as well as satisfaction of social needs (love, nurturance, and approval).

During the school years, one of the primary motives directing the child's behavior is achievement. The **achievement motive** results in "behavior directed toward attainment of approval or the avoidance of disapproval . . . in situations where standards of excellence are applied" (Crandall, 1963, as quoted in Cohen, 1976). Thus, the achievement motive includes aspects of such other motives as **effectance** (see Chapter 8) and *approval*.

It is not surprising that the achievement motive should become such a dominant force in the schoolchild's life. After all, in the school setting, mastery is stressed and reinforced heavily: formal approval and nurturance by teachers are primarily dependent upon the child's continued demonstration of school achievement. The strength of this force on even the youngest child is illustrated by a kindergarten girl who asked her parents, "Will you still love me if I get a bad report card?" When they answered, "Of course we will. You did your best, didn't you?", the child responded "Yes. But what if I get a bad grade?"

The achievement motive is one very important part of the schoolchild's developing personality. Clearly, the extent to which the child achieves or excels in school will have a direct impact on his self-concept. Poor achievers tend to have more negative self-concepts and lower self-esteem than do high achievers. This relation between achievement and self-worth tends to create a cycle for the child. The child with a poor self-concept and low self-esteem will not strive to achieve, since he expects failure. His resulting failure in turn reinforces his negative evaluation of himself.

ISSUE

Are there racial differences in the development of self-concept and self-esteem?

We have seen that the way a child comes to view and evaluate himself is strongly influenced by his parents' evaluations of themselves and by his peers' evaluations of him. Thus, it is not hard to imagine how a child belonging to a minority group that is evaluated negatively by the majority of society might also come to view himself negatively, and behave in ways that are likely to reinforce negative evaluations of him by others. By 4 or 5 years of age, children are aware both of their own racial identity and of society's attitudes toward that race (Clark, 1955). How does this awareness affect the child's emerging self-concept?

Early research published from the 1930s to the 1950s suggested that even very young Black children in the United States had already begun to develop negative self-concepts. Especially striking were the findings of Clark (1955) that both Black and White children aged 2 to 7 tended to say that a Black doll "looked bad."

Fortunately, recent years have brought some decline in overt prejudice against Blacks and an increase in racial pride among Blacks. This cultural change seems to have created a more positive self-concept in young Black children. Indeed, a recent replication of Clark's study (Hraba & Grant, 1970) found that, while White children were still more likely to say that the Black doll "looked bad," Black children were now more likely to say that the White doll "looked bad." Increased racial awareness and pride among Blacks living in the United States thus appear to have had a positive impact on the self-esteem of these young children.

Unfortunately, this recent research also demonstrates that arbitrary color lines are still being drawn, even among young children. The errors of the past are, regrettably, very difficult to overcome.

Summary of Understanding Oneself

During the school years, the child begins to construct an articulated concept of himself (*self-concept*) and of his own worth (*self-esteem*). This heightened self-awareness is largely a reflection of how others see him, so that, for example, the schoolchild who is popular with his peers will have a positive self-concept and high self-esteem, while the unpopular child will have a negative self-concept and low self-esteem. In addition, the schoolchild's self-concept and self-esteem largely reflect the extent to which the child is able to *achieve*. Again, high achievers view themselves more positively, as they in turn tend to be more highly evaluated by others. Low achievers, in contrast, tend to view themselves, and to be viewed by others, in a negative light.

UNDERSTANDING OTHERS: SOCIAL COGNITION DURING THE SCHOOL YEARS

Children's newfound ability to understand themselves points to another advance in their social growth: namely, in their ability to understand others. The school-aged child (Piaget's *concrete operational* child) leaves much of his **egocentrism** behind and shows an ever-increasing ability to take another person's point of view (**perspective-taking**) and to understand the emotions of others (**empathy**). In addition, school-aged children show greater maturity in judging the rightness or *morality* of their own behavior and that of others. Thus, school-aged children are much more accurate in answering questions about what someone else sees, or knows, or feels, or thinks (Shantz, 1975).

"What Does Another Person See?"

As we mentioned in Chapter 8, *perspective-taking* refers to the ability to adopt another person's point of view: to understand the other person's thoughts, emotions, intentions, and viewpoints. As such, it is the exact opposite of *egocentrism*, or the tendency to project one's own point of view onto others.

At a simple, visual level, one can assess a child's perspective-taking ability by examining how well he or she responds to the question, "What does another person see?" Does the child realize that what another person sees is not the same as what he sees? If so, can he then predict what the other person actually does see?

As we saw in Chapter 8, even the preschooler can sometimes realize that another person sees something differently than he does. However, the preschooler is still unable to specify just what it is the other person actually sees and simply describes his own perspective. The school-aged child is much more accurate in describing another person's point of view, as illustrated in a classic study by Piaget.

As you will recall, visual perspective-taking ability was first studied in Piaget's "mountains" experiment, where the child sees a scene comprised of three mountains and must describe how the scene looks to a doll located at various positions around this scene. Piaget found three separate stages in which children produced different answers to this problem. In the first stage (ages 4 to 6), children described the doll's viewpoint as their own. Children aged 6 to 7 (the beginning of the concrete operational period) did much better but still made mistakes. Children in this second stage realized that near and far objects had to be reversed for the doll across the table, but did not reverse objects to their immediate left or right. Finally, at the third stage (after 7 years), the children were able to completely and accurately describe the scene from any of the doll's perspectives (Flavell, 1968; Laurendeau & Pinard, 1970; Piaget & Inhelder, 1956).

Piaget's straightforward results have, however, been somewhat clouded by more recent studies. Other research on perspective-taking has found that preschoolers can accurately describe what someone else sees if the scenes are very simple, while even adolescents have difficulty with very complex scenes (see Shantz, 1975, for a review). Thus, it appears that the preschool child is not completely egocentric, while the school-aged child is not completely nonegocentric. Children in both age groups may or may not be egocentric, depending upon the child and the complexity of the task. Nevertheless, it is generally believed that, as children grow older, they become less prone to egocentrism and are better able to take another person's point of view in ever more complex situations.

"What Does Another Person Know?"

One area in which the school-aged child continues to show vestiges of egocentrism is in his answer to the question "What does another person know?" The school-aged child's limitations in this area are most clearly seen in his referential communication skills. **Referential communication** refers to those situations in which the child (the "speaker") must construct a message in such a manner that some other person (the "hearer") knows what he is talking about or "referring to." For example, if a mother asks a child "Where are you?" and the child answers "I'm here," the mother does not know where "here" is and, hence, cannot understand the child's message; the child is clearly lacking adequate referential communication skills.

Research on referential communication skills involves a fairly straightforward situation. Usually, there are two people, a speaker and a hearer, who cannot see each other. Both speaker and hearer sit in front of an identical set of objects that go together in some way but are discriminable from one another: for example, several marbles of different sizes and colors. The speaker's task is to communicate to the listener which of these objects he is thinking about. Obviously, if the speaker says simply "It's a marble," his communication will fail, since all of the objects are marbles. If he says "It's a blue marble," the listener will do better but will still make mistakes if there are several blue marbles. Only if the speaker says "It's the large blue marble on your left side" will the communication be assured of success.

To date, research on referential communication skills has shown a clear developmental trend that is quite similar to the trend for visual perspective-taking already described. Young school-aged children can be found to communicate effectively when the task involves very simple, familiar objects. However, tasks involving more complex, unfamiliar objects result in communication breakdown. Even school-aged children communicate poorly in this task. It is not until the early teens that the child masters these more complex and unfamiliar tasks (Glucksberg, Krauss, & Higgins, 1975). Thus, the school-aged child finds some difficulty communicating to another some piece of knowledge that he possesses. In this sense, the child lacks an appreciation for what other people know or need to know in order to understand him.

"What Does Another Person Feel?"

A clearly important social skill related to perspective taking is the ability to appreciate the emotions of others—in other words, the capacity to feel *empathy*. Among other things, empathy enables the child to understand and predict the effects of his own behavior on the emotions of others.

Figure 11-1.   An example of Borke's Interpersonal Perception Test, 1971. (From *Interpersonal Perception Test*, 1971, by H. Borke. Reprinted by permission of the author.)

Interestingly, parents seem to have an intuitive grasp of the young child's limited capacity to understand the feelings of others. Many parents consider the child's egocentrism by saying "How would *you feel* if Sally hit you?" instead of "How do you think *Sally feels* when you hit her?"

Most psychological studies of the development of empathy use a picture-story format (as in Borke's Interpersonal Perception Test, 1971). The child is told a short story. He is then asked to pick out from a group of face pictures the one that reflects how the person in the story feels. (See Figure 11-1.) The results of these studies show that children as young as 4 years are quite accurate in identifying happy faces for simple happy stories. However, even 7-year-olds have difficulty identifying situations involving fear, sadness, and anger. Moreover, it is not until late childhood and early adolescence that children become adept at identifying the emotions of people unlike themselves in unfamiliar situations. Once again, then, we see that only gradually do children acquire the ability to consider another person's perspective—in this case to understand how someone else feels (Shantz, 1975).

"What Is Another Person Like?"

The question "What is another person like?" really includes everything we have discussed up to this point—and much more—since it includes how one perceives and understands the characteristics of others. This ability has been aptly called **person perception.** In general, there are two sorts of things that we can say about other people. We can describe their *overt* characteristics: what they look like, what they do, where they live, how much wealth they possess, and so on. We can also describe their *covert* characteristics: what they think, what they feel, what they believe, and what their motives and goals are. An adult usually describes others by mentioning both overt and covert characteristics. For example, John Doe might be described as a "brilliant young lawyer from San Francisco, a man with high ambitions and great self-confidence." But what about children? Do children's descriptions of others include both types of characteristics and, if so, to what degree?

In one study, W. J. Livesley and D. B. Bromley (1973) asked 320 children (aged 7 to 15) to write descriptions of themselves and eight other people they knew. The children were told to describe the people carefully and not to describe physical characteristics. Interestingly, analysis of these descriptions revealed that the 7-year-old children tended to concentrate on overt physical characteristics in their descriptions, even though they had been instructed *not* to do so. For example, a boy (aged 7) describes another boy he dislikes:

> "He is very tall. He has brown hair, he goes to our school. I don't think he has any brothers or sisters. He is in our class. Today he has a dark orange jumper and grey trousers and brown shoes" [Livesley & Bromley, 1973, p. 213].

Children aged 8 and older, in contrast, used more covert characteristics in their descriptions. For example, a boy (aged 9) describing another boy he dislikes said:

> "He smells very much and is very nasty. He has no sense of humour and is very dull. He is always fighting and he is cruel. He does silly things and is very stupid. He has brown hair and cruel eyes. He is sulky and 11 years old and has lots of sisters. I think he is the most horrible boy in the class. He has a croaky voice and always chews his pencil and picks his teeth and I think he is disgusting" [Livesley & Bromley, 1973, p. 217].

Another interesting finding of this study was that a majority of children at all ages tended to "evaluate" others as "good" or "bad," "nice" or "horrible." This brings us to the final aspect in the child's developing understanding of others—namely, what criteria are used by children in evaluating the *morality* of others and their behavior?

"Is Another Person Good or Bad?"

The ability of the child to evaluate the *morality* of behavior—his own or that of others—has been studied in some depth by Jean Piaget (1932) and Lawrence Kohlberg (1964). Both Piaget and Kohlberg studied moral development by having children evaluate the actions of characters in stories. The child's evaluations of these characters—and the reasons given by the child for his evaluations—were then used by Piaget and Kohlberg to assess the child's understanding and level of morality.

Piaget's Theory

Piaget's early work (1932) described the key ways in which the preoperational child's concepts of morality differ from those of older children. These differences center around the child's notions of *intentionality, relativism,* and *punishment.*

Intentionality.   The *intentions* that guide behavior are one of the most important things that a child must learn. Of course, even the very young preschooler has some sense that intentions are important, manifested in statements like: "I didn't hit her on purpose! It was an accident!" However, the preschooler has little deep understanding of what intentions are and how to evaluate them.

Piaget found that young children under 7 or 8 years tend to judge another person's (and their own) behavior as good or bad mainly in terms of its actual consequences, rather than in terms of the person's good or bad intentions. For example, a 5-year-old would see a child who accidentally broke an expensive vase as "worse" (that is, less moral) than a child who deliberately kicked the vase but didn't damage it. Older, school-aged children, like adults, are more likely to view the intentional act as "worse," regardless of the extent of the damage.

Relativism.   The *relativism* of good and evil is a further concept to be mastered by the school-aged child. Adults are well aware that things are neither "all good" nor "all bad," but usually a mixture of both. This is less the case for the preschool child, who tends to evaluate people and behavior in absolute terms, as all good or all bad. Moreover, the young child believes that everyone judges the morality of people and behavior in exactly the same way he does. Thus, a 4-year-old would argue that a woman who stole a car in order to take someone who was dying to the hospital is utterly and completely bad—and would expect everyone else to agree. A child of 10, however, would realize that the woman is not completely evil: she did a "bad" thing in stealing the car, but her motives were "good."

Punishment.   Comprehending the nature of punishment is a final aspect in the child's understanding of morality. The young child is punished when he is "bad"; hence, he comes to believe that the delivery of punishment means that some bad behavior must have occurred. The child who is punished, whether by a spanking or by falling and breaking his arm, must have behaved badly and is simply receiving his just rewards from daddy, teacher, or some other force.

The importance of punishment in the child's moral evaluations can be seen in research by Kohlberg (1963a, 1963b). In this study, 4- to 7-year olds were asked to evaluate the "goodness" or "badness" of a child in a story. The child was described as being both helpful and obedient by watching a baby brother when his mother was away. However, the baby-sitting child was spanked when his mother returned. Many of the 4-year-olds decided that the child in the story was bad—after all, he was spanked, wasn't he? Some 4- and 5-year-olds even invented a misdeed to account for the punishment. It was not until 7 years of age that children argued that the child was good and that he was wrongly punished.

In sum, Piaget's discussion of the development of morality reflects rather directly the *cognitive* functioning of the child. The young child's egocentrism and his inability to coordinate different thoughts prevent him from realistically considering the intentions of others, from appreciating the relativism of morality, and from separating punishment from "evil."

Kohlberg's Theory

Kohlberg's theory (1964) of moral development represents an extension and refinement of Piaget's earlier work. While Piaget cataloged general age trends in

Table 11-1. Kohlberg's stages of moral reasoning

Stage I. Premoral
    Type 1. Punishment and obedience orientation
    Type 2. Naive instrumental hedonism

Stage II. Morality of Conventional Role Conformity
    Type 3. Good-boy morality of maintain good relations,
        approval of others
    Type 4. Authority maintaining morality

Stage III. Morality of Self-accepted Moral Principles
    Type 5. Morality of contract, of individual rights,
        and of democratically accepted law
    Type 6. Morality of individual principles of conscience

moral thinking during the school years, he did not specify the precise transitions that occur. Kohlberg, on the other hand, has attempted to delineate three major *stages* in the development of moral judgments (see Table 11-1).

The Premoral Stage.   The first stage is the *premoral stage* and encompasses the age period from 4 to about 10 years. There are two main types of moral reasoning at this stage: Type 1, *punishment or obedience orientation;* and Type 2, *naive instrumental hedonism.* During this first stage, both the child's behavior and his judgments of morality are based on his expectation of punishment (Type 1) and future enjoyment (Type 2). Examples of the two types of moral reasoning are reflected in the responses of two boys who were asked "Should Joe tell on his older brother to his father?" after Joe had gone somewhere he wasn't supposed to go.

> Type 1: Danny. "In one way it would be right to tell on his brother or his father might get mad at him and spank him. In another way it would be right to keep quiet or his brother might beat him up" [Kohlberg, 1964, p. 401].

> Type 2: Jimmy. "I think he should keep quiet. He might want to go someplace like that, and if he squeals on Alex, Alex might squeal on him" [Kohlberg, 1964, p. 401].[2]

In the first example, Danny's primary concern was with the possibility of *punishment;* if he acted one way, his father would punish him, but if he acted the other way, his brother would punish him. In the second example, Jimmy's reaction was *hedonistic;* his primary concern was with how his action might affect his own future enjoyment.

---

[2]This and all other quotations from this source are from "Development of Moral Character and Moral Ideology," by L. Kohlberg. In M. L. Hoffman and L. W. Hoffman (Eds.), *Review of Child Development Research,* Vol. 1. © 1964 Russell Sage Foundation, New York. Reprinted by permission of Basic Books, Inc.

The Stage of Conventional Rule-Conformity.   Kohlberg's second stage (about ages 10 to 13) is also characterized by two types of moral reasoning: Type 3, *good-child morality of maintaining good relations and the approval of others;* and Type 4, *authority-maintaining morality.* In this second stage, the child believes that morality resides in conformity to peers, parents, and authorities. The motive behind his conformity is to gain approval and avoid disapproval and dislike. An example of this type of reasoning is seen in Andy:

> "I try to do things for my parents; they've always done things for me. I try to do everything my mother says: I try to please her" [Kohlberg, 1964, p. 401].

Here, Andy's principal concern is neither with whether he'll be punished (Type 1 behavior of the "premoral stage") nor with whether his actions might jeopardize some pleasurable thing that he himself might want to do in the future (Type 2 behavior of the "premoral stage"). Rather, he is now concerned with how he can go about maintaining good relations with his parents.

The Stage of Self-Accepted Moral Principles.   The final stage of morality in Kohlberg's theory does not begin to emerge until about age 13 and continues to develop throughout adulthood. Kohlberg has called this final stage the *morality of self-accepted moral principles.* A child at this stage considers the morality of obligations, individual rights, and democratically accepted law (Type 5), as well as individual principles of conscience (Type 6). Again, a few examples are the best method of illustrating this final level of morality:

> Bill, in response to "Should the husband steal the expensive drug needed to save his wife's life?": "Lawfully no, but morally speaking I think I would have done it. It would be awfully hard to live with myself afterward, knowing that I could have done something which would have saved her life and yet didn't for fear of punishment to myself" [Kohlberg, 1964, p. 401].
>
> Steve, to the same question: "By the law of society he was wrong but by the law of nature or of God the druggist was wrong and the husband was justified. Human life is above financial gain. Regardless of who was dying, if it was a total stranger, man has a duty to save him from dying" [Kohlberg, 1964, p. 401].

In the above examples, both Bill and Steve have undertaken the difficult task of weighing two different and conflicting sets of sophisticated moral considerations. On the one hand, both are aware that certain moral judgments have been set down in the formal laws of society. On the other hand, both have concluded that these formal laws are not carved in stone and must sometimes give way to the moral dictates of conscience.

Evaluation of Kohlberg's Theory.   Kohlberg bases his theory of morality on how children assess the morality of others. He believes that children pass through three distinct stages of morality, and that each stage is characterized by its own particular types of moral reasoning. Moreover, Kohlberg argues that, although children may occasionally rely on earlier forms of moral reasoning, this occurs with less and less frequency as they mature.

One might well question the extent to which children's ability to reason about the morality of the *behavior of others* influences the morality of their *own behavior.* Just because children have notions of right and wrong that they can use to evaluate the behavior of others does not necessarily mean that they will make similar evaluations of their own behavior and then use these evaluations to guide their behavior (Hoffman, 1970).

Very little research has attempted to relate moral reasoning to moral behavior. However, existing research does *not* reveal any strong connection between moral judgments and moral behavior. For example, Grinder (1964) found that moral reasoning in boys 7 to 11 years of age was not related to their willingness to resist temptation—although it was for girls. Similarly, Hoffman (1970) found that moral reasoning ability in 13-year-old girls was not related to their feelings of guilt—although it was for 13-year-old boys.

Results of research on the connection between moral reasoning and behavior thus far remain obscure. One thing is clear: the ability to use higher levels of reasoning in judging the morality of others does not guarantee that children will use high levels of morality in their own behavior.

Summary of Understanding Others

School-aged children show major gains in their understanding of others. These accomplishments are reflected in their evolving ability to take another person's point of view (*perspective-taking*) and to understand the emotions of others (*empathy*)—an ability that is in turn reflected in their growing awareness of "what another person sees," "what another person knows," "what another person feels," "what the other is like," and "whether the other is good or bad." In large part, these gains in social understanding reflect the child's departure from *egocentrism* and growing *perspective-taking* ability. However, this egocentrism does not disappear abruptly when the child enters school, but gradually diminishes from preschool to adolescence. Even the older schoolchild displays egocentrism in situations that are complex or unfamiliar, just as even the preschool child shows some perspective-taking ability in very simple, familiar tasks.

Another interesting qualification to the work we have reviewed on social understanding is that it is not as closely linked to behavior as one might think. Some relationship between moral reasoning and moral behavior does exist, but the exact nature of this relationship is not only unclear and complex but relatively weak, indicating that social understanding is only one part of the overall picture. Let us turn now, then, to a discussion of some of the other factors that may be relevant to the development of social *behavior* during the school years.

INDIVIDUAL DIFFERENCES

Thus far we have focused on the general course of socialization in the average American child, while ignoring any differences that exist among individual children. (See Figure 11-2.) In reality, however, differences among individual children in social behavior and development are marked. Some children are shy and inhibited in the presence of other children and are very dependent on adults. Some children are careful to obey all the rules; others flagrantly break all the

Figure 11-2. Although it is possible to speak of the "normal" development of the child, it is important to remember that every child is an individual, with unique qualities that will affect his or her development and socialization.

rules. One might well ask, then, what causes individual differences in social behavior? Not surprisingly, explanations for these individual differences are as complex as the differences themselves. Some factors seem to lie within the child: his or her behavioral predispositions, or "personality" traits, and sex. Other factors seem to lie outside the child in the environment: parental practices and *socioeconomic class.*

The Child's Personality

Parents have long been generally aware of something that psychologists have only recently begun to explicitly recognize: namely, the fact that every child is different, even from the moment of birth. Newborn infants are not empty vessels simply waiting for the environment's impression to be stamped upon them. Rather, the newborn comes equipped with certain behavioral predispositions: a primitive "personality." One newborn may be quiet, passive, and seemingly content, spending most of her time sleeping. Another newborn may be active, irritable, and loud, spending most of her time crying.

That individual children show differences in temperament and behavior from very early in life—if not from birth—has now been documented in a number of studies. On the simplest level, we know that infants differ in activity level, and such differences may be related to activity level later in life (Janis et al., 1969). On a more complex level, we know that infants as young as a few weeks differ in their degree of social responsiveness to their parents (Schaffer & Emerson, 1964). Some infants are "cuddlers," who respond well to being held and cuddled. Other infants are "noncuddlers," who fight off the parent who tries to hold them too close or too long.

At present, there is no strong direct evidence that these early differences in temperament predict later personality. Nevertheless, logic suggests that there must be some relation. The existence of such a relation seems especially likely in light of the fact that the way in which parents respond to their infants depends in large part upon the infant's temperament. For example, the mother with a "non-cuddler" infant may feel rejected by her child. These feelings of rejection could then interfere with the development of normal interaction patterns between her and her child. An abnormal interaction between mother and child could in turn affect the nature of the child's feelings about the mother and later about others, thereby causing the personality traits of early infancy to ultimately affect the child's later social and emotional development.

The Child's Sex

There is little question that the sex of a child affects parents' interactions with him or her, and these interactions in turn shape the course of the child's later growth. By school age, the child's sex has come to color and affect almost all aspects of his or her life.

An exhaustive review of available literature on the development of sex differences is provided by Eleanor Maccoby and Carol Jacklin (1974). In this review, the authors attempted to describe how girls differ from boys. In terms of social behavior, the main differences that they discerned appear to be in *activity level*, *aggression*, and *compliancy*. Let us look first at activity level.

There are no clear-cut differences in the overall level of activity of boys and girls during infancy. Children first begin to diverge in activity level during the preschool period and continue into the school years. By preschool age, boys are often rated as more active than girls. This high activity in boys occurs predominantly in short, high bursts of energy that often make the child's behavior appear to be "out of control" or "wild." Interestingly, these high bursts of activity tend to occur predominantly when boys are interacting with peers.

The heightened activity level of young boys has been frequently suggested as a possible explanation for their high levels of aggression—*aggression* being the second key difference between boys and girls. This difference in aggressiveness is possibly one of the clearest and most universal features distinguishing the two sexes. Boys are more aggressive than girls on an average in almost all cultures that have been studied and in all ways. Boys are more aggressive physically, verbally, and in fantasy. Moreover, evidence for heightened aggressiveness in boys is present from their earliest interactions with others, at around 2 years of age.

In addition to activity level and aggression, sex affects the child's willingness to follow the instructions of others, a trait called *compliancy*. Little girls tend to be more compliant with adults and conform quite closely to instructions given by adults. Little boys, on the other hand, comply less with adult demands but are more compliant when they receive instructions from other children.

The origin of these sex differences in social behavior is not easy to specify. There are, of course, many biological differences between girls and boys, in addition to the obvious genital differences. Biological differences between the sexes may be responsible in part for some of the behavioral differences. For example, infant boys are larger and stronger than infant girls, and these initial differences may be responsible for the heightened activity and aggressiveness shown later by boys.

Biological differences between the sexes do not, however, tell the whole story. Boys and girls are treated differently from the moment of birth. As we saw in Chapter 8, parents tend to interact more with infant boys than they do with infant girls. Moreover, the quality of interaction between parent and infant differs for the two sexes. Thus, infant boys receive more intense forms of stimulation, especially in rough-and-tumble play; infant girls receive more soothing stimulation, with parents' talking gently to them. There can be little doubt that many of the commonly observed sex differences are learned through the differential treatment received by little girls and little boys.

Parental Practices

Individual differences in temperament and sex tend to be reinforced by the parents' reactions to these differences. The intertwining of these early differences with parental behavior makes it difficult to determine just what is primarily responsible. Would original temperament and sex differences manifest themselves in the absence of parental influences? Or is it simply that the parents' responses to the early differences augment later differences in behavior? One thing is clear. Parental practices can have a major impact on the course of socialization of the child. We saw in Chapter 8 how parental behavior and disciplinary techniques affect the child's social behavior. Parents who rely heavily on **power-assertive techniques** (for example, yelling, threatening, physical punishment) tend to produce less socialized children who are more aggressive, less able to resist temptation, and less likely to feel guilt over transgressions. Parents who use **love-oriented techniques** (for example, praise and reasoning) tend to produce more socialized children who are less aggressive, more able to resist temptation, and more likely to feel guilt over transgressions.

In addition, parental practices can influence the child's level of social *understanding*. Parents who rely on love-oriented techniques and provide reasons for why the child should behave in certain ways tend to produce children with higher levels of perspective-taking ability and higher levels of moral reasoning (Bearison & Cassel, 1975; Hoffman, 1970; Shantz, 1975). Moreover, giving reasons that emphasize the feelings and intentions of others (that is, *empathy*) is most effective in developing the child's social understanding.

In short, then, it appears that parental practices can have major effects on the social development of the child. Love-oriented techniques that stress reasons for the child's behaviors seem to be most effective in fostering both social behavior and social understanding.

Socioeconomic Class

Children from different socioeconomic classes behave differently in some respects. Whether this influence comes directly through the family (since different parental practices tend to be associated with different socioeconomic classes) or indirectly through the child's peers is not yet clear.

The concept of **socioeconomic class** refers to a number of different variables, including parents' educational levels, type of employment, and income. Although children in the middle class differ considerably on these variables, this is less true of children from the lowest socioeconomic class. These are the children of poverty: the children whose parents are uneducated and work irregularly—if at all—and hence have little money.

What, then, are the effects of being reared in an environment of poverty on the social development of the child? The first—and perhaps most important— difference between lower- and middle-class children lies in the nature of their *peer relationships*. The poor child spends more time in the company of his peers, and his activities with peers are unlikely to be supervised by adults (Hess, 1970; Psathas, 1957). The peer group thus takes on an extremely important role in the poor child's socialization.

Lower- and middle-class children also differ in the development of *self-concept* and *self-esteem*. It is hardly surprising that, in a competitive society such as ours, poor children rapidly become aware of their position in social status and that this awareness then results in negative self-concepts and low self-esteem. The poor child's negative sense of self-worth in turn produces a child who expects not to achieve. These expectations of failure often materialize in actual failure (Hess, 1970).

Lower-class children seem less mature than their middle-class peers in their level of *social understanding*. For example, on tests of moral reasoning, such as Kohlberg's, lower-class children show less mature levels of moral reasoning than do middle-class children (Kohlberg, 1963a and b, 1964).

These less mature levels of moral reasoning need not necessarily imply less "socialized" behavior. Let us turn, then, to a discussion of the effect of socioeconomic class on social behaviors such as aggression, ability to resist temptation, and the tendency to behave prosocially.

Aggression is often seen as characteristic of the poor child. It is not startling, then, that research has shown that lower-class children view aggression as more acceptable than do middle- and upper-class children (Pope, 1953) and also behave more aggressively (Hess, 1970). Similarly, lower-class children also appear to be less able to resist temptation (Hartshorne, May, Mallie, & Shuttleworth, 1928–1930).

On the other hand, some research has found that lower-class children are more likely to show *prosocial behaviors*. For example, lower-class children have been found to be more sympathetic to others and more willing to share with other children (Hess, 1970). One cannot therefore conclude that lower-class children are necessarily less "socialized" than middle-class children. Perhaps they have simply been socialized to a culture with different values and standards than the middle class.

Summary of Individual Differences

We have seen that individual differences in children's social development can stem from a number of sources. Some of these sources reside within the children themselves: their temperament at birth, and their sex. Other sources reside outside the children within their families and their environments: their parents, their peers, and their socioeconomic class. It is seldom if ever possible to look at particular children and determine the precise effects of these individual factors, since they are all interrelated. Children who are not cuddly are not only different from "cuddlers" at birth but are also likely to be treated differently by their parents, quite possibly resulting in long-term effects on both their understanding of themselves and their understanding of others. Similarly, children of poverty are faced with a myriad of environmental factors that set them apart from their middle- and upper-class counterparts: differences in income, parental interactions, peer relationships, expectations, and societal values. As these factors interact with one another, they, too, are likely to have a lasting effect on children's understanding of themselves and others.

CREATING THE OPTIMAL ENVIRONMENT

The task of creating the optimal environment for social development during the preschool years is difficult enough. This task becomes even more complex, however, during the school years, since the child's social development is now influenced by many more factors than any one person can reasonably expect to control. Teachers come to replace the parents as a major socializing force, while the peer group becomes increasingly important in shaping the child's awareness of himself and his behavior toward others. Nonetheless, parents continue to play a central role, directly and indirectly, in the socialization of their child.

Parents can continue to provide a warm and nurturant environment for their child. Such an environment will help the child to develop a positive self-concept and high self-esteem. The very fact that the child can no longer depend so completely on the parents for immediate protection and reassurance makes it especially important that the parents provide a secure home base from which to approach and confront the outside world.

To the extent possible, parents can also help by taking an active interest in checking the quality of their children's teachers. Do these teachers rely only on power-assertive techniques of teaching, or do they use the far more effective love-oriented techniques? Are they hypercritical and overly harsh in their contacts with students, or are they careful to nurture the child's budding self-concept and self-esteem through praise and support? Ideally, these are the types of questions that school administrators themselves should be asking. However, parents should not assume that there is nothing they can do about whom their child has for a teacher. Many schools allow parents to request particular teachers; most schools are willing to change a child's teacher if the parents make their objections clear.

Both parents and teachers alike have a responsibility to oversee and supervise the child's interactions with his peers. Adults should encourage cooperative activities while discouraging highly competitive activities drawn along "group" lines. In this way, children can hopefully be taught to work with and for one another—rather than against each other.

CHAPTER SUMMARY

In this chapter, we discussed several factors that bear upon the social development of the child during the school years. Parents still influence their child's behavior, not only directly, but also indirectly through the child's "internalization" of many of their rules, standards, attitudes, and beliefs. However, the child now spends a great deal of time at school and away from the direct influence of the parents. Two other socializing forces therefore take on great significance: the teachers and the peer group. The teachers largely—but by no means completely—replace the parents as the direct governors of prosocial behavior, while the child's peers provide particularly forceful role models.

The child's peers also join the parents and the teachers as important factors in the child's developing understanding of himself (*self-concept*) and feelings about his own worth (*self-esteem*). The child comes to view himself largely as others see him. Thus, the evaluations of parents, teachers, and peers will have a direct impact on the child's conception of himself. If parents or teachers are overly harsh and hypercritical in their interactions with children, the children's developing feelings of self-concept and self-esteem are likely to be undermined; if, however, the parents and teachers are warm and supportive in these interactions, children are far more likely to develop positive assessments of their own self-worth.

As children come to understand themselves, they also come to better understand others. In part, this is made possible by declining egocentrism and increasing ability to take another person's point of view (*perspective-taking*) and to *empathize* with him. The school years thus show increasing awareness of what other people sense, know, feel, think, and are like. In addition, there is an increasing sophistication in judging the morality of other people's actions (*moral reasoning*). This increased social and moral understanding does not, however, mean that the child's own behavior will exactly mirror that understanding. *Prosocial* and *moral behavior* seem to require more than simply being able to understand others and being able to distinguish good from bad; it is linked to such individual factors as differences in *temperament, sex, parental disciplinary style,* and *socioeconomic class.*

SUGGESTED READINGS

Cohen, S. *Social and personality development in childhood.* New York: Macmillan, 1976. A good review of several important topics in social development. It is rather technical, however.

Kohlberg, L. Development of moral character and moral ideology. In M. L. Hoffman & L. W. Hoffman (Eds.), *Review of child development research.* New York: Russell Sage Foundation, 1964. A detailed presentation of Piaget's and Kohlberg's theories. It is, however, difficult to read.

Shantz, C. U. The development of social cognition. In E. M. Hetherington (Ed.), *Review of child development research.* Chicago: University of Chicago Press, 1975. An excellent, thorough, well-written, and up-to-date review of the literature on social cognition or social understanding.

GLOSSARY

achievement motive. The desire or motive to gain approval and avoid disapproval in situations where behavior is evaluated against some standard.

compliancy. The willingness to follow the instructions of others.

effectance motive. The child's desire or motive to master and control his environment.

egocentrism. Term used by Piaget to describe the child's self-centered tendency to project his own perspectives, beliefs, motives, and so forth, onto others.

empathy. The ability to identify and understand the emotions of others.

love-oriented. Disciplinary techniques that tend to rely heavily on praise and reasoning.

motive. An internalized goal that directs behavior.

person perception. The ability to know what another person is like. It includes both overt and covert characteristics.

perspective-taking. The opposite of egocentrism; refers to the child's ability to understand the point of view, beliefs, motives, and so forth, of others.

power-assertive. Disciplinary techniques that tend to rely heavily on threats, yelling, and physical punishment.

referential communication. The ability to construct a message in such a manner that it communicates precisely to someone else.

self-concept. A person's sense or image of himself. It includes what he looks like, what he believes, and what he can and cannot do.

self-esteem. A person's feelings about his own worthiness or value.

socioeconomic class. A rough scale that groups families in terms of education, income, and employment.

REFERENCES

Anderson, H. H., & Anderson, G. L. Social development. In L. Carmichael (Ed.), *Manual of child psychology* (2nd ed.). New York: Wiley, 1954.

Bearison, D. J., & Cassel, T. Z. Cognitive decentration and social codes: Communicative effectiveness in young children from differing family contexts. *Developmental Psychology,* 1975, *11,* 29–36.

Berenda, R. W. *The influence of the group on the judgments of children.* New York: King's Crown Press, 1950.

Borke, H. Interpersonal perception of young children: Egocentrism or empathy? *Developmental Psychology,* 1971, *5,* 263–269.

Bryan, J. H. Children's cooperation and helping behaviors. In E. M. Hetherington (Ed.), *Review of child development research,* Vol. 5. Chicago: University of Chicago Press, 1975.

Campbell, J. D. Peer relations in childhood. In M. L. Hoffman & L. W. Hoffman (Eds.), *Review of child development research.* New York: Russell Sage Foundation, 1964.

Clark, K. B. *Prejudice and your child.* Boston: Beacon, 1955.

Cohen, S. *Social and personality development in childhood.* New York: Macmillan, 1976.

Coopersmith, S. *The antecedents of self-esteem.* San Francisco: W. H. Freeman, 1967.

Crandall, V. J. Achievement. In H. W. Stevenson (Ed.), *Child psychology. The sixty-second yearbook of the National Society for the Study of Education* (Part 1). Chicago: University of Chicago Press, 1963.

Flavell, J. H. *The development of role-taking and communication skills in children.* New York: Wiley, 1968.

Gage, N. L. Desirable behaviors of teachers. *Urban Education.* 1965, *1,* 85–95.

Glucksberg, S., Krauss, R., & Higgins, E. T. The development of referential communication skills. In F. D. Horowitz (Ed.), *Review of child development research.* Chicago: University of Chicago Press, 1975.

Grinder, R. E. Relations between behavior and cognitive dimensions of conscience in middle childhood. *Child Development,* 1964, *35,* 881–891.

Hartshorne, H., May, M. A., Mallie, T. B., & Shuttleworth, F. K. *Studies in the nature of the character* (Vols. 1–3). New York: Macmillan, 1928–1930.

Hartup, W. W. Peer interaction and social organization. In P. H. Mussen (Ed.), *Carmichael's manual of child psychology.* New York: Wiley, 1970.

Hartup, W. W., & Coates, B. Imitation of a peer as a function of reinforcement from the peer group and rewardingness of the model. *Child Development*, 1967, *38*, 1003–1016.

Hess, R. D. Social class and ethnic influences upon socialization. In P. H. Mussen (Ed.), *Carmichael's manual of child psychology.* New York: Wiley, 1970.

Hicks, D. J. Imitation and retention of film-mediated aggressive peer and adult models. *Journal of Personality and Social Psychology*, 1965, *2*, 97–100.

Hoffman, M. L. Moral development. In P. H. Mussen (Ed.), *Carmichael's manual of child psychology.* New York: Wiley, 1970.

Horowitz, F. D. The relationship of anxiety, self-concept, and sociometric status among fourth, fifth and sixth grade children. *Journal of Abnormal and Social Psychology.* 1962, *65*, 212–214.

Hraba, J., & Grant, G. Black is beautiful: A reexamination of racial preference and identification. *Journal of Personality and Social Psychology*, 1970, *16*, 398–402.

Janis, I. L., Mahl, G. F., Kagan, J., & Holt, R. R. *Personality.* New York: Harcourt Brace Jovanovich, 1969.

Kagan, S., & Madsen, M. C. Cooperation and competition of Mexican, Mexican-American, and Anglo-American children of two ages under four instructional sets. *Developmental Psychology*, 1971, *5*, 32–39.

Kohlberg, L. The development of children's orientations toward a moral order: I. Sequence in the development of moral thought. *Vita Humana*, 1963, *6*, 11–33.(a)

Kohlberg, L. Moral development and identification. In H. Stevenson (Ed.), *Child psychology. 62nd yearbook of the National Society for Studies in Education.* Chicago: University of Chicago Press, 1963. (b)

Kohlberg, L. Development of moral character and moral ideology. In M. L. Hoffman & L. W. Hoffman (Eds.), *Review of child development research.* New York: Russell Sage Foundation, 1964.

Laurendeau, M., & Pinard, A. *Development of the concept of space in the child.* New York: International Universities Press, 1970.

Livesley, W. J., & Bromley, D. B. *Person perception in childhood and adolescence.* London: Wiley, 1973.

Maccoby, E. E., & Jacklin, C. N. *The psychology of sex differences.* Stanford, Calif.: Stanford University Press, 1974.

Piaget, J. *The moral judgment of the child.* Glencoe, Ill.: Free Press, 1932.

Piaget, J., & Inhelder, B. *The child's conception of space.* London: Routledge & Kegan Paul, 1956.

Pope, B. Socio-economic contrasts in children's peer culture prestige values. *Genetic Psychology Monographs*, 1953, *48*, 157–220.

Psathas, G. Ethnicity, social class and adolescent independence from parental control. *American Sociological Review*, 1957, *22*, 415–423.

Rosen, S., Levinger, G., & Lippitt, R. Desired change in self and other as a function of resource ownership. *Human Relations*, 1960, *13*, 187–193.

Rubin, K. H., & Schneider, F. W. The relationship between moral judgment, egocentrism, and altruistic behavior. *Child Development*, 1973, *44*, 661–665.

Schaffer, H. R., & Emerson, P. E. Patterns of response to physical contact in early human development. *Journal of Child Psychology and Psychiatry*, 1964, *5*, 1–13.

Sears, R. R. Relation of early socialization experiences to self-concepts and gender role in middle childhood. *Child Development*, 1970, *41*, 267–289.

Sears, R. R., Maccoby, E. E., & Levin, H. *Patterns of child rearing.* New York: Harper & Row, 1957.

Shantz, C. U. The development of social cognition. In E. M. Hetherington (Ed.), *Review of child development research.* Chicago: University of Chicago Press, 1975.

Sherif, M., Harvey, O. J., White, B. J., Hood, W. R., & Sherif, C. W. *Intergroup conflict and*

cooperation: The Robbers Cave experiment. Norman, Okla.: University of Oklahoma
  Press, 1961.
Sherif, M., & Sherif, C. W. *Groups in harmony and tension.* New York: Harper & Row, 1953.
Sherif, M., & Sherif, C. W. *Reference Groups.* New York: Harper & Row, 1964.

PART FOUR
ADOLESCENCE

12

Beyond the Child: Psychological Development during Adolescence

We have focused in the preceding pages on psychological growth in the child. As we have seen, complex and important changes transpire during the childhood years. For those interested in the broader sweep of human development, however, growth and change do not cease with the child. Equally fascinating and complex changes occur during the adolescent and indeed the adult years. We do not have space here to delve into the adult years, having chosen the young child as our major focus; however, we would like to discuss adolescent development in some detail, since many of the concerns and conflicts that arise during adolescence characterize adult development as well. Concerns about the self, family relations, sexuality, and friendships and choices about careers arise to a great degree during the adolescent years.

THE ADOLESCENT: THE CENTRALITY OF SELF

ISSUE

Why are adolescents so preoccupied with themselves?

One adolescent characteristic on which there is almost universal agreement, at least for youths in the United States, is adolescents' preoccupation with themselves. This concern for the "inner self," however, does not spring from nowhere. As we shall see shortly, major changes in adolescents' way of thinking and their basic personalities (not to mention in physical and sexual makeup) all come together to focus adolescents on themselves, on their appearance, on their feelings, and on their thoughts—in short, on their identity. These new preoccupations are a natural outgrowth of the changes that have occurred throughout childhood and that converge on the adolescent psyche.

A Framework for Understanding Adolescent Identity: Erikson's Eight Ages of Man

Erik Erikson, a psychoanalyst by training, has devoted his professional career to the study of the life cycle and the conflicts throughout that cycle with which humans have to contend. In Erikson's view, one of life's central conflicts comes during adolescence and concerns the question of identity. Since he sees the construction and establishment of a healthy personal identity as crucial to psychological health, Erikson thus regards adolescence as a critical phase of human development.

Erikson describes the human life cycle as a series of eight stages (or ages) individuals pass through. Each stage is characterized by a unique psychosocial conflict that people face. How they resolve each of the earlier conflicts has a significant impact on their later development and ultimately on their psychological health (Erikson, 1968).

Figure 12-1 illustrates Erikson's theoretical framework. The diagonal from bottom-left to top-right shows the eight stages (or ages) of human development described by Erikson. Stage 1 centers on the infant, whose basic conflict is between trust and mistrust. In particular Erikson stressed the importance of the feeding situation, particularly that the outcome of feeding experiences has the psychological effect of instilling in the infant either a basic sense of trust in the world or a fundamental feeling of mistrust. A regular feeding schedule allows the child to predict accurately how certain aspects of his world operate. Being able to predict how the world will react results in the child developing a basic sense of trust in his surroundings and ultimately in himself. In contrast, an irregular feeding schedule or some other serious disturbance will cause a low degree of predictability and a feeling of mistrust of the world.

For Erikson, then, the young infant's first psychosocial conflict is in the area of *trust/mistrust*. Successful resolution of this conflict (developing a sense of basic trust) serves as a positive building block in the child's construction of a healthy personality.

Stage 2 (from about 18 months to 3½ years) is characterized by a conflict between *autonomy* and *shame* (or *doubt*). At this age the child is becoming more active both motorically and cognitively and begins to experience the autonomy of free choice. He can show stubborn refusal and repeatedly say no to his parents' commands. In reality the child is learning self-control, and for Erikson the primary battleground of this conflict is that of toilet training. The child must learn when to "let go" or "hold on." Successful development of self-control during toilet training gives the child a sense of autonomy and achievement. However, if the child fails to develop self-control, he is likely to be consumed with feelings of shame and self-doubt.

Stage 3, which lasts from about 3½ to 6 years of age, heralds yet another conflict, this time between *initiative* and *guilt*. Further advances in the child's motor, language, and cognitive skills produce a much more active, curious,

	1	2	3	4	5	6	7	8
VIII								INTEGRITY vs. DESPAIR
VII							GENERATIVITY vs. STAGNATION	
VI						INTIMACY vs. ISOLATION		
V	Temporal Perspective vs. Time Confusion	Self-Certainty vs. Self-Consciousness	Role Experimentation vs. Role Fixation	Apprenticeship vs. Work Paralysis	IDENTITY vs. IDENTITY CONFUSION	Sexual Polarization vs. Bisexual Confusion	Leader- and Followership vs. Authority Confusion	Ideological Commitment vs. Confusion of Values
IV				INDUSTRY vs. INFERIORITY	Task Identification vs. Sense of Futility			
III			INITIATIVE vs. GUILT		Anticipation of Roles vs. Role Inhibition			
II		AUTONOMY vs. SHAME, DOUBT			Will to be Oneself vs. Self-Doubt			
I	TRUST vs. MISTRUST				Mutual Recognition vs. Autistic Isolation			

Figure 12-1.   Erikson's theoretical framework of the eight stages of human development. (Reprinted from *Identity, Youth and Crisis,* by Erik H. Erikson, with the permission of W. W. Norton & Company, Inc. Copyright © 1968 by W. W. Norton & Company, Inc.)

exploring creature who is always getting into things and continually asking questions ("where, why") about things. In short, for Erikson, the child is showing initiative in dealing with the world. The opposite of *showing initiative* is *developing guilt*. A child who, for whatever reason, does not explore or who is not permitted to be curious or active will develop feelings of guilt, fear, and withdrawal.

The task of Stage 4 (comprising the elementary school years) is to deal with the conflict between a sense of *industry* and a feeling of *inferiority*. Clearly, the child's mastery of school experiences such as reading, arithmetic, sports, and other extracurricular activities results in a sense of industry; a feeling that one knows how to do things; in short, a feeling that one is a competent human being. Alternatively, failure in these areas can result in a distinct feeling of inferiority and worries about one's competence.

By adolescence (Stage 5), then, the child has already had to cope with a number of major conflicts, the outcomes of which have become part of his personality and which contribute to his growing *sense of identity*, the major area of conflict faced during the fifth stage. If the child has formed a basic sense of trust, followed in successive stages by feelings of autonomy, initiative and industry, he will as an adolescent view himself positively and feel confident about his future: he will, in short, have a positive identity. Major failures during these early stages can result in **identity confusion** (that is, negative feelings about oneself as a person and doubts about the future).

These developmental principles (or as Erikson calls them, **epigenetic principles**) are illustrated in Figure 12-1 in the column 5, row V squares. The (vertical) column 5 entries refer to personality characteristics developed in the child that contribute to his later sense of identity. Thus, mutual recognition and trust of oneself and others (having been resolved in Stage 1), followed by the will to be oneself and the ability to anticipate roles and identify important tasks, all contribute to a positive sense of identity. Autistic isolation, followed by self-doubt, role inhibition, and a sense of futility likewise contribute to a confused identity. The horizontal row V squares refer to the sorts of characteristics shown by the adolescent depending upon the degree of resolution of earlier conflicts and the type of identity evolved. Hence, lack of worry or suspicion about time, certainty about oneself, and a flexible ability to experiment with different roles and to serve as a cooperative apprentice all characterize the adolescent with a positive identity. Confusion or consternation about time (for example, being late), self-consciousness, rigid adherence to a role, and inability to work characterize the adolescent with identity confusion.

In the next stage (Stage 6), Erikson postulates that following adolescence the young adult must come to grips with *intimacy* versus *isolation*. Once a personal identity has been established there is a strong push toward intimacy, in the form of sharing one's feelings and experiences with others, and in a desire to be close to other people and to go outside of one's self. However, confusion or uncertainty about one's identity will preclude intimacy with others and result in a sense of isolation. At this point it is easy to see how identity is central to human development: it is both the culmination of early growth and the cornerstone for later healthy development. The young adult without a clear sense of identity will shy away from meaningful interpersonal relationships and may seek promiscuity without intimacy, sex without love.

Stage 7, *generativity* versus *stagnation*, occurs in mature adulthood. Successful development of a mature identity followed by sharing and intimacy with another, usually in marriage, results in a period of generativity or creativity. Though producing offspring is the most obvious form of generativity, Erikson felt that all forms, including vocational and artistic generativity, are involved at this stage of life. The opposite outcome to generativity, *stagnation*, results in little being created during this period, with boredom predominating, and the person becoming egotistical, self-absorbed, and self-indulgent.

Finally, the last stage (Stage 8) encompasses the later years of life, when the individual either achieves a full sense of *integrity* or experiences a chilling sense of *despair*. The aging adult who achieves integrity can look back on his life's experiences and appreciate them as worthwhile and can come to terms with the finality of the human life cycle without regret. For those experiencing despair, however, there is a feeling that life has been wasted, accompanied by an inordinate fear of death and a pervading sense of regret and bitterness.

Clearly the outcome of these later stages depends in part on how conflicts during earlier stages were resolved. Central to all stages of the life cycle lies the development of a sense of one's own identity. Since the identity conflict flowers during adolescence it is easy to appreciate the importance that adolescents attach to this domain of their lives. In a very real sense, adolescence revolves around the world of personal identity.

Through Erikson's work we have seen how personality development culminates during adolescence in a certain preoccupation with self and identity. However, the realm of personality and emotions is not the only one propelling the adolescent in this direction. Patterns of cognitive growth and changes in physical/sexual functioning act in like fashion to focus adolescents upon themselves and on the meaning of their lives. We will examine these two domains in the following sections.

Summary of Identity Development

Developing a sense of self is a crucial task of adolescence. Erik Erikson's theory of the eight stages (or ages) of human development places central importance on the adolescent years. The four conflict stages leading up to adolescence (trust/mistrust, autonomy/shame, initiative/guilt, and industry/inferiority) all contribute to the adolescent's construction of a personal identity. Further, the resolution of the identity conflict during stage 5 (identity versus identity diffusion) determines, in part, the outcome of the three subsequent stages in adulthood (intimacy/isolation, generativity/stagnation and integrity/despair). Thus, according to Erikson, the development of a sense of identity is a pivotal event in the human life cycle and explains adolescents' characteristic preoccupation with themselves.

ADOLESCENT COGNITION: PIAGET'S FORMAL-OPERATIONAL PERIOD

It is during adolescence that we see the last period of cognitive growth, according to Piaget; namely, the **formal-operational period.** Recall from our earlier discussion that the period immediately preceding this, the concrete-operational period, saw a number of important advances in the child's thinking: a decrease in egocentrism accompanied by an increasing ability to take different perspectives on things; development of a fully integrated system of classification; and conservation of various dimensions such as number, quantity, and volume. More generally, we saw that the great achievement of this period lay in coordinating previously separate thoughts into an integrated and coherent system. We called this the *system of concrete operations*. Nevertheless, for Piaget there are still some definite limits on the child's cognitive capabilities. The limitation is perhaps best summarized in the name he gave to the period; that is, *concrete operations*. The child at this age is limited to coordinating concrete objects or ideas in actual situations. He cannot yet coordinate possible objects or ideas in a hypothetical and abstract situation. The concrete-operational child can coordinate various physical dimensions (for example, the height and width of a beaker of water) and thereby show conservation of liquid quantity. In like manner, the concrete-operational child can conserve mass, number, volume, distance, and weight; in short, most dimensions of the concrete physical reality in front of him. What he cannot yet do, though, is coordinate these separate concrete-operational systems effectively. The concrete-operational child is limited to dealing with one system at a time; for example, volume or number or distance or weight. By this time you may anticipate the general nature of the advance made during the formal-operational period: progressive integration and coordination of previously isolated concrete-operational systems.

Coordinating Concrete-Operational Systems

An example will help illustrate the above point. Looking at Figure 12-2, you see a balance beam with various weights that can be placed in various positions on either side of the beam. The goal is to balance the beam and there are two ways to accomplish it: by changing weights on either side of the beam or by moving weights closer to or farther from the central balance point (fulcrum). The concrete-operational child can solve the balance problem easily when working with only one dimension. For example, he can discover that if one side has more weights on it than the other side, he can restore the balance by removing the extra weight from one side or by adding a weight to the other side. The concrete-operational child can also discover the effect of moving weights different distances from the fulcrum. But the concrete-operational child does not understand that these two systems of operations are related to each other. He does not know, for example, that adding extra weight to one side can be compensated for by moving the weights on the other side further away from the fulcrum. In short, he cannot coordinate these two systems into a higher-order "system of systems." Stated another way, since the concrete-operational system is a system of transformations, the formal-operational system is a transformation of a transformation; that is, it is the ability to transform one system, such as weight, into another system, such as distance. This is the goal of the formal-operational period: namely, the coordination of previously isolated systems of concrete operations into a higher-order system of formal operations.

As a result, the adolescent can evoke systems of operations that are not directly involved at all in the concrete situation before him. Since he has a more fully coordinated set of systems, he is not dependent upon the immediate concrete reality for dealing with problems. He is less tied to the prevailing context

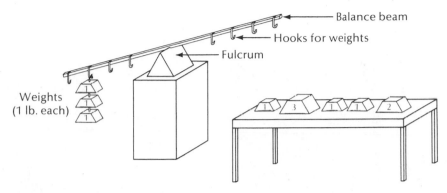

Figure 12-2.   How to balance the beam. A typical balance-beam problem in which a series of weights is attached to one end of the beam. The child is presented with a variety of weights (on the nearby table) and must decide how to restore balance to the beam. The child must decide where on the beam (at what distance from the fulcrum) to place the proper weight.

and can think about questions in a much more systematic, thorough, and formal manner. One illustration of this new ability can be seen in the adolescent's greater reliance on *systematic experimentation*.

Systematic Experimentation

Piaget presented children of various ages with four beakers of colorless, odorless liquid, like those shown in Figure 12-3, along with a smaller beaker also holding a colorless, odorless liquid. First the child is given two unmarked glasses that he is told contain liquid from some of the four beakers. Piaget then adds a few drops of the liquid from the smaller beaker to each glass and the liquid in one turns yellow while the other stays clear. At this point the child is given some empty glasses himself and is told to produce a yellow liquid by combining liquids from the four beakers.

In our example the combination that produces the yellow-color liquid is liquid 1 plus liquid 3. Liquid 2 is plain water having no effect and liquid 4 actively prevents the yellow from appearing. In order to be absolutely sure which liquids are solely responsible for producing the yellow color, the child must systematically try out all possible combinations. Piaget found that while concrete-operational children start out quite systematically, trying 1, then 2, then 3, then 4, they are apt to give up when none of them works. When they do try to combine liquids (for instance, 1 and 2, 2 and 4), they do so in a haphazard fashion. If they accidentally produce the yellow color (for example, with 1 and 3, or 1 and 2 and 3), they don't realize why, nor can they always reproduce the effect again. In contrast, formal-operational children go about the task quite differently. They systematically try out single liquids, followed by combining two liquids together. Even after one correct solution is obtained, they continue to experiment with all possible combinations in order to verify that 1 plus 3 is the essential way to produce the yellow color.

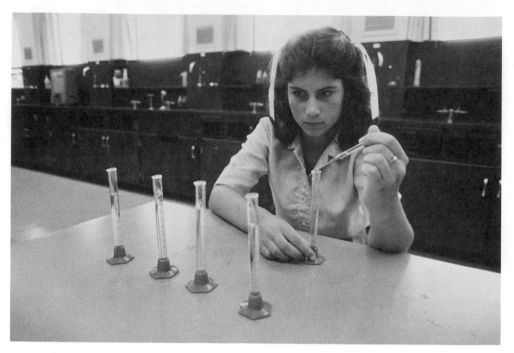

Figure 12-3.

The above behavior of the formal-operational child is referred to by Piaget as **systematic experimentation.** The adolescent in this period exhaustively tries out all possible combinations of liquids. This characteristic also stems from the newly acquired ability to coordinate and utilize mental operations in a totally complete way.

Thinking about the Hypothetical and Abstract

The coordination of systems of thought into higher systems also permits the child to move beyond the actual concrete world of physical reality and to consider hypothetical worlds or other realities. The formal-operational child as a result asks questions like "What if rain fell upward?", "What if I could fly?" "What if there were no poverty or illness?" and "What if they gave a war and nobody came?" These "what if" questions, so characteristic of adolescent thought, stem directly from the ability to bring new, hypothetical dimensions to an otherwise concrete reality. The propensity toward **hypothetical thinking** is also closely allied to the burgeoning tendency to think at a more abstract level. The formal-operational adolescent can consider general issues such as morality, love, phoniness, nationalism. Indeed, one of the abstract issues he can begin to consider is "self." "Who am I?" "Where am I going?" "What do I want from life?" "How do I feel about love, commitment, sex?" A good number of the questions which emerge during adolescence center around the adolescent's sense of and quest for personal identity.

The child's intellectual development parallels and may even pave the way for upheavals seen in his life, namely, concentration on general, abstract concepts, the most personal and important of which is the meaning of his own personal self, or identity.

Summary of Adolescent Cognition

Adolescence marks the final period in Piaget's theory of cognitive growth, the formal-operational period. Among the more important changes occurring in the child's thought processes are an increasing ability to coordinate systems of thought into a higher system, systematic experimentation, and the ability to engage in hypothetical and abstract thinking. The advances made by the adolescent over his concrete-operational counterpart reflect the same general advances made from one period of development to the next—in this case, the coordination of previously isolated systems of thought into higher-order systems. Finally, the propensity of the formal-operational child to engage in hypothetical and abstract thinking may underlie the previously discussed emergence of the adolescent's preoccupation with self-identity.

PHYSICAL AND SEXUAL CHANGES: THE SPOTLIGHT TURNS INWARD

Were it not enough that adolescents' personal and intellectual growth were leading them to focus more on themselves, they are in a very direct and dramatic way thrown back on themselves due to the physical and sexual upheaval they begin to experience. Growth changes, sexual changes and stirrings, acne, beards, menstruation; all in their way focus attention on the changing adolescents' selves. In the next section we will briefly review some of the major physical and sexual changes occurring during adolescence and try to point out their psychological and social impact.

THE BIOLOGY OF ADOLESCENCE

Bodily Changes

Although the onset of puberty is primarily associated with changes in a few salient physical and sexual features, in actuality the changes are so widespread that hardly any bodily tissues are unaffected by it. In general the changes that make up puberty have been classified (Marshall & Tanner, 1974) as:

1. Acceleration and then deceleration of skeletal growth (the adolescent growth spurt).
2. Altered body composition resulting from skeletal and muscular growth, together with changes in the quantity and distribution of fat.
3. Development of the respiratory and circulatory systems, resulting in increased strength and endurance.
4. Development of the gonads, reproductive organs, and secondary sex characteristics.
5. Changes in a variety of other structures (particularly the pituitary gland and the hypothalamus) and their functioning.

Changes in these areas during adolescence are responsible for the major biological changes we see in adolescents' physical and sexual appearance and in behavior. As universal as the changes are, nevertheless a very important fact should be emphasized here. *There are important differences in the order, onset, and rate of growth at puberty.* Though the end result is almost invariably the same, many adolescents and parents suffer great anxiety over how adolescents are progressing through these changes. As we shall see shortly, the concerns and anxieties attending early and late maturation are strong and potentially hazardous to an adolescent's identity, self-esteem, and subsequent psychological growth.

Among contemporary Western youth puberty as judged by its external manifestations (that is, changes in height, weight, and so forth) begins at around age 10 or 11 in girls and 11 or 12 in boys. However by the time these external signs have become apparent, internal events have been changing for some time. In particular hormonal changes that trigger external bodily changes start around 8 or 9 years of age, and changes in the brain that control the hormonal changes have begun even earlier. For these reasons we cannot say for certain when puberty really begins.

Changes in Body Size and Shape

The major physical transformations occurring during puberty include changes in fat distribution, height, weight, and body proportions.

Body Fat.   Subcutaneous fat, which is located under the skin and contributes to our body contours, increases just prior to adolescence, causing the characteristic "chubby" or "baby fat" look of prepubertal children. During the adolescent growth spurt, however, there is a progressive loss of this subcutaneous fat, especially from the arms and legs of teenage boys. Since this loss occurs concurrently with rapid increases in height, it contributes to the "gangly, stringbean" look of some teenage boys. Adolescent girls, in contrast, do not lose fat as markedly as do boys, and therefore enter adulthood with more subcutaneous fat than boys, especially in the region of the pelvis, the breasts, the upper back, and the backs of the upper arms. As a consequence, women's bodies look generally more rounded, while men's bodies appear more muscular, largely because they have less subcutaneous fat.

Height.   One of the more obvious physical changes is the adolescent growth spurt. Somewhere between 10 and 15 years of age, adolescent boys and girls show a dramatic increase in the *rate of growth* (see Figure 12-4, bottom) in height (resulting in the typical heights shown in Figure 12-4, top). As is evident from the curves, there are consistent differences between girls and boys in the growth spurt. Among girls, the growth spurt typically starts at around 10½ years of age, reaches a peak at 12, and ends at 14—though it may start as early as 9½ and end as late as 15 (Marshall & Tanner, 1970). For boys, the spurt usually starts between 12 and 13, peaks at 14, and ends at 16—though it may begin as early as 10½ or as late as 16 and end as early as 13½ or as late as 17 (Katchadourian, 1977). These differing patterns between boys and girls produce the situation where, temporarily at least, girls are slightly taller on the average than boys, a situation that sometimes produces psychological and social difficulties for both boys and girls. However, this temporary height advantage in girls is short-lived since boys

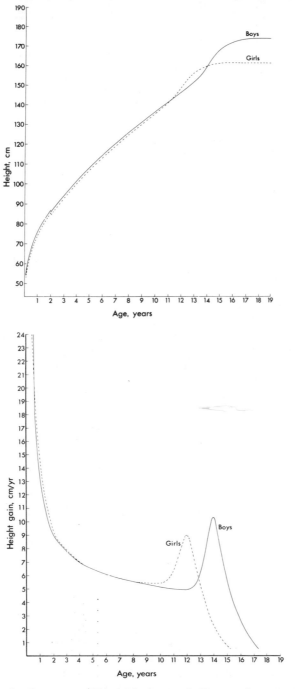

Figure 12-4. At about age 10½, girls begin their growth spurt and are temporarily taller than their male peers (see bottom graph). However, when boys (at about age 12) begin their growth spurt, they typically grow faster and for a longer period of time than girls. The graph on the top depicts the typical heights for boys and girls. (From *Archives of the Diseases of Childhood, Vol. 1*, by J. M. Tanner, R. H. Whithouse, and A. Takaishi. Copyright 1966 by the Institute of Child Health, University of London. Reprinted by permission.)

grow faster and for a longer period of time. In his year of fastest growth a boy normally adds about 3 to 5 inches (7 to 12 centimeters) to his height while a girl adds slightly less (6 to 11 centimeters), resulting eventually in the characteristic difference in adult height between males and females.

Increases in height occur primarily through lengthening of the bones, which also increase in thickness. The legs accelerate in length first (specifically, first the foot, then the calf and the thigh), followed almost a year later by increases in arm length (hands and forearms first, then upper arm). Eventual height is caused more by changes in the trunk than in the legs (Katchadourian, 1977). But because the feet and hands grow first, they cause the adolescent for a short time to have disproportionately larger hands and feet, a potentially disturbing and self-absorbing fact.

Weight.   In general terms the patterns of growth for weight parallel those for height. Thus, the growth curves for weight gained (a weight spurt) and eventual weight attained look very much like the height curves of Figure 12-4. (For details on weight, see Katchadourian, 1977.)

Body proportions.   In the growth spurt the feet and hands grow first, followed by the hips, chest, shoulders, and finally the trunk. All of these individual changes produce noticeable variation in the overall proportioning and the general look of the body. For example, the head, which develops earlier in the child's life, begins to appear much smaller relative to the rest of the body.

In addition to the above changes, the profile straightens, the nose projects more, the jaw becomes more prominent, the lips become fuller, and the hairline begins to recede (predominantly in males). Boys and girls begin to take on a characteristically different appearance, boys having somewhat broader shoulders, narrower hips, and larger legs relative to trunk length (Katchadourian, 1977).

Internal changes.   Finally, there are a variety of less noticeable but equally important changes in the body's internal organs. The heart undergoes a growth spurt, more pronounced in boys, nearly doubling in weight. The number of red blood cells also rises, again more dramatically in boys. Adult men have about 1 million more red blood cells per milliliter of blood than do women. The respiratory system, specifically the size of the lungs, and subsequent respiratory capacity show increases similar to those of the heart/circulatory system, again more strongly in boys. The overall result of these internal changes is to increase the ability of the body to exert itself physically. Physical endurance and exercise tolerance thus increase dramatically during the adolescent period.

Somewhat surprisingly, gross changes in the brain do not occur during adolescence, despite the relatively marked changes in intellectual functioning of the kind noted by Piaget that were just discussed. Possibly there are increases in the number of new connections made between cells that account for increased intellectual capacity in the absence of increased brain size.

Sexual Changes and Maturation of the Reproductive System

Sexual organs are obviously part of the physical makeup of the body and undergo changes during adolescence like other physical structures. For purposes of discussion, we shall review the sexes separately.

Female Reproductive Maturation

Breasts.   The first visible sign of puberty in a girl is the growth of her breasts. Starting somewhere between 8 and 13 (usually at around 11) and completed between 13 and 18 (on the average at about 15), breast development follows a fairly predictable sequence (Tanner, 1962; see Figure 12-5).

Pubic Hair.   Commonly the appearance of pubic hair follows breast development, though it may precede changes in the breast. Pubic hair begins to grow at around 11 or 12 and takes on the adult look by about age 14.

External Sexual Organs.   The most prominent aspect of the female genitals is the mons pubis (also called the Mount of Venus), which consists of the soft protuberance over the pubic bone. Somewhat less visible are the major lips, located below the mons, that in turn enclose the minor lips; the clitoris; and the vaginal opening, usually covered partly by the hymen in virgins. All of these structures enlarge during puberty and become sensitive to sexual stimulation, especially the clitoris (Katchadourian, 1977).

Internal Sexual Organs.   These organs include the ovaries, the fallopian tubes, the uterus, and the vagina. Changes in the uterus during puberty include enlarging of the muscular wall and development of an intricate and powerful set of muscles (needed to accommodate a fetus during pregnancy and force it out during birth). The vagina also becomes larger. The growth of the ovaries is less dramatic, being essentially complete at birth. They contain in immature form about half a million eggs (ova), from which all those subsequently needed (about 400) will be developed. At puberty, eggs begin to be produced in monthly cycles.

Menarche.   The monthly cycle of egg production normally culminates in menstruation, an important biological milestone for adolescent women and one often imbued with strong psychological significance. It is often felt that menarche marks the true beginning of puberty, but in reality it is a rather late event; for example, it sometimes occurs a full two years after the onset of breast development and after the growth spurt in height. In the United States at present, menarche occurs usually at around 12.8 years of age, with a normal range of from 9 to 18 years (Katchadourian, 1977).

Male Reproductive Maturation

Testes.   Initial enlargement of the testes begins at between 10 and 13½ years of age. The testes are the reproductive glands that produce sperm. Unlike the ovaries, however, the total population of sperm produced by a male does not exist from birth. Sperm continue to be produced from cells in the testes. The testes connect to a set of tubes (epididymis, vas deferens, ejaculatory duct, and urethra) that convey sperm, and the penis, which delivers the ejaculate.

The ability to ejaculate develops during adolescence along with the ability to experience orgasm, although the capacity to experience orgasm precedes ejaculatory ability.

Pubic Hair.   Pubic hair in males may begin to appear at any time between 10 and 15 years of age. In contrast to women, whose pubic hair produces a rather

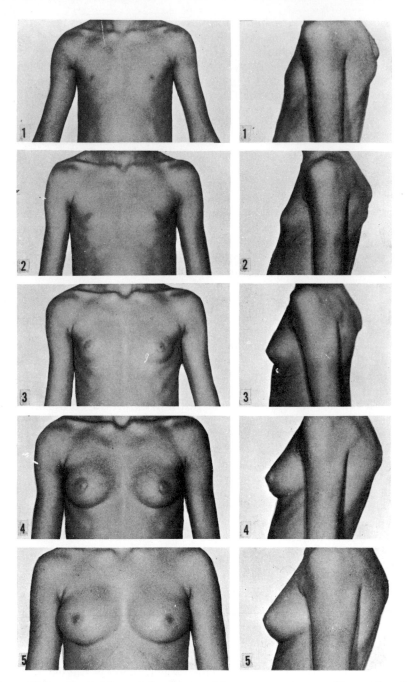

Figure 12-5. Typical breast development in a young woman. (From *Growth at Adolescence* (2nd ed.), by J. M. Tanner. Copyright 1962 by Blackwell Scientific Publications, Ltd. Reprinted by permission.)

uniform triangular shape, male pubic hair continues to spread over the central region of the abdomen, producing a less sharply defined pattern.

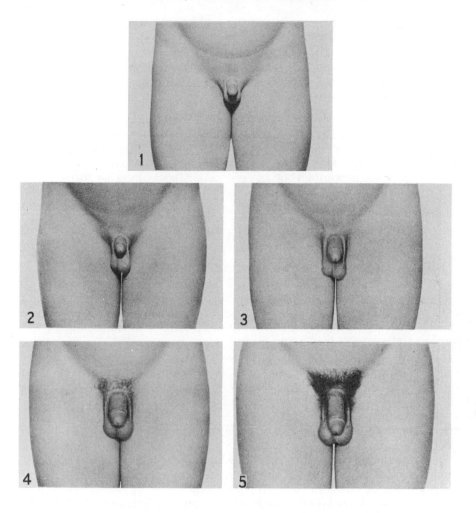

Figure 12-6. Typical genital development in a young man. (From *Growth at Adolescence* (2nd ed.), by J. M. Tanner. Copyright 1962 by Blackwell Scientific Publications, Ltd. Reprinted by permission.)

External Genitals.   Included as external genitals are the penis and scrotum (the sac that encompasses the testes). The penis grows during adolescence and, like breasts in females, follows a relatively predictable pattern (see Figure 12-6). Changes in external genitals begin usually at between 10 and 13½ and are completed between 13½ and 16½.

Voice Changes.   During adolescence the larynx enlarges more dramatically in males than in females, causing a characteristic deepening of the male voice. A rather late development of puberty, it may occur abruptly or gradually, and there is usually a period of time where the voice is breaking, that is, occasionally changing rapidly from a low-pitched adult baritone to a high-pitched squeaky soprano.

Facial and Other Hair.   One of the more obvious badges of manhood is the emergence of the beard. The first strands of facial hair usually begin to grow at the corner of the upper lip, spreading first to form a mustache, eventually spreading to the cheeks and lower lip and finally to the chin and lower face. Body hair, including under the arms, shows some concurrent growth during this period but it continues to spread for a while during early adulthood.

Breasts.   There is in some boys normal breast development for a time. Beginning in the majority of cases at around 14 to 14½ years of age, the breast area shows some enlargement. This usually disappears within one to two years, though in a small percentage of cases it may take as long as three years.

Hormonal Regulation of Pubertal Changes

Much of the responsibility for the varied and complex physical/sexual changes occurring during the adolescent period goes to a very complex system of regulation that includes structures in the brain as well as in other parts of the body. The prime movers in these changes are a number of **hormones**, or complex chemicals secreted directly into the blood stream. It is the action of these hormones on their targets (for example, bones or sex organs) that causes the changes in adolescent physical and sexual makeup. Figure 12-7 graphically shows this complex hormonal system. Essentially, the system is divided into three levels of control: (1) the *hypothalamus*, the highest level of brain control, regulates (2) the *pituitary gland* (located lower in the brain), which, by secreting a number of hormones that act on different parts of the body, controls (3) the specific hormones secreted by the target organs themselves, which control the changes in the organs.

The main avenue of control for adolescent physical and sexual change is from the hypothalamus to the anterior pituitary (see Figure 12-7). From the anterior pituitary six hormones are secreted to different organs: (1) **growth hormone** (GH), which regulates body growth; (2) **thyrotropic hormone** (TSH), which controls the thyroid gland; (3) *adrenocorticotrophic hormone (ACTH)*, which controls the adrenal cortex; (4) *follicle-stimulating hormone (FSH)* and (5) *lutenizing hormone (LH)*, both of which act on the reproductive organs; and (6) *prolactin (PRL)*, which acts on the breasts.

The above hormones regulate the production of other hormones that act directly on the tissues and bring about the changes we have described. With one exception (growth hormone, which is produced by the pituitary itself), they are produced by the ovaries, testes, thyroid glands, and adrenal cortex.

Growth Hormone

The primary function of growth hormone is to stimulate body growth. It acts throughout childhood in regulating growth, but its precise role in pubertal growth is not yet established.

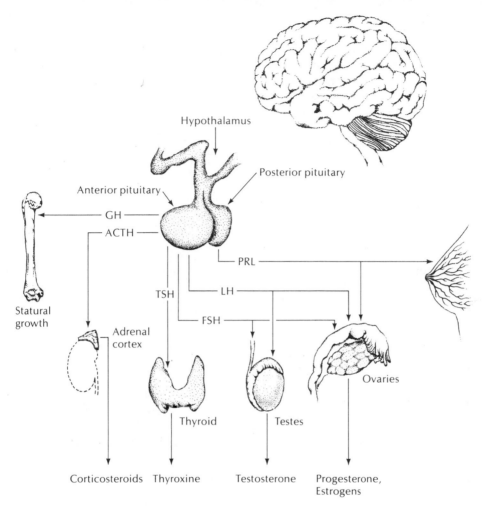

Figure 12-7. Hormones of the pituitary and their targets.[1]
GM—Growth Hormone
ACTH—Adrenocorticotrophic Hormone
TSH—Thyroid Stimulating Hormone
FSA—Follicle Stimulating Hormone
LH—Lutenizing Hormone
PRL—Prolactin

Thyroxine

This hormone, produced in the thyroid gland, is most important in skeletal maturation, and though it does contribute to growth somewhat, it is not considered essential to the growth spurt (Tepperman, 1973).

[1]From "The Hormones of the Hypothalamus" by Roger Guillemin and Roger Burgus. Copyright © 1972 by Scientific American, Inc. All rights reserved.

Testosterone

This hormone, produced primarily in the testes, promotes growth and development of the male reproductive system and enhances the development of muscles. Thus testosterone is both a sex hormone and a growth hormone and is the primary agent in producing male pubertal changes. Testosterone causes enlargement of the testes and growth of the penis as well as the change in voice and growth of pubic and other hair. It is even responsible for predisposing the skin to acne.

Estrogen and Progesterone

These two hormones that are secreted by cells in the ovaries control physical and sexual changes in females and are intimately involved in setting up the menstrual cycle.

Estrogen causes growth and development of the reproductive organs (ovaries, uterus, and vagina), and controls breast enlargement, skeletal growth, and fat distribution, and the development of pubic and other hair.

Progesterone has a more limited range of effects than does estrogen but it is responsible for the vital functions of ovulation and maintenance of the embryo.

The Menstrual Cycle

During puberty the production of estrogen and progesterone begin to follow a cyclical pattern. Menstruation consists of the shedding of the lining of the uterus, which, since it is rich in blood vessels, accounts for the presence of blood in the menstrual flow. This event triggers estrogen production, which starts the maturation of a new egg and the formation of a new uterine lining. This phase continues for about two weeks, or for half of the regular 28-day cycle. At around the midcycle point ovulation occurs; that is, a mature egg is expelled from the ovaries. If fertilization does not occur, the production of estrogen and progesterone decreases markedly and the uterine lining loses its sustenance and is shed once again.

Menstrual cycles are initially quite irregular during puberty and even in young adulthood they may vary at between 26 and 34 days, though 28 days constitutes the average length of the cycle.

The Psychological Impact of Pubertal Changes

The above physical and sexual changes are not without their psychological effects. As stressed throughout this chapter, these changes direct the adolescents' focus of concern back on themselves and ultimately on who they are becoming. Coupled with the emotional and cognitive changes, the physical changes force a process of self-evaluation. Naturally many of these changes cause the adolescent to be temporarily different from others; taller, shorter, fatter, skinnier, and so forth. At a minimum these changes will make adolescents more self-conscious and prone to embarrassment at their physical appearance. More critically, excessive preoccupation with physical differences may cause an impaired self-concept that can contribute negatively to the adolescent's growing sense of identity.

In addition to the general impact on adolescent identity, there are specific effects relating to individual realms of change.

The Impact of Menstruation

A girl's psychological reaction to menstruation can span the spectrum from rather calm, curious anticipation to extreme worry. Negative reactions can stem in part from the physical discomfort that sometimes occurs, including cramps, headaches, and muscle pains. In addition, the appearance of blood in the menstrual flow may frighten some girls, especially those who have had little information in preparation for menstruation. Finally, negative reactions can be conditioned by the reactions of others and by lingering social stereotypes. Hearing menstruation called "having the curse" or "being unwell" or "being unclean," a young girl can hardly be expected to wait for menstruation with joyous anticipation. Most of these negative reactions can be minimized. Emphasizing how natural menstruation is, making sure the girl knows what is actually happening and what to do about it, and making provision for medical care in the event of physical problems will go a long way toward alleviating anxieties.

Erection and Nocturnal Emission

Comparable anxieties can arise in boys when they experience frequent and spontaneous erections as well as when they first experience nocturnal emissions (sometimes called "wet dreams," since they are frequently accompanied by erotic dreams). Though most adolescents today understand better than their parents did how normal these events are, some contemporary adolescents still experience anxiety and guilt.

Psychological Effect of Maturing Early or Late

One salient factor influencing adolescents' psychological development is whether they mature early or late. A host of complex effects surrounds this developmental attainment, and it is different in boys and girls.

For boys, the early maturer is the taller, heavier, more muscular, and sexually advanced boy. He is advanced in ways that will consistently receive rewards in adulthood—bigger, stronger, more "macho." Late maturers often suffer in comparison for a time and both groups show different psychological characteristics. Studies have shown that late-maturing boys (measured objectively by skeletal age) were rated as less attractive, less well-poised, and more tense, talkative, and attention-seeking. Early maturers, in contrast, were rated as more attractive, poised, calm, and socially adept (Jones & Bayley, 1950). These differences can persist into adulthood. In one follow-up study of men age 33, late maturers scored lower than early maturers on personality measures of self-control, responsibility, and dominance (Jones & Bayley, 1957).

For girls, the advantages and disadvantages of early versus late maturation are less straightforward. For young girls, early maturing girls may suffer socially (Faust, 1960), at least in terms of how other girls will respond to them. They are different and hence somewhat ostracized. However, as most girls begin to show signs of maturing, the balance shifts to favor those who are at a more mature stage. Thus the psychological value of early versus late maturation appears to be determined more by the level of maturation of the immediate social group for girls, rather than by some general societal standard, as it is for boys.

Summary of Physical and Sexual Maturation

A host of physical and sexual changes take place in all adolescents, though the onset, order, and rate of change may differ dramatically among different adolescents. The outward, observable manifestations of change are preceded by internal hormonal changes that set up and direct the external changes.

Major changes in body size and proportion occur, including redistribution of body fat, a growth spurt in height, weight, and some internal organs, and a shift in body proportions.

Sexual maturation in girls includes appearance and development of breasts, pubic hair, external genital organs, and internal genital organs, particularly the uterus and vagina.

Sexual maturation in males includes enlarging of the testes and penis, growth of pubic and facial hair, voice changes, and, in some cases, temporary breast development.

The many changes that occur in adolescent physical and sexual development are guided by a complex, integrated regulation system that includes the hypothalamus, the pituitary gland, and target organs. Signals from the hypothalamus cause the pituitary to secrete six hormones that, in turn, act on target organs to secrete their own hormones. Some of these target-organ hormones (especially testosterone in males and estrogen in females) are directly involved in producing the characteristic changes noted in adolescent physical and sexual maturation.

These dramatic changes work to focus adolescents on their bodies and eventually on their "selves." Pubertal changes can and do have a psychological impact on the adolescent. Anxieties in girls about the menstrual cycle and in boys about nocturnal emissions are often easily eliminated through proper instruction.

Maturing early or late can also produce some anxieties in adolescents, and there appear to be differences in personality and social skills between adolescents who mature early and those who mature late. To some extent, though, the benefits of maturing early versus late differ in boys and girls. Whereas for boys early maturation is consistently regarded with high esteem, for girls early maturation initially may be a social handicap among their female peers, although eventually physically more mature girls are preferred socially to physically less mature girls.

SEXUAL BEHAVIOR, ATTITUDES, AND VALUES

ISSUE

Are we in the midst of a sexual revolution?

Much has been made in recent years about changes in sexual behavior and attitudes among young people; some have called these changes a "sexual revolution." However, it is important to realize that the most dramatic aspect of the revolution has been not in the area of sexual behavior, but in attitudes toward sex. According to data collected by Kinsey and his colleagues (Kinsey, Pomeroy, Martin, & Gebhard, 1953), only 2% of females born before 1900 had premarital intercourse prior to age 16 and 8% prior to age 20. In contrast, for the mother of today's adolescents, 4% had sexual intercourse prior to 16 and 21% prior to age 20. As we shall see, these figures approximate those found among today's females, although they are somewhat lower, indicating that premarital sexual behavior has been increasing in the recent past (Simon, Berger, & Gagnon, 1972). Thus the greatest increase in premarital sexual behavior occurred over the first two or three decades of this century. For today's youth, then, the more dramatic changes have occurred not in sexual behavior so much as in attitudes and values about sexual activity. There is a greater openness to sexual matters, especially sex education, and greater emphasis on incorporating sex into the total spectrum of emotional and social involvement.

Sexual Behavior among Contemporary Adolescents

A study of the sexual experiences of college students (Simon, Berger, & Gagnon, 1972) conducted around 1967 indicated a moderate increase in sexual intercourse beyond that found by the Kinsey et al. (1953) study. Over all years of college, 56% of males and 32% of females had sexual experience. In addition, the first experience of many of those responding had taken place during college. Thus by 1967, more than half the males and a third of the females had sexual intercourse prior to marriage. Since that time the greatest increase in sexual intercourse has occurred among females. While by 1970 the percentage of males having experienced sexual intercourse had leveled off at about 80%, the percentage of females reported having had intercourse is still rising (51% in 1970, 56% in 1971). It is clear that sexual experiences are increasing at a faster rate for women than for men. No doubt the availability of contraceptive devices has contributed to this trend. But even so, there has been a serious increase in teenage pregnancy.

It is important to point out, however, that the numbers above are general figures and do not take into account large numbers of factors that greatly influence sexual activity. For example, *age* is an important factor determining sexual behavior. In the above study, only 36% of college freshman males reported having had sexual intercourse, while 68% of seniors reported having had sexual intercourse. Comparable figures for females were 19% and 32% respectively. Thus, younger adolescents are less sexually experienced (and more conservative in attitude) than are older adolescents. In addition, as the above figures indicate, *sex* differences are strong in regard to sexual experience. Girls report less overall incidence of sexual intercourse at all ages (Simon, Berger, & Gagnon, 1972). Beyond age and sex, *social* and *educational* factors play a role in sexual attitudes. Those youths from economically more advantaged backgrounds and of higher education are less conservative and more tolerant of premarital sexual experiences (Yankelovich, 1974). Finally, political and religious beliefs obviously influence sexual beliefs and, to some extent, behavior. Politically conservative youths are also more conservative in sexual attitudes than are politically liberal youths and have more limited sexual experience (Wilson, 1971). With regard to religious beliefs, among contemporary youth 13 to 19 years of age, 60% of virgins report that they attend religious services fairly often, while only 36% of nonvirgins so state.

In summary, it does appear that premarital sexual intercourse has increased among contemporary adolescents to the point where a clear majority of males and females have experienced intercourse.

Masturbation

In addition to intercourse, an adolescent's sexual experience extends to other forms of behavior (including petting, embracing, and kissing), but perhaps the most emotionally charged activity centers on masturbation. This activity provides a sexual outlet for many adolescents and, although figures are divergent, it appears that the incidence of masturbation is relatively high, especially in males (Kinsey, Pomeroy, & Martin, 1948; Sorensen, 1973). At the same time, strong feelings of fear and guilt appear to accompany masturbation activity (Sorensen, 1973), although all available evidence indicates that masturbation is a relatively normal, enjoyable activity that is harmful only in extreme cases.

Sexual Attitudes and Values

As stated earlier, the real revolution that appears to be happening in this country centers primarily on attitudes, feelings, and values toward human sexuality. There is greater interest in and less fear of sexual matters, particularly among females.

Accompanying this new openness is an increased desire for education on all aspects of sexual activity, not just the physical mechanics but also the relation between sex and love. In a recent survey (Sorensen, 1973), 85% of females and 75% of males agreed that more sex education courses were needed in the nation's schools. In addition, nearly 75% of adolescents concurred that the most important thing about the morality of sex concerned how people treated each other, not just what they did. This last piece of data reveals strongly that contemporary youth place as much or more emphasis on the meaning of a relationship that includes sex as on the sexual activity itself. Most adolescents thus are tolerant of sexual behavior between two people who care about each other (Sorensen, 1973), but are less tolerant of purely casual sex devoid of any emotional involvement.

To the extent that these changing attitudes and values in the United States reflect a trend toward incorporating sex into the total scheme of emotional and social development, it can be seen as a healthy development. Sex divorced from every other aspect of one's life can have damaging effects on personal growth. Nevertheless, although for the majority of adolescents sex appears to be integrating itself more comfortably into the general scheme of life, this is not the case for everyone. There is still a significant percentage of youth who are not part of the sexual revolution, who have not had much sexual experience, and who may be fearful of sex. In a cultural climate where sexual activity is relatively common and where certain adolescents may look upon sexual experience as a badge of status, an inexperienced adolescent may begin to feel unattractive, strange, or otherwise inadequate, resulting in self-denigration and depression. We know very little about the possible negative psychological effects of the sexual revolution, if any. We must not just focus on its beneficial effects, however; we must also be cautious about potential hazards, particularly in the adolescent.

Teenage Pregnancy

One consequence of the sexual revolution appears to be an alarming increase, among adolescent girls especially, in the number of illegitimate births (Vincent, 1966), despite the availability of contraceptive measures. It has been estimated that between 1957 and 1969, the number of illegitimate births among girls under 20 rose from about 80,000 in 1957 to 135,000 in 1969 (Vincent, 1966; Pannor, Massarik, & Evans, 1971).

Why is this happening? One reason is obvious—a large percentage of adolescents are not taking adequate contraceptive precautions. This is all the more surprising since the vast majority of college-age adolescent women appear to be in favor of having birth control devices available on campus to anyone who wants them (Koenig & Falkenstein, 1972). Despite such attitudes and generally available knowledge about contraceptive techniques, the number of unplanned pregnancies has increased. Part of the reason may have to do with how good the adolescent's sex education really has been. One study (Zelnick & Kantner, 1973) found that only 40% of sexually active adolescent females knew the time of greatest pregnancy risk during the menstrual cycle; most thought it occurred during menstruation. However, most pregnancies of adolescents, as with adults, probably result from carelessness, the impulsiveness of the moment, and the naive belief that "it can't happen to me!"

There has been much controversy recently surrounding whether a pregnant teenager should have an abortion, should give up her baby for adoption or should keep the baby. Regardless of how one views this issue, it is clear that much more is needed in the area of prevention: more sex education, in particular, is needed on the facts of intercourse and pregnancy as well as on the availability and use of contraceptive devices.

Summary of Adolescent Sexual Behavior and Attitudes

It has been said that our society is witnessing a sexual revolution among youth. Careful examination reveals that the revolution at present is focused more on changing sexual attitudes than on changing sexual behavior. Radical change in sexual behavior appears to have occurred around the turn of the present century. Since then there has been a gradual but steady increase in the number of adolescents (especially females) having premarital intercourse. More critically, today's youth appear to be relatively more open about sexual matters, more interested in sex education, and more desirous of integrating sexual behavior into general personality and social growth. Nevertheless, some adolescents are quite uncertain and anxious about sexual matters. In addition, there has been an alarming rise in teenage pregnancy over the previous two decades. These two facts point up the need for more intensive sex education in general and more education concerning the use of contraceptive devices in particular.

THE ADOLESCENT IN THE FAMILY: THE QUEST FOR INDEPENDENCE

As the search for and construction of a personal identity proceed, the adolescent simultaneously moves toward developing greater control over his life. Whereas the child is relatively more dependent upon his parents and they control many of the decisions that affect his life, in adolescence the balance begins to shift toward greater responsibility on the individual in decision-making. The push to independence comes from two sources: from within the individual, and from society as a whole. Hence the individual seeks to gain a greater say in many aspects of his life. At the same time, parents and others begin gradually to shift their expectations of the adolescent in similar ways. However, the transition to independence can be a tense and trouble-filled period for both adolescents and their parents. An important determinant of success or failure in this area lies within the parents and how they interact with and guide their children toward greater independence and responsibility for their actions.

Dimensions of Parental Behavior

Two dimensions of parental behavior and attitudes that we described in earlier chapters continue to be particularly important in dealing with adolescent development (Schaefer, 1959; Martin, 1975). The first dimension we called "love/hostility," "acceptance/rejection," and "loving/rejecting." Essentially this dimension refers to the general atmosphere that parents provide. Are they affectionate and understanding, do they respond warmly and reason with the child; or are they cold, distant, and rejecting? There seems to be little doubt that an atmosphere of warmth and acceptance is necessary for an adolescent's healthy development. Parental hostility and rejection are commonly found in the backgrounds of children with various social and psychological problems. For the adolescent to develop a healthy self-esteem and to be an active, confident, and positive person, he or she must grow up in an atmosphere of love and caring.

The other important dimension is "autonomy/control" (sometimes called "permissiveness/restrictiveness"). Here we refer to how the parent views his or her own power over the child. Does the parent place severe restrictions on the child with regard to obedience, neatness, and other behaviors, or does the parent allow the adolescent some degree of self-control and autonomy in making decisions about his personal habits, friends, and behavior? *Restrictiveness* here means an inordinate amount of parental control; as we shall see, some degree of parental control, in the sense of clear expectations of acceptable behavior and the subsequent exercise of authority to reinforce that behavior, is probably beneficial to adolescent development.

Most critical in terms of how adolescents react to parental characteristics is the combination of the two dimensions (Schaefer, 1959). For example, a child with a *hostile* and *restrictive* parent is likely to develop covert angry feelings toward the parent but hide his true feelings out of fear of a hostile reaction from the parent. A child whose parents are *hostile* but also overly *permissive* or lax in control is likely to be overtly rebellious and resentful. Children reared in a *warm* but *restrictive* environment are likely to be agreeable, friendly but also somewhat passive and conforming with their friends. In contrast, the children of parents who provide a warm, accepting atmosphere, and in addition allow some degree of autonomy in their children are likely to be more active, friendly, and flexible themselves. Thus the parental environment plays a salient role in shaping how the adolescent responds to his family and ultimately in molding the kind of young adult he will become.

Parent/Child Interaction and the Growth of an Independent Adolescent

The nature of the personal interaction between parent and child, coupled with the foregoing basic dimensions of parental behavior, ultimately determines how well the adolescent will progress toward a greater sense of independence. Elder (1962) asked a large number of adolescents to describe how their parents interacted with them. He found seven basic styles of interaction, which varied in the degree of parental versus self control:

Autocratic.   Autocratic parents control all decisions affecting their child, giving the child no say.

Authoritarian.   These parents always have the final word, although the child is occasionally consulted.

Democratic.   Here the child contributes freely to important decision-making matters, but the parents ultimately make or approve of the final decision.

Equalitarian.   Both parents and children contribute equally to decision-making and have an equal vote in the final outcome.

Permissive.   Here the adolescent assumes a more active and influential role in determining decisions.

Laissez-faire.   Here not only does the adolescent contribute equally, but he has final say in accepting or rejecting the parents' opinions and decisions.

Ignoring.   Here the parents are actively out of the picture and the adolescent has free rein to decide issues for himself.

The above styles of interaction range from absolute parental domination to complete parental absence in directing the adolescent's behavior. What are the outcomes of these different kinds of interaction? When adolescents were asked about how reasonable or fair their parents were, children from democratic homes rated their parents most fair, while children from autocratic homes rated their parents least fair. The former children tended to identify more with their parents, while the latter group tended to show more resentment toward their parents (Block & Turula, 1963).

One important difference was that children from both autocratic and ignoring parents felt less desired or wanted by their parents than did children from homes where the parents were more involved (that is, democratic, equalitarian, and permissive parents). Thus, it appears that too little control, as well as too much control, can have negative effects. Adolescents appear to thrive best in an atmosphere where their opinions are respected and where they feel some degree of influence over their lives, but where the parents clearly care enough about their children to involve themselves in making decisions about their children's lives. Complete ignoring of the child results in feelings of rejection and lower self-worth.

In Defense of Parents

The foregoing discussion may have left the impression that the growth of independence is a one-way street with parents determining and ultimately being responsible for the kind of adolescent or young adult that is produced. Nevertheless as we have repeatedly emphasized in the book with regard to parent/child interaction, the characteristics of the child can hold equal weight in influencing the parents' behavior and attitudes. It is quite possible in some cases that parents, faced with a strong-willed and resentful adolescent son or daughter (for whatever reasons), may opt to let the child go his own way, thereby seeming to ignore him. The numerous rapid changes in adolescent cognitive, sexual, and emotional functioning can in themselves produce individual characteristics to which the parent has to adjust. We must be careful not to always imply that parents are responsible for how their children turn out. Changes within the adolescent as well as other influences outside the family (school, peers, work) can affect the adolescent just as strongly. Nevertheless, the family environment is a very important soil in which adolescent growth can be influenced for better or worse.

Summary of Adolescent-Family Relations

A major task facing the adolescent in our society is the growth of independence. Parents play an essential role in how the adolescent solves this task. Parents who provide an environment that is loving and accepting but in which restrictions exist appear to foster independence, friendliness, and flexibility in their children. In contrast, a cold, hostile family milieu that at the same time is overly permissive can produce rebellious, resentful children.

Styles of parent-adolescent interaction also contribute to the adolescent's sense of autonomy and well-being. Overly autocratic or ignoring parents tend to make children feel unwanted and rejected by their parents. Parents who take their adolescent children's opinions seriously but who then exercise final say in making a decision affecting their lives foster greater feelings of independence in their children. In emphasizing the importance of parents we should not lose sight of the fact that adolescents themselves and other outside influences (school and peers) also contribute heavily to the child's growing independence.

REORIENTING TO NEW SOCIAL WORLDS: THE PEER GROUP

Clearly one social influence outside the family that exerts itself rapidly and strongly is the "peer group." This is a loosely defined concept that encompasses many different realms. Hence the peer group may be very large and may include all other adolescents in the culture; somewhat smaller and encompass all those in a particular school or neighborhood; or still smaller and include a close-knit group of friends, or even some few very close friends. As we shall see, adolescents generally progress from orienting and operating on a large scale (being one of a *crowd* of peers) to developing closer, more intimate relations with a few special friends and a very close relationship with one special person of the opposite sex in particular.

ISSUE

Do all adolescents rebel against their parents?

It is common to view the adolescent as progressing away from parental control toward the influence of the peer group. This has sometimes been viewed as adolescent "rebellion" toward parental dominance. In some realms, especially personal dress or recreational interests (music, movies, dancing), peers clearly begin to exert more influence. But parental influence does not cease nor do adolescents appear to completely abandon or ignore the advice or counsel of their parents (Brittain, 1963; Bandura, 1964). As several studies have documented, in general adolescents appear to get along quite well with their parents, show substantial respect and affection for them, and solicit their opinions when they feel they would be valuable; for example, in understanding some aspect of the adult world with which they are unfamiliar (Bandura, 1964; Douvan & Adelson, 1966). Thus it is important not to go overboard in viewing how the typical adolescent moves from a predominantly parental orientation to a peer orientation. There are many subtle shadings and complexities to this change.

Changes in Peer Groups with Age

Across the adolescent years, there appears to be a natural and understandable change in the kinds of groups in which adolescents participate (Dunphy, 1963). Figure 12-8 shows how one investigator has tried to graphically illustrate this change. Generally, adolescents emerge from an initial preference for a small group of same-sex friends (Stage 1) to participation in relatively large groups (here called the crowd), also initially isolated by sex. Eventually, however, males and females begin to interact with each other, though the groups remain separated (Stage 2) (see figure 12-9). The next stage (3) evolves when some upper-status members of each same-sex clique begin to interact with each other to form the first heterosexual cliques. These cliques become more firmly established until there is a fully integrated crowd of people made up of different heterosexual cliques (Stage 4). Finally, during late adolescence generally, this crowd organization begins to deteriorate, resulting in friendships consisting primarily of groups of boy/girl couples who are dating exclusively, who are going steady, or who are perhaps even engaged (Dunphy, 1963).

The above description is meant to provide only a general picture of the nature and formation of adolescent peer groups. There is obviously wide individual variation across adolescents. Nevertheless, there does appear to be a gradual evolution from large groups to smaller, more intimate groups, culminating in the exclusive heterosexual couple, at least in our society. The end result obviously is the development of relationships with fewer people and reliance on these friendships for personal satisfaction and growth. Very often these more intimate friend-

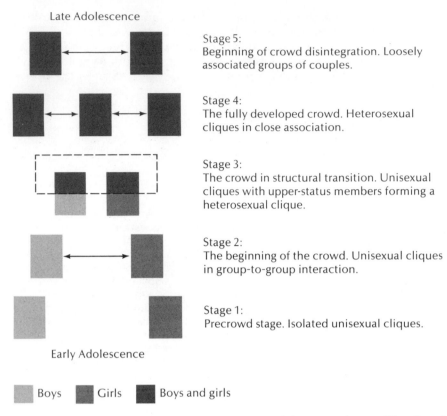

Late Adolescence

Stage 5:
Beginning of crowd disintegration. Loosely associated groups of couples.

Stage 4:
The fully developed crowd. Heterosexual cliques in close association.

Stage 3:
The crowd in structural transition. Unisexual cliques with upper-status members forming a heterosexual clique.

Stage 2:
The beginning of the crowd. Unisexual cliques in group-to-group interaction.

Stage 1:
Precrowd stage. Isolated unisexual cliques.

Early Adolescence

Boys   Girls   Boys and girls

Figure 12-8. Stages of group development in adolescence. (From "The Social Structure of Urban Adolescence Peer Groups," by D. C. Dunphy, *Sociometry*, 1963, *26*, 236. Copyright 1963 by The American Sociological Association. Reprinted by permission.)

ships develop between individuals who are similar to each other and share a lot of common interests (Hartup, 1970).

Conformity to Peer Groups

One of the implications that emerges from the above analysis is that in the process of moving toward fewer and more intimate friendships, the adolescent begins to more actively select those people with whom he chooses to associate. In this sense he will become less conforming to the fads and fashion of the more general adolescent culture or crowd (Costanzo & Shaw, 1966). He will, in short, become more of an individual.

SOCIAL AND BEHAVIORAL PROBLEMS OF ADOLESCENTS

There is probably no greater area of interest or concern regarding adolescence than the problems that adolescents encounter on their way to becoming adults. The list of serious problems that begin in adolescence or plague adoles-

Figure 12-9. Adolescents gradually begin to interact in small groups with members of the opposite sex.

cents is long and worrisome. Anorexia nervosa, suicide, depression, schizophrenia, acute anxiety, introversion, alcoholism and other excessive drug use, juvenile delinquency, and others are all disorders that haunt the period of adolescence. Needless to say we cannot treat all of these here. We would, however, like to highlight two problem areas that seem particularly prominent at the present time: alcoholism and juvenile delinquency.

Alcoholism

We have chosen to focus on alcoholism for several reasons. One is that the incidence of alcoholism is increasing rather rapidly among contemporary adolescents. Secondly, and more critical, is the fact that alcohol is legal and widely accepted in our society. As such, we tend to minimize its potential hazards in contrast to other drugs (like marijuana). Nevertheless, given the potentially self-destructive powers of alcohol as well as its level of acceptance and availability, we feel it important to select this chemical for discussion over others. In so doing, it is not our intention to ignore or diminish the potential danger of abuse of other chemicals like tobacco, marijuana, amphetamines, or the various psychedelic compounds.

Incidence of Alcohol Use

The statistics on alcohol use reveal that by the end of adolescence most teenagers have tried alcohol (Bacon & Jones, 1968). More revealing is the fact that the incidence of use seems to have increased since the late 1960s (Johnston & Bachman, 1975). Although in previous years fewer girls than boys had tried alcohol, that difference has diminished, indicating increased use of alcohol by adolescent girls.

Though most adolescents drink moderately and at least initially within the family context, there is a substantial and *increasing* number of adolescents who drink to excess. In one recent survey, 6% of seniors in high school admitted to drinking practically every day (Johnston & Bachman, 1975), while another study revealed that about 5% of students in ninth grade get drunk at least once a week. Needless to say these youngsters are not off to the best start with regard to moderate alcohol use!

Juvenile Delinquency

Delinquency among adolescents in the United States is certainly not a modern phenomenon (Conger, Miller, & Walsmith, 1965), though it is escalating. A juvenile delinquent is legally defined as a person under 16 or 18 years of age who engages in activities that are against the law. A recent survey found that from 1961 to 1973, the rate of juvenile delinquency almost doubled (Bronfenbrenner, 1975). In fact, it is estimated that 12% of all adolescents (and 22% of adolescent boys) will eventually wind up in juvenile court. Further, although juvenile delinquency is more prevalent among boys than girls, the difference is diminishing due to a dramatic increase in recent years in arrests of girls under 18. Also, youths from lower socioeconomic backgrounds show a higher incidence of arrests for delinquent behavior. Although some of the social class differences may be attributable to discrimination against lower-class youths by authorities, it does appear that the actual rate of delinquency may be higher in this group.

Social Factors in Delinquency

In searching for the causes of delinquent behavior, several social and environmental factors have been identified. One of these factors is a high rate of **social mobility.** Rates of delinquency are highest in those areas and among those families where close ties to relatives or to other community members are missing. Although recent years have seen the greatest percentage increase in delinquency in the suburbs, the highest absolute rate of delinquency occurs in the central urban sections of large cities. Characterized often by social deterioration in housing and economic conditions and by a disorganized social and family structure, these areas are fertile breeding grounds for the despair and alienation that characterize delinquent youth.

Nevertheless social factors alone cannot account for all delinquency. Most children growing up under social conditions similar to those above never become delinquents. In an attempt to uncover other factors, investigators have looked at individual characteristics of delinquent and non-delinquent children. In general, delinquents have been found to be less intelligent (though only slightly so as measured by IQ); they appear more hostile, less motivated academically, and are more mistrustful of authority than are non-delinquents (Caplan & Siebert, 1964; Tutt, 1973). They also show lower self-esteem and self-knowledge (Fitts & Hammer, 1969). A general picture emerges of the delinquent individual as isolated, hostile, without standard academic or vocational motivation, and with a very poor opinion of himself.

As might be expected, parent/child relations differ between delinquent and non-delinquent adolescents. Parents of delinquents are likely to be autocratic or ignoring, and more restrictive and hostile at some times, while indifferent and apathetic at other times. It is of course possible that the parents' behavior may be as much a reaction to the delinquent child's behavior as a cause of it.

Coping with Delinquency

Given the serious nature of the delinquency problem, it seems imperative that actions be taken to treat and ultimately to prevent most delinquency.

Taking a hard line, some have proposed that delinquents be treated like any other adult criminal. They cite evidence that delinquents know that they won't be punished because of their special status and that therefore there is no deterrent to the delinquent acts. Furthermore, they cite evidence that traditional forms of youth rehabilitation—work/study and other educational and vocational programs, recreational programs, and so forth—have not been very successful (Dixson & Wright, 1975). Though these arguments do have some merit, it seems rash and premature at present to simply dump adolescent delinquents into the same categories as adult offenders. This would necessitate similar forms of punishment by imprisonment, which has generally only exacerbated the lawbreaking problem.

Sadly, there are no clear or easy answers to the problems of juvenile delinquency. Problems both in segments of the social environment (school, home, work-place, neighborhood) and probably in the delinquent adolescents themselves all contribute, and adjustments in all of these domains are no doubt needed.

PROVIDING AN OPTIMAL ENVIRONMENT

As most parents will testify, adolescents are, to a great degree, masters of their own fates. Moving beyond childhood dependence on and identification with the family, adolescents begin to forge their own identities, to think their own thoughts, and otherwise to begin the journey toward an independent adulthood. Hence, prescriptions for how to provide an optimal environment for adolescents are less directive and more suggestive in nature.

Perhaps the first thing to suggest is *patience*, not only in the adolescent's parents but in all those people who interact or work with adolescents. Patience is needed often to cope with the dramatic and rapidly changing behaviors adolescents are prone to. Constructing a formal-operational system of abstract thought may result in alternating periods of fervent dogmatism (in which the adolescent may exclaim "Love is everything") with equally intense uncertainty (in which every claim or opinion is challenged, such as "What do you mean by love?"). Such displays can be exasperating to adults or others who are impatient or who may have forgotten their own adolescent displays of similar behavior. Patience is needed in many realms: when adolescents are sure they will never grow or develop like the other kids; when all that comes out of their mouths is criticism of everyone and everything; and when they display little sympathy toward others but demand total sympathy for themselves from others.

By and large, these changes represent a natural outgrowth of adolescents' striving for identity, of their experimenting with newly acquired intellectual power, and of the physical and sexual maturation they are undergoing. Patience will see them through this period without serious conflict or damage. Nevertheless, when the adolescent's behavior is severely disruptive and/or prolonged, professional help should be sought.

With regard to the physical and sexual changes that are occurring, the adolescent should receive information and assurance about how normal these events are, in particular with regard to menstruation in girls and nocturnal emissions in boys.

Information and education are vital in helping the adolescent understand his or her sexuality. Many fears, anxieties, uncertainties, and outright misunderstandings can be avoided if adolescents receive some basic information on sexuality. Some intensive instruction on birth-control methods would seem particularly appropriate at this time, given the findings on teenage pregnancy.

Finally, with regard to the adolescent quest for independence, parents and other adults should take care to be neither too domineering nor too distant. Forcing decisions on the adolescent as well as leaving the adolescent completely on his own appear detrimental to the growth of a sense of autonomy and well-being. A warm, accepting environment that provides direction and, on occasion, restrictions will provide the balance that adolescents need to develop a mature sense of independence.

CHAPTER SUMMARY

Adolescence represents the transition in our culture from childhood to adulthood. Several important changes can be noted during this period that separate adolescents from their childhood and prepare them for their adulthood.

A major change centers on the adolescent's growing sense of self or identity. Erik Erikson has charted eight stages in the life of humans, in which identity formation is seen as the major task of adolescence following resolution of earlier conflicts in childhood and also paves the way for successful growth in adulthood.

Coupled with the adolescent's emerging sense of personal identity are major advances in his intellectual skills. Piaget describes this period as formal-operational thought. It is characterized by coordination of systems of thought into a high-order system, systematic experimentation, and hypothetical and abstract thinking. The adolescent begins to think on a more formal level and can deal with abstract concepts such as truth and love. One crucial concept is that of the "self"; the cognitive advances of the formal-operational child thus help to explain part of the adolescent's preoccupation with "self" or "identity."

A host of physical and sexual changes take place during adolescence. Changes occur in fat distribution, height, weight, body proportions, and even internal organs like the heart and lungs. Sexual maturation likewise involves a number of external and internal changes.

Physical and sexual maturation is under the control of a complex, integrated system involving brain and body structures and hormones. Centers in the hypothalamus send signals to the pituitary gland, which secretes six hormones that in turn direct a series of target organs to produce their own hormones. The target-organ hormones, especially testosterone in males and estrogen in females, carry primary responsibility for adolescent physical and sexual maturation. Some have said that our society is in the midst of a sexual revolution. However, available evidence suggests that the revolution in *behavior* occurred around the turn of the century.

In contrast, a revolution in *attitude* does seem to be occurring. Adolescents appear more open about sex and interested in sex education, especially with regard to the meaning of sexual behavior in interpersonal relationships.

A major task of adolescence is the development of independence. In this regard it appears that parents play a central role in fostering or hindering a sense of independence in their adolescent children. A warm but somewhat restrictive environment seems to best foster a sense of independence, while a cold, permissive family environment fosters rebelliousness and resentment in adolescent children. Likewise, autocratic and ignoring parents can thwart the growth of independence. A better strategy for parents to promote independence seems to be to allow the child to contribute to decisions that affect his life while reserving final judgment for themselves.

Peers begin to take on greater importance in the lives of adolescents. Nevertheless, parents do not cease to be important. They are consulted when adolescents feel uncertain and their parents can offer valuable advice.

Relations with peers during adolescence progress from initial dependence on large groups of same-sex friends to smaller groups, eventually resulting in formation of a close friendship with a few people and in development of a love relationship with one person of the opposite sex.

Finally, a large number of potentially serious psychological and social problems arise during adolescence. We focused on two problems that have emerged recently: alcoholism and juvenile delinquency. Both are serious and difficult to deal with. Hopefully, exposure to the magnitude and complexity of these problems will contribute to their eventual alleviation.

SUGGESTED READINGS

Conger, John Janeway. *Adolescence and Youth: Psychological Development in a Changing World* (2d ed.). New York: Harper & Row, 1977. A good basic text on adolescent development.
Erikson, Erik H. *Identity: Youth and Crisis.* New York: Norton, 1968. An excellent presentation of Erikson's theory of psychosocial development.

GLOSSARY

authoritarian. Parents who always make the final decisions affecting their child but who may consult child before arriving at decisions.
autocratic. Parents who control all decisions affecting their child and who give the child no role in these decisions.
democratic. Parents who allow child to contribute fully to important decisions. However, parents ultimately make or approve final decision.
epigenetic principles. Developmental principles postulated by Erikson.

equalitarian. Both parents and child contribute equally to decisions and have equal vote in outcome.

estrogen. A hormone secreted by the cells of the ovaries that controls physical and sexual changes in females at puberty and is involved in the menstrual cycle.

formal operations. According to Piaget, an overriding mental operation that results from the coordination of previously isolated concrete operations.

growth hormone. A complex chemical secreted by the anterior pituitary that stimulates body growth throughout childhood.

hormones. Complex chemicals secreted by the glands to regulate body functions.

hypothetical thinking. According to Piaget, a characteristic of formal-operational thought. It refers to the ability to move beyond physical reality and to consider other possible worlds.

identity confusion. In Erikson's theory, refers to the adolescent who has negative feelings about himself and doubts about the future as a result of failure to satisfactorily resolve earlier psychosocial conflicts.

ignoring. Parents who are completely uninvolved in child's decision-making process.

laissez-faire. Parents who discuss matters with child but allow child to make final decisions.

permissive. Parents who allow child to play major role in decision making.

progesterone. A hormone secreted by the cells of the ovaries that controls physical and sexual changes in females at puberty and that is involved in the menstrual cycle.

social mobility. The extent to which one can move from one social group or class to another.

systematic experimentation. According to Piaget, a characteristic of formal operational thought. It refers to the use of strategic, planful and exhaustive attempts to solve problems.

testosterone. A hormone produced by the testes that promotes development of the male reproductive system.

thyrotropic hormone. A complex chemical secreted from the anterior pituitary that controls thyroxine production by the thyroid gland.

thyroxine. Hormone produced by the thyroid gland that controls skeletal maturation and, to some extent, general body growth.

REFERENCES

Bacon, M., & Jones, M. B. *Teen-age drinking*. New York: Crowell, 1968.

Bandura, A. The stormy decade: Fact or fiction? *Psychology in the Schools*, 1964, *1*, 224–231.

Block, J., & Turula, E. Identification, ego control and adjustment. *Child Development*, 1963, *34*, 945–953.

Brittain, C. V. Adolescent choices and parent-peer cross-pressures. *American Sociological Review*, 1963, *23*, 385–391.

Bronfenbrenner, U. The challenge of social change and public policy and developmental research. Paper presented at the biennial meeting of the Society for Research in Child Development, Denver, April 1975.

Caplan, N. S., & Siebert, L. A. Distribution of juvenile delinquent intelligence test scores over a thirty-four year period. *Journal of Clinical Psychology*, 1964, *20*, 242–247.

Conger, J. J., Miller, W. C., & Walsmith, C. P. Antecedents of delinquency, personality, social class and intelligence. In P. H. Mussen, J. J. Conger, and J. Kagan (Eds.), *Readings in child development and personality*. New York: Harper & Row, 1965.

Costanzo, P. R., & Shaw, M. E. Conformity as a function of age level. *Child Development*, 1966, *37*, 967–975.

Dixson, M. C., & Wright, W. E. *Juvenile delinquency prevention programs: An evaluation of policy-related research on the effectiveness of preventive programs*. Nashville, Tenn.: Office of Educational Services, Peabody College for Teachers, 1975.

Douvan, E., & Adelson, J. *The adolescent experience*. New York: Wiley, 1966.

Dunphy, D. C. The social structure of adolescent peer groups. *Sociometry*, 1963, *26*, 230–246.

Elder, G. H., Jr. Structural variations in the child-rearing relationship. *Sociometry*, 1962, *25*, 241–262.

Erikson, E. *Identity: Youth and crisis*. New York: W. W. Norton, 1968.

Faust, M. S. Developmental maturity as a determinant in prestige of adolescent girls. *Child Development*, 1960, *31*, 173–184.

Fitts, W. H., & Hammer, W. T. *The self-concept and delinquency*. Nashville, Tenn.: Nashville Mental Health Center, 1969, Monograph No. 1.

Hartup, W. W. Peer interaction and social organization. In P. H. Mussen (Ed.), *Carmichael's manual of child psychology* (3rd ed.). New York: Wiley, 1970.

Johnston, L., & Bachman, J. Monitoring the future: A continuing study of the life styles and values of youth. Ann Arbor, Mich.: Institute for Social Research, 1975.

Jones, M. C., & Bayley, N. Physical maturing among boys as related to behavior. *Journal of Educational Psychology*, 1950, *41*, 129–148.

Jones, M. C., & Bayley, N. The later careers of boys who were early or late maturing. *Child Development*, 1957, *28*, 113–128.

Katchadourian, H. *The biology of adolescence*. San Francisco: W. H. Freeman, 1977.

Kinsey, A. C., Pomeroy, W. B., & Martin, C. E. *Sexual behavior in the human male*. Philadelphia: Saunders, 1948.

Kinsey, A. C., Pomeroy, W. B., Martin, C. E., & Gebhard, P. H. *Sexual behavior in the human female*. Philadelphia: Saunders, 1953.

Koening, F., & Falkenstein, H. Female undergraduate attitudes toward distribution of the birth control pill on the campus. *Journal of Youth and Adolescence*, 1972, *1*, 197–201.

Marshall, W. A., & Tanner, J. M. Variations in the pattern of pubertal changes in girls. *Arch Dis Child*, 1969, *44*, 291–303.

Marshall, W. A., & Tanner, J. M. Variations in the pattern of pubertal changes in boys. *Arch Dis Child*, 1970, *45*, 13–23.

Marshall, W. A., & Tanner, J. M. Puberty. In J. A. Douvis and J. Dobbling (Eds.), *Scientific foundations of pediatrics*. London: William Heinemann Medical Books, 1974.

Martin, B. Parent-child relations. In F. D. Horowitz (Ed.), *Review of child development research* (Vol. 10). Chicago: University of Chicago Press, 1975, pp. 463–540.

Pannor, R., Massarik, F., & Evans, B. *The unmarried father*. New York: Springer, 1971.

Schaefer, E. S. A circumplex model for maternal behavior. *Journal of Abnormal and Social Psychology*, 1959, *59*, 226–235.

Simon, W., Berger, A. S., & Gagnon, J. H. Beyond anxiety and fantasy: The cortical experiences of college youth. *Journal of Youth and Adolescence*, 1972, *1*, 203–222.

Sorenson, R. C. *Adolescent sexuality in contemporary America*. New York: World, 1973.

Tanner, J. M. *Growth at adolescence* (2nd ed.). Oxford: Blackwell, 1962.

Tepperman, J. *Metabolic and endocrine physiology* (3rd ed.). New York: Year Book Medical Publishers, 1973.

Tutt, N. S. Achievement motivation and delinquency. *British Journal of Social and Clinical Psychology*, 1973, *12*, 225–230.

Vincent, C. E. Teenage unwed mothers in American society. *Journal of Social Issues*, 1966, *22*, 22–23.

Wilson, W. C., et al. Technical report of the Commission on Obscenity and Pornography, Vol. 6, 1971.

Yankelovich, D. *The new morality: A profile of American youth in the 1970s*. New York: McGraw-Hill, 1974.

Zelnick, M., & Kanter, J. F. Sex and contraception among unmarried teenagers. In C. F. Westoff et al. (Eds.), *Toward the end of growth: Population in America*. Englewood Cliffs, N.J.: Prentice-Hall, 1973.

PART FIVE

ABNORMAL DEVELOPMENT

13

Childhood Psychopathology

In the preceding chapters, we focused most of our attention upon normal children and normal processes of development. While we explored certain aspects of abnormal development where they were relevant, we have yet to squarely address the important questions of "Who is normal?" and "What does one do with a child who appears not to be normal?" This final chapter is devoted to abnormal development in childhood. There are a multitude of problems besetting children, ranging from such temporary behavior problems as bed-wetting to severely debilitating and fairly permanent disorders, such as childhood psychosis. We will describe briefly some childhood disorders, their causes (where known), and the different techniques of treatment or therapy that have been developed for children who suffer from these disorders.

ISSUE

How serious are psychological problems in childhood?

An estimated 500,000 American children are afflicted with psychoses and borderline psychotic conditions. Another million suffer from other severe mental disorders. Of the 50 million elementary school children in the United States, it is estimated that between 10 and 12 percent have moderate to severe emotional problems requiring some kind of mental health care. Among the 15 million youngsters in the United States who are reared in poverty, one out of three has emotional problems that need attention. The number of young patients being admitted to mental hospitals is increasing steadily. Many long-term patients were first admitted as children or young adults. Drug abuse and delinquency are growing problems. Less than one percent of the disturbed youngsters in the United States receive any kind of treatment, and less than half of these receive adequate help [National Clearing House for Mental Health Information, 1970, p. 7].

WHAT IS ABNORMAL DEVELOPMENT?

As you have already learned, the field of child development is still in its infancy, with many unanswered questions about normal growth. Not surprisingly, the study of abnormal development is surrounded by even greater uncertainty. Difficulties in discussing abnormal development arise at the very outset, when trying to define just what one means by *abnormal development*, or *childhood psychopathology*.

The term *childhood psychopathology* has been defined in different ways by different people. These definitions are not necessarily inconsistent, but differ in what they would include in the term *abnormal behavior*. Some people would include all children who are extremely unhappy, who have unrealistic fears, or who wet their beds. If we were to adopt this position, the prevalence of childhood psychopathology would be almost half of all children. In contrast, we might tightly limit our definition of *abnormal development* by including only those children who are so seriously affected by their conditions that they cannot be expected to care for themselves and live independently of their families or the state. Under this provision the prevalence of childhood psychopathology in the United States would be only 1 to 2% of our children.

Most child psychologists fall somewhere between these two extremes. They would define childhood psychopathology to include moderate and severe disorders that (1) handicap the child to some extent, and (2) require treatment. Given this definition, the prevalence of such disorders is about 10 to 12% of the child population (Kessler, 1966; Engel, 1972). Even this intermediate position is shocking; it means that literally between 5 and 6 million of our elementary school children can be considered in some sense abnormal. Clearly, childhood psychopathology is a serious problem, deserving special attention and concern.

Referral: This Child Seems "Different"

The first step in discovering some problem is often the observation that this child seems "different." He may seem slow in acquiring major developmental milestones such as walking, talking, or toilet training. He may seem moody and withdrawn. Or he may seem overly active and aggressive. In some respect, the child's pattern of behavior and development differs from that of siblings and friends. However, as we have seen, each child is different from every other child and there is no easy rule regarding just *how different* a child must be before some real pathology is suspected. We have all seen children who seem a little slow at first, but later catch up; or who seem overly active, but later calm down. We have also seen children who don't catch up and don't calm down. Often the first response upon observing that a child seems different is to wait and see if the problem goes away.

The length of the waiting period, however, varies considerably, depending on factors such as how deviant and disruptive the child's behavior is, how much experience the parents have had with children, and how fearful they are of the mental health community. If the child's behavior is extremely deviant—and parents have had enough experience with children to realize it—they will often seek expert advice relatively early. In cases where the behavior is only mildly troublesome or parents are inexperienced, no action may be taken until someone else—a friend, a pediatrician, or a teacher—steps in and recommends that they seek expert advice.

The decision to seek professional advice is not an easy one for parents. It requires first that they admit that their child may have a problem that they cannot handle alone and that may not go away. The whole issue often carries with it a heavy burden of guilt. Regardless of whether it is in fact true, involved parents cannot help but wonder whether their child's problems are somehow due to them and their treatment of the child.

Differential Diagnosis: The Search for a Label

When a child goes to a physician with a physical illness, the physician will first attempt to determine just what the illness is. Is it chicken pox, measles, mumps, or something else? The doctor will examine the child's medical history and his current symptoms in making this determination. The resulting diagnosis will be of critical importance, since it will dictate the type of treatment the child receives.

Traditionally, psychologists have adopted a similar medical approach in examining the child's psychological problems. Like physicians, they have tried initially to distinguish among different types of these children, so as to label, or **differentially diagnose,** their disorders. Similarly, they have focused on symptoms of abnormality in arriving at a diagnosis. This approach has, however, met with only limited success, due to a number of confounding factors.

Consider, for example, a 4-year-old child who is brought to a psychologist's office because she does not speak. Clearly, lack of speech in a child of 4 is abnormal. However, there are many possible causes for a particular child's muteness. She may be deaf, or she may be mute because while she can hear, her parents are mute and she has never been exposed to language. She may suffer from mental retardation; even if such a determination is made, the retardation itself may stem from a number of causes, including genetic or biological difficulties within her central nervous system or problems with her environmental upbringing. She may be brain-damaged as a result of prenatal, perinatal, or postnatal accident or illness. Finally, she may be psychotic. The search for a label, or diagnosis, to explain her symptoms is thus much like opening Pandora's box. The symptom itself is fairly obvious: she cannot speak. However, finding the cause is far from obvious or easy.

The example given above is not unusual. It is quite common for children suffering from a wide variety of different disorders to show symptoms that appear quite similar. The similarity of symptoms across very different disorders makes the process of differential diagnosis quite difficult.

Even in cases with a fairly distinct set of symptoms or physical traits, accurate diagnosis may be thwarted if the child suffers from several different disorders at the same time. For example, a mentally retarded child may develop some degree of emotional disturbance due to "being different" and frequent experiences with failure. In such a case, the child is said to have a *primary disorder* of mental retardation, with a *secondary disorder* of emotional disturbance. To the unknowing clinician, a child suffering from such a multiple disorder is especially difficult to diagnose.

Differential diagnosis of childhood psychopathology is thus complicated by at least two factors: first, *the same symptoms are often shared by different underlying disorders;* and second, *multiple disorders can appear in the very same child.* It is not unusual, then, that different psychologists can look at the same child and come up with radically different diagnoses. In fact, the likelihood of agreement among different psychologists in diagnosing a particular child is extremely low (Mehlman, 1952; Raines & Rohrer, 1955; Schmidt & Fonda, 1956).

In recent years, new diagnostic classifications have been suggested to increase the accuracy of differential diagnosis (for example, GAP, 1974). More and more, however, child psychologists are moving away from use of rigid disease labels (the medical model) and toward use of descriptive paragraphs emphasizing the child's unique problems (Ross, 1974).

Treatment: The Search for a Cure

The term *mental illness* has a regrettably deceptive effect upon most lay people. They often assume that mental illness, like physical illness, can be "cured" once it has been properly diagnosed and given the appropriate method of treatment. For this reason families often drag their children from clinic to clinic and therapist to therapist in search of the right label for the child's problems and, hence, the right treatment technique for that particular label. Unfortunately, just as methods of diagnosis are at best imprecise, methods of treatment are inexact and their outcome unpredictable.

Many forms of therapy can be used by clinical child psychologists. Some clinicians rely exclusively on one form of therapy over others, while other clinicians favor an eclectic approach. There is little evidence, however, that any particular therapy should be preferred over any other (Feldman, Solomon, Levinson, & Lasky, 1974). To quote Jane Kessler: "There is no empirical evidence that any one method is better than the others; in fact, *there is as yet no statistical proof that psychotherapy is better than leaving the child alone*" (Kessler, 1966, p. 368, emphasis added).

Despite the large number of approaches, for our purposes, different therapies can be grouped into one of two broad categories. First, there are therapies that follow a basically *psychoanalytic orientation.* Secondly, there are those that prefer the techniques of *behavior modification.*

Psychoanalytic Therapies

The term "psychoanalysis" should immediately bring to mind the name of Sigmund Freud. Freud is generally assumed to be the "father of psychoanalysis," and most current psychoanalytic theories rely on Freud's now-classic work. A discussion of psychoanalytic therapy should therefore begin with a brief review of Freud's theory of development.

Freud argued that the human personality develops through several fairly distinct stages. Each of these stages is characterized by the child's predominant involvement with a particular body region that provides him with sensual pleasure when stimulated. These pleasurable areas of the body Freud labeled **erogenous zones.** In normal development, the child's involvement in particular erogenous zones increases and then diminishes as he moves from stage to stage.

The first stage in Freud's scheme of *psychosexual development* is the *oral stage.* During the oral stage, the child's primary source of sensual pleasure is his mouth.

As the young infant sucks—and later bites—he receives both basic biological gratification for his hunger drive and pleasurable stimulation of his mouth. Indeed, one of the infant's primary sources of contact with his world is through his mouth.

As the infant matures, however, he discovers new means of contact with his world and, at the same time, new demands are placed upon him by his environment. In particular, sometime during his second year, toilet training is instituted and much of his contact with his parents focuses on his eliminative functions. During this period, the child learns that his toileting habits can result in his mother's pleasure or displeasure—and, as a result, he discovers that for the first time he has a means of control over her. Also, the process of toilet training makes the child acutely aware of the pleasurable—and sensual—experiences that are associated with anal stimulation, both in terms of retention and release. As a result, the child becomes increasingly interested in anal stimulation and moves into the *anal stage*.

After the discovery of anal pleasures, the child quickly learns that there is another nearby part of his body that also produces very pleasant feelings when stimulated: namely, the genitals. Once the 3-year-old discovers his genitals, masturbation becomes commonplace. Freud argued that during this *phallic stage* the child also tends to engage in sexual fantasies about his opposite-sex parent— hence the **Oedipal conflict.** According to Freud's notion of the Oedipal conflict, little boys (or girls) wish to involve their mothers (or fathers) in their sexual and other activities. The child's resulting hostile feelings of jealousy toward his same-sex parent, and his fear of retaliation from that parent, are so frightening to him that they are **repressed,** or pushed into his *unconscious*, and the child moves into the next stage: the *latency period*.

The latency period is a time in the child's life when all sensual desires and interests essentially move underground into the unconscious. The latency period usually begins at about the age of 5 and continues until adolescence. At adolescence, the child rediscovers the pleasures of genital stimulation. However, during this final stage, the *genital stage*, sexual pleasures are restricted to mature love objects.

Inherent in the above scheme of development is the notion that things can go wrong at any stage of psychosexual development. The child may receive *too much* gratification and, hence, be reluctant to move on to the next stage. *Too little* gratification during any period of development may likewise prevent the child's orderly progression from one stage to the next. This failure to pass from one stage to the next is called **fixation.** The child who remains fixated at any of the earlier stages may either continue to seek gratification for his more infantile desires or totally deny any interest in those particular forms of gratification (a **reaction formation**).

According to psychoanalytic theory, if the environment provides either too much or too little gratification of a particular need, fixation occurs and *psychopathology may result*. Moreover, the type of psychopathology that emerges reflects the stage at which the fixation occurred. Successful psychotherapy must somehow reach back to the original problem causing the fixation and resolve it before mental health can be restored. There are however different methods for searching out early causal factors and resolving them and, hence, many different types of psychoanalytic therapy.

All therapies do share a number of characteristics in common—in particular, a belief in **psychic determinism.** They believe that every thought, feeling, and action has a cause and can be understood. Thus, abnormal behavior, as well as normal behavior, can be explained—and the same basic mechanisms of explanation apply to both. For example, everyone *represses* (or pushes into the unconscious) those thoughts and feelings that are unpleasant and cause anxiety; the main distinction between the psychologically normal and the psychologically abnormal is in the extent to which different events are anxiety-producing (as a result of past fixations) and, hence, are repressed.

A second common belief shared by different psychoanalytic therapies concerns the source of anxiety. Psychoanalysts feel that anxiety—and therefore repression—can arise from conflicts within the personality as well as conflicts with the outside world. Thus, a young boy's fantasies of sexually possessing his mother can be as real and frightening as the real thing and can, in themselves, result in serious emotional difficulties during later life.

Different psychoanalytic theories also share the idea that memories that are unconscious do not completely disappear from the child's mind. Rather, unconscious memories of childhood events and fantasies can linger and produce long-lasting effects on the development of the personality.

One final thread linking the various psychoanalytic theories is a special emphasis on self-awareness and introspection as a method of treatment. Since visible symptoms of psychopathology are viewed as resulting from repressed inner conflicts, psychoanalysts believe that any truly successful therapy must first make the child aware of these conflicts and help him to resolve them. Role-playing, storytelling, drawing, and discussion of dreams are often used as means for discovering repressed feelings, since unconscious thoughts can often "slip" through in disguised form during such activities. It is believed that once the child becomes aware of his inner conflicts, he can *confront and resolve them*, and, as a result, the symptoms of his disorder will disappear.

Behavior Modification Techniques

Diametrically opposed to the traditional psychoanalytic therapies is the newer behavior modification approach. Behavioristic therapies rely on behavior modification techniques derived originally from learning theory. As with psychoanalytic therapies, however, behavior modification techniques vary widely.

To a behaviorist, psychology is the *study of behavior*. All behavior can be explained in terms of a few basic principles of learning: namely, classical and operant conditioning. (See Chapter 4 for a discussion of the principles of operant and classical conditioning.) Behaviorists view human development as the gradual building up, through conditioning, of associations among events, behaviors, and consequences. If a particular child's development is abnormal, a behaviorist would argue that some faulty associations have been learned as a function of experience. Therapy consists, then, of "unlearning" these incorrect associations and relearning more appropriate ones.

The use of conditioning principles to explain the development of psychopathology began as early as 1928, with Watson's famous experiment with "Little Albert." When Little Albert first entered Watson's laboratory, he was a normal, healthy child of 9 months with no fear of animals. When he left the laboratory, he exhibited a severe animal **phobia** (or irrational fear of animals) that **generalized** to other furry objects, such as his mother's fur coat, and even to

Santa Claus. What had happened to destroy this child's original love of animals? Watson had used *classical conditioning* to produce a phobia.

Recall that **classical conditioning** begins with an *unconditioned reflex,* an innate connection between some biologically potent stimulus (that is, the **unconditioned stimulus**) and a particular response (that is, the **unconditioned response**). The unconditioned stimulus is then repeatedly presented at the same time as some other, neutral stimulus. After a number of such pairings, the originally neutral stimulus comes to elicit a response similar to the original unconditioned response. When this happens, a **conditioned reflex** has been established: the child has learned to produce a **conditioned response** to the **conditioned stimulus.**

In the case of Little Albert, Watson sounded a loud gong whenever Little Albert approached a white furry rabbit. The rabbit was originally a neutral stimulus. Loud noises, however, are normal elicitors of fear (that is, an unconditioned stimulus). The continued pairing of the noise (unconditioned stimulus) with the rabbit (neutral stimulus) resulted in the formation of an association between the two. As a result, the sight of the white furry rabbit became a conditioned stimulus that elicited a conditioned fear response. The learned fear of the rabbit then *generalized* to other similar furry animals and objects (see Figure 13-1).

Watson's experiment demonstrated how easy it is to produce a strong fear reaction through classical conditioning. From examples such as this, Watson argued that *all* such fears are created through a similar process of association of events in the child's environment. Watson therefore denied that such fears reveal the presence of underlying internal conflicts and repression (the psychoanalytic viewpoint); for him, they are simply the direct outcome of classical conditioning. Behaviorists have since learned that just as classical conditioning may cause a fear to develop, classical conditioning can also be used to reduce the same fear by gradually associating the feared object with some pleasant event. This process of treatment, called **desensitization,** is discussed later in the chapter, in conjunction with the discussion of irrational fears—or *phobias,* as they are technically known.

Other childhood disorders appear to follow the laws of **operant conditioning.** Recall that in operant conditioning, the frequency of a particular behavior is modified by its consequences, or *reinforcers.* Consequences that are **positively reinforcing** increase the frequency of behaviors that they follow (or are *contingent* on); consequences that are **negatively reinforcing** decrease the frequency of behaviors that they follow. Positive reinforcers include both the presentation of pleasant events and the removal of unpleasant events. Negative reinforcers include both the presentation of unpleasant events and the removal of pleasant events.

Behaviorists have used the principles of operant conditioning to explain abnormal behavior in terms of inappropriate **reinforcement contingencies.** For example, a child will often get attention and sympathy from parents, teachers, and peers when she acts withdrawn and unhappy. Though intended to alleviate the child's problem, this attention may actually serve as a positive reinforcer, and increase the child's tendency to act withdrawn and unhappy. The following selection from Harris, Wolf, and Baer (1964) illustrates how such a child might be treated.

> The study dealt with a three-year-old girl who had regressed to an excessive amount of crawling. . . . By "excessive" is meant that after three weeks of

A

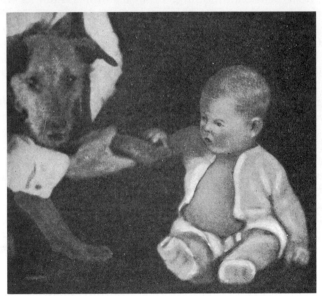

B

Figure 13-1.   The series of pictures shown above illustrates Watson's experimental creation of a phobia in "Little Albert," a normal 9-month-old. The first three pictures (*A, B, C*) show Albert at the start of the experiment. In these pictures, Albert shows no sign of fear of rabbits, dogs, or white rats. The last three pictures (*D, E, F*) show Albert after the rabbit has been associated with a loud gong. Now, Albert cries and tries to crawl away when he sees the rabbit, a fur muff, and even Santa Claus. (From *Psychological Care of the Infant and Child,* by J. B. Watson. Copyright 1928, 1956 by W. W. Norton & Company, Inc. Reprinted by permission.)

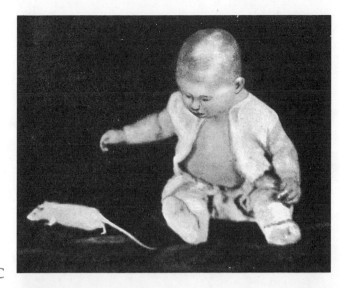

C

D

school she was spending most of her morning crawling or in a crouched position with her face hidden. The parents reported that for some months the behavior had been occurring whenever they took her to visit or when friends came to their home. The teachers had used the conventional techniques . . . for building the child's "security."

Observations recorded in the third week at school showed, however, that more than 80% of the child's time was spent in off-feet positions. The records also showed that the crawling behavior frequently drew the attention of teachers. On-feet behaviors, such as standing and walking, which occurred infrequently, seldom drew such notice.

A program was instituted in which the teachers no longer attended to the child whenever she was crawling or crouching, but gave her continuous warm attention as long as she was engaging in behavior in which she was standing, running, or walking. Initially the only upright behaviors that the teachers were able to attend to occurred when the child pulled herself almost to her feet in order to hang up or take down her coat from her locker, and when she pulled herself up to wash her hands in the wash basin. Within a week of the initiation

E

F

of the new attention-giving procedure, the child acquired a close-to-normal pattern of on-feet behavior.[1]

In the preceding example, operant conditioning was not only used to explain how the child developed the abnormal behavior; it was also used to modify and correct that behavior. This approach typifies the behaviorist belief that basic learning principles underlie both the development and treatment of childhood

[1]From "Effects on Adult Social Reinforcement on Child Behavior," by F. R. Harris, M. M. Wolf, and D. M. Baer, *Young Children*, October 1964, 20(1), 9–10. Copyright © 1964, National Association for the Education of Young Children, 1834 Connecticut Avenue, Washington, D.C. 20009. Reprinted by permission.

disorders. Typically, giving and withholding social *attention* (that is, physical contact, praise, warmth) are used as positive and negative reinforcers. In some cases of severely disturbed behavior, however, more basic biological reinforcers, such as food, may be given to the child for appropriate behavior, while physical punishment may be used as a negative reinforcer for inappropriate behavior. Using these techniques, behaviorists have successfully treated some very severe forms of abnormal behavior, as we shall see shortly.

Behavior modification relies initially on careful observation of the child and the development of a detailed plan for treatment. The first step consists of defining the behaviors that are inappropriately present or absent and of pinpointing the contingencies that maintain those behaviors at a high frequency. During the second step, the contingencies are reversed. Inappropriate behavior is deliberately not reinforced and may even be punished, while appropriate behavior is explicitly rewarded. As a result, inappropriate behaviors gradually disappear while appropriate behaviors increase, until the child finally displays normal patterns of behavior.

A Comparison of Psychoanalysis and Behavior Modification

The differences between psychoanalytic therapies and behavior modification techniques run deep. Psychoanalytic therapies view a child's symptoms as simply an outward manifestation of a basic and underlying internal conflict. They argue that the symptoms will disappear once the underlying conflict is resolved and that until the conflict has been resolved, symptoms will simply continue to appear. Treatment therefore consists of making the child consciously aware of the underlying conflict, so that he can confront it and resolve it. Upon resolution of the inner conflict, the symptoms will, according to the psychoanalyst, likewise disappear.

Behavior modification therapists, in contrast, do not view symptoms as being mere signs of an underlying problem. Rather, they regard symptoms very directly as the core of the child's problems. Because they believe that removal of the child's symptoms will eliminate the pathology, they treat the symptoms directly.

Given the great gap between the two theories, it is not surprising that attempts to reconcile them have not been successful. Behavior modification therapists claim rapid and fairly universal success for their method of treatment, and note that the cure rates for psychoanalysts do not differ substantially from cure rates in the *untreated* population—and that the few cures that do occur take place only after years of extensive, and expensive, psychotherapy. Practioners of behavior modification further argue that traditional psychoanalytic therapy, with its emphasis upon understanding and resolving internal conflicts, focuses too much attention on the child's inappropriate behavior, often reinforcing the very symptoms they are supposedly trying to eliminate. Psychoanalysts retort that behavior modification merely alters the surface of the child's behavior, leaving the deep-seated psychopathology untouched. Until the underlying conflict has been resolved, they argue, removal of one symptom will simply cause other symptoms to develop (a condition known as **symptom substitution**).

PSYCHOPATHOLOGIES OF CHILDHOOD

In the sections that follow, we will highlight some important problems that children experience. For each problem we will describe the major symptoms, causes, and methods of treatment, contrasting, whenever possible, the leading interpretations and treatment techniques.

Specific Disorders

"Specific disorders" are pathologies only in the loose sense of the term. Many normal children experience at least one of these disorders at some point but typically outgrow the problem without any treatment. In other children, however, specific disorders may set the stage for more serious problems later on, making treatment desirable. The need for treatment will thus vary from child to child. Nevertheless, children with specific disorders, despite their often temporary nature, account for the great majority of cases referred to psychologists. Some common disorders in this category involve eating problems, toileting problems, compulsive habits, and irrational fears.

Eating Problems

There is no simple way to describe or classify eating problems. A child may eat too much or too little. Many eating problems arise from psychological difficulties, rather than biological disorders. Nevertheless, prolonged eating problems can result in serious biological harm to the child. In fact, few psychological disorders present as much threat to life and health as do eating disorders.

Obesity. The overweight, or *obese*, child is not an uncommon problem in the United States. Available statistics (Heald, 1967) indicate that 10 to 15% of our childhood population is obese, or at least 15% over normal weight. Given the high frequency of the problem, our current understanding of obesity is surprisingly limited.

It has been suggested (for example, Newburgh, 1944) that obesity is directly due to overeating and underactivity, and that obesity can be "cured" by appropriate dietary controls. However, there are many cases in which obesity does not appear to result solely from dietary problems. In fact, research has shown that the daily caloric intake of obese adolescents is often significantly *less* than the caloric intake of their normal-sized peers (Heald, 1967; Johnson, Burke, & Mayer, 1956). Not surprisingly, dietary programs have limited and short-lived success in treating obese children.

Within the framework of psychoanalytic theory, Hilde Bruch (1941, 1967) has claimed that obesity is merely a symptom of a more basic psychological disturbance. Bruch's original study examined 225 children who ranged from 25% to 150% overweight. These childreen were described as unhappy, maladjusted in social relations, timid, retiring, and clumsy. Bruch claimed that the same underlying psychological disorders that caused these emotional and social problems had preceded and caused the obesity.

Clearly, however, when one observes a 10- or 12-year-old child who is not only obese but unhappy, withdrawn, and maladjusted as well, it is not always a simple matter to determine which came first. It is not unreasonable to assume that obesity itself will cause a child to be unhappy, to withdraw, and to get along poorly with other children—who make fun of her or him. Obesity and emotional disturbance do tend to go together, but one should be cautious in deciding which caused which for a particular child.

Starvation. In direct contrast to the obese child is the child who literally starves himself. This child starves not because there is an inadequate supply of food, but, rather, because he simply refuses to eat the food that is available and literally "wastes away." Children starve themselves at all ages and for a variety of reasons. We shall focus our attention on two of the most common syndromes: *failure to thrive* and *anorexia nervosa.*

The newborn infant's primary contact with the world is through the mother or other caretaker, and focuses on feeding. Feeding per se is not the basis for development of the infant's attachment to the caretaker (see Chapter 5). However, any problems in the relationship between infant and caretaker are likely to occur initially within the context of the feeding situation and thus affect the infant's eating habits. It is this disruption in the caretaker/infant relationship that is now believed to be responsible for failure-to-thrive infants.

Failure to thrive is a relatively rare condition that occurs in quite young infants. Typically, infants suffering from failure to thrive have good appetites but are plagued by chronic and severe diarrhea and vomiting. Medical examinations fail to show the presence of any disease or physical abnormality that might account for the infant's digestive problems. Moreover, failure-to-thrive infants typically show marked improvement and weight gain if they are separated from their parents and placed in the hospital—only to show further relapses upon returning home. Not surprisingly, the cases of failure to thrive that have been documented to date show severely inadequate caretaker/infant relationships. The mothers of these infants appear to treat them coldly, mechanically, and sometimes with open hostility. In particular, the mother's feedings of the infant are often erratic and inappropriately scheduled (Barbero, 1974; Fraiberg, 1974; Fullerton, 1967).

Failure to thrive primarily affects infants. In contrast, **anorexia nervosa** is a syndrome that (usually) affects adolescents and that is more clearly related to pathology in the child, rather than deficiencies in the parent/child relationship (although, of course, this pathology may stem from preexistent problems in the parent/child relationship).

Literally speaking, *anorexia nervosa* means "nervous loss of appetite." It occurs primarily in adolescent and young adult women. The onset of the disorder is often preceded by a self-enforced diet and fears (or the actuality) of being overweight. As one group of investigators put it:

> The most striking aspect of the starved children of our study was their denial of their emaciation. Although most of the patients resembled the starved inmates of a Nazi concentration camp, not one expressed the slightest concern over being so thin. On the contrary, many insisted that they were too fat, being especially concerned about their "stomachs" . . . and breasts [Blitzer, Rollins, & Blackwell, 1967, p. 170].

Anorexia nervosa is generally viewed as a symptom of a serious underlying psychopathology. It occurs frequently in adolescents whose parents also have eating problems and is often associated with long-term eating conflicts between the parents and the child (Blitzer, 1967; Kessler, 1966). Some psychoanalysts have argued that it is also an indication of fixation at the oral stage of psychosexual development; the adolescent girl exhibits her fear of growing beyond the oral stage by trying to prevent the development of secondary sex characteristics, such as the breasts, through self-induced starvation.

Treatment of Eating Disorders. There are many possible causes of eating disorders. In many cases, the eating disorder may be directly linked to such biological disorders as metabolic deficiency. In many cases, however, psychological or emotional distress is also evident, either as a primary or secondary problem. In addition, eating problems seem to often reflect problems withing the family.

There is no question but that persistent eating disorders should be brought to a psychologist's attention. However, treatment techniques for different eating problems vary widely from psychologist to psychologist and patient to patient. The treatment techniques chosen are partly determined by the orientation of the therapist and partly by the therapist's interpretation of the nature of the problem in a particular patient. Generally speaking, if the eating problem seems to stem from problems within the family—as, for example, is the case with the failure to thrive infant—some form of therapy involving the whole family will probably be chosen. In such cases, the therapist not only works with the child and his particular eating problem but, in addition, works with the parents and helps them to understand how their attitudes and behaviors are affecting the child. In other cases, the family structure may be relatively intact and the parent/child relationship adequate. In these cases, individual psychotherapy with the child alone is a likely method of treatment.

The particular form of therapy used may also vary widely, depending on the orientation of the therapist. Many psychoanalytically oriented therapists view eating disorders as secondary symptoms of primary emotional problems. These psychoanalytic therapists would, therefore, choose a method of therapy designed to help the child unravel his basic emotional problem—the assumption being that the child's eating problems will disappear once the primary problem has been discovered and resolved.

Other therapists tend to view the child's eating problem itself as the primary problem, with the child's emotional distress evolving as a secondary symptom. These behaviorists would instead attempt to directly eliminate the eating disorder by appropriate manipulation of the environment. Thus, the starving child might be denied any attention or coaxing when he refuses to eat. Attention would be given to the child only when appropriate eating behavior occurs. These behaviorists assume that any emotional problems of the child will disappear once the primary symptom of refusal to eat has disappeared.

Toileting Problems

Like eating disorders, problems involving toilet training occur with some frequency in our society. Even for the healthiest and best-adjusted children, the conquest of bladder and bowel is often achieved slowly and with major conflicts between the child and the parents. Most children in our society become toilet trained somewhere between their second and third birthdays. Some children, however, have severe difficulties in acquiring bowel or bladder control.

Enuresis

Enuresis, or bed-wetting, is a common problem in our society. One estimate (Lapouse & Monk, 1959) reports that 8 to 10% of the elementary schoolchildren in the United States wet their beds once a month or more. Many of the younger bed-wetting children show no other symptoms of emotional distress (Tapia, Jekel, & Domke, 1960). Persistent bed-wetting after the age of 7 or 8 is, however, often associated with other symptoms of psychological distress (Kessler, 1966). As we mentioned in connection with eating problems such as obesity, however, it is not always possible to determine which came first—since persistent bed-wetting can be a source of much embarrassment and can result in unusual conflicts in the parent/child relationship.

Encopresis

Encopresis, or soiling, is similar to enuresis in that both involve failures in toilet training. Soiling, however, is a much rarer condition and is more serious. Persistent failure in bowel control in older children is almost always associated with more serious personality disorders (Kessler, 1966).

Withholding

Children who soil themselves also tend to have periods during which they withhold their bowel movements for prolonged periods of time. Still other children have a tendency to withhold their bowel movements even though they have no problems with soiling. Withholding can result from quite different circumstances. It may occasionally result simply from a child's bad experience with constipation. After a long bout with constipation, the child's bowel movements are often quite painful. In an attempt to avoid this pain, the child may try to prevent or withhold future bowel movements—which, of course, only further aggravates the problem. In cases such as this, the child generally exhibits no other signs of emotional distress.

Long-term problems with withholding in older children seem, however, to be associated with more serious psychopathology. As mentioned earlier, many of these children alternate between periods of withholding and periods of soiling. Many of these children also exhibit other signs of emotional distress, such as withdrawal and violent temper tantrums.

Treatment of Toileting Problems.   Generally speaking, if the child's problem is short term and appears to exist in the absence of any other symptoms, a behavior modification technique is probably the most appropriate form of treatment. Using this technique, the therapist verbally explains to the child that he should use the "potty" and that rewards will be forthcoming whenever he does so. This verbal explanation is then followed by the straightforward application of operant conditioning: that is, the child is rewarded for each successful trip to the potty. The case of Roger (Peterson & London, 1966) provides a nice illustration of the treatment of such a case.

> The child's name is Roger, and at the time of treatment he was three years, four months old. . . . Roger had displayed no serious difficulties prior to his referral. . . . As far as anyone could tell, he was loved by his parents, liked by his siblings, and enjoyed by most others with whom he came in contact.
>
> The presenting problem, in brief, appeared circumscribed and limited to the fact that Roger did not defecate with either the frequency or aplomb that seemed meet in an otherwise normal and happy three-year-old. The interlude between eliminations was generally about five days, enough to concern the family pediatrician, and when they did occur, bowel movements were so painful that the child was reluctant to complete them. Eventually he would defecate, under increasing physical pressure, but he would hide under a bed (if indoors) or a bush (if outdoors) to perform the act. At the time of referral, he had not had a normal bowel movement in the usually appropriate . . . location for more than three months.
>
> The therapeutic strategy . . . consisted of (1) the generation of insight (cognitive stimulation) to facilitate the initiation of the eliminative sequence, and (2) reinforcement of the adaptive, that is, "target" behavior, upon its occurrence.[2]

Roger saw his therapist for a total of three sessions, during which it was explained that "Everybody likes Roger to go potty, 'cause then he'll feel real good." Between therapy sessions, successful eliminations in the potty were reinforced by praise and a popsicle. Using this technique, the problem was quickly corrected and disappeared by the end of the eighth day.

Behavior modification is an obvious choice for treatment of short-term problems such as Roger's. However, the choice of a particular therapy becomes more difficult when the child's toileting problems seem to be only one symptom of a serious psychopathology. Some clinical psychologists would continue to use behavior modification techniques with their more serious cases.

Psychoanalytically oriented therapists would, however, see a serious toileting problem as a sign of fixation at the anal (soiling or withholding) or phallic (bed-wetting) stages of psychosexual development. They would argue that successful therapy would require that the child resolve his long-standing conflicts through the procedures of psychoanalysis. Such treatments are generally intensive and long-term. Consider, for example, the case of Tony (Kessler, 1966):

> Tony was the younger of two boys, both of whom had been enuretic. Tony had many other problems, including general immaturity, learning difficulty, low tolerance for frustration, and fearfulness. He soiled until he was five, and enuresis persisted into his tenth year. His mother was a dominating person; his father was weak and passive. This mother scorned her husband, and the parents lived a chronic cold war, with no affection and little cooperation.
>
> At the age of four, Tony was accepted for intensive psychotherapy. He

---

[2]From "A Role for Cognition in the Behavioral Treatment of a Child's Eliminative Disturbance," by D. R. Peterson and P. London. In L. P. Ullman and L. Krasner (Eds.), *Case Studies in Behavior Modification*. Copyright 1966 by Holt, Rinehart and Winston. Reprinted by permission.

soon expressed his fear that wild animals might bite off his penis during the night. Much later, it became clear that these persistent nightmares and terrifying images were kept alive by his halfhearted wish that they might come true. In his view, there were definite advantages to losing his penis: He would not wet his bed, and besides his mother would like him better if he were a girl. Moreover, the prospect of growing up to be like his father was not appealing. He believed he would have to lose his penis, anyhow, because he thought that the penis makes babies by some magical transformation within the woman's body. All of this made his penis a definite handicap, something to put out of his mind as much as possible. In his case, bed-wetting was an expression of his wish to be a girl. Until he accepted a boy's role, he had little motivation to fight the symptom [Kessler, 1966, p. 122].[3]

Compulsive Habits

Another frequent—and often specific—disorder of childhood is the presence of **compulsive habits.** Of course, highly repetitive and stereotyped behavior is a normal occurrence in most children and is generally not cause for alarm. Who among us cannot remember a time when we carefully avoided stepping on the sidewalk cracks, or insisted on having a particular story read to us before we could go to sleep? Such common compulsions are generally not, of themselves, worthy of much concern. A psychologist should, however, be consulted if a child's compulsions occupy an inordinate amount of his time or if the child shows other signs of psychological distress. A good example of a serious compulsion is provided by Jane Kessler:

> Peter, age 10, was in treatment for a number of problems. He developed fleeting compulsions and had many superstitions regarding the magic meaning of numbers. His compulsions were usually to check on something. He reported that he had to check on whether the freezer door was closed; he might do this 20 or 30 times and still feel uneasy [Kessler, 1966, p. 253].

The type of treatment given for compulsive habits varies considerably, depending upon who happens to be giving the treatment. Psychoanalysts tend to view compulsive habits as symptoms of extreme emotional distress, with treatment therefore consisting of long-term psychoanalysis. Behaviorists, on the other hand, view compulsive habits as "self-reinforcing" behaviors. Thus, the behaviorist would argue that the mere repetition of the act provides pleasure to the child. The pleasure associated with the act serves as a positive reinforcer and keeps the child engaged in the behavior for long periods of time. The therapist's role, therefore, is to diminish the positive reinforcement value of the act by associating it with punishment. For example, a compulsive thumb-sucker might have this thumb painted with a foul-tasting liquid to diminish the pleasure derived from sucking his thumb, thereby breaking the habit by counteracting its self-reinforcing value.

[3]This and all other quotations from this source are from *Psychopathology of Children*, by J. W. Kessler, © 1966 by Prentice-Hall, Inc. Reprinted by permission.

Childhood Phobias

Fear is a frequent companion of children. As early as 6 to 8 months of age, children know the fear of strangers. As they grow older, children continue to fear things that they cannot understand and learn to fear things that have upset or hurt them in the past. The presence of many of these fears is quite adaptive, for it keeps children away from situations in which they might be harmed.

Children may, however, come to be excessively preoccupied by fears, some of which appear to have no realistic basis. For example, a girl's fear of strangers may keep her from ever leaving home. Her fear of separation may prevent her from attending school. Such extremely pervasive, irrational fears have been called **phobias** and can be serious when they interfere with the child's normal activities.

It is now commonly believed that most phobias are the result of *classical conditioning*, or the pairing of some object with a fear response. As a result of this pairing, a previously neutral object comes to elicit fear.

In the simplest case, the association of a neutral object with fear occurs as the result of a direct experience. For example, a child may develop a dog phobia after having been bitten by a dog. In other cases, the association of a neutral object with fear occurs more indirectly. Thus, a child's fantasies may be fearful and anxiety-producing. This fantasy-based anxiety may, in turn, become associated with some neutral object in the environment. Freud's classic study of Little Hans (Freud, 1909/1953) provides an excellent illustration of a psychoanalytic interpretation of such an "indirect association." Little Hans suffered from a phobic fear of horses. Freud theorized that this phobia was not the result of frightening experiences with horses, but instead resulted from Hans' Oedipal fantasies. These fantasies, argued Freud, caused Hans to unconsciously feel sexual attraction for his mother and fear of his rival for his mother's attentions: his father. Hans could not consciously accept and confront these fantasies and fears, and instead, projected them onto more neutral objects, namely horses. The association between his unconscious fears and horses resulted in the creation of a phobia.

Treatment of Childhood Phobias.   Simple phobias can generally be treated using the same principles of classical conditioning that caused them to arise in the first place. Treatment consists of pairing the neutral object with a pleasurable, rather than a fear, response. This process, called **desensitization,** has proven highly successful in the treatment of many simple phobias (for example, see Lazarus & Abramovitz, 1966; Wolpe, 1958).

In *real-life desensitization*, the child engages in some pleasurable acitivty, such as eating, while being gradually exposed to the feared object. For example, if a child has a fear of dogs, she might first be seated in a pleasant room eating ice cream. After a few minutes, she sees a small dog through a window in the room, but the window is closed and the dog is across the street and behind a fence. At each session, the dog is brought closer and closer, until finally the dog is sitting at the child's feet. Such real-life desensitization is a direct application of the principles of classical conditioning: an event (such as eating ice cream) that normally produces pleasant feelings in the child is continually paired with the feared object; this continued pairing results in the formation of an association between the pleasant object and the feared object, so that the originally feared object also comes to elicit pleasant feelings. Obviously, the use of desensitization requires some skill, lest the therapist produce a new phobia by associating the originally pleasant object with the fear response: for example, a fear of ice cream as well as of dogs.

In recent years, behavior modification therapists have learned that desensitization can occur without having to carry out real-life actions such as actually eating ice cream. A child can instead simply imagine the feared object while in a state of deep relaxation (*cognitive desensitization*). Desensitization has also been successfully accomplished by having the child watch another child learn to approach the feared object (*modeling*).

For most simple phobias, treatment is thus relatively straightforward. Some phobias are not, however, so easily treated. In these more complex phobias, it is not clear that the phobic fear was brought about by a direct, real-life association. Rather, it appears that the phobia was the result of an "indirect association" between some internal conflict and an originally neutral object: for example, Freud's case of Little Hans. In these complex cases, one must be concerned not only with removal of the particular phobic response; one must further attempt to alleviate the underlying anxiety. Most psychoanalysts believe that this anxiety often revolves around the Oedipal conflict. Treatment therefore consists of unearthing and resolving this basic conflict. The complexities and time-consuming nature of such treatment can hardly be overstated and are well illustrated by the following example:

> Mary Ann was referred to a child psychiatry clinic when she was five years and nine months old, because she could not attend first grade. She cried, refused to go, and vomited if forced. . . .
>
> On the whole, treatment was stormy, with great excitement and outpourings of emotion. In order to maintain a clear view of the separation problem, Mary Ann attended a private kindergarten for the rest of the year.
>
> The first stage of treatment dealt with her feelings about her teacher and mother. She declared that she was afraid of the teacher, but it soon became clear that she was jealous and envious of the teacher. . . . The displacement from the mother to teacher then became obvious. . . .
>
> On the other hand, she said that her mother was not really pretty, that she just had pretty clothes. She suggested that her mother might sleep with someone other than the father, and dreamed that her mother was sleeping with Davy Crockett. Her constant fear that her mother was angry with her was interpreted as a projection of her own anger and expectation of punishment. . . .
>
> In about the third month of treatment, Mary Ann made a rash of confessions to her mother. The first crimes confessed were unimportant ones, but they were soon followed by confessions of sexual games with an older boy. . . .
>
> For a period of about a month, the excitement continued on and off. Confessions of wanting to steal everything, to disrobe, that her private parts felt "stiff", and wishes to destroy herself and everyone else were repeated constantly.
>
> During this period, the therapist reviewed with Mary Ann the details of her sexual games. . . . Her jealousy and rage at almost everyone was discussed. She was angry at her brother because he was a boy and had something she didn't have. She was angry at her mother because she had both a husband and a baby. She was angry at her father because he preferred the mother. . . . To add to her sorrow, she had the sneaking suspicion that she was somehow to blame. She feared that she had damaged herself with her sexual experimentation, and that no one loved her because of her badness. . . . A better explanation of sex differences was provided for her, and it was also necessary to set her

straight on the origin of babies. She had some idea of the father's part, but imagined it as a sadistic attack on the woman.

After the spate of confession and the turmoil of excitement, things settled down. Mary Ann began to take great interest in school, particularly in writing, where she excelled. . . . The next fall, she entered first grade and proceeded to do well [Kessler, 1966, pp. 241–243].

Summary of Specific Disorders

A number of so-called specific disorders of childhood exist. These include eating disorders such as obesity, failure to thrive, and anorexia nervosa. Children can also suffer from toileting disorders such as enuresis (wetting), encopresis (soiling), and withholding. We also discussed compulsive habits and childhood phobias. The interpretation and form of treatment of each of these disorders can vary widely, depending upon the theoretical orientation of the particular therapist. Specific disorders frequently appear to be nothing more than extreme forms of some normal problems of growing up. As such, they require relatively simple and short-term treatment, with behavior modification techniques being particularly successful. In other cases, however, the term *specific disorder* appears to be something of a misnomer, for the specific problems appear to be symptoms of some more serious and more general underlying emotional disturbance. In these cases, therapists may differ sharply about the most appropriate therapy to use. Psychoanalysts will favor a psychoanalytic approach, while behaviorists will continue to prefer behavior modification techniques.

Childhood Psychosis

True childhood psychosis is a rare condition. In fact, it is estimated that there are less than half a million psychotic children in the United States (National Clearing House for Mental Health Information, 1970, p. 7). Yet, more has been written about childhood psychosis than any other form of childhood mental illness. Fascination with this relatively rare condition is not hard to explain. The behavior of a psychotic child is extremely bizarre and often begins early in the child's life, so that it is extremely difficult to guess, let alone actually determine, what could have produced the psychosis. The uncertainties that are thus inherent in the study of childhood psychosis make it a fertile and fascinating subject for research and discussion.

General Description of Psychosis

Psychosis refers to the severe condition in which a person has "lost touch with reality." In fact, most psychotic children appear never to have established contact with reality in the first place. A child's psychosis will probably have become apparent quite early in life (usually before the age of 2), with symptoms that are both bizarre and numerous. As the child grows older, these symptoms will interfere with almost all aspects of development, including the ability to form meaningful relationships with other people, perceptual development, and motor coordination.

Over the years, there have been several attempts to distinguish different types of psychoses, such as **autism, childhood schizophrenia,** and **symbiotic psychosis.** Seldom, however, have psychologists been able to clearly discriminate these different forms of psychoses (Rutter, 1978). In this section, therefore, we will focus on autism, which is the best described and most easily identified of the childhood psychoses.

Autism

In 1943, Leo Kanner first described a unique cluster of symptoms under the label of *early infantile autism.* Kanner argued that autism is distinct from other types of childhood psychoses, because the autistic child, unlike other psychotics, does not actually *withdraw* from his relationships with others. Rather, the autistic child *fails to establish* normal relationships with others in the first place.

The failure of the autistic child to establish normal relationships with the other people in his environment is sometimes apparent as early as 4 months of age. At 4 months, most babies are showing the beginnings of interpersonal relationships through the creation of attachments to their mothers. The normal 4-month-old begins to exhibit a variety of behaviors that serve to bring him in close physical contact with his mother. He will adjust his posture when he anticipates being picked up; once picked up, he will cuddle or mold his body to the contours of his mother's body. These early signs of social responsiveness often do not appear in the autistic child. In contrast, the autistic child tends to rigidify his body when being held. He may even arch his back away from his mother, or he may bang his head against her chest.

Between 4 and 18 months of age, numerous other symptoms of disturbance emerge. One of these is the child's failure to develop normal patterns of speech—which further prevents him from establishing any sort of relationship with other people in his environment. About half of the children diagnosed as autistic remain functionally mute. The remaining 50% may acquire some speech, but their speech patterns are bizarre and essentially noncommunicative. For example, an autistic child may walk around mechanically labeling all of the objects in a room but not be able to answer a simple question such as "What is that?" Many autistic children who do speak simply parrot, or mechanically repeat, whatever they have heard. This condition, called **echolalia,** gives the impression that speech is not being used for purposes of communication.

The autistic child also shows excessive and unusual motor patterns. These patterns are often highly repetitive and include rocking, head-banging, arm-waving, and rapidly moving the fingers in front of the eyes. Occasionally, they may even include a variety of self-destructive behaviors. These self-destructive behaviors may be so severe that the child must literally be restrained from biting and digging into his own flesh.

Autistic children also can suffer from a variety of perceptual disorders. In extreme forms, these children may even go so far as to perceive things that simply do not exist in reality. This tendency to perceive objects in the absence of any sensory stimulation is called **hallucination.** Hallucination is believed to occur very rarely in autistic children.

For the most part, the autistic child remains centered on his own body, showing little interest, if any, in his environment—and especially in people. There

are, however, two respects in which the autistic child shows at least some awareness of what goes on around him. First, it is common for an autistic child to react
with extreme fear or frustration to any changes in his environment, even though
he seems otherwise relatively oblivious to that environment. This *insistence on the
preservation of sameness* may be so intense that it becomes extremely difficult to
even change the child's clothes or alter the height of a window shade.

Second, the child may have an obsessive interest in certain objects in that
environment. Usually, this obsessive interest is directed toward mechanical objects, such as clocks, vacuum cleaners, light switches, and faucets. Autistic children may spend hours at a time engaged in highly repetitive, stereotyped interactions with these objects, staring at them, grasping them, and manipulating them.

A more common, yet still extreme, form of perceptual disorder found in
autistic children is at the opposite extreme from hallucination: namely, the tendency to block out, or fail to perceive, events that have actually occurred. Some
autistic children show no evidence of pain as they quite literally tear at their own
skin and inflict various tortures upon themselves. Other autistic children fail to
show any response to even loud noises and, thus, give the appearance of being
deaf. Still other autistic children may misinterpret or misperceive events that are
actually present. For example, an autistic child may perceive a harmless object
such as a lamp as terrifying.

Finally, recent evidence (Rutter & Schopler, 1978) suggests that in addition to
the other severe psychological problems, 75 to 85% of autistic children may also
suffer some form of mental retardation.

The Environmental Hypothesis.   Autism has received a great deal of attention, for it is the most severe of the emotional disturbances of childhood, with the
first symptoms of the disease appearing quite early in life. One of the most widely
known psychologists studying the disorder is Bruno Bettelheim (1967). Bettelheim
believes that autism is caused by environmental conditions. His explanation for
this complex and bizarre disorder is that it is a desperate attempt on the part of
the child to blot out an environment that the child has found painful and frustrating. Bettelheim argues that "autism is the last fortress"—meaning that it is a massive plan of defense set up by the child to avoid a world that the child views as
being painful. It is, however, Bettelheim argues, an "empty fortress," because it
cuts the child off completely from the world around him and prevents him from
establishing "a dialogue with reality."

A central point in Bettelheim's environmental explanation of autism lies in
the concept of *critical periods*, or specific times during development during which
environmental factors can have an unusually strong and pervasive effect on the
course of all of later development. In Bettelheim's view, there are at least three
periods during the first two years of life that are *critical* for the development of
autism. Frustration and insensitivity to the child's needs during any or all of these
three periods can result in autism. The first critical period extends from birth until
6 months of age: the time in the child's life when people have not yet become
clearly differentiated for the child. The second critical period extends from 6 to 9
months of age: the time during which the child normally becomes increasingly
interested in people and, in particular, in such "special" people as his mother. The
third critical period occurs between 18 and 24 months of age: the time when the
child learns how to interact effectively with his environment and begins to learn
how he can himself have an effect on that environment. Bettelheim argues that

frustration during any of these critical periods can result in autism, because the child is thereby discouraged from developing normal patterns of interaction with his environment. Rather than attempt to overcome these frustrations, the child instead turns inward and refuses to further interact with his environment.

It is difficult to find hard evidence in support of Bettelheim's position. The problem in obtaining such evidence is that the causal factors suggested by Bettelheim are highly personal, subjective events that occur prior to the actual development of the disease and, hence, before the child and his parents are under trained observation. As a result, one can only infer the infant's experiences from the parents' later reports or from observations of their later treatment of the child. There can be little doubt, however, that both the parents' memory of their past behavior and their current behavior will have been affected deeply by their experiences with such a seriously disturbed child, thereby further confounding the problem of collecting reliable data.

Nonetheless, early evidence did seem to provide some support for Bettelheim's position. The parents of autistic children, as compared with the parents of other disturbed and retarded children, did seem to reveal several striking shared characteristics, such as high intelligence, detachment, obsessiveness, and coldness (Bettelheim, 1967; Eisenberg & Kanner, 1956; Kanner, 1949; Rimland, 1964).

On the surface at least, the type of parent reflected in these early studies is one that could well fit into Bettelheim's model of autism: a parent who is insensitive to his or her child's needs and therefore discourages the child from developing normal patterns of interaction with the environment. However, in more recent studies, parents of autistic children have not been found to be insensitive (Reichler & Schopler, 1976; Rutter, 1971; Wing, 1972). Moreover, the environmental position is further weakened by the fact that many parents are extremely insensitive—if not downright cruel—to their children, but have children who nevertheless do not become autistic. In fact, autism is no more common among abused children, and among the neglected children who grow up in institutions, than in children who grow up under more normal conditions (Dennis, 1941; Eisenberg & Kanner, 1956; Keeler, 1958; Rimland, 1964). At the other extreme, there are many children who appear to have been well cared for physically during infancy but, nonetheless, become autistic. If it is correct that frustrating events during certain critical periods cause autism, then why do many seriously abused children escape autism, while many seemingly well-nurtured children become autistic? In summary, evidence for a solely environmental cause of autism is extremely weak.

The Biological Hypothesis. Even if the parents of autistic children were more rigid and insensitive than other parents it is hard to believe that rigidity and insensitivity alone could create a disorder as serious as autism. Furthermore, autism appears to develop quite early in the child's life, before he has had extensive interaction with his environment. These and other considerations have led many psychologists to reject a purely "environmental" interpretation of autism. They argue instead that some biological problems are responsible (Rutter & Schopler, 1978).

The earliest proponent of a biological explanation for autism was Bernard Rimland (1964). Rimland stressed the lack of universality in the "cold parent/ autistic child" pattern (Chapman, 1957; Eisenberg & Kanner, 1956; Keeler, 1958;

Schachter, 1958). He noted that many cold and rigid parents who fit the stereotype exactly—and therefore might be expected to have autistic children—have perfectly normal children (Dennis, 1941; Kanner, 1957). Even within a single family, it is unusual to find more than one autistic child—except in the case of identical twins, who are likely to be either both affected or both unaffected (Kanner & Lesser, 1958; Keeler, 1958; Rattner & Chapman, 1959).

Rather than viewing autism as an affective or emotional disorder, Rimland argues that autism can be better understood as a more general cognitive disorder. According to this notion, the autistic child's problems stem from a basic difficulty in relating current events to remembered experiences in the child's past:

> To make a mechanical analogy, it seems very much as though the material had entered the nervous system on a single track, proceeded to a point of storage without ever having been analyzed or supplemented, then later emerged from storage in virtually its original condition, on a parallel track, as an all-or-none response to some subsequent stimulus. There appear to be no switches or sidings along the track which would permit the input to be sorted, segregated, redistributed, or integrated with prior or subsequent input. If we may be permitted to change analogies, the autistic child's brain functions as though it were operated by a clerk rather than a chemist; raw material comes and goes, but the parcels are never opened and their contents are never mixed to form any useful compound [Rimland, 1964, p. 85].

In other words, the autistic child cannot analyze or relate current events to past events and, therefore, experiences his environment as continually changing, unpredictable, and incomprehensible. According to Rimland, this basic cognitive disorder is primarily responsible for the autistic child's various symptoms. For example, the child does not develop a normal relationship with his mother because he does not form the normal associations and memories that link her with pleasant experiences.

Rimland's notion of autism as a cognitive disorder, like Bettelheim's environmental explanation, is at present speculative. Rimland suggests that the child's cognitive problems stem from specific damage to the brain and that the *reticular formation* (an area of the brain believed to be involved in the formation of associations between events and the creation of memories) may be the site of this damage. Although clear support for Rimland's theory is still to come, there is a growing trend among experts toward viewing autism as some form of biological disorder, rather than a disorder caused by a maladaptive environment (Rutter & Schopler, 1978). At present, though, we cannot specify with any certainty exactly what that biological disorder is.

Treatment of Childhood Psychosis

The prognosis for the psychotic child is not encouraging. Under the best of circumstances, extensive long-term treatment may produce some improvement in the child's basic social and behavioral skills. Full recovery is, however, extremely rare and seems to be unrelated to the use of any particular form of treatment (Eisenberg, 1956; Eisenberg & Kanner, 1956; Kessler, 1964; Rimland, 1964; Wing, 1976).

While it appears that no one form of therapy can produce a cure, there is evidence that some therapies are better in improving the child's condition (for example, Lovaas, Schreibman, & Koegel, 1976). Behavior modification techniques in particular have been more effective in the treatment of psychotic children than traditional psychoanalytic methods.

Psychoanalytic therapies, such as Bettelheim's, view childhood psychoses as stemming from a seriously impaired parent/child relationship. Hence, psychotherapy begins by having the therapist take on the role of a parent substitute who is more understanding and supportive of the child than the real parent is capable of being. "We meet the child's needs at whatever level he presents himself, avoiding frustration whenever possible and providing a maximum of gratification" (Rank, 1955, p. 499). Psychoanalysts believe that the creation of such a supportive and nonfrustrating environment enables the psychotic child to let down his barriers and establish an initially tenuous contact—and dialogue—with reality.

Psychoanalytic treatment of psychotic children has not, however, resulted in much success. In fact, Kanner (1957b) noted that autistic children who receive the most intensive psychotherapy often show poorer progress than do children who receive little or no treatment. Behaviorists have argued that this lack of progress stems from the fact that the psychotic child receives attention and comfort from the psychoanalyst whenever he exhibits his psychotic behaviors. Thus, argue the behaviorists, the therapist may inadvertently be positively reinforcing and, hence, maintaining the child's behavioral problems.

In behavior modification, the tables are turned. An environment is created in which only appropriate behaviors are positively reinforced (in order to increase their frequency), while inappropriate behaviors are negatively reinforced (in order to decrease their frequency). This form of therapy must, of necessity, begin on the simplest of all levels, since the psychotic child is often extremely withdrawn and isolated from his environment. For example, therapy may begin by discouraging self-destructive behaviors or by teaching the child to look at his therapist. In addition, basic biological reinforcers, such as food and pain, may be used, since the psychotic child may not respond to *secondary reinforcers* such as praise or criticism. The search for effective and potent positive reinforcers has occasionally resulted in some fairly extreme forms of treatment. For example, Ivar Lovaas has placed children in a room, the floor of which is an electrified grid through which continuous low voltage shock is applied to the children's feet. Appropriate behaviors are then *positively reinforced by turning off the shock*. This treatment was extremely effective, even though it was used only once or twice on the most severely disturbed children (for example, see Lovaas, Freitag, Kinder, Rubenstein, Schaeffer, & Simmons, 1964).

In addition to the difficulties in finding effective positive reinforcers for severely psychotic children, the behavior modification therapist is often at a loss to find appropriate behaviors to reinforce. Many severely psychotic children, being mentally retarded, exhibit few, if any, appropriate behaviors at the outset of treatment. It becomes necessary at times to gradually create those behaviors through **shaping** procedures in which the child is reinforced for increasingly closer approximations to the desired behavior. For example, consider how the behavior modification therapist might go about establishing eye contact with the severely psychotic child. The therapist would begin by giving the child a positive reinforcer, such as a candy, each time the child moved his head in the general direction of the therapist. As the child begins to make an increasing number of general head movements, the therapist might increase his criteria for reinforcement by requiring the child to maintain a head-to-head orientation for one second. On successive trials, the time duration for the head-to-head orientation would gradually be increased. Once a relatively steady head-to-head orientation is maintained, the therapist would again increase the criteria for reinforcement: now the child must at least glance in the direction of the therapist's face. Finally, the child must look directly into the therapist's eyes if he is to be reinforced (Lott, 1968). This process may take literally hundreds of attempts—and weeks of work—to complete. It has, however, proven successful.

Behavior modification techniques have been used successfully to eliminate self-destructive and self-stimulatory behaviors and to create self-help skills, social-interaction skills, and even language skills in severely psychotic children (Lovaas, Freitag, Kinder, Rubenstein, Schaeffer, & Simmons, 1964). Behavior modification techniques do not, however, result in cures. The improvements that are achieved are extremely time-consuming and require almost continuous one-to-one treatment for the child. There is simply not enough time to create perfectly normal behavior in such severely disturbed children. Even more discouraging is the rapidity with which the child's gains are lost. If returned to an institutional setting, the children often regress to their initial state (Lovaas et al., 1976). (See Figure 13-2.) More refinement of behavior modification techniques with psychotic children is needed if the child's hard-won gains will ever generalize to a normal environment without structured reinforcement. Programs that include some form of parent training are most likely to be effective in this regard (Lovaas et al., 1976).

Summary of Childhood Psychosis

Childhood psychosis is the most serious and infrequent form of emotional disturbance in childhood. Though different subcategories of childhood psychosis have been hypothesized, the clearest and most easily identified is that of autism. The most basic characteristic of autistic children is their failure to develop contact with reality. However, autism affects other fundamental aspects of the child's behavior, such as perceptual processes and motor coordination, and is particularly apparent in the child's complete inability to establish normal relationships with other people. The autistic child may adamantly reject and avoid others in his environment.

The treatment of childhood psychosis mirrors the difference of opinion concerning its cause. Psychoanalysts like Bruno Bettelheim, who favor an environmental explanation, view the disorder as stemming from a seriously impaired parent/child relationship. They seek to treat the child by creating a supportive and nonfrustrating environment. Others, like Bernard Rimland, have pointed to an altogether different causal explanation: the biological hypothesis. They view autism as resulting from an actual physical disorder of the brain—and suggest that the other psychoses may also be biologically based. The method of treatment that they favor positively reinforces only the desired behaviors, while negatively reinforcing inappropriate behaviors. This behaviorist approach has, regrettably, not produced outright cures. However, it has proved far more successful than the psychoanalytic approach in at least improving the child's behavior.

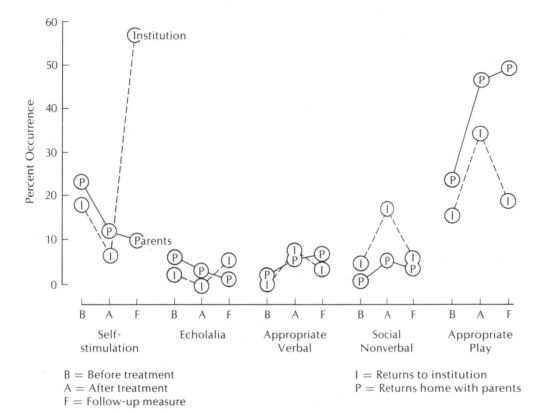

B = Before treatment
A = After treatment
F = Follow-up measure

I = Returns to institution
P = Returns home with parents

Figure 13-2.   This figure well illustrates how fragile the fruits of behavior modification can be if an autistic child is returned to a nonsupportive institutional environment (I). For the most part, all treatment gains were lost for these children and, in some areas, behavior was actually worse than before treatment (for example, self-stimulation).

This figure also illustrates, however, that, if the child returns home and if his parents are trained in behavior modification techniques (P), the autistic child is able to retain therapeutic gains and even show further improvement. (From "A Behavior Modification Approach to the Treatment of Autistic Children," by O. J. Lovaas, L. Schreibman, and R. L. Koegel. In E. Schopler and R. J. Reichler (Eds.), *Psychopathology and Child Development.* Copyright 1976 by Plenum Publishing Corporation. Reprinted by permission.)

CREATING AN OPTIMAL ENVIRONMENT

Obviously, this section is in a sense a summary statement for the entire book. The optimal environment is clearly not one that selects the appropriate form of therapy for a child's problems, but one that prevents such problems from arising in the first place. Knowledge of children and the course of their development is certainly an important aspect of creating such an environment. Ideally, then, we would like to know precisely why some children develop normally, while others develop mental and emotional disorders.

As has been apparent throughout this chapter, we unfortunately have limited knowledge of the causes of childhood psychopathology. In some cases, such as failure to thrive, the problems seem to stem from extremely maladaptive parenting practices early in the child's infancy. In other cases, such as obesity and infantile autism, more basic biological disorders in the child are probably at least partly responsible. In most cases, however, the actual cause is unknown.

It is nevertheless obvious that the creation of an optimal environment should occur long before the child is even conceived. The child's parents—and the mother primarily—must themselves be free from both physical and emotional disease. The mother must maintain her physical and emotional health throughout her pregnancy—and, indeed, throughout her child's life. Once the child is born, his or her environment must be stimulating, rewarding, and happy. His parents must treat him with love and be sensitive to his emotional, as well as his physical, needs. If these steps are taken, then, hopefully, he will develop as a healthy and normal human being.

SUMMARY OF CHILDHOOD PSYCHOPATHOLOGY

It is estimated that between 5 and 6 million of the elementary-school-age children in our country suffer from childhood psychopathology. This means that if all of the disturbed children in the United States were brought together in one place, they would fill a city roughly the size of Chicago. Clearly, childhood psychopathology is a serious problem.

What, then, is childhood psychopathology? How is it treated? And what are its causes? These are the questions that we have examined in this chapter. We have focused on the severity of the problem (10 to 12% of the child population) and the difficulties in making accurate diagnoses of children suffering from psychological disorders. The two principal forms of therapy currently in use were reviewed and contrasted: psychoanalysis and behavior modification. We saw that while psychoanalysis emphasizes introspection and awareness of the underlying cause of the child's disorder, behavior modification attempts to treat the symptoms of the disorder directly, through the procedures of classical and operant conditioning. The distinction between the psychoanalytic and behaviorist methods of treatment was discussed many times during the remainder of the chapter, in which we examined the symptoms, possible causes, and leading methods of treating a number of childhood disorders. These included a number of specific disorders and childhood psychoses. The wide gap between the psychoanalytic and behaviorist viewpoints became particularly apparent in our discussion of the most severe of the childhood psychoses: autism. At the one extreme, we saw psychoanalysts such as Bruno Bettelheim favoring an environmental explanation of the disorder and methods of treatment designed to support the child and shield him from frustration. At the other extreme, we saw Bernard Rimland and Ovar Lovaas positing a biological explanation and favoring treatment techniques designed to encourage desirable behavior and discourage undesirable behavior.

The two schools of thought could hardly be further apart. This is not, however, to say that one position is correct and the other false. Rather, the difference of opinion simply reflects the largely speculative nature of our study of these disorders.

The fact that we are at least asking questions about childhood psychopathology is, however, in itself a very encouraging note. In the opening chapter of this book, we saw that the child has only recently received special attention. In prior centuries, the question was never "What is best for the child?" but, rather, "How can the child best serve others?" The past century has witnessed a major shift in our perception of children, so that we are now very much concerned with what is in the best interests of our children. The scientific study of children and their normal, and abnormal, development is one facet of this changing attitude toward our children. Hopefully, our modern attitude will continue well into the future. If so, then we should eventually be able to at least diminish, if not completely eliminate, the problem of childhood psychopathology.

SUGGESTED READINGS

Kessler, J. W. *Psychopathology of childhood.* Englewood Cliffs, N.J.: Prentice-Hall, 1966. An extremely thorough review of the literature on childhood psychopathology. Although Kessler's orientation is clearly psychoanalytic, she gives a very unbiased view.

Rimland, B. *Infantile autism.* Englewood Cliffs, N.J.: Prentice-Hall, 1964. Although much of the book is highly speculative, it is a classic because of its attempt to put forth a biological interpretation of autism.

Engel, M. *Psychopathology in childhood.* New York: Harcourt Brace Jovanovich, 1972. A simple introduction to childhood psychopathology.

Ullman, L. P. & Krasner, L. *Case studies in behavior modification.* New York: Holt, Rinehart & Winston, 1966. An excellent collection of case studies treated by behavior modification techniques.

Hall, C. S. *A primer of Freudian psychology.* New York: Mentor Books, 1954. A very simple and readable introduction to Freudian theory.

GLOSSARY

anorexia nervosa. Self-enforced starvation. Common in women during adolescence and young adulthood.

autism. Believed to be a particular type of childhood psychosis in which a child fails ever to establish normal relations with others.

childhood schizophrenia. A type of childhood psychosis that differs from autism in that the child initially establishes relations with others and then withdraws.

classical conditioning. The process whereby a new *conditioned reflex* can be created through the continued pairing of a neutral stimulus (for example, a bell) with an unconditioned stimulus (for example, food).

compulsive habit. An extremely repetitive and stereotyped behavior.

conditioned reflex. A learned connection between stimulus and response. Conditioned reflexes are created through the process of classical conditioning.

conditioned response. A response that either has become associated with an originally neutral stimulus through the procedures of classical conditioning or has changed in likelihood as a function of having been reinforced in operant conditioning.

conditioned stimulus. An originally neutral stimulus that comes to elicit a conditioned response through the procedures of classical conditioning.

desensitization. A treatment for phobias used by behavior modification therapists. It consists of gradual and repeated pairings of the feared object with some pleasant event.

differential diagnosis. A process by which a psychologist attempts to precisely label a particular disorder.

echolalia. A language disorder in which the child mechanically repeats, or echoes, whatever is spoken to him or her. Common in autism.

encopresis. The technical term for persistent soiling.

enuresis. The technical term for persistent bed-wetting.

erogenous zones. In Freud's theory, those parts of the body that provide sensual pleasure when stimulated (for example, mouth, genitals).

failure to thrive. An illness of infants who tend to "thrive" in the hospital but not at home. Failure-to-thrive infants are severely underweight due to chronic and severe diarrhea and vomiting with no known biological cause. It is assumed that the problem stems from a faulty mother/infant relationship.

fixation. Failure to move on completely from one psychosexual stage to the next; Freud argued that this occurs when a child receives too much or too little stimulation at any particular psychosexual stage.

generalization. A process whereby behavior learned or conditioned in one context or stimulus situation comes to be exhibited in similar contexts or stimulus situations.

hallucination. The tendency to perceive objects in the absence of any sensory stimulation.

negative reinforcement. Any event that results in a decrease in the future probability of the particular behavior that it follows. Negative reinforcers include the use of punishment and the withholding of rewards.

Oedipal conflict. In Freudian theory, the child's sexual desire for the opposite-sex parent, which results in fear of punishment from the same-sex parent.

operant conditioning. A form of learning in which behavior changes as a function of its consequences, or of reinforcement.

phobia. An irrational fear.

positive reinforcement. Any event that results in an increase in the future probability of the particular behavior that it follows. Positive reinforcers include the use of rewards and the removal of unpleasant stimuli.

psychic determinism. A basic tenet of all psychoanalytic theories, stating that every thought, feeling, and action of every person has a cause.

reaction formation. In Freudian theory, a condition occurring as a result of fixation, in which a child totally denies any interest in a particular form of gratification.

reinforcement contingencies. The factors present in a child's environment that positively and negatively reinforce the child's behavior.

repression. A psychological process or "defense mechanism" in Freudian theory that results in certain thoughts and memories being pushed into the unconscious.

shaping. A technique of behavior modification therapists for creating totally new behaviors by reinforcing the child for increasingly closer approximations to that behavior.

symbiotic psychosis. Believed to be a particular type of childhood psychosis in which the child forms such an intense relationship with one person, usually his mother, that he is unable to separate himself from her or even discriminate himself as a being separate from her.

symptom substitution. The psychoanalytic theory that if one treats and removes a particular symptom without treating the underlying psychopathology, new symptoms will continue to crop up.

unconditioned response. In a reflex, the response elicited by the unconditioned stimulus. For example, the pupil of the eye restricts whenever a bright light is shown.

unconditioned stimulus. In a reflex, the stimulus that automatically elicits the unconditioned response.

REFERENCES

Barbero, G. In M. Klaus, T. Leger, & M. Trause (Eds.), *Maternal attachment and mothering disorders*. New Brunswick, N.J.: Johnson & Johnson Baby Products, 1974.

Bettelheim, B. *The Empty Fortress.* New York: Free Press, 1967.

Blitzer, J. R., Rollins, N., & Blackwell, A. Children who starve themselves. Anorexia nervosa. In I. Frank & M. Powell (Eds.), *Psychosomatic ailments in childhood and adolescence.* Springfield, Ill.: Charles C Thomas, 1967.

Bruch, H. Obesity in childhood and personality development *American Journal of Orthopsychiatry,* 1941, *11,* 467–474.

Bruch, H. Obesity. In I. Frank & M. Powell (Eds.), *Psychosomatic ailments in childhood and adolescence.* Springfield, Ill.: Charles C Thomas, 1967.

Chapman, A. H. Early infantile autism in identical twins: Report of a case. *AMA Archive of Neurological Psychiatry,* 1957, *78,* 621–623.

Dennis, W. Infant development under conditions of restricted practice and minimum social stimulation. *Genetic Psychology Monographs,* 1941, *23,* 143–191.

Eisenberg, L. The autistic child in adolescence. *American Journal of Psychiatry,* 1956, *112,* 607–612.

Eisenberg, L., & Kanner, L. Early infantile autism: 1943–1955. *American Journal of Orthopsychiatry,* 1956, *26,* 556–566.

Engel, M. *Psychopathology in childhood.* New York: Harcourt Brace Jovanovich, 1972.

Feldman, R. B. Solomon, M. L., Levinson, E. D., & Lasky, J. C. treatment of the seriously disturbed preschool child. *Canadian Psychiatric Association Journal,* 1974, *19*(2), 127–129.

Fraiberg, S. Billy: Psychological intervention for a failure-to-thrive infant. In M. Klaus, T. Leger, & M. Trause (Eds.), *Maternal attachment and mothering disorders.* New Brunswick, N. J.: Johnson & Johnson Baby Products, 1974.

Freud, S. [Analysis of a phobia in a five-year-old boy] (J. Strachey, Ed. and trans.). London: Hogarth Press, 1953. (Originally published, 1909.)

Fullerton, D. T. Infantile rumination. In I. Frank & M. Powell (Eds.), *Psychosomatic ailments in childhood and adolescence.* Springfield, Ill.: Charles C Thomas, 1967.

GAP (Group for the Advancement of Psychiatry). *Psychopathological disorders in childhood.* New York: Jason Aronson, 1974.

Harris, F. R., Wolf, M. M., & Baer, D. M. Effects of adult social reinforcement on child behavior. *Young Children,* 1964, *20*(1).

Heald, F. Obesity in the adolescent. In I. Frank & M. Powell (Eds.), *Psychosomatic ailments in childhood and adolescence.* Springfield, Ill.: Charles C Thomas, 1967.

Johnson, M. L., Burke, B. S., & Mayer, J. Relative importance of inactivity and overeating in energy balance of obese high school girls. *American Journal of Clinical Nutrition,* 1956, *4.*

Kanner, L. Autistic disturbance in affective contact. *Nervous Child,* 1942–1943, *2,* 217–250.

Kanner, L. Problems of nosology and psychodynamics of early infantile autism. *American Journal of Orthopsychiatry,* 1949, *19,* 416–426.

Kanner, L. General concept of schizophrenia at different ages. *Proceedings of Association for Research in Nervous and Mental Diseases,* 1954, *33,* 451–453.

Kanner, L. Causes and results of parental perfectionism. *Journal of South Carolina Medical Association,* 1957, *53,* 379–383. (a)

Kanner, L. *Child psychiatry* (3rd ed.). Springfield, Ill.: Charles C Thomas, 1957. (b)

Kanner, L., & Lesser, L. I. Early infantile autism. *Pediatric Clinics of North America,* 1958, *5,* 711–730.

Keeler, W. R. Autistic patterns and defective communication in blind children with retrolental fibroplasia. In P. Hock & J. Zubin (Eds.), *Psychopathology of communication.* New York: Grune and Stratton, 1958.

Kessler, J. W. *Psychopathology of childhood.* Englewood Cliffs, N.J.: Prentice-Hall, 1966.

Lapouse, R., & Monk, M. A. Fears and worries in a representative sample of children. *American Journal of Orthopsychiatry,* 1959, *29,* 803–818.

Lazarus, A. A., & Abramovitz, A. The use of "emotive imagery" in the treatment of children's phobias. In L. P. Ullman & L. Krasner (Eds.), *Case studies in behavior modification.* New York: Holt, Rinehart & Winston, 1966.

Lott, D. *The establishment of eye contact in schizophrenic children.* Unpublished master's thesis. University of Southern California, 1968.

Lovaas, O. I., Freitag, G., Kinder, M. I., Rubenstein, D. B., Schaeffer, B., & Simmons, J. B. Experimental studies in childhood schizophrenia: Developing social behavior using electric shock. Paper read at American Psychological Association meetings, Los Angeles, September 1964.

Lovaas, O. I., Schreibman, L., & Koegel, R. L. A behavior modification approach to the treatment of autistic children. In E. Schopler & R. J. Reichler (Eds.), *Psychopathology and child development*. New York: Plenum Press, 1976.

Mehlman, B. The reliability of psychiatric diagnosis. *Journal of Abnormal and Social Psychology*, 1952, *47*, 577–578.

National Clearing House for Mental Health Information. *The National Institute of Mental Health, Information Publication No. 5027*. Washington, D.C.: U.S. Government Printing Office, 1970.

Newburgh, L. H. Obesity; energy metabolism. *Physiological Reviews*, 1944, *24*.

Peterson, D. R., & London, P. A role for cognition in the behavioral treatment of a child's eliminative disturbance. In L. P. Ullman & L. Krasner (Eds.), *Case studies in behavior modification*. New York: Holt, Rinehart & Winston, 1966.

Raines, G. N., & Rohrer, J. H. The operational matrix of psychiatric practice, I: Consistency and variability in interview impressions of different psychiatrists. *American Journal of Psychiatry*, 1955, *110*, 721–733.

Rank, B. Intensive study and treatment of pre-school children who show marked personality deviations or "atypical development" and their parents. In G. Caplan (Ed.), *Emotional problems in early childhood*. New York: Basic Books, 1955.

Rattner, L. J., & Chapman, A. H. Dangers of indiscriminate hospitalization of the preschool child. *Journal of Dentistry for Children*, 1959, *26*, 55–62.

Reichler, R. J., & Schopler, E. Developmental therapy: A program model for providing individual services in the community. In E. Schopler & R. J. Reichler (Eds.), *Psychopathology and child development*. New York: Plenum Press, 1976.

Rimland, B. *Infantile autism*. Englewood Cliffs, N.J.: Prentice-Hall, 1964.

Ross, A. O. A clinical psychologist "examines" retarded children. In G. J. Williams & S. Gordon (Eds.), *Clinical child psychology*. New York: Behavioral Publications, 1974.

Rutter, M. (Ed.). *Infantile autism: Concepts, characteristics and treatment*. London: Whitefriars Press, 1971.

Rutter, M. On the diagnosis of autism. *Journal of Autism and Childhood Schizophrenia*, 1978, *8*, 1–15.

Rutter, M., & Schopler, E. Autism: A reappraisal of concepts and treatment. New York: Plenum Press, 1978.

Schmidt, H. O., & Fonda, C. P. The reliability of psychiatric diagnosis: A new look. *Journal of Abnormal and Social Psychology*, 1956, *52*, 262–267.

Shachter, M. Contribution à l'étude de l'autisme infantile précoce de Kanner. [A contribution to the study of Kanner's early infantile autism.] *Pédiatre*, 1958, *13*, 175–191.

Tapia, F., Jekel, J., & Domke, H. R. Enuresis: An emotional symptom? *Journal of Nervous and Mental Disease*, 1960, *130*, 61–66.

Watson, J. B. *Psychological care of the infant and child*. New York: W. W. Norton, 1928.

Wing, L. K. *Autistic children*. New York: Brunner/Mazel, 1972.

Wing, L. K. *Early childhood autism*. London: Pergamon Press, 1976.

Wolpe, J. *Psychotherapy by reciprocal inhibition*. Stanford, Calif.: Stanford University Press, 1958.

NAME INDEX

SUBJECT INDEX

452